PEACEFUL KINGS

Peaceful Kings

*Peace, Power, and the Early Medieval
Political Imagination*

PAUL J. E. KERSHAW

OXFORD
UNIVERSITY PRESS

OXFORD
UNIVERSITY PRESS

Great Clarendon Street, Oxford OX2 6DP

Oxford University Press is a department of the University of Oxford.
It furthers the University's objective of excellence in research, scholarship,
and education by publishing worldwide in

Oxford New York

Auckland Cape Town Dar es Salaam Hong Kong Karachi
Kuala Lumpur Madrid Melbourne Mexico City Nairobi
New Delhi Shanghai Taipei Toronto

With offices in

Argentina Austria Brazil Chile Czech Republic France Greece
Guatemala Hungary Italy Japan Poland Portugal Singapore
South Korea Switzerland Thailand Turkey Ukraine Vietnam

Oxford is a registered trade mark of Oxford University Press
in the UK and in certain other countries

Published in the United States
by Oxford University Press Inc., New York

British Library Cataloguing in Publication Data
Data available

Library of Congress Cataloging in Publication Data
Data available

Typeset by SPI Publisher Services, Pondicherry, India
Printed in Great Britain
on acid-free paper by the
MPG Books Group, Bodmin and King's Lynn

ISBN 978–0–19–820870–9

1 3 5 7 9 10 8 6 4 2

For my father, Eric, and in memory of my mother
Kathleen Kershaw, née Cribbins
(7. iii. 35–6. ii. 05)

'So I bequeath a happy peace to you
And all good men, as every prince should do.'
Pericles
William Shakespeare(?), *Pericles, Prince of Tyre*, I.1 (*c.* 1606)

'Peace is a very apoplexy, lethargy; mulled, deaf, sleepy, insensible;
a getter of more bastard children than war's a destroyer of men.'
First Servant
William Shakespeare, *Coriolanus*, IV.5. (*c.* 1607)

Acknowledgements

This book has been a long time in the making. The debts I have consequently accumulated are many and widespread, and I am delighted to make some account of them here. It is a distant descendant of a Ph.D. thesis completed at King's College, London, and my first debt is to Jinty Nelson, who oversaw the work and who taught me as an undergraduate presiding over the Special Subject class on 'Alfred the Great and Charles the Bald' in which my interest in the issues explored here first formed.

I suspect that few places have been as conducive to the formation of early medievalists as the University of London in the 1990s, and this book is also a product of the intellectual environment of the Institute of Historical Research's 'Earlier Medieval' seminar and the scholarly community that surrounded it. Amongst its past and present members I owe particular thanks to Paul Fouracre, John Gillingham, Guy Halsall, Christina Harrington, and Geoffrey West. Alan Thacker's criticism and advice have been valued supports across the years. David Ganz has also been consistently generous with his learning and wisdom. Membership of UCL's *Celtic Inscribed Stones Project* as a postdoctoral fellow between 1998 and early 2000 enabled me to remain in the discipline whilst teaching me an immense amount, and I will always be grateful for Wendy Davies's support, her lessons in rigour, professionalism, and the paramount need for grass-roots perspectives on early medieval politics. Appropriate, then, that *CISP* was housed in a basement office in Russell Square where my colleague Mark Handley taught me much about epigraphy and some dubious Antipodean mnemonics for ogham *aicmí*. He also broadened my understanding of the world of Vandal Africa and Burgundy considerably, and the earlier sections of this book are a testament to that impact. Many others have also been remarkably generous with their time and learning. Mary Garrison has long been a good friend and valued critic, and a contemporary who has consistently shown through her own work that the high level of scholarship achieved by earlier generations of scholars remains achievable by members of my own. Many of the above read some or all of the manuscript; some laboured through sequential versions.

In the wider scholarly community I must also thank Richard Abels, Scott DeGregorio, Anton Scharer, and particularly Rosamond McKitterick, under whose guidance I completed my Cambridge M.Phil. thesis and who has offered valuable criticism at key moments thereafter. David Pratt shared his doctoral work on Alfred the Great with me, although his own monograph, *The Political Thought of Alfred the Great* (Cambridge, 2007) came out too late in the final preparations of this book for me to respond fully to his insights into early medieval political thought, Solomon's place within it, and the achievements of the Alfredian court. Energetic readers might derive some sporting pleasure from exploring the respective ways in which we have approached some common issues. Similarly, Ildar Garipzanov's *The Symbolic Language of Authority in the Carolingian World (c. 751–877)* (Leiden, 2008) emerged in the final stages of the text's editorial emendation. Where particularly pertinent I have sought to engage, albeit briefly, with his thoughts.

In Virginia from 2001 onwards my departmental colleagues Bob Geraci, Chuck McCurdy, Duane Osheim, Ted Lendon, and Elizabeth Meyer have all given generously of their time and knowledge. The latter pair in particular smoothed the translation from NW3 to 22904 considerably. Matthew Gillis gave valuable research assistance in summer 2004, whilst Michael Alexander and Christopher Lundgren provided crucial research assistance at points, and all helped improve the finished product immeasurably. Despite such support, I am acutely aware that errors, omissions, and flaws remain. They are mine alone.

I owe a major debt of thanks to A. J. Woodman, Basil L. Gildersleeve Professor of Classics at the University of Virginia, for his generous help and critical assistance at very many points in the text, and for saving me from innumerable errors.

There are two scholars with whom I would have very much wished to have shared this book. Not least because their comments would have undoubtedly improved it: Tim Reuter and Patrick Wormald. Both offered vital support and advice during the preparation of the Ph.D. thesis and after. Their scholarship continues to teach, and the focus of this book can rightly be said to show evidence of their joint influence upon English early medieval studies.

It is a particular pleasure to acknowledge the incredible work of the Alderman library staff at the University of Virginia, in particular George Crafts and the staff of the ILL/LEO office. My own work is built upon their labours and those of their colleagues in libraries at other institutions. Portions of this book were written and revised whilst I held a Sesquicentennial Fellowship from the University of Virginia in 2004–5. Beth Ostergaard in New York and John T. Schroll in Charlottesville offered support of a different but crucial character. I have had the benefit of a sequence of supportive editors at Oxford University Press: Ruth Parr originally commissioned the book; latterly Anne Gelling, Rupert Cousens, and particularly Seth Cayley have overseen it with almost limitless patience. The anonymous readers of the Press offered much valuable advice and many suggestions which have improved the final version immensely.

I am grateful to Jess Smith, who copy-edited my text for the Press. Karen Parker provided outstanding support during the proofing process and I am deeply grateful for her rigour, patience, and professionalism at the eleventh hour, and well after. Similarly, Fiona Vlemmicks oversaw the final phase of work with a blend of patience and authority any medieval ruler would have been lauded *ad caelum* for processing. I am also grateful to the Bodleian Library,

University of Oxford, for kind permission to reproduce elements of MS. Auct. D. 4. 8, fol. 349r. on the cover.

A study as broad chronologically and geographically as this necessarily rests upon foundations laid by many other scholars. I have striven to signal my debts fully in the chapters that follow but remain acutely conscious that the need for a highly selective citation of modern scholarship precludes an exhaustive settlement of intellectual obligations. Unless otherwise indicated the translations that follow are my own, but nevertheless I am aware that they cannot fail in many cases to have been influenced by those of earlier translators. To those I may have slighted of recognition, I offer my grateful thanks here.

I must thank Adrienne Ghaly, to whom I owe a great debt for her love, support, and criticism. She has not only lived with this book over several years but with its author as he attempted to finish it. (I will now take Bear for his walk.)

My greatest debt, as the dedication of this book makes clear, is to my parents. The deepest roots of my interest in the past are set into distant childhood holidays spent exploring the remains of ancient, medieval, and wartime Greece and Sunday trips across the Pennines to York and the Coppergate excavations of the late 1970s. This book is slight repayment for their support over the years. I offer it nonetheless.

Paul Kershaw

Charlottesville
Virginia

Contents

Abbreviations

Abbreviations for all Anglo-Saxon law codes follow the conventions established in F. Liebermann, *Die Gesetze der Angelsachsen* (Halle, 1903–16).

AA SS	*Acta Sanctorum*
AB	*Annales Bertiniani*, ed. F. Grat, J. Vielliard, S. Clémencet, and L. Levillain, *Annales de Saint-Bertin* (Paris, 1964)
AF	*Annales Fuldenses*, ed. F. Kurze, *MGH SRG* 7 (Hanover, 1891)
AfD	*Archiv für Diplomatik*
AHR	*American Historical Review*
AL	*Annales Laureshamenses*, ed. G. H. Pertz *MGH Scriptores* I (Hanover, 1826)
ALMA	*Archivam latinitatis medii aevi*
ALR	*Anthologia Latina*, ed. Alexander Reise (Leipzig, 1894)
Ambrose, *Ep.*	Ambrose, *Epistolae*
Anton, *Fürstenspiegel*	H. H. Anton, *Fürstenspiegel und Herrscherthos in der Karolingerzeit. Bonner Historische Forschungen* 32 (Bonn, 1967)
ANQ	*American Notes and Queries*
ARF	*Annales regni Francorum,* ed. G. H. Pertz and F. Kurze, *MGH SRG* 6 (Hanover, 1895)
ASC	*Two of the Saxon Chronicles Parallel: with Supplementary Extracts from the Others*, ed. C. Plummer and J. Earle, 3rd edition (Oxford, 1965). MS 'A' unless otherwise stated
ASE	*Anglo-Saxon England*
ASPR	*The Anglo-Saxon Poetic Records*, ed. G. P. Krapp and E. V. K. Dobbie (New York, 1931–53), 6 volumes
AX	*Annales Xantenses et Annales Vedastini*, ed. B. von Simson, *MGH SRG* 12 (Hanover, 1909)
BAR	British Archaeological Reports
Bell.Goth.	Procopius, *Wars*, Books 5–7, *De bello Gothico*
Bell.Van.	Procopius, *Wars*, Books 3–4, *De bello Vandalico*
BMGS	*Byzantine and Modern Greek Studies*
BN	*Bibliothèque nationale*
BZ	*Byzantinische Zeitschrift*

CCCM	Corpus Christianorum Continuatio Mediævalis
CCSL	Corpus Christianorum, Series Latina
CH	*Charlemagne's Heir: New Perspectives on the Reign of Louis the Pious (814–840)*, eds, P. Godman and R. Collins (Oxford, 1990)
De Civ.Dei	Augustine, *De Civitate Dei*, ed., B. Dombart and A. Kalb, *CCSL* 47–8 (Turnhout, 1955), 2 volumes
CIL	*Corpus Inscriptionum Latinarum*
CISP	*Celtic Inscribed Stones Project Database, http://www.ucl.ac.uk/archaeology/cisp/*
CSEL	Corpus Scriptorum Ecclesiasticorum Latinorum
DLH	Gregory of Tours, *Decem Libri Historiarum,* ed. W. Arndt and B. Krusch, *MGH SRM* 1 (Hanover, 1885)
DOP	*Dumbarton Oaks Papers*
ECBPP	F. Dvornik, *Early Christian and Byzantine Political Philosophy* (Washington DC, 1966), 2 volumes
EETS	*Early English Text Society*
EHR	*English Historical Review*
EME	*Early Medieval Europe*
Etym.	Isidore of Seville, *Etymologarium sive Originum Libri XX*, ed. W. M. Lindsay (Oxford, 1911)
FmSt	*Frühmittelalterliche Studien*
GCS	*Die Griechischen Christlichen Schriftsteller der ersten Drei Jahrhunderte*
HBS	*Henry Bradshaw Society*
HE	*Bede's Ecclesiastical History of the English People*, ed. B. Colgrave and R. Mynors (Oxford, 1969)
HJ	*Historisches Jahrbuch*
HS	*Historische Studien*
HTR	*Harvard Theological Review*
HZ	*Historische Zeitschrift*
I&R	P. Wormald, D. Bullough, and R. Collins (eds), *Ideal and Reality in Frankish and Anglo-Saxon Society Presented to J. M. Wallace-Hadrill* (Oxford, 1983)
ILCV	*Inscriptiones Latinae Christianae Veteris*

IuE	*Die Iren und Europa im Früheren Mittelalter,* ed. H. Löwe (Stuttgart, 1982), 2 volumes
Jackson, *Ordines*	R. Jackson (ed.), *Ordines coronationis Franciae. Texts and Ordines for the Coronation of Frankish and French Kings and Queens in the Middle Ages* (Philadelphia, 1995–2000), 2 volumes
JEGP	*Journal of German and English Philology*
JEH	*Journal of Ecclesiastical History*
JMH	*Journal of Medieval History*
JÖB	*Jahrbuch der Österreichischen Byzantinistik*
JRS	*Journal of Roman Studies*
JTS	*Journal of Theological Studies*
LdM	*Lexicon des Mittelalters*
Liber	Sedulius Scottus, *Liber de Rectoribus Christianis,* ed. S. Hellmann, *Sedulius Scottus. Quellen und Untersuchungen zur lateinischen Philologie des Mittelalters* I.1 (Munich, 1906)
Lib. Sacr. Aug.	*Liber sacramentorum Augustodunensis,* ed. O. Heiming CCSL 159B (Turnhout, 1987)
Lib. Sacr. Eng.	*Liber sacramentorum Engolismensis: manuscript B.N. lat. 816. le sacramentaire gélasien d'Angoulême,* ed. P. Saint-Roch, CCSL 159C (Turnhout, 1987)
Lib. Sacr. Rom.	*Liber sacramentorum Romanae aecclesiae ordinis anni circuli (Sacramentarium Gelasianum)* ed. L. C. Mohlberg, L. Eitzenhöfer, and P. Siffrin (Rome, 1960)
LP	*Le Liber Pontificalis,* ed. L. Duchesne (Paris, 1955), 3 volumes
MEC	M. Blackburn and P. Grierson (eds), *Medieval European Coinage* I: *the Early Middle Ages (5th to 10th Centuries)* (Cambridge, 1986)
MGH	*Monumenta Germaniae Historica*
AA	*Auctores antiquissimi*
Capit.	*Capitularia regum Francorum*
Conc.	*Concilia*
Const.	*Constitutiones et acta publica imperatorum et regum*
D	*Diplomata*
DD	*Diplomata regum et imperatorum; Die Urkunden der deutschen Könige und Kaiser*
DK	*Diplomatum Karolinorum*

Epp.	*Epistolae*
Epp. sel.	*Epistolae selectae in usum scholarum*
Fontes	*Fontes Iuris Germanici Antiqui in usum scholarum separatim editi*
LdL	*Libelli de lite imperatorum et pontificum saeculis XI et XII conscripti*
LL nat. Germ	*Leges nationum Germanicarum*
Poetae	*Poetae Latini Aevi Carolini*
SRG	*Scriptores rerum Germanicarum in usum scholarum separatim editi*
SRM	*Scriptores rerum Merovingicarum*
SS	*Scriptores*
SSDM	Scriptores des deutsches Mittelalters
MIÖG	*Mitteilungen des Instituts für Österreichische Geschichtsforschung*
NCMH	*The New Cambridge Medieval History.* vol. I, ed. P. Fouracre (Cambridge, 2005); vol. II, ed. R. McKitterick (Cambridge, 1995); vol. III, ed. T. Reuter (Cambridge, 1999)
P&P	*Past and Present*
RB	*Revue Bénédictine*
REA	*Revue des Études Augustiniennes*
Reydellet, *Royauté*	M. Reydellet, *La Royauté dans la littérature latine de Sidoine Apollinaire à Isidore de Séville* (Paris, 1981)
RIC	H. Mattingley (ed.), *Roman Imperial Coinage* (London, 1913–56)
SC	*Sources Chrétiennes*
SCH	Studies in Church History
Settimane	*Settimane di studio del centro italiano di studi sull'alto medioevo*
SuT	*Studien und Texte*
T&T	L. D. Reynolds (ed.), *Texts and Transmissions. A Survey of the Transmission of the Latin Classics,* revised edition (Oxford, 1986)
TLL	*Thesaurus Linguae Latinae*
TRHS	*Transactions of the Royal Historical Society*
TRW	Transformation of the Roman World
TTH	Liverpool Translated Texts for Historians

Var.	Cassiodorus, *Variae*
VuF	*Vorträge und Forschungen*
ZfKG	*Zeitschrift für Kirchengeschichte*
ZRG GA	*Zeitschrift der Savigny-Stiftung für Rechtsgeschichte germanistische Abteilung*
ZRG KA	*Zeitschrift der Savigny-Stiftung für Rechtsgeschichte kanonistische Abteilung*
ZRG RA	*Zeitschrift der Savigny-Stiftung für Rechtsgeschichte römanistische Abteilung*

Nomenclature and Conventions

The names of individuals, places, and texts are given in the form most familiar to anglophone readers. I have attempted to follow common sense and convention in my choice of names throughout, and to privilege clarity above consistency. Hence, St-Denis, San Paolo fuori le mura, Winchester, and Rome will be found on the following pages. So, too, will Charlemagne, Alfred the Great, and Hrabanus Maurus.

Psalm numbering follows that of the Roman Psalter, R. Weber, *Le Psautier romain et les autres anciens psautiers latins, Collectanea Biblica Latina* 10 (Vatican City, 1953). Translations from the Vulgate come from the Douai-Rheims, though on occasion I have altered the translation to reflect the wording of specific texts and liturgical variations and modernized an occasional archaism. Similarly, faced with a range of orthographic conventions I have for consistency's sake altered occasional discrepancies.

Introduction

After the end of Rome's control over its western provinces in the fifth century, thoughts of peace occupied many minds. This book is about the changing character of that engagement and its place in the formulation of post-Roman political ideas. Poems celebrating Vandal bath-houses that evoked Stoic notions of cosmic order; Burgundian church dedications in the language of the Heavenly Jerusalem, archetypal city of peace; Gregory of Tours' account of the misdeeds of the kings of his age; the acclamations at Charlemagne's coronation ('great and peacemaking emperor'): in all of these, peace emerges in these centuries as a matter for kings and emperors, their celebrants, critics, and advisors, and many who aspired to such roles. More than that, it was a key theme in early medieval culture, evoked through the words hammered into coin blanks, murmured in liturgies, asserted in law-codes; its attainment, character, and consequences explored in a range of vernacular epic and Latin verse.

Such sources have been well studied, and doubtless will continue to be. We will visit many on the pages that follow. But peace, and concerns about it, also turns up in less expected places in the early medieval record. In, for example, the eighth-century Anglo-Saxon Tatwine's trivial but telling observation in one of his *Ænigmata* that the great benefit of the squirrel's agility and its choice of a tree as a home was that it avoided the dangers of war (*discrimina Martis*) that threatened the earthbound.[1] Or, later, in a set of skaldic verses in which an unnamed Viking looks forward to the day when his shield would no longer be bloodstained, war would eventually end, and he and his girl might settle peacefully in 'fair London' (*fogrum Lundúnum*).[2] Such glimpses beyond the face of rulership reveal widely held anxieties about peace and well-being in individual lives, anxieties to be found, for example, in the range of votive prayers in early medieval liturgy: blessings for safe travel and new homes, for victory against outsiders, and for prevailing peace for both rulers and the ruled. That rulers needed to make the case for their ability to create and maintain peace hints at wider expectations on the part of those over

---

[1] *Tatuini Opera Omnia*, ed. M. de Marco, CCSL 133 (Turnhout, 1968), Aenigmata no. 17, 'de sciuro', p. 184, with English translation by E. Van Erhardt-Siebold.
[2] R. G. Poole, *Viking Poems on War and Peace. A Study in Skaldic Narrative* (Toronto, 1991), 90.

whom they ruled. Rulers emphasized their authority as peacemakers, and with it their ability to create and to sustain peace within their lands. The business of a king (*res regia*), wrote an anonymous churchman of the 830s in a poem in qualified praise of a minor Bavarian count, Timo, 'is wholly to support peace'.[3]

Why did sixth-century Frankish, Burgundian, and Gothic kings feel the need to articulate their authority in terms of peacekeeping? Why, beginning in Louis the Pious' reign, do we see an increasing emphasis upon kings in both Francia and Anglo-Saxon England as Solomonic rulers, wise, just, and anointed, but consistently peaceful? Part of the answer, at least, lies in a prevailing need for legitimacy, and for rulers to project—or to have projected on their behalf—an image of themselves as able to maintain social order at a basic level. Sometimes this meant emphasizing continuity, whether with the public face of late Roman provincial authority or the inherited order of a forebear. At other moments the notional restoration of lost peace was the dominant idiom, as it would be for Alfred the Great.

Specifics apart, what was repeatedly underscored was peace as rulership's central purpose—our Bavarian poet's *res regia*—to the point where, by the later tenth century, firm assumptions existed across Western Europe that responsibility for keeping the peace rested with royal authority. The evident failure to do so propelled the development of new strategies to maintain peace and to fill the vacuum perceived to have been created by its collapse.[4] What did it mean, and to whom, to invoke 'peace' in the years after the end of Roman authority? Why talk about peace, as many did, in a world often characterized by endemic violence? Such questions drive this book. Viewed another way, this is an extended meditation upon the relationship between an idea—peace—and an institution—kingship—through the formative centuries of the medieval West, and the historical circumstances, and political and cultural issues that dictated the shifting terms of that relationship. Ideas of peace and of peaceful rulership are key to understanding post-Roman Europe's development of distinct political languages, indebted not only to scriptural ideals and antique models but also informed by new notions of what power was and should be.

SOLOMON IN METZ, 869

In September 869 Sedulius Scottus, the Irish-born polymath who quit his homeland for the opportunities of Francia, composed a poem for the West

---

[3] *MGH Poetae* II, p. 121, lines 15–16: 'Regia prorsus enim res est succurrere paci, / Discreta et regni sceptra movere manu.'

[4] T. Head, 'Peace and Power in France around the year 1000', *Essays in Medieval Studies* 23 (2006), 1–17; R. Landes and T. Head (eds), *The Peace of God: Social Violence and Religious Response in France around the Year 1000* (Ithaca, 1992).

Frankish king Charles the Bald.[5] The occasion was Charles' assumption of the Lotharingian throne, vacant after the death of his nephew, Lothar II, from fever in Piacenza only weeks before.[6] Eight years later Charles would himself succumb to such a fever, a perennial danger of campaigning in the unhealthy air of a late Italian summer.[7] In 869, however, Charles' fortunes seemed high. Lothar's death offered him the chance to reunite two of the three kingdoms created from the Carolingian empire by the treaty of Verdun in 843. This fusion was to be sealed by Charles' coronation in the basilica of St Stephen in Metz, a city long associated with the Carolingian cause and home to St Arnulf's relics, the dynasty's patron and putative founder.[8] Sedulius' verses fêted Charles' arrival in the city. He was the glory of the age, the hero of the Franks, and a worthy heir to both Charlemagne and Louis the Pious.[9] Cleaving to the conventions of *adventus* verse, Sedulius compared Charles to a shining star, inviting his listeners to strew petals in his path and to acclaim him:

'Blessed King Charles comes', let us shout in celebration,
'Holding the paternal sceptre, a peacemaker, like Solomon'.[10]

The world revered Solomon for building a single temple but Charles' fame, observed Sedulius in full panegyric flight, rested upon the construction of a thousand.[11]

The poem was an exercise in the poetic *pièces d'occasion* that embellished Frankish political life, one of several composed by the Irishman that blended the Virgilian with the scriptural to the mixture considered tasteful in ninth-century court circles. In its later lines Sedulius compared Frankish kings and Israel's leaders: Charlemagne was an appropriately patriarchal Abraham, Louis a new Isaac, and Charles, in his turn, Jacob.[12] By 869 such parallels were scarcely

---

[5] On Sedulius Scottus' continental career see L. Mair Davies, 'Sedulius Scottus (*fl.* 840x51–860x74)', *Oxford Dictionary of National Biography* (Oxford, 2004) <http://www.oxforddnb.com/>; P. Godman, *Poets and Emperors, Frankish Politics and Carolingian Poetry* (Oxford, 1987), 155–65, 167–70; M. Lapidge and R. Sharpe, *A Bibliography of Celtic-Latin Literature, 400–1200* (Dublin, 1985), 177–80.

[6] *AB s.a.* 869, pp. 152–68; *AF s.a.* 869, p. 68. J. L. Nelson, *Charles the Bald* (London, 1992), 219–25.

[7] *AB s.a.* 877, pp. 211–21. For a contemporary Carolingian perspective on such matters see the categorical statement of Alcuin, *Epp.* IV, no. 281 (793–804), p. 439: 'Italia infirma est patria . . .'.

[8] O. Oexle, 'Die Karolinger und die Stadt des heilige Arnulf', *FmSt* 1 (1967), 250–364.

[9] Sedulius Scottus, *Carmina*, ed. I. Meyer, CCCM 117 (Turnhout, 1991), no. 12, p. 28, lines 1–10. Commentary: N. Staubach, *Rex Christianus. Hofkultur und Herrschaftspropaganda im Reich Karls des Kahlen, Teil II: Die Grundlegung der 'religion royale'*, Pictura et Poesis, II/2 (Cologne, 1993), 200–10; R. Düchting, *Sedulius Scottus. Seine Dichtungen* (Munich, 1968), 60–4.

[10] *Carm.* no. 12, p. 28, lines 11–12: ' "Rex benedictus adest Carolus", resonemus ovantes, / "Pacificer ut Salemon sceptra paterna tenens".' On the conventions of late antique *adventus* verse see S. MacCormack, *Art and Ceremony in Late Antiquity* (Berkeley, 1981), 17–61 esp. 19–20, 45–6; and C. E. V. Nixon, 'Panegyric in the Tetrarchic and Constantinian Period', in B. Croke and A. M. Emmett (eds), *History and Historians in Late Antiquity* (Sydney, 1983), 88–99.

[11] *Carm.* 12, p. 28, lines 13–14.

[12] *Carm.* 12, p. 29, lines 45–8.

novel.[13] That year, though, the allusion carried specific weight. Solomon had ruled the kingdoms of Israel and Judea. 869 saw Charles extending his authority from West Francia into Lotharingia—a peaceful ruler ready to preside over two Carolingian realms.[14] The world of the first anointed kings provided Carolingian poets with one lexicon of praise. But Sedulius was adept at switching terms and frameworks and, later in the poem, Israelite *regna* gave way to Roman *imperium*. Charles was also a new Augustus, and Sedulius, who seems rarely to have shied from self-promotion, his new Virgil, praising *arma virumque*.[15] The allusion was hardly subtle, but subtlety was not what the occasion demanded for this was public poetry, intended to play its part in the ceremonial sequence of *adventus*, reception, coronation, and celebration that day in 869, and it is not unlikely that Sedulius himself recited this piece of spirited hyperbole before the assembled nobility of West Francia and Lotharingia. Amongst their number was Sedulius' patron, Bishop Franco of Liège, whose support for Charles' planned annexation of Lotharingia goes far to explaining Sedulius' own presence in Metz that autumn.[16] Franco had a role to play on the day, too, taking his place as one of six Lotharingian bishops who officiated at the coronation rite, helping Hincmar of Rheims bless the new ruler as part of the liturgical sequence Hincmar had devised.[17] The blessing that Franco was selected to offer asked God for the new king of Lotharingia's health in mind and body.[18] Had the assembled magnates listening to Sedulius' poetry, possessed the skill to understand his Latin, the will to apply it and, mundanely, been in a position in the congregation that allowed them to hear, they might have been surprised to learn of the extent of Charles' accomplishments.[19] Had their attention held firm as the coronation rite unfolded they might also have noted the reiteration of Sedulius' theme of peace as Hincmar, in the seventh and final blessing, prayed that Charles' enemies be converted to 'the benevolence of peace and charity' and that, amongst other

[13] M. Garrison, 'The Franks as the New Israel? Education for an Identity from Pippin to Charlemagne', in Y. Hen and M. Innes (eds), *The Uses of the Past in the Early Middle Ages* (Cambridge, 2000), 114–61.

[14] On the importance of Charles' dual rule see Nelson, *Charles*, 219–20.

[15] *Carm.* no. 12, p. 29, lines 63–4. For Sedulius' apparent opportunism see Godman, *Poets*, 167–70.

[16] *AB s.a.* 869, p. 157.

[17] Text and commentary: Jackson, *Ordines*, 87–109; *idem*, 'Who Wrote Hincmar's Ordines?', *Viator* 25 (1994), 31–52, at 37–45; A. Sprengler, 'Die Gebete der Krönungsordines Hinkmars von Reims für Karl den Kahlen als König von Lothringen und für Ludwig den Stammler', *ZfKG* 53 (1950/1), 245–67.

[18] Jackson, *Ordines*, 106, no. 21.

[19] C. Pössel, 'The Magic of Ritual', *EME* 17.2 (2009), 112–25, raising at 122–3 the question of the potential variability of individual participant receptivity. For lay attitudes to learning see P. Wormald and J. L. Nelson (eds), *Lay Intellectuals in the Carolingian World* (Cambridge, 2007), with a consideration of Sedulius Scottus' relationship to a particular Carolingian layman, Eberhard of Friuli, offered by me in 'Eberhard of Friuli, a Carolingian Lay Intellectual', at 77–105, esp. 80–8; R. McKitterick, *The Carolingians and the Written Word* (Cambridge, 1989), 211–71.

benefits, peace and tranquillity would flourish in his day.[20] Sedulius had evoked images of peaceful rulership that stretched into antiquity. Here, Hincmar too drew from a long tradition of prayers for rulers. His own innovations would, in turn, enjoy a long life as part of the shared liturgical stock of medieval kingship.

Both poem and *ordo* display a repeated concern that Charles' acceptance as king in Lotharingia would usher in a reign of peace and harmony. The qualities praised by Sedulius the poet and Hincmar the archbishop were formalized into the conceptual core of Charles' new Lotharingian kingship. The Irishman, it would seem, had picked his theme with care. Expatriate poets, after all, must please their patrons.

Peace was a subject for public poetry and petitionary prayer, but for Sedulius Scottus it was also a subject for private reflection. Away from the pomp of the Carolingian court, perhaps back in his dingy lodgings in Liège—a home fit only for moles and owls, he claimed—Sedulius culled definitions of peace from his extensive reading, entering them in a collection that survives as one of the Carolingian period's most extensive *florilegia*.[21] The volume of excerpts and the diversity of texts from which they originated suggest this was an enterprise that spanned years, and one that may well have begun before Sedulius left Ireland.[22] Lines of scripture, and fragments of classical authors (Statius, Publilius Syrus) and church fathers (Augustine, Gregory the Great), as well as a number of homegrown works, were carefully collected and many were organized together beneath the rubric, 'On Peace'.[23] Understanding what peace had meant for earlier generations, for the poets of empire and the fathers of the Church, and the ways in which they had sought to capture its qualities and portray its creation and maintenance, was an enterprise in which Sedulius invested considerable effort. The fruit of some of that study is apparent in his verse, where phrases and images from earlier authors that had caught his eye were reset within the matrix of Sedulius' own words.[24] But they are also apparent in Sedulius' political tract, the *Liber de Rectoribus Christianis* ('the Book of Christian Rulers'), composed around the same time that he produced the Metz panegyric and, like it,

[20] Jackson, *Ordines*, 107–8, nos 27 (turn enemies to peace); 30 (that the king may triumph over visible and invisible enemies, and end his days in peace); 32 (that peace and tranquillity may flourish *in praesenti saeculo*). Staubach, *Rex Christianus* II, 200–10.

[21] *Carm.* no. 4, pp. 8–9, lines 30–1.

[22] Sedulius Scottus, *Collectaneum Miscellaneum*, ed. D. Simpson, CCCM 67 (Turnhout, 1988), best approached with the additional indices of F. Dolbeau, *Supplementum*, CCCM 67 (Turnhout, 1990); see also *idem*, 'Recherches sur le *Collectaneum Miscellaneum* de Sedulius Scottus', *ALatMA* 48–9 (1990), 47–84.

[23] *Collectaneum*, XIII.28, 101–3; LXXX.19, 339.

[24] D. Simpson, 'Sedulius and the Latin Classics', in B. Hudson and V. Ziegler (eds), *Crossed Paths. Methodological Approaches to the Celtic Aspect of the European Middle Ages* (Lanham, MD, 1991), 25–38; J. Meyers, *L'art de l'emprunt dans la poésie de Sedulius Scottus* (Paris, 1986).

intended for the West Frankish king and his intimates.[25] Here, again, his thoughts settled upon peace and peaceful rulership.

The 'Book' was a work of advice and observations on good kingship, one of a number of such 'mirrors' presented by scholars to kings in the course of the ninth century, a largely Carolingian revival of a dormant Latin genre. Peace, wrote Sedulius, was the state for which a ruler should strive. The key to its realization lay in his establishment and maintenance of a right relationship with God. It was this primary personal relationship, based around steadfast faith, merciful, just, and wise rule, and the ruler's pious inner life that brought as its benefit the gift of grace to the kingdom as a whole.[26] Only through the possession of this gift could human society achieve peaceful existence. Even in such ideal circumstances, though, such earthly peace was inherently unstable.[27] Under the cover of its tranquillity, dissent might grow, observed Sedulius, expressing a distrust of peaceful society with deep roots. Peace was, in any case, always susceptible to disruption.[28] Poor or malicious counsel could draw a king from the path of righteousness. Divergence dammed the flow of grace. The Franks may have seen themselves as the New Israel but for Sedulius Scottus theirs was a finely calibrated covenant. When the calibration worked and righteousness reigned, peace was the result, both the sign and substance of communion with God, as the Psalmist made clear: 'For He will speak peace unto His people: And unto His saints: And unto them that are converted to the heart' (Ps. LXXXIV.9).

In some ways 'the Book of Christian Rulers' accorded with the general conventions of Carolingian *specula*, setting out the virtues of the good ruler and addressing the actual practices of correct rulership. For Sedulius, as for his ninth-century contemporary the West Saxon king Alfred the Great, earthly rulership was a matter of technique and *industria*, the craft of governance.[29] Right rule was a man-made thing. Although he was born and educated in Ireland, Sedulius Scottus' surviving writings reveal a grasp of contemporary Carolingian political ideas as firm as his understanding of Carolingian poetic tastes. The 'Book' also revealed the breadth of his historical knowledge, invoking

[25] Staubach, *Rex Christianus*, II, 105–97.
[26] *Liber* cc. 3–4, pp. 27–33.
[27] *Liber* c. 3, pp. 27–8.
[28] *Liber* cc. 3, 6, pp. 28, 37–41.
[29] *Liber, praef.*, 19, lines 1–2. N. Guenther Discenza, 'Power, skill and virtue in the Old English *Boethius*', *ASE* 26 (1997), 81–108; D. Pratt, 'Persuasion and Invention at the Court of King Alfred the Great', in C. Cubitt (ed.), *Court Culture in the Early Middle Ages: The Proceedings of the First Alcuin Conference, Studies in the Early Middle Ages* 3 (Turnhout, 2003), 189–221; J. L. Nelson, 'The Political Ideas of Alfred of Wessex', in A. Duggan (ed.), *Kings and Kingship in Medieval Europe* (London, 1993), 125–8; *eadem*, 'Wealth and Wisdom: the Politics of Alfred the Great', in J. L. Rosenthal (ed.), *Kings and Kingship*, Acta 11 (Binghamton, NY, 1986), 31–52.

a host of figures from the scriptural and classical past from David and Solomon to Leonidas and Theodosius II.[30] An acute sense of the impermanence of earthly peace and, implicitly, of power more generally runs through Sedulius' work. The glory of this world, he observed, was as brilliant and fleeting as a rainbow.[31] The entries in his commonplace book reveal that Sedulius had read and transcribed Augustine's views on the transitory nature of peace in human society. Four centuries divorced master and pupil, but the 'Book' reveals that Sedulius had learnt Augustine's lessons well. They shaped his own political thinking at a fundamental level, contributing to a work that set out a programmatic image of good kingship and its benefits, but which carried, on a deeper level, a sense of the evanescence of any form of effective earthly rule. The contrast between the bombast of his panegyric and the sobriety of his political theorizing is sharp.

Sedulius was an Irish scholar living in the Carolingian middle kingdom, a polity created by the treaty of Verdun, and one almost unique in the early Middle Ages in that its form was brought into being neither by conquest nor colonization but by committee. Its annexation by Charles threatened to end its independent existence less than a quarter century later. Most of Sedulius' time was not spent writing panegyric, composing programmatic political treatises, or reading, but teaching. Grammatical instruction and scriptural rather than political exposition comprise the bulk of his surviving writings, and almost certainly occupied the bulk of his working day.[32] These would earn him the lodging about which he complained, the food, and, more particularly, the drink he portrayed himself fond of.[33] Sedulius' abilities as an exegete and grammarian, rather more than his powers as a poet or as a political theorist, were what made him, and those like him, marketable in the Frankish world.[34] Why had Sedulius quit his homeland? His departure for Francia in the mid 840s has been linked, plausibly, to the

---

[30] *Liber* c. 1, pp. 21–5 (Solomon), c. 3, pp. 27–30 (Saul), c. 4, pp. 30–3 (Solomon), c. 5, pp. 34–7 (Theodosius and Placilla), c. 8, pp. 43–6 (Antiochus, Herod, Pontius Pilate, Pharaoh, Nero, Julian the Apostate, Theoderic), c. 9, pp. 46–9 (Solomon, the Antonines, Constantine, the Theodosii), c. 11, pp. 50–3 (Constantine, Valentinian, Jovian), c. 12, pp. 54–8 (David, Theodosius, Solomon), c. 14, pp. 62–6, (Leonidas, Xerxes), c. 14, pp. 62–6 (Antoninus Pius, Saul, Solomon, David), c. 15, pp. 66–72 (Moses, Hezekiah, the Maccabees, the Theodosii, St Germanus), c. 16, pp. 72–7 (Constantine), c. 17, pp. 77–80 (Julian the Apostate, David), c. 18, pp. 80–4 (David, Constantine, Alexander). For some observations on Sedulius' use of historical exemplars see P. J. E. Kershaw, 'English History and Irish Readers in the Frankish World', in D. Ganz and P. Fouracre (eds), *Frankland. The Franks and the World of Early Medieval Europe* (Manchester, 2008), 126–51, at 129–39.

[31] *Liber* c. 3, p. 28.

[32] Lapidge and Sharpe, *Bibliography*, 177–80.

[33] *Carm.* 9, pp. 23–4, no. 32, pp. 59–60.

[34] Notker, *Gesta Karoli Magna Imperatoris*, ed. H. F. Haefele, *MGH SRG* n.s. 12 (Berlin, 1959), I.1, pp. 1–2, on which see D. Ganz, 'Humour as History in Notker's *Gesta Karoli Magni*', in E. B. King, J. T. Schaefer, and W. B. Wadley (eds), *Monks, Nuns and Friars in Medieval Society*, Sewanee Medieval Studies 4 (1989), 171–83, at 175–6.

intensification of Viking attacks upon Ireland.[35] Whatever his hopes may have been, the Carolingian lands offered little security. Viking, Muslim, and Slavic attacks wracked Western Europe in the middle decades of the ninth century, and Sedulius found himself composing poems celebrating successes over them, including one won by his own bishop.[36] Sedulius praised peace and explored its meaning in his own writings and those of others. It seems to have been a fleeting presence in his own life.

SCOPE OF THIS STUDY

In his praise of Charles the Bald, Sedulius adhered to conventions of Carolingian panegyric and *adventus* verse. So this preface adheres to the conventions of genre, for it is often a commonplace of studies such as this to begin with a single image, event, or episode, and for their authors to argue that in it one might see, condensed, the issues *pars pro toto*. The figure of Sedulius Scottus, reflecting upon the rulers of the scriptural, classical, and earlier medieval past, sifting his reading and considering what peace meant to earlier thinkers, stands as emblematic of the focus of this book and the process of its composition. What Sedulius asked of his sources I ask of mine: how was peace thought of and described? What role did it play in the wider conception of rulership in the early Middle Ages?

Others before me have noted the emphasis placed upon peace in the language of post-Roman rule at particular moments or in specific texts: Alexander Callender Murray for earlier Merovingian Francia, Paul Fouracre and Richard Gerberding for its later form, Karl Schnith for the early eleventh century, Hartmann, Hattenhauer, Ewig, and Renna for the period as a whole.[37] For the Carolingian period, Roger Bonnaud-Delamare's *L'idée paix à l'époque*

---

[35] D. Ó. Cróinín, *Early Medieval Ireland 400–1200* (London, 1995), 226. James Carney's suggestion, that it was the ascendance of the rigorous Céli Dé that drove Sedulius away, remains at least as plausible: 'Sedulius Scottus', in R. E. McNally (ed.), *Old Ireland* (New York, 1965), 230–5.

[36] *Carm.* no. 15, pp. 32–3; no. 25, pp. 48–9; no. 30, pp. 55–7; no. 39, pp. 68–70; no. 45, pp. 80–2; no. 53, pp. 90–1; no. 60, pp. 100–1; no. 67, pp. 109–10. Bishop Hartgar's victory over the Norsemen, *Carm.* no. 8, pp. 21–2. For *Carm.* nos 39, 53, and 67, see Kershaw, 'Eberhard', *Lay Intellectuals*, 83–5.

[37] A. Callender Murray, ' "*Pax et disciplina*": Roman Public Law and the Merovingian State', in T. F. X. Noble (ed.), *From Roman Provinces to Medieval Kingdoms* (London, 2006), 376–88, at 385; P. Fouracre and R. Gerberding, *Late Merovingian France, History and Hagiography 640–720* (Manchester, 1996), 3–4; K. Schnith, 'Recht und Fried. Zum Königsgedanken im Umkreis Heinrichs III', *HJ* 81 (1962), 22–57; H. Hattenhauer, *Pax et iustitia*. Berichte aus den Sitzungen der Joachim Jungius-Gesellschaft der Wissenschaften 3 (Hamburg, 1983); W. Hartmann, *Der Frieden im früheren Mittelalter. Zwei Studien* (Sbuttgart, 1992); E. Ewig, 'Zum christlichen Königsgedanken im Frühmittelalter', in T. Mayer (ed.), *Das Königtum*, VuF 3 (Sigmaringen, 1956), 7–73; H. Kamp, *Friedensstifter und Vermittler im Mittelalter* (Darmstadt, 2001). T. Renna, 'The Idea of Peace in the West', *JMH* 6 (1980), 143–67.

carolingienne spoke both of the early Middle Ages and to contemporary circumstance.[38] Much more recently Ian Wood, reviewing the prayers found in the
Bobbio Missal of c. 700 and their potential origin in Gibichung Burgundy,
expressed some surprise that, 'for a barbarian *regnum*, peace was a central part of
propaganda'.[39] What this book seeks to show is that such surprise might seem
less warranted when set against the substantial position peace occupied in the
political languages of the early medieval West. These emergent kingdoms' drive
for survival and legitimacy led them to develop a political language that stressed
harmony and effective rulership and leaned heavily on an inherited late Roman
political vocabulary that implicitly invoked solidarity and established authority.

The need for a ruler to make and maintain peace, and the legitimacy that often
accrued from its achievement, were hardly ideas peculiar to the early medieval
West. The same decades that saw Charlemagne place heavy emphasis upon peace
and harmony in his legislation and witnessed him acclaimed as a peaceful
emperor in the *laudes* that echoed around St Peter's on Christmas Day 800,
also saw the construction of the new Abbāsid capital at Baghdad, Madīnat al-
Salām, the vizier al-Mansūr's 'City of Peace'. Its name was intended to evoke
Paradise, the paradigmatic place of earthly tranquillity and order for all faiths of
the Book.[40] Similarly, the name of Ch'ang-an, the T'ang capital and, in the
centuries under investigation here, the largest city on the planet, meant 'Long-
lasting Peace'.[41] These were, as Western medievalists have been reminded, the
real places 'where the shots were called' in early medieval Eurasia.[42] Between the
two lay the Uighar empire of Qočo, one of the very few polities to have settled
upon Manichaeism as its official religion, and whose rulers were themselves the
subjects of prayers and hymns that, as might be expected from a religion with

[38] R. Bonnaud-Delamare, *L'idée de paix à l'époque carolingienne* (Paris, 1939), p. i: 'Étudier la
Paix semble répondre à l'une des plus graves préoccupations de l'heure présente'. F. Paxton,
'History, Historians and the Peace of God', in R. Landes and T. Head (eds), *Peace of God*, 21–40.
Bonnaud-Delamare spent the war writing a second thesis, at the École des Chartres, studying peace in
the eleventh and twelfth centuries. Concurrently, in Oxford, Arnaldo Momigliano, was working on
peace and liberty in the ancient world. Neither saw print at the time, but see R. Di Donato (ed.), *Pace
e libertà nel mondo antico. Lezioni a Cambridge: gennaio-marzo 1940* (Florence, 1996); O. Murray,
'Momigliano in England', *History and Theory* 30.4 (1991), 49–64, at 53; C. Dionisotti (ed.), *Ricordo
di Arnaldo Momigliano* (Bologna, 1989), with the text of his inaugural lecture at the University of Pisa
in December 1936 on peace in the ancient world at 109–30.

[39] I. Wood, 'Liturgy in the Rhône Valley and the Bobbio Missal', in Y. Hen and R. Meens (eds),
The Bobbio Missal. Liturgy and Religious Culture in Merovingian Gaul (Cambridge, 2004), 206–18,
at 218.

[40] J. Lassner, *The Shaping of 'Abbasid Rule* (Princeton, 1980), 180. A. Stoclet, 'From Baghdād to
Beowulf: Eulogising "Imperial" Capitals East and West in the Mid-Eighth Century', *Proceedings of
the Royal Irish Academy* C, 105: 4 (2005), 151–95, esp. 166–9.

[41] T. Eckfeld, *Imperial Tombs in Tang China, 618–907: the Politics of Paradise* (London,
2005), 12.

[42] J. L. Nelson, 'England and the Continent in the Ninth Century, I: Ends and Beginnings',
TRHS, 5th series, 12 (2002), 1–21, at 2.

such strident opposition to violence, made much of peace's importance.[43] Closer
to the Carolingian world, ideas of peaceful rule also had their place in Byzantine
political thought: Eastern emperors were acclaimed as *eirenopoios*.[44] Educating
the recently baptized Bulgarian Khan Boris-Michael into the ways of Christian
kingship in the same decade that saw Charles the Bald crowned in Metz, Photios,
Patriarch of Constantinople, emphasized the place of peacefulness amongst a
ruler's qualities.[45] The following year Pope Nicholas I dispatched a long letter to
Boris, written in apparent response to the Khan's own queries about Christian
rulership, revealing that this newly minted member of the family of kings was
concerned, amongst other matters, about quite how he should keep the peace.
When could war be waged? When was one obliged to keep peace with Christian
neighbours? Might a sworn treaty with a Christian neighbour be broken? If so,
when? What, above all, did it mean to be a *Christian* king? Boris was almost
uniquely placed in the later ninth century to assay the visions of kingship offered
by both Rome and Constantinople.[46]

Peace had its place in the political visions of many early medieval cultures, and
other examples could doubtless be added to this brief list. Having acknowledged
the existence of such broad horizons, for the remainder of this book I shall turn
away from them and towards the much more limited territories of the kingdoms
of post-Roman, north-western Europe. That said, such horizons are the wider
setting within which the more focused study takes place, for by seeking to
understand how, where, and why the idea assumed different forms in different
cultures, and more specifically how it found particular expression in early
medieval Europe, this book aims to explore what was distinctive about the
developing political cultures of the post-Roman West. But if geography fails to
set natural limits to my subject neither does chronology. 'What is the greatest
thing in royalty?' Ptolemy II asked the seventy-two Jewish sages who, according
to the Hellenistic confection known as the 'Letter to Philocrates', had visited him
in order to deposit a copy of the Septuagint in Alexandria's library. 'It is that the
subjects may enjoy peace and obtain justice promptly in the courts', came their

[43] H. J. Klimkeit, *Gnosis on the Silk Road. Gnostic Parables, Hymns and Prayers from Central Asia*
(San Francisco, 1993), 156–7; *idem*, 'Manichaean Kingship; Gnosis at Home in the World', *Numen*
29 (1982), 17–32; D. Christian, *Inner Eurasia from Prehistory to the Mongol Empire. A History of
Russia, Central Asia and Mongolia*, I (Oxford, 1998), 266–7.
[44] *Constantini Porphyrogeniti imperatoris De ceremoniis aulae byzantinae*, ed. J. J. Reiske (Bonn,
1829), col. 373.
[45] J. A. Munitz, Jr, 'War and Peace Reflected in Some Byzantine Mirrors for Princes', in *Peace
and War in Byzantium. Essays in Honor of George T. Dennis*, ed. T. S. Miller and J. Nesbitt
(Washington, 1995), 50–61, at 52–3; G. Prinzing, 'Beobachtungen zu "integrierten"
Fürstenspiegeln der Byzantiner', *JÖB* 38 (1988), 1–31; D. Stradouki White, *The Patriarch and
the Prince, the Letter of Patriarch Photios of Constantinople to Khan Boris of Bulgaria* (Brookline, MA,
1982), nos 56, 58, pp. 66–7.
[46] J. Shepard, 'Symeon of Bulgaria—Peacemaker', *Annuaire de l'université de Sofia 'St. Kliment
Ohridski'*, 83 (1989), 9–48; I. Bozhilov, 'L'idéologie politique du Tsar Syméon: Pax Symeonica',
Byzantinobulgarica 8 (Sofia, 1986), 73–88.

collective reply.[47] By Ptolemy II's day, such ideas were already ancient in the respective political traditions to which both parties were heirs.[48] Some aspects of this inheritance will be present in the following pages. For, as we have already seen in the events of Metz in September 869, elements of that deeper history were also exploited by early medieval thinkers. The cultures to which they belonged consistently framed themselves in ways that looked backwards to the classical and scriptural past, drawing extensively upon ideas and images developed in earlier societies with which they sometimes sought vigorously to identify. Kingship is, fundamentally, a retrospective institution.

Sedulius Scottus' historical range reached to ancient Israel and Thermopylae. Mine, here, is less ambitious. This study addresses the world of political ideas and political practice from the late fifth century to the end of the ninth century. This is self-evidently a long period, and many of the issues touched upon in the following chapters could be made—and in some cases have been made—the subject of monographs. Consequently my approach, like Sedulius', will be highly selective. References to peace are plentiful in the early medieval record, something that can be readily established by anyone with a little time, a sense of the synonyms for the 'peace' and its various Latin and vernacular forms, and a few minutes' access to the digital resources that are now key parts of the scholarly armoury. The problem with such tools—beyond the basic issue that for many early medieval texts we possess problematic editions, and in some cases none at all—is that they offer the promise of establishing the location of every reference and the context for none. Nowhere is such a danger more present that in the study of a concept as dangerously diffuse as 'peace'. Moreover, notions of war and peace, indeed some might say many of the abstractions with which early medieval thinkers articulated royal power and the states it generated, can often seem trite until they are grounded in specific circumstance. Such circumstances inflected this language of peace in different ways: shifting emphases, some associations heightened at the expense of others, and so on. There was no single language of peaceful rulership in early medieval Europe. It had many dialects across time, several regional inflections, and it is heard invariably in single voices. Geography, Chris Wickham once observed, works like grace—through people.[49] I hold it as axiomatic that the same can be said of political ideas. Sedulius, balancing scriptural notions and classical ideals, working through the received forms of panegyric, deploying very different ideas of peace as circumstance

[47] F. W. Walbank, 'Monarchies and monarchic ideas', in *idem, et al* (eds), *The Cambridge Ancient History* 7.1, *The Hellenistic World* (Cambridge, 1984), 62–100, at 78–83. See further V. Tcherikover, 'The Ideology of the Letter of Aristeas', *HTR* 51 (1958), 59–85.

[48] J. Baines, 'Origins of Egyptian Kingship', in *Ancient Egyptian Kingship*, ed. D. O'Connor and D. Silverman (Leiden, 1995), 95–156, esp. 142–3.

[49] C. Wickham, *The Mountains and the City* (Oxford, 1981), 6, evoked, colophonically, by P. Horden and N. Purcell, *The Corrupting Sea. A Study of Mediterranean History* (Oxford, 2000), 51.

demanded, and with a sense of the immediate audience for his verse, is the first of
the voices we will hear. It is perhaps worth stressing this last point because there
has been a tendency to write the history of early medieval political thought as a
bloodless subcategory of the history of ideas, shorn of any considerations of their
individual proponents or the precise historical circumstances within which they
existed. In some of its more extreme forms this has led to narratives of development in which hypostasized ideas resemble historical actors, possessing a degree
of independent life verging on the uncanny.[50] Early medieval artists illustrating
Psalm LXXXIV.11 ('Justice and Peace have kissed'), or Prudentius' *Psychomachia*, personified PAX as a female figure, veiled with flowing clothes, who
embraced Justice or dismissed a crowd of similarly personified troubles with a
wave of the hand.[51] Such personifications are best quarantined to the sources
themselves.

This is not to say that ideas were unimportant. Recent work on early medieval
politics has rejected earlier 'statist' interpretive models that linked central authority to the locality through formal bureaucratic state structures, replacing them
with visions of circuits of power in which centre and locality were bonded
through complex meshes of obligation, self-interest, coercion, and, perhaps one
of the more important aspects if also one of the least recoverable, lived experience.[52] Less the product of 'modern' bureaucratic state institutions, successful
early medieval polities might be said to be in large part 'states of mind',
constructed and maintained by allegiances and identities themselves nurtured
by means both formal and informal: from participation in military campaigns or
the exercise of daily duties arising from royal commission through to participation or attendance at the highest and most formally scripted rituals of rulership,
such as Charles the Bald's coronation. In essence, power was a product of
communication above institutionalization, albeit communication whose contexts were made possible by hard material circumstances. Methodologically,
this shift in perspective from agents and agencies signals both an implicit return
to 'mentalités'—albeit in hyper-politicized form—and a renewed engagement
with the vocabulary and the grammar of authority, its concepts, symbols, and
vessels of meaning, as signs of rule and authority in 'real time'. This latter
engagement encompasses both a widened sense of the categories of possible
'symbolic communication', notably through Gerd Althoff's work on the gestural

[50] C. Fasolt, 'Visions of Order in the Canonists and the Civilians', in T. A. Brady, Jr,
H. Oberman, and J. Tracy (eds), *Handbook of European History, 1400–1600: Late Middle Ages,
Renaissance and Reformation* (Leiden, 1995), II, 31–59, at 32–3.

[51] H. Woodruff, 'Illustrated Manuscripts of Prudentius', *Art Studies* 7 (1929), 38–9, 48,
68–9, 73.

[52] H. Hummer, 'Politics and Power', in E. English and C. Lansing (eds), *Companion to the
Medieval World* (Oxford, 2009), 36–67, esp. 36–40. M. Innes, *State and Society in the Early Middle
Ages: The Middle Rhine Valley, 400–1000* (Cambridge, 2000), 4–12, 259–63.

and performative,[53] and the beginnings of a revisiting of its traditional objects of study: an incipient new engagement with the study of *Herrschaftzeichen*, charged with amplified importance as devices for actively generating political authority rather then passively emblematizing it.[54] Further, in the wake of intense debate about 'political ritual' as a category of study, there is a heightened sense of the extant written accounts of such rituals as texts possessing both political content and envisaged political purpose on the part of their authors.[55] Early medieval rulers may not have overseen pre-Geertzian 'theatre states'—both Tim Reuter and Philippe Buc have offered penetrating critiques of those who might confuse Javanese *kraton* with Carolingian *capella*—but their political lives rested upon the articulation of hierarchy, legitimacy, and authority. However, where once such processes were seen as maintaining equilibrium or easily reflective of order, current scholarship would see them as interventions and assertions in an ongoing, fundamentally unstable, debate over power. Nor are current scholars as willing to see strong political content scattered across texts and across distinct media, for example, book art or liturgy, as constituting instrumental programmes of political image propagation with quite the coherence a scholar such as Percy Schramm once did.[56] To understand how early medieval political communication did its work, how rituals and symbols were comprehensible and possessed the possibility to change or confirm attitudes as the subject of contended assertions of meaning ('*this* is what this object or image reveals about the world', '*this* action reveals that this is our current political situation'), we must first understand something of the range and resonances of the ideas being evoked, and the grounds for interpretive divergence and pliancy, as well as the authorities invoked in such readings.[57] Hincmar's carefully constructed *ordo* of 869 was thick with political meaning.

[53] G. Althoff, 'Zur Bedeutung symbolischer Kommunikation für das Verständnis des Mittelalters', *FmSt* 31 (1997), 370–89, and the collected papers, *Die Macht der Rituale. Symbolik und Herrschaft im Mittelalter* (Darmstadt, 2003); *idem, Spielregeln der Politik im Mittelalter. Kommunikation in Frieden und Fehde* (Darmstadt, 1997); *idem, Verwandte, Freunde und Getreue. Zum Politischen Stellenwert der Gruppenbindungen im früheren Mittelalter* (Darmstadt, 1990). J. Barrow, 'Demonstrative Behaviour and Political Communication in later Anglo-Saxon England', *ASE* 36 (2008), 127–50.

[54] I. Garipzanov, *The Symbolic Language of Authority in the Carolingian World (c.751–877)* (Leiden, 2008). S. Maclean and B. Weiler, 'Introduction', *Representations of Power in Medieval Germany*, 800–1500 (Turnhout, 2006), 1–14, esp. 1–7, 11–14.

[55] P. Buc, *The Dangers of Ritual. Between Early Medieval Texts and Social Scientific Theory* (Princeton, 2002), and the responses of A. Walsham, 'Review Article: The Danger of Ritual', *P&P* 180 (2003), 277–87; G. Koziol, 'The Dangers of Polemic: Is Ritual Still an Interesting Topic of Historical Study?' *EME* 11.4 (2003), 367–88. P. Buc, 'The Monster and the Critics: a Ritual Reply', *EME* 15.4 (2007), 441–52. Pössel, 'Magic' offers a commentary on the debate.

[56] D. Warner, 'The Representation of Empire: Otto I at Ravenna', in MacLean and Weiler (eds), *Representation*, 121–40; *idem*, 'Ideals and Action in the Reign of Otto III', *JMH* 25 (1999), 1–18.

[57] Pössel, 'Magic', 113–14, 119–20; S. MacLean, 'Ritual, Misunderstanding and the Contest for Meaning: Representations of the Disrupted Royal Assembly at Frankfurt (873)', in S. MacLean and B. Weiler (eds), *Representations of Power in Medieval Germany, c.800–1500* (Turnhout, 2006), 97–120; Buc, *Ritual*, 79–88.

No less was Sedulius' verse. Part of the work both performed texts did—and in the case of Sedulius' poetry arguably the entire purpose of his occasional verse— was to offer an authoritative reading of immediate events and the politics behind them, and to weave them into a broader fabric, of salvation history, of the Franks' own history, of the worlds of the classical and scriptural past, and the symbolic universe through which early medieval minds made sense of the world and their place within it.

My intention in the chapters that follow is not to attempt to collect every example of peacemaking from the early medieval record, nor to create by aggregation a treatment of the peacemaking processes themselves. Nor is it an attempt to deal with peacemaking in the broadest sense that medieval historians have applied to the phrase, although aspects of this particularly fruitful avenue of research, dispute settlement and conflict resolution, will be raised in the chapters that follow.[58] I am not primarily concerned with kings as lawgivers or lawmakers, an aspect of early medieval rulership whose ideological charge Patrick Wormald so forcefully explored. The continuum between 'peace' and 'law' is particularly well marked for scholars of early English history, where a vision of the 'King's Peace' gradually expanding from immediate proximity of the king and his household in early seventh-century law to encompass additional social and physical spaces (churches, alehouses, assemblies, roads) replaced processes of private redress over which royal overseers presided with something far broader, reorchestrating 'the whole symphony of feud in a royal key'.[59]

In as much as the notion of peacemaking could be seen as encompassing notions of victory, the administration of justice, the creation and maintenance of a harmonious society, it can be read in a loose sense, as a metonym of rulership itself. Our pithy Bavarian poet captured this well: peace was indeed the very stuff of rulership. After all, when a ruler failed to foster or defend it, or at the very least convince others that he did, his days on the throne were numbered, whether the ruler in question was Childeric III or Æthelred *Unraed*. Whilst mindful of these wider resonances of the relationship of peace and early medieval kingship, my focus here is restricted to the explicit depiction of peaceful rulership and specific acts of royal peacemaking. Nor, finally, is this book envisioned as an intervention

---

[58] W. Brown and P. Górecki, 'What Conflict Means: The Making of Medieval Conflict Studies in the United States, 1970–2000', in *eadem* (eds), *Conflict in Medieval Europe. Changing Perspectives on Society and Culture* (Aldershot, 2003), 1–36; S. D. White, 'From Peace to Power: The Study of Disputes in Medieval France', in E. Cohen and M. de Jong (eds), *Medieval Transformations. Texts, Power and Gifts in Context* (Leiden, 2001), 203–18, both of which carry extensive reflections on earlier works. The contribution of the Bucknell group is essential: W. Davies and P. Fouracre (eds), *The Settlement of Disputes in Early Medieval Europe* (Cambridge, 1986); *eidem*, (eds), *Property and Power in the Early Middle Ages* (Cambridge, 1995).

[59] P. Wormald, 'Giving God and King His Due. Conflict and its Regulation in the Early English State', in *idem*, *Legal Culture in the Early Medieval West: Law as Text, Image and Experience* (London, 1999), 333–58, 341. B. R. O'Brien, *God's Peace and King's Peace: The Laws of Edward the Confessor* (Philadelphia, 1999), 73–84 with extensive references.

in the ongoing debates on the so-called 'Peace of God' movement, though by attempting to offer an analysis of early medieval ideas of what peace was, and how the central figure of the ruler created and maintained it, I hope that this study might contribute to a better understanding of the prehistory of the ideas, rhetorical strategies, and expectations of its participants. The notion that in the earlier Middle Ages kings were traditionally responsible for peace is often treated as a given by scholars of the Peace Movement, as it was for the later tenth-century churchmen whose writings they analyse, and as it was already for our Bavarian poet with his pithy definition of *res regia*, but that notion has no intrinsic independent life of its own and 'tradition' is not to be taken on trust. If it *was* a commonplace, how had it come to be so? What historical processes and cultural assumptions propounded and affirmed it?

COWS, CLOAKS, SWORDS, AND HOSTAGES

Peace may have been seen as a general royal responsibility, but at crucial moments it became an issue of paramount importance. Amongst such moments of condensed interest we might number times of unrest, threat, or political transition, insecurity and contention, meetings between kings and diplomatic activities, and peace agreements ending frontier skirmishes and open war.

In the same autumn of 869, while Sedulius celebrated Charles the Bald as a new Solomon, just such peace agreements were being agreed to elsewhere across Western Europe. Several weeks after Charles the Bald's coronation, Roland, archbishop of Arles, was buried. He had been kidnapped by 'Saracens'—Muslim raiders from the Camargue—whilst overseeing the preparation of defences against the possibility of just such an attack. A deal was eventually struck between Franks and raiders and ransom terms set for his return. Under Muslim threats to break off the parley, the price of Roland's redemption was fixed at 150 pounds of silver, 150 cloaks, 150 swords, and 150 slaves. His supporters may well have felt the satisfaction of a job well done as they saw the raiders, once paid, fulfilling their part of the bargain and carrying the Archbishop, dressed in his vestments and mounted on his throne, through the waves to the safety of the Frankish shore. Their delight was short-lived. Roland had died three days before. It was his corpse, propped in his throne, that had been set upon the shore.[60]

Sedulius' notion of peace as a man-made thing is repeatedly borne out by episodes such as these, though few quite so Bergmanesque. One such settlement had been made between the Breton *dux* Salomon (his name itself proof that the Carolingians did not have a monopoly upon Solomonic allusions) and a group of Vikings based on the Loire.[61] According to Regino of Prüm, writing in the early

[60] *AB s.a.* 869, pp. 165–6.
[61] W. Davies, 'Alfred's Contemporaries: Irish, Welsh, Scots and Bretons', in T. Reuter (ed.), *Alfred the Great* (Aldershot, 2003), 323–39, at 332–3.

tenth century, this peace had cost the Breton king 500 cows, no small outlay in ninth-century Brittany, but one that crucially enabled his subjects to return to the harvest.[62] Elsewhere that year, in the Eastern Frankish kingdom in the city of Regensburg, Charles' other brother, Louis the German, lay ill. For the East Frankish author of the *Annals of Fulda* it was the news of this illness that had spurred Charles on to his opportunistic seizure of Lotharingia in contravention of an earlier agreement between the two.[63] Louis' sickness also meant that oversight of the eastern frontiers of the Carolingians' territories had fallen to his sons, Charles—known to later centuries, although not to contemporaries, as 'the Fat'—and Carloman, his older brother.[64] From his sickbed Louis had made peace with the Wends, a Slavic tribe, 'on some kind of terms' (*sub quadam conditione*) in the dismissive words of the West Frankish *Annals of St Bertin*. Charles the Fat, together with the *marchiones* of his territory, confirmed the treaty.[65] Elsewhere on the eastern borders Louis' other son Carloman was campaigning in Bohemia. In defeat the Bohemians asked for and were granted his right hand (*dextras... dari petunt et accipiunt*)—a handshake—the long-established gesture for making peace or establishing a formal political relationship.[66]

Late summer 869 saw similar peace agreements being reached or enforced elsewhere in the early medieval landscape. In Anglo-Saxon England an uneasy peace prevailed between the English and the 'great Viking army' that had arrived on their shores in 865, a peace manifest in a terse entry in the *Anglo-Saxon Chronicle*. 'This year the army (*here*) went back to York, and stayed there a year'.[67] Battle between the allied forces of Wessex and Mercia and the Scandinavian invaders the previous year had ended in deadlock and a settlement. The West Saxon leaders King Æthelred and his younger brother Alfred then returned home. The Viking army moved north to Northumbria, giving those to the south a respite, albeit one that the *Chronicle*'s author, looking back with the hindsight of the early 890s, knew would be brief before nine years of recurrent war. Far to the south in Rome, Pope Hadrian II was less concerned with Vikings or Slavs than with the independent Arab powers of southern Italy, and particularly the Muslim stronghold of Bari, and the terms under which Italy's king Louis II would come to an agreement with Sawdan, its emir. In February 869 Hadrian

---

[62] W. Davies, *Small Worlds. The Village Community in Early Medieval Brittany* (London, 1988), 22–4.

[63] *AF s.a.* 869, p. 69.

[64] S. MacLean, *Kingship and Politics in the Late Ninth Century. Charles the Fat and the End of the Carolingian Empire* (Cambridge, 2003), 2.

[65] *AB s.a.* 869, p. 164.

[66] *AF s.a.* 869, p. 68. For an exhaustive treatment of the handshake in ancient history see S. Knippeschild, *'Drum bietet zum Bunde die Hände': Rechtssymbolische Akte in zwischenstaatlichen Beziehungen im orientalischen und griechisch-römischen Altertum* (Stuttgart, 2002), 16–52.

[67] *ASC s.a.* 869: 'Her for se here eft to Eoforwicceastre 7 þær sæt an gear.'

had asked a visiting delegation of Byzantine monks to pray for him and for Louis II, 'that, for our everlasting peace, Almighty God might make the nation of the Saracens subject to him'.[68] Concerns about war to the south were matched by worries about events north of the Alps. Charles' Lotharingian ambitions had led Hadrian to dispatch several anxious letters about the threat they posed to the empire's peace.[69] The Pope contrasted West Frankish aggression against fellow Christians with Louis II's righteous campaigns against the Saracen 'sons of Belial', and Hadrian's own struggle as Peter's heir to preserve the peace and quiet of the Church. Where Sedulius Scottus praised Solomonic unity, Hadrian II saw discord. But both looked for peace.

In the later ninth century earthly peace may have been praised in verse that evoked the achievements of Solomon, Aeneas, and Augustus, but it was bought with cattle on the hoof, wine, and expensive gifts, such as the prized Frankish cloaks with which Viking raiders kept themselves warm through the extreme cold of ninth-century winters.[70]

The following chapters trace the place of peace in the thoughts of a wide range of minds. For all that, the actual mechanisms for making and keeping peace between polities changed relatively little across this period. Two elements stand central to the early medieval peacemaking process: oath-swearing and the giving up or exchanging of hostages. Both belong to the deep grammar of pre-modern politics, and both were common features of political life from the Atlantic to the Danube in the early Middle Ages.[71] These were shared forms of peacemaking, their basic character readily recognized and applied by very different groups. Together, oath-swearing and hostage-giving fused the threat of divine sanction, however construed by the contracted parties, with the tangible risk of injury or death for those serving as hostages. For a ruler, their failure threatened a visible and dangerous breach of his commitment to prevailing values of honour, obligation, and protection. The coercive power of hostage-taking might seem self-evident, but several early medieval authors' sources sought to clarify its purpose. 'Hostages were given up as assurances that promises would be kept', commented the early ninth-century reviser of the *Annales regni Francorum*. His approximate contemporary, the Lombard Paul the Deacon, was even more explicit. His edition of Pompeius Festus' *De verborum significatu*, assembled after his return to Monte Cassino in the mid 780s, was intended by Paul as a

---

[68] *LP* II, p. 176, 'Oretis pro christianissimo filio nostro Hlodowico imperatore Augusto, ut ei Deus omnipotens ad nostram perpetuam pacem Sarracenorum faciat subditam nationem'.

[69] *MGH Epp.* VI nos. 16, 17, pp. 717–19, 719–20.

[70] M. McCormick, P. E. Dutton, and P. A. Mayewski, 'Volcanoes and the Climate Forcing of Carolingian Europe, A.D. 750–950', *Speculum* 82 (2007), 865–95, esp. 884–7.

[71] For hostages (*géill*) in Sedulius' homeland of early Ireland and the system of *cáin* (clientage), see R. Stacey, *The Road to Judgment: From Custom to Court in Medieval Ireland and Wales* (Philadelphia, 1994), 98–111.

little gift (*munusculum*), a minor addition to Charlemagne's growing library.[72] Festus' substantial original seems to have been stripped of what Paul considered irrelevancy. Nevertheless he kept, as part of the discussion of the preposition *ob*, Festus' etymology of the word *obsides*, 'hostages', with its invocation of a familiar phrase of Roman historians (*fidem praestare*): ' "*obsides*" from "*ob fides*" ', 'those who are given to prove the loyalty of their country'.[73] Charlemagne scarcely needed written instruction on the uses of such hostages; they were long a key means with which he had tied his conquered neighbours into political clientage, though the fact that Paul's brother may well have arrived at the Frankish court as just such a pledge may have given the entry a more private charge.[74] Other explanations were less lofty and far more pragmatic. 'Take hostages from all, that you may be a keen prince, and be able to chastise', was the advice of one metrical Middle Irish wisdom text. Even if the people seem steadfast all will be in vain until their hostages are in your hands, it added. A king without hostages was like ale in a leaking vessel, commented another, possessed of dwindling potency.[75]

In practice, a sliding scale governed the respective investments of the contracting parties. When one side had the upper hand this could turn into one-sided hostage donation, often with the number and selection of close family members of leading men left to the dominant party.[76] With few exceptions all were adult, aristocratic men. Theoderic, famously, had served his time as a hostage, as did countless others.[77] Few were as famous as he and the legendary Walter, or culted like the ill-starred St Pelagius, taken by the Umayyad caliph 'Abd-ar-Rahmān III in the 920s as a surety for Asturian quiescence, executed (according to his Christian hagiographers) for spurning the Caliph's sexual advances and made both the focus of a cult by Sancho of Léon and a verse *vita* by Hrotsvitha of Gandersheim.[78]

[72] Sextus Pompeius Festus, *De verborum significatu quae supersunt cum Pauli epitome*, ed. W. M. Lindsay (Leipzig, 1913). For Paul's dedicatory letter see *MGH Epp.* IV, 508. D. Bullough, 'Charlemagne's court library revisited', *EME* 12.4 (2003), 339–63 at 347.

[73] Festus, *De verborum significatu*, 187: 'obsides pro ob fides, qui ob fidem patriae praestandam dantur'.

[74] A. J. Kosto, 'Hostages in the Carolingian World (714–840)', *EME* 11.2 (2002), 131–2.

[75] T. O'Donoghue, '*Cert cech ríg co réil*', in B. Osborn and C. Marstrander (eds), *Miscellany presented to Kuno Meyer* (Halle, 1912), 258–77, at 261. idem, 'Advice to a Prince', *Ériu* 9 (1923), 43–54, at 51.

[76] For Alfred in 876 see *ASC* A *s.a.* 876; Asser, *Rebus*, c. 49, pp. 36–8, at 37. For Charlemagne, *ARF s.a.* 775, 776, 787, 789. Louis the Pious: *ARF s.a.* 818; Charles the Bald, *AB s.a.* 862, pp. 88–9; Louis the German: *AF s.a.* 864, p. 62. When hostages were not drawn from the highest social order annalists sometimes felt compelled to comment, for example, *Annales Mosellani*, ed. J. M. Lappenberg, *MGH SS* 16 (Hanover, 1859), 494–9, *s.a.* 794, p. 498.

[77] Jordanes, *Getica*, 271, *MGH AA* 5.1 (Berlin, 1882), 128. J. Shepard, 'Manners maketh Romans? Young Barbarians at the Emperor's Court', in E. Jeffreys (ed.), *Byzantine Style, Religion and Civilization. In Honour of Sir Steven Runciman* (Cambridge, 2006), 135–58, at 138–41.

[78] For the cult of Pelagius: R. Collins, 'Queens-Dowager and Queens-Regent in Tenth-Century León and Navarre', in J. C. Parsons (ed.), *Medieval Queenship* (New York, 1993), 79–92. For the tenth-century *vita* by Raguel, see C. Rodriguez Fernández, *La Pasión de S. Pelayo: Edición critica con traducción y comentarios* (Santiago de Compostela, 1991); J. Bowman, 'Beauty and Passion in Tenth-century Córdoba', in M. Kueffler (ed.), *The Boswell Thesis: Essays on 'Christianity, Social*

Pelagius' fate is a reminder that hostagehood in the service of political relations raised issues of honour, obligation, and adaption on the part of the individual hostage. Pelagius was remembered for his resistance to the Caliph's advances. Walter of Aquitaine became, as we shall soon see, more Hunnish than the Huns. In Anglo-Saxon England we see various instances of hostages fighting loyally for the lords in whose trust they were placed, an accommodation that ran with, rather than against, their own values.[79] And when agreements went wrong? If not rape, then mutilation and death. Our sources are, however, strikingly silent on such matters.[80] Within the Carolingian world, military expansion created tangible logistical problems for a Frankish court faced with a substantial inflow of foreign hostages, leading to their dispersal to aristocratic and ecclesiastical households.[81]

To these we must add a set of additional acts: gift-giving, and the transitory activities that metonymically represented a harmonious, well-ordered, and notionally coherent household; feasting, drinking, hunting, and other shared activities; adoption by various means, including weapon bestowal, baptismal sponsorship, and marriage alliances.[82] The latter category raises the question of

---

Tolerance, and Homosexuality' (Chicago, 2006), 236–53; L. A. McMillan, ' "Weighed down with a thousand evils": images of Muslims in Hrotsvit's *Pelagius*', in P. A. Brown, L. A. McMillan, and K. Wilson (eds), *Hrotsvit of Gandersheim: Contexts, Identities, Affinities, and Performances* (Toronto, 2005), 40–55.

[79] For Anglo-Saxon England: *ASC* A *s.a.* 755 (the 'Cynewulf and Cyneheard episode') and Æscferth, 'son of Ecglaf', a hostage in Byrhtferth's entourage who went down fighting at Maldon in 991, *The Battle of Maldon*, lines 265–7, in D. Scragg (ed.), *The Battle of Maldon AD 991* (Oxford, 1991), 29. On his identity, M. Locherbie-Cameron, 'The Men Named in the Poem', in Scragg (ed.), *Maldon*, 242. For just such a realignment of loyalties taking place in Charlemagne's Francia, and the concern that it was happening at the local rather than the central level see *MGH Capit.* I, no. 32 (800), c. 12, p. 86.

[80] For other such silences see Halsall, *Warfare*, 1–9. Some exceptions: Thietmar of Merseburg also noted the Vikings leaving mutilated hostages in the wake of their retreat from Athelstan, *Chronicon*, ed. R. Holtzmann, *MGH SRG* 9 (Berlin, 1935), VIII, c. 40, p. 217. Heming's cartulary recorded a dispute involving one Æthelwine, 'he who had his hands cut off by the Danes whilst a hostage' (*a Danis obses manibus truncatus est*), T. Hearne (ed.), *Hemingi Chartularium Ecclesiae Wigorniensis* (Oxford, 1723), I, 259–60. In 1014 Cnut abandoned the English hostages his father had demanded the previous year on the shore at Sandwich. The E *Chronicle* noted that they had lost their hands and noses. The C and D versions added that they had also lost their ears *ASC s.a.* 1014. For a literary treatment of capture by Vikings as a situation for (justified) sexual fears see the tenth-century satirical poem *Moriuht: A Norman Latin Poem From the Early Eleventh Century*, ed. and trans. C. J. McDonough (Toronto, 1995), 77.

[81] J. L. Nelson, 'Charlemagne and Empire', in J. Davis and M. McCormick (eds), *The Long Morning of Medieval Europe. New Directions in Early Medieval Studies* (Aldershot, 2008), 223–34, at 224–8; R. Lavelle, 'The Use and Abuse of Hostages in Later Anglo-Saxon England', *EME* 14.3 (2006), 269–96. For Frankish issues of hostage dispersal, see the Mainz hostage *indiculus*, *MGH Capit.* I no. 115 (c. 805/6), 233–5; no. 32 (800), c. 12, p. 86; no. 45 (February, 806) c. 13, p. 129; no. 99 (781 x 810), c. 10, p. 207.

[82] The bibliography on all these subjects is extensive. Entry points include B. Jussen, *Spiritual Kinship as Social Practice: Godparenthood and Adoption in the Early Middle Ages* (Newark, DE, 2000); J. Lynch, *Godparents and Kinship in Early Medieval Europe* (Princeton, 1986); B. Effros, *Creating Community with Food and Drink in Merovingian Gaul* (New York, 2002); G. Althoff, *Family, Friends and Followers. Political and Social Bonds in Early Medieval Europe*, trans. C. Carroll

gender. Paradoxically, perhaps, given that peace personified was consistently represented as female, the majority of the peacemaking procedures we see in our sources were the province of ruling male elites. Royal women had important roles to play, however, as participants in the ceremonial life of a royal household and hospitality, and were self-evidently central to political marriages. Such tasks come together in the familiar figure of 'the peaceweaver', the *freoðuwebbe*, a type drawn from the *Beowulf*-poet's image of queens, Hild, Freawaru, and particularly Wealhtheow, the *friðusibb folca* ('peace relation of the peoples'), hostess at Hrothgar's court who bonded host and guest, created community and, through the prioritization of her attention, enacted hierarchy.[83] Whilst marriage alliances are not uncommon outside the Old English poetic corpus they largely occur as a means of fostering and furthering pre-existing positive relationships, often at potentially dangerous moments, rather than establishing a sharp transition from outright hostility to peace.[84] Nor did they exist in isolation, but were in tension with other bonds, obligations, and potentially other marriages, factors of partic-ular importance at moments such as the early sixth century or the early tenth, when we see a web of marriages linking ruling houses.[85] Often such alliances seem to have been possible only where perceptions existed of cultural or political commonalities, or by the willingness of the dominant party to countenance the

(Cambridge, 2004), 152–6; *idem*, 'Der frieden-, bündnis- und gemeinschaftsstiftende Charakter des Mahes im früheren Mittelalter', in I. Bitsch, T. Ehlert, and X. Von Ertzdorff (eds), *Essen und Trinken in Mittelalter und Neuzeit* (Sigmaringen, 1987), 13–25; D. Bullough, *Friends, Neighbours and Fellow-Drinkers: Aspects of Community and Conflict in the Early Medieval West* (Cambridge, 1991). F. Curta, 'Merovingian and Carolingian Gift Giving', *Speculum* 81 (2006), 671–99. I. Voss, *Herrschertreffen im frühen und hohen Mittelalter. Untersuchungen zu den Begegnungen der ostfränkischen und westfränkischen Herrscher im 9. und 10. Jahrhundert sowie der deutschen und französischen Könige vom 11. bis 13. Jahrhundert* (Cologne, 1987); M. Wielers, 'Zwischenstaatliche Beziehungsformen im frühen Mittelalter (Pax, Foedus, Amicitia, Fraternitas)', Habilitationsschrift (University of Münster, 1959).

[83] L. Sklute, '*Freoðuwebbe*', in H. Damico and A. Hennessy Olsen (eds), *New Readings on Women in Old English Literature* (Bloomington, IN, 1990), 204–10, modified by the observations of A. Hall, 'A Present, a Potentate and a Peaceweaver in *Beowulf*', *Studia Neophilologica* 78.1 (2006), 81–7, at 85, whose translation I follow here. M. J. Enright, *Lady with a Meadcup. Ritual, Prophecy, and Lordship in the European Warband from La Tène to the Viking Age* (Dublin, 1996), 1–37.

[84] R. Abels, 'Paying the Danegeld: Anglo-Saxon Peacemaking with Vikings', in Philip de Souza and John France (eds), *War and Peace in Ancient and Medieval History* (Cambridge, 2008), 173–92. For the limited and non-gender-specific occurrence of the compound in the Old English record see Sklute, '*Freoðuwebbe*', in *New Readings*, 204–10. A. Welsh, 'Branwen, *Beowulf*, and the Tragic Peaceweaver Tale', *Viator* 22 (1991), 1–13; J. Chance, *Woman as Hero in Old English Literature* (Syracuse, NY, 1986), 1–11. L. Eshelman, 'Weavers of Peace, Weavers of War', in D. Wolfthal (ed.), *Peace and Negotiation: Strategies for Coexistence in the Middle Ages and the Renaissance*, (Turnout, 2000) 15–37; C. Parrish Jamison, 'Traffic of Women in Germanic Literature. The Role of the Peace Pledge in Marital Exchanges', *Women in German Yearbook* 20 (Lincoln, NE, 2004), 13–36.

[85] S. MacLean, 'Making a Difference in Tenth-Century Politics: King Athelstan's Sisters and Frankish Queenship', in Fouracre and Ganz, *Frankland*, 167–90, at 180–1.

notion that the other side might indeed possess such shared ground or have the potential to do so. Marriages to seal peace between Anglo-Saxon kings and Vikings are noticeably absent from the ninth-century record as, for that matter, is evidence of similar strategies between the Franks and Saxons in the century before. Arguments from absence these both may be, but it remains striking that it is not until Athelstan's reign that we have a firm record of a marriage compact with a Scandinavian ruler. In 927, one of Athelstan's daughters married Sihtric *Cáech*, the newly baptized king of Jorvik, an indicator to Richard Abels that 'the House of Wessex now regarded Scandinavian kings as no different from other territorial rulers'.[86]

In certain cases the marriage itself might have been both a recognition of shared value and a means by which it might be further inculcated, bringing with it religious and cultural change as much as it affirmed a political relationship. Nelson has suggested this was the case of Theoderic's unnamed niece ('a one-woman civilizing process'), sent by her uncle to marry the Thuringian king Hermenfrid around 506 and dispatched with a letter written by Cassiodorus making clear to her new husband and his court the added value she brought to the rough Thuringians.[87] The contrast with male hostages is noteworthy: men in foreign households were acculturated, women in foreign households were agents of culture. For royal women seeking to foster peace under their own initiative and free from a male-dominated framework a further strategy was available: prayer, either their own or the formal commissioning of prayers for peace from religious communities, an approach favoured by both Radegund and Balthild in the later seventh century, according to their biographers.[88]

Many of these activities broadcast simple political signals of their own that required little learning and only basic life experience to grasp.[89] Carefully constructed 'rituals' were not always necessary in a world in which early medieval royal and aristocratic power was, by its very lived materiality, enunciative, particularly when considered against the prevailing background of the marginal existence of the majority.[90] Peacemaking of the kind we have seen from 869 took place across that landscape in late autumn precisely because the campaign season was drawing to a close. Armies could no longer be kept in service, and the demands of harvest-time, to pick grapes or gather crops (or to skim surplus from

---

[86] R. Abels, 'Peacemaking', 189.

[87] J. Nelson, 'Gendering Courts in the Early Medieval West', in L. Brubaker and J. M. H. Smith (eds), *Gender in the Early Medieval World* (Cambridge, 2004), 185–97, at 186–7, 192–3.

[88] *Vita Sanctae Balthildis*, ed. B. Krusch, *MGH SRM* 2 (Hanover, 1888), 477–508, cc. 5, 9, 487–8, 493–4. Y. Hen, *The Royal Patronage of the Liturgy in Frankish Gaul to the Death of Charles the Bald*. HBS *Subsidia* 3 (London, 2001), 37–41.

[89] Pössel, 'Magic', 122.

[90] A. Al-Azmeh, *Muslim Kingship: Power and the Sacred in Muslim, Christian and Pagan Politics* (London, 1997), 3; K. Leyser, 'The Tenth Century Condition', in *idem*, *Medieval Germany and its Neighbours 900–1250* (London, 1982), 1–9.

those who did) exerted a steady homeward pull that kings had to contend with.[91] Sedulius Scottus' own public theorizing was itself undertaken in the hope of similar reward with food and drink, for the same hard realities governed the lives of early medieval ideologues, too.[92] The record for 868/9 reflects this. According to the *Annals of Xanten*, written by an anonymous Lotharingian vehemently hostile to West Frankish ambition, the year before Charles the Bald was crowned in Metz many of his subjects were, as a result of floods and famine, surviving on a diet of dog meat and the flesh of their dead.[93]

IDEAL, REALITY, AND TEXTUALITY

The contrast between starving peasants and a king lauded for initiating a new golden age of peace sharply evokes 'the tensions between the cultivated image and the brutal realities of early medieval western society' that has informed much work over the last few decades.[94] That such harsh conditions existed on the ground we can have no doubt, as physical anthropology and historical osteology make clear.[95] Nevertheless, the depiction of such apparent brutal realities could be no less artless nor any less politically directed than Sedulius' hymn to the creation of Charles the Bald's new Israel. For 868 the *Xanten* author set out the contrast between the king's claim of peacefulness and the realities of life away from court in stark and wholly intended terms. It offered the image of a world in profound disorder: severe weather, the appearance of a comet 'on the holy night of Septuagesima', followed by 'winds and a great flood'.[96] Charlemagne's empire was split between a number of rulers, of which Louis the German was, in the annalist's opinion, 'wiser and more just than the rest'.[97] The division was the result of collective misbehaviour, he continued, turning to scripture to give his opinion weight, and citing Proverbs XXVIII.2: 'For the sins of the land many are the princes thereof'. For early medieval readers Proverbs was one of the five Solomonic books. While Sedulius praised Charles as a new Solomon, the anonymous *Xanten* annalist levelled criticism imbued with the weight of authority and wisdom of Solomon's own words.[98]

---

[91] K. Leyser, 'Money and Supplies on the First Crusade', in T. Reuter (ed.), *Communications and Power. The Gregorian Revolution and Beyond* (London, 1994), 77–97; G. Halsall, *Warfare*, 149–51.

[92] *Carm.* no. 9, pp. 23–4; no. 32, pp. 59–60.

[93] *AX s.a.* 869 [868], pp. 26–7.

[94] P. Wormald, 'Foreword', *Ideal and Reality*, x.

[95] R. Fleming, 'Bones for Historians: Putting the Body back in Biography', in D. Bates (ed.), *Writing Medieval Biography: Essays in Honour of Frank Barlow* (Woodbridge, 2006), 29–48.

[96] S. Ashley, 'The Power of Symbols: Interpreting Portents in the Carolingian Empire', *Medieval History* 4 (1996), 34–50.

[97] *AX s.a.* 869 [868], p. 27: 'Ludewicus filius . . . qui sapientior et iustior caeteris'.

[98] W. Horbury, 'The Wisdom of Solomon', in J. Day, P. Gordon, and H. G. M. Williamson (eds), *Wisdom in Ancient Israel* (Cambridge, 1995), 182–96, at 186–9.

The *Annals of Xanten*'s entry for 869 recounting the previous year's events, hints at just how pervasively politicized and allusive even seemingly straightforward accounts might be. Ostensibly a spare account of earthly collapse and poor weather—life on the ground—the annalist deployed Solomonic language and Israelite motifs in a very different way from Sedulius in order to encode potent political criticism. Implicit in his image of natural disaster was the commonplace contemporary notion, articulated in a range of prayers and political tracts, perhaps most famously the Irish work *De XII Abusivis Saeculi* ('On the Twelve Abuses of the World') that the order of the natural world reflected, and could be affected by, a ruler's personal qualities.[99] In particular, ninth on the tract's list of 'abuses', which were archetypal instances of flawed members of society such as the youth without obedience, the irreligious elder, the immodest woman, and so on, was the *rex iniquus* ('the unjust or unfair king') whose own failure to apply self-rule brought crop failure, famine, war, infertility, and no peace for his people. The *Xanten* annalist offered not only his own but also the cosmos' criticisms of Charles' kingdom, the very inverse of the Hincmar and Sedulius portaits.

PEACE IN THE EARLY MEDIEVAL IMAGINATION

Poems, prayers, individual annal entries recording partisan perspectives of 'what happened': all were products of the early medieval imagination, a term I use here to recognize that all sources, however seemingly prosaic, are contingent products of human creativity. Some outlets afforded greater imaginative play, others less. To get a sense of that range, and with it the pervasiveness of our theme in early medieval culture, let us close by looking at two very different types of text: heroic epic and peace treaties. Peacemaking and peacekeeping were recognized categories for those working and thinking in the epic mode that audiences could be expected to recognize and respond to. Some sense of the degree to which they marble the early medieval literary record might be gained by a brief consideration of two of the more substantial literary monuments of the early Middle Ages: the *Waltharius* and *Beowulf.*

---

[99] Text: *De XII Abusivis Saeculi*, ed. S. Hellmann. *Texte und Untersuchungen zur Geschichte der altchristlichen Literatur* 34.1 (Leipzig, 1909), 1–61. A. Breen, 'The Date, Provenance and Authorship of the Pseudo-Patrician Canonical Materials', *ZRGKA* 81 (1995), 83–129; idem, 'Pseudo-Cyprian *De Duodecim abusivis saeculi* and the Bible', in P. Ní Chatháin and M. Richter (eds), *Irland und die Christenheit. Bibelstudien und Mission/Ireland and Christendom. The Bible and the Missions* (Stuttgart, 1987), 230–45; H. H. Anton, 'Pseudo-Cyprian: *De duodecim abusivis saeculi* und sein Einfluss auf den Kontinent, insbesondere auf die karolingischen Fürstenspiegel', in H. Löwe (ed.), *Die Iren und Europa im Frühen Mittelalter* (Tubingen, 1982), II, 568–617. On the cosmic consequences of kingship see R. Meens, 'Politics, Mirrors for Princes, and the Bible: Sins, Kings and the Well-being of the Realm', *EME* 7.3 (1998), 345–57; M. Blattman, 'Ein Ungluck für sein Volk: der Zusammenhang zwischen Fehlverhalten des Königs und Volkswohl in Quellen des 7.–12. Jahrhunderts', *FmSt* 30 (1996), 80–102.

Peace agreements between the Franks, Burgundians, and Aquitanians with Attila's Huns provided the collective premise behind the ninth- or tenth-century epic the *Waltharius*, and the adventures of its eponymous hero, Walter.[100] In the poem's opening lines the Franks, under the rule of King Gibich, gripped with terror in the face of the Huns' onslaught, agree to make immediate peace with Attila, 'clasping right hand in right hand' (like Carloman's Bohemians in autumn 869), and offering hostages and tribute.[101] Similar decisions were made at the courts of Burgundy and Aquitaine, and it is the direct consequence of these decisions to sue for peace with Attila that the poem's three central figures— Walter, the Aquitanian prince, Hiltgund, the daughter of the Burgundian king Heiric (and Walter's betrothed), and the Frankish noble Hagan—come to the Hunnish court. Walter's experiences there, his rise to pre-eminence as he out-performs his Hunnish peers, his friendship with Hagan, and his eventual escape and subsequent adventures all take place within the context of the experience of hostagehood at a former enemy's court. Indeed the *Waltharius* might be read as a working through, in heroic mode, of the consequences of hostage donation. The existence of fragments of what appears to be the poem's Old English analogue, *Waldere*, together with the appearance of several of the *Waltharius*' protagonists in other surviving verse, notably the Old English *Widsið* from the Exeter Book, hints that the Walter narrative was but one strand of a much larger and more complex skein of Germanic narratives that mixed the mythic and the quasi-historical, albeit one which, for its written expression, was heavily indebted to scripture and the Latin hexameter tradition.[102]

Kingship's complex relationship to peace is also explored in *Beowulf*.[103] From Scyld Scefing's arrival at the poem's beginning, through the flawed peace of the ageing Hrothgar's reign—prematurely crowned by the construction of Hrothgar's

---

[100] *MGH Poetae* VI, 26–83. The bibliography on the *Waltharius* is sizeable and key issues remain vexed. Recent studies, with reference to earlier literature, include J. Ziolkowski, 'Fighting Words: Wordplay and Swordplay in the Waltharius', in K. E. Olsen, A. Harbus, and T. Hofstra (eds), *Germanic Texts and Latin Models. Medieval Reconstructions, Germania Latina* 4 (Leuven, 2001), 29–52.

[101] *Waltharius*, *MGH Poetae* VI, p. 25, lines 22–4.

[102] A. Bisanti, 'Il Waltharius fra tradizioni classiche e suggestioni germaniche', *Pan* 20 (2002), 175–204; A. Hennessey Olsen, 'Formulaic Tradition and the Latin Waltharius', in H. Damico and J. Leyerle (eds), *Heroic Poetry in the Anglo-Saxon Period. Studies in Honor of Jess B. Bessinger Jr.* Studies in Medieval Culture 32 (Kalamazoo, 1993), 265–82; G. F. Jones, 'The Ethos of the Waltharius', in F. E. Coeenan, W. P. Friederich, G. S. Lane, and R. P. Rosenberg (eds), *Middle Ages—Reformation—Volkskunde, Festschrift John G. Kunstmann* (Chapel Hill, 1959), 1–20; P. Dronke, 'Functions of Classical Borrowing in Medieval Latin Verse', in *Classical Influences on European Culture A.D. 500–1500* (Cambridge, 1971), 159–64, at 160–2. For the text of the *Waldere* fragments, *ASPR* VI, 4–6.

[103] M. Lapidge, 'The Archetype of Beowulf', *Anglo-Saxon England* 29 (2000), 5–41, on which see R. Frank, 'A Scandal in Toronto: The Dating of Beowulf a Quarter Century On', *Speculum*, 82.4 (2007), 843–64. For the cultural common ground of the *Waltharius* and *Beowulf* see A. Orchard, *A Critical Companion to Beowulf* (Woodbridge, 2003), 136–7; F. P. Magoun, 'A Note on Old West Germanic Poetic Unity', *Modern Philology* 43 (1945), 77–82.

hall, Heorot, and ruptured by Grendel's raiding—to Beowulf's fifty-year service as protector of his people whose death inaugurates an age of war, in *Beowulf* kingship is repeatedly framed in terms of the ability of a ruler to keep his people's peace and protect them from attack, supernatural or otherwise. Grendel's attacks, in this context, are profoundly disruptive because they are prosecuted without the possibility of settlement and directed with vehemence against Heorot, the very place above all where a king's peace should hold good, undermining Hrothgar's authority even as they served to define Grendel's bestial inhumanity.[104] Little wonder, then, that one commentator has seen in the figure of Beowulf, the defender of Heorot and the Geatish restorer of the Danish king Hrothgar's peace, as the poet's 'heathen prince of peace'.[105] In *Beowulf*'s poetic universe kings brought peace through force of arms, defending their people and overseeing harmony amongst their followers within the hall.[106] And it is *Beowulf*, too, that is one of the three works that gives us the figure of the *freoðuwebbe*, 'the peaceweaver', whom we have already encountered.

In *Beowulf* peaceful reigns come to their natural conclusion or are abruptly interrupted by external savagery. The ageing Hrothgar is unable to uphold the peace of his hall and the safety of his subjects. Peaceweaving marriages ultimately fail.[107] Beowulf's own account of the Danish princess Hildeburh, is a 'tale within a tale' in which Hildeburh's marriage to the Frisian Finn ended in carnage with the death of Finn, their son, and her brother, and Hildeburh's return from the disastrous alliance to Denmark.[108] Similarly, the other peacemaking marriage of *Beowulf*, that of Hygelac's daughter Freawaru to the Heathobard prince Ingeld, founders at the wedding feast. There, recognition by one Heathobard warrior that the arms and armour borne by a young Dane were once the possessions of a dead comrade (slain in the very strife the marriage sought to terminate) sparks renewed violence.[109] *Beowulf*'s consistently dark treatment of peace also finds expression in the act that initiates the sequence of events culminating in Beowulf's own death in battle with the dragon. The theft of a goblet from its hoard provokes the dragon's attack—ironically, an act intended to provide a peacemaking gift for the thief to present to his estranged lord. Intended to re-establish good relations, the goblet's theft instead precipitates destruction on a massive scale, provoking the dragon's attack and leading directly to Beowulf's death and,

---

[104] *Beowulf and The Fight at Finnsburg*, ed. F. Klaeber, 3rd edn (Boston, 1950), lines 150–65.

[105] R. Frank, 'Skaldic Verse and the Date of Beowulf', in C. Chase (ed.), *The Dating of Beowulf* (Toronto, 1981), 123–39, at 133. On Hrothgar's kingship and its weaknesses, see R. Derolez, 'Hrothgar, King of Denmark,' in H. Maes-Jelinek, P. Michel, and P. Michel-Michot (eds), *Multiple Worlds, Multiple Words. Essays in Honour of Irène Simon* (Liège, 1987), 51–8; M. Brennan, 'Hrothgar's Government', *JEGP* 84 (1985), 3–15.

[106] J. W. Earl, *Thinking about Beowulf* (Stanford, 1994), 100–36.

[107] G. Overing, 'The Women of Beowulf', in P. Baker (ed.), *The Beowulf Reader* (New York, 2001) at 219–60, at 224–48.

[108] *Beowulf*, lines 1066–159.

[109] *Beowulf*, lines 2024–69.

with it, the end of the peace for the Geats as a whole.[110] What began as an individual's search for peace ends with its destruction for a community. Peace, the kings who created it, the processes that brought it about (or at least sought to), and the constant presence of forces that threatened to end it, both supernatural (Grendel, the dragon) and natural (enemy tribes, old age), provided the *Beowulf*-poet with key material for his interlocking themes.[111]

Taken together, these poems reflect something of the sensibilities, interests, and concerns to be found in the ambient cultures that produced them.[112] For the moment, this sketch should make the case that the subjects of this book were ones that also attracted early medieval exploration. The family of early medieval thinkers on peace to which Sedulius and the unnamed figures behind *Beowulf* and the *Waltharius* belonged will be the one that we shall track in the chapters that follow. As a theme, a historically significant act, and a manifestation of rulership with its place in the wider theories of royal power and the qualities of an ideal ruler, peace had its place in the literature of early medieval Europe and in particular moments of specific lives and political events, when it became the subject of concerted interest.

Comparably demanding in human ingenuity, though less free in the range of its application, was the production of written peace treaties between early medieval leaders. Here the imaginative enterprise was not to frame past events for a political purpose so much as to shape future events by pragmatic planning in the present.

Whilst narrative references to rulers making and keeping peace are not uncommon, the same cannot be said of extant early medieval peace treaties. Responding in August 599 to a request by the Visigothic king Reccared for copies of the Visigoth's treaties (*pacta*) with Justinian kept in Constantinople's imperial archives, Gregory the Great was negative.[113] The request could not be fulfilled, he replied: the *cartofilacium* keeping the records of Justinian's reign were lost to fire.[114] Gregory's inability to recover the requested text of the Visigothic-Byzantine treaty is emblematic of the poverty of extant early medieval peace treaties. If our narratives carry frequent references to treaties and to agreements,

---

[110] *Beowulf*, lines 2278–86.

[111] E. Wilson, 'The Blood Wrought Peace: A Girardian Reading of *Beowulf*', *English Language Notes* 34 (1996), 7–30. C. R. Davis, *Beowulf and the Demise of Germanic Legend in England* (New York, 1996), 113–17.

[112] P. Wormald, 'Bede, *Beowulf*, and the Conversion of the Anglo-Saxon Aristocracy', in S. Baxter (ed.), *The Times of Bede* (Oxford, 2006), 30–100, with additional notes at 100–6. J. M. Hill, *The Cultural World in Beowulf* (Toronto, 1995).

[113] M. Vallejo Girvés, 'The Treaties between Justinian and Athanagild and the Legality of Byzantium's Peninsular Holdings', *Byzantion* 66 (1996), 208–18. A. D. Lee, 'Treaties in Late Antiquity, in Philip de Souza and John France (eds), *War and Peace in Ancient and Medieval History* (Cambridge 2008), 107–19.

[114] *Ep.* IX.299c, pp. 225–6.

some no doubt committed to writing, only a handful survive. That many more once existed there can be little doubt. Reccared's request to Gregory reveals that he, for one, believed several copies to have been produced in the past and subsequently held by both parties, a practice we know occurred in contemporary Byzantine relations with the Sasanids.[115]

The handful of treaties that survive for the post-Roman West differ markedly in date, path of survival, specific historical context, form, and vision. That all reveal concerted efforts to articulate ideas of harmony and peaceful coexistence between distinct groups, and enshrine concrete procedures by which that might come about, ought not to be lost to us. However, any attempt to analyse a body of texts as a textual category in its own right is fraught. No treaty survives in what can be shown to have been its original form. Those that survive have been transmitted in one of two ways. The treaty of Andelot survived embedded in the text of Gregory of Tours' *Ten Books of History* whilst that between the Byzantines and the Sasanids survived in the fragments of Menander Protector's histories found in the *Souda*.[116] The remainder have been transmitted through their inclusion in legal manuscripts, such as the post-Conquest collection of Anglo-Saxon treaties and law-texts in Cambridge, Corpus Christi College, MS 383, or in Carolingian capitulary compilations such as Hague 10 D 2, a Rheims product of the later ninth century. Unsurprisingly, the few treaties we have neither conform rigidly to a uniform structure nor form part of an easily identifiable treaty tradition. Coming as they did at the end of negotiations, they served as both an idealized portrait of the relationship created between the parties and the terms upon which it was meant to continue. They necessarily followed the meeting, discussion, and, however coerced or mutually decided, the agreement. The written terms of a peace treaty might be referred to later, as by Gregory of Tours in his confrontation with Guntram, for example, or cross-referenced by other codes, such as Edward's laws' reference to the written 'peace treaties' (*friðgewritu*) in tenth-century Anglo-Saxon England. The Carolingian treaties of the ninth century reveal a level of textual interplay that hints at an awareness of an ongoing tradition of treaty production. Some of the surviving treaties do contain occasional references to the ritual context of peacemaking, at least in terms of individuals present, the location where the agreement was made, the specific terms reached, or the means by which the compact was sealed. It is clear that, at least in sixth-century Italy and Francia, rulers signed a copy of the treaty.[117] During the Gothic wars Belisarius infamously refused to sign a treaty with Wittigis in 540, on the grounds that peace would have robbed him of the

---

[115] J. Wiesehöfer, 'From Achaemenid Imperial Order to Sasanian Diplomacy: War, Peace, and Reconciliation in Pre-Islamic Iran', in K. Rauflaab (ed.), *War and Peace in the Ancient World* (London, 2006), 121–40, esp. 132–3.

[116] Lee, 'Treaties', 106–8.

[117] On issues of late antique and early Byzantine treaties and diplomacy see A. D. Lee, 'Byzantine Treaties', in *idem, Information and Frontiers. Roman Foreign Relations in Late Antiquity* (Cambridge,

chance to present a Gothic king before Constantinopole's crowds.[118] The wary Goths in their turn demanded that Belisarius both formally sign and swear to uphold the treaty's terms. Similar dual practices are evident in Gregory of Tours' account of Andelot: oath-swearing and written subscription were seen as complementary processes.[119]

A shared function was common to these texts, which may be approached as belonging to a recognizable common category: each endeavoured to set out notional patterns of behaviour and interaction in a fashion that afforded those involved the opportunity to engage in political image-building. As such, these treaties are discussed here primarily as articulations of political ideas. In the chapters below I address the extant treaty texts that fall within this book's limits: the Frankish agreement of Andelot (587), the numerous ninth-century Carolingian intra-familial treaties from the middle decades of the ninth century, and Alfred's treaty with the Viking leader Guthrum from the 880s. With so sparse a corpus upon which to base any analysis it is hard to engage in a credible way with issues of origins and development.[120]

As this initial sketch hopes to show, the relationship between peace and power that lies at the heart of this book was one that could be explored by many authors working in many different genres to a similarly broad range of purposes. Before we address these relationships we have an even more basic question to ask: what was meant by peace in the early Middle Ages?

1993); A. Gillett, *Envoys and Political Communication in the Late Antique West, 411–533* (Cambridge, 2003), with references.

[118] *Bell. Goth.* VI.29.5–6.

[119] For the relationship of oath and subscription in Greek and Roman treaties, E. Meyer, *Legitimacy and Law in the Roman World. Tabulae in Roman Belief and Practice* (Cambridge, 2004), 96–7.

[120] Gillett, *Envoys*, 249.

1

Solomon's Temple, Augustus' Altar, and Edwin's Roads: Peace in the Political Imagination

> For I know the thoughts that I think towards you, saith the Lord, thoughts
> of peace, and not of affliction, to give you an end and patience.
>
> Jeremiah XXIX.11

Hrabanus Maurus, warning the Emperor Lothar against the false claims of false prophets, diviners, and dream interpreters in his commentary on Jeremiah, reminded him that God's thoughts were His alone.[1] But early medieval men and women had thoughts about peace, too. Can we recover them? More specifically, what was the peace that peaceful rulership created or maintained? The attempt to recover conceptual fields that were meaningful to early medieval minds is a vexing one. Concrete definitions of even quite technical terms are highly problematic for the early Middle Ages, those of abstractions such as 'peace' even more so. There was no single definition, no authoritative conception of peace in the early Middle Ages. Peace was a concept present in a number of fields of thought, religious, liturgical, political, and legal, many of which had deep roots. Such vocabularies did not exist in conceptual quarantine but interconnected and overlapped, or were inadvertently or intentionally confused. This potential for polyvalency makes it imperative that we address these ideas at some length, not least to establish what might be called the tonal complexity that even seemingly simple statements possessed.

Common to many was their frequent use of the Latin word that recurs with inevitable frequency in these chapters: *pax*, and its many derivatives, notably *pacificus*.[2] To these must be added a cluster of vernacular terms, such as Old English *sibb* (OHG *sibba*, Gothic *sibja*) and *frið* (OHG *fridu*, OS, *frithu*, ON *friðr*), some of which occur in the legal texts of early medieval Europe and in works which sought to render the word of God into Germanic vernacular. Etymologically, both Old English *frið* and *sibb* and their continental relatives

---

[1] Hrabanus Maurus, *Expositionis super Jeremiam prophetam libri viginti*, c. 29, PL 111, cols 793–1272 at 1018–19.
[2] On *pacificus* and *pax* see *TLL* X.1.vi, pp. 12–18; X.i.I, pp. 863–78.

have their roots in notions of kinship and friendship, a semantic bond implying not only that peace was the notional state of order within a family, but also that kin ties were, in some basic sense, a model for positive bonds between unrelated individuals.[3] The relationship between a language and the norms of the society that employed it is less straightforward than was once thought, and the social models of nineteenth-century philology have been the targets of withering criticism.[4] That said, this powerful and persistent set of associations frequently recurs in our sources, often in contexts in which the resonances of kinship are apparent in other elements of the text.

The resulting mix of ideas and the absence of clear definitions have driven some to exasperation. 'Men of the earlier middle ages knew what they meant by war and peace. Their definitions are not hard to find', wrote Michael Wallace-Hadrill, 'even though when found, they prove to be inconsistent.'[5] Personal circumstance, the dictates of poetic form and metre, and individual originality (by women as well as men) were all factors in the selection and presentation of certain meanings of peace. Such factors rarely promoted consistency. In the pages that follow I am less interested in consistency than with establishing core meanings, reference points, and main reservoirs of ideas and imagery from which early medieval ideas of peace and peaceful rulership were drawn. As we shall see, there existed a number of key texts and figures that were touchstones for those who turned their minds to the matter. Such common ground not only provided the raw material for theorists, it also offered the possibility of shared conceptions between theorists and their audiences, a 'textual community' in the loosest sense.[6]

I begin not with the earliest but with the best-known and in many ways the most accessible image of early medieval peaceful rulership: Bede's account of Edwin of Northumbria's reign from book two of the *Historia ecclesiastica*.[7] By so doing I intend to offer not only an analysis of Bede's image of the Northumbrian king in itself but also to use it as an entry point into the constituent elements of the image of peaceful kingship.

---

[3] D. H. Green, *Language and History in the Early Germanic World* (Cambridge, 1998), 52–62, with references. For kinship and community in early Germanic society see A. Callendar Murray, *Germanic Kinship Structure: Studies in Law and Society in Antiquity and the Early Middle Ages* (Toronto, 1983). The problems with philologically grounded models of ur-Germanic society are well acknowledged; see *inter alia* P. J. Geary, *The Myth of Nations. The Medieval Origins of Europe* (Princeton, 2003), 15–40; J. L. Bloomfield, 'Benevolent Authoritarianism in Klaeber's *Beowulf*: An Editorial Translation of Kingship', *Modern Languages Quarterly* 60.2 (1999), 129–59; P. Amory, *People and Identity in Ostrogothic Italy, 489–554* (Cambridge, 1997), 326–31.

[4] Amory, *People*, 326.

[5] J. M. Wallace-Hadrill, 'War and Peace in the Early Middle Ages', *TRHS*, 5th series, 25 (1976), 157–74, reprinted in *idem, Early Medieval History* (Oxford, 1975), 19–38, at 19.

[6] F. Theuws, 'Introduction: Rituals in Transforming Societies', in F. Theuws and J. L. Nelson (eds), *Rituals of Power. From Late Antiquity to the Early Middle Ages* (Leiden, 2000), 1–15 on the balance between individual interpretation and wider cultural forms.

[7] See, for example, Halsall, *War*, 18–19; J. E. Damon, *Soldier Saints and Holy Warriors: Warfare and Sanctity in the Literature of Early England* (Aldershot, 2003), 35–52, esp. 35–40.

FROM SEA TO SEA: BEDE AND EDWIN

Bede's prose is famously spare. Equally restrained is his deployment of rich imagery. In his account of Edwin's reign over Northumbria in the second quarter of the seventh century this dryness lapsed as Bede described a ruler for whom he had evident warmth and admiration. The results are among two of the most arresting vignettes in early medieval literature. The first, the vision of a man's life as the passage of a sparrow's flight through a royal hall, whilst an vision placed in the mouth of one of Edwin's followers, was clearly Bede's own.[8] The second, and the motif that concerns us here, is that which opens Bede's summary of the achievements of Edwin's reign:

> It is told that at that time there was so much peace in *Britannia*, that wherever King Edwin's power extended, as is said proverbially right up to today, even if a woman with a recently born child wanted to walk across the whole island, from sea to sea, she could do so without anyone harming her.[9]

At face value, Bede's decision to couch Edwin's peace in proverbial terms offers what to some might seem a chilling insight into the levels of lawlessness accepted in eighth-century England. Only in the reign of a king as exceptional as Edwin, we learn, might an unaccompanied mother and child countenance leaving the safety of the family home and the protection of armed male kin.[10] Less subjectively, the passage offers us an initial insight into what peace at its most basic might mean for an early medieval author: freedom from robbery, rape, or violence; security to travel at will, and to literally 'go in peace'.[11] It also hints

---

[8] M. Toswell, 'Bede's Sparrow and the Psalter in Anglo-Saxon England', *ANQ* 13.1 (2000), 7–12; D. K. Fry, 'The Art of Bede: Edwin's Council', in M. H. King and W. M. Stevens (eds), *Saints, Scholars and Heroes: Studies in Medieval Culture in Honour of Charles W. Jones*, 2 vols (Collegeville, MN, 1979), I, 191–207, noting scriptural and patristic debts.

[9] *HE* II.16, pp. 192–3: 'Tanta autem eo tempore pax in Britannia, quaquaversum imperium regis Æduini pervenerat, fuisse perhibetur ut sicut usque hodie in proverbio dicitur, etiam si mulier una cum recens nato parvulo vellet totam perambulare insulam a mari ad mare, nullo se ledente valeret.' R. Cramp, 'Eadwine (c.586–633)', *Oxford Dictionary of National Biography*, Oxford University Press, Sept 2004; online edn, Oct 2005 http://www.oxforddnb.com/view/article/8567, accessed 21 Nov 2008, with further references.

[10] For comparable continental anxieties see T. Reuter, 'The Insecurity of Travel in the Early and High Middle Ages: Criminals, Victims and their Medieval and Modern Observers', in J. L. Nelson (ed.), *Medieval Polities and Modern Mentalities* (Cambridge, 2006), 38–71. Adomnán, *Cáin/Lex innocentium*, ed. and trans. K. Meyer, *Cáin Adamnáin: An Old-Irish Treatise on the Law of Adamnan* (Oxford, 1905), with comments in T. O'Loughlin (ed.), *Adomnán at Birr, AD 697. Essays in the Commemoration of the Law of the Innocents* (Dublin, 2001); M. Ní Dhonnchadha, 'The *Lex Innocentium*: Adomnán's Law for Women, Clerics and Youths, 697 AD', in M. O'Dowd and S. Wichert (eds), *Chattel, Servant or Citizen: Women's Status in Church, State and Society* (Belfast, 1995), 58–69.

[11] G. Halsall, 'Violence and Society in the Early Medieval West: an Introductory Survey', in *idem* (ed.), *Violence and Society in the Early Medieval West* (Woodbridge, 1998), 1–45, esp. 4–12; R. V. Coleman, 'Domestic Peace and Public Order in Anglo-Saxon Law', in J. Woods and D. Pelteret (eds.), *The Anglo-Saxons: Synthesis and Achievement* (Toronto, 1984), 49–56.

at the wider early medieval anxiety over travel, an anxiety manifest most pointedly in the various votive masses for those undertaking a journey (*missa pro iter
agentibus*).

This motif of the king's peace indexed by travellers' safety finds numerous
analogues. It was already present, for example, in the eulogistic account of
Theoderic's reign in the *pars anterior* of the mid-sixth century *Anonymous
Valesianus*, and would be revisited by later authors.[12] It occurs, to cite a single
example, nearly a century and a half after Bede's death, in a pilgrimage account of
the 860s, written by one Bernard, a Frankish or perhaps Breton monk who
together with several companions journeyed from Rome to Jerusalem. His short
account of the journey reveals his own understandable concerns with personal
safety and peaceful travel in a foreign land. He recorded with shocked delight
the peaceful relations between Christian and non-Christian in Egypt, and also
the law and order that prevailed in the Egyptian countryside. If the donkey or
camel upon which he rode died, and he was forced to abandon his goods by the
roadside whilst he found a replacement mount, they would still be there when he
returned: 'such peace exists there' (*talis pax est ibi*).[13] Bernard contrasted Abbasid
Egypt's order, and the piety of its Christians, with the disorder he had witnessed
in *Romania*—Rome and its outlying districts. There, violence was common,
theft and robbery widespread, and pilgrims travelled to St Peter's with armed
protection.[14] Lombardy and Brittany, conversely, enjoyed good levels of peace,
the former, like Benevento, under Louis the German's control.[15] Bernard's
travels allowed him to do what few were capable of in the intensely local world
of the early Middle Ages: gauge the uneven topography of peace and social order
across a wide landscape and so implicitly assess the relative success of the different
rulers responsible for it. Like Bede before him, he assessed political efficacy (and
offered criticism) through concrete experience of peace.[16]

It is this immediate sense of peace that underpins and often gives deeper
resonance to some of the more sophisticated notions we will shortly encounter.
Self-evidently it is also the same core notion of personal safety and social peace
implicit in many of the extant early medieval law-codes with their penalties
against murder, injury, or theft. Julius Goebel, commenting upon the use of the
word peace (*frið*) in the Anglo-Saxon legal corpus, has left us a usefully loose
definition of this type of peace: 'an unartful sense of public order or general

---

[12] *Anonymous Valesianus*, T. Mommsen (ed.), *Chronica Minora* I *MGH AA* 9 (Berlin, 1892),
306–28, on the peace afforded to travellers, XII. c. 59, p. 322. J. N. Adams, *The Text and Language
of a Vulgar Latin Chronicle* (London, 1976), 111–12, and S. J. Barnish, 'The Anonymous
Valesianus II as a Source for the Last Years of Theoderic', *Latomus* 42 (1983), 572–96.

[13] *Itinerarium Bernardi monachi Franci*, ed. T. Tobler and A. Molinier, *Itineraria Hierosolymitana
et descriptiones terrae sanctae bellis sacris anteriora et Latina lingua exarata* (Geneva, 1879), 309–20,
c. 23, at 319.

[14] *Itineraria*, c. 24, pp. 319–20.

[15] *Itineraria*, c. 24, p. 320.

[16] Reuter, 'Insecurity', 45.

security'.[17] This is not to say that there was a shared notion of what constituted a peaceful society. The level of ambient violence acceptable within specific environments differed substantially even within a single society. The early medieval landscape was characterized by the existence of places in which peace was an especially valued commodity: the king's hall, the sanctuary of a church, the numinous precincts of the saint's tomb, and the rightly ordered monastery.[18] Rupturing the heightened peace of such places could breach fundamental rules of social hierarchy, propriety, and purity, as well as specific royal laws. At various times the peace and order of such places might spread out into wider society: a king's peace might cover his territories, like Edwin, or a saint stand guard over a kingdom's peace. Our sources also reveal that such shifts in levels of violence and its threat were perceptible to at least some of its members, and it is against the backdrop of such violence that Bede's profile of the king who could establish and maintain peace for his subjects stands in such sharp relief.

What ought we to make of Bede's central image of mother and child? Bede's own claim is that the image, and the sense of the golden age of peace that Edwin's reign represented, was proverbial amongst eighth-century Northumbrians. Leaving aside objections that Bede's contact with the common folk of Northumbria was probably minimal at best, might his statement contain a kernel of truth? Perhaps. The brief existence of a cult of Edwin at Whitby, presided over by his daughter, Eanflæd, following his death in battle in 633, suggests that some remembered his reign fondly, or at least were encouraged to do so, though the fact that Whitby's attempt to transform slain king into culted saint faltered suggests, ultimately, too few.[19] That said, the arresting image of mother and child as we have it was Bede's own, and consequently carries the possibility of dependencies on other works. One aspect of this intertextuality has been long-recognized: behind his image of Edwin's rule stand several passages drawn from the Old Testament's account of the peace Israel enjoyed under Solomon's rule.[20] Echoes of several other scriptural and patristic passages might also be heard here. The introductory phrase of 'so much peace' (*tanta pax*), used repeatedly by Bede to introduce the different elements of his description, echoed the words of

[17] J. Goebel, *Felony and Misdemeanor: A Study in the History of English Criminal Procedure* (New York, 1937), 423.

[18] R. Meens, 'The Sanctity of the Basilica of St Martin. Gregory of Tours and the Practice of Sanctuary in the Merovingian Period', in R. Corradini, R. Meens, C. Pössel, and P. Shaw (eds), *Text and Identities in the Early Middle Ages*, Forschungen Zur Geschichte des Mittelalters, 12 (Vienna, 2006), 275–88; W. Davies, 'Protected Space in Britain and Ireland in the Middle Ages', in B. Crawford (ed.), *Scotland in Dark Age Britain* (St Andrews, 1996), 1–19. J. L. Nelson, review of T. Head and R. Landes, *The Peace of God*, in *Speculum* 69 (1994), 163–9, at 169.

[19] For the culting of slain Anglo-Saxon kings see C. Cubitt, 'Sites and Sanctity: Revisiting the Cult of Murdered and Martyred Anglo-Saxon Royal Saints', *EME* 9.1 (2000), 53–83; A. T. Thacker, '*Membra Disjecta*: the Division of the Body and the Diffusion of the Cult', in C. Stancliffe and E. Cambridge (eds.), *Oswald: Northumbrian King to European Saint* (Stamford, 1995), 97–127; D. Rollason, 'The Cults of Murdered Royal Saints in Anglo-Saxon England', *ASE* 11 (1983), 1–22.

[20] J. McClure, 'Bede's Old Testament Kings', *I&R*, 76–98, at 88, citing III Kings IV.21, 24–5.

Hezekiah, king of Judah to the prophet Isaiah. Here, in the wake of his victorious defence of Judah against the Assyrian armies of Sennacherib, and his healing by God working through Isaiah, Hezekiah gave thanks to God for his twin deliverances from his enemies and from sickness: 'And Hezekiah said to Isaiah: "The word of the Lord, which he hath spoken, is good." And he said: "Only let peace and truth be in my days."'[21]

There are other telling resonances between Hezekiah, king of Israel, and Edwin, king of Northumbria.[22] After a protracted period of idolatry it was only during Hezekiah's reign that Israel returned to the worship of the one God. Similarly, it was only under Edwin that Northumbria became, at least for Bede, Christian once again. Baptized by Paulinus, Edwin was Northumbria's first Christian Northumbrian ruler. Political parallels between Hezekiah and Edwin might also be drawn. Edwin's rule was founded upon his reunification of Deira and Bernicia under his authority and the expansion of Northumbria across large swathes of northern Britain and as far south as Kent. Under Hezekiah's rule Judah was reunited with the remains of Israel, an echo of Solomon's unificatory authority. And in this newly reunified kingdom the Temple, purified and rededicated, also regained its place at the centre of collective devotional life. This, together with his successes in warfare, his defeat of the Philistines and the peace that his strong rule brought, led Hezekiah to be seen as something of a second David or Solomon.[23] The precise extent of Edwin's peace, 'from sea to sea' (*a mari ad mare*) itself carries a biblical resonance, recapitulating the terms of two biblical descriptions of peace in Israel, Psalm LXXI.7–8, which, as we shall soon see, was a key passage for the framing of peaceful rule, and Zechariah IX.10. In both cases the extent of peace is defined explicitly 'from sea to sea' (*a mari usque ad mare*).[24]

Here, then, Edwin's peace conformed to established and well-recognized scriptural forms. Such conformity was intentional. Edwin may have been Northumbria's first Christian king but underlying Bede's portrait lay the notion that

---

[21] Isa. XXXIX.8. For Bede's own knowledge of Isaiah see *De eo quod ait Isaias*, PL 94, cols 702–10, translated in A. G. Holder and W. Trent Foley, *Bede: A Biblical Miscellany* TTH 28 (Liverpool, 1999), 39–45.
[22] The Old Testament books in which Hezekiah appears (Isaiah, Kings, Chronicles) were ones Bede knew thoroughly, and whose understanding of them was part of his reputation in the eighth-century English Church. *In regum librum XXX quaestiones* was written in response to questions submitted to him by Nothelm of London (CCSL 119, pp. 289–322, at 289), whilst the work known as *De eo quod ait Isaias* was a response to questions sent by Acca of Hexham (PL 94, col. 702).
[23] The scriptural background of the interrelationship between these figures is delineated by M. A. Throntveit, 'The Relationship of Hezekiah to David and Solomon in the Books of Chronicles', in M. P. Graham, S. L. McKenzie, and G. N. Knoppers (eds), *The Chronicler as Theologian. Essays in Honour of R. Klein* (London, 2003), 105–21, and for insights to Bede's own understanding of the Old Testment see P. Meyvaert, '"In the Footsteps of the Fathers": The Date of Bede's Thirty Questions on the Book of Kings to Nothelm', in W. Klingshirn and M. Vessey (eds), *The Limits of Ancient Christianity: Essays on Late Antique Thought and Culture in Honor of R. A. Markus* (Ann Arbor, 1999), 267–86.
[24] Reuter, 'Insecurity', 44–5.

the novelty of his reign was offset by its relationship to ancient but ongoing patterns of righteous rule. More concretely, elite members of that culture possessing some familiarity with the Fathers might well have heard a different association, for in the words with which he described mother and child Bede echoed Augustine.[25]

Finally, if Bede's description raised associations with the Old Testament, for some at least it may also have called to mind the New, and the image of another journeying mother and newborn child, Mary and the infant Christ on the flight into Egypt (Matt. II.13–15), protected in their case by God, the most powerful of all lords.[26] Such associations were explicitly cited in a seventh-century source that reminds us that others in the insular world looked to kings to protect women and the young, Adomnán's *Cáin Adomnán* or *Lex innocentium* ('The Law of the Innocents').[27]

At Birr in early 697 Adomnán, abbot of Iona, gathered the great and the good, ecclesiastical and secular, headed by Loingsech, newly established high king of Tara, to promulgate a collective undertaking to guarantee the protection of women, clerics, youths, and church property. Conventionally, responsibility for the protection of a mother and child would have fallen to their immediate, weapon-bearing male kin, by whose own status the mother and child's was often determined.[28] In Bede's account, however, Edwin took on this role of protector. This, indeed, is an image of the ruler as head of household writ large, and one that also recalls something of the conceptual linkage between kin and peace implicit in its Old English vocabulary: mother and child are safe with the distant patriarchal figure of the king watching over them.[29] In a sense this image transformed kingdom into household, an idea developed in the next detail Bede offered of life under Edwin's rule:

That king took such care for the good of his people that in very many places where he saw clear springs near public highways he ordered stakes to be fixed with bronze vessels

---

[25] Augustine, *Enchiridion*, ed. M. P. J. van den Hout et al., CCSL 46 (Turnhout, 1969), I.13.43: 'A parvulo enim recens nato usque ad decrepitum senem, sicut nullus est prohibendus a baptismo, ita nullus est qui non peccato moriatur in baptismo'. Similar phrases are also to be found in *Serm.* 294, PL 38, cols 1335–48, at 1348. Not for the first time would Bede silently insert phrases from Augustine into his own prose. G. Brown, 'Bede, Venerable', in A. Fitzgerald and J. C. Cavadini (eds), *Augustine through the Ages: An Encyclopedia* (Grand Rapids, MI 1999), 95–6, at 96. F. M. Biggs, 'Bede's Use of Augustine, Echoes from Some Sermons?', *RB* 108 (1998), 201–13. A. T. Thacker, 'Bede and Augustine: History and Figure in Sacred Texts', (Jarrow Lecture, 2005).

[26] For Anglo-Saxon treatments of the Flight into Egypt see M. Clayton, *The Cult of the Virgin Mary in Anglo-Saxon England* (Cambridge, 1990), 145–6, 150–1, and its treatment by Bede, 'Homily on the Feast of the Holy Innocents', *Homiliae Evangelii*, ed. D. Hurst, CCSL 122 (Turnhout, 1965), I.10, 68–72.

[27] See above n. 10.

[28] M. P. Richards and B. J. Stanfield, 'Concepts of Anglo-Saxon Women in the Laws', in H. Damico and A. H. Olsen (eds), *New Readings on Women in Old English Literature* (1990), 89–99, esp. 92–3; A. Klinck, 'Anglo-Saxon Women and the Law', *JMH* 8 (1982), 107–21.

[29] P. E. Dutton, *The Politics of Dreaming in the Carolingian Empire* (Lincoln, NE, 1994), 5–22.

hanging from them for the refreshment of travellers. No one touched these save for its proper use—either not daring to, through great fear of Edwin, or not wishing to, through great love for him.[30]

Edwin's wayside opulence mapped the image of the household and the duties of a lord across the entire kingdom. Northumbria's roadsides became theatres for a form of absent but ever-present royal hospitality. As Rosemary Cramp has observed, Bede's account calls to mind the high-prestige bowls recovered from a number of high-status graves directly contemporary with Edwin's reign (most recently Prittlewell) and which presumably played their part in the same high-status feasting for which many of the objects also buried were intended.[31] As Edwin's protection reached out from his household so, too, did his hospitality.

In large part this general definition of peace as played out in the example of Bede's Edwin is negative. It was the absence of strife, the curbing or cessation of violence. Somewhat problematically for the historian, this means a state where some things, at least, did not happen. 'This being a time of peace, nothing which is mentioned by *historia* occurred', wrote Sulpicius Severus in his *Chronicle* in the later fourth century, explaining away the scarcity of evidence for one period of Israel's past.[32] It is apt, then, that one of the concepts most consistently linked with peace is silence, whether the peace of the study, the cloister, or of an individual.[33] Other comparable associations, many of considerable antiquity, connect peace with justice, mercy, order, truth, and harmony (*concordia*) as elements in a larger web of associated meanings.[34] Often, as in these examples, the association is complementary, occasionally to the point where two spheres

---

[30] *HE* II.16: 'Tantum rex idem utilitati suae gentis consuluit, ut plerisque in locis ubi fontes lucidos iuxta puplicos viarum transitus conspexit, ibi ob refrigerium viantium, erectis stipitibus, aereos caucus suspendi iuberet, neque hos quisquam, nisi ad usum necessarium, contingere prae magnitudine vel timoris eius auderet, vel amoris vellet.'

[31] Cramp, 'Edwin'. See, for example, the recently discovered Coptic bowl from Prittlewell, S. Hirst, *The Prittlewell Prince: The Discovery of a Rich Anglo-Saxon Burial in Essex* (London, 2004). For Sutton Hoo see R. L. S. Bruce-Mitford, *The Sutton Hoo Ship Burial* (London, 1983), III, pp. 732–57. For another passage with possible relevance here see Gregory the Great's discussion of life as a road and the danger from robbers to those carrying silver vessels (*vascula argenti*) in a letter to the recently converted King Reccared of the Visigoths in Spain, *Ep.* IX. 229b (August 599).

[32] Sulpicius Severus, *Chronica*, ed. A. Lavertujon, *La Chronique de Sulpice Sévère* (Paris, 1896), I.26, p. 64.

[33] To hold one's peace in scripture see Exod. XIV.14; Deut. XX.9; II Kings VII.9; Neh. V.8, VIII.11; Esther IV.14; Job VI.24, XI.3, XIII.5, XIII.13, XXXIII.31, XXXIII.33; Ps. LXXXII.2; Prov. XVII.28; Isa. XXXVI.21, XL.14; LXII.6, LXIV.12; Jer. IV.19, XXXVII.5; Lam. II.10, III.28; Dan. X.15; Amos VI.11; Obad. I.5; Hab. I.13; Matt. XX.31, XXVI.63; Mark III.4, IV.39 (where Christ's injunction of 'Peace' calms the Sea of Galilee), XIV.61; Luke IV.35, IX.36; Ecclus. XIII.4, XIII.28, XIX.28, XX.6; Judith VII.22, XIII.16; II Macc. XII.2; Tobit V.8; Wisd. VIII.12.

[34] For peace and justice see II Tim. II.22; Heb. XII.11; Jas. III.18; Baruch VI.2: Ecclus. V.12. On peace and truth see Jer. XXXIII.6; Zech. VIII.6, VIII.19; Mal. II.6, Luke XIV.32, XVIII.39, XIX.40, XX.26; Acts XII.17, XV.13, XVIII.9; I Cor. XIV. 28. Peace and security see I Thess. V.3; peace and mercy see I Tim. I.2; II John I.3.

interpenetrate, are mutually supporting, such as peace and justice, or function as loose synonyms for each other. One might think of the Psalmist's words: 'Mercy and truth have met each other: justice and peace have kissed' (Ps. LXXXIV.10), or the Christological chain REX—LEX—LUX—PAX ('KING—LAW—LIGHT—PEACE') that occurs in various early medieval inscriptions and illuminations.[35]

Of all these associations it is the fundamental duality of war and peace that is the most frequently encountered in our sources, perhaps set out most explicitly in the words of Ecclesiastes III.8 ('A time of love, and a time of hatred. A time of war, and a time of peace').[36] That said, the two could still exist in the same kind of directional relationship as we have seen with the relationship of justice to peace. For Augustine and for others war itself might be the route to peace. Oscillations between war and peace were the governing principle behind many views of human activity in the early Middle Ages. An important bridge between the two, and one with its own ceremonies, imagery, and ideological charge was victory, an idea whose close associations with peace, forged in Roman imperial ideology, found its own place in post-Roman politics and has been explored by Michael McCormick in a classic study.[37] This relationship of victory and peace is a further presence, too, in Bede's image of a seventh-century king. Edwin's peace was the fruit of a hard-won political dominance that, as we have seen, extended across large swathes of Britain. His conquest of Elmet, and establishment of his authority in Anglesey and Man, meant that Bede's image of a peace 'from sea to sea' was not simply a trope. It accurately reflected the hegemony that stretched from the Deiran shore to the Irish Sea.[38] How that political unity was maintained, and how great was the peace that existed within it, is evident from the third and final section of Bede's description. This gives us a further clue to the realities that underpinned periods of peace in early medieval society. Peace was kept, wrote Bede, by Edwin's constant movement through his kingdom, in what amounted to a parade of continuous self-celebration:

He kept such a state of excellence in his kingdom that not only were banners carried before him in battle, but also in time of peace a standard-bearer was wont to go before him as he rode about his cities, towns, and provinces with his followers. Furthermore,

---

[35] R. Favreau, "*Rex, lex, lux, pax*": jeux de mots et jeux de lettres dans les inscriptions médiévales', *Bibliothèque de l'École des Chartes* 161.2 (2003), 625–35; I. Barros-Dios, '*Pax, Lux, Lex, Rex*', in D. Buschinger and W. Spiewok (eds), *Die Ritterorden im Mittelalter—Les ordres Militaires au Moyen Age* (Greifswald, 1996), 31–45. For Ps. LXXXIV.11 see K. Schreiner, 'Gerechtigkeit und Frieden haben sich geküßt (Ps. 84, 11): Friedenstiftung durch symbolisches Handeln', *TuI*, 37–86.

[36] G. Fasoli, 'Pace e Guerra nell' Alto Medioevo', in F. Bocchi, A. Carile, and A. Pini (eds), *Scritti di Storia Medievale* (Bologna, 1974), 79–104.

[37] McCormick, *Eternal Victory*.

[38] *HE* II.5.

when he walked anywhere along the streets a banner of the kind which the Romans call a *tufa* and the English *thuuf*, used to be borne before him.[39]

For Edwin the cost of peace was indeed eternal vigilance, and a willingness to impress his authority upon the kingdom through his presence in a fashion that left little doubt military might underpinned his reign. Bede's account of Edwin's procession, its standards, and in particular his reference to the *tufa* hint that Edwin's mode of ceremonial was a vernacular interpretation of a late imperial triumphal procession. It was an appropriate form for a ruler whose *villa regis* at Yeavering, built upon a Romano-British site, with its wooden amphitheatre or *cuneus*, reveals a mode of kingship alive to the possibilities of Roman forms of political symbolism, perhaps wisely so in a polity that may well have included a sizeable Romano-British descendant population for whom Saxon rule was more acceptable in sub-Roman style.[40]

Edwin's peace was seemingly built upon military victory and sustained by the constant reiteration of that fact. To be a king who maintained peace was not to be a king who avoided violence altogether. For Bede, as for many others, peace was predicated upon effective war leadership on the part of rulers. A peaceful king was one who was able to limit internal domestic 'illegitimate' violence whilst success-fully engaging in 'legitimate' violence, often raids and war on an organized scale. Kings who refused to fight presented those around them with a frustrating and dangerous novelty. In political cultures in which war created opportunities to gain status and wealth, kings who refused to fight not only endangered their own position, but also jeopardized the ambitions of others.[41] Edwin's contemporary, Sigeberht of East Anglia, was one such figure. According to Bede his voluntary withdrawal to the quiet of a monastery came to an abrupt end when his kingdom faced attack by Penda, and his subjects demanded his presence amongst their ranks, to inspire confidence. Dragged from his cell to the battlefield, Sigeberht's refusal to take up weapons and his decision to arm himself with a staff ended in forseeable disaster.[42] The tale hints at Bede's evident distaste for piously pacifist kings who refused to behave in appropriately royal fashion.

Edwin's own end came, as we have seen, in 633. His severed head, taken to York, was placed in the portico of St Peter's, the church he had founded.[43] His

[39] *HE* II.16: 'Tantum vero in regno excellentiae habuit, ut non solum in pugna ante illum vexilla gestarentur, sed et tempore pacis equitantem inter civitates sive villas aut provincias suas cum ministris, semper antecedere signifer consuesset; nec non et incedente illo ubilibet per plateas, illud genus vexilli, quod Romani tufam, Angli appellant thuuf, ante eum ferri solebat.'

[40] B. Hope-Taylor, *Yeavering. An Anglo-British Centre of Early Northumbria* (London, 1977); P. Frodsham, 'Forgetting *Gefrin*. Elements of the Past in the Past at Yeavering', *Northern Archaeology* 17/18 (1999), 1–21.

[41] Halsall, *War*, 2, 26–30.

[42] *HE* II.15, II.18.

[43] *HE* III.24. *Vita Gregori*, ed. B. Colgrave, *The Earliest Life of Gregory the Great* (Cambridge, 1968), cc. 18–19, pp. 100–5.

body rested in Whitby. Neither place became a centre of pilgrimage, nor did Edwin join the growing ranks of early Anglo-Saxon royal saints. Edwin's reputation as a peaceful ruler long outlived his failed cult. In the tenth century the *Historia*'s account of Edwin would be reused by Wulfstan *Cantor* in his depiction of Edgar, the *rex pacificus* of his own day.[44] In the twelfth century William of Malmesbury described the peace of Alfred's reign in terms of the safety of the public roads, where golden dishes could be left without being stolen, in words indebted to Bede's image of Edwin.[45] For Wulfstan and for William, as for us here, Edwin became a touchstone for thinking about peaceful rulership.

Bede's image of Edwin was woven from the central strands of thought to which we shall repeatedly return: scriptural typology (Solomon and, to a lesser degree, Hezekiah), the imagery and ceremony of the later Roman Empire, and, not least, the indigenous political forms of Rome's heirs. To these fields must be added, as Bede demonstrates with more finesse than most, individual authorial invention. Taken together they present the core bodies of thought from which early medieval notions of peaceful rulership emerged. Any effort to understand them is an exercise more akin to political ecology than taxonomy for, as here in the *Historia*'s image of Edwin, they exist not in isolation but in interaction and complex coexistence. But before we understand their interaction, we must examine the elements in greater detail.

FORGETTING THE ARA PACIS

The relationship of *pax* to *imperium* that Bede's image of Edwin's progress through the Northumbrian countryside sought to evoke has its roots in the Roman past. Since its dedication on the 30th January 9 BC the Ara Pacis had played a significant role in Roman celebrations of prosperity and peace.[46] Every year on that day and on the 4th of July, the anniversary of the altar's *constitutio* by the Senate, the city's magistrates and priests offered annual sacrifices. Ovid, exiled the year after the altar's dedication, was an early witness to the rites, and left a brief account of the ceremony in the *Fasti*.[47] The altar was built to celebrate Augustus' victorious return in 13 BC from three years' successful active campaigning in Spain and Gaul, a statement of the peace and order he had brought

---

[44] *Frithegodi Monachi Breuiloquium Vitae Beati Wilfredi et Wulfstani Cantoris Narratio Metrica de Sancto Swithuno*, ed. A. Campbell (Zurich, 1950), lines 440–65, pp. 154–5, borrowing general sentiments from *HE* II c. 16. Commentary: D. Whitelock, 'Wulfstan "Cantor" and Anglo-Saxon Law', in A. H. Orrick (ed.), *Nordica et Anglica. Studies in Honour of Stéfan Einarsson* (The Hague, 1968), 83–92, at 84.

[45] R. H. C. Davis, 'Bede After Bede', in C. Harper-Bill, C. Holdsworth, and J. L. Nelson (eds), *Studies in Medieval History Presented to R. Allen Brown* (Woodbridge, 1989), 103–16.

[46] P. A. Brunt and J. M. Moore (eds), *Res Gestae Divi Augusti* (Oxford, 1981), c. 12, pp. 101–2.

[47] *Fasti*, trans. J. G. Frazer (London, 1967), lines 709–22, pp. 54–5.

to the provinces as well as his effective suppression of the civil wars that had wracked Rome for decades.[48] The Ara's much-discussed friezes, with their richly carved foliage, scenes of growth and abundance, and images of Aeneas and Augustus himself drove home both the link between peace and abundance and echoed the notion, found elsewhere in the Augustan artistic programme, that his rule was a *saeculum aureum* for Rome and its citizens.[49] The Ara's consecration marked Augustus' intervention into the narrative of Rome's past and the city's ceremonial geography, a major moment in his journey from Actium to acclamation as *pater patriae* in 2 BC, and his eventual metamorphosis from Octavian to Augustus. To the west of the Ara Pacis stood the obelisk of Psammetichus II, imported by Augustus from Heliopolis in 10 BC as a symbol of Egypt's importance in his personal rise to power. The obelisk served as the *gnomon* for an *horologium* inscribed in a double-axe design that covered over a kilometre of the Campus. Bronze letters sunk into the travertine pavement spelled out the names of the hours and the days, the forms of the constellations, and the dates of the solstices and autumn equinox.[50] Together, sundial and altar formed a ritual complex within the wider ceremonial space of the Campus Martius, standing as a monument to peace in an environment traditionally defined by war, and in implicit material dialogue with an immediate environment that included some of Rome's oldest cult sites.[51] The altar invited a web of associations that touched upon the rhythms of the seasons, fertility, social order, peace at home and dominance abroad, and, above all, upon a notion of cosmic order in which Augustus himself occupied the central place.[52] Sundial and altar also worked together to commemorate him. On his *dies natalis*, 23 September, the *gnomon*'s shadow fell towards the altar.

[48] The literature on the Ara Pacis is extensive and, ironically, rich in disagreement. Recent entry points include P. Rehak, *Imperium and Cosmos. Augustus and the Northern Campus Martius* (Madison, WI, 2006), 96–137; J. C. Anderson, 'The Ara Pacis Augustae: Legends, Fact and Flights of Fancy', in M. T. Boatwright and H. B. Evans (eds), *The Shapes of City Life in Rome and Pompeii: Essays in Honor of Lawrence Richardson Jr. on the Occasion of His Retirement* (New Rochelle, 1996), 27–51.

[49] D. Castriota, *The Ara Pacis Augustae and the Imagery of Abundance in Later Greek and Early Roman Imperial Art* (Princeton, 1995); P. Zanker, *The Power of Images in the Age of Augustus* (Ann Arbor, 1988), 172–9. P. J. Holliday, 'Time, History and the Ara Pacis Augustae', *The Art Bulletin* 72.4 (1990), 542–57, at 544.

[50] N. De Grummond, 'Pax Augusta and the *Horae* of the *Ara Pacis Augustae*', *American Journal of Archaeology* 94 (1990), 663–77, at 676–7; E. Buchner, *Die Sonnenuhr des Augustus* (Mainz, 1982); idem, 'Solarium Augusti und Ara Pacis', *Mitteilungen des Deutschen Archäologischen Instituts, Römische Abteilung* 83 (1976), 319–65.

[51] J. Elsner, 'Cult and Sculpture: Sacrifice in the *Ara Pacis Augustae*', *JRS* 81 (1991), 50–61, at 52; H. Kähler, 'Die *Ara Pacis* und die Augusteische Friedensidee', *Jahrbuch des Deutschen Archäologischen Instituts* 69 (1954), 67–100; M. K. Thornton, 'Augustan Genealogy and the *Ara Pacis*', *Latomus* 42 (1983), 619–28.

[52] On the wider question of the Augustan definition of peace see E. Simon, 'Eirene und Pax. Friedensgöttinnen in der Antike', *Sitzungsberichte der Wissenschaften Gesellschaft an der Johann-Wolfgang-Goethe-Universität Frankfurt am Main* 24 (1988), 55–69; A. Momigliano, 'The Peace of the Ara Pacis', *Journal of the Courtauld and Warburg Institutes* 5 (1942), 228–31.

At some point in late antiquity the Ara Pacis disappears from view. Its sporadic appearance in the numismatic record, on coins issued by Nero and Domitian, and arguments for the subsequent recarving of its panels in late antiquity show its continued place in later imperial political imagery.[53] We might postulate that, like many of the other civic sites that remained in use during the fourth century, it finally ceased to function in its fullest fashion in the early 390s, the result of Theodosius' suppression of all pagan cults in 391–2.[54] Its gradual drift from visual prominence seems to have begun as early as Hadrian's reign, however, when the Campus' ground level was raised, leaving the Ara's own floor considerably lower than the ground around it and the complex as a whole sunk inside a shallow banked depression.[55] From the second century onwards, building encroached upon the Campus Martius and this, together with the effects of flooding from the Tiber and considerable earthquake damage, did little to maintain the altar's prominence in the fashion originally intended.[56] It is not known for certain when the altar finally vanished but by the sixteenth century, when it was rediscovered, it lay beneath several layers of silt and soil.

The Ara's disappearance at late antiquity's close was clearly physical, but its path into obscurity might also be said to have been the result of changes in the values and mental landscape of Romans as much as in the topography of the city itself. Over the course of the fourth and fifth centuries the Ara became a site stripped of meaning as the ritual topography of imperial Rome, like those of other, lesser towns and cities across the western provinces, was gradually over-written by that of a Church whose bishops were rapidly redefining both its identity and their own in processes as complex as any in the shift from antiquity to the early Middle Ages.[57] The sanctoral cycles of Rome's martyrial churches came to overshadow, if not fully occlude, the earlier Roman calendars; the rites of *pax deorum* gave way to the liturgies of *concordia apostolorum*.[58] Something of this transformation was captured in Ambrose's and Symmachus' respective

[53] D. A. Conlin, *The Artists of the Ara Pacis: The Process of Hellenization in Roman Relief Sculpture* (Chapel Hill, 1997), 47–51.
[54] R. Curran, *Pagan City and Christian Capital: Rome in the Fourth Century* (Oxford, 2000), 209–16.
[55] M. T. Boatwright, *Hadrian and the City of Rome* (Princeton, 1987), 33–73, esp. 40, 66–73.
[56] F. Rakob, 'Die Urbanisierung des nördlichen Marsfeldes. Neue Forschungen im Areal des Horologium Augusti', *L'Urbs. Espace urbain et histoire. Collection de l'École française de Rome* 98 (Rome, 1987), 687–712; D. Manacorda, 'Trasformazioni dell'abitato nel Campo Marzio: l'area della "Porticus Minucia"', in L. Paroli and P. Delogu (eds), *La storia economica di Roma nell'alto Medioevo alla luce dei recenti scavi archaeologici* (Florence, 1993), 31–53.
[57] See, for example, M. Humphries, *Communities of the Blessed: Social Environment and Religious Change in Northern Italy. AD 200–400* (Oxford, 1999) and his introduction to B. Lançon, *Rome in Antiquity. Everyday Life and Urban Change, AD 213–609* (Edinburgh, 2000), xvi–xxii.
[58] Lançon, *Rome*, 133–40; C. Pietri, 'Concordia apostolorum et renovatio urbis (culte des martyrs et propagande pontificale)', *Mélanges d'Archéologie et d'Histoire de l'École Française de Rome* 73 (1961), 275–322; J. Huskinson, *Concordia Apostolorum: Christian Propaganda at Rome in the Fourth and Fifth Centuries. A Study in Early Christian Iconography and Iconology*, BAR Int. Ser. 148 (Oxford, 1982).

contributions to the debates over the restoration of the altar of Victory in the
Senate in 384. Symmachus' petition to Valentinian II carried a late call for pagan
tradition, the continued respect for the peace of the gods of the city's forefathers,
'the gods of our native land'.[59] Ambrose's response takes us to the heart of the
shift in the meaning of peace and its ceremonies over the course of the fourth
century: 'You beg peace for your gods from the emperors. We ask for peace for
the emperors themselves from Christ!'.[60] Ambrose won, although the traditional
language of the *res publica* would find a new context within the language of a
developing Roman liturgy in which those prayers for the emperors, and their
successors in the early medieval West, would be made.[61]

In the ceremonial precincts of the Ara Pacis such conceptual and devotional
shifts took appropriately physical form. Already by the late 360s the basilica and
baptistery of San Lorenzo in Lucina had been built in the Campus Martius, their
walls fracturing the already disturbed coherence of the sundial's grid.[62] Christian
liturgy and rites of initiation, the passions of the martyrs and the lives of the
saints provided very different narratives of triumph, divinity, and destiny to those
encoded by the sculptors of the Ara Pacis, offering new Christianized meanings
of peace. The processions of pious worshippers to the sacrifice on the altar's
friezes and those of other pagan sites gave way to new processions, and new
constellations of sacrifice and remembrance, and the displacement of a pagan
saeculum aureum by Christ's eternal reign of peace in his Heavenly Kingdom.
The handful of inscriptions recovered from San Lorenzo attest to this change in
meaning, for example the fragmentary third- or fourth-century inscription
recording that an unnamed individual was 'receptus in pace'.[63] Such inscriptions
serve as indicators of this shift in ritual and meaning for both individuals and
communities. Anniversaries of saints' deaths and not emperors' birthdays became
the familiar days for celebration and remembrance.[64] It was they who came to

[59] R. H. Barrow, *Prefect and Emperor: The Relationes of Symmachus, A.D. 384* (Oxford, 1973),
40–1.

[60] J. H. W. G. Liebeschütz, with C. Hill, *Ambrose of Milan. Political Letters and Speeches*, TTH
43 (Liverpool, 2005), *Ep.* 18, 78–94, at 83.

[61] For the early post-Apostolic adoption of the Roman language of *pax* by Christian thinkers see
O. M. Bakke, *'Concord and Peace'. A Rhetorical Analysis of the First Letter of Clement with an
Emphasis on the Language of Unity and Sedition* (Tübingen, 2001).

[62] R. Krautheimer, *Corpus Basilicarum christianarum Romae. The Early Christian Basilicas of
Rome* (Vatican City, 1959), II, pp. 178–9; Rakob, 'Die Urbanisierung', 687–712 on the German
excavations of the early 1980s; O. Brandt, 'Sul battistero paleocristiano di S. Lorenzo in Lucina',
Archeologia laziale 12, *Quaderni di archeologia etrusco-italica* 23 (Rome, 1995), 145–50; M. E.
Bertoldi, *S. Lorenzo in Lucina, Le chiese di Roma illustrate*, new series 28 (Rome, 1994).

[63] *ILCV* 429. Photograph and text of this inscription (S6) by A. Blennow at <http://
spazioinwind.libero.it/lucina/inscriptions.htm>. For the 'receptum in pace' formula and related
forms, M. Handley, *Death, Society and Culture: Inscriptions and Epitaphs in Gaul and Spain, AD
300–750*, BAR Int. Ser. 1135 (Oxford, 2003), 11–14; I. Kajanto, 'The Hereafter in Ancient
Christian Epigraphy', *Arctos* 12 (1978), 27–53.

[64] J. Elsner, *Art and the Roman Viewer: The Transformation of Art from the Pagan World to
Christianity* (Cambridge, 1997), 244–5.

populate the landscape of the early Middle Ages, and they who anchored the interpretative frameworks of those who travelled through this post-Roman landscape.

In the case of the Ara Pacis this is striking. Some time in the seventh or eighth century one such traveller composed a list of Rome's religious and historical sites to be seen on a number of routes through the city, a guide for other pious travellers.[65] The author of the 'Einsiedeln itinerary' was selective, recording some, but far from all, of Rome's major sites. Listing many of the major stations of Rome's new religious landscape—churches such as San Lorenzo in Damaso, San Clemente, and the Lateran—it included earlier sites with their own places in western Christianity's apostolic and post-apostolic narratives, like the Colosseum, the site of St Peter's prison, and Constantine's Arch. Also present were some sites with no clear Christian associations, but considerable claim on the pilgrim's eye: the baths of Caracalla, Trajan, and Commodus, and various aqueducts. Passing by the complex of the northern Campus Martius, plotting an eastward route from the Porta San Pietro to the Porta Salaria the 'Einsiedeln itinerary' noted, minimally, an *oboliscum*.[66] The ritual complex that had once fanned out from this axis, like the Ara Pacis itself, went unmentioned. It had ceased to exist in an early medieval pilgrim's eyes. A core commemorative site of the Roman past had been forgotten.

The Ara Pacis was not the only site in Rome dedicated to the cult of peace and the celebration of Rome's triumphs over outside peoples. In AD 71 Vespasian, mindful of Augustus' precedent, had begun the construction of the great Templum Pacis upon his return from the capture of Jerusalem. Dedicated four years later, the temple's precincts contained spoils from Jerusalem, Greek sculpture, and, in due course, a library, the Bibliotheca Pacis.[67] Amongst those spoils were objects looted from the Temple (Herod's, the second structure to occupy the site of Solomon's original building), including its golden seven-branched candelabrum, whose display in the subsequent triumphal procession was shown on the arch that celebrated Vespasian's victory on the Via Sacra.[68] Until Rome's successive sacks by Alaric's Goths in 410 and Geiseric's Vandals in 455, the

---

[65] *Itinerarium Einsidlense, Itineraria et alia geographica*, ed. R. Weber, CCSL 175 (Turnhout, 1965), 331–43.

[66] *It. Ein.* p. 335, line 106. Usefully mapped by D. Manacorda, *Museo Nazionale Romano Crypta Balbi* (Rome, 2000), 50–2. On the sacred topography of Rome and its early medieval written record McKitterick, *Perceptions of the Past in the Early Middle Ages* (Note Dame, IN, 2006), 42–6.

[67] C. F. Noreña, 'Medium and Message in Vespasian's Templum Pacis', *Memoirs of the American Academy in Rome* 48 (2003), 25–43.

[68] On Vespasian's emphasis upon peace, Philip de Souza, '*Parta victoriis pax*: Roman Emperors as Peacemakers', in *idem* and J. France (eds), *War and Peace in Ancient and Medieval History* (Cambridge, 2008), 76–106, 98–9; M. Harrison, 'From Jerusalem and Back Again. The Fates of the Treasures of Solomon', in K. Painter (ed.), *'Churches Built in Ancient Times'. Recent Studies in Early Christian Archaeology*, Occasional Papers from The Society of Antiquaries of London 16 (1994), 239–48, at 239–41.

riches of the Temple, relics of the site of the united Israel's cultic heart and reminders of Solomon's peaceful rule, stood within the precincts of the Templum Pacis: the furniture of one culture's Temple of Peace housed inside another's.[69] Razed in Commodus' reign, and probably rebuilt in the reign of his successor Septimius Severus, the Templum Pacis enjoyed a protracted and, unlike the Ara Pacis, a partially recoverable late antique half-life. Ammianus Marcellinus recorded Constantius II visiting it in 357, on a ceremonial circuit in which the pagan imperial cult of Peace was seemingly considered less offensive than that of Victory, whose statue he removed from the Senate.[70] It retained its identity through the fifth and into the earlier sixth century.[71] Procopius recorded that statues were still standing within its precincts in the 520s, although his description makes evident that for him it was a place whose meaning lay in a distant past rather than the reality of Justinian's empire.[72] Very shortly thereafter part of the Templum complex was refigured by Felix IV as the Church of Saints Cosmas and Damian, whose sixth-century apsidal mosaics depicted Christ and his saints in a scene of celestial peace, and upon whose feast the congregation offered petitionary prayers for peace.[73] Here, again, the *pax Romana* had been supplanted by the peace and order of the community of the saints, and the promise of heavenly peace for the saved.

Procopius is also the source for a final witness to sixth-century Rome's dislocation from its classical past, an account of a Roman attempt to reopen the doors of the Temple of Janus during the Gothic wars of the 530s. The *porta Janualis* had its own place in the way in which notions of peace had been given physical form in classical Rome. It was long-regarded by Romans as an 'indicator of peace and war' (*index pacis bellique*) shut in times of peace, but opened for war.[74] The ritual's roots were attributed to the celebrations following Rome's victory in the first Punic war. Famously, the doors were shut three times in Augustus' reign, as he proudly recalled in the *Res Gestae*, and at various moments

[69] Josephus, *Jewish War* VII.158. For discussion, see Noreña, 'Medium and Message'.
[70] Ammianus Marcellinus XVI.10.20. Curran, *Pagan City*, 191–3; R. Klein, 'Der Rombesuch des Kaisers Konstantius II im Jahre 357', *Athenaeum* 57 (1979), 98–115.
[71] Marcellinus, *Comes, Chronicon*, ed. T. Mommsen, *MGH AA* 11 (Berlin, 1894), *s.a.* 408, p. 69, echoed by the so-called Copenhagen Continuator of Prosper, *MGH AA* 9 (Berlin, 1892), *s.a.* 408, p. 299. On which see S. Muhlberger, 'Heroic Kings and Unruly Generals: The "Copenhagen" Continuation of Prosper Reconsidered'; *idem*, 'The Copenhagen Continuation of Prosper: A Translation', *Florilegium* 6 (1984), 50–70; 71–95, at 74.
[72] *Bell.Goth.* LV.21.
[73] Krautheimer, *Rome*, 92; C. Belting-Ihm, 'Theophanic Images of Divine Majesty in Early Medieval Italian Church Decoration', in William Tronzo (ed.), *Italian Church Decoration of the Early Middle Ages and Early Renaissance* (Bologna, 1989), 43–61. J. Deshusses (ed.), *Le Sacramentaire Grégorien. Principles formes d'après les plus anciens manuscrits* (Freiburg, 1992), I, no. 438, p. 204.
[74] J. Blair DeBrohun, 'The Gates of War (and Peace): Roman Literary Perspectives', in K. A. Raaflaub (ed.), *War and Peace in the Ancient World* (Oxford, 2007), 256–78; R. Taylor, 'Watching the Skies: Janus, Auspication, and the Shrine in the Roman Forum', *Memoirs of the American Academy in Rome* 45 (2000), 1–39, esp. 7–8.

thereafter.[75] They, too, seem to have had continued life in the Christian period. It is Procopius, once more, who gives us the final glimpse of the doors of Janus in his account of the siege of 537–8 during the Gothic wars. Starving, the aqueducts cut, and with too many civilians and too few soldiers to face Wittigis' Goths, a secret party of Romans inside the Byzantine-held city attempted to force open the temple doors. The attempt to reopen the doors was presumably intended as an attempt to invoke traditional Roman ideals: a morale boost to the fighting spirit of an embattled citizenry against a Gothic enemy who had, over the previous decades, come to appropriate the language of imperial peace for themselves, and a final plea to the gods who had protected the city *ab urbe condita*. Such pleas, and the fabric of belief that made them possible, were already becoming part of a lost world. In the course of the diplomatic overtures between the Gothic court and Constantinople that preceded the outbreak of hostilities, Cassiodorus, adopting the voice of 'Rome' herself, had written to Justinian reminding him who the real defenders of Rome's *securitas* were: the Apostles Peter and Paul.[76] For his part Procopius was explicit that the temple's abandonment had been the result of conversion. 'When the Romans came to honour Christianity', he noted, 'as truly as any others, they gave up the custom of opening these doors, even when they were at war'.[77] The attempt failed. The doors, Procopius relates, could barely be moved. No rallying gesture could be given. Time and rust had intervened.

If this process of effacement coupled with Rome's decreasing importance as a political centre in the later fourth and fifth centuries shrank the presence of peace in public political life, in the East, at least, the cult of peace remained vital, though deeply changed, through the transformations of the fourth century and after. Soon after Constantinople's foundation in November 324, building began on a church dedicated to St Eirene under Constantine's direct patronage in the heart of his new capital.[78] It is unlikely that the foundation was intended to celebrate a specific martyr. Early Christianity generated a number of passions of martyrs named Eirene, though none enjoyed the importance or popularity that such a prominent foundation demanded, and it is best seen as a dedication to a personification, Hagia Eirene ('Holy Peace').[79] Augustus established the Roman cult of Pax. Constantine christianized it. The Church of Hagia Eirene was a central fixture in Constantinople's topography, serving as the city's cathedral

---

[75] *Res Gestae*, c. 13; S. Platner, *A Topographical Dictionary of Ancient Rome* (Oxford, 1929), 278–80.

[76] *Var.* XI.13.6.

[77] *Bell. Goth.* V.25.

[78] W. S. George, *The Church of Saint Eirene at Constantinople* (London, 1913).

[79] R. Krautheimer, *Three Christian Capitals, Topography and Politics* (Berkeley, 1983), 46. For the background of this building policy see *idem*, 'The Ecclesiastical Building Program of Constantine', in G. Bonamente and F. Fusco (eds), *Costantino il Grande dall'antichità all'umanesimo* (Macerata, 1993), II, pp. 509–52. On the possible identities of Eirene see A. Khazdan, 'Irene', *ODB*, II, p. 1008. D. M. Nicol, 'Byzantine Political Thought', *CHMPT*, 51–79 at 53–4.

until its central role was usurped by Hagia Sophia's completion in 537. Despite its overshadowing, the original church was rebuilt by Justinian after being burnt down in the Nika riots.[80]

Hagia Eirene's construction was but one element of a broader programmatic commitment to peace by Constantine. He evoked peace in his public political statements not only through church-building but also through his speeches and coinage.[81] Numerous emperors and, particularly in the later third century, a number of would-be emperors, had issued coins carrying variants on the formulae PAX AUG(G).[82] So, in his turn, did Constantine, whose coinage also bore the legend PAX PERPET from late 312 onwards.[83] Whilst both words had appeared on earlier coins, their appearance together was a Constantinian innovation, perhaps the influence of Lactantius, who deployed the phrase, and whose notions of a Christian empire informed Constantine's own.[84] Ambiguous in precise meaning, alluding as much to the Augustan tradition of peaceful rule as to the peace of the Church or the arrival of a divinely sanctioned era of peace, Constantine's PAX coinage, like those coins bearing LIBERTAS and VICTORIA, anticipated the later deployment of a reduced range of pointedly vague legends that came to dominate later imperial coinage.[85] This numismatic lexicon, as we shall shortly see, found its imitators in the West. The deployment of a language and imagery of peace had, in fact, begun before the Edict of Milan and the peace of the Church. The anonymous panegyrist who spoke in praise of Constantine at Trier in late 310 chose to close his presentation by lauding him as a god who had brought a new golden age of peace.[86] Following the Edict of Milan peace was a theme to which Constantinian propaganda frequently returned: in Constantine's own 'Oration to the Saints', with its invocation of the Christian interpretation of

---

[80] U. Peschlow, *Die Irenenkirche in Konstantinopel* (Berlin, 1978).

[81] R. Longtin, 'Constantine and Christianity: the Numismatic Evidence', *Journal of the Classical and Numismatic Society*, series 2, 1.2 (2000), 5–27; P. Bruun, 'Victorious Signs of Constantine: a Reappraisal', *Numismatic Chronicle* 157 (1997), 41–59.

[82] See for examples the PAX issues from AD 68–9, *RIC* I, p. 190, and the issues of Galba, 203, 205–6, and Otho, 226, PAX ORBIS TERRARUM. The numbers are too numerous to list comprehensively here. See de Souza, '*Parta*', 98–100. A. Casagrande, 'Commodus used PAX as Propaganda to Instill the Confidence of Roman Citizens in their Emperor', *The Celator* 5.4 (1991), 28–9; J. A. Garzón Blanco, 'La evolución de la iconografía de la diosa PAX a través de la numismática imperial romana', *Gaceta Numismática* 119 (1995), 33–8.

[83] *RIC* 6: 355; 7: 143.

[84] *Divine Institutes*, VII.26. On which see C. M. Odahl, *Constantine and the Christian Empire* (London, 2004); T. D. Barnes, 'Lactantius and Constantine', *JRS* 63 (1973), 29–46.

[85] J. M. C. Toynbee, 'Roma and Constantinopolis in Late-Antique Art from 312 to 365', *JRS* 37 (1947), 135–44.

[86] R. A. B. Mynors, *XII Panegyrici Latini* (Oxford, 1964), VI.21. For the Constantine/Augustus identification see B. S. Rodgers, 'Constantine's Pagan Vision', *Byzantion* 50 (1980), 259–78, recapitulated in C. E. V. Nixon, R. A. B. Mynors, and B. S. Rodgers, *In Praise of Later Roman Emperors. The Panegyricii Latini* (Berkeley, 1994), 248–51. See also R. R. R. Smith, 'The Public Image of Licinius I: Portrait Sculpture and Imperial Ideology in the Early Fourth Century', *JRS* 87 (1997), 170–202, at 187.

the peace-bringing child of Virgil's Fourth Eclogue;[87] in the panegyric *carmina figurata* of Publilius Optatianus Porfyrius; and in both of Eusebius' *Vita* and *Laus Constantini*.[88] Inaccessible to Latinate western readers, these Greek works went untapped by theorists of power in the successor kingdoms.[89] Despite this, the figure of Constantine cast a shadow in the early medieval West: the mix of imperial authority, Christian piety, and military victory he represented made him an appealing figure for some. Publilius Optatianus Porfyrius' *carmina*, like their subject's brand of Christian emperorship, would gradually spawn later eighth- and ninth-century imitators, and at least one claim would be made that a Carolingian emperor wore Constantine's own crown.[90]

In Byzantium these imperial ideas were the foundations for an ongoing tradition of political ideas and ceremony. But what survived into the early Middle Ages of these political languages and cultural frameworks? Not the sites, clearly: but the idea of imperial peace held a value for rulers like Edwin and Charles the Bald, and for the men who wrote for and about them. In the former western provinces the association of Roman rule and peace was transmitted by a number of routes, some more recoverable than others. Isidore's widely read *Etymologies* kept alive some notion of the Gates of Janus in early medieval classrooms, if only in his account of the derivation of the word 'door' (*ianua*) from Janus.[91] Early medieval poets, notably those at Carolingian courts, revisited Virgil's verse in order to shape their own idealized imperial images, and to praise new golden ages of peace. Charlemagne, and many who followed him, was praised, like Augustus, as another Aeneas.[92] Also important was the template of royal ideals offered by Roman panegyric, a genre whose image of imperial

---

[87] T. D. Barnes, *Constantine and Eusebius* (Cambridge, MA, 1984); M. Edwards, *Constantine and Christendom. The Orations of the Saints; The Greek and Latin Accounts of the Discovery of the Cross; The Edict of Constantine to Pope Silvester* TTH 39 (Liverpool, 2003).

[88] Eusebius, *Life of Constantine*, trans. A. Cameron and S. Hall (Oxford, 1999), 155, 156–8; 311–12. H. Drake, *Constantine and the Bishops. The Politics of Intolerance* (Baltimore, 2002), 244–5. On Publilius see U. Ernst, *Carmen figuratum: Geschichte des Figurengedichts von den antiken Ursprüngen bis zum Ausgang des Mittelalters* (Cologne, 1991); T. D. Barnes, 'Publilius Optatianus Porfyrius', *American Journal of Philology* 96 (1975), 173–86.

[89] E. Ewig, 'Das Bild Constantins des Großen in den ersten Jahrhunderten des abendländischen Mittelalters', *HJ* 75 (1956), 1–46; S. N. C. Lieu, 'From History to Legend and Legend to History: The Medieval and Byzantine Transformation of Constantine's *Vita*' and J. Stevenson, 'Constantine, Aldhelm and the Loathly Lady', both in S. Lieu and D. Montserrat (eds), *Constantine: History, Historiography, and Legend* (London, 1998), 136–76; 189–206.

[90] E. Faral, *Ermold le Noir. Poème sur Louis le Pieux et Épitres au Roi Pépin. Les classiques de l'histoire de France au moyen âge* 14 (1932, repr. 1964), lines 848 *et seq.*; C. M. Chazelle, *The Crucified God in the Carolingian Era: Theology and Art of Christ's Passion* (Cambridge, 2001), 31–2; V. H. Elbern, 'Liturgisches Gerät in edlen Materialien zur Zeit Karls des Großen', in W. Braunfels and H. Schnitzler (eds), *Karl der Große. Lebenswerk und Nachleben* (Düsseldorf, 1965), III, pp. 115–67, at 137–8.

[91] *Etym.* XV.7.

[92] C. Ratkowitsch, *Karolus Magnus—alter Aeneas, alter Martinus, alter Iustinus* (Vienna, 1997); M. Tanner, *The Last Descendant of Aeneas. The Hapsburgs and the Mythic Image of the Emperor* (New Haven, 1993).

authority also owed a debt to the Augustan archetype, and which found its last generation of exponents at the Vandal, Ostrogothic, and Merovingian courts. Historical narratives were similarly significant. The accounts of the Roman past in Latin historical digests of the later empire, collections such as Justinus' epitome of Pompeius Trogus' lost *Historiae Philippicae* and Eutropius' *Breviary*, found later readers, and by so doing also played their part in keeping the idea of Augustan peace alive and accessible.[93]

Liturgy proved equally important for maintaining a memory of Roman peace in the post-Roman centuries. Despite surviving in a Frankish copy dating from the mid eighth century, the Old Gelasian Sacramentary contains in large part prayers conventionally seen as characteristic of the liturgy of certain Roman basilicas in the seventh and early eighth centuries.[94] Its well-known '*missa pro regibus*' shows that the relationship was still invoked in the services with its appeal to God, 'protector of all kingdoms, and especially of the Roman Empire'.[95] The *secreta* of the Mass, the prayer spoken over the sacraments, invoked the same linkage between Rome and peace:

Accept, O Lord, the supplicant prayers and sacrifices of your Church for the safety of Your servant and to work the old miracles of Your arm for the protection of faithful peoples and, the enemies of peace overcome, may the secure Roman freedom let them serve You.[96]

And, here, in the final post-Communion prayer:

O God, You who have prepared the Roman Empire for the preaching of the Gospel of the Eternal Kingdom, hold out to Your servants, our princes, heavenly weapons, that the peace of the Church will not be disturbed by the storm of wars.[97]

---

[93] 'Justinus', *T&T*, *s.n.*, 197–9, Eutropius, 7–10. On the MSS tradition see *T&T*, 159–62. For the early medieval reception of these, and other, works see R. McKitterick, 'The Audience for Latin Historiography in the Early Middle Ages: Text, Transmission and Manuscript Dissemination', in A. Scharer and G. Scheibelreiter (eds), *Historiographie im frühen Mittelalter*, Veröffentlichungen des Instituts für Österreichische Geschichtsforschung 32 (Vienna, 1994), 96–114.

[94] Scholarship on the Old Gelasian Sacramentary is substantial and vexed, and cannot be entered into with any detail here. See, however, the summary of arguments for a Roman attribution over a Merovingian place of composition of Garipzanov, *Symbolic Language*, 58–68, who reviews the arguments and affirms, to my mind correctly, a Roman origin for the *missa* with a summary of its sources and an English translation at 327–9. For the case for Frankish origin see Y. Hen, *The Royal Patronage of Liturgy in Frankish Gaul to the Death of Charles the Bald (877)* (London, 2001), 39–40. Even if a case could be sustained for a Frankish hand behind this *missa pro regibus* it would, in any case, only be a Frankish reflex of a late imperial practice.

[95] *Lib. Sacr. Rom.*, 1505: 'Deus, regnorum omnium et romani maximae protector imperii, da servis tuis regibus nostris illis triumphum virtutis tuae scienter excolere, ut cuius constitutione sunt principes, eius semper munere sint potentes. Per.'

[96] *Lib. Sacr. Rom.*, 1507: 'SECRETA: Suscipe, domine, praeces et hostias aecclesiae tuae pro salute famuli tui illius subplicantes et protectione fidelium populorum antiqua brachi tui operare miracula, et superactis pacis inimicis secura tibi serviat romana libertas. Per.'

[97] *Lib. Sacr. Rom.*, 1509: 'POST COMMUNIONEM: Deus, qui praedicando aeterni regni evangelio romanum imperium praeparasti, praetende famulis tuis illis principibus nostris arma caelestia, et pax aecclesiarum nullo turbetur tempestate bellorum. Per dominum.'

Later hands would emend these prayers, dropping *imperium* and *libertas* for less anachronistic terms, but before that point the services of an unknown number of early medieval religious centres invoked Roman peace in their prayers.[98]

The Old Gelasian Mass' final prayer signals one of the last and most important contexts within which a sense of the *pax Romana* was transmitted to the early Middle Ages: the notion that the creation of earthly peace through Rome's conquests was the necessary prelude to the dissemination of Christ's teachings and that the birth of the Prince of Peace and the establishment of the *pax Romana* was a divinely inspired conjunction.[99] Philo of Alexandria first propounded this idea which was developed by later apologists, including Melito of Sardis, Origen, Lactantius, and Eusebius.[100] Adherents of this perspective—and there were many—held that it was only Rome's unification of different peoples under a single authority that rendered the apostolic mission possible.[101] Not all, however, saw the constellation of Incarnation and Augustan authority working in divine concert. In the later second century Hippolytus had read the relationship not as one of harmony but of dissonance: the Roman Empire was nothing less than a satanically inspired counterfeit of the true kingdom of Christ.[102] Nor would the straightforward optimism of this imperial Christology survive long into the fifth century, when the relationship of Christianity and a faltering empire provoked its reconsideration, and would find in Augustine a mind unwilling to light upon easy answers in historical coincidence.[103] Nevertheless, the synchrony of Augustan peace and Incarnation continued to inform later generations through works such as Rufinus' translation of Eusebius and, above all, by Orosius' immensely influential *Seven Books of History Against the Pagans*.[104] Bede, for example, would

[98] McCormick, *Eternal Victory*, 342–7; *idem*, 'The Liturgy of War in the Early Middle Ages: Crises, Litanies and the Carolingian Monarchy', *Viator* 15 (1984), 1–23. See also Hen, *Royal Patronage*, 39–41.

[99] K. Wengst, *Pax Romana: and the Peace of Jesus Christ*, trans. John Bowden (London, 1987), 7–54.

[100] Origen, *Contra Celsum*, ed. and trans. H. Chadwick (Cambridge, 1965). For Eusebius see A. P. Johnson, *Ethnicity and Argument in Eusebius' Praeparatio Evangelica* (Oxford, 2006), 180–90, with references.

[101] E.g., Origen, *Contra Celsum*, II. c. 30, p. 92.

[102] R. A. Markus, 'The Roman Empire in Early Christian Historiography', *The Downside Review* 81 (1963), 340–53, at 342; P. Beskow, *Rex Gloriae: The Kingship of Christ in the Early Church*, trans. E. J. Sharpe (Stockholm, 1962), 176–7; P. Prigent, 'Hippolyte, commentateur de l'Apocalypse', *Theologische Zeitschrift* 28 (1972), 391–412.

[103] Markus, 'Empire'.

[104] Rufinus, *Die Kirchengeschichte mit der lateinischen Übersetzung der Rufinus*, ed. A. Schwarz and T. Mommsen (Leipzig, 1903), I, pp. 385–9. Earlier studies include J. E. L. Oulton, 'Rufinus' Translation of the Church History of Eusebius', *JTS* 30 (1929), 150–74; A. J. Droge, 'The Apologetic Dimensions of the Ecclesiastical History', in H. W. Attridge and G. Hata (eds), *Eusebius, Christianity and Judaism* (Leiden, 1992), 492–509, esp. 489. On Orosius see A. Merrills, *History and Geography in Late Antiquity* (Cambridge, 2005), 35–99, esp. 47–8, 57–9, with references.

see a connection between Christ's birth at a time of the highest earthly peace (*pax summa*) and his gift of heavenly peace (*pax superna*).[105]

TESTAMENT AND COMMENTARY

When Roman ideas of peace survived into the early Middle Ages they often did so within the matrix of Christian thought. All the authors of many of the works under discussion here were, like Bede, the products of a Latin Christian education, although the precise character of that education varied widely. That education meant that for them, too, the idea of peace would lead toward a sequence of associated scriptural passages, episodes, and figures, such as Hezekiah but particularly Solomon, and ultimately, Christ: peacemaker between man and God, foretold by Isaiah (Isa. IX.6), anticipated by Solomon, and identified by Paul as Prince of Peace (Rom. V.1, Eph. II.14).[106] For our purposes, peace revolved around the use of one key term, *pax*, the Vulgate translation of the Greek *eirene* and, in turn, the Hebrew *salom*, each of which possessed their own distinct semantic range and related fields of meaning.[107]

The individual books of scripture are highly diverse in form, content, and style, no less the range of ideas of peace they contain. The Vulgate offers around 500 explicit references to *pax* and its derivatives in one form or another. Isolating such passages makes it possible to sketch something of this range, but is, however, dangerously artificial, for such passages were rarely encountered in isolation. More likely they would instead have been read or heard as part of a larger tapestry of scripture, in a homiletic or liturgical context, or encountered within a work intended for a new and specific purpose, alongside other related passages. Exegesis turned on the principle of explication of scripture by scripture, a process that impelled commentators to generate latticeworks of associated and mutually amplifying passages, each of which provided context and depth to the other, creating a self-supporting system of scriptural truth. Scriptural treatments of peace were subject not only to interpretation but also to translation, whether through interlinear glosses or through vernacular translations such as Wulfila's Gothic text (thus Luke II.14: '*wulþus in hauhistjam guda jah ana airþai gawairþi in mannam godis wiljins*') or the *Heliand*, the early ninth-century Old Saxon treatment of the Gospels in which Christ, *friðubarn godes* ('the peace-child of

[105] Bede, 'In nativitate Domini', CCSL 122, p. 37.

[106] For Hezekiah's deployment as an ideal for kingship in the tenth century, H. Wolfram, *Conrad II, 990–1039. Emperor of Three Kingdoms*, trans. D. A. Kaiser (University Park, PA, 2006), 148–53.

[107] 'Frieden', *s.v. Theologisches Realenzyklopädie*, IX, 605–46. *Eirene* see E. Dinkler, 'The Early Christian Conception of Peace', in P. Yoder and W. Swartley (eds), *The Meaning of Peace* (Louisville, 1992), 164–212; G. Haufe, 'Eirene im Neuen Testament', *Communio viatorum* 27.1–2 (1984), 7–17.

God'), was transplanted into a wild landscape of hill forts and warrior re-
tinues.[108]

A comprehensive treatment of scriptural notions of peace is impossible here.
That said, a brief sketch remains useful. Scriptural treatments of peace can be
loosely grouped into a number of general categories. First, inner peace, the inner
harmony and calm of a person. Second, peace between people, whether at the
individual or collective levels. Essentially political in character, this notion of
peace is applicable both to peace within and between social units: individuals,
families, tribes, cities, peoples, or kingdoms. By the very nature of subject matter,
these larger, more formally political types of peace have a presence in the Old
Testament that they lack in the New.[109] Shifting the focus brings us to peace
with God, a state of harmony that can exist on the individual or the collective
level, the latter being invariably linked to God's Covenant with Israel. Old and
New Testament alike, however, share strong elements of peace as an eschatological concept, with the notion of the Messiah as a bringer of peace or its creator,
and the defining notion of heavenly peace, the reward of the just and faithful.
This messianic notion, fulfilled, was a defining theme of the Gospels, where
peace and peacemaking are presented as a quality and an activity of particular
importance to both the individual Christian and the Christian community. The
New Testament also recast the Covenant, reshaping the relationship that Christians had with God through the Crucifixion, the central reconciling act between
man and God.[110]

In general terms we can identify a core of scriptural passages that early
medieval authors repeatedly drew upon. In Reydellet's succinct appraisal: 'la
théorie du prince chrétien s'appuie sur un corpus de textes relativement réduit'.
More reduced, still, when, as here, we are dealing with a single aspect of Christian
rulership.[111] The historical books of the Old Testament offer their respective
accounts of Israel, its rulers, and the times of peace and war that both underwent.
In terms of personal relations with God, the Psalms and the Book of Job both

---

[108] For *frið* and its compounds, the Toronto *Dictionary of the Old English Corpus, s.v.*; Bosworth
and Toller, *Dictionary*, S.V., 338–9; C. Fell, '*UnFrið*: An Approach to a Definition', *Saga-Book of
the Viking Society for Northern Research* 21 (1982–3), 85–100. For peace and its cognates in OHG
see Green, *Language*, 52–62, and for Gothic G. H. Balg, *A Comparative Glossary of the Gothic
Language* (New York, 1887), 131. For the *Heliand* E. E. Sievers, *Titelauflage vermehrt um das Prager
Fragment des Heliand und die Vaticanischen Fragmente von Heliand und Genesis* (Berlin, 1935), lines
1156, p. 82; 3899, p. 266. On the latter's recasting of Christian concepts D. H. Green, 'Three
aspects of the Old Saxon biblical epic, the *Heliand*', in D. H. Green and F. Siegmund (eds), *The
Continental Saxons from the Migration Period to the Tenth Century: An Ethnographic Perspective*
(Woodbridge, 2003), 247–63, with discussion at 264–9, and J. Cathey, *Hêliand, Text and
Commentary* (Morgantown, WV, 2002), 167–8.
[109] V. P. Furnish, 'War and Peace in the New Testament', *Interpretation* 38 (1984), 363–79.
[110] Chazelle, *Crucified God*, and B. Raw, *Anglo-Saxon Crucifixion Iconography* (Cambridge,
1990).
[111] M. Reydellet, 'La Bible miroir des princes du ive au viie siècle', in J. Fontaine and C. Pietri
(eds), *Le monde latin antique et la Bible*, Bible de tous les temps 2 (Paris, 1985), 431–53, at 432.

offered passages that set out the individual's relationship with the Almighty, and the condition of fallen man more generally. In the case of the Psalms their centrality was underlined by their prominent position in early medieval devotional life, from monastic rounds to lay private prayer, and the particular relationship they defined between man and God, a relationship rendered all the more charged because of the early medieval conviction of their royal, Davidic character. From our perspective it is worth noting that notions of peace of varying types run through the Psalms: as an ideal state to be sought out and struggled for (Ps. XXXIII.15, 'seek peace and pursue it'), but also as an inner state (Ps. CXXII.7). Certain psalms, such as Psalms LXXI and CXXI, offered images of both peaceful rule and the character of the peaceful kingdom. In the case of Psalm LXXI we have already seen something of its importance at work in Bede's construction of the peace of Edwin's reign. It is here also that we see repeated the notion that peace comes from God and is His gift: 'The Lord will give strength to his people: the Lord will bless his people with peace' (Ps. XXVIII.10), a sentiment also present elsewhere, for example, Proverbs XVI.7: 'When the ways of man shall please the Lord, he will convert even his enemies to peace', and at its most unequivocal in Isaiah XLV.7: 'I form the light, and create darkness; I make peace, and create evil. I the Lord that do all these things.' God was in the words of many a prayer for peace, *largitor pacis*. Proverbs offered a wealth of comments on the practical benefits of peace and the advantages of being peaceful, for example, Proverbs XII.20: 'Deceit is in the heart of them that think evil things: but joy followeth them that take counsels of peace'.

Certain passages offered instances of peace that early medieval men and women would have found readily comprehensible within the terms of their own lives. The accounts of war and peace found in Joshua, Kings, Chronicles, and Maccabees, for example, in which peace settlements were made and treaties established (I Macc. VIII.20–2, IX.70; II Macc. XII.11–12) had immediate relevance in a world where such procedures remained commonplace activities. Similarly, Genesis contained what early medieval readers would have recognized as the first case of hostage suretyship (Gen. XXXXII.19–33).[112]

The Deuteronomist's statements on the right conduct of war ('If at any time thou come to fight against a city, thou shalt first offer it peace') also touched upon the concrete question of peace settlements and the issue of correct conduct in war.[113] Related to this, and on the simplest level, are the scriptural notions of peace already familiar to us from Bede: absence of violence, coercion, freedom to travel, contained in the commonplace statement 'to go in peace' found

[112] See also Gen. XII–XXV; Josh. IX.15; I Kings IV.24 V.12, XXII.45; I Chron. XII.18, XVIII.10; Ezra IV.17. S. Morschauser, 'Hospitality, Hostiles and Hostages: On the Legal Background of Genesis 19:1–9', *Journal for the Study of the Old Testament* 27.4 (2003), 461–85, esp. 476–7.

[113] Deut. XX.10–12. See also, on collective oath-swearing: Josh. IX.15, XXI.42.

throughout the books of the Bible and the liturgy.[114] Common to many of these references was the core notion that peace, whether individual, collective, or even in the natural world, was a gift from God, a notion fundamental to the many petitionary prayers for peace in the early medieval liturgy, and to theorists of ideal rulership. Peace won through battle came, for example, through the right relationship of the ruler and the people of Israel with God, and the fulfilment of Abraham's Covenant with God (Exod. XV.1–27). Other books offered less triumphalist passages, notably Lamentations and Jeremiah (Jer. VI.14, VIII.11: 'Peace, peace: and there was no peace'), whose cry of despair more than one medieval churchman would reach for. In the early 840s, as the Carolingian lands slid into conflict in the wake of Louis the Pious' death, Hrabanus Maurus dispatched the commentary on Jeremiah, which heads this chapter, to Louis' eldest son, Lothar, 'an appropriate and timely gift', as Mayke de Jong noted.[115] In prophecy, despair and hope run close, and in a number of the prophetic books peace was framed eschatologically, as the hope of the world to come. The prophecies of Micah and Isaiah, for example, provide one of the paradigmatic passages on this final peace after Christ's return: 'And he shall judge amongst the nations, and shall rebuke many people: and they shall beat their swords into ploughshares, and their spears into pruning hooks: nation shall not lift up sword against nation, neither shall they learn war any more' (Mic. IV.2–4; Isa. II.2–44).[116]

Complex interpretive traditions developed around such passages that sought to place the prophesied time of peace in historical time.[117] For many they spoke of the period that followed the Parousia and Antichrist's defeat, a period preceded by a time of tribulation, famine, and 'wars and rumours of wars' (Mark XIII.5–8, developing Dan. II.28–9). Some saw this foretelling Christ's thousand-year reign on earth, when the blessed would enjoy earthly peace and prosperity, conditions that offered the opportunity for final penance for some and a gentle acclimatizing to the heady pacific atmosphere of the imminent Heavenly Kingdom for others.[118] Jerome, working from discrepant figures given in the Book of Daniel, calculated this period's length as precisely forty-five days, a pause for the faithful to be tested.[119] By so doing he established the idea of a brief episode of earthly peace which became the focus for subsequent

[114] Exod. IV.18; Judg. XVIII.6; I Sam, I.17; XX.13; II Sam, III.23 XV.9 XV.27; II Kings V.19; Mark V.34; Luke VII.50, VIII.48; Jas. II.16; Judith VIII.34. Travel in peace: Gen. XXVI.31.
[115] M. de Jong, 'Exegesis for an Empress', in E. Cohen and M. de Jong (eds), *Medieval Transformations. Texts, Power, and Gifts in Context* (Leiden, 2001), 69–100, at 72.
[116] Mic. IV.3, V.3–4; Hos. II.20; Zech IX.10; Pss. XXXXVI.9–10, LXII.3, LXII.14.
[117] E. A. Matter, 'The Apocalypse in Early Medieval Exegesis', in R. K. Emmerson and B. McGinn (eds), *The Apocalypse in the Middle Ages* (Ithaca, NY, 1992), 38–50.
[118] R. E. Lerner, 'Refreshment of the Saints. The Time after Antichrist as a Station for Earthly Progress in Medieval Thought', *Traditio* 32 (1976), 97–144. B. Daley, *The Hope of the Early Church. A Handbook of Patristic Eschatology* (Cambridge, 1991), 20–2, 31.
[119] Daley, *Hope*, 133. Lerner, 'Refreshment', 101–2.

embroidery. Augustine dismissed any attempt to assess the exact length of this reign of peace, though he conceded that it was a time free of sin watched over by a reigning Christ. Others, such as Bede, shared Augustine's hesitancy over chiliasm, but conceded that whilst there might be a brief, peace-filled pause between Antichrist's defeat and the Last Judgement, its precise length was not for man to know.[120]

Undoubtedly the most politicized eschatological scenario, and the one in which a variant of the peacemaking ruler of earthly origin figures most prominently, is that of 'the Last Emperor'. In the words of Bernard McGinn, this shadowy end-time ruler, 'usually appears as a war-like ruler who will defeat all Rome's and God's enemies, vindicate the good of the just by his provision of a messianic time of plenty, and achieve supreme imitation of Christ before handing over world domination to him'.[121] Thus, the Last Emperor's actions recapitulated the Augustan imperial peace that preceded Christ's first coming, creating a second terminal peace at the close of the salvational arc. The tangled roots of the Last Emperor 'King of Peace' tradition lie in late antique apocalyptic texts such as the Oracle of Baalbek and the Coptic Apocalypse of Elijah, but came to prominence and eventual influence in the West through the later seventh-century Syriac apocalyptic tract ascribed to Methodius of Patara, and conventionally known as the Revelations of Pseudo-Methodius.[122] Translated into Latin in Merovingian Francia around 720, and extant in several eighth-century manuscripts from centres including Corbie and St-Gall, Pseudo-Methodius enjoyed considerable popularity in the earlier Middle Ages.[123] Conclusive evidence of the figure of the Last Emperor emerging into new works before Adso of Montier-en-Der has not been authoritatively identified and he is not, as Kevin Hughes has pointed out, a presence in some of the period's more extensive treatments of Antichrist.[124] That said, there are fleeting hints that the image of the peace-bringing Last Emperor had some currency in the Carolingian world: at least one figure in the Utrecht Psalter, produced perhaps at Rheims in the 820s, and dressed in a manner strikingly similar to some contemporary images of rulers, has been plausibly identified as him.[125] Few, however, have gone so far as Richard Landes, who has suggested that Charlemagne's imperial coronation, dateable to the

[120] Lerner, 'Refreshment', 104–5.
[121] B. McGinn, *Antichrist: Two Thousand Years of the Human Fascination with Evil* (New York, 2000), 88–9.
[122] B. McGinn, *Visions of the End. Apocalyptic Traditions in the Middle Ages* (New York, 1979), 39–49.
[123] W. J. Aerts and G. A. A. Kortekaas, *Die Apokalypse des Pseudo-Methodius: die ältesten griechischen und lateinischen Übersetzungen* (Leuven, 1998).
[124] K. Hughes, *Constructing Antichrist: Paul, Biblical Commentary, and the Development of Doctrine in the Early Middle Ages* (Washington, DC 2005), 162.
[125] McGinn, *Antichrist*, 104–6; A. Belkin, 'The Antichrist Legend in the Utrecht Psalter', *Rivista di Storia e Letteratura Religiosa* 23 (1987), 279–88.

first day of the year 6000 by *annus mundi* calculation, was intended to fulfil the promise of the thousand-year peace ushered in by the Last Emperor's reign.[126]

The New Testament, in its turn, provided its own distinct treatments of peace, and distinct legacies. The political peace of the Old Testament books comes to be less relevant and to be supplanted by a no less powerful sense of community and collective peace: that of the members of the Church joined in Christ. This, too, we shall see deployed by early medieval authors, in particular Paul's powerfully influential language of community, *caritas*, 'bonds of peace' (*vincula pacis*), and of unity (Gal. III.28), key terms in the development of early medieval discourses of political collectivity and deployed with special force by the Carolingians in the creation of a public language of political relations. Paul's emphasis upon peace in his epistolography was also highly influential.[127] Other principal passages include Luke II.14 ('Glory to God in the highest, and on earth peace to men of good will'), which served in the 790s as the tag to the mosaic celebrating Charlemagne and Leo III in the Lateran *triclinium*, and John XIV.27 ('Peace I leave with you, my peace I give unto you'), in which peace refers not only to the community, and to the hope for salvation that Christ's incarnation makes possible, but also serves as a metonym for his teachings as a whole, and for the state of eternal life that the Incarnation both promised and provided the path towards. A further pivotal passage, and one that leads to another aspect of peaceful rulership in its christological or christomimetic aspect, is to be found in the Ninth Beatitude, 'Blessed are the peacemakers: for they shall be called children of God'. This image of the peacemaker as the son of God opened up parallels between Christ, the literal *filius Dei*, and those who followed his teachings.

At the centre of this latticework stood Christ. He was the true peacemaker, the Prince of Peace, the reconciler of man to God through his Incarnation and Crucifixion.[128] The Cross, symbol and instrument of his sacrifice, was itself a symbol of peace. Christ *was* peace: 'For he is our peace, who has made two into one' (Eph. II.14). Christ may have been the ultimate Prince of Peace, but it would not be until the ninth century that explicit parallels between Christ and living rulers would emerge fully into royal theory. Christian culture constantly

---

[126] S. Shimahara, 'Peut-on parler de millénarisme à l'époque carolingienne?: l'apport de quelques sources exégétiques', *Temas Medievales* 14 (2006), 99–138 offers a recent overview of attitudes to Carolingian eschatology. For the case for Carolingian apocalyptic concerns see W. Brandes, '*Tempora periculosa sunt*. Eschatologisches im Vorfeld der Kaiserkrönung Karls des Grossen', in R. Berndt (ed.), *Das Frankfurter Konzil von 794. Kristallisationspunkt karolingischer Kultur* (Mainz, 1997), I 49–79; R. Landes, 'Lest the Millennium be Fulfilled: Apocalyptic Expectations and the Pattern of Western Chronography, 100–800 CE', in W. Verbeke, D. Verhelst, and A. Welkenhuysen (eds), *The Use and Abuse of Eschatology in the Middle Ages* (Leuven, 1988), 137–211; J. Gil, '*Los terrores del año 800'*, *Actas del Simposio para el estudio de los codices del "Comentario al Apocalipsis" de Beato de Liebana* (Madrid, 1977), 215–47.

[127] On peace in the greetings of the early Church see J. Lieu, '"Grace to you and peace": the Apostolic Greeting', *Bulletin of the John Rylands University Library of Manchester* 68.1 (1985), 161–78.

[128] II. Cor. V.20; Gal. I.15; Eccles. XXXXIV.17.

affirmed Christ's kingship, and in as much as it also emphasized Christ's peacemaking, it underscored those same characteristics in earthly kingship.[129] Simultaneously, the kingship of Christ legitimized not only individual rulers but also reaffirmed kingship as the prevailing political model.[130]

For most early medieval theorists, however, it was the safer figure of Solomon with whom peaceful rule was most commonly associated. Solomon prefigured Christ. Both were 'sons of David' and for many commentators the building of Solomon's Temple foreshadowed Christ's own greater creation of 'the living temple' of the Church. Solomon's peaceful reign was a figure for Christ's own endless reign of peace.[131] Here is Bede fusing all these elements in the first chapter of his commentary on the Temple:

> The House of God which King Solomon built in Jerusalem was made as a figure of the holy universal Church which, from the first of the elect to the last to be born at the end of the world, is daily being built through the grace of the king of peace, namely its Redeemer.[132]

Understandably, perhaps, given its power, the end point of the syllogism implicit in this identification—that if the king is like Solomon and Solomon, in turn, a type of Christ, then the king is himself comparable to Christ—was used by political commentators hesitantly, albeit with growing confidence from the second quarter of the ninth century onwards.[133] Often the assocation was unspoken but present, perhaps nowhere more powerfully than in the Aachen chapel, where Charlemagne's throne stood immediately beneath a cupola bearing the image of Christ in majesty.[134]

What, then, of Solomonic kingship itself? The Old Testament's centrality as a storehouse for models of early medieval rulership hardly needs restating.[135]

---

[129] Beskow, *Rex Gloriae*. Beskow's work comes under attack as a contributor to the 'Emperor mystique' from T. F. Matthews, *The Clash of the Gods: A Reinterpretation of Early Christian Art*, 2nd edition (Princeton, 1999), 15, 194 n. 22, on which see P. R. L. Brown's review, *The Art Bulletin*, 77.3 (September, 1995), 499–502 of the first edition.

[130] P. D. King, 'The Barbarian Kingdoms', in J. H. Burns (ed.), *The Cambridge History of Medieval Political Thought, c. 350–1450* (Cambridge, 1988), 126–7.

[131] Gregory the Great, *Hom Ez.* II. 3.13.

[132] Bede, *De templo*, 1.1.1: 'Domus Dei quam aedificavit rex Salomon in Jerusalem, in figuram facta est sanctae universalis Ecclesiae, quae a primo electo usque ad ultimum, qui in fine mundi nasciturus est, quotidie per gratiam regis pacifici, sui videlicet Redemptoris, aedificatur'. (Translation from Connolly and O'Reilly, *Temple*, 5, with comments on the typology of the Temple at pp. xxii–xxviii.)

[133] For the case of Thegan's portrait of Louis the Pious, M. Innes, '"He never even allowed his white teeth to be bared in laughter": the Politics of Humour in the Carolingian Renaissance', in G. Halsall (ed.), *Humour, History and Politics in Late Antiquity and the Early Middle Ages* (Cambridge, 2002), 131–57, at 147–51.

[134] Noble, *Iconoclasm*, 239. For Solomon's throne Garrison, 'New Israel?' 154–6 with references.

[135] P. Riché, 'La Bible et la vie politique dans le haut Moyen Âge' and M. Reydellet, 'La Bible miroir des princes' 385–400, 431–53; P. E. Schramm, 'Das alte und das neue Testament in der Staatslehre und Staatssymbolik des Mittelalters', in *La Bibbia nell'alto Medioevo, Settimane* 10, 229–55; E. Ewig 'Königsgedanken', *Das Königtum*, 7–73; R. Kottje, *Studien zum Einfluss des alten*

Within the coterie of ideal rulers that the Old Testament offered, Solomon was both a powerful and a versatile figure, drawing together an unparalleled number of the faces of rulership: just judge, anointed and divinely chosen monarch, warrior, prophet, peacemaker, builder, exorcist, and a king renowned for his wealth and famed, above all, for his wisdom, God's gift at Solomon's request.[136] Nor was Solomon simply scripture's subject. As we've already seen many viewed him as its author; Proverbs, Ecclesiastes, Ecclesiasticus, Wisdom, and the Song of Songs were all ascribed to his authorship.[137]

Biblical texts offered powerful vignettes of Solomon's many-sided character: the messianic ruler, entering Gihon on David's mule in a prefiguration of Christ's own entry into Jerusalem (I Kings XXXIII); Israel's anointed ruler (I Kings XXIX–XL); as a ruler devoted to the pursuit of wisdom; a wise judge, notably in the case of the infant jointly claimed by the two harlots (I Kings XXXIX–XL); and, in his meeting with the Queen of Sheba, a peaceful and diplomatic lord, an admired friend of other rulers (I Kings X.1–13).

It is in Paralipomenon, in particular, that Solomon figured as a king not merely associated with peace but defined by it: 'The son, that shall be born to thee, shall be a most quiet man: for I will make him rest from all his enemies round about: and therefore he shall be called Peaceable: and I will give peace and quietness to Israel all his days'.[138] Yoking Solomon to peace-giving, besides drawing upon the narratives of Solomon's reign, was fostered by the etymology of his name. 'Solomon' derived from the Hebrew for peace 'shalom' and, through Jerome's *On the Interpretation of Hebrew Names* and Isidore's *Etymologies*, this

Testaments auf Recht und Liturgie des frühen Mittelalters (6. bis 8. Jahrhundert) (Bonn, 1965, 2nd edition 1970). David's place in early medieval political thought has captured the majority of scholarly interest: S. Hamilton, 'A New Model for Royal Penance? Helgaud of Fleury's *Life of Robert the Pious*', *EME* 6.2 (1997), 189–200; P. Buc, 'David's Adultery with Bathsheba and the Healing Power of the Capetian Kings', *Viator* 24 (1993), 101–20; H. Steger, *David Rex et Propheta: König David als Vorbildliche Verkörperung des Herrschers und Dichters im Mittelalter, nach Bilddarstellungen des achten bis zwölften Jahrhunderts*, Erlanger Beiträge zur Sprach- und Kunstwissenschaft 6 (Nuremberg, 1961).

[136] L. K. Handy, *The Age of Solomon: Scholarship at the Turn of the Millennium* (Leiden, 1997). P. A. Torijano, *Solomon. The Esoteric King, From King to Magus, Development of a Tradition* (Leiden, 2000); K. I. Parker, 'Solomon as Philosopher King? The Nexus of Law and Wisdom in I Kings 1–11', *Journal for the Study of the Old Testament* 53 (1992), 75–91.

[137] A. Lemaire, 'Wisdom in Solomonic Historiography' and W. Horbury, 'The Wisdom of Solomon', in J. Day, R. P. Gordon, and H. G. M. Williamsom (eds), *Wisdom in Ancient Israel* (Cambridge, 1995), 106–18, 182–96, at 186–9.

[138] I Chron. XXII.9–10. On the image of Solomon in Chronicles see R. B. Dillard, 'The Literary Structure of the Chronicler's Solomon Narrative', *Journal for the Study of the Old Testament* 30 (1984), 85–93; idem, 'The Chronicler's Solomon', *Westminster Theological Journal* 43 (1980), 289–300; S. Abramsky, 'The Chronicler's View of King Solomon', *Eretz Israel* 16 (1982), 3–14. On Solomon and the Psalms see J. M. Carrière, 'Le Ps. 72 est-il un psaume messianique?', *Biblica* 72 (1991), 49–69; J. Brière, 'Salomon dans la Psaumes', *Supplement au Dictionnaire de la Bible* 11 (1987), cols 456–8.

derivation became a commonplace of early medieval exegesis.[139] 'Nobody doubts', emphasized Bede, 'that Solomon, which means "Peacemaker", signifies both by his very name and the extremely peaceful state of his reign, the one of whom Isaiah said "His Empire shall be multiplied, and there shall be no end of peace."'[140] Etymology unlocked essentials. Solomon symbolized peaceful rule, a state that was the culmination of his own military successes, his dominion over neighbouring peoples, the unity of Israel under his wise rule, and administration of justice that kept that unity intact. Added to this, however, and crucial to the complete image of him, was Solomon's right relationship with God, manifest in the building of the Temple, an activity made possible by the peace that Solomon established and held. The Temple's construction was not only the central event of Solomon's reign, it was also the key event in Israel's collective relationship with God.[141] This special relationship was apparent from his early request for the gift of wisdom from an approving Almighty (I Kings III.4), and it was such wisdom that, in turn, was often presented as the key to Solomon's rulership, enabling him to administer justice correctly, to seek out, create, and maintain Israel's peace. Crucially peace, then, was itself the outcome of wisdom, as much as any of the other benefits Solomon's subjects enjoyed, such as wealth. This bond between wisdom and peace, *sapientia* and *pax*, became, literally, proverbial, and was taken up in the early medieval West's home-grown wisdom literature, such as Ireland's sixth- or seventh-century *Proverbia grecorum* and the Old English *Maxims*.

For all this Solomon was not flawless. He amassed wealth, horses, and the multitude of wives who in his old age succeeded in turning his heart 'to follow strange gods' (III Kings II.4). Divine punishment for these sins and the breach of the Covenant they entailed left Israel divided and beset by enemies. Augustine was more attentive than most to Solomon's failings, devoting several chapters of book XVII of the *City of God* to a rejection of him as either the focus of the christological prophecy or as anything more than a 'kind of shadowy sketch' of Christ.[142] This was not least because Solomon's kingdom did have an end, as Israel's history made evident.[143] As in many things Augustine's dissonant note did not carry far, and whilst these failings were occasionally drawn upon by early medieval moralists—Theodulf of Orléans held him up as an example of how idleness led first to fornication and then to idolatry—Solomon was considered an exemplary king.[144] In the Bible of San Paolo fuori le mura, produced at Rheims

[139] *Liber Interpretationis Hebraicorum Nominum*, ed. P. Antin, CCSL 72 (Turnhout, 1959), 59–161, at 85, on which see D. Brown, *Vir Trilinguis. A Study in the Biblical Exegesis of Saint Jerome* (The Hague, 1992), 77. Isidore, *Etym.* VII.vi.65. Hincmar, *Explanatio in Ferculum Salomonis*, PL, 125, cols 817–34, at 817.

[140] *De Templo*, I.2.2, citing Isa. IX.7.

[141] R. Braun, 'Solomonic Apologetic in Chronicles', *Journal of Biblical Literature* 92 (1973), 505.

[142] *De Civ. Dei* XVII.8–11.

[143] *De Civ. Dei* XVII.11.

[144] Theodulf, *Fragmenta Sermonum Aliquot*, PL 105, cols 275–82, at 280.

in the early 870s at Charles the Bald's request, figures such as Pharaoh and Saul embodied bad kingship. Solomon stood firmly on the side of the good.[145]

Solomon's emergence as a model for Christian rulership was early. Athanasius, writing his *Apologia* to Constantius II in 356 held him, alongside David, as a model for the emperor, specifically to warn him against bad counsel.[146] His range of qualities made him a particularly appealing ideal for those wishing to praise their rulers, qualities invoked in late Merovingian Francia, Alfred's Wessex, and particularly in the Carolingian world where, in the middle decades of the ninth century we see what Nicholas Staubach has termed 'Solomon typology' become increasingly central to political imagery.[147] The Frankish and Anglo-Saxon kingdoms did not have a monopoly on Solomon. The seventh-century inscription from Llangadwaladr, memorializing Cadfan, king of Gwynedd as REX SAPIENTISSIMUS OPINATISSIMUS OMNIUM REGUM ('wisest (and) most renowned of all kings') carries a clear Solomonic resonance.[148] Few territories, however, went as far as the ruling houses of early medieval Brittany and the central medieval Hungarian kingdom in adopting the name as one appropriate for rulers. The identification of certain rulers with Solomon did not end with their own reigns. In later centuries Oswald, Edwin's successor on Northumbria's throne, Alfred the Great, and Charlemagne would all be remembered as rulers in the mould of Solomon as time blurred the figures of ideal and actual ruler into one.[149]

Solomon's memory survived in material as well as textual form even though the sites in Jerusalem with which he was associated were, like Augustus' Rome, reconfigured and overwritten. Constantine's Church of the Holy Sepulchre became the primary focus of Christian pilgrimage, leaving the Temple abandoned and largely in ruins until the later seventh century. In the 330s, however, it was still possible for the so-called 'Bordeaux pilgrim' to see the remains of the *cubiculum* where Solomon had written the Book of Wisdom.[150]

The *cubiculum* seems to have remained a stop on the sixth-century tour circuit when an unknown author produced an emended version of the short (probably) fourth-century list of holy sites, the *Breviarius de Hierosolyma*. The later emendations are characterized by consistent interest in Jerusalem's Solomonic and

---

[145] W. J. Diebold, 'Ruler Portrait of Charles the Bald in the S. Paolo Bible', *Art Bulletin* 76 (1994), 12–14.

[146] Dvornik, *ECBPP* II, 644–5; 736.

[147] Staubach, *Rex christianus*.

[148] CISP no. LGADW/1 <http://www.ucl.ac.uk/archaeology/cisp/database/> with full references.

[149] *Vita sancti Oswaldi regis auctore Drogone*, AA SS. Aug, II, 94–102; G. Klaniczay, *Holy Rulers and Blessed Princesses: Dynastic Cults in Medieval Central Europe* trans. Éva Pálmai (Cambridge, 2002), 84. G. Rauschen, *Die Legende Karls des Grossen im 11. und 12. Jahrhundert* (Leipzig, 1890), 119.

[150] *Itinerarium Burdigalense*, ed. P. Geyer and O. Cuntz, *Itineraria et alia geographica*, CCSL 175 (Turnhout, 1965), 591.4–30; Milner, 'Image', p. 75 n. 12.

Constantinian sites, though their author, echoing the Bordeaux pilgrim, noted gloomily of the Temple site, 'nothing remains there but a single cave'.[151] In the later seventh century the Temple Mount was extensively reconfigured with the building of both the Dome on the Rock and the al-Aqsa mosque in the early Islamic period. When Bernard the Monk, our Frankish traveller with the keen sense of tourist safety, passed through in the early 870s he seems to have mistaken one or both of these complexes for Solomon's Temple containing, confusedly, 'a Saracen synagogue', a misidentification many later western visitors, including the early Crusaders, would follow.[152]

The treasures of the Temple were, as we have already seen, in Vespasian's Temple of Peace until the fifth century. Traditions differ over whether it was Alaric's Goths or the Vandals who seized them, but Procopius relates that some, at least, were kept by Vandal rulers in North Africa until recovered by Belisarius' conquest. The objects paraded by Vespasian in 70 were carried by imperial troops in triumph once again, though this time through the streets of Constantinople, not Rome, in a procession that ended in the Hippodrome. Procopius relates what happened next:

And one of the Jews seeing these treasures, approached one of those known to the emperor and said, 'These treasures I think it is inexpedient to carry into the palace in Byzantium. Indeed, it is not possible for them to be anywhere other than in the place where Solomon, the King of the Jews, formerly put them'.[153]

The improper possession of the Temple's objects had precipitated Rome's sack in 455, he explained. The destruction of the Vandal kingdom in its turn was a further result of wrongful possession and implicit pollution of the Temple's holiest objects. According to Procopius, the tale rattled Justinian: 'When this had been brought to the ears of the Emperor, he became afraid and quickly sent everything to the sanctuaries of the Christians in Jerusalem'.[154] But not all the treasures were believed to have made their way to Jerusalem. Embellishing Gregory of Tours' account of Childebert I's defeat of Amalric in 531, the anonymous author of the *Liber historiae Francorum* added that amongst the booty the Merovingians took from Toledo were chalices that were once Solomon's.[155] In the ninth century a cup believed to have once belonged to Solomon was kept in Hagia Sophia.[156] Another vessel, the so-called 'Dish of Solomon' (in fact a late Sasanian object, as its current name 'the Chosroes Dish' makes clear)

---

[151] *Breviarius de Heirosolyma* A, *Itineraria et alia geographica*, CCSL 175, 109–12, at 116: 'Inde venis ad templo quod fabricavit Salomon, non inde remansit nisi una cripta.'

[152] *Itinerarium Bernardi*, c. 12, p. 316.

[153] *Bell. Van.* IV. 9, 5–9.

[154] *Bell. van.* IV. 9.9.

[155] *LHF* 23, pp. 278–9.

[156] S. Tougher, 'The Wisdom of Leo VI', in P. Magdalino (ed.), *New Constantines: The Rhythm of Imperial Renewal in Byzantium, 4th to 13th Centuries* (Aldershot, 1994), 174; I. Ševčenko, 'The Greek Source of the Inscription on Solomon's Chalice in the *Vita Constantini*', in *To Honor Roman*

was almost certainly in Francia at the same time, owned by Charles the Bald and perhaps his predecessors before being given to St-Denis.[157]

'PEACE IN OUR TIME': LITURGICAL PETITIONS FOR PEACE

It is perhaps an obvious fact, but one worth restating, that many of the key figures and passages we have just met were themselves encountered by medieval Christian communities over the course of the liturgical year as the temporal cycle, patterned on Christ's life, moved through the sequence of feasts from Advent to Pentecost, celebrating Incarnation, Crucifixion, and Resurrection, each with appropriate prayers, readings, hymns, and homilies. Not simply a place to hear of peace, churches physically enacted peace collectively through the Mass, manifest in the kiss of peace (*osculum pacis*) which reaffirmed the earthly peace of the Christian community.[158] Preceding this, the Eucharist, in which the members of the community are joined through bread and wine, body and blood, in the one body of Christ is simultaneously an act of anamnesis, recalling Christ's Passion, reconciliation between man and God, and Christ's gift of peace (I Cor. 10–17). Whilst early medieval Eucharistic theology lies beyond my scope here, it is important to stress that one of the central lessons of the Mass was the reiteration that true peace could only come from God. This theme lies at the heart of many of the individual prayers for peace found in the early medieval liturgy: 'Give' (*Da*) is the driving imperative that opens many of these brief prayers. 'Give to us your peace in our days', in the words of a recurrent phrase of early medieval sacramentaries. Prayer, after all, sought to bridge the gap between fallen humanity and the heavenly kingdom, the very gap to which the lack of peace in earthly society bore witness. Together with other equally valuable commodities—*lux, salvus, veritas, abundantia*—it was a gift from God. 'Direct us in the ways of truth and peace' runs a prayer from the early seventh-century Leonine or Verona Sacramentary.[159] 'Free (Your people) from evil days and thought of war', reads one prayer from the Carolingian Sacramentary of Angoulême, 'and give times of tranquillity and peacefulness to them'.[160]

Jakobson: Essays on the Occasion of his Seventieth Birthday, 11th October 1966 (The Hague and Paris, 1967), III, 1806–17.

[157] L. Webster, '*Aedificia nova*: Treasures of Alfred's Reign', in T. Reuter (ed.), *Alfred the Great* 79–103, at 96–8. G. A. Kornbluth, *Engraved Gems of the Carolingian Renaissance* (University Park, PA, 1995), 13–14.

[158] K. Petkov, *The Kiss of Peace. Ritual, Self and Society in the High and Late Medieval West* (Leiden, 2003), esp. 120–4; Y. Carré, *Le baiser sur la bouche au Moyen Âge: Rites, symboles, mentalités à travers les textes et les images, XIe–XVe siècles* (Paris, 1992), all with references.

[159] *Sacr. Ver.* no. 251.

[160] *Lib. Sacr. Eng.* no. 1829: 'Libera eam a diebus malis et cogitatione bellorum et da eis tempora tranquilla atque pacifica'.

Such petitionary prayers are found in a variety of forms throughout the liturgical record of the early Middle Ages and many were simply part of the stock of daily worship. Some, however, were intended for times of unrest, war or threatened attack—*in tempore belli* as one rubric explained.[161] Such sentiments can be seen in the following sequence of 'prayers for peace' (*Orationes pro pace*) drawn from the Old Gelasian Sacramentary.

O God, from whom holy desires, right counsels, and just works derive, give to Your servants that peace which the world is unable to give, so that hearts might be devoted to Your instruction and times, with fear of the enemy removed, might be tranquil through Your protection.[162]

O God, Founder of the World, under whose jurisdiction the succession of all the ages flows, kindly hearken to our invocations and grant the tranquillity of peace to the present times, so that in the praises of Your pity we might rejoice with unceasing exultation.[163]

O God, You who does not allow those believing in You to be harmed by any terrors, condescend to accept the prayers and sacrifices of a people devoted to You, so that the peace granted by Your devotion might keep the Roman territories secure from every enemy.[164]

Again, the theme returns in the final, post-Communion prayer:

O God, originator and lover of peace, whom to know is to live, and whom to serve is to rule, protect your suppliants from every attack, so that we who trust in your protection might fear the arms of no hostile power.[165]

For many of these prayers the peace asked for was quite general, usually communal and often temporally circumscribed, *in nostros dies*.[166] Several, though, possessed particular focus.[167] The anxious relationship between peace and travel that we have seen repeatedly finds its place in the liturgical record. In the eighth-century Sacramentary of Autun we find a prayer for someone undertaking a journey (*missa ad proficiscendum in itinere*) and with it the request that an

---

[161] *Had.* no. 997.

[162] *Lib. Sacr. Rom.* no. 1472: 'Deus, a quo sancta desideria et recta sunt consilia et iusta sunt opera, da servis tuis illam quam mundus dare non potest pacem, ut et corda mandatis tuis dedita et hostium sublata formidine tempora sint tua protectione tranquilla: per.'

[163] *Lib. Sacr. Rom.* no. 1473: 'Deus, conditor mundi, sub cuius arbitrio omnium saeculorum ordo decurrit, adesto propitius invocationibus nostris et tranquillitatem pacis praesentibus concede temporibus, ut in laudibus misericordiae tuae incessabile exultatione laetemur: per.'

[164] *Lib. Sacr. Rom.* no. 1475: 'SECRETA: Deus, qui credentes in te populis nullis sinis nocere terroribus, dignare praecibus et hostiis decate tibi plebis suscipere, ut pax a tua pietate concessa Romanos fines ab omni hoste faciat esse securos: per.'

[165] *Lib. Sacr. Rom.* no. 1476: 'POST COMMUNIONEM. Deus, auctor pacis et amator, quem nosse vivere, cui servire regnare est, protege ab omnibus inpugnationibus supplices tuis, ut qui defensione tua fidemus, nullius hostilitatis arma timeamus: Per.'

[166] See for example *Lib. Sacr. Rom.* nos 1247, 1258; *Lib. Sacr. Eng.* no. 20.

[167] *Lib. Sacr. Aug.* nos 413, 414.

angel of peace protect the traveller. (Like the Angel Raphael protected Tobias, Tobit's son, in a foreign land, comments one variant, adding the strut of biblical precedent to its general appeal.)[168] If travel fostered fear, home held the promise of peace, as this prayer for a new house makes clear:

Praying with one heart to the Eternal and Omnipotent God, let us beg on behalf of this house and all living in it that the Lord should condescend to assign an angel of peace, an angel of light, and an angel of protection.[169]

Others, however, deserve the label more formally: prayers that requested peaceful reigns, explicitly linking peace and kingship, offered occasionally, daily, or at specific junctures: as part of a royal mass, a ruler's inauguration, or reconsecration.

The origins of such prayers in the Christian tradition are early, beginning with St Paul's injuction 'that all supplications, prayers, intercessions, and thanksgivings be made for all men, for kings, and for all that are in high station: that we may lead a quiet and a peaceable life (*quietam et tranquillam vitam*) in all piety and chastity' (I Tim. II.1–2). By Constantine's reign such prayers were both expected by the emperor, who actively sought out prayers for the public well-being, and offered to him as signs of loyalty. Petitioning for his restoration in 327, Arius wrote to Constantine, the agent of his potential reconciliation with the Orthodox Church ('through your peacemaking and your piety'), affirming his adherence to Nicaea and closing by offering his hopes that, once reintegrated into the community of the *ecclesia*, 'we all in common may offer the customary prayer for your peaceful and pious empire and for your entire family.'[170] By the end of the fourth century, as Ambrose's response to Symmachus makes evident, prayers for peace for rulers were a part of Christian self-awareness.

It was this broader tradition to which early medieval prayers for rulers found in our Italian and Frankish collections belonged, such as the probably Merovinigan benediction, *Benedic domine hunc presulem principem*. This prayer's roster of biblical types signals a developing tendency to invoke scriptural figures characteristic of the later Merovingian period:

O Lord, who governs all the kingdoms of the world, bless, we beseech You, our king. Amen.

And bless him with such glory that he may hold the sceptre with such sublimity, rule like David, and through Your mercy obtain his reward. Amen.

---

[168] *Lib. Sacr. Aug.* nos 413, 414. On the 'angel of peace' see P. de Clerck, 'L'ange de paix', in K. G. Cushing and R. F. Gyug (eds), *Ritual, Text and Law. Studies in Medieval Canon Law and Liturgy Presented to Roger E. Reynolds* (Aldershot, 2004), 11–22.

[169] *Lib. Sacr. Aug.* no. 424: 'Aeternum atque omnipotentem deum unanimiter orantes petamus pro hanc domum atque omnes habitantes in ea uti eas dominus angelum pacis angelum lucis angelum defensionis assignare dignetur'.

[170] Sozomen, *Historia Ecclesiastica*, ed. J. Bidez and G. C. Hansen, GCS 50 (Berlin, 1960), II.27. Drake, *Constantine and the Bishops*, 260.

Grant that he, through Your inspiration, may rule his people with mercy, and grant that he will establish and maintain a peaceful kingdom like Solomon. Amen.

Grant that he may serve You always with fear, and fight for you with peace. Protect him and his nobles with Your shield, and let him remain victor without end. Amen.[171]

From the earlier ninth century onwards prayers such as this were assembled together with newer material into larger sequences, coronation *ordines*, beginning with the so-called First English *Ordo*, and continuing with the sequence of Carolingian *ordines* initiated with that for Charles the Bald's marriage to the Anglo-Saxon Judith in 856. From there, they would pass into the general body of royal liturgy.

A full exposition of the place of peace in the early medieval liturgy demands a substantial study of its own. Before moving on, however, it is important to note not only the theme's prevalence in early medieval devotional life, and more specifically the repeated quest for peace that these prayers carried, but also this central fact: when kings made and kept the peace 'in their days' they offered a response, however fleeting, to an insistent petition in the prayers spoken in the holy places of their realms.

THE LIMITS OF EARTHLY PEACE, AUGUSTINE
AND HIS EARLY MEDIEVAL READERS

It is a truism that Augustine's intellectual legacy is central to any consideration of early medieval thought.[172] 'It is often assumed that the early middle ages were a period profoundly influenced by Augustine', James O'Donnell has written, 'but in just what way this influence was exercised, what its limits were, and how it came to be, these are questions that still deserve attention.'[173] These are, self-evidently, questions both deep and wide, and ones that engage with multiple processes of reception as well as the emergence of Augustine as an authority in the minds of many early medieval thinkers on a multitude of subjects.[174]

---

[171] *Lib. Sacr. Aug.* no. 1642. Translation based on that of Wickham Legg, *Coronation Records*, 11.
[172] F. Oakley, 'Celestial Hierarchies Revisited: Walter Ullmann's Vision of Medieval Politics', *P&P* 60 (1973), 3–49.
[173] J. J. O'Donnell, 'The Authority of Augustine', St Augustine Lecture at Villanova University, *Augustinian Studies* 22 (1991), 7–35.
[174] M. Gorman, *The Manuscript Traditions of the Works of St Augustine* (Florence, 2001). For the influence of Augustine in specific early medieval thinkers see John Cavadini's exemplary close readings in *idem, The Last Christology in the West: Adoptionism in Spain and Gaul 785–820* (Philadelphia, 1993); *idem*, 'The Sources and Theology of Alcuin's Treatise *De Fide Sanctae et Individuae, Trinitiatis*', *Traditio* 46 (1991), 123–43; see J. L. Nelson, 'The Intellectual in Politics: Context, Content and Authorship in the Capitulary of Coulaines, November 843'; H. Mayr-Harting, 'Ruotger, The Life of Bruno and Cologne Cathedral Library', in L. Smith and B. Ward (eds), *Intellectual Life in the Middle Ages: Essays presented to Margaret Gibson* (London, 1992), 1–14, 33–60. W. Otten, 'The Texture of Tradition: The Role of the Church Fathers in Carolingian Theology', in I. Backus (ed.), *The Reception of the Church Fathers in the West from the Carolingians to the Maurists* (Leiden, 1997), I, 3–50; J. J. Contreni, 'Carolingian Era, Early', and J. Kelly, 'Carolingian Era, Late', in *Augustine through the Ages*,

My focus here is very restricted, addressing as it does a specific and important aspect of Augustine's intellectual legacy to his early medieval readers, listeners, and excerptors: how he thought about peace. Here, again, there is need of caution. 'It is quite likely', commented Donald Bullough on the tenuous manuscript tradition of the final books of the *City of God*, 'that to many of them [i.e., early and high medieval writers] even Augustine's celebrated definition of peace, the one beginning "peace between mortal man and God is ordered obedience, in faith to eternal law; peace between men is ordered concord" was unknown'.[175]

It is valuable at this stage to sketch out Augustine's own theories of peace, and the ways in which they interrelated, for several reasons. First, because taken on his own terms he offers the most sophisticated model of what constituted peace. Second, because a schematic sense of Augustine's thought serves as a further framework for understanding early medieval conceptions. Third, because in order to understand the distinct reception of Augustine's writings, and to be able to contextualize those individual readings and to chart divergence from Augustine's original thought, we need to establish a baseline.

Like Kantorowicz's king, modern scholarship's Augustine is a creature of multiple forms. We have the 'historical' Augustine, whose ideas were susceptible to growth and to change, and whose elucidation has been one of the achievements of Augustinian scholarship in the last half-century.[176] The second is the adjective Augustinian, the abstracted Augustine of synthetic studies of his thought, whose ideas float free from the grounding of specific texts. Unsurprisingly, he has been placed prominently in the upper reaches of many studies of Christian thinking on peace, and its related field, the just war.[177]

Early medieval readers—even those armed with a copy of the *Retractiones*— had little notion of a historicized Augustine, and even less of an awareness of the value of such a figure. While commentators have often seen them espousing 'Augustinian' ideas, they also had no easy access to the kind of modern syntheses that allow such views to be readily and accurately digested and deployed.[178]

124–9, 129–32; E. Dekkers, 'Quelques notes sur des florilèges augustiniens anciens et médiévaux', *Augustiniana* 40–1 (1990), 27–44; J. N. Hillgarth, 'L'influence de la *Cité de Dieu* de saint Augustin au Haut Moyen Age', *Sacris Erudiri* 28 (1985), 5–24.

[175] Bullough, 'Peace', 368.

[176] An approach embodied by two works, P. R. L. Brown, *Augustine of Hippo: A Biography*, (London, 1967, 2nd edn, 2000), R. A. Markus, *Saeculum: History and Society in the Theology of St Augustine* (Cambridge, 1970, 2nd edn, 1988), and now J. J. O'Donnell, *Augustine. A New Biography* (New York, 2005). On these developments C. Leyser, *Authority and Asceticism from Augustine to Gregory the Great* (Oxford, 2000), 5–8.

[177] C. A. J. Coady and J. Ross, 'St. Augustine and the Ideal of Peace', *American Catholic Philosophical Quarterly* 74 (2000), 153–61; R. H. Bainton, *Christian Attitudes to War and Peace. A Historical Survey and Critical Reevaluation* (Nashville, 1960), 91–9; F. H. Russell, *The Just War in the Middle Ages* (Cambridge, 1975).

[178] Contreni, 'Carolingian Era, Early', in J. C. Cavadini and A. D. Fitzgerald p. 125.

This is not to say that the early Middle Ages did not have Augustinian abstractions and digests of its own. Augustine was an authority to be invoked in argument and deployed as a kind of patristic trump card in debate (*Si Augustinus adest, sufficit ipse*).[179] Coupled with such reverence was an often remarkable willingness to excerpt, edit, and reframe his words.[180] This sense of Augustine as *auctoritas* contributes to his name being attached, accidentally or intentionally, to the writings of others. Digests or collations of his thought also came in the form of florilegia.[181] Prosper's early fifth-century *Liber sententiarum*, for example, organized selected statements of Augustine's on peace beneath a number of discrete rubrics, some explicit—'On the observance of peace' (*De observantia pacis*), 'On the fullness of peace' (*De plena pacis*), 'On the kind of peace which is sought from God' (*Qualiter pax a Deo quaeretur*)—and others less so.[182] Contrastingly, Eugippius, the still only partially understood compiler of Augustine's works, seems to have made little use of Augustine's more developed pronouncements on peace, although in the ninth century scholars like Sedulius Scottus and Florus of Lyons would both pick the threads on peace from the writings of Augustine they could access, and weave them into their own collections.[183]

Mindful of such complexities, and equally aware that what I am undertaking here is itself an act of synthesis that rests firmly on the work of others, we must still ask what peace meant to Augustine. His comments on the subject range from brief observations through to extended reflection, and they occur across a range of his works. Sustained treatments are to be found in the *Explanations of the Psalms*, several sermons and letters, and book XIX of the *City of God*, the key, late work of Augustine's meditation on the nature of peace, in which the discussion of peace is central to Augustine's broader discussions of the ends of the two cities. Augustine's works contain over 2500 individual references to peace, a number that confounds easy synthesis.[184] It was a subject that occupied him to the end. In one of his final letters, written in winter 429/30, the septuagenarian bishop wrote warmly to Darius, commander and imperial ambassador, in response to the news that he had brokered a treaty with Geiseric that had seemingly stemmed the Vandal onslaught along the North African coast. Augustine was

[179] E. Rauner, 'Notkers des Stammlers "Notatio de illustribus viris", Teil I. Kritische Edition', *Mittellateinisches Jahrbuch* 21 (1986), 34–69, at 63.
[180] Contreni, 'Reception', *Augustine through the Ages*, 216–18.
[181] Dekkers, 'Quleques notes', 21–31.
[182] *Prosperi Aquitani Opera*, ed. M. Gestaldo, CCSL 68A (Turnhout, 1972), XXIX, 'De observantia pacis', 264; CXLIII, 'De concordia et obedientia', 295; CLXIX, 'De plena pacis', 297; CLXXXVI, 'Qualiter pax a Deo quaeretur', 301; CCXLVIII, 'De simulatione pacis cum inimico', 315; CCCLXXIII, 'De pace Christi', 356.
[183] Florus, *Expositio in Epistolas Beati Pauli ex Operibus Sancti Augustina Collecta* PL 119, cols 279–420, on which see C. Charlier, 'La compilation Augustinienne de Florus sur l'Apôtre: sources et authenticité', *RB* 57 (1947), 132–86.
[184] D. X. Burt, 'Peace', in. Cavadini and Fitzgerald (eds), *Augustine*, 629.

full of praise for Darius' achievement: ' . . . it is a higher glory still to stay war itself
with a word than to slay men with the sword, and to procure or maintain peace
by peace, not by war'.[185]

Most who have considered the issue have placed notions of peace close to the
centre of the sprawling edifice of Augustine's thought.[186] 'Peace', one reader of
Augustine has recently observed, 'is the pivotal term in Augustine's understanding of both cities'.[187] It certainly lay close to his conception of humanity's fallen
state and hunger for reunification with God: 'For every man is in search of peace',
he wrote, 'even when waging war, whereas no one is in quest of war when making
peace'.[188] It lay at the heart of his own sense of his journey's end, recounted,
famously, in the *Confessions*: 'Restless is my heart, until it rests in you'.[189] For
Augustine thoughts about peace led to notions of order, harmony, collectivity.
Order was the key: 'peace of all things', he wrote, 'is the tranquillity of order'
(*Pax omnium rerum tranquillitas ordinis*).[190] From order came peace: in a person's
heart, in a household and family, in an earthly polity, in the Church and,
ultimately, in the Heavenly Jerusalem. Consequently, the term *pax* is made to
work hard in Augustine's thought, encompassing a variety of conditions. This
feature of his thought has frequently fostered confusion amongst his readers. It
also caused concern for Augustine who, in a discussion of the perfect peace of the
Heavenly Jerusalem was acutely conscious of the semantic range the word had
already had to bear.[191] But it was the peace of Heaven, the *pax caelestis*, and of
the Heavenly Jerusalem, that was for Augustine true peace. It alone was permanent and free from disruption, the product of 'a perfectly ordered and
perfectly harmonious fellowship in the enjoyment of God': the final fixed
order, the 'crystalline stasis' in Caroline Walker Bynum's words, of the
saved.[192] In heaven the body and its appetites no longer threatened to disturb
minds: true immutable order creating full and perfect peace, final firm foundations for eternal peace.

---

[185] *Ep.* 229, CCSL 57, pp. 497–8.
[186] R. L. Wilken, *The Spirit of Early Christian Thought. Seeking the Face of God* (New Haven,
2003), 192–9; Burt, 'Peace', *Augustine*, 629–32; J. Laufs, *Der Friedensgedanke bei Augustinus.
Untersuchungen zum XIX. Buch des Werkes 'De Civitates Dei'* (Wiesbaden, 1973); C. Cary-Elwes,
'Peace in the City of God', *La Ciudad de Dios* 167 (1955), 417–33; H. Rondet, 'Pax tranquillitas
ordinis (de civitate dei, 19, 13)', *La Ciudad de Dios* 167.2 (1956), 343–65.
[187] Wilken, *Spirit*, 192.
[188] *De Civ. Dei* XIX.13.
[189] G. Lawless, 'Interior Peace in the "Confessiones" of St. Augustine', *REAug* 26 (1980), 45–61.
[190] *De Civ. Dei* XIX.13.
[191] *De Civ. Dei* XIX.11. 'Sed quoniam pacis nomen etiam in his rebus mortalibus frequentatur,
ubi utique non est vita aeterna, propterea finem civitatis huius, ubi erit summum bonum eius,
aeternam vitam maluimus commemorare quam pacem'. See also *De Civ. Dei* XIX.12.
[192] C. Walker Bynum, *The Resurrection of the Body in Western Christendom, 200–1336* (New York,
1995), 61.

Peace on earth presented a paradox. The drive for peace was a fundamental aspect of life in the fallen world: all men, indeed all living things, sought peace. Wild animals wanted peace for themselves. Even monsters, such as Cacus, the monstrous cave-dwelling son of Vulcan, wished for peace in the cave he called home. All human societies, by various laws and systems of regulation, endeavoured to create and maintain peace. The motives behind such a drive were mixed. The Roman Empire, Augustine noted, and with it presumably the Roman peace—though Augustine, famously, avoided the concept—was the product of the human desire for dominion. For all that, peace was ephemeral, not least because it rested upon the actions and desires of fallen humanity, and those foundations were inherently unstable, riddled as they were with the rot of human frailty and bodily weakness. This sense of the flawed quality of earthly peace fostered a highly ambivalent attitude to its creation and maintenance, an attitude that found tangible expression in Augustine's refusal to see in Solomon's reign any simple reflection of the peace of the Heavenly Jerusalem. The mechanics of how peace was made and maintained on the earth is a subject for which Augustine had little sustained interest, but some contempt. Resorting to an image he drew upon elsewhere in discussions of the vitiated value of political organization, Augustine famously cited the case of the robber who, despite his socially disruptive character, nevertheless wished for peace with his fellow robbers.[193] At best, earthly peace created an opportunity—the preconditions that would allow the cultivation of the modes and practices that might help smooth the path to the individual Christian's journey towards his eternal end. Earthly desires, rather than a love of God and a desire to live in fellowship with one's fellow men, led to a state that might resemble peace, but was really only a shadow of its true form.

PEACE OUTSIDE THE *PAX ROMANA*

Early medieval political thought was long considered the product of three components: the classical, the scriptural, and the 'Germanic'.[194] Bede's portrait of Edwin, in particular, has been read as an image of 'the sacred king in war and peace', a manifestation of kingship maintaining deep continuities with pagan tradition.[195] Arguments for such pagan continuity carry little weight today though there is little doubt the cultures of late Iron Age Europe and Scandinavia possessed notions of peace and social order of their own, and, so far as we can

---

[193] *De Civ. Dei* XIX.12.
[194] Wallace-Hadrill, 'Peace', 19.
[195] W. A. Chaney, *The Cult of Kingship in Anglo-Saxon England: The Transition from Paganism to Christianity* (Manchester, 1970), 93–4.

glimpse them, valued rulers who could provide peace, stability, and fertility for the land. Indeed, these early northern cultures seem to have had an ideal peace king of their own in the figure of the legendary Fróði, or *frið-Fróði* ('Peace-Fróði'), a Danish king invoked in a number of sources, from late tenth-century skaldic verse to Snorri's *Prose Edda* (*Skáldskaparmál*) and Saxo Grammaticus' *Histories* in the thirteenth century. 'Fróði' was a name shared by a number of early rulers (Saxo listed five) some of whom came to be associated and conflated with the qualities of their mythical namesake.[196]

We have a few problematic accounts of Germanic belief that suggest concerns for peace played a significant role in pagan cult practice: Tacitus, at the close of the first century, and Adam of Bremen, in the last quarter of the eleventh, both recorded Germanic deities whose benefits included peace. The *Germania* recorded the collective devotion to the goddess Nerthus of the seven tribes of the Anglii. Her statue, carried in an ox-cart through the countryside, stopped war and brought *pax et quies* as she passed; weapons were put away and peace, briefly, reigned between the tribes.[197] Nerthus has often been identified with the Old Norse deity Njorðr, recorded in very much later Scandinavian sources and, notionally, in Swedish and western Norwegian place names.[198] Fricco, the ithyphallic deity recorded by Adam of Bremen as standing between Woden and Thor in the pagan temple at Uppsala, was, according to Adam, responsible for a rather different pair of blessings, *pax* and *voluptas*. Fricco has, in his turn, been identified with Freyr, the Norse fertility god associated with peace and prosperity, himself linked to the figure of Fróði, the legendary peaceful ruler of Danish myth.[199]

Roman historian and German bishop offer problematic accounts, but both share the notion that peace played some part in the beliefs of late Iron Age Germans and early medieval Scandinavian pagans. There is some fragmentary early medieval evidence to give this support. Writing his life of the missionary-bishop Anskar in the 860s, Rimbert recorded a wave of diabolically inspired apostasy in the trading town of Birka. The old gods had been displeased by the arrival of Christianity. If the people of Birka wanted a new god they could have one: not Christ, though, but one of their own, their former king, Eric III. The messenger of the gods offered their reflection on the good old pre-Christian days:

---

[196] A. Ebenbauer, 'Fróði und sein Friede', in H. Birkhan (ed.), *Festgabe für Otto Höfler zum 75. Geburtstag*, Philologica Germanica, 3 (Vienna, 1976), 128–81.

[197] *Germania*, c. 40.

[198] R. North, *Heathen Gods in Old English Literature* (Cambridge, 1997), 1–25 offers a comprehensive recent treatment. See also E. C Polomé, 'A propos de la déesse Nerthus', *Latomus* 13 (1954), 167–200; R. Simek, *Dictionary of Northern Mythology*, trans. A. Hall (Cambridge, 1993), 233–5; G. Schütte, 'The Cult of Nerthus', *Sagabook of the Viking Society* 8 (1913–14), 29–43. For Nerthus and Merovingian kingship see P. Barnwell, 'Einhard, Louis the Pious and Childeric III', *Historical Research* 78 (2005), 129–39, at 130.

[199] North, *Heathen*, 30, 236.

'You, I say, have long enjoyed our goodwill and under our protection you have dwelt in
the land you hold for a long time with much abundance (*multa abundantia*) and had
peace and prosperity (*pace et prosperitate*). You have also duly sacrificed and performed the
vows made to us, and your worship has been very pleasing to us.'[200]

In a more general sense the notion of 'Germanic peace' has a history of its own,
one with roots in nineteenth-century German legal scholarship, and in particular in the work of the so-called *Rechtsschule*, scholars such as Wilda, Brunner,
and Waitz.[201] For them and for many who followed their lead, early medieval
codes carried earlier layers of 'primal German law'.[202] The sense of social peace
found in these codes was nothing less than the archaic notions of ancient
Germanic peace. The idea that early medieval law might be used to speak of
late Iron Age 'Germanic' social norms and ancient cultural notions has had its
day. But like the philologically framed models of Germanic society that
emerged from the same scholarly culture, it has been a long time dying.
Only in recent years, for example, has Julian Goebel's groundbreaking attack
of 1937 upon *Rechtsschule* perspectives emerged into general discussions of
early medieval law, and with it Goebel's destruction of one of the central
elements to the *Rechtsschule*'s model of Germanic law, the folk peace.[203]
Goebel's response to this model might be characterized as a rejection of the
systematic and the synthetic, a wholesale exorcism of what he termed the
Rechtsschule's attachment to an 'all-pervading undifferentiated Germanic *Volks-
geist*'.[204] In place of the 'systematic structure of great seeming perfection',
Goebel offered an image of early medieval law that was contingent and
pragmatic, as well as far more alive to distinctions of dating and geography,
and the importance of later Roman legal forms. In short, his understanding
was one that in many ways directly anticipated much recent scholarship. In this
model there was a place for peace, and a place too for the peace given by the
king, but whilst earlier generations of Germanic scholars had seen references to
peace in the early medieval record as tips of a vast legal iceberg, Goebel, wisely,
was content to see them as limited phenomena that shed light only upon their
immediate contexts.

     The one area of Western Europe where we can, with some claim, speak of
tangible traces of indigenous modes of peaceful rulership is early Christian

---

[200] *Vita Anskarii*, c. 26, ed. G. Waitz, *MGH SRG* 55 (Hanover, 1884), 56. On this passage
J. T. Palmer, 'Rimbert's *Vita Anskarii* and Scandinavian Mission in the Ninth Century', *JEH* 55
(2004), 235–56, at 246–7.
    [201] W. Wilda, *Das Strafrecht der Germanen* (Halle, 1842); H. Brunner, *Grundzüge der Deutschen
Rechtsgeschichte* (1925); G. Waitz, *Deutsche Verfassungsgeschichte. Die Verfassung des deutschen Volkes
in ältester Zeit* (Graz, 1953).
    [202] P. Wormald, *The Making of English Law: King Alfred to the Twelfth Century* (Oxford, 1999),
11–28; Amory, *People*, 326–7.
    [203] J. Goebel, *Felony and Misdemeanor. A Study in the History of English Criminal Procedure* (New
York, 1937, reprinted Philadelphia, 1976), 1–61.
    [204] Goebel, *Felony*, 3.

Ireland. Recent scholarship has come to see surviving Old Irish kingship tracts (*tecosca*) less as fossilized accounts of pre-Christian kingship and more as products of specific political circumstance, self-conscious archaizing, and scholarly dialogue between traditional and contemporary biblically informed notions of kingship. In this respect early Irish kingship tracts might be said to be another instance of 'active' political texts. They were intended to assert an essentially ecclesiastical vision of good kingship through the manipulation of traditional forms, images, and the authority figures from whom the texts recordes much of this material came 'an antique shell', to quote Kim McCone, 'sometimes more fake than genuine, capable of housing a new or significantly modified ideology . . .'.[205]

That peaceful rule was considered important from an early date is clear from the seventh-century vernacular kingship tract known as *Audacht Morainn* ('The Testament of Morann').[206] Like several later *tecosca* this takes the form of advice from an elder to a younger man, in this case the judge and *fili* Morann to the young king, Feradach Find Fechtnach. The well-being of his people, Morann explains, rests upon a ruler's *fír flaithemon*, a term with no direct English equivalent, but which included notions of justice, truth, and righteousness.[207] This both guards his people from natural disaster (plague, great lightning), fosters fertility (fruit in the forest, abundance of milk, corn, fish), and maintains peace and order within them:

> It is through the justice of the ruler that he judges great tribes [and] great riches.
> It is through the justice of the ruler that he secures peace, tranquillity, joy, ease, [and] comfort.
> It is through the justice of the ruler that he dispatches (great) battalions to the borders of hostile neighbours.
> It is through the justice of the ruler that every heir plants his house-post in his fair inheritance.[208]

The same quality will ensure that violence is controlled in assemblies, during hostings, and drinking-bouts. Morann counsels the young king Feradach to be economic with his own use of violence: 'let him not redden many forecourts, for bloodshed is a vain destruction of all rule and of protection of kin for the

---

[205] K. McCone, *Pagan Past*, 218; C. Doherty, 'Kingship in Ireland', in E. Bhreathnach (ed.), *The Kingship and Landscape of Tara* (Dublin, 2005), 3–31, esp. 6, 26–9, quoting McCone, *Pagan Past*, at 6 n. 21.
[206] F. Kelly (ed.), *Audacht Morainn* (Dublin, 1976). Discussions of the text include B. Jaski, *Early Irish Kingship and Succession* (Dublin, 2000), 72–5; P. L. Henry, 'The Cruces of Audacht Morainn', *ZCP* 39 (1982), 33–53. For the 'classic formulation of early Irish kingship as a hangover from the remote Indo-European past' see D. Binchy, *Celtic and Anglo-Saxon Kingship* (Oxford, 1970), and on it, P. Wormald, 'Celtic and Anglo-Saxon Kingship: Some Further Thoughts', in P. Szarmach and V. D. Oggins (eds.), *Sources of Anglo-Saxon Culture* (Kalamazoo, 1986), 151–84.
[207] C. Watkins, '*Is trefir flathemon*: Marginalia to Audacht Morainn', *Ériu* 30 (1979), 181–98.
[208] *Audacht Morainn*, cc. 12–21 (quoting cc. 13–16), p. 7.

ruler'.[209] Vigilant, equitable, measured, generous: Morann's ideal king—the true ruler (*fírflaith*)—stood in contrast with a series of royal antitypes, culminating in the violent, uncontrolled, and animalistic *tarbflaith*, 'the bull ruler'.[210]

A number of other early Irish kingship tracts display a striking coolness to martial values. 'Peace is better than a successful war', runs one of the 'Sayings' ascribed to Flann Fína, Aldfrith of Northumbria (d. 705), in a text of the later eighth or ninth century. 'Wisdom is better than weapons', it adds, while a sequence of later maxims explores the limits of warriorhood: 'The martial life is a distressful occupation. It is not renowned.'[211] The intensity with which the advice-giving *fili* of these texts, and the actual scholars that spoke through them, offer an ideal of kingship in which peace, prosperity, and justice took precedence over warfare and raiding, has been viewed, plausibly, as an ecclesiastical initative to reshape rulership along Christian lines, emphasizing peace, amongst other qualities, at the expense of aggressive, predatory war leadership.[212]

In one instance intervention took an even more direct form. As we have seen already at Birr in early 697, Adomnán oversaw a collective agreement—*Cáin Adomnán* or *Lex innocentium* ('The Law of the Innocents')—which sought to curtail certain categories of violence and which was confirmed by some ninety-one guarantors headed by Loingsech, newly established high king of Tara, and including many kings and leading churchmen.[213]

The tract whose influence stretched furthest from Ireland is one we have already encountered, the anonymous seventh-century *De XII Abusivis Saeculi* ('On the Twelve Abuses of the World'), commonly ascribed in the early Middle Ages to either Augustine, Cyprian, or St Patrick.[214] Its enumeration of social aberrations or 'abuses', archtypal instances of flawed members of society—the youth without obedience, the irreligious elder, the immodest woman—and their positive alternatives provided short, accessible, and widely applicable passages to would-be theorists of social order. Most pertinent for present concerns is the ninth abuse, the *rex iniquus* ('the unjust king'), that the order of the natural world reflected, and could potentially be affected by, a ruler's personal qualities and that

---

[209] *Audacht Morainn*, cc. 28–49, pp. 9–11.

[210] *Audacht Morainn*, c. 62, pp. 18–19.

[211] C. Doherty, 'Ireland and Rome in the Seventh Century', in É. Ó. Carragáin and C. Neuman de Vegvar (eds), *Roma Felix—Formation and Reflections of Medieval Rome* (Aldershot, 2007), 277–86, at 284–6.

[212] Dhonnchadha, 'Birr', in T. O'Loughlin (ed.) *Adomnán*, at 20.

[213] Charles-Edwards, *Early Christian Ireland*, 568–9.

[214] Breen, 'Text and transmission', 84–9.

his failure to apply self-rule brought crop failure, famine, war, infertility, and the disruption of the peace of the people (*pax populorum*).[215] Deceptively simple in its exposition of good and bad social types, *De XII abusivis* was, as Aidan Breen has shown in a series of painstaking studies, a careful distillation of scriptural passages (often filtered through commentary) with complex thematic structuring influenced by both monastic notions of order and the image of Jacob's Ladder (Gen. XXVIII.11–19).[216]

Such concerns were not restricted to explicitly political works. Sometime shortly after its production in the late eighth or early ninth century, probably at the monstery of Tallaght, a scribe, one Moél Cáich, made extensive alterations to the liturgical collection now known as the Stowe Missal. Amongst his emendations he expanded the prayer *Memento vivorum*, a prayer of remembrance for the living, inserting several further requests into the text for 'mild weather and fertility of fruits of the lands, for the return of peace and an end to differences, for the well-being of the kings and the peace of peoples and the return of captives...'.[217]

From *Audacht Morainn* and other *tecosca* literature, through *De XII abusivis* and on into the writings of Sedulius Scottus in the ninth century, Irish political tracts show their authors to possess a shared and pervasive concern with the theme of peaceful rulership. This concern emerged from the complex weaving together of Christian concerns, scriptural concepts, and notions of traditional modes of rule and produced a body of political material quite distinct from forms to be found elsewhere. From the middle decades of the eighth century onwards some of this material would be taken up by new generations of scholars, including Cathwulf, Alcuin, and Hincmar, who shared with their Irish predecessors a wish to intervene in and to shape contemporary kingship. The depth of the Irish contribution to early medieval Europe's scholarly culture has been a contentious issue in recent years but when we examine the various currents of thought that flowed into images of the peaceful ruler, it cannot be underestimated.[218]

Early medieval culture has more claim than many in European history as one defined by an intense engagement with the inheritances from past cultures. Often the results of that retroactive process were strikingly, if unintentionally, innovative, as for example, in the sophisticated pseudo-paganized *Audacht Morainn*, or

[215] *De XII Abusivis saeculi*, c. 9, 51–3.

[216] Breen, 'Text and Transmission' 80–1; *idem*, 'Bible', 231–6; *idem*, 'Irish exegesis', 72–6.

[217] S. Meeders, 'The Early Irish Stowe Missal's Destination and Function', *EME* 13.2 (2005), 179–94, esp. 186, from where this translation derives.

[218] C. D. Wright, 'Bischoff's Theory of Irish Exegesis and the Genesis Commentary in Munich Clm 6302: A Critique of a Critique', *Journal of Medieval Latin* 10 (2001), 115–75.

Edwin's progress through his kingdom with its Roman overtones. To understand how early medieval kingship was constructed we need to understand the nature of the materials in use, as well as the particular histories of each. Having done so, and thus having mapped our foundations we can move forward to look at the ways in which these ideas came together in specific configurations.

2

After the *Pax Romana*

When the ways of man shall please the Lord,
He will convert even his enemies to peace.

Proverbs XVI.7

PEACE IN TRANSITION

Writing around 439 Salvian of Marseilles lamented the absence of peace and security in the Roman world of his own day.[1] Compounding his misery was his sense that, whilst its benefits had disappeared, peacetime's vices had robustly survived into his own disordered day. If Salvian claimed the death of peace in the provinces of the West, many who came after would view reports of its end as highly premature. When we turn to the earliest post- or sub-Roman political cultures what becomes immediately apparent is the intensity with which we see claims made of maintaining, creating, or upholding peace, be it the Ostrogothic emphasis upon *civilitas* and *tranquillitas*, Gibichung assertions of PAX ET ABUNDANTIA, or Merovingian kings' claims to be the upholders of peace, protectors of the Church, and social order. In recent years a complex but fluid notion of 'transformation' has become the dominant—if not the uncontested—mode by which the shift from the late empire to the early successor kingdoms has been understood. It is tempting to conclude that this was just how the rulers of those kingdoms wished their reigns to be seen, as they sought legitimacy for fledgling regimes emerging in the shadow of imperial power and whose constitutional validity, from a traditional imperial perspective and from that of local Roman elites, was suspect, to say the least.[2] The disjunct between reassurances of peace and life 'on the ground' may well have rendered such claims hollow at particular times and places and later commentators would share Salvian's pessimism, but those reassurances continued to be made, often as elements of larger

---

[1] Salvian, *De gubernatione Dei*, ed. C. Halm, *MGH AA* 1 (Berlin, 1987), VII.1, pp. 84–5.
[2] A. H. M. Jones, 'The Constitutional Position of Odoacer and Theoderic', *JRS* 52 (1962), 126–30.

political programmes of integration and control.[3] Such programmes were responses to fundamental challenges for a new ruling class: how were these new
kings to maintain social order? Newborn kingdoms had to learn to communi-
cate: how were their kings to deal with each other or to create and maintain
political relations; to organize peaceful interaction between 'barbarian' and
Roman; to settle conflicts?[4]

In this chapter it will be these claims towards maintaining peace, and perceptions of a ruler's obligations to do so, that concern us. Rulers desired to speak
with a recognizable language of political power to assert and secure authority,
and frequently emphasized peace at times of acute political stress. For their part,
churchmen sought to shape and channel barbarian kingship along Christian
paths.

These centuries also fostered theories of peace in their own right, perhaps most
significantly those of Gregory the Great whose pontifical career, lived out
between the pull of monastic retreat and the constant demands of overseeing a
city beset by Lombard pressure, would prompt some sustained reflection on our
theme. This environment also generated a further phenomenon: the tendency for
some early medieval historians to identify periods of peace and order, often in the
form of specific reigns of peace, in their own peoples' pasts, new golden ages
within their own barbarian narratives. We have already encountered one such
moment, Edwin of Northumbria's reign in the pages of Bede, and we shall
shortly meet other 'peaceful kings' such as Dagobert, 'peaceful like Solomon' in
the words of the anonymous author of the eighth-century *Liber historiae Francorum*.

The underlying lesson of these various explorations is that the post-Roman
period was a world of sustained uncertainty in which peace was a significant
commodity—political, social, and personal. Kings, and men who would be
kings, from the Brittonic West to the northern hem of the Sahara, broadcast
images of themselves as the embodiments of good rulership, as keepers of the
peace.

VANDAL VARIATIONS

Reviewing Lapeyre's edition of Ferrandus' *Vita Fulgentii*, Charles Saumagne
reflected upon the *Vita*'s image of later fifth-century North Africa and coined a
phrase that has enjoyed a vigorous afterlife: 'la paix vandale'. Others took it up,
notably Charles Courtois, *doyen* of Vandal studies, who recognized in it an

---

[3] M. Innes, 'Land, Freedom and the Making of the Early Medieval West', *TRHS*, 6th series, 16
(2006), 39–74.
[4] A. Gillett, *Envoys and Political Communication in the Late Antique West, 411–533* (Cambridge,
2003).

arresting inversion of the conventional duality of Roman order and barbarian chaos.[5] Behind the apparent oxymoron stood the notion that under Vandal rule, peace and order—and the governmental system that supported both—continued to flourish in the later fifth and earlier sixth centuries in the conquered provinces of the North African littoral in implicit contrast to deteriorating conditions elsewhere in the western Mediterranean. Recent scholarship has done much to confirm that the rhythms of late antique North African life continued through the Vandal interlude. In the centres of power no less than in the fields and hinterlands Vandal kings appropriated many of the trappings of the late Roman state: continuity, of a kind, was their goal.[6] Despite its brief life, Vandal Africa holds a unique place in the development of sub-Roman political ideas. It was here that barbarian rulers first found themselves praised in the style of later Roman emperors, and where the early steps were taken in the fusion of scriptural ideals and classical poetic forms for political purpose.

Following Geiseric's crossing into North Africa in 429, successive treaties between the empire and Vandal kings formalized the latter's control of Numidia Africa Proconsularis, and Byzacena. Procopius recorded that as part of the agreement between Geiseric and Valentinian III, the Vandals offered annual tribute and a hostage, Geiseric's son and future heir, Huneric (477–84).[7] Ties would be further strengthened between the Hasdingi and the empire through Huneric's marriage in 456 to Eudocia, Valentinian's eldest daughter. These treaties recognized an essentially independent Vandal kingdom that was to be ruled by consecutive members of the Hasdingi dynasty until 533/4, when Belisarius dragged the North African provinces back under imperial rule.[8] Many of the troops who sought to rejoin Carthage and its territories to Justinian's empire had, perhaps, a weaker grasp on late Roman high culture than

[5] C. Saumagne, 'La paix vandale. Apropos de documents relatifs à la domination vandale en Afrique', *Revue tunisienne* (1930), 167–84, reprinted in *Les Cahiers de Tunisie* 10 (1962), 417–25; C. Courtois, *Les Vandales et l'Afrique* (Paris, 1955). See also the comments of L. Maurin, 'Thuburbo Majus et la paix vandale', *Les Cahiers de Tunisie* 15 (1967), 225–54, at 225, reflecting upon the term and its implications. For an overview of Vandal studies, A. H. Merrills, 'Vandals, Romans and Berbers: Understanding Late Antique North Africa', in *idem* (ed.), *Vandals, Romans and Berbers. New Perspectives on Late Antique North Africa* (Aldershot, 2004), 3–28.
[6] Michael McCormick, *Eternal Victory: Triumphal Rulership in Late Antiquity, Byzantium, and the Early Medieval West* (Cambridge, 1986), 261–6; J. H. W. G. Liebschütz, '*Gens* into *regnum*: the Vandals', in H.-W. Goetz, W. Pohl, and J. Jarnut (eds), *Regna and Gentes: The Relationship Between Late Antiquity and Early Medieval Peoples and Kingdoms in the Transformation of the Roman World*, TRW 13 (Leiden, 2003), 55–83; A. Cameron, 'Vandal and Byzantine Africa', in A. Cameron, B. Ward-Perkins, and M. Whitby (eds), *Late Antiquity: Empire and Successors, A.D. 425–600*, Cambridge Ancient History 14 (Cambridge, 2000), 552–69.
[7] *Bell. Van.* I.4.13. On this agreement, F. M. Clover, 'Emperor Worship in Vandal Africa', in G. Wirth et al. (eds), *Romanitas-Christianitas: Untersuchungen zur Geschichte und Literatur der römischen Kaiserzeit* (Berlin 1982), 661–74, at 667–8.
[8] F. M. Ausbüttel, 'Die Verträge zwischen den Vandalen und Römern', *Romanobarbarica* 11 (1991), 45–67. A recent overview of Vandal settlement is given by A. Schwarz, 'The settlement of the Vandals in North Africa', in Merrills (ed.), *Vandals*, 49–59.

some of the Vandal elite that they sought to dislodge. These Vandals were men who built baths, patronized poets, and oversaw an intellectual environment that produced many of the poems later gathered in the so-called *Latin Anthology*, as well as several biblical epics, most notably Dracontius' *De laudibus Dei*.[9]

A sequence of five poems in the *Anthology* ascribed to one Felix focused their flattery upon the baths built by Trasimund (d. 523) at Alianae, an unidentified site seemingly favoured by Vandal kings for their villas and 'leisure complexes'.[10] They reveal, as sharply as any aspect of life in early medieval North Africa, some of the cultural continuities under the Vandal interlude.[11] For Felix, Trasimund's authority was such that he could make peace between the elements themselves:

> A royal order has raised an illustrious building,
> The heat, the stone, the water, the brazier, all equally feel his *imperium*.
> Here Vulcan is imprisoned by the ice of the waters.
> And the fire is at peace with the fountain's flow.
> There is harmony between the icy water and the flames,
> And the nymph of the cold water is stunned by the blazing pools.[12]

Felix's verses portray Trasimund as a ruler in the Stoic tradition, capable of reconciling cosmic opposites and balancing the elements with the same authority with which he ruled a mixed society comprising similarly oppositional communities, Roman and Vandal.[13] Such sentiments were not uncommon in late fifth-century Africa.[14] This backwards glance towards a model of rulership with its roots in a Hellenistic past also characterizes the Vandal awareness of the possibilities of exploiting the imagery of past power. Some Vandal coins, after all, carried the images of a horse's head and palm tree, symbols first found on Phoenician coinage and linked to myths of Carthage's foundation.[15]

---

[9] G. Hays, ' "*Romuleis Libicisque Litteris*": Fulgentius and the "Vandal Renaissance"', in Merrills (ed.), *Vandals*, 101–32, esp. 125–6; G. Chalon, M. Devallet, P. Force, P. Griffe, J.-M Lassère, and J.-N. Michaud, '*Memorabile factum*. Une célébration de l'évergétisme des rois vandales dans l'Anthologie Latine', *Antiquité africaine* 21 (1985), 207–62. For the assembly of the *Latin Anthology* see A. Cameron, 'Byzantine Africa—The Literary Evidence', in J. H. Humphrey (ed.), *Excavations at Carthage*, 7 (Ann Arbor, 1978), 29–62.

[10] R. Miles, 'The *Anthologia Latina* and the Creation of Secular Space in Vandal Carthage', *Antiquité Tardive* 13 (2005), 305–20, 305 n. 1. E. Courtney, 'Observations on the Latin Anthology', *Hermathena* 129 (1980), 37–50, at 39.

[11] Miles, '*Anthologia*', 310–12.

[12] *ALR* 212, lines 1–6: 'Regia praeclaras erexit iussio moles, / Sensit et imperium calx, lapis, unda, focus./ Inclusus Vulcanus aquis algentibus hic est, / Et pacem liquidis fontibus ignis habet./ Cum lymphis gelidis gestat concordia flammam / Ac stupet ardentes frigida nympha lacus.'

[13] Chalon et al., '*Memorabile*', 227–36.

[14] D. J. Nodes, *Doctrine and Exegesis in Biblical Latin Poetry* (Leeds, 1993), 109–10. See also the comparable treatment of the unification of the elements by Ennodius in his verses on the baths of Aponus, *MGH AA* 7, 178–9.

[15] For Vandal coinage G. M. Berndt and R. Steinacher, 'Minting in Vandal North Africa: Coins of the Vandal Period in the Coin Cabinet of Vienna's Kunsthistorisches Museum', *EME* 16.3 (2006), 252–98, esp. 266–7 (on horse iconography); F. M. Clover, 'Felix Karthago', *DOP* 40 (1986), 1–16, at 5–8; *MEC*, 19–21, 422.

Similar themes of harmony can be seen in the verse of Luxorius, the poet in whom Carthage found its Fellini.[16] His poems, populated by trained animals, dwarf pantomimists, and the dissipated, are tableaux of late antique indulgence, and might seem at first to offer little direct insight into the political culture of the Vandal kingdom, save as evidence for the seductive loucheness of North African culture.[17] One of Luxorius' poems, however, does carry a plausible political charge, although the subject—an after-dinner animal act—may seem at first sight unpromising political material:

After a long time a wonderful pleasure has been granted to the Carthaginians.
A gentle monkey is sitting on the back of a dog it fears.
What great things the times presage for the happy kingdom when wild animals learn to observe the law of peace.[18]

Some commentators have seen a reference here to political conditions in the Vandal kingdom: the 'wild animals' (*ferae*) of the poem are an allusion to the Vandals themselves, and perhaps the Goths, their ferocity tamed by the *lex pacis* of Roman ways.[19] This would not be the last time that Roman culture was viewed as a curb on barbarian beastliness.[20] The Vandal poet Dracontius would see a similar process at work not in a *triclinium* but in the classroom, where his teacher, *grammaticus* Felicianus, worked wonders worthy of Orpheus on the mixed class of Romans and Vandals in his charge.[21]

Felix celebrated its cosmic creation within the walls of a Vandal warlord's bath-house whilst Luxorius coded political commentary and disdain for his new masters into a poetic account of a postprandial entertainment. But not all would praise the Vandal kings for their pacific qualities or unite in approval of the new regime. For the Catholic bishop of Vita, Victor, the Vandal conquest was little less than a second Fall. His *Historia persecutionis Africanae provinciae*, written, and probably rewritten, in the 480s offers an image of a landscape of peace

---

[16] On Luxorius see Hays, 'Romuleis', 112–14; J. George, 'Vandal Poets in their Context', in Merrills (ed.), *Vandals*, 133–43, esp. 140–2; M. Rosenblum, *Luxorius. A Latin Poet Among the Vandals* (New York, 1961).

[17] Miles, '*Anthologia*', 306 n. 3. For Procopius' account of Vandal excess see *Bell. Van.* IV.6.6–9.

[18] *ALR* 330: 'Reddita post longum Tyriis est mira voluptas, / Quem pavet ut sedeat simia blanda canem. / Quanto magna parant felici tempora regno, / Discant ut legem pacis habere ferae'. The translation here is, with minor alterations, Rosenblum's, *Luxorius*, 137–8, with discussion at 209–10.

[19] M. Chalon et al., '*Memorabile*', 207–62, at 208 n. 6. Rosenbaum, *Luxorius*, 209–10, drawing upon O. Schubert, *Quaestionum De Anthologia Codicis Salmasiani, Pars I, De Luxorio* (Weimar, 1875), 16–17.

[20] T. E. J. Wiedemann, 'Between Men and Beasts: Barbarians in Ammianus Marcellinus', in I. S. Moxon, J. D. Smart, and A. J. Woodman (eds), *Past Perspectives. Studies in Greek and Roman Historical Writing* (Cambridge, 1986), 189–201.

[21] D. Shanzer, 'Two Clocks and a Wedding: Theoderic's Diplomatic Relations with the Burgundians', *Romanobarbarica* 14 (1996–7), 225–58, at 234–5.

destroyed by the Vandals' very arrival.[22] For Victor it was the years before their advent when the land had been rich and fertile; then peace reigned. After 429, however, the Vandals torched and murdered, driving Romans to seek refuge in caves.[23] Drought and famine ensued as nature—directed by a wrathful God rather than held in equilibrium by a neo-Stoic Vandal king—punished Catholic Roman and Arian Vandal alike for the persecution of His Church.[24]

Between the explicitly literary and the consciously pious, stands Blossius Aemilius Dracontius, arguably Vandal Africa's pre-eminent literary figure, who offers a more tempered and certainly more personal treatment of the theme of peace and power.[25] Dracontius combined the pursuit of letters with the responsibilities of public office, serving as *advocatus* to Carthage's Proconsul.[26] Peace, Dracontius realized, was neither to be celebrated nor to be mourned. Its flux was simply one current in the flow of life itself:

> Though all things return, a man's life does not come back to him.
> But it flies, a fugitive, like a swift bird.
> There are fixed times for peace and for bloodshed.
> Leisure, and the toil of soldiering, each has its time.
> There are fixed times for rejoicing and for grieving.
> Some times yield gain, others, losses.[27]

The work from which this is taken, the *Satisfactio ad regem Gunthamundum* was a verse apology and Dracontius' attempt to win back favour and secure release from prison, his punishment for composing verse lauding an 'unknown lord' (*dominus ignotus*). Considerable ink has been spilled in attempts to identify this figure, with candidates ranging from Zeno or Anastasius I to figures nearer at hand (Odoacer? Theoderic?), consensus settling upon an eastern emperor over a Gothic leader, though a plausible case has recently been made for Huneric

---

[22] *Victoris Vitensis, Historia persecutionis Africanae provinciae sub Geiserico et Hunirico regibus Wandalorum*, ed. K. Halm, *MGH AA* 3.1 (Berlin, 1879), 1–58. D. Shanzer, 'Intentional Audiences: Historiography, Hagiography, Martyrdom in Victor of Vita's *Historia Persecutionis*', in Merrills (ed.), *Vandals*, 271–90, with references; W. E. Fahey, 'History, Community and Suffering in Victor of Vita', in D. Kries and C. Brown Tkacz (eds), *Nova Doctrina Vetusque. Essays on Early Christianity in Honor of Frederic W. Schlatter* (New York, 1999), 225–41.

[23] *Historia*, c. 3.

[24] On dating see J. Moorhead, *Victor of Vita: History of the Vandal Persecution*, TTH 10 (Liverpool, 1992), pp. xvi–xviii.

[25] A. Merrills, 'The Perils of Panegyric: The Lost Poem of Dracontius and its Consequences', in *idem* (ed.), *Vandals*, 145–6; M. Edwards, 'Dracontius the African and the Fate of Rome', *Latomus* 63.1 (2004), 151–60 offers a crisply underwhelmed response to Dracontius.

[26] *PRLE* II, pp. 379–80; F. Clover, 'The Symbiosis of Romans and Vandals in Africa', in E. K. Chrysos and A. Schwarcz (eds), *Das Reich und die Barbaren, Veröffentlichungen des Instituts Für Österreichische Geschichtsforschung* 29 (Vienna, 1989), 57–73, at 62–3; D. F. Bright, *The Miniature Epic in Vandal Africa* (Norman, OH, 1987), 14–20.

[27] Dracontius, *Satisfactio*, ed. F. Vollmer, *MGH AA* 14 (Berlin, 1905), 114–31, at 128, 255–9. Here, and below, I draw from the translation of Sister M. St Margaret, *Dracontii Satisfactio with Introduction, Text, Translation and Commentary* (Philadelphia, 1936).

(478–94).[28] The importance of Dracontius' *Satisfactio* lies in the evidence it contains of how an educated North African could praise the power of his Vandal king. Dracontius' authorial affect was innocent confusion: why was the poem's lowly author even categorized as a fitting target for Gunthamund's royal anger?[29] Dracontius' twisting argument for freedom blended with a sequence of historical precedents for royal mercy, particular praise for Gunthamund, and broader reflections on God's mercy and man's fallen state. By invoking their shared experience of sin and weakness, Dracontius sought to collapse the distance between Vandal king and disgraced prisoner.

The *Satisfactio* began with an address not to Gunthamund but to God, the highest of kings, in the explicit hope that the Almighty would direct the king to restore him to his former position. Lowering his sights, Dracontius then addressed the king directly, emphasizing his mercy, justice, and generosity. Gunthamund even treated prisoners of war fairly, Dracontius observed. Only rebels faced the prospect of execution.[30] He pressed into service a roster of classical and biblical figures, either to demonstrate the quality of royal mercy or, more often, to stress that the dispensers of past royal mercy had themselves been sinners. David was an adulterer, Dracontius noted, yet had he not spared his enemies from death? He was penitent. His sins were forgiven.[31] Similarly, Solomon, son of David and Bathsheba (whose sin was equal to David's own) held the highest office.[32] Solomon, moreover, asked the Lord for wisdom, not for his enemies' deaths:

Solomon himself did not demand the neck of his enemies when he prayed to the Lord, but the ability of a wise man. He appeared as prudent, because he refused to be bloodthirsty, and was a peacemaker and consistent in his counsels.[33]

Solomon was followed in quick succession by Stephen Protomartyr (pardoning his killers from beneath a volley of stones), Julius Caesar, Augustus, Titus, even Commodus. Each, in their own way, observed Dracontius, was forgiving.[34] Whilst for many, including Augustine and Isidore, a king was one who ruled rightly, for Dracontius he was one who ruled mercifully.[35] A man's a king, he observed, who pardons those beneath him, controls his anger, masters his heart.[36] Inner, not cosmic, equilibrium was the core of Dracontius' vision of royal power.

---

[28] Merrills, 'Dracontius', in *idem* (ed.), *Vandals*, 146; Clover, 'Symbiosis', 62–3.
[29] *Satis.*, lines 265–6.
[30] *Satis.*, lines 125–9.
[31] *Satis.*, lines 158–60.
[32] *Satis.*, lines 161–2.
[33] *Satis.*, lines 167–70.
[34] *Satis.*, lines 171–90.
[35] J. Balogh, '*Rex a Recte Regendo*', *Speculum* 3 (1928), 580–2.
[36] *Satis.*, lines 209–10.

The political reflections found in the *Satisfactio* may well have been heartfelt, but few would call them sophisticated. For example, when his list of mighty animals who show mercy to lesser prey moves from eagles spurning sparrows to the somewhat less likely refusal of dragons to attack moles, or the observation that lightning targets trees not blades of grass, we might perhaps hear something of a desperate author's scramble for material.[37] Viewed from our perspective, however, the importance of the *Satisfactio* lies in its deployment of classical and biblical types of ruler in close succession. Dracontius stands in the vanguard of the first generation of theorists of post-Roman rulership, and one of the very first to bring the figures of Augustus and Solomon together in a work that espoused the desirability of mercy and peacefulness as qualities to a new generation of kings, a vision, as Michael McCormick noted, some distance from traditional notions of 'Germanic *Heerkönigtum*'.[38] Above all, the *Satisfactio* is a highly personal and contingent piece of political theory, though one that would find responsive later readers; Eugenius II in Visigothic Spain would rework it in seventh-century Toledo, as would members of Carolingian court circles.

Vandal Africa failed. Equally evanescent were the neighbouring Berber kingdoms that came into being in the later fifth century onwards, and whose elites, like those of their Vandal neighbours, also adopted the titles and political modes of late Rome.[39] The evidence is fragmentary but suggestive that late Roman notions of peace played their part in the political language here too. In the Aures mountains of North Africa, for example, an epitaph erected in the fifth century's final years to one Masties, *dux* and self-styled *imperator*, recorded his virtues: he had never sworn falsely, nor broken faith with either Roman or Moor. In war and in peace he had been prepared.[40] Grandly asserting his independent authority whilst simultaneously memorializing his qualities—those of a loyal and dependable federate client of a lost western emperor—Masties' epitaph is a snapshot of rulership caught in transition between sub- and post-Roman forms.

PAX ET ABUNDANTIA: GIBICHUNG BURGUNDY

534 was a bad year for fledgling kingdoms. Not only was Vandal Africa crushed by Belisarius, Gibichung Burgundy finally fell to Clovis' heirs. Amongst all the experiments in sub-Roman politics the kingdom of Burgundy is unique in failing

[37] *Satis.*, lines 267–80.
[38] McCormick, *Eternal*, 266.
[39] Merrills, 'Introduction', in *idem* (ed.), *Vandals*, 5–7.
[40] Text: *PLRE II*, p. 734. Discussion: M. Handley, 'Disputing the End of African Christianity', in Merrills (ed.), *Vandals*, 291–310, at 299; P. A. Février, 'Masuna et Masties', *Antiquité africaine* 24 (1998), 141–7.

twice in little over a century.[41] Settled initially in the Rhineland in the 410s, the Burgundians were resettled by Aëtius in the early 440s in Maxima Sequanorum.[42] The sources for early sixth-century Burgundian history are fragmentary. At least under the better documented rule of the Arian Gundobad (474–516) and his Catholic son, Sigismund (516–23)—rulers with whom we will be particularly concerned—the image that comes into focus is of a kingdom characterized by peaceful cultural and religious coexistence between Burgundian and Roman, a balancing act comparable to Ostrogothic Italy's regime of *civilitas*, a term also employed in contemporary Burgundy.[43] Though an Arian, Gundobad seemingly enjoyed cordial relations and intellectual exchange with Avitus, Catholic bishop of Vienne. Theological debate between the two appears to have been conducted with civility and even some personal warmth. Similarly, the Burgundian laws, the *Liber Constitutionum*, in the form we have them issued by Sigismund in April 517, reveal at least on the prescriptive level, a high degree of Romano-Burgundian cooperation.[44] That coexistence is also evident in the form of Burgundian rulership. *Patricius*, *magister militum*, and *rex*, Burgundian kings balanced the identities of imperial office and barbarian ruler in their own layered authority.[45]

For all the brevity of its political existence, several of the cultural forms pioneered in sixth-century Burgundy would have a long career in the West, the idea of peaceful rule not least amongst them.[46] In Gundobad it had a ruler who appears to have had a genuine concern for peace itself, manifest as much in his theological reflections as in his political posturing. Sixth-century Burgundy has also been identified as a plausible point of origin for the development of new prayers for peaceful reigns, part of the developing liturgy of western rulership.

[41] I. N. Wood, '*Gentes*, Kings and Kingdoms—The Emergence of States: The Kingdom of the Gibichungs', in H.-W. Goetz, J. Jarnut, and W. Pohl (eds), *Regna and Gentes*, 243–69; I. N. Wood and D. Shanzer, *Avitus of Vienne. Letters and Selected Prose* TTH 38 (Liverpool, 2002), 3–27; J. Favrod, *Histoire politique du royaume burgonde (443–534)* (Lausanne, 1997).

[42] Wood and Shanzer, *Avitus*, 14–15; Favrod, *Histoire*, 100–17. On the vexed matter of Burgundian settlement see I. Wood, 'Ethnicity and the Ethnogenesis of the Burgundians', in H. Wolfram and W. Pohl (eds), *Typen der Ethnogenese unter besonderer Berüksichtigung der Bayern* (Vienna, 1990), 53–69, esp. 65–9.

[43] Shanzer and Wood, *Avitus*, 11: '. . . remarkably liberal'. D. Boyson, 'Romano-Burgundian Society in the Age of Gundobad: Some Legal, Archaeological and Historical Evidence', *Nottingham Medieval Studies* 2 (1988), 91–118, noting at 113: '. . . a settled, well-ordered, hierarchical and *essentially peaceful* society' (my italics).

[44] P. Amory, 'Names, Ethnic Identity, and Community in Fifth- and Sixth-Century Burgundy', *Viator* 25 (1994), 1–30; idem, 'Ethnographic Rhetoric, Aristocratic Attitudes and Political Allegiance in Post-Roman Gaul', *Klio* 76 (1994), 438–53; idem, 'The Meaning and Purpose of Ethnic Terminology in Burgundian Laws', *EME* 2.1 (1993), 1–28; D. Frye, 'Gundobad, the *Leges Burgundionum*, and the Struggle for Sovereignty in Burgundy', *Classica et Mediaevalia* 41 (1990), 199–212.

[45] P. Barnwell, *Emperors, Prefects and Kings: The Roman West, 395–565* (Chapel Hill, 1992), 82–9.

[46] B. Rosenwein, 'Perennial Prayer at Agaune', in S. Farmer and B. Rosenwein (eds), *Monks and Nuns, Saints and Outcasts. Religion in Medieval Society* (Ithaca, 2000), 37–56.

Gundobad was the first known post-Roman ruler to identify his rule explicitly with the concept of peace: a silver coin minted in Lyons in the early sixth century bearing the legend PAX ET ABUNDANTIA around the monogram GVB, with the figure of Victory on the reverse.[47] This was one of two coins issued in the earlier sixth century to bear the word peace as material propaganda.[48] Further, the presence of the king's monogram, an innovation to Burgundian coinage under Gundobad, marks a step away from the sub-imperial coinage (issued by rulers but bearing the emperor's monogram rather than their own) and towards an independent ideological apparatus.[49]

How ought we to read Gundobad's slogan? Was it Roman? Scriptural? Both, probably. From Constantine onwards, evocations of PAX on coins could register powerful and almost certainly intentionally ambiguous associations with both imperial tradition and Christian soteriology. ABUNDANTIA, as much as PAX, had its roots in Augustan political imagery. Antique depictions of PAX conventionally showed a female figure, grasping a cornucopia, olive branch, staff, or sceptre, crowned with a laurel wreath, often looking down—as she does on the Ara Pacis—upon the infant Ploutos, 'Plenty'. Gundobad was a presence in the politics of the imperial court in Constantinople under two successive emperors prior to becoming king of Burgundy in 473, and thus knew about both the media and the messages of late Roman political imagery.[50] Notions of abundance had their place in the Christian lexicon, too, often carrying messianic overtones—the plenty of the New Jerusalem, the land of milk and honey, the abundance of Solomon's kingdom. And it is in this context that we find PAX and ABUNDANTIA linked in Psalm CXXI.7: 'Let peace be in thy strength: and abundance in thy towers' (*fiat pax in virtute tua et abundantia in turribus tuis*).[51] As a political slogan from an Arian king to a population that was both Roman and Catholic the phrase might best be read as an elegantly economic means by which Gundobad could reassure his subjects in doubly familiar terms. Explicitly religious legends are relatively rare in the sixth-century West. But that one occurs in the early sixth-century Burgundian kingdom ought not to surprise us. The level of scriptural engagement at Gundobad's court was high, with the Psalms

[47] *MEC* I.338, with discussion at 76. On this coin, and other Burgundian silver issues see J. Tricou, 'Légendes et symboles chrétiens des monnaies burgondes', *Studi di Antichità cristiana* 26 (1965), 551–5.

[48] J. P. Callu, '*Pax et Libertas:* une légende monétaire de Théodebert Ier', *Mélanges de numismatique, d'archéologie et d'histoire offerts à Jean Lafaurie* (Paris, 1980), 189–99, at 194; E. K. Chrysos, 'The Title BASILEUS in Early Byzantine International Relations', *DOP* 32 (1978), 29–75, at 53. For the deployment of VICTORIA inscriptions in successor coinages see McCormick, *Eternal*, 318–19 (Visigothic), 339 (Burgundian and Frankish).

[49] Frye, 'Gundobad', 205.

[50] Wood, 'Burgundian', 255; 261–9, with the quotation at 266; Amory, 'Names', 8, 13. *PLRE* II. pp. 524–5.

[51] H. Donner, 'Psalm 122', in W. Claasen (ed.) *Text and Context: Old Testament and Semitic Studies for F. C. Fensham* (Sheffield, 1988), 81–91; A. Strus and L. Alonso-Schökel, '*Salmo* 122: Canto al nombre de Jerusalén', *Biblica* 61.2 (1980), 234–50.

particularly so.[52] Psalm CXXI was one of the so-called Zion Psalm sequence, and generations of commentators on this psalm served as the focus for meditations upon the Heavenly Jerusalem, the earthly Church, and the nature of peace itself.[53] In 515, Sigismund had founded St-Maurice d'Agaune, a monastic centre whose devotions were constructed around an intense programme of constant psalmody.[54] Avitus of Vienne delivered the dedication homily at St-Maurice and had been closely involved in its establishment.[55]

At what point in the early sixth century was this coin minted? If the general position of the coin's issue in the development of a distinct post-Roman ideology is relatively clear, the precise circumstances of its production are not. Its assertion of peace might hint at a time following disorder or war, perhaps the early 500s, in the wake of Gundobad's suppression of his brother's revolt. If the latter, it might be read as a restatement of Gundobad's authority and a reminder of the benefits his rule promised to restore.[56] Ian Wood has plausibly suggested just such a context for Gundobad's issue of the 'milder laws' (*leges mitiores*) that Gregory of Tours recorded as issued in the early sixth century, and it is not implausible to see lenient laws and promotional coinage forming joint components in a concerted exercise in hearts and minds.[57] A later date for the coin is also possible, however, and, on balance, perhaps more likely. Most of Gundobad's surviving coinage has been dated towards his reign's end in 516. Such a dating also accords with the suggested date of 513–16 given by Peiper for Avitus of Vienne's delivery of a homily for the dedication of a unnamed basilica, identified variously as a church in Geneva or more plausibly, St Irenaeus in Lyons, in the presence of Gundobad and his son and co-ruler Sigismund.[58] This homily contains an apparent allusion to the coin's legend, as Avitus both celebrated the new foundation and used the opportunity to fête the rulers in whose presence he spoke.[59] Whilst it is by no means automatic that the phrase had to be deployed within a single time frame, and our fragmentary knowledge of Burgundian history and its coinage limits the certainty with which we might place the coin's issue in a specific context, it is

---

[52] *Ep.* 1, pp. 12–15; 4, pp. 290–32, 21–2, 54–5. Shanzer and Wood, *Avitus*, 8–10, 163–207, offer detailed analyses and translation of Gundobad's correspondence with Avitus and its theological content.

[53] Prosper of Aquitaine, *Expositio Psalmorum*, CCSL 68A, 128–30; Hilary of Poitiers, *Tractatus super Psalmos*, PL 9, cols 660–7. On the early medieval commentary tradition of the Zion Psalms see T. Renna, 'Zion and Jerusalem in the Psalms', in F. Van Fleteren and J. C. Schnaubelt (eds), *Augustine: Biblical Exegete* (New York, 2001), 279–98.

[54] Rosenwein, 'Prayer', 40–1.

[55] Avitus of Vienne, *Homilia*, ed. R. Peiper, *MGH AA* 6.2 (Berlin, 1883), no. 25, pp. 145–6.

[56] Wood, 'Burgundians', 253–4.

[57] *DLH* II.33; Wood, 'Burgundians', 253.

[58] *Hom.* 25. C. Perrat and A. Audin, 'Alcimi Ecdicii Viennensis Episcopi Homilia Dicta in dedicatione superioris basilicae', *Studi in onore di Aristide Calderini e Roberto Paribeni* (Milan, 1957), II, 433–51. Reydellet, *Royauté*, 133–4 opts for Sigismund, while Perrat and Audin, 'Alcimi', 442–4, Shanzer and Wood, *Avitus*, 8–9 opt for a date during Gundobad's lifetime.

[59] *MEC*, 76.

perhaps more probable that the coin issue and dedication homily were intended as in some sense complementary and concelebratory.

Avitus' homily survives only in a corrupt and incomplete text. Having praised the form of the finished church he moved on to celebrate the power of the saints whose relics it contained. The city was impregnable because of the basilica as much as by its walls. The saints were its doorkeepers. Like Jerusalem, which is built like a city, wrote Avitus, the newly completed church was encircled by towers, albeit towers devoted to the cult of the saints. Turning from the building to the Burgundians themselves, Avitus hoped that it would a bastion of peace for them, a place where there would be 'peace in strength, and strength in peace', strength for the rulers, those who command, and peace for the ruled, who serve. Claiming to speak frankly Avitus praised the unnamed king before him (Gundobad?) the father of the Catholic peoples, as a light of religion and the pillar of the province—apposite imagery for the location—as well as a model of virtue, the surety of the Church, glory of the age, exalted in *civilitas*.[60] In its evocation of virtue (*virtus*) and *civilitas* Avitus' lexicon of praise for his king shared key elements with his Ostrogothic contemporaries, although the considerable emphasis upon the king's provision of peace, and the *virtus* upon which it rested, is noteworthy. Peace, it appears, played a particularly important part in the formation of the royal Burgundian self-image, broadcast in coinage and reiterated in homilies delivered before the Burgundian elite. Through liturgy and on coinage the Burgundian kingdom in the 510s was framed in terms of the Psalms, and as nothing less than a New Jerusalem.

Avitus occupied a key position as advisor, author, and celebrant of Burgundian kings Gundobad and Sigismund.[61] His relationship with the former was also the context in which the king could express his own concerns about peace, not only in terms of his own reign and its propaganda but with regard to Christian history as a whole. In a letter of uncertain date, but probably in the first decade of the sixth century, one passage in particular captured the Burgundian king's eye, Micah IV.2–4:

For the law shall go forth out of Zion, and the word of the Lord out of Jerusalem. And he shall judge among many people, and rebuke strong nations afar off: and they shall beat their swords into ploughshares, and their spears into spades: nation shall not take sword against nation: neither shall they learn war any more. And every man shall sit under his vine, and under his fig tree, and there shall be none to make them afraid.[62]

---

[60] Avitus, *Hom.* 24, p. 145. Perrat and Audin 'Alcimi', 437–9 provide a French translation of this problematic and fragmentary text and an edition of it at 448–51. For the context and content of Avitus' dedication homilies I. Wood, 'The Audience of Architecture in Post-Roman Gaul', in L. A. S. Butler and R. K. Morris (eds), *The Anglo-Saxon Church. Papers on History, Architecture and Archaeology in Honour of Dr. H. M. Taylor* (London, 1986), 74–9.

[61] Shanzer and Wood, *Avitus*, 8.

[62] *Ep.* 21 p. 54. My understanding of this letter is strongly indebted to the translation and commentary of Shanzer and Wood, *Avitus*, 202–3.

Gundobad's question to Avitus was one of periodization. Had the time evoked by the prophet Micah already passed? Or was the prophecy still awaiting fulfilment? The question betrays concern on the king's part about the very nature of salvation history: would such a time of peace come in the future, was a divinely ordained kingdom of peace coming? Did the span of time covered by Micah's prophecy include his own day, or had it passed?

In reply Avitus, in addition to misidentifying the passage as Isaiah II.3—doubtless on account of the 'swords to ploughshares' motif both share—invoked the familiar reading of the synchrony of Christ's birth and Augustus' peace. Yes, he explained, the prophecy had been fulfilled by Christ's Incarnation, and with it the advent of the New Law. Developing this theme in his reply to the Arian king, Avitus explained that to some extent it could be understood as referring to the earthly life of Christ during which undisturbed peace flourished throughout the world. But more likely, he added, it referred to the peacefulness of faithful Christians, 'since the majority of them lack, and have lacked, the use of the sword', a weapon that symbolized the first crime, Cain's slaying of Abel, and underlined the violent nature of fallen man.[63] Mic IV.3's references to nations *not* lifting up sword against nation led Avitus to invoke Mark XIII.8—'For nation shall rise against nation and kingdom against kingdom'—a sign of the final days foretold by Christ, and a situation he seems to have seen in his own day as it led him to inform Gundobad that 'the end of the world is nearly upon us'.[64]

As we have already seen, Avitus is also our link with another Burgundian foundation of the 510s, St-Maurice, Agaune, and another type of material: liturgy. St-Maurice, with its *turmae* of monks engaged in endless recitation of the psalms, would have meant the daily reiteration of the peace and abundance of Jerusalem celebrated on Gundobad's coinage. The monks prayed for the world from which they had fled. They kept vigil over the realm. Agaune, it now seems clear, had a long tradition of devotion to warrior-saints. Prior to 515 it had been the centre for devotion to St Ferreolus and there is evidence that similar devotion was focused upon the saints of the Theban Legion at Agaune even before the 515 refoundation.[65] In terminology—the notion of *turma*, a term with a primarily military meaning—and in the treatment of the institution in Avitus' homily in which the *exercitus felix* of the martyred legion elided with the community of St-Maurice, the overall impression of Agaune is, to quote Barbara Rosenwein, one of 'inverted militarism'.[66] It is tempting to see this sublimation of the martial in the pious as a further aspect of the emphasis upon peace present elsewhere in Gibichung Burgundy, a kingdom that looked to its

---

[63] *Ep.* 22, p. 54: 'quorum cum maiori numero desit ac defuerit ferri usus'.
[64] *Ep.* 22, p. 55: '. . . et ex ipsis malorum indiciis imminere iam paene mundi terminum colligamus'.
[65] Rosenwein, 'Perpetual', 46–53.
[66] Rosenwein, 'Perpetual', 53–4.

saints as its gatekeepers and its monks, not its *milites*, as the guardians of its security and stability.

A final piece of evidence of prayer in the service of power remains to be considered. Ian Wood has suggested that the *Missa pro principe* found in the Bobbio Missal might plausibly be seen as a product of St-Maurice, Agaune.[67] The Mass placed considerable emphasis upon peace, and the relationship between it and kingship, as the opening lines of the *Collectio* make clear:

God, Omnipotent Lord, who through incalculable wisdom so disposed the world that without kings and rulers no epochs of the world should exist in peace, so that with the justice of good men flourishing, all things subjected to the evil of wicked men should wither away . . .

The prayer goes on to ask for divine support for the king and his army against his enemies, as was once given to Moses. The *post nomina* prayer asked for peace for the dead alongside salvation for the living, before invoking Joshua in a reiterated request for his support of the king against his foes. It is in the *ad pacem*, however, that the theme receives its most extensive treatment:

Mediator of Heaven and earth, Omnipotent God, Jesus Christ who loves the pacified and peaceful hearts of men, as suppliants we beseech you that peace [which] must be maintained which you left to your apostles, enduring ceaselessly may it flourish in our hearts and just as the strong hand of David once, with Goliath smitten, made peace for the people of Saul, so may our ruler, with you helping, with nations on all sides conquered, shine peacefully in his rule, prosperously for countless years.[68]

Ian Wood has suggested that a similar Burgundian origin, and a common concern for peaceful rule, is evident in the interest shown by the compiler of the Missal.[69] 'Peace', he concluded, 'was something that the Burgundians made much of, on occasion, and the emphasis to be found on *pax* in the Bobbio Missal may perhaps reflect a particular concern of the Burgundian royal house—a piece of political ideology which then crept into the liturgy of the Rhône valley'.[70] Allusions to peace on the coinage, a dedication homily in which peace and *virtus* were given prominence in the thematic treatment of the glories of the Gibichung house, and a letter seemingly from Gundobad's own hand expressing direct concern over the deeper meaning of a scriptural passage foretold by Micah: all attest to precisely such an interest at the Gibichung court. Whether Gundobad was a ruler whose interest in peace stretched beyond words to actions is a moot

[67] I. Wood, 'Liturgy', in *Bobbio Missal*, 206–18. For commentary and translation (cited here) see '*Missa*', in Garrison, *Bobbio Missal*, 187–205. The original text in E. A. Lowe (ed.), *The Bobbio Missal: A Gallican Mass-Book*, HBS 58 (London, 1920), 151–3.

[68] Garrison, '*Missa*', in *Bobbio Missal*, 202–3, 209.

[69] Wood, 'Liturgy', in *Bobbio Missal*, 209.

[70] Wood, 'Liturgy', in *Bobbio Missal*, 213.

point. In Ennodius' near contemporary life of Epiphanius, diplomat-bishop of Pavia, the image of Gundobad lecturing the saint on the nature of life in war and peace, and consenting to a peace agreement with the Goths, suggests that it did.[71] Others, however, offered a different image. Gregory of Tours was far from complimentary, whilst Marius of Avenches' account of the many exquisite tortures by which he exterminated his brother's supporters in 500 casts a rather darker light.[72] Nevertheless the association of peace and the Gibichungs endured past the end of their kingdom. Shortly after his death in 523 Sigismund, founder of St-Maurice, Agaune, would become the focus for a cult that emphasized his qualities as both a man of peace and a healer, bringing health and relief to the fevered.[73]

How, ultimately, can we account for the stress placed upon peace in Burgundian political culture? Needless to say there is no reason to see this emphasis upon peace as anything innately 'Burgundian'. Curiously, however, it was a characteristic that some observers associated particularly with Burgundian kingship. For Ammianus Marcellinus in the later fourth century, the benefits of peace and abundance were key to the success of a Burgundian king's rule. In a brief excursus on fourth-century Burgundian society, he noted the limits that 'ancient custom' placed upon the *hendinos*, one of the tribe's two rulers. If wars were lost or crops failed, the king would either surrender his power or be deposed. Ammianus, professional soldier and camp-stool ethnographer, saw parallels between the Burgundians and the Egyptians.[74] Ammianus' account cannot be taken at face value. Nor, as Ian Wood has noted, can corroborating evidence be found to give support to his image of bipartite Burgundian sacral kingship nor, indeed, to the conditional character of the *hendinos*' authority. That said, it remains a curious coincidence that Gundobad's coins proclaimed precisely the qualities that Ammianus' kings needed to provide their subjects. Several decades later, and writing from a radically different perspective, Orosius, as part of his attempt to show the mollifying effects of Christianity, made considerable play of the fact that, once converted, the Burgundians lived 'peacefully, mildly and innocently'.[75] The image can be more assuredly assigned to the category of accounts of

---

[71] *Vit. Ep.* cc. 154–70, with Gundobad's approval and wish for divine assent at 166–7.

[72] *DLH* II.28; Marius of Avenches, *Chronicon imperiale*, ed. T. Mommsen, *MGH AA* 11 (Berlin, 1894), p. 234.

[73] *DLH* III.4. On Sigismund's cult see F. S. Paxton, 'Liturgy and Healing in an Early Medieval Saint's Cult: The Mass *In honore sancti Sigismundi* for the Cure of Fevers', *Traditio* 49 (1994), 23–43, esp. 28–9; *idem*, 'Power and the Power to Heal. The Cult of St Sigismund of Burgundy', *EME* 2.2 (1993), 95–110; R. Folz, *Les saints rois du Moyen Âge en Occident (VIᵉ-XIIIᵉ siècles)* (Brussels, 1984), 23–5. For Sigismund's pacific qualities in the *Massa Sancti Sigismundi* see Wood, 'Liturgy', in *Bobbio Missal*, 206–18.

[74] Ammianus Marcellinus, *Res Gestae*, XXVIII.5.14, ed. J. C. Rolfe (Cambridge, MA, 1935–9), 169. On the historical value of this passage see Wood, '*Gentes*', 243–4; Wiedemann, 'Men and Beasts', 189–201.

[75] Orosius, *Hist.* I.7.32.

Christianity's benefits than to any firmly grounded early history of Burgundian belief, although Orosius' account of the Burgundian conversion to Catholic orthodoxy has recently received serious reconsideration.[76] Nearly a century later Ennodius, in keeping with panegyric convention, addressed the subject peoples of Theoderic, praising the Burgundians for their *constantia* in holding to their peace with the Ostrogoths.[77] Such views were not universal. Looking back from later sixth-century Byzantium Agathias singled the Burgundians out as an exceptionally bellicose people, recounting the crushing impact the display of King Chlodomer's severed head had upon Frankish morale before battle in 524.[78]

Part of the answer to the emphasis on peace at Gundobad's court lies in the key fact that Burgundian kings ruled over a mixed population with a sizeable Roman element whose interests and expectations had to be addressed and anxieties allayed about new forms of rule, and new types of ruler. Matthew Innes was undoubtedly right when he noted that '[t]o be seen as legitimate by the provincial populace, authority had to be articulated and exercised in the appropriate terms ... they were useful precisely as they helped cope with substantial change'.[79] External pressures, however, may have been no less paramount. Burgundy's history across the turn of the sixth century is marked by intermittent periods of war. Clovis invaded in 500, allied with Gundobad's brother, Godegisel, capitalizing upon civil war within the Gibichung house. Godegisel would ultimately be defeated at Vienne.[80] Theoderic, in his turn, would invade in 508 during a period of continuing internal tensions.[81] The Gibichung emphasis upon peace emerged in a kingdom subject to repeated pressure and outright attack from larger, predatory neighbours, attacks that would ultimately remove the beleaguered kingdom from the political map. Squeezed between the Franks and Theoderic's Italy, wary of both, this might be termed the Swiss paradigm of Burgundian ideology. Faced with larger neighbours whose size, strength, and own predatory ambitions made pre-emptive aggression unwise—although campaigns such as Sigismund's against the Franks in 518 were occasionally mounted—we may well see in the Burgundian theme of peace an attempt to polish up a virtue from a political necessity.

[76] M. Handley, 'Inscribing Time and Identity in the Kingdom of Burgundy', in S. Mitchell and G. Greatrex (eds), *Ethnicity and Culture in Late Antiquity* (London, 2000), 83–102, at 83, citing *IL CV* no. 44.

[77] Ennodius, *Panegyric*, ed. C. Rohr, *Der Theodericus-Panegyricus des Ennodius*, MGH SuT 15 (Hanover, 1995), c. 54, p. 234. On which see Shanzer, 'Two Clocks', 232.

[78] Agathias, *The Histories*, tr. J. Frendo (Berlin, 1975), I. 5, pp. 11–12.

[79] Innes, 'Freedom', 63.

[80] *DLH* II.33.

[81] *DLH* II.32–3. Shanzer and Wood, *Avitus*, 15–17.

'BRAVE MEN ARE ALWAYS MODEST IN PEACE . . .': [82]
OSTROGOTHIC ITALY

'The holy laws of kinship have purposed to take root among monarchs for this reason: that their tranquil spirit may bring the peace which people long for.' The words are Cassiodorus', from a letter written on Theoderic's behalf to Clovis around 507 when mounting tensions between the dominant rulers of the former western provinces made peace a pressing concern for rulers and ruled alike.[83] And if kinship failed to maintain peaceful relations between kingdoms, continued Cassiodorus, what chance had the lesser bonds created by hostage exchange?

In the opening decade of the sixth century kin ties did indeed bind the Ostrogothic and Frankish courts. Theoderic was married to Audefleda, Clovis' sister. Theoderic's daughter Amalasuintha, married Eutharic, while another, Theodegotha, was the wife of the Visigothic King Alaric II: it was he who was the target of Clovis' threatened aggression in 506–7.[84] A fragile peace had held between Visigoth and Frank since summer 502, when the two had met on an island at Amboise on the Loire, continuing a tradition of midstream summits initiated by several late fourth-century emperors in their dealings with barbarian leaders.[85] At Amboise Alaric II and Clovis sought to settle their differences, and subsequently celebrated their amity.[86] Yet for all Theoderic's apparent nurturing, the ties of kin failed to hold early sixth-century Western Europe in a state of *quies*. By spring 507 the escalating tension between Frank and Visigoth would culminate in the battle of Vouillé.[87]

Theoderic's letter to Clovis, famously, is found in the *Variae*, the twelve-book collections of official correspondence and chancery paperwork drafted by Cassiodorus on behalf of several Ostrogothic kings and assembled around 538

---

[82] *Var.* XII.3.3 ('*viri fortes semper in pace modesti sunt*'). In the discussions that follow I have drawn from the partial translations of S. J. Barnish, *Cassiodorus, Variae,* TTH 12 (Liverpool, 1992), and T. Hodgkin, *The Letters of Cassiodorus* (London, 1886).

[83] *Var.* III.4.1. Translation from Barnish, *Variae,* 48. On Cassiodorus' involvement in Ostrogothic diplomacy see Gillett, *Envoys,* 174–219. The *Variae*'s form and function is discussed in *idem,* 'The Purposes of Cassiodorus' *Variae*', in A. C. Murray (ed.), *After Rome's Fall. Narrators and Sources of Early Medieval History: Essays Presented to Walter Goffart* (Toronto, 1998), 37–50; J.-L. Jouanaud, 'Pour qui a-t-il publié les *Variae*?', *Teoderico il Grande,* II, pp. 721–41. A. J. Fridh, *Terminologie et formules dans les Variae de Cassiodore: études sur le développement du style administratif aux derniers siècles d'l'antiquité,* Studia graeca et latina Gothoburgensia 2 (Stockholm, 1956). For sixth-century diplomacy see also Shanzer, 'Two Clocks', 225–58.

[84] Gillett, *Envoys,* 208–12.

[85] For Valentinian I's meeting mid-Danube with the Alaman leader Macrianus see Ammianus Marcellinus *Res Gestae,* XXX.3; for Valens' similar conference with Athanaric of the Tervingi in 369 see *Res Gestae,* XXVII.5.

[86] *DLH* II.35.

[87] I. N. Wood, *The Merovingian Kingdoms, 450–751* (London, 1994), 46.

during the beginning of Belisarius' campaigns in Italy.[88] Cassiodorus clearly reworked and excerpted the collection, though the extent of this process is impossible to gauge without the control of his originals. Cassiodorus' letters undoubtedly offered a consciously constructed image of rulership, more formal portrait than informal snapshot.[89] The final face of Ostrogothic kingship that emerges from the *Variae*, and specifically Theoderic's, is patriarchal, dispensing wisdom, ever respectful of Roman tradition and order, counselling self-restraint and nurturing peace. In many ways it was an imperial ideal in action, as Procopius acknowledged.[90] Recently, Genevra Kornbluth has plausibly read the sapphire seal ring in the Kunsthistorisches Museum in Vienna bearing the legend ALARICVS REX GOTHORVUM and an image of a strikingly unarmed ruler as a diplomatic gift from Theoderic. If so, his peacemaking words of the early 500s may well have been complemented by gifts offering their own image of pacific rule.[91]

More generally, Cassiodorus'/Theoderic's letters stand in the vanguard of diplomatic overtures between the rulers of the successor states of the West. When we hear the earliest generation of post-Roman rulers speak to each other they often speak, as here, about peace.

Other letters drafted by Cassiodorus contain comparable portraits of Theoderic as a lover of peace and a king keen to avert conflict. As tensions mounted in the early 500s, Theoderic wrote to remind Alaric II that war was a terrible thing, and victory uncertain.[92] Similar letters were dispatched to Gundobad of Burgundy and to Clovis.[93] Theoderic's interest in securing peace across large expanses of the former western provinces may well have come from a genuine sense of responsibility, although such peacemaking—the carefully paternalistic choreography of good relations between Franks, Burgundians, Visigoths, and Vandals—carried with it an inescapable political charge, as an implicit assertion not only of Ostrogothic authority, but also of self-conscious superiority and the right to instil order. Theoderic's gifts to Gundobad of a sundial and *clepsydra* were objects heavily imbued with *romanitas*, intended to order and civilize, distant descendants of Augustus' horologium.[94] Other letters from the *Variae* cast further light on Theoderic's belief in a ruler's love of peace. 'Universal love for peace wins praise for the ruler', Theoderic wrote to the patricians Caelianus

[88] Gillett, 'Purpose', 48–9. Barnish, *Variae*, xiv–xvii.

[89] S. Bjornlie, 'What have Elephants to do with Sixth-Century Politics? A Reappraisal of the "Official" Governmental Dossier of Cassiodorus', *Journal of Late Antiquity* 2.1 (2009), 143–71.

[90] *Bell. Goth.* V.1.25–9. P. Heather, 'The Barbarian in Late Antiquity. Image, Reality, and Transformation', in R. Miles (ed.), *Constructing Identities in Late Antiquity* (London, 1999), 234–56, esp. 236–7, 249–50.

[91] G. Kornbluth, 'The Seal of Alaric, *rex Gothorum*', *EME* 16.3 (2008), 299–332, esp. 326–32.

[92] *Var.* III.1.2.

[93] *Var.* III.4.5.

[94] *Var.* I.46 makes the civilizing character of the gifts explicit. See Shanzer, 'Two Clocks', 241–5, with the date of the gifts discussed at 251–2.

and Agapitus around 510, and a peaceful and tranquil society was itself an adornment to royal authority.[95] More than this, its creation reflected glory upon anyone in a position of power. Writing to Agapitus, a city prefect struggling with rowdy circus factions, Theoderic spoke as one ruler of men to another: 'Your public praise', Agapitus learned, 'is a people at peace'.[96] Regardless of status, peace added lustre, and legitimacy, to all in authority. In Theoderic's eyes peacemaking and peacekeeping were vital components of power, at least as we see it represented in the official image of Cassiodorus' prose. 'It's your duty to repress all violence and injustice in the provinces over which you preside', the Rhaetian *dux* Servatus was told. In practical terms this duty meant dampening the martial vigour of the warlike tribe of the Breones, who were, the letter went on, 'continuing in peace the habits and maxims of war'.[97]

That the *Variae* were assembled during the opening stages of Justinian's war against the Ostrogoths gives these aspects of the collection additional resonance, not least the collection's famous opening letter from Theoderic to the Emperor Anastasius, written in 508 in the months following Vouillé, when a Byzantine alliance with the Franks reconfigured the political map and heightened tensions between Ravenna and Constantinople. Here, Theoderic voiced his belief that the quest for peace was a core element of a ruler's duty: 'It is proper for us, most clement emperor, to seek for peace, we who are known not to have reasons for anger'.[98] Tranquillity, he continued, was a state from which all nations profited:

Every kingdom ought to desire tranquillity, in which both peoples benefit and the interests of nations is protected. For tranquillity is the fair mother of the liberal arts, renewing the mortal race with multiple generations. Tranquillity encourages opportunity and develops character, and he is recognized as being ignorant of such great things who is perceived not to have sought it.[99]

Cassiodorus would voice similar sentiments for Theoderic's successors until the eventual outbreak of war with the Byzantines in 535. One of the earliest letters from Athalaric to the Emperor Justin in 526 was a similar request for peace which cast the overture as part of Athalaric's inheritance:

I would be justly blamed, most benevolent of princes, if I were to ask in a lukewarm way for your peace, which my forebears, as is known, demanded with so burning a desire. In what respect would I be a worthy heir, if I were found to be unequal to my predecessors in so glorious a concern?[100]

---

[95] *Var.* I.23.
[96] *Var.* I.32. See also *Var.* VI.24.
[97] *Var.* I.11.
[98] *Var.* I.1.1.
[99] *Var.* I.1.1. Heather, 'Barbarian', 253–4; for context J. Moorhead, *Theoderic in Italy* (Oxford, 1992), 142–4.
[100] *Var.* VIII.1.1. Translation: Barnish, *Variae*, 101.

Last in the sequence of peacemakers in the *Variae*'s pages we find Theodehad,
faced with an aggressive Byzantium (Sicily had just fallen to Belisarius) and
mounting unpopularity in Italy, who offered the plausible if scripturally un-
moored observation in a letter to Justinian of 534 that God 'always welcomes
tranquillity between kings'.[101] The theme is consistent, though less confidently
employed than in Theoderic's day. With good reason: war was imminent, and
for the next few decades he would have found little to welcome as the armies of
the Goths, 'Greeks', and Franks made a battlefield of Italy.

    The notion that war and peace placed different demands upon a people was at
the core of the way in which Ostrogothic rulers theorized about the society they
ruled—the much-discussed concept of *civilitas*: the regime of Gothic-Roman
coexistence in which each party adhered to its own laws, and were responsible for
distinct activities within a single society.[102] Thus, in the words of a letter written
by Cassiodorus in Athalaric's name, both nations might share jointly in the sweet
otium of tranquillity.[103] At the heart of *civilitas* lay implicit notions of
peace: between Goths and Romans, but, as importantly, within Roman civic
society itself. Regardless of how we view the actual ethnicity of the two named
groups (were some 'Goths' Romans? Some 'Romans' Goths?) on the notional
level, defence of the Ostrogothic kingdom fell to the Goths that the Romans
might live in peace. 'Whilst the army of the Goths wages war, the Romans are at
peace' (*Dum belligerat Gothorum exercitus, sit in pace Romanus*) as Cassiodorus
put it in a letter of around 535.[104] This ethnographically determined division of
responsibilities, with notions of Roman domestic peaceability and the surviving
association of the *pax Romana* alongside the Gothic elite's prevailing sense of
themselves as warriors, fused into a notion of a single society, seeking to satisfy
the self-image and allay the anxieties of both communities. This division of
responsibility was repeatedly voiced by Theoderic, adopted by his heirs and
imitators, and suggested to others.[105] Writing to the Pannonians on the occasion
of the appointment of Colossaeus as governor around 510, Theoderic advised
them to be like his Goths, waging war abroad but exercising self-discipline at
home.[106]

[101] *Var.* X.19.1.
[102] This regime, and its conceptual roots in late Roman ethnography, has been the subject of
much recent analysis, see P. J. Heather, 'Theoderic, King of the Goths', *EME* 4.2 (1995), 145–73;
Amory, *People and Identity*; McCormick, *Eternal Victory*, 266–84. This list makes no claims to be
comprehensive. On *civilitas* in particular see C. Schäfer, 'Probleme einer multikulturellen
Gesellschaft. Zur Integrationspolitik im Ostgotenreich', *Klio* 83 (2001), 182–97; M. Reydellet,
'Théoderic et la *civilitas*', in A. Carile (ed.), *Teoderico e i Goti tra Oriente e Occidente* (Ravenna,
1995), 285–96, also treated in his *Royauté*, 222–4.
[103] *Var.* VII.3.2.
[104] *Var.* XII.5.4, on which see Amory, *People and Identity*, 50–1.
[105] *Var.* I.24; *Var.* VIII.3.
[106] *Var.* III.24.4.

Cassiodorus' highly fragmentary *laudes* depicted Theoderic as a pacifier, his justice bringing tranquillity to his provinces even as his *imperium* reined in haughty foreigners.[107] Ennodius' prose panegyric, delivered to Theoderic at Ravenna in spring 507 does survive, however, and provides crucial further evidence of the vigorous projection of his quasi-imperial image through this most imperial medium as Ennodius twisted the conventions of the form into a resemblance of contemporary Ostrogothic *civilitas*.[108] Theoderic had restored true order and peace to Italy. The peace of his reign allowed scholars to study and their works would, in return, make him immortal.[109] Theoderic, for his part, recognized that his wisdom came not from himself but from God.[110] Working within the panegyrical form, Ennodius praised Theoderic's martial prowess. To number his wars was to count as many victories.[111] To see him in battle was to be overpowered; to see him in peacetime was to fear nothing. His reputation was defence enough.[112] It protected his people in peacetime, but, noted Ennodius, he built fortresses all the same.[113] The peace he preserved allowed the young Goths to practise war games and train for war.[114]

For numerous early and central medieval chroniclers as well as several recent ones, Theoderic's reign was seen as a time of peace and prosperity, benefits represented to later generations through his raising of new buildings and restoration of old ones.[115] This afterimage emerged early. The author known as the Anonymous Valesianus, writing in mid-sixth-century Ravenna, looked back with nostalgia to the early years of Theoderic's reign as a period of peace and stability.[116] The Anonymous wrote during the later years of the Gothic wars, a

---

[107] *Orationum reliquae*, ed. L. Traube, *MGH AA* 14 (Berlin, 1905), 466, lines 9–11.

[108] Amory, *People and Identity*, 113–14; S. G. MacCormack, *Art and Ceremony in Late Antiquity* (Berkeley, 1981), 230–4.

[109] Ennodius, *Panegyricum*, ed. C. Rohr, *Der Theoderich-Panegyricus des Ennodius, MGH SuT* 12 (Hanover, 1995), c. 2, p. 196.

[110] *Pan.* c. 3, p. 196.

[111] *Pan.* c. 5, p. 198.

[112] *Pan.* c. 2, p. 200.

[113] *Pan.* c. 59, p. 238. Compare with *Var.* I.28.

[114] *Pan.* c. 83, p. 256.

[115] C. La Rocca, 'Perceptions of an Early Medieval Urban Landscape', in Peter Linehan and J. L. Nelson (eds), *The Medieval World*, vol. 10 (London, 2001), 416–30, at 417–21. M. J. Johnson, 'Towards a History of Theoderic's Building Program', *DOP* 42 (1988), 73–96, esp. 89; B. Ward-Perkins, *From Classical Antiquity to the Middle Ages. Urban Public Building in Northern and Central Italy, AD 300–850* (Oxford, 1984), 28–32; Barnish, *Cassiodorus: Variae*, pp. xiii-iv; T. S. Brown, *Gentlemen and Officers. Imperial Administration and Aristocratic Power in Byzantine Italy A.D. 554–800* (Rome, 1984), 4–5.

[116] *Anonymi Valesiani pars posterior*, ed. T. Mommsen, *Chronica Minora* I, *MGH AA* 9 (Berlin, 1892), 306–28. Translation: *Anonymous Valesianus pars posterior*, ed. and trans., J. C. Rolfe in *Ammianus Marcellinus* III (Cambridge, MA, 1939), 530–69. For recent commentary see V. Neri, 'La legittimatà politica del regno teodericiano nell' *Anonymi Valesiani Pars Posterior*', in A. Carile (ed.) *Teoderico ei i Goti tra Oriente e Occidente* (Ravenna, 1995), 313–40; G. Zecchini, 'L'Anonimo Valesiano II: genere storiografico e contesto politico', *Settimane* 13 (1993), II, 809–18; S. J. Barnish, 'The *Anonymous Valesianus* as a Source for the Last Years of Theoderic', *Latomus* 42 (1983),

time when disorder and war weariness made the peace of previous decades already resemble a lost golden age, a comparison the contemporary images of Theoderic would have done much to foster.[117] The Anonymous' account of Theoderic has come in for some criticism. An initially positive attitude to Theoderic shifts in the work's later chapters, becoming deeply critical of a ruler whose actions against the Roman population and the Catholic Church revealed a man who had, its author maintained, fallen into the Devil's hands.[118] Our concerns, however, are less with its reliability as a source for the reconstruction of the events of Theoderic's reign and more with its author's construction of the Ostrogothic ruler himself:

Hence, Theoderic was a man of great distinction and of goodwill towards all men, and he ruled for thirty-three years. In his times Italy for thirty years enjoyed such good fortune that his successors also inherited peace.[119]

This equation is worthy of note: it was specifically Theoderic's goodwill (*bona voluntas*) that led to peace. For the Anonymous his reign amounted to a practical lesson in the sentiments of Luke II.14. Nearly three centuries later the same passage would rubricate the image of another ruler—Charlemagne—the admirer of Theoderic, on the walls of Leo III's *triclinium* at the Lateran.

As has long been recognized, the Anonymous' portrait of Theoderic carries a notably Solomonic resonance.[120] Although illiterate, Theoderic's innate wisdom was such that he coined a number of aphorisms that the Anonymous claimed were still circulating in the 540s.[121] Similarly, he was remembered as a capable judge, resolving a question of contested maternity in a fashion reminiscent of the Judgement of Solomon (III Kings III.16–18).[122] Through the marriages of his sisters Amalafrida and Amalbirga to the Vandal Trasimund and the Thuringian king Herminifrid, Theoderic made peace with the neighbouring peoples, behaving in such a way that other cities sought out treaties with him, as earlier kingdoms had sought out Solomon.[123] And it is in the Anonymous' appraisal of Theoderic's achievements that we find an early variant on a motif already met, peace and security on the roads. Gold and silver sent through the country were as

---

572–96; J. N. Adams, *The Text and Language of a Vulgar Latin Chronicle. (Anonymus Valesianus II)* (London, 1976).

[117] Barnish, '*Anonymous Valesianus*', 572–96.

[118] *Anon. Val.* 83.

[119] *Anon. Val.* 59: 'Ergo praeclarus et bonae voluntatis in omnibus, qui regnavit annos XXXIII. Cuius temporibus felicitas est secuta Italiam per annos triginta, ita ut etiam pax pergentibus esset.'

[120] N. Tammasia, 'Sulla seconda parte dell'Anonimo Valesiano', *Archivio storico italiano* 71.2 (1913), 3–22, esp. 8–9, 12. Whilst Tammasia's deductions on the identity of the work's author are refuted by Adams, *Text*, 5, the case for a Solomonic element to the portrait remains hard to dismiss.

[121] *Anon. Val.* 61. Moorhead, *Theoderic*, 103–5.

[122] *Anon. Val.* 62.

[123] *Anon. Val.* 68, 70, 72, 73.

safe as if they were within city walls.[124] The Anonymous' evocation of a Solomonic ideal in the middle years of the sixth century took place not only a time of conflict but also at a moment when the figure of Solomon enjoyed particular currency as an image of authority in contemporary Byzantium. At a Good Friday service sometime between 532 and the end of 537, Romanos the Melode delivered his fifty-fourth *kontakion*, a verse sermon, 'On Earthquakes and Fires', which identified Justinian as a new Solomon, praising him for the rebuilding of both Hagia Sophia and Hagia Eirene after the Nika riots against a backdrop of a sequence of military successes over the Goths, including the retaking of Rome.[125] Jerusalem's Temple was never rebuilt, Constantinople's was: proof of God's favour, despite natural disasters and difficulties. Three decades later the *kontakion* delivered at the rededication service in 562, following four years of rebuilding in wake of the dome's collapse, restated the Solomonic theme even more explicitly.[126] Later again, in 566 or early 567, Corippus' panegyric framed Justin II in similar terms.[127] If sixth-century Constantinople could claim its Solomons, why not Ravenna?

Ennodius also left us another work that casts light on the deep tensions of the years around the turn of the sixth century, and something of the broader anxiety over peace in the immediate post-Roman world. His *Vita* of St Epiphanius offers a rather different insight into the way in which the relationship between peace and royal power could be conceived. Written within a decade of its subject's death in 496, the *Vita* offers a portrait of the saint as peacemaking diplomat, employed on repeated diplomatic missions between the Burgundian, Ostrogothic, imperial and Visigothic courts.[128] Indeed, Epiphanius' first episcopal act was to command his flock to be peaceful and to preserve unity.[129] Ennodius' work

---

[124] *Anon. Val.* 72.

[125] *Bell.Goth.* VIII.33.15–38. R. J. Schork, *Sacred Song from the Byzantine Pulpit: Romanos the Melodist* (Gainesville, FL, 1995), 184–96, esp. 193–4. For context and discussion E. C. Topping, 'On earthquake and fires', *BZ* 71 (1978), 22–35. J. Moorhead, *Justinian* (London, 1994), 58–60. For Hagia Sophia's Solomonic associations see G. Scheja, 'Hagia Sophia und Templum Salomonis', *Istanbuler Mitteilungen* 12 (1962), 44–58. For these associations as the response to an earlier archaeological evocation of the Temple and its builder by Anicia Juliana in the construction of her church of St Polyeuktos in the mid 520s see R. M. Harrison, *A Temple for Byzantium. The Discovery and Excavation of Anicia Juliana's Palace Church in Istanbul* (London, 1989), esp. 33–40; idem, 'The Church of St Polyeuctos in Istanbul and the temple of Solomon', in C. Mango, O. Pritsak and U. M. Pasicznyk (eds), *Okeanos: Essays presented to Ihor Ševčenko on his Sixtieth Birthday by his Colleagues and Students*, Harvard Ukrainian Studies 7 (1984), 276–9. F. B. Flood, *The Great Mosque of Damascus: Studies on the Makings of an Umayyad Visual Culture* (Leiden, 2001), 75–88, 104–9, offers an overview of Solomonic architectural themes in Constantinople and sets them in their wider eastern Mediterranean context. For Justinian's (apocryphal?) statement. 'O Solomon, I have outdone you!' recorded in the eleventh (or twelfth?) century, *Narratio de Aedificatione Templi Sanctae Sophiae*, ed. T. Preget, *Scriptores Originum Constantinopolitanarum* (Leipzig, 1901), I, 105. For Justinian's 'Solomon complex' see I. Shahid, *Byzantium and the Arabs in the Sixth Century. II. 1* (Washington DC, 2002), 361.

[126] A. Palmer, with L. Rodley, 'The Inauguration Anthem of Hagia Sophia in Edessa: A New Edition and Translation with Historical and Architectural Notes and a Comparison with a Contemporary Constantinopolitan Kontakion', *BMGS* 12 (1988), 117–67.

[127] Corippus, *In Laudem*, IV.283.

[128] *Vita Beatissimi viri Epifani episcopi Ticinensis ecclesiae*, ed. F. Vogel, *MGH AA* 7 (Berlin, 1885), 84–109.

[129] *Vit. Ep.* 21–6, p. 87 (an early act of peacemaking with the violent Burco); *Vit. Ep.* 44, p. 89 (*estote pacifici estote unianimes*).

has been the subject of searching and sustained analysis by Andrew Gillett as one of a number of fifth- and sixth-century treatments of 'the saint as envoy'.[130] My interest here, however, is less with episcopal authors of concord such as Epiphanius and more with those with whom he conversed, the recipients of his embassies, and the figures that Ennodius portrayed in the court conversations his peacemaking engendered: the kings themselves.

Ennodius' *Vita* comprises a sequence of diplomatic episodes, from his first steps as a representative of the church of Pavia settling a land dispute with a violent and acquisitive neighbour through to his final embassy to Theoderic, undertaken on behalf of the people of Liguria. Persuasion and practical *pietas*, rather than miracle-working, lay at the core of Epiphanius' saintliness. Neither ascetic nor miracle worker Ennodius' Epiphanius is, as Reydellet observed, 'un homme de la parole'.[131] Ennodius' portrait is of a bishop and a *beatus pacificus*, an image of the diplomat-bishop that gained currency in tandem with the rising importance of episcopal authority in the post-Roman world, and one that we shall also meet at the sixth century's close in Gregory of Tours' portrait of his own diplomatic activities in his *Ten Books*.

At the *Vita*'s core lies a sequence of first-person exchanges between Epiphanius and various rulers: the Emperor Anthemius, Gundobad, and Theoderic. His capacity initially is as a representative of the citizens of Liguria (who, like the people of Theoderic's letter to Clovis, want peace) or, later, on behalf of rulers, including Theoderic himself. In an early section of the Life Ennodius recounted an episode in which Epiphanius undertook an embassy between the general Ricimer and the western Roman emperor Anthemius. Received by the emperor, whose purple robes and riches, symbols of fleeting power (*insignia potestatis fugitivae*) Ennodius sketched in sharp contrast to Epiphanius' own immutable *virtus*, the encounter offered Ennodius the opportunity to offer a brief sermon on a ruler's obligations to God, to peace, and to his subjects. Anthemius had been entrusted with responsibility of so great a state by God, who through the teachings of the Catholic Church Anthemius recognized as the originator and lover of devotion 'through whom the weapons of peace break the madness of war'. Concord, 'Epiphanius' continued, trampling on pride's neck, overcomes when bravery could not prevail. Mercy, not vengefulness, made David praiseworthy. To be merciful to suppliants was to share something of the face of heavenly rule, as prefects, kings, and secular lords had learned.[132] The peace that Epiphanius asked from Anthemius was not simply a benefit to Ricimer, but also a gift to God. 'To have conquered without

---

[130] Gillett, *Envoys*, 148–71.

[131] Reydellet, *Royauté*, 149.

[132] *Vit. Ep.* 63, p. 92: 'Summa coelestis Domini, venerande princeps, est ordinatione dispositum, ut cui tantae reipublicae cura mandabatur, per catholicae fidei dogma Deum et auctorem et amatorem pietatis agnosceret; per quem bellorum furorem pacis arma confringunt, et calcans colla superbiae concordia superat, quod fortitudo non praevalet. Sic namque David praedicabilem parcendi magis inimico animus reddidit, quam intentio vindicandi. Sic perfecti

bloodshed', Epiphanius added, 'will be a triumph which will bring special glory to the annals of your reign', and a triumph made particularly sweet by the fact that it was a victory of kindness over the fierce and warlike Goths.[133]

As victory for Anthemius was a certainty, to go to war would risk not only his own troops, but also Ricimer's, and they, shortly, would be Anthemius', too. Why risk double losses? asks Epiphanius. Finally, he reminded Anthemius, 'he who first offers peace furthers his own best interests'.[134] In reply Anthemius argued that, in fact, *he* was a peace-seeking ruler. Who, after all, amongst his predecessors had been willing to marry their daughter to a mere barbarian, 'a pelt-clad Goth' (*pellito Getae*)? It was Ricimer, he countered, talking peace but preparing for war, who was the real aggressor. Epiphanius' piety and persuasive speech won the reluctant emperor over: 'I dare not refuse the peace for which you ask'. Epiphanius was pleased by the result, offering thanks to God who had given His peace to the emperor's heart.[135]

The pattern established by this initial encounter repeats in later chapters of the *life*. Tensions between Nepos and Euric, for example, elicit a further Epiphanian embassy, and an encounter between bishop and bellicose Visigothic king elicits from Epiphanius a further articulation of the close relationship of earthly and heavenly authority. Condemning Euric's reputation for violence, Epiphanius noted that such acts of violence neither engendered God's blessings nor offered security from divine wrath. Euric, Epiphanius observed, is a subject of the heavenly sovereign, who, when he was about to ascend to heaven, left peace to his disciples (John II.14). 'We must be guardians of his precepts', Epiphanius continued, 'especially when we know that no man can be called strong who has been overcome by anger.'[136] Epiphanius taught that kings were themselves subjects of the Almighty. They ought to follow his teachings, defend and protect peace, and nurture it within themselves. The schematic relationship of the kingdom's welfare and the ruler's inner life, as well as the tangible state of peace in which both could exist that will characterize much early medieval political thought is becoming apparent for the first time in these interchanges.

Others also fell under the spell of Epiphanius' counsels of peace. According to Ennodius, Epiphanius' diplomatic skills caught the attention of Theoderic himself, from whom the bishop accepted a commission to undertake a diplomatic mission to the court of the Burgundian king Gundobad to secure peace and recover captives. The commission elicited praise from Epiphanius: 'Shall I recall first that you have surpassed all previous emperors in justice or in the

---

saeculorum reges et domini, supplicantibus indulgere coelesti arte didicerunt. Supernae namque dominationis instar possidet, qui imperium suum pietate sublimat.'

[133] *Vit. Ep.* 64, p. 92.
[134] *Vit. Ep.* 65, p. 92.
[135] *Vit. Ep.* 70–71, p. 93.
[136] *Vit. Ep.* 87, p. 95.

pursuance of war or in devotion?'[137] Theoderic's willingness to seek peace with the Burgundians Epiphanius compared favourably to David's treatment of Saul (I Kings XXIV.4–13).

In Ennodius' figure of Gundobad, though, Epiphanius' pleas for peace found their counterblast. However much the Burgundian king might have projected an image of peacebility for Ennodius the Gallo-Roman Bishop of Pavia King Gundoba was a proponent of war, aware of the demands it placed upon a ruler:

> You are an advocate of peace, and are ignorant of the laws of war, and in bringing about concord you eviscerate terms decided by the sword. What you consider wrong is law for those at war. O bright star of Christianity, enmities know not the restraint that you advocate. Nobody in battle employs the moderation that you, O excellent mediator, extol with the polish of your mouth. The law of those at war permits everything that at other times would be illegal. In times of peace, one might perhaps adopt measures such as those you have suggested, but in war he who does not injure an enemy aids him.[138]

Much like Cassiodorus' Theoderic, Ennodius' Gundobad was a king fully aware of the conflicting demands of life in the times of war and peace. For all his point-for-point rejection of Epiphanius' arguments and justification of his own aggression ('I have done nothing more than take the precaution of recognizing open enemies'), Gundobad—like all the recipients of Epiphanius' embassies—eventually conceded to his arguments for peace, ordering the release of a throng of captive Italians. Epiphanius, a conqueror whose weapon was persuasion, returned to Italy with even more captives than ever followed Alexander, 'whom empty praise called "the pacifier of the world", and who led a swarm of nations'. Empty praise indeed: Epiphanius was the true pacifier of his world.[139]

As the *Variae* reveal, Ostrogothic kings sought to nurture peace with other post-Roman rulers, with Constantinople, at least until the advent of war, and within the mixed society over which they reigned. Simultaneously, Ostrogothic Italy was a place in which traditional notions of the *pax Romana* were seized upon by both Gothic rulers and their spokesmen, who were seeking to annex established ideology and present political and social models that secured their legitimacy, as well as by loyal Romans with a vivid sense of civic continuity. Whilst Wittigis peddled notions of *civilitas* and the Gothic protection of Roman peace in besieged Rome, as we have seen, loyalists to the emperor attempted to open the doors of Janus, evoking the same traditions of imperial war and peace that the

---

[137] *Vit. Ep.* 143, p. 102.
[138] *Vit. Ep.* 165–7, p. 105: 'Belli iura pacis suasor ignoras, et condiciones gladio decisas concordiae auctor evisceras. Lex est certantium quem putas errorem. Frenum nesciunt inimicitiae, quem tu, Christianae lucis iubar, ostendis. Proeliis temperantiam nullus adnectit, quae oris tui nitore, egregie moderator, adtollitur. Statuta sunt dimicantium, quicquid non licet tunc licere. Ista sibi forte quies vindicet, quae narrasti: hostem suum qui non laesit, adiuvit.' This translation draws heavily from *Vita Epiphanii*: G. M. Cook, *The Life of St Epiphanius by Ennodius* (Washington DC, 1942), 99.
[139] *Vit. Ep.* 176, p. 106.

Amal elite invoked. Peace became the subject of immediate ideological value, but also of nostalgic remembrance; a prize of such value that its establishment and maintenance became the province of saints such as Epiphanius and the possession of the kings with whom they spoke.

'DISPOSE OUR DAYS IN YOUR PEACE':
GREGORY THE GREAT

Overseer of Rome and its wider territories, pastor of a flock often beset by material hardship and the threat of attack by Lombards, with whose leaders he found himself in frequent and often vain negotiations, Gregory the Great had more reasons than most to reflect upon the manifold meanings of peace.[140] His duties also included the maintenance of the peace and order of the Church in the widest sense, a task that demanded his involvement in matters ranging from local disputes to complex dealings with the clergy of Ravenna and Constantinople.[141] Emblematic of Gregory's concerns for earthly peace, and hopes for the eventual attainment of the peace of the Heavenly Jerusalem, are the words of the three petitions that tradition remembered him adding to the Canon of the Roman Mass: 'And dispose our days in Your peace, and may You order us to be snatched from eternal damnation and be numbered in the flock of Your Elect'.[142] Gregory's writings show him exploring how the gift of the first petition might lead, ultimately, to the last.

For all the clarity of these requests, Gregory has left us no systemic treatment of peace. His thought has to be recovered from several of his works: the sprawling *Moralia*, his *Homilies* on the Gospels and Ezekiel, the *Pastoral Care*, the sketchy commentary on the Song of Songs, and the *Register*.[143] To explore Gregory's treatment of the notions of peace across this corpus is to move from pragmatism

---

[140] For 'the swords of the Lombards' see *Ep.* I.3, p. 34, I.30, p. 37, VI. 61, pp. 434–4, XIII.39, pp. 1042–3.

[141] See, for example, *Ep.* VII.29, pp. 487–9 (dispute between monastery of Neas and the Archbishop of Jerusalem); VIII.12, pp. 530–1 (wrangle between Candidus, abbot of Gregory's own monastery of St Andrew and Maurentius over a will); IX.54, pp. 612–3 (Gregory as an advocate for peace in a domestic dispute). Letters explicitly addressing peace include V.41, pp. 320–5 (with a particularly detailed discussion of peace supported by a catena of scriptural passages); V.42, pp. 325–7, V.44, pp. 329–57, VII.28, pp. 486–7 (with citations), IX.197, pp. 752–4 (with extensive citations), and the discussions of Markus, *Gregory*, 91–6; *idem*, 'Gregory the Great's Europe', *TRHS* 5th series, 31 (1981), 21–36; *idem*, 'Papal Primacy: Light from the Early Middle Ages', *The Month* 229 (1970), 352–61.

[142] *LP* I, p. 66 *HE* II.1.

[143] Mindful of the serious doubts raised over the authenticity of the commentary on I Kings attributed to Gregory, I omit it here. See F. Clark, 'R. A. Markus, Gregory the Great and *In I Regum*', *The Heythrop Journal* 40.2 (1999), 207–11; *idem*, 'The Authorship of the Commentary in I Regum: Implications of Adalbert de Vogüé's Discovery', *RB* 108 (1998), 61–79; A. de Vogüé, 'L'Auteur du Commentaire des Rois attribué à saint Grégoire: un moine de Cava', *RB* 106 (1996), 319–31.

to abstraction within a single body of thought. Occasionally the two came together. In one of his initial homilies on the Gospels delivered in the very early 590s, for example, and which introduced the recently elevated pope to the congregations of Rome's martyrial churches, Gregory quoted Luke XIV.31–2 with the observation that a king outnumbered by his enemies on the eve of battle was wise to sue for peace. The passage, Gregory explained, was an allegory of mankind's relationship with Christ: Christian practice was a form of spiritual diplomacy; tears of contrition for sin and acts of mercy were embassies sent heavenward.[144] Alms-giving and participation in the Eucharist amounted to peacemaking actions by the individual Christian, establishing positive relations with the Heavenly King, drawing him closer. Diplomacy with a very different kind of king, the Lombard Agilulf, also occupied Gregory at just this time, with a far less positive outcome. Writing to a correspondent in Constantinople in early 591, Gregory commented that peacemaking with the Lombards was an exercise in futility. Their 'treaties' (*sinthiciae*) were swords (*spatae*), he wrote. Their gratitude? Revenge.[145]

As these two instances suggest, Gregory distinguished categorically between earthly and heavenly peace. The former, he observed whilst glossing John XIV.27 ('my peace do I leave to you, my peace I give to you'), was the peace Christ left to the members of the Church on earth. The latter, the true peace (*pax vera*) of the Heavenly Kingdom, was a community defined by endless happiness and total love.[146] Earthly peace was unstable, and rich with danger and opportunity; danger, in that it could foster false Christians and allow heresies to flourish. Further, the potential pleasures of peacetime could distract from the serious business of reflection upon personal sin, the contemplation of God, and the individual Christian's preparation for judgement.[147] Such pleasures threatened to blind Christians, and, thus blinded, they would rush into hellfire.[148] For this very reason, Gregory observed, the truly holy were warier of times of prosperity than of trouble. And opportunity? Inasmuch as it afforded a chance for those sins to be overcome, self-correction to take place, and the individual Christian to foster the inner peace that led, ultimately, to membership of the heavenly community.[149] In such endeavours the good preacher was a vital guide, directing and fortifying the individual Christian's mind, telling of the peace of the

[144] *Hom. Ev.* XXXVII.6–7, pp. 352–4.
[145] *Ep.* I.30, p. 37. For commentary see W. Pohl, 'The Empire and the Lombards: Treaties and Negotiations in the Sixth Century', in *idem* (ed.), *Kingdoms of the Empire: The Integration of Barbarians in Late Antiquity*, TRW I (Leiden, 1997), 75–134, at 75.
[146] *Hom. Ev.* XXX.10, p. 268.
[147] P. Catry, 'Amour du monde et amour de Dieu chez Saint Grégoire le Grand', *Studia Monastica* 15 (1973), 253–75.
[148] *Hom. Ev.* XXXIX.7, pp. 386–7.
[149] *Mor.* III.9.15, pp. 123–4. See also *Hom. Ez.* I.10.43–4, pp. 165–7, in which Gregory presents a chain of actions from the recognition of sin by conscience through self-accusation, penitence, inner conflict, and finally peace with God. See also *Mor.* VI.33.51, pp. 320–1.

Heavenly Jerusalem, and revealing its joys.[150] More specifically, as Gregory explained in his homily on Ezekiel XL.1–4 the preacher offered his listeners a comprehensible image of the celestial peace, the *pax superna*, of the Heavenly Jerusalem on which they could focus their thoughts and direct their efforts. This 'vision of peace' (*visio pacis*) was a schematic of the path to salvation, Gregory explained, like a diagram scratched onto a tile.[151] Ideally, the inner vision of peace (*visio intimae pacis*) would orient the observant and reflective Christian to higher heavenly peace.[152] But even in this process of reflection danger lurked. The Christian ought not to confuse map with territory, earthly traces for heavenly reality. Earthly peace, he pointed out, was but a *vestigia*, a footprint of eternal peace. Who would be mad enough to love footprints, rather than He whose feet made them?[153]

For Gregory the contemplative life of the monastery was the ideal environment for the cultivation of inner peace, for it removed the demands and the temptations of the active life: wealth caused dissent, idle gossip extinguished inner peace.[154] This monastic peace lay close to the heart of Gregory's own sense of self. Shortly after his papal elevation, in October 590, Gregory wrote to Theoctista, sister of Emperor Maurice, lamenting his forced return to the world. He had lost the peace and quiet of monastic withdrawal that had brought him joy and once again found himself in the tumult of the world. Externally he had risen but, he added, inside he had experienced a fall. Like Adam he had been expelled from Paradise; driven from the face of the Lord.[155]

For those like Gregory himself, holding positions of power in the world and unable to retreat to a life of contemplation, he offered counsel. The *Pastoral Care* contains a sequence of specific injunctions by which a ruler could ensure peace. Indeed, the *Pastoral Care* can be seen as a work intended to offer insights into the means by which the able *rector* could sustain a peaceable and ordered Christian community, maintaining Christian unity in a world of diversity and flux, and might be considered a guide to peaceful rulership *in toto*. (Alfred the Great and his circle of helpers seem to have read it this way.) Many of Gregory's injunctions, on how to admonish, correct and teach various types of character, for example, sought to stabilize Christian community. 'Have salt in you, and have peace among you', taught Christ, Gregory noted, 'but by salt the wisdom of speech is meant'. A ruler's words should be wise and well chosen, lest his intentions are misunderstood.[156] And, Gregory added, returning to the theme later in the work, he must also choose

---

[150] *Hom. Ez.* I. XII.23, pp. 196–7.
[151] Ibid. For the nature of the *visio internae pacis* see *Hom. Ez.* II.1.5, pp. 210–12.
[152] *Hom. Ez.* II.5.2, pp. 275–7, II.8.20, pp. 351–2.
[153] *Reg. past.* III.22., I, pp. 408.
[154] On the disruptive influence of wealth see *Mor.* I.7.9. p. 29.
[155] *Ep.* I.5, pp. 5–6. Markus, *Gregory*, 17–23.
[156] *Reg. past.* II.4, pp. 186–94, esp. at 192.

wisely the moment to speak.[157] Misspoken or mistimed words, as well as too many words chosen unwisely, threatened to extinguish the peace of the heart. Behind such sentiments lurked a monastic distrust of unmonitored speech. Within his social taxonomy Gregory found a place for both the inherently 'pacified' (*pacati*) and those who were actively peacemakers (*pacifici*), opposing the former with the quarrelsome (*discordes*) and the latter with the equally active sowers of discord.[158] Peacemakers and sowers of discord possessed distinct genealogies. The former, of course, were *filii Dei*. The latter, Satan's children. Gregory cautioned the *pacifici*, as we have seen he cautioned the peaceful, against making peace with or between the wicked. When united evildoers are more powerful they form a greater threat against the good.[159] Gregory also offered some concrete advice for the peacemakers: they should seek to instil a love of inner peace (*pax interior*) in the minds of the wicked, so that in time they will realize the benefits of external peace (*pax exterior*). The wicked, in their turn, should be allowed to come to appreciate this inner peace. Pushing them too sharply towards external peace ran the risk of propelling them into wickedness.

Having established external, earthly peace (*pax terrena*), rulers ought to be careful not to endanger their hopes of heavenly peace (*pax superna*) through the pitfalls and moral dangers such a state created, dangers we have already glimpsed. But, conceded Gregory, pragmatically, it is better to establish some kind of earthly peace amongst the perverse even before they have reached the point where they might begin to understand the notion of heavenly peace. By so doing they might begin to behave in a more loving way towards their neighbours, in the process becoming better people, and so moving nearer to that which is still a long way from them: the peace of the Creator.[160] Even so, he cautioned against over-attachment to peace in the present, not least because it hampered contemplation of the eternal. 'Peace, therefore, as we now have it, is to be treated as something to be both loved and condemned'.[161] Over-affection for peace and quiet could lead to a general reluctance to identify, confront and to reprove the sinful when needed.[162] Alternatively, those who sought short-term peace at any price ran the risk of causing long-term harm. To maintain peace with the wicked was itself sinful, as those who entered into peace with evil men shared in their guilt. (It is a moot point whether, later in his pontificate, Gregory's words would come back to him as he made pacts with Rome's Lombard attackers.) Love for peace could lead to hell, not heaven, if earthly peace rested not on righteousness but on sin. After all, poor circumstances could produce good order, observed Gregory,

---

[157] *Reg. past.* III.14, pp. 340–8.
[158] *Reg. past.* III.22, pp. 402–12.
[159] *Reg. past.* III.23, pp. 412–19.
[160] *Reg. past.* III.23, p. 419.
[161] *Reg. past.* III.22, p. 408.
[162] Ibid.

quoting Jeremiah XLVIII.11: 'He hath rested upon his lees, because he lay untroubled in his sins'.[163]

It was one thing to theorize about rulers, another to deal with specific individuals. What image of peaceful rulership do we see in Gregory's letters to contemporary kings and emperors? Writing to Maurice in June 595, Gregory flatteringly observed that Maurice understood the pre-eminent importance of the Church, noting that Maurice rightly grasped that 'nobody can rule earthly things righteously unless he learns how to handle things divine'. A polity's health was gauged by the welfare of the Church: the peace of the *res publica* was judged by the peace of the universal Church.[164] Gregory recognized that it fell to the emperor to protect the Church, and conceded that it fell to himself to foster peace within the body of the Church, although in the application of this right, as for example, when Maurice counselled Gregory to make peace with the patriarch of Constantinople, he could chafe under the injunction.[165] Nevertheless, it was in the execution of that responsibility that Maurice fulfilled his duty to God, thereby receiving in return God's gift of peace, as Gregory wrote at the close of a letter of September 595:

May Almighty God, who sees your clemency loving and defending the integrity of Catholic righteousness which is pleasing to Him, allow you to rule here over a pacified state, with its enemies defeated, and to reign with His saints in eternal life.[166]

This was a notion of Christian emperorship that looked back to the fourth century, and to a model that Gregory had held up to Maurice elsewhere when addressing the case of the ecumenical patriarch, Constantine.[167] It placed the emperor in a hierarchy in which each rank had obligations to those both above and below them, a point Gregory made explicit in a letter to Maurice of October 596: 'Almighty God, who has made your Majesty the guardian of the peace of our Church, preserves you with the very faith which you preserve in the unity of the priesthood, and when you subject your heart humbly beneath the yoke of heavenly piety, through heavenly grace, it is brought about that you tread on your enemies with the foot of fortitude.'[168] A similar, if less exalted notion of royal responsibility informed Gregory when he wrote to Virgilius of Arles and evoked the memory of Childebert I ('of blessed memory') as a king who had safeguarded the rights and the peace of Arles' monastic communities.[169]

---

[163] *Hom. Ez.* I.X.27, p. 157, XII.18, pp. 193–4, on the dangerous influence of the *pacem peccatorum* on those not firmly on the path to salvation (Ps. LXXII.2–3).
[164] *Ep.* V.37, pp. 308–11, at 308.
[165] *Ep.* V.39, pp. 314–18, writing to the Empress Constantina in June 595.
[166] *Ep.* VI.16, pp. 385–6, at 386. For the notion that peace on earth came only with God's permission see *Ep.* IX.112.
[167] *Ep.* V.36, pp. 304–7.
[168] *Ep.* VII.6, pp. 452–3.
[169] *Ep.* IX.217, pp. 780–1.

Indeed, in a letter of November 602 to Brunhild, Gregory saw this willingness to protect the peace of 'venerable places' together with a love of divine worship as the secret behind the Franks' political success.[170] The theme was not new. Already in June of the previous year Gregory had stressed the intimate correlation of piety and political success, quoting Solomon: 'Righteousness exalts a nation, but sin makes any people wretched'.[171] Faith and peace came together elsewhere, as in Gregory's letter to the Lombard King Agilulf in late 598, in the wake of a further truce between the two. Here Gregory praised the Lombard king's love of peace, explicitly connecting it to his love of God: 'because by loving peace you show that you love God, who is its author'.[172] Similar sentiments can be seen in a companion letter to the Catholic Theodelinda, wife of the Arian Agilulf, praising her true faith and exhorting her, in turn, to encourage Agilulf to maintain the Christian state of peace.[173]

In the cases of both Maurice and Agilulf, Gregory's motivation for counselling peace might be readily understood: both rulers' adherence to peace had immediate implications for Rome and for Gregory's own position. The same encouragement, however, can be found in Gregory's overtures to rulers whose actions posed far less of an immediate political threat. Writing to King Reccared, Gregory cited Luke II.14 and praised his correspondent's *bona voluntas*, which had brought him into the peace of the universal Church following his conversion to Catholic orthodoxy. Gregory, conscious when dealing with kings and military leaders that fame could well be the spur, went on to exhort the Visigothic king to pursue peace not for any spiritual benefit but rather in order that his reign would be remembered, and praised, in ages to come.[174] Gregory cannily realized that the profound nostalgia for peaceful reigns that we have already seen displayed by such writers as Bede and the *Anonymous Valesianus* could be made to dovetail persuasively with early medieval rulers' concern for fame and reputation.

Augustine and Gregory are often contrasted. Gregory initiated the tradition.[175] That the two lived in vastly different worlds has escaped nobody, nor that they perceived their respective worlds in equally divergent fashion. However, both shared a profound sense that a key element of the existence of peace was order. Notions of order underpinned Gregory's objections to the patriarch of Constantinople's claims to the title of ecumenical patriarch, but they informed his notion of social and ecclesiastical peace, too. Writing to the bishops of Gaul in August 595 Gregory spelled out in basic terms the need for inferiors to show appropriate reverence for their superiors, and for those superiors to act with appropriate affection for those beneath them. The survival of the Church,

---

[170] *Ep.* XIII.5, pp. 997–1001, at 997.
[171] *Ep.* XI.46, pp. 943–4, citing Prov. XIV.34.
[172] *Ep.* IX.66, pp. 621–2.
[173] *Ep.* IX.68, p. 624.
[174] *Ep.* IX.229. pp. 805–11.
[175] The habit began with Gregory himself, *Ep.* X.16, pp. 844–5, at 845.

Gregory explained, was entirely dependent upon the existence of different ranks. Peace and love emerged from such a system.[176]

'THE OIL OF PEACE AND THE WINE OF THE LAW': VISIGOTHIC SPAIN

The birth and death of the Visigothic presence in the late antique West were marked by two very distinct peace treaties. The first, initiating nearly three centuries of political independence, was the *foedus* by which Constantius ceded land around Toulouse to the Gothic king Wallia in 418. Modern commentators have debated the treaty's impact.[177] For Iberian natives, Orosius and, later, Isidore, 418's meaning was clear: the pacification of the warlike Goths revealed Divine Providence at work in the history of their own land.[178] The 418 *foedus* was, however, but one of a sequence of treaties between Visigoths and Romans stretching back to the 370s. This sustained exposure to Roman political structures, of which the negotiation of such treaties was an important part, may itself have played a role in the Goths' own increasingly hierarchic conception of kingship in the later fourth and fifth centuries.[179]

The earliest extant document to capture post-Visigothic political realities was also a treaty, the so-called *pactus* of Theodemir of 713.[180] The *pactus* was an agreement between a member of the Umayyad elite, Abd al Aziz, son of Musa ibn Nusair, *wali* of Ifriquiya, and one Theodemir, a local count overseeing several settlements in Baetica. The *pactus* was one of many such *dhimma*—'treaties of protection'—that bound local Christian communities to Muslim authorities across a reconfigured Mediterranean world.[181] Regional powerbrokers like

---

[176] *Ep.* V.59, pp. 357–60.

[177] P. Rousseau, 'Visigothic Migration and Settlement, 376–418. Some Excluded Hypotheses', *Historia* 41 (1992), 345–61; T. S. Burns, 'The Settlement of 418', and P. Heather, 'The Emergence of the Visigothic Kingdom', both in J. Drinkwater and H. Elton (eds), *Fifth-Century Gaul: A Crisis of Identity?* (Cambridge, 1992), 53–63 and 84–94 respectively.

[178] Orosius, *Adv. Pag.* VII.43.10, p. 300: '. . . ad hoc ordinatus a Deo, ut pacem confirmaret'. Isidore of Seville, *Historia de regibus Gothorum, Vandalorum et Suevorum*, ed. C. Rodríguez Alonso, *Las historias de los Godas, Vándalos y Suevos de Isidoro de Sevilla: estudio, edición crítica y traducción* (León, 1975), *s.a.* 416.

[179] P. Heather, *Goths and Romans, 332–489* (Oxford, 1991), 196–7; P. C. Díaz, 'Visigothic Political Institutions', in P. Heather (ed.), *The Visigoths. From the Migration Period to the Seventh Century. An Ethnographic Perspective* (Woodbridge, 1999), 321–57, esp. 324–30.

[180] A. M. Howell, 'Some Notes on Early Treaties Between Muslims and the Visigothic Rulers of al-Andalus', *Actas del I Congreso de historia de Andalucía, diciembre de 1976, Andalucía medieval 5.1* (Córdoba, 1978), 3–14. Questions of transmission in Arabic sources are addressed by A. Carmona González, 'Una cuarta versión de la capitulación de Tudmir', *Sharq al-Andalus* 9 (1992), 11–17; P. Balaña Abadia, 'La fecha exacta de la capitulación de Tudmir, un error de transmisión', *Awraq Revista editada por el Instituto Hispano-Arabe de Cultura* 4 (1981), 73–7.

[181] D. R. Hill, *The Termination of Hostilities in the Early Arab Conquests A.D. 634–656* (London, 1971); M. Khadduri, *War and Peace in the Law of Islam* (Baltimore, 1955).

Theodemir were the men whom successive Visigothic rulers had themselves
sought to control and convince, local elites who formed a dispersed Visigothic
political community. For anyone with hopes of establishing effective central
authority in the Iberian peninsula in the first millennium, whether emperor,
Visigothic king, or Umayyad emir, problems of distance and geography, and the
issues of communication and cohesion they created, were fundamental. It was
Leovigild (569–86) who was the first post-Roman ruler to weld some form of
unity from sub-Roman Spain's constituent cities and localities. Political coherence was the product of conquest.[182] Isidore portrayed Leovigild and his son and
successor Reccared as an exercise in contrast. The Arian father, irreligious, 'eager
for war' (*bello promptissimus*), his Catholic son and successor, distinguished by his
peace and piety (*fide, pius et pace praeclarus*).[183] Conversion to orthodoxy and the
maintenance of the political unity his father had won in battle fused in Isidore's
portrait of Reccared: what his father had attained by conquest the son preserved
in peace through his fairhandedness and moderation.[184]

From Leovigild's reign onwards, successive rulers employed numerous strategies to bolster their central authority: oaths of fidelity, threats of excommunication, and frequent broadcasts of persuasive public language of unity and
collectivity. This was expressed through law-codes and through the national
Visigothic church councils, as both formal occasions and in their carefully
recorded scripts. Visigothic kingship was characterized by distinct forms, ritual,
and court ceremony informed by contemporary eastern practice.[185] Visigothic
rule has conventionally been seen as an unstable institution defined by a lack of
lineal royal continuity, 'occupative' rather than elective in Grierson's formulation, and beset by the threat of internal rebellions and coups.[186] The latter could
occasionally attain levels of internecine violence sufficient to supposedly
shock even Gregory of Tours whose cynical label for the Visigothic practice of
rebellion—*morbus Gothicus*, 'the Gothic disease'—historians from Fredegar's
continuator onwards have lifted for themselves.[187]

---

[182] M. Kulikowski, *Late Roman Spain and its Cities* (Baltimore, 2004), 283–6, 306–7.
[183] Isidore, *Historia*, c. 52, p. 261. John of Biclarum had no trouble seeing Leovigild's campaigns
as a path towards peace, whose campaigns paved the way for the peace and quiet of Leovigild's reign,
Chron., cc. 50, 54, pp. 70–1.
[184] *Hist. Goth.* cc. 52–5, pp. 261–3.
[185] M. R. Valverde Castro, *Ideología, simbolismo y ejercicio del poder real en la monarquía visigoda:
un proceso de cambio* (Salamanca, 2000), 180–253; P. Díaz, 'Rey y poder en la monarquía visigoda',
Iberia 1 (1998), 175–95; McCormick, *Eternal*, 297–327.
[186] P. Grierson, 'Election and Inheritance in Early Germanic Kingship', *Cambridge Historical
Journal* 7 (1941), 1–22 on 'occupative' rule. On the issue of succession see R. Collins, 'Julian of
Toledo and the Royal Succession in Late Seventh-Century Spain', P. H. Sawyer and I. N. Wood
(eds), *Early Medieval Kingship* (Leeds, 1977), 30–49; J. Orlandis, 'La iglesia visigoda y los problemas
de la sucesión al trono en el siglo VII', *Settimane* 7 (1960), 333–51; *idem*, 'La sucesión al trono en la
monarquía visigoda', in J. Orlandis (ed.), *Estudios visigóticos III. El poder real y la sucesión al trono en
la monarquía visigoda* (Rome, Madrid, 1962), 57–102.
[187] *DLH* III.30.

Captains may have changed but the ship sailed on, the institution of kingship itself buoyed rather than broken by the surrounding turbulence. Visigothic kings played heavily upon the language of peace, in particular the peace of the Christian community, to assert legitimacy and to bind together a divided political community.[188] As such, Visigothic Spain has often been seen as a foreshadowing of Carolingian political culture.[189] The engine for development in both cases, it might be said, was political insecurity and fears about longer-term legitimacy. These concerns find expression in both the sequence of major church councils following the Third Council of Toledo, and in the liturgy. Visigothic church councils, like their late imperial predecessors, were in both enacted and written forms displays of a unified, ordered, and orthodox Church.[190] Few councils either opened or closed without a collective articulation of the pre-eminent importance of orthodoxy and peace, whether for the Church, Iberian society, or some fusion of the two. Throughout these councils the notion of *ecclesia*'s peace and orthodoxy, maintained under the tutelage of an equally orthodox ruler, blended with a wider notion of peaceful society. As the closing statement of the Fourteenth Council of Toledo (684) put it, with epigrammatic concision: 'Our glorious king Erwig, under whose peace the peace of the Church is safeguarded (*sub cuius pace pax servatur ecclesiae*)'.[191]

The Third Council of Toledo set the ideological script for those that followed. Reccared and his wife Baddo made joint statements of orthodoxy. In turn, the assembled churchmen responded, affirming the king's responsibility to provide the peace and unity for his Holy Catholic Church.[192] Reccared, in reply, then formally explained his responsibilities, setting out a creed of royal *ministerium* his successors would also be bound by:

A king's concern ought to extend and be directed in this way, namely, in a manner which, it should be agreed, takes its reasoning full of truth and knowledge. For just as in human affairs royal power excels more gloriously, as he watches over his co-provincials' advantage, so too ought his foresight to be greater as well. But now, most blessed priests, we not only apply our skill to those things by means of which the peoples placed under our rule may be governed and live most peaceably, but with the help of Christ we also think

---

[188] S. Castellanos, 'The Significance of Social Unanimity in a Visigothic Hagiography: Keys to an Ideological Screen', *Journal of Early Christian Studies* 11.3 (2003), 387–419; R. L. Stocking, *Bishops, Councils, and Consensus in the Visigothic Kingdom, 589–633* (Ann Arbor, 2000), 12–22, 69–74.

[189] M. de Jong, 'Adding Insult to Injury: Julian of Toledo and his *Historiae Wambae*', in Heather (ed.), *The Visigoths*, 373–402, at 373.

[190] Toledo V (636), Vives, 226. See also, from the close of the Visigothic period, the opening of Toledo XVI (693), Vives, 482.

[191] Toledo XIV (684), c. 12, Vives, 447.

[192] Toledo III (589), Vives, 116. Echoed in Merida (666), Vives, 325; Saragossa III (691), Vives, 480.

forward to what is heavenly and we strive not to be ignorant of those things which make peoples faithful.[193]

Royal power, Reccared continued, was intended to rein in human madness and to check human nature; to spread peace and tranquillity, and to enlighten those dwelling in error through the *lux serena* of truth.[194] The king provided security, peace, and quiet, conditions in which the Church could flourish.[195]

In his closing homily to Toledo III, Leander of Seville took up the theme as he praised the newfound unity of the Church.[196] 'You assuredly proclaim, as in the psalms, "peace to the haters"', Leander told the assembled churchmen, 'saying "Magnify the Lord with me and let us exalt His Name as one."'[197] Leander's homily was, as Rachel Stocking has noted, a celebration of Catholic unity.[198] 'Therefore, preach only the union of nations, yearn for the oneness of all peoples', he advised his fellow churchmen, 'spread abroad only the blessings of peace and love'.[199] The Visigoths' conversion within the wider framework of salvation history Leander saw as an event that moved the world one stage nearer to the state of universal faith and with it one step nearer the final days. His closing peroration drove home the binding power of the Christian community, and the nature of the newly orthodox kingdom:

The peace of Christ has destroyed the wall of discord that the Devil built, and the house that was split by mutual slaughter is now joined by a single cornerstone, Christ. Therefore, let us say: 'Glory to God in the highest; and on earth peace to men of good will'. For no reward outweighs love. Therefore it is placed before all joy, because peace and love have come about, and they hold the first place of all virtues. It remains, however, that having all unanimously become one kingdom, we should approach God with prayers, as much for the stability of the earthly kingdom as for the happiness of the heavenly kingdom, so that the kingdom and the people who have glorified Christ on earth should be glorified by Him not only on earth but also in Heaven. *Amen.*[200]

---

[193] Toledo III (589), Vives, 123: 'Regia cura usque in eum modum protendi debet, et dirigi, quem plenam constet veritatis et scientiae capere rationem; nam sicut in rebus humanis gloriosa eminet potestas regia, ita et prospiciendae commoditati conprovincialium maior debet esse et providentia. At nunc, beatissimi sacerdotes, non eis tantummodo rebus diffundimus solertiam nostram quibus populi sub nostro regimine positi pacatissime gubernentur et vivant, sed etiam in adiutorio Christi extendimus nos ad ea quae sunt coelestia cogitare et quae populos fideles efficiunt satagimus non nescire.' King, *Law,* 30 n. 1.
[194] Toledo III (589), Vives, 123–4.
[195] Toledo VI (638) c.16, Vives, pp. 11–12; Toledo XIV (683) c.12, p. 447. In his *Sententiae* Isidore offered a comparable vision of the ruler's responsibility to guard the peace and discipline (*pax et disciplina*) of the Church emphasizing their accountability before God for their proper discharge of the power given to them, *Sententiae,* ed., P. Cazier CCSL 11 (Turnhout, 1998), III.51, p. 304.
[196] On Leander's role at Toledo III Stocking, *Bishops,* 48–54.
[197] Toledo III (589), Vives, 141, citing Ps. CXIX.7; XXXIII.4.
[198] Stocking, *Bishops,* 86.
[199] Toledo III (589), Vives, 141: '...non nisi connexionem gentium praedicas, non nisi unitatem populorum suspiras, non nisi pacis et caritatis bona disseminas'.
[200] Toledo III (589), Vives, 144: 'Parietem enim discordiae quem fabricaverat diabolus pax Christi destruxit, et domus quae divisione in mutuam certabat caedem, uno iam Christo lapide

Visigothic church councils offered a theatre within which notions of community were articulated until virtually the kingdom's fall. At the close of both Toledo XVI and Saragossa III, held in 691 and 693, the council prayers were offered that Egica's reign would continue for many years to come, that all the people of the *patria* would enjoy *tranquillitas* and that the king would be victorious over his enemies. Egica would echo them himself to support the Church, to rule in peace and govern with piety, discernment, and moderation.[201] A decade after his death Muslim armies snuffed out any future dreams of Visigothic tranquillity.

Let us, for the moment, stay in the later sixth century and the world of the Third Council of Toledo, but turn from the councils themselves to the writing of history. Leander's notion of the Gothic conversion forming an important episode in the spread of orthodoxy and peace across the world was one shared by his contemporary, John of Biclarum.[202] John's medium was not the homily but universal history. In his short chronicle John saw Reccared as a new Constantine or Marcian, his defeat of Guntramn's invading army and its Septimanian allies in 587 his Milvian, and Toledo III his Nicaea or Chalcedon. Toledo III had, John wrote, 'given peace to the universal Church everywhere'.[203] Had the later 580s not witnessed Khusrau II of Persia entering into a peace treaty with the Emperor Maurice, converting to Christianity in the process?[204] This was Christian history as chaos theory: convocations in Toledo reconfigured the Near East from Armenia to the Euphrates.

The image of Reccared in John's *Chronicle* leads us to the figure that must loom large in any discussion of Visigothic intellectual culture and political thought: Isidore of Seville. Isidore, it must be said, saw little value in peaceability for its own sake. Closing his *Historia Gothorum* he saw, not without admiration, that the secret of the Goths' success lay in their unwillingness to sue for peace and their commitment to war. 'Most peoples', he wrote, 'are scarcely permitted to rule through pleas and gifts, the liberty of the Goths has come about more by joining battle than asking for peace'.[205] As in his balanced appraisal of Leovigild, the war-keen father, and Reccared, his peace-loving son, Isidore saw a place for

angulari coniungitur. Dicamus ergo omnes: "Gloria in excelsis Deo et in terra pax hominibus bonae voluntatis." Nullum enim praemium caritati compensatur. Ideo omni gaudio praeponitur, quia pax et caritas facta est, quae omnium virtutum optinet principatum. Superest autem ut unanimiter unum omnes regnum effecti tam pro stabilitate regni terreni quam felicitate regni caelestis Deum precibus adeamus, ut regnum et gens, quae Christum glorificavit in terris, glorificetur ab illo non solum in terris sed etiam in caelis. Amen.'

[201] Toledo XVI (693), 484.
[202] For an overview of John's life and writing see now Roger Collins' commentary in CCSL 173 A, 110–48. K. Baxter Wolf, *Conquerors and Chroniclers of Early Medieval Spain,* TTH 9 (Liverpool, 1990), 1–11.
[203] John of Biclarum, *Chronicon,* ed. C. Cardelle de Hartmann CCSL 173A (Turnhout, 2001), cc. 90–1, pp. 80–2 '... catholica ubique pace data ecclesiis'.
[204] John of Biclarum, *Chron.* c. 92, p. 82 with the comments of Collins, 'Historical Commentary', 147.
[205] *Hist. Goth.,* c. 69, pp. 285–6.

both war and peace in the patterns of politics. In general terms his thinking rested within a familiar framework. In his *Mysticorum expositiones sacramentorum seu Quaestiones in Vetus Testamentum* Isidore offered short and accessible allegorical interpretations of Old Testament figures and events from the expulsion from Eden to the age of the Maccabees, interpretations often informed by his own anti-Jewish perspective. Absalom, he pointed out, following Jerome, meant 'father of peace'; surprising, Isidore added dryly, when it was recalled that he waged war upon David, his father.[206] Absalom was also understood to be Jerusalem, itself meaning peace, but for Isidore, whose motive in writing was as much to polemicize as elucidate, it represented those Jews who had fled from the face of Christ, showing themselves to be faithless, and Judas, Christ's betrayer.[207] Isidore also touched upon notions of peace at various points in the *Etymologies*, from citing Cicero's definition ('Peace is tranquil freedom') in his treatment of philosophical categories through to his discussion 'Laws and times' of treaties and pacts: *pactum*, coming, he explained because it is made from peace (*ex pace factum*).[208] Alongside conventional etymologies of Solomon and Jerusalem, Isidore offered insights into the role of the *caduceatores* in Roman diplomacy, and the meaning of the handshake: 'The right hand (*dextra*) is so called from 'giving' (*dare*), for it is given as a pledge of peace.'[209]

It is in the seventh century's central decades that the theme of peace comes into its own in Visigothic political culture. The historical context is specific. As part of a wider attempt to shore up his authority Chindaswinth (r. 642–53) pursued a two-pronged policy. First, he insisted upon loyalty oaths to protect the throne against usurpers, rebels, and conspiracies. Divine punishment for perjury was buttressed by secular laws that promised harsh punishment, exile, and death, for those who acted 'against the people or the homeland'.[210] By the oath's terms there was to be no way back for such conspirators. Mercy could not be shown to those who broke their word, nor pardon given. Second, Chindaswinth raised his own son, Recceswinth, to joint rule in 649. This seems to have been in response to growing concern about political stability. In a letter of 648 Braulio and Eutropius had written to the aging Chindaswinth expressing concern about the future peace of the kingdom. They reflected upon past crises, their own desire for tranquillity of life, and revealed their awareness of the dangers to which the kingdom remained exposed.[211] It was this sense of present danger that had driven them to overcome their fear of writing to the king with the suggestion that Chindaswinth make Recceswinth co-ruler. Age was on their minds, and

[206] Isidore of Seville, *Mysticorum expositiones sacramentorum seu Quaestiones in Vetus Testamentum. In regum secundum*, PL 83, cols 409–14, c. 3, at 412–13. See also *Etym.* VII.vi.67.
[207] Ibid.
[208] *Etym.* II.xxix.13; V.xxiv.18.
[209] *Etym.* VIII.xi.48; XI.i.66.
[210] *LV* II.1.8. King, 'Law', 40.
[211] PL 80, cols 684–5.

Recceswinth's youth made him a stronger potential protector of the peace than the older Chindaswinth. If peace was to be preserved, power had to rest with a capable war leader. Braulio reached for biblical precedents for an illustrious leader passing power to his son. Moses passed on power to Joshua, he added, and David to Solomon. So, too, should Chindaswinth to Recceswinth.

Despite all this Chindaswinth's death in 653 was followed by open rebellion. Froia, a local leader from the Ebro valley, in alliance with the Basques, attempted to wrest power from Recceswinth. The rising was eventually put down, but not before considerable damage had been caused and many lives lost. In the prologue to his *Sententiae*, Taio of Saragossa recalled his own experience of the rebellion's consequences, the looting, abductions, desecrations; the bodies left unburied in the streets to be eaten by dogs and carrion birds. Yet relief had eventually come, he recalled to the work's dedicatee, Quiricus, because of prayer.[212]

One of the apparent consequences of the violence of Recceswinth's early reign was a greater stress upon the theme of peace in the legislation, poetry, and liturgy of the Toledan court—for example, in the closing chapter of Recceswinth's *Liber Iudiciorum*, promulgated in 654, and itself an unequivocal statement of the reestablishment of royal order. Its first book, 'On the Law' closed with a powerful statement of the benefits of peace to the kingdom:

And so with domestic peace established and the plague of contention having been entirely taken from first, prince, second, the citizens, and then the people and the homeland, we must go forth against our enemies, and meet them powerfully and confidently, certain of victory outside the kingdom, as there is nothing to fear, or to anticipate fearing, from dissension at home.[213]

With 'the oil of peace and the wine of law' mixed together, it continued, the salavation of the whole people was assured. Men were better protected by equity than by weaponry, justice enforced by the good king a better defence than his soldiers' spears. Justice bound together a kingdom, and fostered a shared desire to defend it.[214] The consequent concord of the citizens, as much as the modesty of princes or the temperance of kings, was itself a victory over the enemy, a concord that was itself the result of 'the mildness of princes'.

And thus the good prince, ruling internally and conquering externally, while he possesses his own peace and crushes another's quarrel, is celebrated as a ruler over his citizens, and a victor over his enemies, and is destined to have eternal repose after the passage of time, a heavenly kingdom after the diadem and the purple, a crown of glory, not of yellow gold.

---

[212] Taio of Saragossa, *Sententrâe*, PL 80, cols. 727–999, at 728.
[213] *LV* I.2.6, p. 42: 'His in domestica pace ita perfectis, at totaque primo a principibus, secundo a civibus, exhinc a populis et a domo iurgiorum peste seclusa, eundum in et in adversis et obviandum hostibus potentialiter ac fidenter, tanto in externis spe fida victorie, quanto nil erit, quod ex internis formidari valeat aut timeri.'
[214] *LV* I.2.6, p. 42: 'Pacis enim oleo et legum vino tota plebium massa in statu salutari concreta exeret hostibus indevictos, unde inlesos artus, producentur iustis adiuta legibus tela.'

Moreover, nor will he cease then to be a king, for whilst he leaves the earthly kingdom and seeks the heavenly one, he will not have lost his glory, but rather increased it.[215]

The *Liber Iudiciorum*'s emphasis upon peace did not exist in isolation. The previous year Toledo VIII had familiar recourse to a language of peace and unity. The council began, pointedly, with the assembled bishops, laymen, and king singing the Gloria, with its collective reiteration of peace and goodwill. The bishops then blessed Recceswinth who, in turn, addressed the assembly. Having stressed the collective peaceability of the assembled group, the council turned to the problem of the rebels who, according to the terms set out by Chindaswinth at Toledo VII (646), were to be permanently excluded and anathematized. The need to reconcile a dangerously marginalized section of the nobility with the Toledan elite, however, carried the day. At the formal level the debate pitched royal mercy against the consequences of perjury, and the need to harmonize justice, mercy, and truth led the council to reach for Psalm LXXXIV.11, 'Mercy and truth have met each other: justice and peace have embraced'.[216] Scriptural authority provided a convenient fig leaf for an exigent policy change.

Kings praised peace and bishops invoked it. In the writings of Eugenius II of Toledo (d. 657) the mid-seventh-century emphasis on peace finds a third mode of expression: poetry.[217] Eugenius, the teacher of Julian (who remembered his skills as a liturgist), predecessor of Ildefonsus as the metropolitan of Toledo, had close links to the court, and was himself a prominent participant in several national church councils.[218] According to Ildefonsus' account in *De Viris Illustribus*, Eugenius' career had begun as a member of Chindeswinth's palace chapel. His brief retreat to Saragossa to study and pray ended abruptly with his enforced appointment to the see of Toledo, a position he held under both Chindeswinth and Recceswinth.[219]

Eugenius' compositions reveal a man with a keen sense of the body's frailty, the mind's mutability, and the fleeting nature of life. He combined treatments of all three with sharp observations on Visigothic court life. His evident interest in

---

[215] *LV* I.2.6, p. 42: 'Sicque bonus princeps, interna regens et externa conquirens, dum suam pacem possidet et alienam litem obrumpit, celebratur et in civibus rector et in hostibus victor, habiturus post labentia tempora requiem sempiterna, post luteum aurum celestem regnum, post diadema et purpuram gloriam et coronam; quin pocius nec deficiet esse rex, quoniam, dum regnum terre relinquid et celeste conquirit, non erit amisisse regni gloriam, sed ausisse.'

[216] Toledo VIII (653), Vives, 261.

[217] On Eugenius' poetry R. Collins, 'Julian of Toledo and the Education of Kings in Late Seventh-Century Spain', in *idem, Law, Culture and Regionalism in Early Medieval Spain* (Aldershot, 1992), III, 1–22, at 8–11; C. Codoñer Merino, 'The Poetry of Eugenius of Toledo', in F. Cairns (ed.), *Papers of the Liverpool Latin Seminar*, 3 (Liverpool, 1981), 323–42.

[218] Collins, *Visigothic*, 167–8.

[219] Ildefonsus of Toledo, *De Viris Illustribus*, ed. C. Codoñer Merino, *El 'De Viris Illustribus' De Ildefonso de Toledo* (Salamanca, 1972), c. 13, pp. 133–4. On Eugenius' appointment King, *Law*, p. 126 n. 7; J. F. Rivera Recio, '¿Cisma episcopal en la iglesia Toledana-visigoda?', *Hispania Sacra* 1 (1948), 259–68. C. H. Lynch, *Saint Braulio, Bishop of Saragossa (631–51) His Life and Writings* (Washington DC, 1938), 56–60.

peace occupies the point where all overlapped. It is in a fragmentary abecedarial hymn that we see Eugenius' desire for peace at its most trenchant.[220] The verses that do survive (letters H through to T) are an admission of sin and a plea for forgiveness in desperate times:

> With friends imprisoned and estates burnt,
> To God let us pray with heartfelt sighs,
> That He should make enemies yield to us, and resist the wicked.
> > Spare, Redeemer.
>
> Light of the angels, now kindly undertake
> To stop the wars. Bring back the joys of peace,
> Let the sorry heart be healed by kindness.
> > Spare, Redeemer.
>
> Look, fearful death strikes at our hearts,
> Famine crushes, the weapons of battle clash,
> Grant us now, O Christ, a time of quiet.
> > Spare, Redeemer.
>
> Let anger not endure, but let the remedy draw near
> By which the sins we have committed might be destroyed,
> And the hardships we fear ended.
> > Spare, Redeemer.
>
> O peace everlasting, O everlasting glory,
> We ask for peace, bring in the plenty of peace;
> Let the barbarian peoples be calmed by the favour of peace.
> > Spare, Redeemer.[221]

Eugenius' verse bears echoes of Psalms XVIII.14 and CXLII.5, and also Joel II.16–17, with which it shares a combined sense of collective abandonment and the same request: 'Gather together the people . . . Between the porch and the altar the priests, the Lord's ministers, shall weep, and shall say: "Spare, O Lord, spare thy people: and give not thy inheritance to reproach, that the heathen should rule over them. Why should they say among the nations: Where is their God?"' Eugenius, in effect, styled himself as a seventh-century Joel for a new nation beset by adversity.[222] Was it prayers such as this that Taio felt had finally brought peace to his war-wracked kingdom?

---

[220] Ildefonsus *Vir. Ill.* c. 13. On masses attributed to Eugenius see M. C. Díaz y Díaz, 'Literary Aspects of the Visigothic Liturgy', in E. James (ed.), *Visigothic Spain: New Approaches* (Oxford, 1980), 63, 73 n. 2.

[221] *MGH AA* 14, *carm.* no. 20, pp. 247–8: '<K>aptis amicis et perustis praediis / Deum precemur corde cum suspiriis, / Ut curvet hostes et resistat inprobis. Parce redemptor,/ <L>ux angelorum, iam benignus accipe: /Compesce bella, redde pacis gaudia, / Contrita corda sanet indulgentia. Parce redemptor. / Mors, ecce, dira nostra pulsat pectora, / Fames perurguet, tela belli concrepant; / Concede, Christe, iam quieta tempor<a. Parce redemptor>. Non ira duret, sed medella prox<imet, / Qua deleantur prava, quae commis<imus, / Et finiantur dura, quae pavescim<us. Parce redemptor.> / O pax perennis, o perennis gloria, / Pacem rogamus, pacis infer copiam; / favore pacis gens quiescat barbara. <Parce redemptor>.'

[222] J. N. Hillgarth, 'Popular Religion in Visigothic Spain', *Visigothic*, 3–60, at 40.

Eugenius returned to the theme of peace in a second poem, one composed, perhaps, in quieter times:

You who desire always to shun the hostile snake repel by peace its trickery from affecting your heart.
The mind of he who has Christ in his heart glows with peace.
He who spurns peace, this mad one will perish.
Peace is the life of the soul, peace is virtue and peace is healing.
Peace is the order of things, peace is love of goodness.
Peace is rest for the weary, peace is the sure end of toil.
Persuasive peace unites, good peace conciliates.
Peace suppresses quarrels, peace sweetens all joys.
Peace rules devout hearts, peace puts to flight all evils.
The peace of the highest threefold God is the best reward for the peaceful,
Let the peace of the highest threefold God end strife.[223]

The poem's emphasis upon the prophylactic properties of a peaceful heart, which drives out evil and keeps its bearer clear of the Devil, and the closing lines' Trinitarian emphasis find parallels elsewhere in Eugenius' work.[224] Of particular importance here, however, we might note Eugenius' reference to 'peace is the ordering of things', quoting Augustine's *pax ordo rerum*: the sentiments of book XIX of the *City of God* recast in Visigothic verse.

These lines would also be influential, producing imitations that would themselves influence ninth-century writers with Spanish connections writing two centuries later in the Carolingian world. The figure linking Toledo and Francia was the anonymous author of twenty-five brief verses addressing various virtues, some with explicitly royal associations, others with more general application for one in power, together with comments on the obligations of other members of society (priests, bishops, monks).[225] In short, a Visigothic verse *speculum principis*. Vollmer, Eugenius' editor at the *MGH*, included them with the other Eugenian *spuria*. Current general consensus attributes them to an anonymous seventh-century Toledan poet. Our poet works through a range of directives,

---

[223] *MGH AA* 14 *carm.* no. 4, pp. 234–5: 'Qui cupis infestum semper vitare chelydrum, / Cordis ab affectu pace repelle dolum. / Mens pace rutilat, quae Christum pectore gestat: / Quae pacem spernit, haec furibunda perit. / Pax animae vita, pax virtus paxque medella, / Pax ordo rerum, pax bonitatis amor. / Pax fessis requies, pax denique certa laboris, /Pax blanda sociat, pax bona conciliat. / Pax lites reprimit, pax gaudia tota remulcet, / Pax pia corda regit, pax mala cuncta fugat. / Pax tria summa Deus pacatis praemia praestet, / Iurgantes perimet pax tria summa Deus.' For the Prudentian overtones of *pax tria summa* see A. A. R. Bastiaensen, 'Prudentius' *Hymnus de Trinitate*', *Studia Patristica* 28, 3–14.
[224] For Eugenius' prophylactic poems against demonic night attack see *MGH AA* 14 *carm.* nos. 77–9, p. 264. Ildefonsus and the author of the *Chronicle of 754* would both remember him as an expositor of the Trinity see *De Viris Ill.* c. 13, p. 134. *Crónica mozárabe de 754, Edición crítica y traducción*, ed., J. E. López Pereira (Saragossa, 1980), c. 26, p. 46.
[225] N. Messina, *Pseudo-Eugenio di Toledo. Speculum per un nobile visigoto. Introduzione, edizione critica e traduzione. Concordanze e lista di frequenze*, Monografías de la Universidad de Santiago de Compostela 85 (Santiago, 1984).

from the need to love God and obey the commandments through the desirable qualities of kings (*sapientia, prudentia, simplicitas, patientia*) and all those in power (*iustitia, misericordia, clementia,* amongst others). The twenty-fifth and final virtue was on the benefits of peace to the kingdom. The placement of peace as the subject of the final verse in the sequence, serving as the culmination of the virtues adumbrated in the previous stanzas, is structurally evocative of the patterning of the vision of peace as the *summa* of the virtues' collective work in Prudentius' *Psychomachia.* The verse's greatest stylistic debt, however, is to Eugenius' own verse:

> Let peace be with you, king. Love peace always.
> Peace strengthens a kingdom; peace strengthens a kingdom's flanks,
> Peace nourishes the soul, harmony preserves the peace.
> Peace checks quarrels, and binds the harmonious likewise.
> Quarrels fear peace, discord flees from peace.
> Peace drives out hatreds, peace nourishes pure love.[226]

Elsewhere in the sequence the poet advised his reader to remind the monks of his kingdom of the need to be free of goods, and to follow the examples of Elias, Paul, Anthony, and John. The man who loves peace needs nothing more.[227] He was equally direct when it came to advice on judges, stressing that they should neither deceive the people by mixing pure gold with other metals, nor be swayed by love of money. 'Thus', he concluded, 'shall peace be maintained throughout your entire kingdom and your power and glory will always be praised. Here, and in Eternity, you will be honoured.'[228]

There is little in this exploration of the qualities of lay authority that is of theoretical sophistication. The importance of these poems, however, lies in what they reveal of the pervasive presence of our theme in the seventh-century political imagination. That said, they struck a chord with later writers offering guidance to new generations in places of power. Smaragdus of St-Mihiel sent a version of them to an unidentified son of Louis the Pious in 817, Dhuoda, whilst offered her own variant on some of their lines to her young son William in her *Liber Manualis* of 841 when counselling him 'to do his utmost to be at peace with all men'.[229]

---

[226] *Carm.* no. 15, p. 41: 'Pax tecum maneat, rex, pacem semper amato. / Pax regnum solidat, regni pax cornua firmat. / Pax anim/am nutrit, retinet concordia pacem, / Pax reprimit litem, concordes nectit et idem. / Lis pacem metuit, refugit discordia pacem. / Odia pax pellit, castum pax nutrit amorem.'

[227] *Carm.* no. 24, p. 53: 'Exemplo Eliae populi consortia vitent / Et Pauli, Antonii atque Iohannis ament. / Propria dimittant, habeant ut propria cuncta, / Vir nihil extraneum pacis amator habet.'

[228] *Carm.* no. 25, p. 55: 'Non hos decipiat auri decoctio pura, / Noxius argenti nec male captet amor. / Censoribus populi obediant ut postulat ordo: / Sic pax obtineat omnia regna tua / Et tibi, <rex>, sit laus virtus et gloria semper, / Hic et in aeternum sit tibi semper honor.

[229] For these poems and Smaragdus see Strecker's comments, *MGH Poetae* IV.3, p. 918. Dhuoda, *Handbook for her Warrior Son,* ed. and trans. M. Thiébaux (Cambridge, 1998), IV. c. 7, p. 146.

In its prayers and laws, in the rhetoric of its national councils, and the private concerns of its kings, Visigothic Spain emerges as a political culture in which the idea of peace played no small part. For the Spanish Christians who lived under Muslim dominance in the centuries after 713 that association would live on in their own sense of the lost Visigothic kingdom, and the peace and freedom that their forefathers had enjoyed before the coming of Umayyad domination. The militant Eulogius—historian and ultimately participant in the Cordoban martyr movement—viewed his people's history in terms set, almost inevitably, in a fundamentally scriptural matrix. Others by then had cast their *gens* as a New Israel, but few had used the parallel to write about failure, captivity, and resistance. For Eulogius the current Emir, Muhammad I (d. 886) was a '*satrap of darkness*'. This phrase made of the Conquest a Baylonian captivity for the Mozarabic Church and people—a captivity made all the worse by the Emir's policy of destroying the churches raised by their forefathers 'in a time of peace' some 300 years previously—the age of Reccared—Eulogius' lost golden age of peace and orthodoxy.[230]

If the Visigothic attachment to peace survived in the memories of Umayyad Spain's Christian community it also survived in that most retentive of genres, liturgy. We find prayers for peace recorded in the *Liber ordinum* and in the rich body of '*ad pacem*' prayers that survive from Visigothic Spain.[231] There is no space here to explore the immensely rich liturgical culture of Christian Spain or its legacy, but something of the prevailing concerns of post-Roman rule can be seen in this invocatory prayer from the so-called 'Antiphonary of Wamba'—an eleventh-century copy of what may well have been a seventh-century original—which captures the spirit of the Visigothic search for peace, with its succesive calls for:

Peace in Heaven. Amen.
Peace on earth. Amen.
Let Your peace and abundance, O Lord, come down upon us. Amen.
Peace to the kings and the powers of this world. Amen.
Peace to your Catholic Church, which is assembled in this place, and is spread, in peace, throughout the globe of the whole earth. Amen.[232]

---

[230] Eulogius, *Memoriale sanctorum*, III.3 ('Destructio basilicarum') PL 115, col. 802: 'Qua occasione satrapae tenebrarum inde capta, etiam ea templorum culmina subruunt, quae a tempore pacis studio et industria patrum erecta, pene trecentorum a diebus conditionis suae numerum excedebant annorum.' See D. Millet-Gérard, *Chrétiens mozarabiques et culture Islamique dans l'Espagne des VIIIe—IXe siècles* (Paris, 1984), 23; J. Fontaine, *L'art mozarabe* (Paris, 1977), 62.
[231] On the survival of Visigothic liturgy see R. Collins, 'Continuity and Loss in Medieval Spanish Culture: the Evidence of MS Silos, Archivo Monástico 4', in R. Collins and A. Goodman (eds), *Medieval Spain: Culture, Conflict and Coexistence. Studies in Honour of Angus Mackay* (Basingstoke, 2002), 1–22.
[232] G. Prado, *Textos Inéditos de la Liturgia Mozárabe* (Barcelona, 1926), 51, cited by Kantorowicz, *Laudes*, p. 48 n. 123: 'Pax in coelo. Amen. / Pax in terra. Amen. / Pax et plenitudo tua, Domine, super nos descendat. Amen. / Pax regibus et potestatibus seculi huius. Amen. / Pax

MEROVINGIAN FRANCIA

In the early sixth century Gundobad was not alone in seeing the propaganda potential of coinage bearing messages that directly associated himself with peace. Sometime in the early years of his reign, Theudebert I (c. 534–48), Clovis' grandson, issued a coin bearing a comparably bold declaration: *PAX ET LIBER-TAS*.[233] Appropriately economic in its evocation of two unequivocally Roman values—in keeping with what we know of Theudebert's appetite for *imitatio imperii*—ambiguity or polysemy was hardly an issue here. The precise circumstances of the coin's issue are, however, unclear. It may perhaps have been part of the propaganda surrounding his invasion and subsequent occupation of Italy in 539, a statement of his intentions to protect traditional Roman order, and a bid for the same ground that Ostrogothic notions of *civilitas* had targeted.[234] More likely is that it was meant primarily for domestic reception, to reassure a Gallo-Roman elite not only of continued order but also of the continued respect for free status, civic identity, and rights of ownership.

That Theudebert's issue shared two of its terms and general form (PAX ET . . .) with the earlier Burgundian issue might suggest, if not the latter's influence upon its larger and politically longer-lived neighbour, at the very least a shared reliance upon coinage as a means for reaffirming continued social order into the sixth century. The primary intention of Theudebert's PAX ET LIBERTAS, however, was not to evoke the political language of a defunct neighbour but rather to speak in the register of imperial authority.[235] As with the message so the medium. It copied both the weight and the material—gold—of eastern imperial coinage.[236] There is no record of the impact this piece of early Frankish *imitatio imperii* made in either Italy or Francia but we do know of one response from Constantinople. Procopius dismissed the Frankish ruler's coinage

---

ecclesie tue catholice, que est in hunc locum constituta, et per /universum orbem terrarum in pace diffusa. Amen.'

[233] M. Prou, *Catalogue des monnaies françaises de la Bibliothèque nationale: Les monnaies mérovingiennes* (Paris, 1892), no. 55, pp. 14–15; R. Collins, 'Theudebert I, *Rex Magnus Francorum*', in P. Wormald (ed.), *Ideal and Reality in Frankish and Anglo-Saxon Society Presented to J. M. Wallace-Hadrill* (Oxford, 1983), 7–33, at 27–30, with reproduction, pl. i, see also *MEC*, 116–17.

[234] Callu, '*Pax*' 189–99.

[235] Collins, ' Theudebert I', 27–8. On Theodebert's other acts of *imitatio*, McCormick, *Eternal*, 338–9, and his claims to extensive rule made in a surviving letter to Justinian of c. 535, *Ep. Aus.* no. 20, *MGH Epp.* III, p. 133. On the changing identity of coinage in the successor states see M. Hendy, 'From Public to Private: The Western Barbarian Coinages as a Mirror of the Disintegration of Late Roman State Structures', *Viator* 19 (1988), 29–78, esp. 61–2.

[236] On the restricted use of gold and the adherence of 'pseudo-imperial' coinage to Byzantine norms of weight and style see Collins, 'Theodebert I', 27–8.

as upstart pretension.[237] Sixth-century Byzantines were possessive not only of the imperial prerogative to issue *solidi* but also of the imperial ideology and iconography they bore. Constantinople's citizens had both liturgy and Hagia Eirene's commanding presence as constant reminders that they, as *Rhomaoi*, were the true heirs of Rome, and with it, Rome's cult of peace.

Theudebert's PAX *solidus* is emblematic of several generations of Merovingian kings' concern with the domestic order and peace of their kingdoms. The extant Frankish legislation of the sixth and early seventh centuries reveals the continuation of late Roman provincial policing strategies under the direction of Frankish kings that sought, at a grass-roots level, to maintain peace and order.[238] The *Pactus pro tenore pacis* (511 x 558), for example, was an agreement drawn up between Chlothar I and Childebert I between 511 and 558, in the form of joint and individual edicts on the regulation of ordeals, the punishment of theft and possession of stolen goods, the role of the *centenarius* and the pursuit of thieves across the borders of kingdoms.[239] The *pactus* sought to preserve the peace at the regional level, placing its local maintenance in the hands of *centenarii*, responsible for the pursuit of criminals and leadership of armed militia (*trustes*).[240] The full text was itself a composite, consisting of legislation from both rulers, eight clauses from Childebert followed by a further seven from Chlothar, the two collectively dispatching a further three.[241] Similar concerns manifest in Chlothar II's Edict of Paris of 614, issued after his assumption of power and in the wake of the Council of Paris.[242] 'That there will be everlasting peace and discipline in our kingdom', runs the title to one chapter, 'through Christ's favour, and that the rebellions and insolences of evil men will be strictly checked'.[243]

Grass-roots pragmatism to lawlessness was one reponse. Guntramn's *Edict* of 585, issued at Péronne and transmitted as an *addendum* to the *capitula* of the Council of Mâcon, itself convened at his initative, offered a different

---

[237] *Bell.Goth.* VII.33, 5–7. On Merovingian imperial attitudes see S. Fanning, 'Clovis Augustus and Merovingian *imitatio imperii*', in K. Mitchell and I. Wood (eds), *The World of Gregory of Tours* (Leiden, 2002), 321–35; C. Morrisson, 'Les insignes du pouvoir impérial au Ve et au VIe siècle', in M. Rouché (ed.), *Clovis—histoire et mémoire. La baptême de Clovis, son écho à travers l'histoire* Paris, 1997) 11, 753–68.

[238] A. Callander Murray, '*Pax et Disciplina:* Roman Public Law and the Merovingian State', in T. F. X. Noble (ed.), *From Roman Provinces to Medieval Kingdoms* (London, 2006), 376–88.

[239] *MGH Capit.* I, no. 3 (511 x 558), 3–8, p. 5. On the role of the *centenarius* see A. Callander. Murray, 'From Roman to Frankish Gaul: *Centenarii* and *Centenae* in the Administration of the Frankish Kingdom', *Traditio* 44 (1988), 59–100.

[240] *MGH Capit.* I, no. 3 (511 x 558), c. 9, pp. 5–6.

[241] The treaty-like character of these joint declarations is noted by Goebel, *Felony and Misdemeanor*, 67 n. 5.

[242] A. Callander Murray, 'Immunity, Nobility, and the Edict of Paris', *Speculum*, 69.1 (1994), 18–39; P. Fouracre, 'Eternal Light and Earthly Needs: Practical Aspects of the Development of Frankish Immunities', in P. Fouracre and W. Davies (eds), *Property and Power in the Early Middle Ages* (Cambridge, 2002), 53–81, at 62–3.

[243] *MGH Capit.* I, no. 9 (614/5), 20–3, at 22, no. 11: 'Ut pax et disciplina in regno nostro sit, Christo propociante, perpetua et ut revellus vel insullentia malorum hominum severissime reprimatur.'

approach.[244] Childebert and Chlothar looked to local officals to keep the peace through practical measures. Guntramn, Gregory of Tours' *rex bonus,* looked instead to his bishops and ultimately to God, 'by whose *imperium* all things are ruled' and who gave support to those who adhered to his commandments.[245] Political stability and collective salvation (*pro regni nostri . . . stabilitate et salvatione regionis*) were therefore less a matter for low level administration than of preaching and pastoral correction, which fostered honesty, a love of justice, and the heavenly gifts of earthly tranquillity (*tranquillitas temporum*) and collective salvation (*salvatio populorum*) granted by God.[246] Sunday observance, a particular problem, was to be enforced, and just judgements given. Ultimately, the apparent differences between Guntramn's ecclesiological vision and his predecessors' *decreta* are the products of genre: memoranda of legislative directives on the one hand, and a quasi-homiletic address to a church council by a presiding ruler on the other.[247]

Alexander Callander Murray's vision of these sixth-century peacekeeping strategies and the Merovingian *centenarius* as heir of the *assertor pacis* and *eirenarch* of the late Empire emphasizes the strength of late Roman provincial practice to early Merovingian kingship.[248] A similar debt is apparent if we turn from law to poetry, and to a figure that perhaps most consciously sought to cast his subjects in a late Roman mode: the panegyrist Venantius Fortunatus.[249]

Peaceful rulership was a subject to which Venantius would return on various occasions over the three decades of his time in Francia. Why did peaceful rule enjoy so prominent a place in Venantius' imagery of sixth-century Frankish kingship? Genre, of course, played its part. A ruler's virtues in peace, like his successes in war, had been commonplaces in Latin panegyric since Pliny first wrote for Trajan.[250] By the fourth century, panegyric could be written, quite literally, by the book, as several late imperial handbooks codified its requirements.[251] This meant that for Venantius—no less than for Ennodius—peace was

---

[244] O. Pontal, *Histoire des conciles mérovingiens* (Paris, 1989), 186.

[245] *MGH Capit.* I no. 5 (585), 11–12, at 11.

[246] *Ibid.* Compare *DLH* VIII.30. For later legislation against Sunday labour *MGH Capit.* I no. 7 (596), no. 17, pp. 15–18, at 17.

[247] *MGH Capit.* I no. 6 (585), 12 n. 4, Boretius suggested 'Peronne in pago Ambiensi', i.e., Péronne, Somme, but Péronne, Saône-et-Loire is surely more likely.

[248] Murray, '*Pax et Disciplina*'; *idem,* 'Roman', 77–80, drawing upon numerous studies of the late Roman East. On local peacekeeping in the eastern empire see R. Bagnall, *Egypt in Late Antiquity* (Princeton, 1993), 164–5.

[249] B. Brennan, 'The Career of Venantius Fortunatus', *Traditio* 41 (1985), 49–78; J. George, 'Venantius Fortunatus: Panegyric in Merovingian Gaul', in M. Whitby (ed.), *The Propaganda of Power: the Role of Panegyric in Late Antiquity* (Leiden, 1998), 225–46; *eadem,* 'Venantius Fortunatus: the End Game', *Eranos* 96 (1998), 32–43; *Venantius Fortunatus: Personal and Political Poems* (Liverpool, 1995); *Venantius Fortunatus: the Role of a Latin Poet in Merovingian Gaul* (Oxford, 1992).

[250] R. A. B. Mynors, *XII Panegyrici Latini* (Oxford, 1964). On peace in later imperial panegyric see M. Mause, *Die Darstellung des Kaisers in der lateinischen Panegyrik,* Palingenesia 50 (Stuttgart, 1994).

[251] D. A. Russell and N. G. Wilson, *Menander Rhetor* (Oxford, 1981).

never far from his pen. In a kingdom comprising Gallo-Roman aristocrats and Frankish kings the *romanitas* of Venantius' panegyrics took on additional importance, framing as it did new and fragile political circumstances in the language of older certainties. Some of the better educated members of the old senatorial elite may even have recalled that panegyric was not just a Roman tradition but also a local one: Gaul's schools of rhetoric had produced a number of late antique panegyrics and it was there, sometime in the late fourth century, that the so-called 'Gallic corpus' was assembled.[252]

Panegyric's form only partly explains the prominence of peace in Venantius' political poetry. As important is the fact that his career, like that of his friend and contemporary, Gregory of Tours, was played out against the backdrop of the later sixth-century's civil war and unrest depicted in Gregory's *Ten Books*.[253] These may be briefly sketched: Chlothar's death in 561 had opened the way for competition between his four sons, Charibert I, Guntramn, Sigibert I, and Chilperic. War between Sigibert and Chilperic opened the 560s. By the decade's close Sigibert had launched an attack upon Guntramn, and conflict between the two simmered into the 570s, leading to an alliance between Chilperic and Guntramn and, in 575, Sigibert's assassination. These years have been claimed, with good reason, as the nadir of Merovingian civil strife.[254] Sigibert's son, Childebert II, backed by Guntramn and his father's own nobles, emerged to take his father's place, although his stepmother, Brunhild, married Chilperic's son, Merovech, who mounted his own failed bid for power against his father. The souring of relations between Guntramn and Childebert II led to a temporary realignment of allegiances that saw Childebert II and Chilperic, the long-standing enemy of his father, come together in the early 580s, before Childebert and Guntramn renewed their alliance. Chilperic's assassination in 584 added a further level of generational complexity, as his son Chlothar II joined the fray, backed (as Childebert had been earlier) by Guntramn. The entry of an additional competitor, Chlothar I's son and long-time exile, Gundovald, into Frankish affairs between 582 and 585, forced a further reconfiguring of priorities and alliances. Guntramn and Childebert II dominated Frankish politics until their deaths in 592 and 596.

Venantius' own career wove through these events.[255] From the mid–560s onwards he produced, alongside hagiography and other works, a range of political poems and verse panegyrics.[256] Understandably, many of the occasions

[252] T. D. Barnes, 'Emperors, Panegyrics, Prefects, Provinces and Palaces (284–317)', *Journal of Roman Archaeology* 9 (1996), 539–42.

[253] Wood, *Kingdoms*, 88–101. My debt to these pages ought to be clear.

[254] Wood, *Kingdoms*, 89.

[255] See the reconstruction of George, *Venantius*, 28–34; *eadem*, 'End Game', 32–43; on Venantius' later poems, Brennan, 'Career', 49–78.

[256] George, *Venantius*; S. Coates, 'Venantius Fortunatus and the Image of Episcopal Authority in Late Antique and Early Merovingian Gaul', *EHR* 115 (2000), 1109–37; J. Kitchen, *Saints' Lives and the Rhetoric of Gender: Male and Female in Merovingian Hagiography* (Oxford, 1998) 25–58.

when Venantius was called upon to recite his poetry were times of tension and uneasy peace, when a formally vocalized sentiment of peace became particularly important in smoothing over and reinforcing the values of consensus and harmony. His praise poems in favour of kings were stripped-down pieces, noticeably shorn of the narrative excurses and mythological embellishments found in much earlier panegyric.[257] In spring 566 Venantius stood before the assembled dignitaries of the Frankish kingdom in Metz to recite his *epithalamium* at Sigibert's wedding to the Visigothic princess Brunhild, daughter of Athanagild, and offered fulsome praise for the era of peace the marriage promised. In his verses Venantius expressed the wish not only that Sigibert and Brunhild would live together peacefully but that that peace would touch every subject under their joint rule, 'May the joy of all arise under your guidance, let the world love peace, let the conqueror Concord rule'.[258] Venantius singled out Sigibert as a peaceful ruler: Cupid's arrows, inflaming his desire for Brunhild, struck into his 'peaceful bones'.[259] Peacefulness was innate in Sigibert—part of his very fibre. In the poem's opening lines Venantius, commenting upon the dukes gathered around the King, had separated him from their warlike character and played upon the meaning of the words *duces* and *decus*: 'Look, Mars has his leaders (*duces*). Look, Peace has her glory' (*decus*).[260]

Sometime later Venantius returned to the theme in a poem celebrating Sigibert's victories in battle against the Thuringians and Saxons. Here, peace came by more conventional means, martial prowess. Venantius could hardly have been blunter:

> Your wars have granted peace with new-found prosperity.
> Your sword has brought forth sure joy.[261]

The theme of peaceful rule was treated most fully, however, in a poem that seems to have been delivered as part of an *adventus* for Charibert in Paris in 567. 'Stifle your long-standing sorrow', Venantius counselled the assembled Parisians, 'for a peaceful king has returned' (*rex placidus rediit*).[262] Venantius went on to explain that whilst Charibert's predecessors had enlarged their kingdoms, they had done so by arms, whilst he had done so peacefully.[263] Venantius' Charibert might also

---

[257] George, 'Panegyric'; Reydellet, *Royauté*, 298.

[258] *MGH AA* IV, *carm.* no. 6.1, lines 140–1, p. 129: 'Auspiciis vestris cunctorum gaudia surgant, / Pacem mundus amet, victrix concordia regnet.' Here, and subsequently, I have drawn heavily from the translations of George, *Personal*, 25–39.

[259] *MGH AA* IV, *carm.* no. 6.1, lines 37–41, p. 125.

[260] *MGH AA* IV, *carm.* no. 6.1, line 20, p. 124: 'Mars habet ecce duces, pax habet ecce decus'.

[261] *MGH AA* IV, *carm.* no. 6.1a, lines 15–16, p. 129: 'Prosperitate nova pacem tua bella dederunt / ET peperit gladius gaudia certa tuus'.

[262] *MGH AA* IV, *carm.* no. 6.2, line 14, p. 131.

[263] *MGH AA* IV, *carm.* no. 6.2, lines 39–40, p. 132: 'Illi auxere armis patriam, sed sanguine fuso: / Tu plus adquiris qui sine clade regis.'

be seen as a distant relative of the Gunthamund of Dracontius' *Satisfactio*. Both conquered without bloodshed, achieving the benefits and glories of military conquest without its cost. Here, too, Venantius paraded Roman and biblical figures, including David and Solomon, the latter singled out for his wisdom, love of justice, and mastery of law.[264]

Venantius adapted the traditions of late imperial panegyric to the political conditions and culture of Merovingian Francia. His contemporary and the bishop in whose entourage Venantius spent time, Gregory of Tours, offered a more original perspective on the conjunction of peace and power. In his *Histories* Gregory treated the relationship of peace and rulership not, as many of the figures we have encountered so far in this chapter, by providing intentionally idealized images of power, but rather through his detailed accounts of political life. Gregory's *Histories* have been seen, at least in part, as a lament for the lost golden age of domestic peace under Clovis, and a sustained critique by account of the *discordia* and *bella civilia* of his own day.[265] As Guy Halsall has recently emphasized, the crux of Gregory's critique, and the point at which the implicit agenda becomes explicit, takes place in the preface to Book Five. This is an axial passage in his work, one of the very few where he dropped third-person narrative for direct speech to lecture the kings of his own day about the divisions within the royal family and the struggles between family members—the fact that the kings chose to wage war against each other rather than against outside enemies, as Clovis had. The kings had wine, grain, oil, gold, and silver but lacked one thing: 'because you do not have peace, you do not have the grace of God'.[266] If the kings wanted to engage in civil wars, Gregory advised them to pursue those of the interior life: spirit against flesh, virtues against vices.[267]

Gregory's *Histories* and the extensive examples of Merovingian violence they contain, from civil wars to urban and monastic unrest to the feud of Sichar and Chramnesind (itself a *bellum civile* for Gregory), move between hostility and amity and end with Sichar's murder. Taken togther, they might be read as a sustained exercise in providing the material evidence of the lack of peace. Gregory's paradox is that whilst he wrote extensively about local feuds and civil wars, with a profoundly far-reaching influence on how later generations have

[264] *MGH AA* IV, *carm.* no. 6.2, lines 76–81, p. 133.
[265] Explicit in the *DLH* V, *praef.*, 193–4. The bibliography on Gregory of Tours is substantial. K. Mitchell and I. Wood (eds), *The World of Gregory of Tours* (Leiden, 2002) offers a comprehensive overview, many new perspectives and considerable references to earlier studies. Other key works include M. Heinzelmann, *Gregory of Tours: History and Society in the Sixth Century*, trans. C. Carroll (Cambridge, 2001); A. H. B. Breukelaar, *Historiography and Episcopal Authority in Sixth-Century Gaul. The Histories of Gregory of Tours Interpreted in their Historical Context* (Göttingen, 1994).
[266] *DLH* V *praef.*, p. 193: 'Unum vobis deest, quod, pacem non habentes.'
[267] *DLH* V *praef.*, 193, citing Gal. V.17 and Tim. VI.10. G. Halsall, 'The Preface to Book V of Gregory of Tours' *Histories*: Its Form, Context and Significance', *EHR* 122 (2007), 297–317.

viewed his own age, his real concern lay with the theme of peace and harmony.[268] The *Histories* is a sustained account of the politics of its absence. Only in recent years have scholars come to see Gregory as a figure influenced by Augustine's formative attitudes to the vicissitudes of earthly rule, or even to concede that, in his acute sense of the failings and fluctuations of earthly rule, there is an Augustinian element to his thought.[269]

LEGISLATING FOR *CARITAS*: THE TREATY OF ANDELOT (NOVEMBER 587)

When not delivering jeremiads against Merovingian violence, Gregory was on occasion himself involved in establishing concord between members of the Carolingian ruling house. At various points in the *Histories*, he offered a portrait of himself as one of Francia's *beati pacifici*, a bishop-diplomat in the same tradition as Epiphanius, involved in summits and deputations between members of the Merovingian ruling house. Gregory clearly had an eye for these events, detailing the sequences of public meetings, communal meals, and symbolic actions—ostentatiously enthroning one another, swapping spears—by which agreements were made and displayed.[270] It was in the context of one of these agreements that Gregory spliced into his narrative the actual text of the agreement made in November 587 between members of the Merovingian *stirps regia* that briefly aligned the Burgundian and Austrasian branches of the royal family.[271] It is, then, to Gregory that we owe the survival of the earliest extant post-Roman peace treaty.[272]

The treaty of Andelot forms an episode in the complex family disputes of the late sixth century, codifying a *modus vivendi* between two kings, the young Childebert II of Burgundy, son of Sigibert, and his uncle, Guntramn, king of Austrasia, and the division of territory between the two. Andelot was simultaneously a division of the kingdom and a response to the specific political

---

[268] Halsall, 'Preface', 317. Attitudes to, and the influence of, the Sichar-Chramnesind episode explored by I. Wood, 'The Bloodfeud of the Franks: a historiographical legend', *EME* 14.4 (2006), 489–504.

[269] Halsall, 'Preface', 304–5. W. Goffart, *The Narrators of Barbarian History (A.D. 550–800): Jordanes, Gregory of Tours, Bede, and Paul the Deacon* (Princeton, NJ, 1988), 181–2, 202.

[270] *DLH* V.17, p. 216; VII.33, pp. 353–4. On which see R. Le Jan, 'Apprentissages militaires, rites de passage et remises d'armes au haut Moyen Âge', in P.-A. Sigal (ed.), *Initiation, Apprentissage, éducation au Moyen Âge* (Montpellier, 1993) 213–32, at 223–4.

[271] *DLH* IX. 20, pp. 434–41.

[272] *DLH* IX. 20, pp. 434–41. Textual variations between the earliest recensions of the treaty are minimal. See P. Bourgain and M. Heinzelmann, 'L' oeuvre de Gregoire de Tours: la diffusion des manuscrits' in N. Gauthier and H. Galinié, eds, *Grégoire de Tours et l'espace gaulois. Actes du congrès international Tours, 3–5 novembre 1994* (Tours, 1997), 273–317, esp. 278–283.

problems of 587.[273] The citation of documents verbatim was a common technique of Christian historiography, which Gregory had probably learned from Eusebius.[274] Why did Gregory reproduce Andelot specifically? Viewed within the broader framework of Gregory's vision of his own day, the treaty had a key rhetorical role in Gregory's work, providing an independent, royally sanctioned model of good relations within the ruling house, the very thing he had hoped for in the Preface to Book Five. Its clauses, with their concern for providing norms governing peaceful interaction and deployment of a language of *caritas*, offered a script for how competing Merovingian royal rivals ought to behave. It also showed the same emphasis upon the need for God's grace in the creation and maintenance of peace that was voiced in the *Histories*. As a 'real' document existing outside the narrative it supported it allowed Gregory to show his idea of peace as shared with others, specifically the rulers of Gaul.

The paradigmatic character of the treaty signalled by its heading in Gregory's text—*exemplar pactionis*—might be said to apply as much to the model it provided for harmonious royal interaction as for potential scribal replication. The *pactio* began with a tableau of pious political cooperation, buttressed by consensus and divinely approved:

When, in Christ's Name, the most excellent lords Guntramn and Childebert and the most glorious lady Queen Brunhild met out eagerness for love at Andelot in order that any matter, in whatever respect, that could potentially produce discord between them might be settled between them with fuller counsel, through the mediation of priests and nobles and with the help of God, it was settled, approved and agreed between them that, as long as Almighty God wished them to live in this world, they would maintain faith between themselves and love, pure and simple.[275]

The treaty set out territorial divisions and enshrined general obligations between members of the royal family. More specifically, its sequential clauses (presented by Gregory as continuous text) addressed particular issues such as the control of territory, whether named *civitates*, legal units of property, such as *morgengabe*, or the future inheritances of the next generation, male and female. Protecting female-owned property was a particular concern: several sections set out safegaurds for the property rights of royal women. Alongside such horizontal

---

[273] For a recent rereading of the treaty and its political contexts as text and as agreement see M. Widdowson, 'Merovingian partitions: a "genealogical charter"?, *EME* 17.1 (2009), 1–22, esp. 15–21.

[274] On documentary evidence in Eusebius see R. L. P Millburn, *Early Christian Interpretations of History* (London, 1954), 54–73, esp. 64. For his influence on Gregory, Halsall, 'Preface', 316.

[275] *DLH* IX c. 20, p. 436: 'Cum in Christo nomen praecellentissimi domni Gunthchramnus et Childebertus regis vel gloriosissima domna Brunechildis regina Andelao caritates studio convenissent, ut omnia, quae undecumque inter ipsis scandalum poterat generare, pleniori consilio definirent, id inter eos, mediantibus sacerdotibus atque proceribus, Deo medio, caritates studio sedit, placuit atque convenit, ut, quamdiu eos Deus omnipotens in praesenti saeculo superesse voluerit, fidem et caritatem puram et simplicem sibi debeant conservare.'

obligations within the royal house Andelot formalized relations between rulers and ruled and seeking to fix a political *status quo*. Individual clauses requried all followers (*leudes*) to return to the positions of loyalty they had held in Chlothar's day. Each contracting ruler formally committed to repatriate those who had defected during the civil wars and undertook that in future neither would attempt to lure away the other's men. Whilst the rulers recevied renewed assurances of loyalty, their nobles were given assurance that their lawful property rights would be recognised, and their general freedom of movement protected. Each kingdom's leading men were, then, both the beneficiaries of elements of the treaty and almost certainly the local political players upon whom the implementation of the treaty's others prescriptions would ultimately rest.

Andelot presented a set of norms and obligations—idealised responses to a specific situation—to which the contracting parties were bound by oath. And whilst the treaty contained specific clauses, these are couched, like those relationships already discussed, in terms of idealized kin relations. Guntramn's obligations to Childebert's sons—should Childebert die—were those of a dutiful father (*pius pater*), with overtones of religious faithfulness and correct Christian behaviour.[276] Similarly, Guntramn's relationship with Faileuba, Childebert II's wife, was as a brother to a sister, informed by spiritual love (*dilectio spiritualis*).[277] Good kin-relations overlapped conceptually with religious observance. The treaty's rhetoric of good relations had scriptural and also liturgical overtones: *caritas*, but also purity and faithfulness were repeatedly invoked. 'Love', its author clearly felt, was a key component of social harmony.[278] In terms of the lifetimes of Guntramn and Childebert II, the text repeatedly emphasized God's ultimate power over future affairs. In terms of the treaty's own role in this narrative, it described itself as the material device through which 'pure and simple harmony' was enjoined.[279]

A final theme of the treaty, present in its care to preserve the property of the individual kings' followers, and their loyalty in a more general sense, was the need for collective action and support from the nobility for both rulers. For as much as it safeguarded the rights of female and junior members of the royal house, Andelot secured the rights of both rulers' *leudes*, whilst the proem emphasized the active role played by both nobles (*proceres*) and priests (*sacerdotes*) in the settlement itself (*mediantibus sacerdotibus atque proceribus*).[280]

Andelot is one of a small group of related documents produced by a largely Gallo-Roman legislative community around the turn of the sixth century. It

---

[276] *DLH* IX c. 20, p. 436. *Pius pater* was the term of address to Guntramn used by Childeric's legates in Gregory's account of their meeting at Chalon-sur-Saône in 583, see *DLH* VII c. 6, pp. 328–9.

[277] *DLH* IX c. 20, pp. 436–7.

[278] On a similar theme see Caesarius of Arles, *Sermones*, ed. G. Morin, CCSL 103, 104 (Turnhout, 1953), no. 39, I, 172–7, esp. 174–5, discussed by W. Klingshirn, *Caesarius of Arles, The Making of a Christian Community in Late Antique Gaul* (Cambridge, 1994), 189.

[279] *DLH* IX c. 20, Andelot, c. 12, p. 436: 'Et quia inter praefatus regis pura et simplex est in Dei nomen concordia inligata.'

[280] On *leudes* see Halsall, *Settlement*, 36.

shares with them both general character and intent, as well as the public language of contemporary Merovingian authority.[281] Its language also finds echoes in the wording of texts preserved in the formularies of Angers and Marculf, a relationship that led Anna Drabek, in what remains the most detailed study of the text to date, to argue both for its place within a tradition of later Roman legislation, and more specifically its kinship with the tradition of 'private pacts' contained in these collections for the division of estates between surviving heirs or the exchange of land parcels between friends.[282]

'IPSE PACIFICUS VELUT SALOMON': THE *LIBER HISTORIAE FRANCORUM*

The *Liber Historiae Francorum*, written around 727 at an unidentified centre somewhere north of Paris, is, hagiography apart, our primary narrative for late Merovingian history.[283] It is based, with some significant divergences, upon the six-book version of Gregory's *Histories*.[284] At first glance the *LHF* appears an unlikely source for material on peace. Its author's martial, not to say secular, interests are prominent throughout.[285] From the account of the Franks' origins as Trojans from the establishing image of the Franks' Trojan ancestors—brave, strong, warlike and restive in Illium—to the final chapters recounting the wars of Chilperic II's reign, the *LHF*'s historical narrative that amounted to a genealogy of Frankish martial virtue to the advent of Theuderic IV around 721, the *LHF* presented an historical narrative that amounted to a genealogy of Frankish martial virtue.[286] Belligerence,

---

[281] A. C. Murray, '"PAX ET DISCIPLINA"', 376–88. I. N. Wood, 'The Code in Merovingian Gaul', in J. Harries and I. N. Wood (eds), *The Theodosian Code*, (Ithaca, 1993), 161–77.

[282] 283 A.M. Drabek, 'Der Merowingervertrag von Andelot aus dem Jahr 587', *MIÖG* 78 (1970), 34–41, esp. 36–41. For recent approaches to formularies, from rather distinct positions, see A. Rio, *Legal Practice and the Written Word in the Early Middle Ages: Frankish Formulae, c. 500–1000* (Cambridge, 2009) and W. Brown, 'Conflict, Letters, and Personal Relationships in the Carolingian Formula Collections', *Law and History Review* xxv.ii (2007), 323–44.

[283] *Liber Historiae Francorum*, ed. B. Krusch, *MGH SRM* 2 (Hanover, 1888), 241–328. The major study remains R. Gerberding, *The Rise of the Carolingians and the Liber historiae Francorum* (Oxford, 1987), addressing the place of the work's composition at 146–59. Fouracre and Gerberding, *Late Merovingian France*, 17–18, 79–87, McKitterick, *History and Memory*, 9–22 address questions of political context, purpose, and in the latter case, important aspects of transmission.

[284] G. Kurth, 'Étude critique sur le *Gesta Regum Francorum*', *Bulletins de l'Académie royale de Belgique*, 3rd series 18 (1889), 261–91, criticized by Gerberding, *Rise*, 3, 32–3, *et passim*. The LHF author worked from the six-book edition of the *Histories*, on the circulation of which see the extended discussion of MSS tradition to be found in W. Goffart, 'From *Historiae* to *Historia Francorum* and Back Again: Aspects of the Textual History of Gregory of Tours', in J. J. Contreni and T. F. X. Noble (eds), *Religion, Culture, and Society in the Early Middle Ages: Studies in Honor of Richard E. Sullivan* (Kalamazoo, MI, 1987), 55–76.

[285] Gerberding, *Rise*, 159.

[286] *LHF* c. 1, p. 241.

the *LHF*'s account stressed, was an immutable element of the Frankish character. Undiminished by Clovis' conversion, it linked the Franks of the author's generation with those of distant times.[287] This bellicosity the *LHF*'s author illustrated by numerous references to raiding, tribute taking, and subjection.[288] The historicity of such embellished accounts is, naturally, questionable but of less relevance in a study of the representation of royal behaviour.[289] For current purposes the most important passage in the *LHF* is its description of Dagobert as 'a pacific king, like Solomon' (*Ipse pacificus, velut Salomon*). Here, too, the *LHF* author's martial preoccupations shaped the work's portrait of Dagobert I, a *rex pacificus*, like Solomon. Tellingly, his description of the Solomonic Dagobert was preceded by a near-epic account of his involvement in his father Chlothar II's campaigns against the Saxons culminating in mass killings of adult males, *pour encourager les autres.*[290]

King Dagobert himself was the strongest king of the Franks, patron of the Franks, most severe in judgement, the benefactor of the Church. For he himself was the first to order that much wealth be distributed as alms to the churches of the saints. He established peace throughout his entire kingdom. His reputation resounded amongst many peoples. He struck fear and dread into all the surrounding kingdoms. He was a peacemaker, like Solomon, he who achieved peace for the kingdom of the Franks.[291]

Much like his (or her) immediate contemporary Bede's treatment of Edwin, establishing peace by conquest and the threat of war, the *LHF*-author's vision of peaceful rulership rested upon effective military leadership. Engendering *timor*, rather than cultivating *caritas* or domestic *dilectio* lay at the heart of our author's notion of royal peacemaking. Inheritance also played its part: the Solomon-like Dagobert inherited the kingdoms won by his father Chlothar II, himself identified on at least one occasion as 'like David'.[292]

The *LHF*'s portrait has to be set within the context of the increasing emphasis upon biblical figures in later Merovingian political culture found in a range of different sources, liturgical, historical, and prescriptive.[293] Taken together these complementary but autonomous representations hint at a coherence of attitudes

---

[287] *LHF* c. 15, pp. 261–4.
[288] Gerberding, *Rise*, 32–8, summarized at 36; 'Gregory's picture was not quite violent enough for the LHF-author', with examples.
[289] McKitterick, *History and Memory*, 10–11.
[290] *LHF* c. 42, pp. 314–15.
[291] *LHF* c. 42, p. 314: 'Fuitque Dagobertus rex fortissimus, enutritor Francorum, severissimus in iudiciis, ecclesiarum largitor. Ipse enim elimosinarum copia de fisco palacii per ecclesias sanctorum primus distribuere censum iussit. Pacem in cuncto regno suo statuit. In multis gentibus rumor eius personuit. Timorem et metum in universis regnis per circuitum incussit. Ipse pacificus, velut Salomon, quietus regnum obtenuit Francorum.'
[292] The opening address of the Council of Clichy of 626/7 described Chlothar 'like David' (*velut ... David*), see *Concilia Galliae A. 511 - A. 695*, ed. C. de Clercq, CCSL 148A (Turnhout, 1963), p. 291.
[293] Hen, 'Bible', 283–9.

towards rulership in the later seventh and earlier eighth centuries, faint traces, perhaps, of wider collective perceptions of royal power.

Several sources suggest that the portrayal of Dagobert here was already current by the later seventh century. The first, written some sixty years before the LHF and less than thirty years after Dagobert's death in 639, is the *Chronicle of Fredegar*.[294] Here the same image of the king is presented in a much less condensed form. Throughout its account of his actions Dagobert was presented in the same light, administering justice to rich and poor alike even while he forced those nations around to submit to him. His military exploits, recounted by *Fredegar* were extensive.[295] The chronicle also noted his fame as an almsgiver, and his attempts to maintain diplomatic contact with the kingdoms around, including Constantinople, for he had made a 'treaty of perpetual peace' with Heraclius.[296] The similarity between the two accounts is striking. The images they create of Dagobert are remarkably coherent, and all the more valuable for their apparent independence from each other.

The *LHF*'s use of Solomon as a model of good rule had also been anticipated in an anonymous letter written to an unidentified young king (Clovis II? Sigibert III?) which presented a series of model rulers, biblical and Frankish.[297] Conventionally dated to the mid-seventh century, and thus within a decade of Dagobert's death, it can be used with some authority as evidence for the perceptions of kingship and the royal office in the first half of the seventh century.[298] The nameless author of the letter to the young king invoked the images of both David and Solomon, their wisdom, eloquence, and fairness in judgement, but also their successes in battle, singling out Solomon's defence of Israel from the surrounding peoples as a model for emulation.[299] He proceeded to invoke St Paul:

'Let not the sun go down upon your anger (Eph. IV. 26).' If the letter's recipient had been stirred to anger he was to immediately recall his heart to the peace of the Lord, 'which', the letter continued, 'the Lord, as it is read in

---

[294] On the date of composition of 'Fredegar' see the comments of J. M. Wallace-Hadrill, *The Fourth Book of the Chronicle of Fredegar with its Continuations* (London, 1960), p. lv.

[295] Fredegar, *Chron.*, IV c. 58, pp. 48–9, 'Avars, Slavs and all the other peoples up to the Frontiers of the Roman empire submitted'; Dagobert's campaign against the Slavs, IV c. 68, pp. 56–8; his use of the Bavarian against the Bulgars, IV c. 72, pp. 60–1; but note also the ending of Saxon tribute to the Franks under Dagobert's rule, IV c. 74, pp. 62–3; Spanish campaigns, subjection of the Gascons and Bretons, IV c. 78, pp. 65–6.

[296] Fredegar, *Chron.*, IV c. 60, p. 50. His patronage of St-Denis, 'in the hope of ensuring the patronage of the saint', recorded at IV c. 79, pp. 67–8.

[297] *MGH Epp.* III, no.15 (c. 645?), pp. 457–60. E. Dümmler, 'Ermahnungsschreiben an einen Karolinger', *NA* 13 (1887), 191–6, addressing its reuse as advice for a young Carolingian prince with a grandfather called Charles, and the possible candidates at 192.

[298] M. Garrison, 'Letters to a King and Biblical *exempla*: the examples of Cathwulf and Clemens Peregrinus', *EME* 7.3 (1999), 305–28, at 311; Hen, 'Bible', 285–6; Reydellet, *Royauté*, 545 n. 160; Anton, *Fürstenspiegel*, 51–2, noting in passing its thematic closeness to the *LHF*.

[299] *MGH Epp*, III, no. 15, p. 458.

scripture, has promised by his words to bestow upon the patient soul of he is who is deemed worthy.'[300]

Look to the Lord, the recipient was advised, let Him guide your path, 'that you might live on the earth in peace'.[301]

Towards the end of the late ninth century the letter would be adapted for a new recipient, a member of one of the Carolingian families. That it could be so reflects the fact that by the late seventh century we begin to see, in the use of biblical *exempla* and increasingly confident moralizing on the nature of rulership, a move towards the general application of these ideas and the emergence of ways of thinking about kingship that the Carolingian intellectuals would develop to new heights. It is to them that we must now turn.

[300] *MGH Epp.* III, no. 15, p. 459: ' "Sol non occidit super iracundiam vestram." Sed si aliquid contigerit, unde ira commotus fueris, cito animus suam recipiat pacem, quia Dominus, sicut legitur in scripturis, super pacientem animum verbum promissionis suae dignatur largiri.'
[301] *MGH Epp.* III, no. 15, p. 459: 'Ergo tu expecta Dominum, ut ipse custodiat viam tuam, ut et tu cum pace inhabites terram . . . '.

3

Dominus Pacificus:
The Age of Charlemagne

'To Charles, Augustus, crowned by God, great and peacemaking emperor of
the Romans, life and victory!'

Coronation *laudes*, Christmas Day 800 (*Annales regni Francorum*, version)

PATTERNS OF PEACE IN CAROLINGIAN CULTURE

In the previous chapter we have seen the prominence of peace in virtually all the local
political idioms of the post-Roman West. Each, in their own fashion, anticipated
certain elements of the Carolingian political deployment of the theme of peace
addressed in this chapter. Some were reflective of the particular interests of
individual rulers and their advisors, such as Gundobad and Avitus, or of perspectives
of particular scholars, such as Eugenius II and his circle of Toledan scholars. In the
later eighth and ninth centuries we move into a far denser political culture. Peace
again became the subject of poetry and political polemic, but was also discussed in
letters of admonition and in numerous Carolingian 'mirrors for princes', prescriptive
works that sought in various ways to cast Frankish rulership, particularly after
Charlemagne's death, into a comprehensible and, more pressingly, a potentially
replicable office. Notions of kingship found expression in increasingly elaborate
king-making *ordines* whose prayers and blessings articulated kingship's aspirational
forms even as they ritually created it. In abstract terms, the long-term legacy of the
rationalized intervention that removed the last Merovingian and installed a Pippinid
in his place would be the continued susceptibility of Carolingian authority to further
interventions of a comparable kind: kingship could be made and potentially un-
made, or argued into and out of existence. The family rebellions of Louis the Pious'
reign of the late 820s and 830s, Louis' enforced penance at Soissons in 833, and the
texts it generated attest to a political culture (one might say in a limited sense a 'public
sphere') increasingly characterized by a fluent and often highly polemical conversation on the nature of power. This conversation was a development not only of a
specific event—the emergence of the Carolingians—but also of the formulation of a
language of political authority under Charlemagne apparent, for example, in the
capitulary record, that was initially intended to promulgate royal authority but

which was rapidly adopted by ninth-century Carolingian intellectuals as a means of independently interrogating and reacting to that authority. And this was, to borrow Dr Johnson's distinction, *conversation*, not just talk. Complicating this process were further historical developments, in particular the partition of Verdun in 843, which added additional layers of potential partisanship and political perspective.

The treatments of peace we will examine here are elements of this broader process. They might also be seen as a component of a Carolingian discourse on ideal forms that included Christian society and practice, monastic community, political unity, and lay life and conduct.[1] Unsurprisingly, bearing in mind the number of figures who turned their minds to the subject, my approach is selective, for the Carolingian period offers a wealth of material.[2] This wealth has not gone unnoticed. 'For the first time in the history of the West', Eugen Ewig observed of this period, 'the idea of peace revealed its revolutionary strength'.[3] Donald Bullough answered his own question ('was there a Carolingian anti-war movement?') negatively, but demonstrated nevertheless that the period undoubtedly witnessed a shifting interest and sustained investment in the idea of peace.[4]

This range of material means that a sketch of those shifts might be useful at this stage. Peace was part of Carolingian claims to power from its birth. In the mid-eighth century, papal sanction of the Pippinid coup rested upon a perception, espoused by some at least, that Merovingian weakness threatened social order as a whole.[5] Carolingian apologists would go on to construct narratives portraying the dynasty as the long-term defenders and keepers of Frankish peace. Einhard's portraits of the capable Charles Martel and the haplessly trundling Childeric III, who was relegated to the reception and dismissal of foreign legates, with their implicit contrast of true political *potentia* realized through activity set against the empty titulature and hollow symbolics of the Merovingian, remain the best known in all Carolingian history.[6] Less commonly noted is the arena in

---

[1] J. L. Nelson, 'Presidential Address IV: Bodies and Minds', *TRHS*, sixth series, 15.1 (2005), 1–27, esp. 3. E. Boshof, 'Einheitsidee und Teilungsprinzip in der Regierungszeit Ludwigs der Frommen', in P. Godman and R. Collins (eds), *Charlemagne's Heir: New Perspectives on the Reign of Louis the Pious (814–840)* (Oxford, 1990), 161–89; H. Beumann, *'Unitas ecclesiae-unitas imperii-unitas regni*. Von der imperialen Reichseinheitsidee zur Einheit der regna', *Settimane* 27 (Spoleto, 1981), 531–71; U. Penndorf, *Das Problem der 'Reichseinheitsidee' nach der Teilung von Verdun (843). untersuchen zu den späten Karolingern* (Munich, 1974); M. Cristiani, *Dall'unanimitas all'universitas: da Alcuino a Giovanni Eriugena: Lineamenti ideologici e terminologia politica della cultura del secolo IX* (Rome, 1978), 7–28.

[2] Bonnaud-Delamare, *L'idée de paix* remains the bridgehead study of the subject.

[3] Ewig, 'Königsgedanken', 63.

[4] D. Bullough, 'Was there a Carolingian anti-war movement?', *EME* 12.4 (2004), 365–76, at 376.

[5] *ARF s.a.* 749, p. 8. H. Büttner, 'Aus den Anfängen des abendländischen Staatsgedankens: die Königserhebung Pippins', *Das Königtum*, VuF 3 (1956), 155–67, at 160–1.

[6] C. Bouchard, 'Images of the Merovingians and the Carolingians', *History Compass* 4.2 (2006), 293–307; P. Fouracre, 'The Long Shadow of the Merovingians', *Charlemagne*, 5–22, at 6. P. Barnwell, 'Einhard, Louis the Pious and Childeric III', *Historical Research* 78 (2005), 129–39.

which Einhard chose to delineate their respective identities. Charles defended the peace of his kingdom, guarding it against both internal usurpation and external conquest. The final duties stripped from Childeric, and by implication the activities through which his authority was most fundamentally expressed, were his exchanges with foreign kingdoms and the establishment of good relations, as he represented the Frankish people as a whole in their dealings with other peoples. The loss of this role was the last act in the pantomime of power Einhard portrayed Merovingian rule as having become. Childeric acted the peacemaker. Charles *was* the peacemaker, the real performer of what the ninth-century author of the poem on Count Timo called the *res regia*.

The ninth century saw war and peace occupying a rather more complex relationship than they had done in the later eighth century. Characterized by slowed and more scattered military activity and the repeated problems of internal violence and interfamilial rivalry, from the late 820s onwards these problems would culminate in the trauma of Fontenoy and in 843 the creation of the three kingdoms.[7] The problem for Charlemagne's grandsons and, in time, his great-grandsons, was that the Franks had become their own neighbours. There had been sub-kingdoms before, of course, usually ruled by cadet Carolingians, but these had always existed in clear subordination to higher, paternal power.[8] Verdun created three notionally equal kingdoms. The ramifications of this change were enormous: war became problematic on several levels when fellow Carolingians and brother kings were one's neighbours, rather than Saxons, Bretons, or Slavs. Charles the Bald, Lothar, and Louis the German, and in time their heirs, were forced to find ways to accommodate their literal *proximi*, maintaining notions of Carolingian unity and developing modes of accommo-dation, a series of ritualized and written treaties in what Anglophone scholars have come to call in a phrase evocative of contemporary Carolingian political language, 'the regime of fraternal concord'.[9] The decades after Fontenoy were characterized by shifting alliances, escalating moments of predatory aggression between neighbouring Carolingian kingdoms and frequent climb-downs.[10] For the remainder of the ninth century, Carolingian rulers were reluctant to allow war to escalate to the scale it had reached in the early 840s, suggesting that the

---

[7] T. Reuter, 'The End of Carolingian Expansion', *Charlemagne's Heir*, 391–405; *idem*, 'Plunder and Tribute in the Carolingian Empire', *TRHS*, 5th series, 35 (1977), 75–94. P. Classen, 'Die Verträge von Verdun und Coulaines 843 als politische Grundlagen des westfränkischen Reiches', *HZ* 196 (1963), 1–35.

[8] B. Kasten, *Königssöhne und Königsherrschaft. Untersuchungen zur Teilhabe am Reich in der Merowinger- und Karolingerzeit*, MGH Schriften, 44 (Hanover, 1997).

[9] The specifics explored most fully in R. Schneider, *Brüdergemeine und Schwurfreundschaft. Der Auflösungsprozeß des Karolingerreiches im Spiegel der Caritas-Terminologie in den Verträgen der karlingischen Teilkönige des 9. Jahrhunderts* (Lübeck, 1964).

[10] J. L. Nelson, 'The Search for Peace in a Time of War: the Carolingian *Brüderkrieg*, 841–843', in J. Fried (ed.), *Träger und Instrumentarien des Friedens im hohen und späten Mittelalter*. Sigmaringen, 42 (*VuF* 1996), 87–114.

horrors of Fontenoy had led to a profound sense of the dangers and damage of
internecine warfare within the Carolingian body politic.[11]

If Fontenoy's carnage cast a shadow so, too, did Charlemagne.[12] By the 830s
at the latest Charlemagne's reign was seen as a past period of peace of the kind we
have seen cherished in the constructed histories of other early medieval peoples.
Nithard, closing his *Histories* disillusioned and dispossessed in late March 843,
voiced this perspective, in the process revealing the degree to which some
members of the Carolingian elite at least had internalized the political theories
of previous decades. 'In the times of Charles the Great of good memory', he
wrote, 'who died almost thirty years ago, peace and concord ruled everywhere
because our people were treading the one proper way, the way of common
welfare, and thus the way of God. But now since each goes his separate way,
dissension and struggle abound. . . . Then', Nithard continued, 'there was abundance and happiness but now there is poverty and sadness everywhere.'[13] Where
once the elements smiled down on the Carolingians now they threatened. As he
wrote, there was an eclipse and a heavy snowfall. Carolingian misrule misordered
nature's rhythms.[14] By the 880s this perspective had developed further. Writing
then, the 'Poeta Saxo' presented an image of Charles that drew heavily upon
Einhard's earlier biography, but with occasional telling additions. Writing of his
troubled relationship with his brother Carloman, for example, the poet offered
an image of Charlemagne as innately pacific, patiently bearing the competition
and quarrelling of his brother, and, to the amazement of all, never losing his
temper.[15] Notker the Stammerer's Charlemagne, dating from the same decade,
was far more irascible, but shared with the Poeta Saxo's the central characteristics
of the ruler as a fixed point of measured order.[16]

In contemporary Carolingian histories peace would also find its place, from
the seasonal rhythm of war and peace found in the *Annales regni Francorum* to
some of the more politically loaded treatments, such as the *Annales Mettenses
priores*. Alongside such larger enterprises we also occasionally glimpse privately
articulated concerns for peace. Writing from Northumbria to his pupil Joseph,

[11] J. L. Nelson, 'Violence in the Carolingian World and the Ritualization of Ninth-Century Warfare',
in G. Halsall (ed.), *Violence and Society in the Early Medieval West* (Woodbridge, 1997), 90–107.

[12] W. Diebold, '*Nos quoque morem illius imitari cupientes*: Charles the Bald's Evocation and
Imitation of Charlemagne', *Archiv für Kulturgeschichte* 75 (1993), 271–300; R. McKitterick,
'Charles the Bald (823–877) and his Library: the Patronage of Learning', *EHR* 95 (1980), 28–47.

[13] Nithard, *Historiarum*, IV.7, pp. 49–50. The translation cited here is Dutton's, *Carolingian
Civilization*, 331, with minor modifications.

[14] S. Airlie, 'World, the Text and the Carolingian: Royal, Aristocratic and Masculine Identities
in Nithard's Histories', in Nelson and Wormald (eds), *Lay Intellectuals*, 51–76; J. L. Nelson, 'Public
Histories and Private History in the Work of Nithard', *Speculum* 60 (1985), 251–93.

[15] *MGH Poetae* IV, p. 59, lines 177–80.

[16] P. J. E. Kershaw, 'Laughter After Babel's Fall: Misunderstanding and Miscommunication in
the Early Middle Ages', in Guy Halsall (ed.), *Humour, History and Politics in Late Antiquity and the
Early Middle Ages* (Cambridge, 2002), 179–202, at 193, with references.

Alcuin asked to be sent the latest news from Francia: was Charlemagne travelling? Was it peace or war?[17] For most of the years leading up to his coronation on Christmas Day 800 the answer to Alcuin's question would have been, unequivocally, war. 790, however, was an exception. 'The Franks were quiet' (*Franci quieverunt*) noted one annalist laconically.[18] Alcuin's pupil Hrabanus shared with a correspondent a quasi-Gregorian lament: he wished he could turn away from the stresses and demands of his current life to work quietly in his *meditatorium*.[19] Writing around 820, Claudius of Turin complained in a letter to his friend Theodimir that, because of Arab attacks upon the Ligurian coast, he was forced to hold a sword by night, books and a pen by day.[20] The cycles of war and peace that characterized Carolingian public life also shaped individual lives.

As these examples suggest, peace had become Charlemagne's legacy to his descendants, part of the burden of Frankish rulership and part of the Carolingians' myth of themselves.[21] This point is significant not simply for how it affected Carolingian self-perception and the tradition of rulership that they were part of, but also because of the way it has influenced how generations of scholars have in their turn viewed the period.[22] 'The Carolingian period hovers in a dream time', Janet Nelson has observed, speaking of many scholars' perceptions, 'when the monarch was on his throne, God was in his heaven, and all was right with the world.'[23] Carolingian rulers would likely have been delighted to know that such a prelapsarian image survived. It was, after all, their intention.[24] The powerful pull of the notion that the Carolingian period was not only a time when there was considerable emphasis on peace in political language and theorizing about peace as a product of right rule, but that it also was a tangible benefit of the regime itself', has had a powerful effect upon broader master narratives of the early Middle Ages. Perhaps most perniciously, this has fostered the image of the eighth and earlier ninth centuries as a time when, for the first time since Rome's end, state-centred institutions restored some semblance of order to western Europe. This image enjoys a currency beyond the usual restricted precincts of scholarly opinion. The annual Karlspreis, for example, is awarded by the city of Aachen to individuals—or in the case of 1986, to the entire population of Luxembourg—judged to have made

---

[17] *MGH Epp.* IV, no. 8(790), 33. Commentary: Bullough, *Alcuin*, 396–8.

[18] *Annales Nazariani, s.a.* 790, *MGH SS* 1 (Hanover, 1826), 44. *Rev ARF s.a.* 790, p. 87.

[19] For Hrabanus' lament for lost *otium* see *Ep.* 28 (840–2), *MGH Epp.* V, 443–4, at 444.

[20] *MGH Epp.* IV, p. 601. M. Gorman, 'The Commentary on Kings of Claudius of Turin and Its Two Printed Editions (Basel, 1531; Bologna, 1751)', *Filologia Mediolatina* 4 (1997), 99–131.

[21] *MGH Capit* I, no. 197 (October 833), 52; *MGH Capit* II, no. 287 (March 884), c. 1 pp. 371–5. See also the Poeta Saxo's portrayal of Charlemagne, *MGH Poetae* IV, 59, lines 159–60.

[22] R. Morrissey, *Charlemagne and France. A Thousand Years of Mythology*, trans. C. Tihanyi (South Bend, IN, 2003). J. L. Nelson, review, *The Peace of God, Speculum* 69.1 (1994), 163–9 at 168.

[23] Nelson, *Peace of God*, 168. Innes, *State and Society*, 6.

[24] P. Fouracre, 'Carolingian Justice: the Rhetoric of Improvement and the Contexts of Abuse', *Settimane* 42, II, 771–803.

an outstanding contribution to 'World Peace and Humanity'.[25] With an awareness of the political resonances of the liturgical year possessed of a genuinely Carolingian charge, the prize is awarded annually on the Feast of the Ascension.[26]

EARLY CAROLINGIAN POLITICAL THOUGHT

As much as Carolingian apologists wished to present a clean break with the Merovingian past, there were substantial continuities across 751 in political imagery and ideas, as in many other fields. Peace had its place also in the earliest works of Carolingian imagery. A notion that the Franks excelled in both peace and war was a core component of their projected self-image. The first, short prologue to *Lex Salica*, dating from the later seventh or early eighth century, claimed that the laws had been established by the Franks and their leaders 'for the sake of keeping peace among themselves'.[27] The longer prologue of *Lex Salica*, composed sometime in the 760s, offered the following catalogue of Frankish virtues: 'The outstanding nation of the Franks, established by the power of God, brave in war, loyal to treaties ... profound in counsel ... wonderfully distinguished in form, bold, swift, and austere.'[28] Appropriating the traditional categories of Roman political praise with a self-image more evocative of classical notions of barbarian vigour, the passage gave prominent place to the Franks as a people of peace.[29] The introduction's later passages drew from a different vocabulary, that of liturgy, and prayers for the Franks' collective well-being: 'May Christ guard their kingdom forever, give them rulers, fill them with the light of His grace, protect their army, support their faith. May Jesus Christ, Lord of Lords, grant them with His gracious love the joys of peace and times of happiness.'[30] Fusing the patterns of panegyric

[25] <http://www.karlspreis.de/>. See also the judicious comments of J. Story, 'Introduction', *Charlemagne*, 2–3. K. Gerner, 'King Arthur, Charlemagne and Soros: Aggression and Integration in Europe', *Yearbook of European Studies* 11. *Expanding European Unity-Central and Eastern Europe* (Amsterdam, 1999), 37–67, esp. 59–61.

[26] M. Sierk, *Festtag und Politik. Studien zur Tagewahl karolingischer Herrscher, Beihefte zum Archiv für Kulturgeschichte* 38 (Cologne, 1995), 95. Charles the Fat was himself crowned king of West Francia on the feast of the Ascension in May 885, see S. MacLean, *Kingship and Politics in the Late Ninth Century: Charles the Fat and the End of the Carolingian Empire* (Cambridge, 2003), 127.

[27] *Pactus Legis Salicae*, ed. K. A. Eckhardt, *MGH LL. nat Germ.* IV.1 (Hanover, 1962), prologue, p. 2.

[28] *Lex Salica* ed., K. A. Eckhardt, *MGH LL. nat. Germ.* IV.2 (Hanover, 1969), prologue p. 3: Gens Francorum inclita, / auctore Deo condita, / fortis in arma, / fidelibus atque amicis suis satisque firma. /profunda in consilio, / nobilitasque eius incolumna / vel forma mirabiliter aegregia, / audax, velox et aspera, / ... '. P. Wormald, 'The *Leges Barbarorum*: law and ethnicity in the post-Roman West', in H.-W. Goetz, J. Jarnut, and W. Pohl (eds), *Regna and Gentes: the Relationship between Late Antique and Early Medieval Peoples and Kingdoms in the Transformation of the Roman World* (Leiden, 2003), 21–54, at 28–30; Garrison, 'Israel', 129–30, both with extensive references.

[29] Garrison, 'New Israel', 129–33.

[30] *Lex Salica*, c.3, p. 7: 'Vivat qui Francus diligit, Christus eorum regnum usque in sempiternum custodiat, rectores eorundem lumen gratiae suae repleat, exercitumque eorum protegat atque

with the language of prayer, the framework of Carolingian political culture was put in place early. Already by the 760s we can see an emergent identification with Solomon in various works of Charlemagne's reign, before becoming a full-blown element in the political imagery of the reigns of Louis the Pious and, most of all, Charles the Bald, where it arguably reached its apogee. In his foundation charter for Prüm in 762 Pippin III, for example, presented himself as an anointed king, ruling by God's will, a king who sought to do His wishes.[31] Moses built the Tabernacle, Solomon the Temple: Pippin had Prüm.

It is with Charlemagne's sole reign after 771 that Carolingian political theory begins to flourish. The (probably) Anglo-Saxon Cathwulf, writing around 775, several years after Charlemagne had finally assumed sole rule of the Franks, enumerated the signs of Charlemagne's blessedness and implicitly his legitimacy, placing considerable emphasis upon the apparent absence of violence that accompanied his rise to power.[32] The divinely inspired death of Carloman in 771, he claimed, paved the way for Charlemagne's peacefully elevation as sole ruler of the Franks.[33] Similarly, the relatively pacific conquest of Lombard Italy of 774, and the wealth of Pavia that it brought, were telling indicators that Charlemagne the ruler and his political policies found favour in God's sight.[34] Cathwulf saw neither struggle nor chance in Charlemagne's rise to sole power. Rather, it revealed the effortless unfolding of right order: Carolingian ambition and divine plan ran smoothly in parallel. God, Cathwulf stressed, was with the Franks, and Charlemagne won the day, like Moses, Joshua, Ezekiel, and Judas Maccabeus. Like them, Charlemagne stood in right relation to the Almighty. Cathwulf was the first of several Carolingian intellectuals to press home the lesson that pious kingship paved the way to victory. He also expended considerable effort explaining what that meant: the need to take counsel, the protection of the Church and the weak, and the recurrent theme of the need to give proper thanks to God for victory. It also included a rather more specific concern for peace of a certain kind: 'that the graves of Christians have peace' (*ut sepulchra christianorum*

---

[31] *DKar* no. 16 (August 762), 21–5, at 22, see Garrison, 'Israel', 131–2; B. Merta, 'Politische Theorie in den Königsurkunden Pippins I', *MIÖG* 100 (1992), 117–32, at 125; I. Heidrich, 'Titulatur und Urkunden der arnulfingischen Hausmeier'; *AfD* 11/12 (1965/6), 71–279, at 164.

[32] *MGH Epp.* IV, 501–5. On this see M. Garrison, 'Letters to a King and Biblical Exempla: the Examples of Cathuulf and Clemens *Peregrinus*', *EME* 7.3 (1998), 305–28; *eadem*, 'The English and the Irish at the Court of Charlemagne', in P. L. Butzer, M. Kerner, and W. Oberschelp (eds), *Karl der Grosse und sein Nachwirken. 1200 Jahre Kultur und Wissenschaft in Europa* (Turnhout, 1997), 97–124; J. Story, 'Cathwulf, Kingship, and the Royal Abbey of Saint-Denis', *Speculum* 74 (1999), 1–20; Anton, *Fürstenspiegel* 75–9; G. Musca, 'Caraterri e compiti del potere sovrano nella lettera di Catulfo a Carlo Magno', *Critica Storia* 2 (1962), 621–37.

[33] *MGH Epp.* IV, 502: '. . . non minimum est beatudinis signum, quod Deus transtulit illum de regno ad alterum et exaltavit te super omne hoc regnum sine sanguinis effusione.'

[34] *MGH Epp.* IV, 502: 'Sexta, quod Langobardorum exercitus ante faciam [tuam] sine publico bello in fugam conversus. / Septima: Alpes intrasti, inimicis [fugient]ibus; opulentissimam quoque civitatem etiam Papiam cum rege sine cruoris [effusione et insuper] cum omnibus thesauris eius adprehendisti.'

pacem habeant.[35] The dead, no less than the living, were protected by Charlemagne. Cathwulf's mode of kingship has been characterized as 'a piety of propitiation derived from Old Testament models'.[36] The theme of bloodless victory, and an image of Charlemagne's kingship that was simultaneously righteous, ambitious, but at heart non-violent was a theme to which he returned in the letter's closing verse, praising God for having increased Charlemagne's kingdom without war, even though impious war (*impia bella*) itself had come to Charlemagne from throughout the world.[37]

Cathwulf's skeletal narrative, needless to say, stands in stark opposition to what we can recover of the far more complex reality, and his insistence upon the peculiar bloodlessness of Charlemagne's rule rings hollow. The precise circumstances of Carloman's death in December 771 are obscure to us (perhaps intentionally so), though the fraught and competitive character of his relationship with his elder brother is clear.[38] Supposedly placid Italy would revolt within a matter of months after Cathwulf wrote. That Cathwulf did so in any case at a time when the Carolingian war-machine was constantly engaged, offensively, against its neighbours, and in 775 in particular against the Saxons, heightens the dissonance between his letter and the world in which it was produced. Cathwulf's letter is an awkward document, stitching together an idealized image of contemporary events with lessons of scripture and notions of kingship drawn from Ambrosiaster and *De XII abusivis*. This seventh-century Irish text served as a key source for several generations of Carolingian scholars, but Cathwulf seems to have been the first.[39] Most pertinent for Cathwulf's purposes was the ninth abuse; the *rex iniquus* (filtered, perhaps through intermediary texts) underpinned Cathwulf's portrait of the idealized path of blessings along which the victorious Charlemagne progressed towards power.[40] Follow the eight pillars of just kingship (*veritas, patientia, largitia*...), counselled Cathwulf, spinning out the cosmic consequences from Charlemagne's authority, and even the winds and storms would be tranquil.[41] Fail to rule rightly, however, and the results would be disastrous: dissent, infertility, storms at sea and, ultimately, destruction.[42] The truth of his lessons Cathwulf saw attested to all around him, in the examples of Waifar of Aquitaine, killed in 768, and the dispossessed King Desiderius. Neither the Aquitanian duchy nor the

---

[35] *MGH Epp.* IV, 504.

[36] Garrison, 'Letter', 327.

[37] *MGH Epp.* IV, 503: 'Laudemus sanctam Trinitatem, sed bello fortiter augens, / Hic Deus adiutor validus tibi semper adinstat; / Impia qui tulit tibi semper bella per orbem.'

[38] R. McKitterick, *History and Memory in the Carolingian World* (Cambridge, 2004), 117.

[39] Story, 'Cathwulf', 2 n. 3, 8; Anton, 'Königsvorstellungen', 298–301; *idem*, 'Einfluß', 598–9.

[40] Bullough, *Alcuin*, 240.

[41] *MGH Epp.* IV, 503: 'Et tunc erit aeris et tempestatum tranquillitas, terre maris cum omnibus in eis nascentibus fecunditas, et dominaberis etiam multis feliciter gentibus et inimici tui ante faciem tuam cadunt et reliqua.'

[42] *MGH Epp.* IV, 503: 'Pro regis iniustitia sui ipsius infelicitas erit, uxoris filiorum quoque dissensio, populorum fames, pestilentia, infecunditas terre, maris quoque tempestatibus fructus terrarum diversis percussis, et ab inimicis suis superatus ex explusus de regno.'

Lombard kingdom had been buttressed by pillars of right rule. Consequently, they collapsed. Nature reflected rulership, and current events gave credence to Cathwulf.

Cathwulf may have evokes Moses in his letter to Charlemagne, but from the 770s onwards it was David, the prayerful warrior king, whom most scholars invoked when offering praise to Charlemagne.[43] Solomon was also invoked in these decades, as an ideal of righteousness, the respectful recipient of God-given wisdom and, with growing frequency, as an ideal of peaceful rule. As part of a general argument for Frankish support for, and Carolingian obligation to, the Papacy, Pope Paul evoked Solomon to Pippin the Short in a letter of the early 760s, albeit alongside the more prominently portrayed David, *rex et propheta.*[44] Solomon, the most multifaceted of rulers, offered an increasingly attractive model to those seeking to invoke a royal ideal in the late 770s. In these years, Charlemagne's court was becoming a powerful political centre, the focus of tribute and diplomatic contacts, and Charlemagne's view of his position, manifest in the mandates he issued at Herstal in March 779, suggests a ruler with a growing interest in peace and order. The capitulary that recorded them shows a king working in harmony with the Church and aristocracy, acting in fulfilment of God's will (*secundum Dei voluntatem*), increasingly concerned with justice, orthodoxy, and the suppression of violence. The latter directives included outlawing the formations of armed bands, sworn associations (save for collective charity, or mutual support after fire or shipwreck), and decreeing that those travelling 'whether going to the palace or elsewhere' (*ad palatium aut aliubi pergunt*) could do so without the risk of assault by armed gangs. For Charlemagne and his churchmen, as for Bede a half-century before, a righteous king ensured peaceful travel for all his subjects. Feuds were to be settled by payment, under threat of royal involvement.[45] It would be going too far to see these injunctions comprising a 'peacemaking' policy on Charlemagne's part but they initiate a deepening concern to address lawlessness and uphold justice within the Frankish territories that might be said to find its counterpart in external relations—the annual reports of treaties, hostages, and tribute-giving that closed the regular campaign season.[46] Together with the anointing of Pippin and Louis in Rome in 781, and the emphasis upon unbroken peace within the kingdom (amongst other royal benefits) in the prayer *Prospice*, these developments

---

[43] Bullough, *Alcuin*, p. 368 n. 116; Garrison, 'Israel', 153. T. F. X. Noble, 'Tradition and Learning in Search of Ideology: the *Libri Carolini*, in R. Sullivan (ed.), *'The Gentle Voice of Teachers': Aspects of Learning in the Carolingian Age* (Columbus, OH, 1995), 227–60, at 239–40.

[44] *Cod. Car.* no. 33, *MGH Epp.* III, p. 540. D. H. Miller, 'The Roman Revolution of the Eighth Century: A Study of the Ideological Background of the Papal Separation from Byzantium and Alliance with the Franks', *Medieval Studies* 36 (1974), 79–133, at 128–9.

[45] *MGH Capit.* I, no. 20 (779), pp. 46–52, c. 14 (*de trustis*), c. 16 (*coniurationes*), c. 17 (*de iterantibus*), c. 22 (*faida*).

[46] T. F. X. Noble, 'From Brigandage to Justice: Charlemagne, 785–794', in C. Chazelle (ed.), *Literacy, Politics, and Artistic Innovation in the Early Medieval West: Symposium on Early Medieval Culture* (London, 1992), 49–75.

contributed to a context in which identifications with Solomon were increasingly appropriate.[47]

Later capitularies of the 780s and 790s would reiterate the concerns of Herstal but it was Alcuin's arrival at court that many have seen as the impetus behind the heightened emphasis upon peace evident in subsequent capitularies.[48] In the *Admonitio generalis* of 789, the key document of Carolingian reform and Alcuin's influence upon it,[49] Charlemagne's opening address to his audience of churchmen and secular dignitaries offered 'the greeting of perpetual peace and blessedness in Christ the Lord, God Eternal'.[50] Beginning in a contemplative mode, the *Admonitio* explained that Charlemagne reflected with 'a peaceful and pious mind' (*pacifico pie mentis*) upon the bond that linked the Franks to God, His clemency, and the need for it to be recognized by prayer and good works.[51] If Charlemagne's decision to pursue reform and correction was the product of the king's peaceful mind, peaceful, too, was the society he sought to create. Chapter 62 of the *Admonitio* expounded how such peace was to exist in Christian society, between 'all persons everywhere', both clerical and lay, great and small. Matthew V.23–4 was invoked: 'For nothing is pleasing to God without peace, not even the offering of the holy sacrifice at the altar.'[52] A sequence of scriptural passages followed (Matt. XIX.19, V.9; John XIII.35), stressing the need for peace and mutual love within society. This exhortation to collective concord closed with a further passage: 'The children of the devil always exert themselves to provoke dissension and discord but the children of God always strive for peace and love.'[53] Conformity to the canons of orthodoxy, expounded at length in the text, was a form of peacekeeping as it maintained the unity of the Carolingian Church. That unity, in its turn, paved the way for 'the eternal joys of peace'.[54] The uniform observance of the Roman chant offered another path to peace and a reminder of the unifying power of prayer.[55] *Pax ecclesiae* would thereafter be a frequent concern in Carolingian legislation.[56] The *Admonitio* revived the theme at its close, in a

---

[47] Jackson, *Ordines*, 458, comment Nelson, 'Kingship', 57–8, with translation at 58.
[48] Nelson, 'Brüderkrieg', 88; J. M. Wallace-Hadrill, *Early Germanic Kingship in England and on the Continent* (Oxford, 1971), 114–15.
[49] On Alcuin's involvement in the drafting of this capitulary, D. Bullough, *Alcuin*, 312–13, noting at 312 that 'Alcuin's direct involvement seems certain'. See also F.-C. Scheibe, 'Alcuin und die *Admonitio Generalis*', *DA* 14 (1958), 221–9. M. Alberi, 'The Evaluation of Alcuin's Concept of the *Imperium Christianum*', in J. Hill and M. Swann (eds), *The Community, the Family and the Saint* (Turnhout, 1998), 3–17.
[50] *MGH Capit.* I, no. 22 (789), 52–62 at 53.
[51] M. de Jong, 'Charlemagne's Church', in J. Story (ed.), *Charlemagne, Empire and Society* (Manchester, 2005), 103–35, at 115.
[52] *MGH Capit.* I, no. 22 (789), c. 62, p. 58.
[53] *MGH Capit.* I, no. 22 (789), c. 62, p. 58, drawing upon I John III.10.
[54] *MGH Capit.* I, no. 22 (789), c. 60, p. 57.
[55] *MGH Capit.* I, no. 22 (789), c. 80, p. 61.
[56] E.g. *MGH Capit.* I, no. 98 (801), c. 2, p. 205; *MGH Capit.* II, nos. 228 (850) c. 21, p. 122; 248 (847), c. 5, p. 177.

succinct tripartite declaration: 'Peace to those who preach. Grace to those who obey. Glory to our Lord, Jesus Christ.'[57]

Beyond the frontiers of Francia different considerations took over. There, pacification took place in its more sinister, euphemistic sense. Pippin III's 768 memorandum for the ordering of the recently subdued Aquitaine is its earliest manifestation,[58] but it also characterized later Carolingian legislation in annexed territories such as in Italy after 774.[59] Similarly, legislation in conquered territory resulted in the first Saxon capitulary (785?) which presented a desire for peace as a prime aim of Carolingian control. The Saxon *comites* were singled out for special attention: 'All counts are to strive to live in mutual peace and concord.'[60] Similar directives were addressed to post-Agilolfing Bavaria.[61]

Court poetry, similarly, had presented an image of Charlemagne as a king *pacificus* in these years. The significance of these references in praise poetry can be overstated. At best they were encountered fleetingly by those present when they were recited, whilst an even smaller number may have encountered them in written form, and they scarcely constitute elements in the development of a coherent 'ideology'.[62] What they do indicate, however, is an awareness on the part of a number of individual authors that peace and notions of pacific rule were not merely acceptable at Charlemagne's court, but were themes worth emphasizing. As such, we might read them as indicators of reception: of an individual's awareness of Charlemagne's own ideological projections, of other authors' preoccupations, and a desire to harmonize with both.

Already in 780 Adam of Masmünster had closed his prefatory verse in the copy of Diomedes he presented to Charlemagne with an image of the king ultimately attaining a place in heaven, 'where concord reigns, joined with

---

[57] *MGH Capit.* I, no. 22 (789), p. 62.

[58] *MGH Capit.* I, no. 18 (768), pp. 42–3, discussed by F. L. Ganshof, 'The Use of the Written Word in Charlemagne's Administration', *The Carolingians and the Frankish Monarchy*, trans. Janet Sondheimer (London, 1971), 125–6.

[59] Note the increased emphasis upon peacemaking found in the Lombard recension of the Capitulary of Herstal, *MGH Capit.* I, no. 20 (779), c. 8, p. 48; c. 12, pp. 49–50. See also the following Italian capitularies which take social order as their central concerns; no. 89 (780 x 790), pp. 188–9; no. 90 (781?), pp. 190–1; no. 91(782 x 786), pp. 191–3. On Carolingian legislation after 774 and the legitimation of Frankish authority: F. Manacorda, *Ricerche sugli inizii della dominazione dei Carolingi in Italia* (Rome, 1968), 38–43. This emphasis upon peace continued into the later ninth century, e.g., Louis II's capitulary prior to his Beneventan campaign, *MGH Capit.* II no. 218 (866), c. 3, p. 95. Peace and order in Bavaria: *MGH Capit.* I, no. 68 (801 x 813), c. 1, pp. 157–8, at 157; no. 69 (810), pp. 158–9.

[60] *MGH Capit.* I, no. 26 (775–90), c. 29, p. 70, echoed in no. 97 (790 x 800), p. 203. Unity and peace within the Saxon lands, and Charlemagne's power over them, was a theme repeated in the less punitive second Saxon capitulary: *MGH Capit.* I, no. 27 (797), c. 1, p. 71.

[61] *MGH Capit.* I, no. 68 (801 x 813), c. 1, pp. 157–8, at 157; no. 69 (810?), pp. 158–9.

[62] On the increasing reluctance to read coherent ideological statements into disparate, and often author-driven, works of art and literature see Bernhardt, 'Concepts', 141–63; Warner, 'Ideal and Action', 1–18.

perpetual peace'.[63] Shortly after, in the dedicatory verse that prefaced his Gospel lectionary produced to mark Pippin's baptism in Rome, Godescalc, writing between 781 and 783, gave prominent place in his praise to Charlemagne 'the good and renowned hero of the whole world', 'trusting in heavenly arms', *pacificus rector*, a 'patient and impartial ruler', before moving on to catalogue his (many) other virtues ('provident and wise, learned in the liberal arts, guardian of justice').[64] 'Hibernicus Exul' offered a comparable poetic meditation upon Charlemagne's successes, marvelling at opulent tributes offered to him by the other princes of the world, before launching, with mock hesitation, into his own poetic tribute.[65] Taking the form of a verse dialogue between poet and Muse, Hibernicus' poem shifts from a description of tribute-giving to poetic self-questioning (what can a poet ever give a king?) to full-throated panegyric. Hibernicus took as his departure point his crushing of Tassilo's 'rebellion' in 787, as he asks his Muse to tell him 'Who is attempting to destroy our father's excellent peace?' Who has pointlessly disturbed the extraordinary peace with violence?'[66] The Devil, the 'slippery serpent' (*lubricus serpens*), comes the answer, a cue for a brief recapitulation of the destruction of Eden's peace that he had also caused, and his continued disruptive influence.[67] In Bavaria as in Eden the Devil, wrote Hibernicus, 'tears apart treaties of perfect peace, and delights to commit peoples to savage war'.[68] Whilst the surviving poem is fragmentary its closing lines returned to the themes with which Hibernicus had begun, gift-giving, the return of proper hierarchy, and right order re-established.[69] Later poets picked up the theme. Fardulf, the Lombard appointed abbot of St-Denis in return for his exposure of Pippin the Hunchback's rebellion in 792, praised '*pacificus*

---

[63] *MGH Poetae* I, p. 94, lines 19–20: 'Pacis ubi iugiter perpes concordia regnat, / Dulcia stelligeri gaudens per pascua celi.'

[64] *MGH Poetae* I, p. 94, lines 1–10: 'Orbe bonus toto passim laudabilis heros, / Inclytus in regno, fretus caelestibus armis, / Laude triumphator, dudum super aethera notus, / Iure patrum solio feliciter inclitus heres, / Pacificus rector, patiens dominator et aequus, / Praelatus multis, humili pietate superbus, / Providus ac sapiens, studiosus in arte librorum / Iustitiae custos rectus, verusque, fidelis, / Pauperibus largus, miseris solacia praestans, / Plenus honore dei et Christi conpulsus amore . . .'. Godman, *Poets*, 46–7.

[65] *MGH Poetae* I, carm. 2, pp. 396–9. For discussion see Godman, *Poets*, 60–2, (with the first 40 lines translated in his *Poetry*, 174–9); A. Ebenbauer, *Carmen Historicum: Untersuchungen zur historischen Dichtung im karolingischen Europa* I, Philologica Germanica, 4 (Vienna, 1978), 18–29. On 'Hibernicus' see Garrison, 'English and the Irish', 100–1.

[66] *MGH Poetae* I, p. 397, lines 42–3: 'Quis pacem eximiam conatus frangere patrum? / Quis frustra egregiam commovit in arma quietem?' Airlie, 'Narratives', 112–13.

[67] *MGH Poetae* I, carm. 2, p. 398.

[68] *MGH Poetae* I, carm. 2, p. 398, lines 56–7: 'Hic solus scindit perfectae foedera pacis, / Et populos saevis gaudet committere bellis.'

[69] The theme of peace was also one to which he would return after 800 see *MGH Poetae* I, carm. 3, p. 399, lines 5–6: 'Summus apex Karolus Caesar, pax orbis opima, / Huic turmas hominum subdere colla docet.' Hibernicus has also been identified as the author of Pippin's epitaph, *MGH Poetae* I, carm. 15, lines 13–15, p. 405: 'Unus amor populi, virtus, pax omnibus una, / Dilexit cunctos, unus amor populi. / Rex bonus et placidus, nulli bonitate secundus'. Airlie, 'Charlemagne', 112–13.

Carolus' in a poem celebrating the king's visit to its newly rebuilt palace complex.[70] And it was an image of Charlemagne as the peacemaker, albeit a Davidic one, that Theodulf reached for in his verse portrait of the court in 795.[71] By late 799 the anonymous author of 'Karolus Magnus et Leo Papa', written on the occasion of the fugitive Leo III's arrival at Aachen, was portraying Charlemagne as 'the *pharos* of Europe', outstripping the sun in the intensity of his brilliance, 'shining with peace and joy' (*pace nitet laeta*), and, as he had been for Theodulf, a force for order.[72]

Against this backdrop the figure of Solomon emerges with growing frequency over the 780s and 790s as several writers pursued the exegetical and etymological treatments of the name of 'Solomon'.[73] Allusions to Solomon as a peaceful ruler invariably brought with them evocations of the typological christology linking Solomon and Christ.[74] Alcuin, in his *Interpretationes nominum Hebraicorum*, restated how the peacemaking Solomon was a type of the peace-giving Christ.[75] Discussing the images of the cherubim in the *Libri Carolini*, Theodulf turned to Bede on the Temple, and his treatment of 'Solomon, which is interpreted as "*pacificus*" and represents the figure of Christ'.[76] These ideas, once restricted to scholarly cliques, began to circulate in the orbit of the royal court. Wigbod, in the heavily derivative prefatory verses to the commentary on the Octateuch that he had compiled at Charlemagne's request, praised its commissioner, happy and

---

[70] *MGH Poetae* I, *carm.* 1, p. 353, lines 11–12: 'Inter quae sancti Dionysi rector ut aulae / Fieret, indulsit pacificus Carolus.' On the palace complex of St-Denis see C. P. Loveluck, 'Rural Settlement Hierarchy in the Age of Charlemagne', in J. Story (ed.), *Charlemagne*, 230–59 at 245–6; M. Wyss, 'Un établissement carolingien mis au jour à proximité de l'abbaye de Saint-Denis: la question du palais de Charlemagne', in A. Renoux (ed.), *'Aux marches du palais': Qu'est-ce qu'un palais médiéval? VIIe Congrès international de la Société d'archéologie médiévale, Le Mans-Mayenne, 9–11 septembre 1999* (Le Mans, 2001), 191–200.

[71] *MGH Poetae* I, *carm.* 27, pp. 490–3, at 492, lines 73–4: 'In medio David sceptro regit omnia, largas / Disponens epulas ordine pacifico.'

[72] *MGH Poetae* I, 365–79, at 366, lines 22–3. For Charlemagne as *pacificus* see p. 367, line 66. On the poem and its contexts see the collected papers in P. Godman, J. Jarnut, and P. Johanek, *Am Vorabend der Kaiserkrönung. das Epos 'Karolus Magnus et Leo Papa' und der Papstbesuch in Paderborn 799* (Berlin, 2002). For a recent discussion see F. Stella, 'Autor und Zuschreibungen des Karolus magnus et Leo Papa', in A. Bihrer and E. Stein (eds), *Nova de veteribus. Mittel- und neulateinische Studien für Paul Gerhard Schmidt* (Munich, 2004), 155–75. In the early 830s Bernowin of Besançon was exploring the same constellation of rulership, light, law, and peace (*rex—lux— lex—pax*) in a *carmen figuratum: MGH Poetae* I, *carm.* 21–2, pp. 420–1. See also Angilbert's epitaph, *MGH Poetae* I, 356.

[73] See for example, Alcuin's Bible-poem 'Dum primus pulchro verat homo . . .', (*MGH Poetae* I, *carm.* 69, pp. 288–92) recently dated by Bullough to the 790s; *Alcuin*, 406–7, with its 'roll-call of Old Testament *duces* and kings . . . as models' (p. 410) including Solomon *pacificus* at p. 290, lines 117–18.

[74] *MGH Poetae* I, *carm.* 40, p. 73, lines 15–16: 'Pacificus servet quae textus littera monstrat, / Rex quoniam Christus pacifer ipse fuit.'

[75] *Interpretationes Nominum Hebraicorum*, PL 101, cols 723–34, at 726–9; 730, linking Luke II.14 with John XIV.27.

[76] *Opus Caroli regis contra synodum, MGH Conc.*, II, I.20, p. 198; for discussion see A. Freeman, 'Opus Caroli regis contra synodum: an Introduction', in *eadem, 'Theodulf of Orléans: Charlemagne's Spokesman against the Second Council of Nicaea* (Aldershot, 2003), 43–4.

famous, triumphant, pious, eager to foster a revival of patristic learning.[77] Who could count the number of books he'd gathered from so many lands?[78] Borrowing wholesale from Avitus of Vienne's verses on virginity, Wigbod offered Charles a parade of scriptural figures, inviting him to reflect upon the reigns of past kings and their achievements, and to remember David's psalms and whatever Solomon the peacemaker had written, 'he who through illuminating proverbs expressed hidden meanings'.[79]

There was almost certainly no single impetus behind this development. In general terms, it was part of a deepening scholarly engagement with the scriptural past. Its particularly political application, however, may have come from Alcuin and his circle. Joseph Scottus, Alcuin's student and the recipient of his questioning letter from Northumbria asking about Francia's state of peace in 790, was himself a poet whose verse celebrated Charlemagne's virtues, comparing him to Solomon *pacificus* in an acrostic poem of the later 780s.[80] Teacher followed pupil: 'Blessed are thy men and thy servants who stand before thee always and hear thy wisdom', wrote Alcuin to Charlemagne in February 798, quoting the Queen of Sheba's words to Solomon.[81] The remarks, at least from Alcuin's account, found favour with Charlemagne and resulted in an invitation that he, too, might wish to join the happy throng.[82] By the time the letter arrived, the Marchfield had convened and Charlemagne and his armies were campaigning in less joyous territory, Saxony. Alcuin was reluctant to join them. The prospect that he might be forced to do so pitched Alcuin into exegetical clarification. When the Queen of Sheba had said those words, he explained, she *was* indeed in Solomon's presence, but in Jerusalem ('that is the vision of peace') rather than the land of the Philistines.[83] Alcuin begged that he might be allowed to enter into the joy of Charlemagne's presence in Francia, the land of peace and happiness (*in terra pacis et laetitiae*), rather than Saxony, one of strife and wars and contentions (*terrra dissensionis et belli*).[84] Like a lamb amongst lions,

---

[77] *MGH Poetae* I, p. 96, lines 19–23. Bullough, 'Court Library Revisited', 339–40; M. Gorman, 'Wigbod and Biblical Studies under Charlemagne', *RB* 107 (1997), 40–76.

[78] *MGH Poetae* I, p. 96, lines 1–10.

[79] *MGH Poetae* I, p. 96, lines 19–20: 'Pacificus quicquid lata inter sceptra Salomon / obscurum sensu praeclara proverbia duxit'. On the poem see Bullough, 'Court Library Revisited', 339–40; M. Gorman, 'Wigbod and Biblical Studies under Charlemagne', *RB* 107 (1997), 40–76. For the poem's debts to earlier verse see L. Munzi, 'Compilazione e riuso in eta carolingia: il prologo poetica di Wigbodo', *Romanobarbarica* 12 (1992/3), 189–210, at 200.

[80] *MGH Poetae* I, p. 156, lines 31–7: 'Morsus es inferni, o rex, cuius celsa tribunal / Astra poli superat, prior a consortibus es tu, / Pacificus Salomon verusque oblatus es Isac, / En homo tuque deus, pensas qui proemia cuique, / Tu stas damnans omne nefas, defensor et ultor, / Rex pie, virtutum tibi gloria, mystice Samson, / Auxiliare decus, flos campi, summaque dextra.' On Joseph see Garrison, 'Irish and English', 105–7.

[81] *MGH Epp.* IV, no. 143 (798), pp. 224–7, at 227, citing III Kings X. 8–9.

[82] *MGH Epp.* IV, no. 145 (798), pp. 231–5.

[83] *MGH Epp.* IV, no. 145 (798), p. 234.

[84] *MGH Epp.* IV, no. 145 (798), p. 254. Bullough, 'Anti-War Movement?', 367.

Alcuin added, he was raised and educated in peace, not in the midst of battle.[85] Alcuin's evocation of Charlemagne as Solomon, and his antitheses between Francia/ Israel and Saxony/Philistia, grew from the contemporary court culture of name play. The message it carried, however, underscored Alcuin's powerful sense of the vastly different experiences of war and peace.[86] And it was in Francia/Israel where, he added, 'God's Temple is being constructed by the art of the most wise Solomon': an explicit allusion to the ongoing construction of the Aachen palace chapel.[87]

In late July of that same year, and as part of the same sequence of exchanges, Charlemagne wrote to Alcuin from Saxony, asking him for some sweet songs with which he might soften the savage fury of 'his boys'.[88] Discipline in the field was seemingly under strain.[89] Alcuin, mindful of the divergent worlds of scholar and warrior, responded to the request that his sweet melodies might be heard amidst 'the horrid clash of weapons and the raucous blast of trumpets'. Nevertheless, he sent the verses accompanied by a letter in which he mockingly referred to himself as a *miles veteranus*, and used the letter as an opportunity to offer Charlemagne advice, counselling him to cultivate his inner peace, to maintain inner moderation—the *via regia* to effective planning lay in such peace.[90] If poetry might settle the nerves of the Carolingian troops, history offered their leader useful advice. Ancient books of history, he informed Charlemagne, stressed self-control, a virtue especially vital for warriors.[91] Three things were to be considered in the face of the enemy: strength, cunning, and peace (*virtus, dolus, pax*). Collective strength could defeat an enemy. If that was not enough for victory, he counselled turning to cunning and deceit. Finally, and implicitly a last resort, let counsels for peace overcome hatred of the enemy.[92]

---

[85] *MGH Epp.* IV, no. 145 (798), p. 235.

[86] M. Garrison, 'The Social World of Alcuin: Nicknames at York and at the Carolingian Court', in L. Houwen and A. MacDonald (eds), *Alcuin of York: Scholar at the Carolingian Court*, Germania Latina III (Groningen, 1998), 58–79, esp. 67–8.

[87] Scholarship on the models for the Aachen chapel is extensive. C. McClendon, *The Origins of Medieval Architecture: Building in Europe, A.D. 600–900* (New Haven, 2005), 108–20; de Jong, 'Carolingian Church', 129; Garrison, 'Israel', 154–6; N. Hiscock, 'The Aachen Chapel: A Model of Salvation', in P. L. Butzer and D. Lohrmann (eds), *Science in Western and Eastern Civilization in Carolingian Times* (Basel, 1993), 115–38.

[88] *MGH Epp.* IV, no. 149 (798), p. 242. For Alcuin's sentiments in this letter see S. Jaeger, '"Seed-sowers of Peace": The Uses of Love and Friendship at Court and in the Kingdom of Charlemagne', in M. Williams (ed.), *The Making of Christian Communities in Late Antiquity and the Middle Ages* (London, 2005), 77–92, at 80–2.

[89] As it had been before, see *ARF s.a.* 782, pp. 58–9.

[90] *MGH Epp.* IV, no. 149 (798), 242: 'Sed inter haec morborum genera medio tramite prudens temperamentum consistit: inde tumentem furorem mitigans, hinc desidem animum erigens: et via regia in pacis consilio cuncta conponit.'

[91] *MGH Epp.* IV, no. 149 (798), 242: 'Quod militantibus virtutis genus maxime necessarium esse in antiquis historiarum libris legimus, ut cuncta sapiens temperantia, quae agenda sint, regat atque gubernet.' On this see Bullough, *Alcuin*, 267.

[92] *MGH Epp.* IV, no. 149 (798), 242: 'Nam tria videntur in hoste consideranda: virtus, dolus, pax. Primo an publica virtute vinci valeat adversarius. Sin autem ad fraudes et ingenia doli res

Having addressed the matter of grand strategy in war, Alcuin moved on to other matters, astronomical, computistical, and his own, less bloody struggle with the Adoptionist, Felix of Urgel.

Alcuin's preference for a land of peace and joy was expressed the following year, when he shied away from joining Charlemagne in a Rome convulsed by factional strife in August 799 by claiming to prefer peaceful, if squalid, Tours over gilded but turbulent Rome, and turning for justification, once more to Solomon, citing Proverbs XXI.9: 'It is better to dwell in a corner of the housetop, than with a brawling woman in a wide house.'[93] Charlemagne's response to this choice of passage has—perhaps mercifully—been lost.

Alcuin's association of the palatine chapel at Aachen with Solomon's Temple brings us to a further, if contentious, context for the growth of Solomonic associations in the later eighth century. Opinions differ as to the degree to which the Temple served as an actual blueprint for the building, though the notion that Charlemagne's throne, like that of Middle Byzantine emperors, imitated Solomon's own seems far less likely than once thought.[94] Nevertheless, whether or not the rising edifice of the Aachen chapel was intended to replicate the Temple, visitors where encouraged to draw the parallel. The verses placed around the rotunda, ascribed by some to Alcuin himself, transformed the chapel into a representation of the living Church, itself prefigured by Solomon's own Temple, evoking I Peter II.2–10:

> When the living stones are linked in peaceful harmony,
> And in even number all stand together.
> The work of the Lord who has built this whole hall shines,
> And the pious labour of mortal men is crowned with success.[95]

As with some other phenomena conventionally seen as Carolingian innovations, a precedent existed for this identification beyond Francia. The long verse inscription upon the chapel of Sant' Anastasis at Corteolona, founded by Liutprand (d. 744) in late 729, made explicit comparisons between it and Jerusalem's Temple. Its anonymous author, speaking through Liutprand, voiced the king's

referenda sit. Et si nec hoc had proficit, tunc pacis consilio inimicitiarum odia esse delenda videntur.'

[93] *MGH Epp.* IV, no. 178 (799), 294–6, at 295.

[94] Garrison, 'Israel', 155–6, with references. For Byzantium, see J. Trilling, 'Daedalus and the Nightingale: Art and Technology in the Myth of the Byzantine Court', in H. Maguire (ed.), *Byzantine Court Culture from 829 to 1204* (Washington, 1997), 217–320, esp. 222–30; G. Brett, 'The Automata in the Byzantine "Throne of Solomon"', *Speculum* 29 (1954), 477–87, at 477–8, 485–6.

[95] *MGH Poetae* I, 432: 'Cum lapides vivi pacis conpage ligantur, / Inque pares numeros omnia conveniunt, / Claret opus domini, totam qui construit aulam, / Effectusque piis dat studiis hominum.' Translation: G. Bandmann, *Early Medieval Architecture as a Bearer of Meaning* (New York, 2005), 271 n. 51; J. C. Plumpe, '*Vivum saxum, vivi lapides:* The Concept of "Living Stone" in Classical and Christian Antiquity', *Traditio* 1 (1943), 1–14.

prayer that Christ, ruling the angels, governor of all, would make 'the Catholic faith grow with me, and that You favour this temple, just as was said unto Solomon himself'.[96] In the 760s Paul the Deacon also invoked Solomon when praising the Beneventan *dux* Arichis II's chapel in Salerno, dedicated to Sophia and itself part of an impressive palace complex, and reflecting the Beneventan ruling house's own Byzantine and more specifically quasi-Justinianic emphasis upon the bond between wisdom and rule.[97]

Alcuin's claimed education in a time of peace was evidently formative: he remained anxious about war and sensitive to its dangers and disturbances.[98] These exchanges with Charlemagne form only one element of the much larger body of documentation that stretches from his early letters onwards and which reveal Alcuin not only as someone with a keen interest in avoiding the less peaceful parts of the Carolingian world, but also as a figure actively attempting to foster peace when and where he could.[99] A comprehensive study of Alcuin's thinking on peace lies beyond my reach here, but it is worth briefly considering what the most influential intellectual at Charlemagne's court thought of when he thought about peace.

Alcuin's notion of peace also clearly informed his vision of the past, and in turn, one might suspect that his sense of the past shaped the vision of his present. In his verse eulogy of the church of York, written sometime in the 780s, Alcuin offered his own treatment of the Saxon, and more particularly the Northumbrian, past and its rulers.[100] Amongst the kings discussed by Alcuin, three were prominent: Edwin, Osuiu, and Oswald. The former was a ruler of considerable importance in Bede's scheme of rule, a preserver of peace, a victor in war. The image of good kingship found in Alcuin's royal sketches suggests, as Donald Bullough noted, a general debt to *De XII abusivis*. Equally, panegyric convention played its part in shaping his treatment's form.[101] Although based upon Bede's account Alcuin developed the image of Edwin in several crucial ways. He wielded the royal sceptre without cruelty, Alcuin wrote, and with mild goodness. In turn, he was loved by his people and called 'Father of the

---

[96] *MGH Poetae* I, p. 106, line 1304, discussed by N. Everett, *Literacy in Lombard Italy, c. 568–774* (Cambridge, 2003), 249–50; C. Calderini, 'Il palazzo di Liutprando a Corteolona', *Contributi dell'Istituto di Archeologia* 5 (Milan, 1975), 174–203.

[97] K. Neff, *Die Gedichte des Paulus Diaconus* (Munich, 1908), no. 4, p. 15. On Arichis' patronage see J. G. Mitchell, 'Arichis und die Künste', in H.-R. Meier, C. Jäggi, and P. Büttner (eds), *Für irdischen Ruhm und himmlischen Lohn: Stifter und Auftraggeber in der Mittelalterlichen* (Berlin, 1995), 47–64.

[98] See, for example, the concern he expressed when writing to Riculf, Charlemagne's court-chaplain, that his friend would return in peace, *MGH Epp.* IV, no. 25 (794?), pp. 66–7.

[99] Jaeger, ' "Seed-sowers" '.

[100] Godman, *Alcuin*, pp. xxxix–xlvii; D. Bullough, 'Hagiography as Patriotism: Alcuin's "York" Poem and the Early Northumbrian *vitae sanctorum*', in E. Patlagean and P. Riché (eds), *Hagiographie, cultures, et sociétés. IVᵉ–XIIᵉ siècles: actes du colloque organisé à Nanterre et à Paris (2–5 Mai 1979)* (Paris, 1981), 339–59.

[101] Bullough, *Alcuin*, 275–6.

homeland' (*pater patriae*), an honorific traditionally bestowed by the Senate upon emperors.[102] Alcuin's Edwin, like Bede's, was a victorious war-leader, bringing many peoples under his *imperium*.

> Meanwhile, whilst the powerfully armed one ruled the tribunal of his kingdom in calm peace, with wars stilled everywhere, he restrained his peoples with the strong reins of justice.[103]

Alcuin's portrait of Edwin omitted several key elements in the *Historia Ecclesiastica*, including two of its best-known images: the image of the sparrow through the hall and Bede's account of bowls by the wayside and the safety of mother and child. Alcuin emphasized instead the king as lawgiver; it was in his concern for justice that the foundations of Edwin's peaceful rule lay.[104] Fear of due punishment prevented acts of violence, and made Edwin's subjects adhere to the law that he had imposed.[105] The shift is significant. Bede had said nothing of Edwin the lawmaker, nor has any other evidence come down for seventh-century Northumbrian law. Either Alcuin knew of such legislation (perhaps) or, more likely, he read Bede's account of Northumbrian peace and order with an implicit assumption that such a state could only be the product of effective and enforced law, of the kind we have seen Charlemagne putting in place at Herstal in 779.

The present was rarely far from Alcuin's image of the past. Looking back from the 780s, a period of bitter division within Northumbria, Edwin's reign represented a high point in insular kingship: 'Britain', he wrote, describing Edwin's death, 'has not had such a ruler again'.[106] The sentiment that his reign amounted to a golden age was underlined by Alcuin's pointed quotation from Book 8 of *The Aeneid*, and Evander's account to Aeneas of Saturn's golden age of peace, a flourish that says perhaps as much about Alcuin's Northumbrian sense of self as it does about his classical learning.[107] *Rex iustus* and *rector*, the ideal embodied by Edwin would also manifest in Alcuin's later theorizing. Oswald was also a ruler whose qualities Alcuin celebrated, again in large part because of his abilities in both peace and war: terrible to his enemies, warm towards his friends, he was 'as unconquerable in war as he was faithful to treaties of peace'.[108] So, too, Osuiu, the third member of Alcuin's triumvirate of Northumbrian kings, the most just, his

---

[102] Godman, *York*, p. 14, lines 115 *et seq.*
[103] Godman, *York*, p. 14, lines 124–6: 'Interea placida regni dum pace tribunal / Rexerat armipotens, sopitis undique bellis, / Iustitiae validis populos frenabat habenis.'
[104] Godman, *York*, p. 14, lines 115–30, see also p. 22, lines 217–18.
[105] Wormald, *Making*, 128 on the absence of any other evidence for Edwin as a lawmaker.
[106] Godman, *York*, pp. 22–4, lines 232–4: 'Eduinus occubuit regum clarissimus ille, / Post quem non habuit praeclara Britannia talem.'
[107] *Aen.* 8.325.
[108] Godman, *York*, p. 26, lines 272–3: 'Hostibus horribilis, cunctis iocundus amicis: / Ut bello indomitus, sic pacta in pace fidelis.' On *fidelitas-perfidia* as qualities see Wallace-Hadrill, *Early Medieval History*, 164–5.

laws equitable, and, like Oswald, both invincible in battle and faithful in peace.[109]
Alongside martial success and, in the case of Edwin and Osuiu, just laws, peace
played a key part in Alcuin's sketches of good kingship in his 'York' verses. It
also underlay his description of another highpoint of the Northumbrian past,
Eadberht's reign, when he and his brother, the archbishop Egbert, oversaw
kingdom and Church together, their regime characterized by *concordia*,[110] each
complementing the other: 'This one was strong, that one pious, this one vigorous,
that one kind. Each in turn preserving the laws of brotherly peace.'[111]

Perhaps of all the theorists under discussion here it is Alcuin's ideas on peace that
have been most studied by scholars, and fitted into models of Charlemagne's so-
called programme of reform.[112] Kleinclausz devoted an entire chapter to 'Alcuin,
défenseur de la paix Chrétienne', a thinker 'nourished' on Augustine's thought.[113]
Above all Anton, in what remains the standard guide to Carolingian prescriptive
political thought, emphasized the importance of what he termed Alcuin's *pax idee*,
and its Augustinian roots.[114] There is room for caution. As we have seen, rendering
down the complexities of Augustine's writings on peace into any kind of coherent
synthesis, and then assuming that that synthesis was one accessible to specific
scholars in the past, is deeply problematic. In the case of Alcuin the difficulties of
easy judgements have been emphasized by Donald Bullough who, reflecting upon
Alcuin's formative years at York, wrote with characteristic caution. 'It is impossible',
he conceded, 'to imagine Alcuin without Augustine. But how much of the Doctor's
massive *oeuvre* he read over his lifetime is only dimly recoverable from his own
writings; and how far he had followed, or endeavoured to follow the sophisticated
argumentation of Augustine's major treatises is hardly clearer.'[115] Bullough's cir-
cumspection extended directly to Augustine's impact upon his political thought:
'Alcuin's familiarity in his York years with all or substantial parts of Augustine's *De
civitate Dei*, and its consequent influence on his thinking about kingship and
emperordom, has been widely *assumed*.'[116]

Such caution is well placed. Alcuin was capable of deploying a variety of
concepts of peace, often within a single text. He was also able to draw ideas

[109] Godman, *York*, p. 48, lines 570–4: 'Legibus ille etiam fuerat iustissimus aequis, / Invictus
bellis nec non in pace fidelis donorum largus misereris, pius omnibus aequus. / Imperium retinens
septenos nam quater annos, / Compositis rebus felix in pace quievit.'

[110] Godman, *York*, p. 100, line 1278: 'Quam rex et praesul concordi iure regebant'.

[111] Godman, *York*, p. 100, lines 1282–4: 'Fortis hic, ille pius; hic strenuus, ille benignus /
Germanae pacis servantes iura vicissim, / Ex alio frater felix adiutus uterque.'

[112] A. Kleinclausz, *Alcuin* (Paris, 1948), 109–37; L. Wallach, *Alcuin and Charlemagne: Studies in
Carolingian History and Literature*, 2nd edition (Ithaca, 1968); J. M. Wallace-Hadrill, 'The *Via
Regia* of the Carolingian Age', *Early Medieval History*, 181–201, at 189–90.

[113] Kleinclausz, *Alcuin*, 110, building upon Bonnaud-Delamare, *L'idée*, at 28–30, restated at 111,
'Les lettres d'alcuin et ses divers ouvrages apparaissent tout imprégnés des idées augustiniennes sur la
paix.

[114] Anton, *Fürstenspiegel*, 99–100.

[115] Bullough, *Alcuin*, 261.

[116] Bullough, *Alcuin*, 262.

of peace from various parts of Augustine's works (and pseudonymous works attributed to him), alongside numerous other sources. Like Cathwulf, for example, he was familiar with *De XII abusivis* in some form, the influence of which informed his views of both contemporary rule and past Northumbrian kings.[117] But, as we saw in his general query to Joseph in 790, Alcuin was equally able to express an interest of his own in the matter, and to express concerns free from any sophisticated patristic underpinning.[118] Writing to Offa, for example, on Charlemagne's behalf, Alcuin expressed a familiar anxiety: that *peregrini* might travel the roads in peace.[119]

Alcuin's conceptions of peace were clearly multiple. To understand something of their range more clearly it is worth considering the ways in which Alcuin thought and wrote about peace in his letters, nearly 300 of which survive from between 790 and his death in 804. At its most straightforward peace was, alongside *amicitia, dilectio,* and, to a lesser degree, *caritas,* a key phrase in Alcuin's lexicon, itself indebted to the traditions of Christian letter-writing.[120] Phrases such as *pax tibi* or *pacifice valete* are not infrequent elements in Alcuin's farewell-clauses, as they are for others.[121] More often, however, in his letters Alcuin wrote of the peace of the Church, specifically of peace between its individual members and harmony within their collective belief; peace created through the collective will.[122] In his polemics against Adoptionism, Alcuin repeated the long-standing notion that heresy ruptured ecclesiastical harmony.[123] No less substantial was his concern over monastic disorder whether writing to his former community at York,[124] or to those elsewhere he repeatedly stressed the importance of peace within the community and within the spiritual lives of individual monks.[125] Without peace as the precondition of monastic life, Alcuin wrote in an admonitory letter to the Murbach community in 796, nothing would please God.[126]

In the wake of Viking attacks upon Lindisfarne Alcuin wrote more schematically to King Æthelred of Northumbria. In as much as the attacks were divine punishment for misbehaviour they offered Alcuin the opportunity to offer advice

---

[117] Bullough, *Alcuin*, 275–6, with citations of the possible impact of Pseudo-Cyprian on the portraits of rulers in his *York* poem.

[118] E.g., Alcuin's presentation of Jerusalem as a vision of peace, *MGH Epp.* IV, no. 145 (798), pp. 231–5, at 234; *MGH Epp.* IV, no. 198 (800?), pp. 326–9 at 327.

[119] *MGH Epp.* IV, no. 100 (796), pp. 144–6.

[120] Bullough, *Alcuin*, 294–5. M. Garrison, 'The Bible and Alcuin's Interpretation of Current Events', *Peritia* 16 (2002), 68–84.

[121] *MGH Epp.* IV, no. 8 (790), pp. 33–4, at 34; no. 55 (782 × 786), p. 99; no. 107 (796), p. 154; no. 112 (796), p. 163; no. 204 (800?), p. 337. C. Lanham, *Salutatio Formulas in Latin Letters to 1200: Syntax, Style, and Theory* (Munich, 1975).

[122] E.g. *MGH Epp.* no. 24 (793), p. 68; no. 139, pp. 220–2.

[123] *MGH Epp.* IV, no. 23 (793), p. 60.

[124] *MGH Epp.* IV, no. 74 (790 × 796), 116–17.

[125] *MGH Epp.* IV, no. 219 (801), p. 363; no. 117 (796), pp. 172–3; no. 74 (790 × 796), 116.

[126] *MGH Epp.* IV, no. 117 (796), 172–3.

for correction to both the monastic community and to the Northumbrian court. In a sequence of letters Alcuin stressed, alongside laments for the moral turpitude of his *patria*, the need for Æthelred to pray regularly, to remember the example of Hezekiah, (protected by the Lord and blessed with long life), and to be a benign ruler, *rector* not *raptor*, *pastor* not *predator*. Alcuin's sketch of good kingship included the need for internal peace, and also the particular bond with priests: 'Let there be united peace and love between you'.[127] In a second letter to Æthelred Alcuin spelt out in greater detail the moral conduct and behaviour of the righteous king, drawing in elements from both *De XII abusivis* and Isidore, and expanding the earlier notion that internal peace was crucial. History, explained Alcuin, has taught that those in the highest positions of authority (*maxima imperia*) have been brought down by internal strife (*dissensiones intestinae*) whilst the smallest state or province could through peaceful concord grow in power until it ruled over those empires that once were powerful.[128]

Alcuin's vision was one in which a strong kingdom, no less than the true monastery, was one in which peace prevailed between its members. Unanimity and social peace, manifest through collective prayer, brought God's grace. This in turn could bring about heavenly peace.[129] Similarly, the peaceful end of Charlemagne's Saxon campaigns served to extend the peace of the Church.[130] The peace of the Church and the teaching of orthodoxy led to eternal peace.[131] On another level, Alcuin made clear that inner peace, and correct observance of Christian precepts, was the path of peace (*via pacis*).[132] Elsewhere he termed this *via regia* the public road (*strata publica*), implying they were the same path, which led man to the kingdom of Heaven.[133]

An entirely conventional distinction between earthly and heavenly peace underlay Alcuin's pronouncements on *pax*.[134] Heavenly peace was true peace, *vera pax*: only it would last.[135] The precise nature of this true peace was unknowable, surpassing all understanding.[136] It came from God and it was God.[137] He, as Alcuin told the Northumbrian king Coenwulf in 797, was the True Ruler.[138] Earthly rulers were responsible for earthly peace. Good kings protected and made safe the realm: their subjects could shelter in their shadow.[139]

[127] *MGH Epp.* IV, no. 16 (793), p. 44: 'Sit una pax et caritas inter vos.'
[128] *MGH Epp.* IV, no. 18 (793), pp. 51–2. This passage discussed Bullough, *Alcuin*, 414–15.
[129] *MGH Epp.* IV, no. 17 (793), p. 48; *Ep.* 23, pp. 60–1.
[130] *MGH Epp.* IV, no. 7 (790), pp. 31–3, at 32. *MGH Epp.* IV, no. 7.
[131] *MGH Epp.* IV, no. 23 (793), p. 61.
[132] *MGH Epp.* IV, no. 256 (802), pp. 413–14, see also *Ep.* 225, p. 369.
[133] *MGH Epp.* IV, no. 193 (800), p. 321.
[134] *MGH Epp.* IV, no. 12 (before 792), pp. 37–8.
[135] Eternal peace: *MGH Epp.* IV, no. 23 (793), 60; no. 91 (794–6), p. 135; no. 205 (800), p. 342.
[136] *MGH Epp.* IV, no. 212 (800/1), p. 353, written to Riculf of Mainz c. 800, citing Phil. IV.7.
[137] *MGH Epp.* IV, no. 136 (798), p. 210; *Ep.* 310, p. 478.
[138] *MGH Epp.* IV, no. 123 (794–5), pp. 180–1.
[139] *MGH Epp.* IV, no. 41 (797), p. 84, echoing Judg. IX.15 on the duties of the anointed king and Mark IV.32 on the Kingdom of God, and hence a further parallel between earthly and heavenly rulership.

Alcuin recognized the need for effective military strength, and the benefits that accrued from terrifying one's enemies.[140] After all, Charlemagne's campaigns extended the size of the Christian peace in Europe.[141] Here, perhaps, we hear Alcuin at his most Augustinian in its commonly understood sense: Carolingian armies might bring peace.[142] Kings, like other leading figures in Christian society, were to live in peace with one another, joined, as Alcuin's letter to Offa on behalf of Charlemagne made clear, by *vincula caritatis*.[143] Christian rulers had obligations not only to their subjects within the societies they oversaw, but also for the collective peace of Christianity. Like individual monastic communities, kingdoms were themselves cells that formed part of a larger unity. The theme of inter-regnal peace was an attitude that in the eighth century seems to have been largely limited to Alcuin. In the decades after 843, however, it emerged as a dominant strand in political thought. Expounding the obligations of rulership to Coenwulf, Alcuin listed peace with friends as amongst the most important.[144] Offa was also exhorted to be peaceable, though Alcuin's writings after his death reveal that he might have found the prospect unlikely.[145] Alcuin repeated the need for peace with, and the peaceful conversion of, the Saxons[146] and later, the Avars.[147] Occasionally in his letters Alcuin addressed Charlemagne as a peaceful ruler directly.[148] In two letters from summer 799 Charlemagne was addressed as both 'David, lover of peace',[149] and as a *dominus pacificus*.[150]

In the wake of the imperial coronation—which seems to have had little impact upon Alcuin's overall perception of Charlemagne's responsibilities—and the slackening in annual campaigning, Alcuin wrote from Tours in 802 setting out what he felt were Charlemagne's duties in a time of peace.[151] The arena for peacetime government was the assembly, the physical representation of the realm, where Charlemagne ought to 'decide what is right for every rank . . . proclaim your enactments and give holy counsel that each may go home happy with the teachings of eternal salvation.'[152]

The belief that Christian communities, whether individual monasteries, the Church, or Christian society in its entirety, needed peace shaped Alcuin's

---

[140] *MGH Epp.* IV, no. 257 (802), pp. 414–16, at 414. The same idea is expressed of the Kingdom of Israel in Alcuin's commentary on the Song of Songs, *Compendium in Canticum Canticorum*, PL 100, cols 642–64, at 657.
[141] *MGH Epp.* IV, no. 7 (790), p. 32.
[142] See also Alcuin's letters to Paulinus of Aquilea, *MGH Epp.* IV, no. 99 (796), pp. 143–4.
[143] *MGH Epp.* IV, no. 100 (796), p. 145.
[144] *MGH Epp.* IV, no. 123 (797), pp. 180–1.
[145] *Ep.* 101 (796), pp. 147–8.
[146] *Ep.* 174 (799), p. 289.
[147] *Ep.* 118 (796), p. 173.
[148] *Ep.* 136 (798), p. 205.
[149] *Ep.* 170 (799), p. 281.
[150] *Ep.* 174 (799), pp. 288–9, at 288.
[151] *Ep.* 257 (802), pp. 414–16.
[152] Ibid.

conception of his own obligations.[153] His description of individual letters bringing *verba pacifica* to their readers was no mere allusion. On several occasions he wrote expressly to resolve disputes, or to counsel for peace.[154] In one of the fullest expositions of the importance of peace, to reconcile an unnamed former pupil to himself, Alcuin taught that it was always better to be the defender than the accuser: 'because the former defends with a view to peace, while the latter accuses with a view to discord'.[155] Alcuin's admonitory writings, letters, and the *Liber de virtutibus et vitiis*, were themselves manifestations of this belief in the need for churchmen to be *seminatores pacis*, preaching and making peace.[156] Writing to Charlemagne in May 799, Alcuin described himself as *pacificus Albinus*, asking Charles, as a Christian ruler, to settle the disruptions convulsing Rome, albeit disruptions in which, as we have seen, he had no stomach to play a direct role.[157] Laymen, too, had to play their part as peacemakers. This was a theme Alcuin addressed in several of his 'admonitions' to lay recipients.[158] One recipient, an unidentified *dux* and his wife, were counselled to love God and one another. By so doing peace, amongst other benefits, would blossom within them.[159]

Perhaps Alcuin's most sustained treatment of the subject, however, comes in his *Liber de virtutibus et vitiis*, a handbook written for Wido, count of the Breton March until his death in 801.[160] The *Liber* consists of thirty-five chapters, the first twenty-six of which deal with a variety of virtues, such as forgiveness and humility, alongside such vices as envy, pride, and anger.[161] The subsequent sections outline eight principal vices, whilst the last chapter contains Alcuin's comments on the four principal virtues: wisdom, justice, courage, and temperance. In its concerns this late work might be viewed as merely an expanded admonitory letter of the kind Alcuin regularly despatched to lay correspondents.[162] Like them it sought to cultivate peace in the Carolingian world at the level of its constituent components, religious communities and individual powerful men. One of the *Liber*'s chapters

---

[153] Jaeger, '"Seed-sowers"'.

[154] *Ep.* 58 (782–6?), pp. 101–2.

[155] Ibid. p. 101: 'Saepe melior est defensor quam accusator; quia ille ad pacem defendit, iste ad discordiam accusat.' On the blessedness of peacemaking see also no. 255 (802), p. 412.

[156] *Ep.* 82 (793–6), p. 125, writing to Beornwin at the Mercian court; *Ep.* 101 (796), p. 147; *Ep.* 158 (798), pp. 256–7; *Ep.* 212, p. 353. On the blessedness of those who taught peace, *Ep.* 158 (798), pp. 256–7. See also *Ep.* 132 (798?), pp. 198–9.

[157] *Ep.* 174 (799), pp. 287–9.

[158] For Alcuin's letters to laymen see D. Bullough, 'Alcuin and Lay Virtue', in L. Gaffuri and R. Quinto (eds), *Predicazione e società nel Medioevo: riflessione etica, valori e modelli di comportamento/ Preaching and Society in the Middle Ages: Ethics, Values and Social Behaviour* (Padua, 2002), 71–91.

[159] *MGH Epp.* IV, no. 69 (789–796?), pp. 112–13 is discussed, and an identification of its recipient made, by Bullough, 'Lay Virtue', 74–6.

[160] On Wido's career see J. M. H. Smith, *Province and Empire: Brittany and the Carolingians* (Cambridge, 1992), 52–3, 67–8.

[161] Text in PL 101, cols 613–38, at 617. Anton, *Fürstenspiegel*, 84–8, Wallach, *Alcuin*, 231–54.

[162] For example *MGH Epp.* IV, no. 33 (793–57), pp. 74–5.

was devoted to peace.[163] This is Alcuin's most detailed exposition of peace, and one that drew from a sermon attributed to Peter Chrysologus, though transmitted through a sermon erroneously ascribed to Augustine.[164] Whilst the text he drew from was not genuinely Augustinian, that Alcuin looked to his authority when seeking a passage on peace's character is not without significance.[165] The passage began with an assertion about the central role of Christ as *mediator* between man and God and his legacy of peace on earth:[166]

The Saviour, returning to the Father, gave the teachings of peace to His Disciples as a special gift, saying: 'My peace I give to you. Peace I leave to you (John XIV.27). In peace I dismiss you, in peace shall I find you.' Departing He wished to give that which, upon His return, He wished to find in everybody.[167]

This concentration upon the nature of Christ's incarnation, and more particularly the quotation from John's Gospel, grounds the *Liber* in the issues that had concerned Alcuin for much of the 790s.[168] The passage from John was a touchstone for Alcuin, occurring also in his treatise on Hebrew names, where it had served as a gateway by which he offered his readers the conventional reading of how peacemaking Solomon was a type of the peace-giving Christ.[169] It was also the subject of a lengthy explanation in Alcuin's commentary on John.[170]

In the course of the Johannine passage Alcuin moved from Christ the son of God as peacemaker to the wider identification of all earthly peacemakers stated in Matthew V.9's assertion that peacemakers will be called the sons of God. The act was implicitly christomimetic:[171] 'He who does not want to embrace peace does

---

[163] PL 101, col. 617.

[164] Pseudo-Augustine, PL 39, cols 1933–4, on which see W. Otten, 'The Texture of Tradition: The Role of the Church Fathers in Carolingian Theology', in I. Backus (ed.), *The Reception of the Church Fathers in the West* (Leiden, 1997), I, 1–51, at 28–9; Wallach, *Alcuin*, 241–2. The core text is Peter Chrysologus, *Sermones*, ed. A. Olivar, CCSL 24 (Turnhout, 1975), no. 53, 293–6, with commentary at 292. For Alcuin's use of Pseudo-Augustinian material in this work, Bullough, 'Lay', 85–7.

[165] On 'the blessed Augustine' see *MGH Epp.* IV, no.178 (799), p. 294. Writing on behalf of Charlemagne Alcuin also cited Augustine to Offa, no. 100 (796), pp. 144–6, at 146. In the debate over the Saxons' forced conversion Alcuin fell back upon Augustine's writings as the final authority, *MGH Epp.* IV, no. 111, (796), pp. 159–62; no. 156 (796), pp. 253–5.

[166] J. C. Cavadini, *The Last Christology in the West. Adoptionism in Spain and Gaul 785–820* (Philadelphia, PA, 1993), 55–9, 65–6.

[167] *Lib. de. Virt*, c. 6, PL 101, col. 617: 'Salvator ad Patrem rediens, quasi speciale munus discipulis pacis dedit praecepta, dicens: "Pacem meam do vobis, pacem relinquo vobis." In pace vos dimitto, in pace vos inveniam. Proficiscens voluit dare, quae desiderabat rediens in omnibus invenire.'

[168] G. Blumenshine, 'Alcuin's *Liber contra haeresim Felicis* and the Frankish Kingdom', *FmSt* 17 (1983), 223–33, at 227.

[169] *MGH Epp.* IV, no. 82 (793–6), p. 125; no. 181 (801), p. 300, citing John XIV.33, *Interpretationes Nominum Hebraicorum*, PL 100, cols 723–33.

[170] PL 100, col. 939.

[171] *Matt.* V.9 also cited to the monks of Wearmouth-Jarrow, *MGH Epp.* IV, no. 19 (793), pp. 53–6, at 54.

not want to be called a son of God. The man who disdains to be a peacemaker denies that God is his father.'[172]

A right relationship to God was predicated upon an individual's wish to be a peacemaker, an idea that also underpinned the belief Alcuin voiced repeatedly in his letters, that peacemaking was a central element in a good Christian life, whether lived by a monk, bishop, king, or, here, a layman. Returning to the benefits of Christ's peace, and his reconciliation of man with God, Alcuin reiterated the message of John, that the peace of Christ led to eternal salvation, whilst Satan's false peace led to perpetual perdition.[173] Wido was also taught the need to maintain inner peace, or at least some kind of conscious inner calibration: 'One must always have peace with [one's] goodness, and always wage war on one's vices.'[174] Alcuin moved on to explain true peace, and the external manifestations of internal peace: 'peace, which is within us, unites harmony between brothers, and affection between neighbours'.[175] Further, he added:

Peace is the mother of love, its presence a sign of holiness, of which God, speaking through the Prophet said, 'Love peace and truth' (Zach. VIII.19).[176] Peace is the purity of the people, the glory of the priests, both the joy of the homeland and the terror of the enemy, whether visible or invisible. Peace must be guarded with all our strength, which rests always in God. Who remains in Holy Peace, remains with the saints of God.[177]

The *Liber* collects many of the ideas of peace expressed elsewhere by Alcuin: peace as an internal state and as a psychomachian metaphor. *Pax* also spoke of the literal truths of Christianity, man's relationship to God. It contained a clear sense of the good Christian's duty to make peace, and the concrete benefits that accrued from the successful performance of such obligations. Alcuin closed his brief handbook to Wido with a peroration drawn largely from Ecclesiastes VI.5–20, offering the words of Solomon to the Frankish count:

---

[172] *Lib. de. Virt.* c. 6, PL 101, col. 617: 'Non vult Filius Dei dici, qui pacem noluerit amplecti. Negat sibi Patrem Deum, qui pacificus esse contemnit.'
[173] *Lib. de. Virt.* c. 6, PL 101, col. 617: 'Pax Christi ad salutem proficit sempiternam. Pax quae in diabolo est, ad perpetuam pervenit perditionem.'
[174] *Lib. de Virt.* c. 6, PL 101, col. 617: 'Pax cum bonis, et bellum cum vitiis, semper habenda est.'
[175] *Lib. de Virt.* c. 6, PL 101, col. 617: 'Pax vero, quae in nobis est, concordiam fratrum, et charitatem copulat proximorum.'
[176] Also cited in *MGH Epp.* IV, no. 312 (800/1), p. 353, and hence contemporary with the composition of the *Lib. de Virt.*
[177] *Lib. de Virt.* c. 6, PL 101, col. 617: 'Pax dilectionis mater est. Pax indicium est sanctitatis, de qua Deus per prophetam ait: "Pacem et veritatem diligite". Pax plebis est sanitas, gloria sacerdotis, et patriae laetitia, et terror hostium sive visibilium, sive invisibilium. Omnibus viribus pax est custodienda, quia semper in Deo manet. Qui in pace sancta manet, cum sanctis Dei manet.'

As Solomon said, 'The sweet word multiplies friends, and appeases enemies, and a gracious tongue in a good man abounds. Be in peace with many, but let only one in a thousand be your counsellor.[178]

Social harmony was Alcuin's final message. Appropriately he closed with Solomon's extended treatment not of *pietas* but of *amicitia*:

If you would have a friend, test him before you claim him, and do not credit him easily. For there is a friend for his own occasion, and he will not abide in the day of your trouble. And there is a friend that goes out to friendship. And there is a friend a companion at the table, and he will not abide in the day of distress. A friend if he continue steadfast, shall be to you as yourself, and shall act with confidence among them of thy household. A faithful friend is a strong defence: and he that has found him has found a treasure. Nothing can be compared to a faithful friend, and no weight of gold and silver is able to countervail the goodness of his fidelity. A faithful friend is the medicine of life and immortality: and they that fear the Lord, shall find him. He that fears the Lord, shall likewise have good friendship: because according to him shall his friend be. My son, from thy youth up receive instruction, and even to your grey hairs you shall find wisdom. Come to her as one that ploughs, and sows, and wait for her good fruits for in her you will toil but little.[179]

In texts like the *Admonitio generalis*, Alcuin helped give voice and form to the conceptualization of an idealized Frankish society. In the *Liber*, it might be said, he pursued the same goal at the level of the individual, attempting to shape not only the right behaviour and moral bearing of an individual but also, in his final sections, turning to the ways in which that individual might then deal with others. Intended for Wido, the *Liber* nevertheless taught lessons about the creation, soul by soul, bond by bond, of that same society, the strong Christian kingdom that he had sought in many of his letters.

---

[178] *Lib. de Virt.* c. 36, PL 101, col. 638: 'Verbum dulce multiplicat amicos, et mitigat inimicos: et lingua eucharis in bono homine abundabit. Multi pacifici sint tibi, et consiliarii tibi sint unus de mille.'

[179] *Lib. de Virt.* c. 36, PL 101, col. 638: 'Si possides amicum, in tentatione posside eum, et non facile credas illi. Est enim amicus secundum tempus suum, et non permanebit in die tribulationis. Est amicus, qui egreditur ad amicitiam. Est autem amicus socius mensae, et non permanet in die necessitatis. Amicus si permanserit fixus, erit tibi coaequalis, et in domesticis tuis attende. Amicus fidelis, protectio fortis: qui autem invenit illum, invenit thesaurum. Amico fideli nulla est comparatio, et non est digna ponderatio auri et argenti contra bonitatem fidei illius. Amicus fidelis medicamentum vitae et immortalitatis; et qui metuunt Dominum, inveniunt illum. Qui timet Dominum, aeque habebit amicitiam bonam, quoniam secundum illum erit amicus illius. Fili, a juventute tua excipe doctrinam, et usque ad canos invenies sapientiam: et quasi is, qui arat et seminat, accede ad illam, et sustine bonos fructus illius; in opere enim ipsius exiguum laborabis.'

CAROLUS MAGNUS ET PACIFICUS

Charlemagne's acclamation as emperor in Rome in 800 as *pacificus* marked the integration of a ruler's peacemaking qualities into formal Carolingian titulature. Its importance cannot be underestimated, inasmuch as Charlemagne's elevation to the imperial title was an event that changed the parameters within which western rulership was conceived. It reasserted an explicitly imperial ideology, investing old ideas with new force in novel contexts.

Precisely because of this wider impact, the question of Charlemagne's assumption of the imperial title remains one of the most vexed in Carolingian scholarship.[180] Complicating matters further are the multiple ideological currents and concrete political processes that converged in the events in St Peter's, and the no less numerous accounts we have of the events of the years 799–800. The consequent range of possible combinations and the interpretations they support are dizzying. Not only are many modern accounts 'collages' of elements from different sources, as Philippe Buc has rightly noted, they can be assembled into different patterns.[181] Was a concern over the integration of the Saxon elites the spur for adopting a usefully inclusive imperial title? Did the real engine lie in the micropolitics of competing local Roman elites, into which Charlemagne was dragged as a useful support by an embattled Leo? And so on. My interest here is limited to a single set of questions: why was Charlemagne called not only great but peacemaking in the acclamation? How ought we to contextualize the terms of his acclamation, and how, by implication, might it have been understood at the time? What can we say about how contemporaries viewed his coronation as a whole in terms of the image of the peacemaking ruler?

The key political events that led Charlemagne to Rome—Alcuin's city of endless quarrels—in the last months of 800 are well known, and need only detain us briefly.[182] Factional tensions within the city had exploded in April 799. Making his way through the streets to San Lorenzo in Lucina, Leo III was

---

[180] J. L. Nelson, 'Why Are There so Many Different Accounts of Charlemagne's Imperial Coronation?', in *eadem, Courts, Elites, and Gendered Power in the Early Middle Ages. Charlemagne and Others* (Aldershot, 2007), XII, 1–27; R. Schieffer, 'Karl der Große, Eirene und der Ursprung des westlichen Kaisertums', in W. Pohl (ed.), *Die Suche nach den Ursprüngen. Von der Bedeutung des frühen Mittelalters* (Vienna, 2004), 151–8; *idem*, 'Der Weg zur Kaiserkrönung 800', *Zeitschrift des Aachener Geschichtsvereins* 104–5 (2002/3), 11–23; M. Becher, 'Die Kaiserkrönung im Jahre 800. Eine Streitfrage zwischen Karl dem Großen und Papst Leo III', *Rheinische Vierteljahrsblätter* 66 (2002), 1–38; H. Mayr-Harting, 'Charlemagne, the Saxons, and the Imperial Coronation of 800', *EHR* 444 (1996), 1113–33.

[181] Nelson, 'Accounts', 8, citing Buc, *Ritual*, 50.

[182] R. Collins, 'Charlemagne's Imperial Coronation and the Annals of Lorsch', in J. Story (ed.), *Charlemagne. Empire and Society* (Manchester, 2005), 52–70; J. Fried, 'Papst Leo III besucht Karl den Großen in Paderborn oder Einhards Schweigen', *HZ* 272 (2001), 281–326; M. Becher, 'Karl der Große und Papst Leo III', in C. Stiegemann and M. Wemhoff (eds), *799, Kunst und Kultur der Karolingerzeit: Karl der Grosse und Papst Leo III. in Paderborn 799* (Mainz, 1999) I, 22–36.

attacked, badly beaten, and imprisoned by members of a rival papal faction, supporters of Popes Hadrian and Paschal.[183] San Lorenzo was his destination as it was the starting point of the Major Litany, the important papal procession to St Peter's that had taken place annually on 25 April every year since at least the sixth century. With an irony certainly lost on the participants, the sequence of events that would culminate in the coronation of Charles *magnus et pacificus* began with a violent attack on the route to the church whose initial third- or earlier fourth-century foundation had disrupted the outer precincts of the *horologium* of Augustus' Ara Pacis, a primary site of the initial conjunction of peace and *imperium*. Indeed, San Lorenzo seems to have been selected as the procession's starting point precisely because the remaining open space of the former *horologium* formed a piazza large enough for assemblies to foregather.[184]

Leo III later fled north, meeting Charlemagne at Paderborn before returning, under Frankish protection, in autumn 799. That November, Charlemagne himself arrived in Rome, with the apparent intention of restoring order in the city and addressing the charges of impropriety against Leo that the Paschaline faction had, if not manufactured, at the very least done their best to publicize. Met by the Pope at the twelfth mile from the city (famously double the distance conventionally accorded emperors) Charlemagne went on to oversee a council to discuss claims of Leo's alleged impropriety. On 23 December Leo swore a public oath of purgation, asserting his innocence. Two days later, Charlemagne entered St Peter's and was crowned by Leo's hand and subsequently acclaimed. It was this acclamation, not the crowning, that made Charles emperor. Two variant forms of the acclamation are extant, one from the *Annales regni Francorum*, the other from the *Liber Pontificalis* account of Leo III's pontificate. This is the Frankish annalist's account:

To Charles, Augustus, crowned by God, great and peacemaking emperor of the Romans, life and victory![185]

And this, the *Liber Pontificalis*:

To Charles, most pious Augustus, crowned by God, great and peacemaking emperor, life and victory![186]

Shortly after Easter 801, Charlemagne and his entourage left Rome, never to return.

---

[183] J. Dyer, 'Roman Processions of the Major Litany (*litaniae maiores*) from the Sixth to the Twelfth Century', in E. Ó Carragáin and C. Neuman de Vegvar (eds), *Roma Felix: Formation and Reflections of Medieval Rome* (Aldershot, 2007), 113–58.

[184] Dyer, 'Roman', 115.

[185] *ARF s.a.* 801, p. 112: 'Carolo augusto, a Deo coronato magno et pacifico imperatori Romanorum, vita et victoria!'

[186] *LP* II, 7: '. . . Karolo, piisimo Augusto, a Deo coronato, magno et pacifico imperatore, vita et victoria!'

How then ought we to understand the emphasis upon Charlemagne as *pacificus* that both versions share, and understand also the ideological, ceremonial, and political contexts of Charlemagne, 'great and peacemaking emperor'? Why not 'great and just', or 'great and wise'?

One context is immediately to hand, for we have already tracked the gradual emergence of an emphasis upon peace in the ambient political culture of the Carolingian court in the later 780s and 790s.[187] On at least two occasions, in the years leading up to the coronation in 800 Alcuin explicitly addressed letters to Charlemagne, his '*dominus pacificus*'. In a letter of 798 Alcuin had already reminded Charlemagne of his 'peaceful and lovable power'.[188] A year later, in June 799, he counselled peace with the Saxons, addressing Charlemagne in similar terms.[189] Those with keen memories or a version of the text to hand might also have recalled the opening words of the *Admonitio generalis* (*Considerans pacifico piae mentis...*).[190] Viewed within terms of formal political rhetoric, the Charlemagne celebrated in the *laudes* of 800 was the striving Josiah of 789 triumphantly affirmed.

Acclamation was an element of the liturgy, and the notion of Carolingian rulers as Solomonic peacemakers was already a familiar element in the Frankish liturgy by the later eighth century. The Carolingian 'Eighth-Century Gelasian' known as the Sacramentary of Angoulême, produced c. 800 probably in Aquitaine, contains two royal benedictions and a mass for a king, including the earliest extant occurrences of both *Prospice omnipotens Deus*, and *Deus inenarrabilis*.[191] Also present in the Sacramentary of Angoulême was *Qui regnis omnibus*, which outlined the need for the king to keep the peace of the people by ruling well and temperately, informed by fear of God, like Solomon, 'who ruled in a time of peace'.[192] Solomonic parallels were made also in a further prayer, *Benedic domine hos presules*, found in both the Sacramentary of Angoulême and Autun. On the grounds of its plural form this prayer has been dated to the years between 768 and 771, the period of the joint rule of Carloman and Charlemagne. It asks for God's blessing for the rulers, that the king would emulate David, ruling with sublimity, and Solomon:

Grant to them that, through your inspiration, each may rule his people with mercy and grant that he will establish and maintain a peaceful kingdom, like Solomon. Amen.[193]

---

[187] For a parallel deepening of interest in the celebration of royal victories in the 790s see McCormick, *Victory*, 362–87, esp. 384–5.

[188] *MGH Epp.* IV, no. 136 (798), pp. 205–10, at 205.

[189] *MGH Epp.* IV, no. 174 (799), pp. 287–9.

[190] *MGH Capit.* I, no. 22 (789), p. 53.

[191] *Lib. Sacr. Eng.* nos 1857, 1858, 2318.

[192] *Lib. Sacr. Eng.* no. 2316.

[193] *Lib. Sacr. Eng.* no. 2317; *Lib. Sacr. Eng.* no. 1642. Dating, Jackson, *Ordines*, 62 n.11.

If liturgical imprecation provides one context, no less important are Carolingian relations with Rome, and the rhetoric within which they were framed.[194] Allusions to *pax, caritas*, and *amicitia* recur frequently in exchanges between Rome and Francia from the 750s onwards, part of a political language whose elements T. F. X. Noble has carefully elucidated.[195] On one level this was the standard vocabulary of political alliance: it was a recurrence of the same lexicon of Christian political relations to be found in Charlemagne's dealings with other western rulers, such as the state of *pax et amicitia* Alchred of Northumbria optimistically hoped Lull of Mainz might broker with Aachen.[196] On another level again it bore a tangible relationship to a different political reality, the Papacy's move away from Byzantium and towards the Franks as their primary source of military support and political security from external pressure. Already in the *Constitutum Constantini*, often claimed as a text concocted in the papal chancery in the formative years of Carolingian relations with the Papacy, we find peace enumerated as one of the benefits (*gratia, pax, caritas, gaudium, longanimitas, misericordia* . . .) which it claimed Constantine had given the Church.[197] In the later 790s, as the rhetoric of peace was being deployed with increasing frequency at the Carolingian court, Charlemagne's relationship with the Papacy was famously schematized—from the papal perspective, at least—in one of the mosaics that decorated Leo III's newly built Lateran *triclinium*, the borders of which carried the words of Luke II.14: 'Glory to God on high and peace on earth to men of good will.'[198] Serving as an audience and banqueting hall, a site for receptions, negotiations, and celebrations, the *triclinium* was an apposite space for such sentiments, where its words glossed the activities below.[199]

---

[194] Noble, *Republic*, 256–76.
[195] Noble, *Republic*, 159, 168, 263–7.
[196] *MGH Epist. select.* I, no. 121 (773), pp. 257–8, on which see Bullough, *Alcuin*, 160–1, 243.
[197] Text: *Constitutum Constantini*, ed. H. Fuhrmann, *MGH Fontes* 10 (Hanover, 1968), 57. For the argument that it was a Carolingian product of Louis the Pious' reign see J. Fried, '*Donation of Constantine*' and '*Constitutum Constantini*': The Misinterpretation of a Fiction and its Original Meaning (Berlin, 2007) with references to earlier studies.
[198] P. Llewellyn, 'Le contexte romain du couronnement de Charlemagne. Le temps de l'Avent de l'année 800', *MA* 96 (1990), 209–25; P. Classen, *Karl der Große, das Papsttum und Byzanz. Die Begründung des karolingischen Kaisertums*. Beiträge zur Geschichte und Quellenkunde des Mittelalters 9 (Sigmaringen, 1988), 54–7; Noble, *Republic* 323–4; P. E. Schramm, *Die zeitgenössischen Bildnisse Karls des Grossen* Beiträge zur Kulturgeschichte des Mittelalters und der Renaissance 29 (Leipzig, 1928), 4–16. See also the place of peace in letters of Leo III, *MGH Epp.*, V no. 3 (April 798), 58–9, at 58; no. 5 (800), 66–9; no. 10 (808), 87–8. H. Belting, 'Die beiden Palastaulen Leos III. im Lateran und die Entstehung einer päpstlichen Programmkunst', *FmSt* 12 (1978), 55–83.
[199] On *triclinia* generally see L. Bek, '*Questiones Conviviales*: The Idea of the *Triclinium* and the Staging of Convivial Ceremony from Rome to Byzantium', *Analecta Romana Instituti Danici* 12 (1983), 81–107. For the wider history of such *triclinia* see I. Lavin, 'The House of the Lord: Aspects of the Role of Palace *triclinia* in the architecture of late Antiquity and the Early Middle Ages', *Art Bulletin* 44 (1962), 1–27, addressing Leo's Lateran at 12–13.

All these, however, are significant but general contexts. The most important and the most immediate precursor to Charlemagne's imperial acclamation and explicit identification of him as *pacificus* is to be found in the oldest set of the Carolingian *laudes*, those entered between 783 and 792 in the Bavarian-produced Mondsee Psalter. Here we find Charlemagne already styled 'the most excellent Charles, crowned by God, great and peacemaking king of the Franks and the Lombards, and *patricius* of the Romans' (*Karolo excellentissimo et a Deo coronato magno et pacifico rege Francorum et Langobardorum, ac patricio Romanorum vita et victoria*).[200] The *rex pacificus* had arrived in the Carolingian political lexicon. These words are echoed by the second oldest set of *laudes*, copied into BN lat. 13159, the so-called 'Psalter of Charlemagne', produced (perhaps) at St-Riquier, generally dated c. 795–800, and certainly before the events of December 800.[201] That the *laudes* might, in some form, have been chanted on several occasions from the 750s onwards raises the possibility that the formal liturgical identification of Charlemagne (and perhaps also Pippin and Carloman) with peace may well have an early origin, though the lack of any extant text prior to the Mondsee text makes this conjecture unprovable.[202] What is more certain is that the date of the *laudes'* entry into the Mondsee Psalter harmonizes with the emergence of celebrations of Charlemagne as *pacificus* in a range of praise poems. How well, and if it all, these poets knew or had heard such acclamations is a moot point, though we might note that in some cases—Godescalc's 781 poem, itself part of a gospel intended as a gift on the occasion of Pippin's anointing in Rome, Fardulf's celebration of Charlemagne's visit to the refurbished St-Denis— the occasions that produced the poems offered themselves as potential moments for liturgical acclamation. Either way, the conclusion is clear: the earliest evidence we have for the formal deployment of Charlemagne as *rex pacificus* points us to circles close to the Carolingian royal family and the court.

Whilst the context for the copying of the Mondsee *laudes* points to the Carolingian elite, its precise wording betrays a debt to the Latin imperial titulature employed by Byzantine emperors, apparent in a number of letters sent from the eastern empire to western rulers, and still current in seventh- and

[200] F. Unterkircher, *Die Glossen des Psalters, von Mondsee (vor 788), Montpellier, Faculté de Médecine MS. 409* Spicilegium Friburgense 20 (Freiburg, 1974), 511. The date and context of manuscript and *laudes* addressed by Garrison, 'Missa', Bobbio Missal, 190–1; *eadem*, 'Israel', 140–2. E. H. Kantorowicz's discussion, *Laudes Regiae. A Study in Liturgical Acclamations and Mediaeval Ruler Worship* (Berkeley, 1958), 33–7, remains important. For the wider context of the manuscript's production and its journey to Francia see R. McKitterick, *The Carolingians and the Written Word* (Cambridge, 1989), 252–5, Garrison, 'Israel', 140–1. On these titles P. Classen, '*Romanum gubernans imperium*: Zur Vorgeschichte der Kaisertitulatur Karls des Grossen', *DA* 9 (1951), 103–21; Kantorowicz, *Laudes*, 21.
[201] Garrison, 'Israel', 140; M. McNamara, *The Psalms in the Early Irish Church* (Sheffield, 2000), 156–60; B. Opfermann, *Die liturgischen Herrscherakklamationen im Sacrum Imperium des Mittelalters* (Münster, 1953), 102–3; Kantorowicz, *Laudes*, 14–15, 33.
[202] For the possibility that the *laudes* had been sung as early as 751 see Garrison, 'Israel', 140, noting that the *Liber Pontificalis* records them performed in Rome on Charlemagne's approach.

eighth-century Italy. The evidence is sparse but significant. Writing to Child-ebert II in the late 580s the Emperor Maurice had styled himself 'Faithful in Christ, Merciful, the Greatest, Generous, Peacemaking' (*'fidelis in Christo, mansuetus, maximus, beneficus, Pacificus . . .'*), appropriate qualities, for the letter itself was intended to foster peaceful relations between emperor and king.[203] Such terms also find occasional expression in dating clauses and even an inscription now lost.[204] In one letter of Pope Zachary, for example, written during the reign of the Byzantine emperor, Constantine V 'Copronymus' (r. 741–75) we find titles that closely anticipate the style of the royal titles afforded Charlemagne in both the Mondsee *laudes* and, subsequently, those of Christmas 800. This letter, written to Boniface in early 748 and addressing a series of questions about baptism, pastoral duties, and synodal issues immediately anticipates the *laudes'* wording, closed with a dating clause 'in the emperorship of the most pious and august Lord Constantine, crowned by God, great and pacific emperor . . .'.[205] Byzantine references of any sort disappeared from papal dating clauses in the pontificate of Hadrian I, replaced by pontifical years, a symptom of both the disengagement with eastern imperial power and the growing sense of papal confidence in the Carolingians as a nearer and more effective ally.

The Greek equivalent of *pacificus* is *eirenopoios*, and there is clear evidence that a practice of acclaiming the Byzantine emperor as a peacemaker, an *eirenopoios*, existed in the eastern court at this time.[206] In John Haldon's words they were ' . . . entirely standard acclamations of formal ceremonial occasions at Constantinople and well beforehand.'[207] The title may have had its deepest roots in the

---

[203] *MGH Epp.* III, *Ep. Aust.* no. 42 (585 × 590), pp. 148–9.

[204] Classen, 'Vorgeschichte', 103, 109–10; K. Brandi, 'Der byzantinische Kaiserbrief aus St Denis und die Schrift der frühmittelalterlichen Kanzleien', *Archiv für Urkundenforschung* 1 (1908), 5–86, at 32, 43–4, 57, 60. For *pacificus* in imperial titulature in late seventh and early eighth-century church councils see Mansi, *Concilia*, XI, 697–8, 719, 737, 909. For epigraphic evidence of its use from the Church of St-Demetrius, Thessaloniki, see A. A. Vasiliev, 'An Edict of the Emperor Justinian II, September, 688', *Speculum* 18.1 (1943), 1–13, at 5–6. For its use in a lost inscription in Sant' Apollinare in Classe, dated to 731 and the joint reign of Leo the Isaurian and Constantine V see Classen, 'Vorgeschichte', 109.

[205] *MGH Epp.* III, no. 80 (748), 360–1, at 361: 'Data Kalendis Maii, imperante domno piisimo augusto Constantino a Deo coronato magno pacifico imperatore anno vicesimo nono, post consulatum eius anno septimo, indictione prima'.

[206] On the origins of this term in imperial titulature see G. Rösch, *Onoma Basileias: Studien zum offiziellen Gebrauch der Kaisertitel in spätantiker und frühbyzantinischer Zeit*, Byzantina Vindobonensia, 10 (Vienna, 1978), 49, 118; L. Berlinger, *Beiträge zur inoffiziellen Titulatur der römischen Kaiser. Eine Untersuchung ihres ideengeschichtlichen Gehaltes und ihrer Entwicklung* (Breslau, 1935), 42–67. On acclamations in Byzantine political life see R. F. Taft, 'The Dialogue before the Anaphora in the Byzantine Eucharistic Liturgy III: "Let us give thanks to the Lord. It is fitting and right"', *Orientalia Christiana Periodica* 55 (1989), 69–72.

[207] J. Haldon, *Warfare, State, and Society in the Byzantine World, 565–1204* (London, 1999), 44.

late Republican period of imperial titulature — in the early third century Cassius Dio claimed Julius Caesar had been acclaimed in precisely these terms after his death—but over the course of the fourth and fifth centuries it had become part of Byzantium's ceremonial language, and a sporadic presence, as we have seen, in its written manifestations. Liudprand of Cremona was a rare western witness to Nicephoras II Phocas' acclamation as a prince of peace and 'the morning star' in just this fashion. Like much in Constantinople, it earned his scorn. Constantine VII Porphyrogenitus' tenth-century compilation of earlier court ceremonial, *De ceremoniis*, carried the text of several acclamations for the emperor as *eireno-poios*.[208] More particularly the text of a coronation contained in *De ceremoniis* also reveals an emphasis on peace in Byzantine court practice. The congregational cry of 'Holy! Holy! Holy! Glory to God in the highest and on earth peace to men of good will' immediately followed the moment of coronation, and was repeated in later acclamations.[209] Augmenting these sung evocations of peace were the moments in the ceremonial sequence when the emperor offered the kiss of peace to both the patriarch and higher clergy in the sanctuary and the leading secular officials outside it, mediating, in George Majeska's words 'between the two worlds, bringing the *pax* of the altar to the lay world of the empire'.[210] Liturgy was, above all, the context in which the conceptual fields of peace, defined by passages of scripture that we have already touched upon, became the spoken rubrics for collective, performed activity. On at least one occasion a foreign ruler, the Bulgar Symeon, also received acclaim as a peacemaker, a title subsequently placed upon his seal.[211] Byzantine evocations of peace in the

---

[208] Cassius Dio, *Roman History*, XLIV.49.2. *Constantini Porphyrogeniti Imperatoris De Ceremoniis Aulae Byzantinae Libri Duo*, ed. J.J. Reiske (Bonn, 1829–30) I. 63, pp. 280–4; I. 77, pp. 372–3; II.43, pp. 650–1; II.47, pp. 682–3. On this see O. Treitinger, *Die oströmische Kaiser- und Reichsidee nach ihrer Gestaltung im höfischen Zeremoniell* (Darmstadt, 1956), 230–1. The argument has been made for the essentially static character of Byzantine coronation from the later eighth into the twelfth century see G. P. Majeska, 'The Emperor in His Church: Imperial Ritual in the Church of St Sophia', in H. Maguire (ed.), *Byzantine Court Culture from 829 to 1204* (Washington DC, 1998), 1–2 n. 3, citing the evidence of the later eighth- and twelfth-century texts of middle Byzantine ceremonial edited by J. Goar, *Euchologion sive rituale graecorum* (Venice, 1730, reprinted Graz 1960), 726–30. See also J. L. Nelson, 'Symbols in Context: Rulers' Inauguration Rituals in Byzantium and the West in the Early Middle Ages', *Politics and Ritual in Early Medieval Europe* (London, 1986), 259–82, at 268 n. 38. For Liudprand of Cremona's cynical view of Nicephoras II Phocas' acclamation as a peacemaker of, *Relatio de legatione Constantinopolitana*, ed. B. Scott (London, 1993), c. 28, p. 10, with commentary at 75.

[209] *De Cerem.* I. 38, pp. 191–6, at 193–4, on which see G. Dagron, *Emperor and Priest. The Imperial Office in Byzantium* (Cambridge, 2003), 54–5; Majeska, 'Emperor', 1–11, at 3 n. 9; P. Yannopoulos, 'Le couronnement de l'empereur à Byzance: rituel et fond institutionnel', *Byzantion* 61 (1991), 71–92; C. Tsirpanlis, 'The Imperial Coronation and Theory in "De cerimoniis aulae Byzantinae" of Constantine VII Porphyrogennitus', *Kleronomia* 4 (1972), 63–91.

[210] Majeska, 'Emperor', 8.

[211] P. Stephenson, *Byzantium's Balkan Frontier. A Political Study of the Northern Balkans, 900–1024* (Cambridge, 2000), 22; J. Shepard, 'Symeon of Bulgaria—Peacemaker', *Annuaire de l'Université de Sofia St. Kliment Ohridski* 83 (1989), 9–48; R. Jenkins, 'The Peace with Bulgaria (927) celebrated by Theodore Daphnopates', in P. Wirth (ed.), *Polychronion. Festschrift F. Dölger*

context of imperial coronation are likely to have possessed contemporary currency when Charlemagne entered St Peter's, at least amongst some present.[212] Peace was a theme that was being given considerable emphasis in contemporary Byzantium. The empress Irene—whose legitimacy some saw as opening the way for Charlemagne's own assumption of the imperial title—sought to project the image of a peacemaker, perhaps unsurprisingly in an eastern empire that had been fundamentally divided by iconoclasm.[213] After all, from baptism she had borne the name that was conventionally given to foreign princes when they joined the Byzantine ruling house as the result of a peace treaty established through marriage.[214]

In conclusion, Charlemagne is identification as great and peacemaking emperor has a clear meaning and a complex provenance. It was simultaneously resonant of Byzantine titulature and the language of acclamations, in circulation in Byzantine-influenced Italy into the eighth century, but also part of the home-grown language of Christian rulership fostered in court circles from the later 780s onwards. Adopted in an early form in Carolingian court ceremonial, evocative of other Frankish prayers for kings, the deployment of these titles in St Peter's as part of a political event that was itself a confluence of multiple political interests and hopes seems apt. It seems appropriate in its own right that the event has generated so many differing interpretations, both medieval and modern.

Can we see this Carolingian concern for peace manifest itself in any of the ninth-century accounts of the event? Perhaps we can. The Annals of Lorsch (*Annales Laureshamenses*) offer the account nearest in time and perhaps closest to Charlemagne's court. The entry for 800 begins with an unambiguous statement of Charlemagne's achievements on the eve of his departure for Rome:

And in the summertime, he gathered together his great men and his faithful men at the city of Mainz. And when he saw that there was peace throughout all his lands (*et cum*

---

zum 75. Geburtstag (Heidelberg, 1966), 287–303; P. Karlin-Hayter, 'The Homily on the Peace with Bulgaria of 927 and the "Coronation" of 913', *Jahrbuch der Österreichischen Byzantinistik* 17 (1968), 29–39. At the conclusion of negotiations between Charlemagne and the emperor Michael III in 812 the *Annales regni Francorum* recorded that the legates Arsafius and Theognostus acclaimed Charles ('laudes ei dixerunt') after receiving the text of a treaty between the Franks and Byzantium in the Aachen chapel. In this context, might Charlemagne, like Symeon a century later, have also been an acclaimed *eirenopoios*? *ARF s.a.* 812, p. 136.

[212] Nelson, 'Symbols in Context', *Politics and Ritnal*, 268 n. 38.

[213] W. T. Treadgold, *The Byzantine Revival, 780–842* (Stanford, 1988), 110–26, esp. 113–14. For the question of Irene's legitimacy and its implications for Charlemagne, J. L. Nelson, 'Women at the Court of Charlemagne: A Case of Monstrous Regiment?', in J. C. Parsons (ed.), *Medieval Queenship* (Stroud, 1994), 434–62, at 446–9.

[214] A. McClanan, *Representations of Early Byzantine Empresses: Image and Empire* (London, 2002), 157; R. Macrides, 'Dynastic Marriages and Political Kinship', in J. Shepard and S. Franklin (eds), *Byzantine Diplomacy* (Aldershot, 1992), 263–80, esp. 276.

cognovisset undique per omnes fines suos pacem), he recalled to mind the injury that the Romans had done to Pope Leo, and he turned his face to go in the direction of Rome....[215]

Charlemagne convokes a great assembly—from bishops and abbots to the rest of the Christian people (*seu reliquo christiano populo*) and collective agreement is reached that Leo should purge himself. This he duly does, responded to by a collective performance of the *Te Deum*, the great hymn of thanksgiving, by Charlemagne, churchmen, and the assembled 'devout Christian people'. With no emperor in Byzantium, and Charlemagne not only occupying Rome but many of the former western provinces (*Italia, Gallia, Germania*) granted to him by God, it seemed just to all that Charlemagne be given the name emperor. The annalist continued:

King Charles himself was unwilling to deny their request: rather, with all humility, subjecting [himself] to God and to the request of the bishops and of all the Christian people, that same day of the Nativity of our Lord Jesus Chirst, he received the name of emperor, with the blessing of the Lord Pope Leo. And there, the first thing of all that he did was to recall to peace and concord (*ad pacem et concordiam revocavit*) the Holy Roman Church from the discord (*discordia*) they had had between themselves. And there he celebrated Easter.[216]

The *Annals of Lorsch* have been the subject of intense scrutiny by several scholars, most recently Roger Collins.[217] Amongst other features Collins has stressed the account's claim of the spontaneity of Charlemagne's visit to Rome, the lack of an eastern emperor, and the collective rather than purely papal initiative behind Charlemagne's elevation to an imperial title. But it is worth stressing also that, as the account above shows, the Lorsch annalist consistently emphasized Charles the peacemaker. Domestic order was his primary interest, Rome's turmoil an afterthought. But domestic peace was not simply Francia's, it was that of the former Roman territories he now ruled. The imperial title, however, was offered to him not by a discrete group but rather by the Christian people as a whole, of which Italy's bishops (and Rome's) were but one element. Finally, Charlemagne's first act was to give to the Church what he had already given to the empire he so clearly ruled in all but title: peace and concord.

If the *Annals of Lorsch* are indeed 'the nearest we can come to the view held by Charlemagne and his advisors' after the event, the fact that they place such a heavy emphasis upon Charlemagne as an imperial peacemaker is significant indeed, not least as important further confirmation that the words of the acclamation, of Charlemagne *pacificus*, reflect how he and his advisors saw

---

[215] *AL*, s.a. 800, p. 38. Translation: Nelson, 'Accounts', 2.

[216] *AL*, s.a. 801, p. 38. Translation: Nelson, 'Accounts', 3–4.

[217] R. Collins, 'Charlemagne's Imperial Coronation and the Annals of Lorsch', in Story (ed.), *Charlemagne*, 52–70, esp. 64–9.

himself, and wished others to see him. They also hint at strong Carolingian input into the form the 'coronation' took.

The growing rhetoric of peace at the court, this specific selection of titles already in use by the 790s, and the retroactive account of the Lorsch Annals collectively reveal something of the degree to which the image of peacemaker had become central in the years before 800. Far from Einhard's surprise coronation, in St Peters Charlemagne was acclaimed in familiar and perhaps even favoured terms, crowned by God, great and peacemaking emperor. And, beginning on his homeward journey when we see it first deployed in a grant to Nonantola issued at Bologna on the 29th May 801, pacificus became a formal and frequent element of Charlemagne's diplomatic titulature until 813.[218]

The Lorsch Annals were not unique in their emphasis. Other later Carolingian historians certainly made the connection between the words of the acclamation and Charlemagne's pacification of Rome and his restoration of Leo; so too did the contemporary Byzantine historian Theophanes.[219] The anonymous author of the entry for 800 in the *Annales Sancti Amandi*, for example, made Charlemagne's peacemaking between Leo and the Romans the key act in the path to the imperial title. After an otherwise unattested fishing trip—recorded by some annalists as a less frivolous inspection tour of Frankish sea defences—Charlemagne 'proceeded to Rome, and made peace between the Romans and Pope Leo; and Leo consecrated him emperor'.[220] Similarly, the 'Poeta Saxo', writing around 890, offered his own verse interpretation of the events of Christmas Day 800 and he too linked the pacification of Rome with the coronation:

> The voice of the Roman people cried out in unison:
> 'To the August Charles the Great, bringing peace.

---

[218] *DK* no. 197 (May, 801), pp. 265–6, at 265. I. H. Garipzanov, 'Communication of Authority in Carolingian Titles', *Viator* 36 (2005), 40–80, esp. 59–61; Classen, 'Vorgeschichte', 103; H. Wolfram, ed., *Intitulatio* II. *Lateinische Herrscher- und Furstentitel in neunten und zehnten Jahrhundert* (Vienna, 1973), 495, 512–4, 519–21. Whilst Charlemagne's diploma for Nonantola was the first to style him *pacificus* it is worth nothing that we see him acting as *de facto* peacemaker in early March 801 when he sought to settle formally the long-standing dispute between Siena and Arezzo, *DK* no. 196 (March, 801), p. 264.

[219] *Chronographia*, in C. Mango and R. Scott, with G. Greatrex, trans., *The Chronicle of Theophanes Confessor. Byzantine and Near Eastern History, AD 284–813* (Oxford, 1997), AM 6289, pp. 647–9, at 649.

[220] 'Carolus rex fuit ad mare, ut piscaret; et Leutgardis regina obiit. Et ille perrexit ad Romam, et pacificavit Romanos et papam Leonem; et Leo benedixit eum ad imperatorem.' On this M. Garrison, '*Praesagum nomen tibi*: The Significance of Name-Wordplay in Alcuin's Letters to Arn', in M. Niederkorn-Bruck, A. Scharer, and W. Störmer (eds), *Erzbischof Arn von Salzburg*, Veröffentlichungen des Instituts für Österreichische Geschichtsforschung 40 (Vienna, 2004) 107–27 at, 118; J. L. Nelson, 'Aachen as a Place of Power', in M. de Jong, E. van Rhijn and F. Theuws (eds), *Topographies of Power in the Ear*, (Leiden, 2001), 236.

> Deservedly holding the sceptre of the Roman Empire.
> Glory, prosperity, kingdom, peace, life, triumph!'[221]

If the title mattered to Charlemagne and his advisors, it remains extremely difficult to know in any substantial sense what impact the term had upon wider political communities.[222] His full imperial title would continue to be a part of the formal terms of address deployed by a number of correspondents, from ambitious Frankish scholars to Greek emperors, writing to the Carolingians well into the ninth century, and continued to be a theme adopted by poets. Hibernicus 'Exul', well attuned to the court's ideological currents pointedly celebrated the glories of the Emperor Charlemagne rather than the age past, in which the peacemaking lord Charles (*dominus pacificus Karolus*) 'rules the Romulean empire with the highest virtue'.[223] Dungal, writing in 811, used the title as the base for his own embroidered variation in the opening to his letter to Charlemagne on the matter of reported eclipses.[224] Similarly, the title was invoked in full by Maxentius, the Patriarch of Aquileia, replying to Charlemagne's request for expositions on baptism in 811.[225] Linked to the imperial title, *pacificus* would turn up in later poems in praise of Charlemagne's heirs. Theodulf, in a late poem dedicated to Louis explicitly compared him to Solomon.[226] So did Brun Candidus in his metrical *vita* of Eigil.[227] Elements of the *laudes* would find echo in later moments of celebration, such as in Walahfrid Strabo's *adventus* verses for Lothar from the 830s. Happiness, fertility and the flowers of a new spring all accompanied the arrival of the peace giving Lothar. Home and away, near and far: harmony reigned everywhere, Breton and Bulgar had yielded alike.[228] Royal advents offered themselves as prime moments for celebrating peaceful rule, not least, as Kantorowicz made clear, on account of

---

[221] Poeta Saxo, *Annalium de gestis Caroli Magni imperatoris libri quinque*, ed. P. van Winterfeld, *MGH Poetae* IV, pp. 1–71 at 46, lines 16–19: 'Romanae sic concordi simul ore canentis: 'Augusto Carolo magno pacemque ferenti, / Imperii merito Romani sceptra tenenti, / Gloria, prosperitas, regnum, pax, vita, triumphus!'

[222] Garipzanov, 'Authority', 56; W. Brown, 'The Idea of Empire in Carolingian Bavaria', in Weiler and MacClean (eds), *Representation*, 37–55, both addressing Wolfram's categories of *Selbstaussage* and *Fremdaussage*.

[223] *MGH Poetae* I, *carm.* 5, p. 401, lines 11–16: 'In quis Romuleum summa virtute gubernat / Imperium dominus pacificus Karolus, / Cui cedunt proceres et gloria celsa priorum, / Solis obumbrantur sidera ceu radiis, / Flumina ceu Nilo, colles vincuntur Olimpo, / Argento obrizum plus velut ore nitet.' Godman, *Poets*, 62–3.

[224] *MGH Epp.* IV, no. 1 (811), pp. 571–8, at 571, on which see B. Eastwood, 'The Astronomy of Macrobius in Carolingian Europe: Dungal's Letter of 811 to Charles the Great', *EME* 3.2 (1994), 117–34.

[225] *MGH Epp.* IV, no. 27 (811–812), p. 537.

[226] *MGH Poetae* I, *carm.* 76, lines 13–14 p. 577: 'Es quoque pacificus, sapiens Salomonis ad instar, / In specie es Ioseph, viribus inque David.'

[227] *MGH Poetae* II, *carm.* 2, p. 100, c. 8: 'Hludvicus rex pacificus Caesarque serenus / Vobis iam propria mandavit voce salutem.'

[228] *MGH Poetae* II, *carm.* no. 63, pp. 405–6, at 406.

royal *adventus* ceremonies' potential evocation of the Advent of Christ, the Prince of Peace, Himself twice hailed explicitly as rex *pacificus* in the Antiphons for the first Vespers of the Nativity.[229] As an element in imperial titulature, its place in Carolingian praise poetry was assured into the later ninth century and beyond. Hrabanus would also deploy the title in a letter to Lothar in 855.[230] Sedulius Scottus would repeatedly marshal the term to praise a number of royal subjects, and it would also find its place in the qualities remembered in the verse epitaph to Louis II in late 875, chiselled on the tombstone still visible in Sant'Ambrogio, Milan and concretely emblematic of its firm integration into the ninth-century political lexicon.[231] In sparser form it occurred in the celebratory rhythmic verse on Odo's assumption of the throne in February 888.[232] Introduced in to Frankish circles in the later eighth century, notions of the *imperator pacificus* would haunt the political imagination of the West, and its thinkers, from the Ottonian and Salian courts through the polemicists of Investiture, and beyond.

It was as 'most serene Augustus, the great and pacific emperor crowned by God' that Charlemagne issued the *Divisio regni* of February 806.[233] An explicit attempt to forestall wrangling after his death, the *Divisio* was intended 'to establish and preserve peace between his sons' in the words of the *Annales regni Francorum* entry for that year, echoing the language of the capitularies, and to ensure that the internal peace would continue to be protected by his heirs.[234] Charlemagne's own voice is not always easy to hear, but we might catch it here in the text of the *Divisio*'s explanations of its goals: that it would prevent confusion, competition, and disorder, and allow his sons to defend the frontiers of their clearly defined kingdoms, preserving 'peace and *caritas*' with their brothers and, crucially, keeping the Carolingian edifice built by Charlemagne intact and strong.[235]

---

[229] Kantorowicz, 'King's Advent', *Selected Studies*, 40–2.
[230] *MGH Epp.* V, no. 57 (855–6), p. 515. 'DOMINO PRAECELLENTISSIMO NOBISQUE DEI MUNERE DATO, MAGNO ET PACIFICO ATQUE CORONATO REGI LOTHARIO ULTIMUS VESTRAE SERVITUTIS FAMULUS MAURUS.'
[231] *Carm.* no. 59, lines 26, p. 99. P. E. Schramm and F. Mütherich, *Denkmale der deutschen Könige und Kaiser*, p. 99. (Munich, 1962), no. 38, p. 128, plate at 243. Text: *MGH Poetae* III, 405.
[232] *MGH Poetae* IV, p. 138: 'Vivendo vivas ut Enohc, / Pacificus uti Sadoc, / Sis benedictus ut Iacob, / Sanctissimus ut fuit Iob.'
[233] Text: *MGH Capit.* I, no. 45 (806), pp. 126–30. Commentary: D. Hägermann, 'Quae ad profectum et utilitatem pertinent: Normen und Maximen zur "Innen- und Außenpolitik" in der *divisio regnorum* von 806', in J.-M. Duvosquel and E. Thoen (eds), *Peasants and Townsmen in Medieval Europe: Studia in honorem Adriaan Verhulst* (Ghent, 1995), 605–17; idem, 'Reichseinheit und Reichsteilung. Bemerkungen zur *Divisio regnorum* von 806 und zur *Ordinatio Imperii* von 817', *HJ* 95 (1975), 278–307; W. Schlesinger, 'Kaisertum und Reichsteilung: zur Divisio regnorum von 806', in R. Dietrich and G. Oesrich (eds) *Forschungen zu Staat und Verfassung Festgabe für Fritz Hartung* (Berlin 1958), 9–51.
[234] *ARF s.a.* 800, p. 121: 'de pace constituenda et conservanda inter filios suos et divisione regni facienda in tres partes'.
[235] *MGH Capit.* I, no. 45, pref. p. 127: '. . . et fines regni sui qui ad alienigenas extenduntur cum Dei adiutorio nitatur defendere, et pacem atque caritatem cum fratre custodire'. J. L. Nelson, 'The Voice of Charlemagne', in R. Gameson and H. Leyser (eds), *Belief and Culture: Studies in the Middle Ages. Studies Presented to Henry Mayr-Harting* (Oxford, 2001), 76–88.

The ideal was 'perpetual peace' between his sons, and the *Divisio* offered concrete provisions for its maintenance.[236] Neither brother was to breach the borders of another's kingdom with the intention of causing disturbance, receive another's subjects, or acquire land in another kingdom.[237] The *Divisio* also addressed the issue of maintaining coherent relations with neighbouring peoples as a multiple rather than a single, political unit, as in the case of hostage-taking. Here, collective responsibility and consensual agreement dictated how hostages were to be taken, kept, and returned only with the consent of the king whose frontiers they secured.[238]

REWRITING A PEACEFUL PAST: *ANNALES METTENSES PRIORES*

The promulgation of the 806 partition has been claimed, plausibly, as the backdrop to the production of a work composed by an author who, regardless of identity or location, was highly ideologically attuned to Charlemagne's inner circle: the *Annales Mettenses priores*.[239] This work's annalistically structured account of the Frankish past offered its audience a genealogy of Carolingian virtue that stretched back into the seventh century.[240] Reworking a range of earlier texts, including Fredegar, his continuators, and the *Annales regni Francorum*, the *Annales Mettenses priores* are as intensely presentist as any other more formal early medieval genealogy, offering in their accounts of Pippin II, Charles Martel, Pippin III, sequential portraits of ideal rulers: pious, measured, humble, always ready to seek the advice of their nobles, reluctant to resort to violence without making peacemaking overtures to their frequently proud and perfidious enemies, whether Saxon, Aquitanian, or Lombard, but always victorious when they did so.[241] Each was in turn portrayed as a leader for whom the peace of their kingdom and peaceful relations with external peoples, were fundamental to his

---

[236] *MGH Capit.* I, no. 45, c. 6, p. 128.

[237] *MGH Capit.* I, no. 45, cc. 6 (the integrity of borders), 7–8 (ban on receiving another's man), 11 (ban on the acquisition of *res immobilis*), at 128–9.

[238] *MGH Capit.*, no. 45 (806) c. 13, p. 129. See also *AB s.a.* 831, p. 3, a parallel instance of Louis the Pious sending captured rebels to be held in custody 'in various places'. This is a subject now handled by A. J. Kosto, 'Hostages in the Carolingian World (714–840)', *EME* 11.2 (2002), 123–47.

[239] *Annales Mettenses priores*, ed. B. de Simson, *MGH SSRG* 10 (Hanover, 1905), and see the overview of Y. Hen, 'The Annals of Metz and the Merovingian Past', in Hen and Innes (eds), *Uses of the Past, 175–90;* P. Fouracre and R. Gerberding, *Late Merovingian France, History and Hagiography 640–720* (Manchester, 1996), 340–9; I. Haselbach, *Aufstieg und Herrschaft der Karlinger in der Darstellung der Sogenannten Annales Mettenses priores. Ein Beitrag zur Geschichte der politischen Ideen im Reiche Karls des Großen*, HS 412 (Lübeck, Hamburg, 1970).

[240] Hen, 'Annals', 176–7.

[241] R. Collins, 'Deception and Misrepresentation in Early Eighth Century Frankish Historiography: Two Case Studies', in J. Jarnut, U. Nonn, and M. Richter (eds), *Karl Martell in Seiner Zeit* (Sigmaringen, 1994), 227–48.

conception of rule.[242] Collectively, the portrait was of a family better equipped and innately better suited for the task than their notional rulers.[243] That these portraits of past Carolingians reflect early ninth-century Carolingian political perspectives rather than later Merovingian actualities has escaped few readers.[244] Whilst the *Divisio*'s prescribed pacific Carolingian cooperation in the future for Charlemagne's heirs the *Annales* offered a complementary but crucially retrospective narrative of the same values enacted by his ancestors.[245]

With an eye for diplomatic detail that recalls the set-piece scenes of diplomatic interchange found in Ennodius' *vita* of Epiphanius and Gregory's *Histories* as much as it anticipates Nithard's account of Fontenoy, the annalist expended considerable time unfolding the build-up to the battle of Tertry and the estrangement of Pippin and Theuderic III. Unjustly dispossessed by Ebroin— Theuderic's mayor—several Neustrian nobles fled to Pippin. Pippin, 'with calm mind', despatched ambassadors to Theuderic requesting that the refugees whom Ebroin, covetously, had expelled from their lands and deprived of their property, be fully restored, by royal law, to their patrimonies.[246] Theuderic was unresponsive. By taking up his servants, he explained to Pippin's ambassadors, Pippin had breached 'justice and the law' (*ius et legem*), breached 'justice and the law' : one king's charity to another's dispossessed nobles read as a director contravention of the directive, present in both Merovingian legislation as well as Carolingian, not to take poach another's follwers.[247] Faced with this response the decision is made by 'all Pippin's leaders' to fight 'for the robbed and the wretched who had safely sought his protection and defence'.[248] Seeking a peaceful resolution, only resorting to arms reluctantly, and only with collective consent, the annalist's Pippin is a reluctant warrior, justifying, in a piece of extended first-person speech, an attack upon Neustria and the circumstances that had forced his hand to war: the need to defend the Church, to protect the *patria*, and the fact that peace through negotiation was not possible: 'Through ambassadors I repeatedly appealed humbly to Theuderic on their behalf, but received nothing in return but a pompous, prideful response.'[249] Even after the two sides reassembled on the battle's eve,

[242] Haselbach, *Aufstieg*, 158–61.

[243] Hen, 'Annals'.

[244] Haselbach, *Aufstieg*, 160. Precise physical location of composition and immediate political purpose, assuming one exists, have both been much debated: H. Hoffmann, *Untersuchungen zur karolingischen Annalistik* (Bonn, 1958), remains the foundational study. Hen, 'Annals', 181–90 stresses the importance of the 806 context. Fouracre and Gerberding, *Late Merovingian France*, 337–48, offer a judicious assessment of these subjects.

[245] Hen, 'Annals',183–6.

[246] *AMP s.a.* 689, p. 7.

[247] *AMP s.a.* 688, p. 6: 'A quo, causa perpetrati homicidii agnita, solita pietate suscipitur et ceteris profugis iure humanitatis cum honore sociatur.' In contrast, Theuderic, *s.a.* 689, p. 7: 'Hanc legationem Theodericus suggerente Berthario superbe recepit suosque profugos servos, quos Pipinus contra ius et legem susceperat, quandoque [a] se requirendos spopondit.' For such concerns in the 806 *divisio* see *MGH Capit.* I, no. 45 (806), cc. 7–8, p. 128.

[248] *AMP s.a.* 689, p. 7.

[249] *AMP s.a.* 689, p. 8.

Pippin once more sent legates to Theuderic, again seeking to settle peacefully the crisis between the two sides, rehearsing his demands, offering gold and silver as an incentive against battle, and expressing a fear as pressing in 806 as in 687 that 'the most noble and related blood of the Franks would be shed under the uncertain impulse of war.'[250] Whilst Pippin argued for peace, Theuderic, heeding the evil advice of Berchar, Ebroin's replacement as *maior domus*, spurned diplomatic overtures. Victorious, Pippin brought peace back to the Franks.

In the wake of his victory the *Annales* show Pippin achieved the same level of order to Francia as a whole that he had created in Austrasia. 'He restored', recorded the annalist under the entry for 691, 'the whole of the fatherland to a most peaceful state, flourishing in Christ's service', overseeing the annual assemblies at which, in addition to receiving 'offerings' and planning the forthcoming campaign, he received assurances of peace from his subjects.[251] External relations were stabilized, the annalist noting the flow of hostages and establishment of agreements between the Franks and their neighbours.[252]

Then, girded in strength, with divine help his companion, he governed the kingdom of the Franks internally with justice and peace and externally with most prudent policies and the unconquerable protection of arms, with the Lord's aid. Delegations of the nations living around about, that is, the Greeks, Romans, Lombards, Huns, Slavs, and Saracens, poured in to him. And the fame of his victory and triumphs went out among all peoples that, deserving on account of his virtue and prudence, all the nations round about sought his friendship with great gifts and rewards. And receiving them kindly, he rewarded them with even greater gifts and sent them home. With no less speed he sent his own legates through the various regions at the right moment for the well-being of the realm, obtaining peace and friendship from the surrounding peoples with the greatest goodwill.[253]

In due course Charles Martel would continue the Pippinid tradition of overseeing Frankish peace: 'in the manner of his ancestors, sends his legates to Chilperic, requesting conditions of peace'. Both Charles and Pippin III, the

---

[250] *AMP s.a.* 690, p. 9: 'Multa quoque pondera auri et argenti se sibi dare spopondit, si eius suggestionibus adquiesceret et pacem cum ipso magis quam prelium habere eligeret, ne forte ipso renuente civile bellum existeret, in quo nobilissimus et cognatus sanguis Francorum sub incerto belli impetu funderetur.'

[251] *AMP s.a.* 691, p. 12: 'Pippinus singularem Francorum obtinuit principatum . . . cunctam illam patriam in Christi servitio florentem pacatissimamque reddidit.'

[252] *AMP s.a.* 692, pp. 13–14.

[253] *AMP s.a.* 692, p. 15: 'Ipse vero precinctus robore, comitante divino auxilio, regnum Francorum interius iusticia et pace, exterius prudentissimis consiliis atque invictis armorum presidiis, auxiliante Domino, gubernat. Confluebant autem ad eum circumsitarum gentium legationes, Grecorum scilicet et Romanorum, Langobardorum, Hunorum quoque et Sclavorum atque Sarracenorum. Exierat enim fama victoriae et triumphorum eius in omnes gentes, ut merito propter virtutem et prudentiam eius cunctae circumsitae nationes amicitiam illius magnis oblatis muneribus implorarent. Quos ille clementer suscipiens maioribus remuneratos donis ad propria dirigebat. Ipse quoque haud segnius oportuno tempore legatos suos pro utilitatibus imperii sui per diversas regiones dirigens pacem et amicitiam circumpositarum gentium cum maximo favore impetrabat.'

annalist made clear, maintained Frankish peace.[254] Both settled domestic peace and external relations with such efficacy that neither led summer expeditions: 'he led an army into no region' (*in nullam partem exercitum duxit*) in the annalist's favoured phrase, and a telling one to be applied to past members of the Carolingian royal house in the opening years of the ninth century. By then Charlemagne had ceded military leadership to his sons. Like the Metz Annalist's image of Pippin after Tertry, he was spending increasing time at home. Diplomacy had replaced war leadership.

[254] For Charles Martel, see *AMP s.a.* 740, p. 30: 'Carolus princeps precellentissimus, devictis in circuitu Francorum hostibus, eo anno interiora regni sui cum pace disponens, nullam in partem exercitum duxit'; *s.a.* 741, p. 30: 'Carolus princeps, domitis circumquaque positis gentibus, dum ea quae pacis erant infra sui regiminis terminos disponeret . . .' For Pippin III see *AMP s.a.* 751, p. 43: 'Exinde omnis terra Francorum sub Pippini dominatione in summa pace quievit.'

4

New Solomons

Just as, after the death of the most warlike King David, the neighbouring peoples, whom his strong hand had subdued, for a long time paid their tribute to his peaceful son Solomon . . . so the monstrous *gens* of the Northmen still loyally paid to Louis the tribute which through terror they had paid to his father, the most august emperor Charles.

Notker, *Gesta Karoli*, II. 19.

As we move into the ninth century, the care taken to ensure both equitable division of the empire in 806 and peace between its constituent kingdoms after Charlemagne's death, the emphasis upon the peaceful face of Carolingian dynastic power evident in the *Annales Mettenses priores*, and the reiterated identification of Charlemagne as *pacificus* in his official titles and in a number of works addressed to and about him, augur the growth of our theme's prominence in Carolingian thought.[1] As we have also seen, Solomon was hardly absent from the cast of Charlemagne's ideology, but it is under Louis that we see him move to the centre of Carolingian political thought.

As Notker's words from his *Gesta Karoli* at the head of this chapter make clear, the frequent identification of Charlemagne with David carried another implicit typological association—Louis, his son, as Solomon. It was a parallel underpinned both by Louis' own interests and the singular historical fact that despite several early military successes Louis' reign was distinguished by an absence of the aggressive campaigning that had characterized the early decades of Charlemagne's.[2] In this way the emphasis upon peace both reflected and to some degree justified a relaxation of the earlier warlike attitudes of the Franks even as it developed in prior patterns of political imagery. This period was also defined

---

[1] K. F. Werner, '*Hludovicus Augustus*. Gouverner l'empire chrétien—Idées et réalités', *CH*, 3–123. Werner, amongst others, has noted that Louis' reign was characterized by little of the yearly aggression that had previously typified Frankish behaviour, 'Gouverner l'empire', *CH*, 7–8.
[2] Werner, 'Gouverner', *CH*, II, 57–8. T. Reuter, 'The End of Carolingian Military Expansion', *CH*, 391–405.

by increasing internal tensions as the early years of promise and optimism gave way to unrest and open rebellion. Louis' authority was contested, and prominent within that contest were issues over who should be responsible for the empire's peace and who should protect it (Louis? Lothar? The Pope?). Louis' reign witnessed not only political dissent from within the Carolingian royal house, it also saw a broadening political discourse, as distinct factions voiced political positions of their own, Hrabanus, Agobard, even Wiggo—Hell's demonic door-man whose strictly non-canonical name had its root in the word for war '*wig*'— all had views on peace in the Carolingian lands (at least according to Einhard) in the later 820s.[3] Louis' own concerns with imperial unity, peace, and order were also shared by a new generation of scholars who slipped into the mode of *magister* and propounded their own perspectives on the essentials of rulership, as well as Louis' failure to realize them. Addressing the purpose of kingship at the great reforming council held in Paris at Pentecost 829 in response to criticism of Louis' rule, the assembled clergy confidently dictated the emperor's job description: 'the royal office is specifically intended to govern God's people, and to rule with equity and justice, and to strive that they may have peace and harmony'.[4] This widening of the political discourse against the backdrop of factional tensions is a core feature of the political culture of Louis' reign: ideas of Christian kingship and collectivity first used coherently as part of the language of rule expressed in court-centred works and directed outwards to the Frankish political community occur, from the 820s onwards, in a larger environment. In the process, the ideals associated with the father came to be used to assess the efforts of the son and, on more than one occasion, to find him wanting.[5] In short, peaceful rule became a yardstick of good, and of legitimate, rule.[6] This was not a one-sided process. Louis shared their concerns. Looking back from the 840s, the anonymous biographer known as the 'Astronomer' made much of Louis' concern for the peace of the Church and of society as a whole. He was, he wrote, 'always devoted to peace, always the lover of peace and friend of unity, he always sought not only for his sons but also for his enemies to be unified with him in charity': a lover of 'true peace'.[7] That he did so in itself validated the criticisms and advice to which he was subject, and rendered him on occasion dangerously susceptible to the models set out for him.

---

[3] *Translatio et miracula sanctorum Marcellini et Petri*, ed. G. Waitz, *MGH Scriptores* 15.1 (Hanover, 1888), no.50 (829) III.14, p. 253.

[4] *MGH Conc.* II. 2, p. 651: 'Regale ministerium specialiter est populum Dei gubernare et regere cum equitate et iustitia et, ut pacem et concordiam habeant, studere.'

[5] Werner, 'Gouverner', *CH*, 56–7.

[6] Ibid.

[7] *Vit. Hlud.* c. 54, p. 506: '. . . qui ut paci semper studens semperque dilector pacis atque amator unitatis, querebat non modo filios, sed et inimicos sibi caritate uniri.' *Vit. Hlud.* c. 60, p. 532 (amator vere pacis).

The association of Louis and Solomon in political rhetoric took place during an intensification of exegetical activity and a deepening interest in the Solomon of scripture, an enterprise that culminated in Hrabanus Maurus' sequence of biblical commentaries for Louis the Pious, Judith, Louis the German, and Lothar.[8] Walahfrid, Claudius of Turin, and Angelomus of Luxeuil would all produce sustained discussions of the peace of Solomon's reign.[9] These commentaries hint at a mutually informing process taking place in these years: the image of Solomon finding wider currency in the contemporary world at the same time at which scholars were expounding at considerable length upon the political world in which the actual Solomon lived and ruled. Mayke de Jong has brilliantly envisaged the reading practices of the court circles within which these treatments of the Old Testament's historical books were discussed and digested.[10] She has stressed that such exegesis addressed not only what happened but also why it happened, offering moral lessons directly applicable to rule in the present even as it simultaneously illuminated textual obscurities and exposed the inner workings of salvation. Inasmuch as the well-being of the kingdom hinged upon the piety and right relationship of their ruler with God, a spiritual understanding of scripture was a political education: the same principles governed ninth-century rulers as much as their biblical predecessors.

Louis' reign was long and its politics complex. There is no space here to deeply contextualize the texts and theorists to which I now turn in the broader narrative of the years 814 to 840. Nevertheless, as the discourse of peaceful rulership flowed along the course dictated by these events, a very brief sketch may usefully orientate us. In 817 Louis, apparently spurred by thoughts of mortality, promulgated the *Ordinatio imperii*, dividing his realm amongst his sons and nephew. He didn't anticipate the birth of Charles the Bald. Attempting to go against his own division and redraw the map, he alienated his sons while at the same time facing the mounting criticism of the later 820s. His sons' unrest, particularly Lothar's estrangement in the wake of Charles' birth in 823, culminated in the reform councils of 829 and the revolts of the earlier 830s that led in turn to Louis' enforced penance at Soissons. Restored to power in 834, Louis' desire to

---

[8] M. de Jong, 'The Empire as *ecclesia*: Hrabanus Maurus and Biblical *historia* for Rulers', in Innes and Hen (eds), *Uses of the Past* 191–226; *eadem*, 'Old Law and New-found Power: Hrabanus Maurus and the Old Testament', in J. W. Drijvers and A. A. MacDonald (eds), *Centres of Learning. Learning and Location in Pre-Modern Europe and the Near East* (Leiden, 1995), 161–76.

[9] Claudius of Turin, *XXX quaestiones super libros regum*, PL 104, cols 623–810, II.7, cols 699–701, III, cols. 722–42. *Walahfrid Strabo's* Libellus De Exordiis Et Incrementis Quarundam in Observationibus Ecclesiasticis Rerum: *A Translation and Liturgical Commentary*, ed. and trans. A. Harting-Correa, Mittellateinische Studien und Texte 19 (Leiden, 1995), pp. 50–2, 58–60, 64–6, 74–6. Angelomus of Luxeuil, *Enarrationes in quatuor librum Regum*, PL 115, cols. 247–552, esp. cc. 6–15, cols. 412–75.

[10] de Jong, 'Hrabanus', 195–6.

provide the teenage Charles with a patrimony incurred a further wave of revolt, led by Louis the German and Pippin II, from whom Louis took lands for Charles, which was eventually settled in 840. Louis' death in June of the same year precipitated a further destabilization, as Lothar, his eldest surviving son, sought to assert himself with the support of the previously dispossessed Pippin II of Aquitaine over his brothers Louis the German and Charles the Bald. The latter two brothers, victorious over Lothar's forces at the infamous battle of Fontenoy, strengthened their alliance with the publicly sworn bilingual oaths of mutual support, locking themselves into this first fraternal agreement with conditional clauses that threatened the dissolution of their subjects' oaths of loyalty if either brother broke his oath of brotherly support. The following year, in 843, the empire was partitioned between the brothers by committee, creating West Francia, Lotharingia, and East Francia, the three fundamental units that will last beyond the end of my range here.

LESSONS IN RULERSHIP: SMARAGDUS OF ST-MIHIEL

Louis was thirty-six when he succeeded to sole power in 814, and had already been a king for about thirty-three years, having been crowned King of Aquitaine in 781. In the years before Charlemagne's death, and certainly before Louis' coronation as co-emperor in 813, Smaragdus of St-Mihiel composed his *Via regia*, almost certainly for Louis.[11] The precise date of the work is uncertain, though internal references to its recipient as a young man (*parvulus*) and Smaragdus' putative origins in Spain, the Spanish March or Aquitaine make an early date plausible. Amongst the multiple arguments for Smaragdus' Iberian origins is his knowledge of texts of limited circulation and Iberian origin, including Taio of Saragossa's Gregorian encyclopedia, the *Sententiae*, Julian of Toledo's grammar, and the set of verses we have already looked at, the seventh-century Visigothic verse *speculum principum*.[12] Smaragdus sent a copy of them to an unidentified son of Louis the Pious in 817, perhaps on the occasion of the *Ordinatio imperii*.[13]

Like Eugenius, Smaragdus engaged with notions of peace repeatedly and in contexts that might not seem at first glance very likely. Already in the preface to his commentary on Donatus of around 805 he had offered a parallel between

---

[11] *Via Regia*, PL 102, cols 931–70. J. Bovendeert, 'Royal or Monastic Identity? Smaragdus' *Via regia* and *Diadema monachorum* Reconsidered', in R. Corradini, R. Meens, C. Pössel, and P. Shaw (eds), *Texts and Identities in the Early Middle Ages* (Vienna, 2006), 239–51; Anton, *Fürstenspiegel*, 132–72; O. Eberhardt, *Via Regia. Der Fürstenspiegel Smaragds von St. Mihiel und seine literarische Gattung* (Munich, 1977).

[12] Smaragdus, *Liber in Partibus Donati*, ed. B. Löfstedt, L. Holtz, and A. Kibre, *CCCM* 68 (Turnhout, 1986), ix–xi, with references.

[13] For these poems and Smaragdus see Strecker's comments, *MGH Poetae* IV.3, p. 918. Dhuoda, *Handbook for her Warrior Son*, ed. and trans. M. Thiébaux (Cambridge, 1998), IV. c. 7, p. 146.

grammar and social order, the binding power of peace in human society, and the
binding power of conjunctions in language: as peace bonded the hearts of
brothers so conjunctions in their turn ordered, joined, united, and adorned
words.[14] (On this point Smaragdus' views on grammar might be said to amount
to a grammarian's variation on Gregory the Great's theme of the vexed relationship of language and social harmony.) Smaragdus' treatment of Donatus is thick
with scriptural passages and categories, a reflection of his attempt at 'Christian
grammar' both elucidated through and revealed by Christian verities.[15] In an
earlier section of the commentary Smaragdus had noted that *pax* was an absolute
noun (*nomina absolutiva*)—'like God, reason, light, discernment, truth, sin,
moon, love'—a word whose meaning was fully intelligible alone.[16]

No less than in his treatment of grammar Smaragdus brought, even by
Carolingian standards, a sensibility steeped in scripture to mapping a king's
path.[17] In the *Via regia*'s second chapter, 'On Keeping the Lord's Commandments', he offered a substantial extract from Leviticus that set out the fundamental relationship between piety and plenty in stark terms:

If you walk in My precepts, and keep My commandments and act upon them, I will give
you rain in due seasons, and the earth will bring forth its seeds, and your orchards will be
replenished with fruit . . . I will give peace to your coasts. You will sleep, and none shall
make you afraid.[18]

As for the Israelites of old so for the new. The words of Isaiah, no less than those
from Leviticus, spoke directly to Frankish kingship: 'O that thou hadst hearkened
to my commandments: thy peace had been as a river, and thy justice as the waves of
the sea.' Observe God's commandments, Smaragdus stressed, 'and your peace will
be happily multiplied'.[19] And the base of that good relationship? Fear of the Lord,
Smaragdus explained in a later chapter: 'Fear of the Lord is a crown of wisdom,
filling up peace and the fruit of salvation'.[20] Covenantal concepts also played their
part in Smaragdus' thought: he cited the Prophet Malachi's words that God's
covenant with Israel was one of life and peace (*vitae et pacis*).[21] Again, the same
qualities ought to characterize God's bond with the Franks.

---

[14] *MGH Poetae* I, *carm.* 13, p. 614, lines 3–5: 'Pax animas fratrum iungit: coniunctio verba /
Ordinat, adnectit, unit et ornat ea. / Pax retinet mentes: apices coniunctio nectit . . .'. J. A. Alford,
'The Grammatical Metaphor: A Survey of its Use in the Middle Ages', *Speculum* 57 (1982),
728–60, addressing Smaragdus briefly at 738.
[15] V. Law, 'The Study of Grammar', in R. McKitterick (ed.), *Carolingian Culture: Emulation
and Innovation* (Cambridge, 1994), 129–54, at 141–3. J. LeClerq, 'Smaragde et la grammaire
chrétienne', *Revue du moyen âge latin* 4 (1948), 15–22.
[16] *Liber in partibus Donatus, De qualitate nominis*, c. 18, p. 27.
[17] Law, 'Grammar', 100–1.
[18] *Via reg.*, c. 2, col. 938, citing Lev. XXVI. 3–6.
[19] *Via reg.*, c. 2, col. 939, citing Isa. XLVIII. 18–19.
[20] *Via reg.*, c. 3, col. 940, citing Ecclus. I. 22.
[21] *Via reg.*, c. 5, col. 945, citing Mal. II.5.

If fear was one component of a right relationship with God, humility also had its place. 'Travel the way of humility and peace', Smaragdus counselled, *that* was the royal road.[22] Patience, too, played its part.

Patience is what commends us to God, and guards and protects us from all bad things. Patience is the thing that tempers anger, it is that which holds the tongue, it is that which governs the mind, it is that which guards peace.[23]

Simplicitas, straightforwardness or openheartedness, was a parallel path to the heavenly robe of peace and glory.[24] Fear of God, humility, patience, *simplicitas:* such qualities maintained peace and stabilized relations with God.

In some of the *Via regia*'s other chapters, Smaragdus outlined the negative qualities which could destroy it. Anger and zeal both threatened disruption to the inner life of the king, his right relationship with God and, in consequence, the kingdom's peace as a whole.[25] Equally key, advised Smaragdus, was the need for a successful ruler to listen to advice, citing a sequence of leaders from Noah, sustained by good advice throughout the years it took for the Ark to be built, through to Solomon, making peace with the nations and building the Temple.[26] But it is in the *Via regia*'s seventeenth chapter that Smaragdus turned to the subject of peace in its own right, and its place in Christians' lives. Having discussed peace in the context of humility Smaragdus now discussed humility in the context of peace:

For nobody exalts himself more greatly in the presence of God than the one who humbles himself before Him. For this reason the humble are exalted by the Lord, in order to be called a son of God and an heir of Christ. He should only strive for peace, because he ought to seek peace and to follow as a son of peace. For in such a manner did the Apostle urge us, saying: 'Follow peace with all men, and holiness: without which you shall not see God' (Heb. XII.14). And also the Lord himself said in the Gospel: 'Blessed are the peacemakers: since they shall be called the sons of God' (Matt. V.9). For by His holy commandment and salvational teaching, the Saviour, His Passion drawing near, commended us to keep this teaching and commandment. For He said: 'My peace do I give you' (John XIV.27). Ascending into Heaven the Lord left us this inheritance, and he ordered us to follow it through his most faithful David king and prophet: 'Turn away from evil and do good. Seek peace and pursue it.' (Ps. XXXIII.15). For if we wish to follow it with a sincere heart we will be the heirs of Christ. But if we desire to be heirs of Christ, we must live in the peace of Christ. If we are the sons of God, we ought to be

---

[22] *Via reg.*, c. 18, col. 958.

[23] *Via reg.*, c. 7, col. 947: 'Patientia est quae nos Deo commendat, et a malis omnibus custodit et servat. Ipsa est quae iram temperat; ipsa est quae linguam refrenat; ipsa est quae mentem gubernat; ipsa est quae pacem custodit . . .'.

[24] *Via reg.*, c. 6, col. 946, 'Curre ergo, rex, firmiter per simplicitatis itinera, ut ad perennem citius pervenias vitam, et immortalitatis cito accipias praemia, et stola induaris pacis et gloriae.'

[25] *Via reg.*, c. 22, cols 961–2, at 961. On Smaragdus' conception of good and bad zeal see Anton, *Fürstenspiegel,* 149–50.

[26] *Via reg.*, c. 20, col. 960. Bovendeert, 'Royal', 249.

peacemakers. For it is right for the sons of God to be peacemakers and humble, with meek minds, simple hearts, chaste speech, innocent in spirit and harmonious in affection, embracing one another with good faith in unity.[27]

In her recent reappraisal of the relationship of the *Via regia* and Smaragdus' other manual of advice, the *Diadema monachorum*, Jasmijn Bovendeert has convincingly repudiated earlier views of the two's perceived interdependence, and the attendant notion that through the *Via regia* Smaragdus sought to repackage monastic virtues to Louis as royal ones, contributing to a putative 'monastic turn' in the the conception of kingship. Rejecting this image of *speculum principum* as a Trojan Horse for the monastic ideal Bovendeert has instead emphasized that the works were distinct, if overlapping, sharing certain Christian fundamentals but also distinct treatments of virtues particularly suited to a lay ruler (justice, mercy) and to a monk (humility), and so on. This chapter on peace, however, is one of the few common to both, evidence not of a specifically monastic ideal so much as a sense of truth applicable to all members, however different their positions, in the order of a single Christian community.[28]

PEACE, ORDER, AND LOUIS THE PIOUS

Louis' legislation after 814 suggests that he was receptive to Smaragdus' lessons for kings to be peacemakers, as well as the inheritor of his father's own capitulary legislation and political rhetoric.[29] At Aachen in July 817 he issued the *Ordinatio imperii* before the assembled elites of his empire.[30] Acknowledging that the empire enjoyed, through God's gift, peace and safety on all sides, Louis acknowledged that his *fideles* had advised him to take pre-emptive steps to address the question of succession. Lothar received the imperial title, his

---

[27] *Via reg.*, c. 17, col. 957: 'Nemo enim se apud Deum magis exaltat, quam qui se apud semetipsum propter Deum humiliat. Ad hoc enim a Domino humilis exaltatur, ut filius Dei et haeres Christi vocetur. Tantum est ut pacem sequatur, quia pacem quaerere debet, et sequi filius pacis. Taliter enim nos admonet Apostolus dicens: "Pacem sequimini cum omnibus et sanctimoniam, sine qua non videbitis Deum." Ipse quoque Dominus in Evangelio ait: "Beati pacifici: quoniam filii Dei vocabuntur." Nam et inter sua divina mandata et magisteria salutaria, passioni iam proximus hoc nobis praeceptum atque mandatum commendavit Salvator custodiendum. Ait enim: "Pacem meam do vobis." Hanc nobis haereditatem ascendens Dominus in coelum reliquit; et sequi eam per suum fidelissimum regem David atque prophetam mandavit: "Diverte a malo, et fac bonum: inquire pacem, et persequere eam." Si hanc enim sincero corde sequi voluerimus Christi haeredes erimus; si autem Christi haeredes cupimus esse, in Christi pace debemus versari. Si filii Dei sumus, pacifici esse debemus: pacificos enim oportet esse Dei filios et humiles, mente mites, corde simplices, sermone puros, animo innocentes, affectu concordes, fideliter sibimet unanimiter cohaerentes.'

[28] Bovenderert, 'Royal', 249–50.

[29] G. Schmitz, 'The Capitulary Legislation of Louis the Pious', *CH*, 428–36, esp. 436.

[30] *MGH Capit.* I, no. 136 (817), 270–3.

brothers their kingdoms (Aquitaine, Bavaria) and the title 'king' (*regiis insigniri nominibus*).[31] Several of the *Ordinatio*'s clauses sought practical solutions as to how they were to deal with each other in order better to preserve not only their own peace but also 'the everlasting peace of the entire Christian people'.[32] Louis prescribed annual visits of Pippin and Charles to Lothar, to renew not only their own fraternal love but also collectively to agree upon matters concerning common utility (*utilitas communis*) and perpetual peace (*pax perpetua*).[33] If one of the brothers could not come, legates were to be sent instead. Lothar, in turn, owed equal responsibility to his younger siblings.[34] Subsequent clauses made clear quite what matters he wished discussed by his sons. War and peace with outside peoples were to be addressed collectively.[35] Other sections sought to prevent discord between the three: after his death his sons' vassals could not hold land in more than one kingdom, though Louis was clear to state that they might choose their wives from any part of the Carolingian territories, in order that such unions might bind the peace between the kingdoms more tightly.[36] Louis went on to address family matters of his own, setting out the intended inheritance patterns for the next generation of Carolingians.[37]

Louis' written request that his sons play nicely may be read as naïvely optimistic, but there is little reason to think it was not heartfelt. Its general concerns are to be found elsewhere in his surviving legislation, for example in his injunction of 819 that counts and abbots alike were to preserve the peace, or in his attempt to control behaviour within the palace-complex of Aachen.[38]

The idea that peace was the province of the Carolingian king was clearly very much alive in the opening years of Louis' reign, and in places far from the inner circuits of imperial authority. However it would end, Louis' reign began in a spirit of optimism, albeit one not unclouded by the sense on the part of both Louis ands his advisors ('*nos fideles nostri ammonerent...*') that the peace he had inherited had to be worked at to be preserved. In the early 820s, Amalarius of Metz in his *Liber officialis* harped heavily in his preface on Louis as a new Solomon, 'the Peace of the World'. 'Let God maintain your power. Let God make your kingdom peaceful', he implored in language evocative of the liturgy of kingmaking, before going on to pray that the empress Judith, 'the most noble and wise Augusta', would enjoy health for many years to come. 'O Lord', Amalarius continued, 'watch over the light of peace. Watch over the light of

---

[31] *MGH Capit.* I, no. 136 (817), 271.
[32] *MGH Capit.* I, no. 136 (817), 271.
[33] *MGH Capit.* I, no. 136 (817), c. 4, 271.
[34] *MGH Capit.* I, no. 136 (817), c. 5, p. 271.
[35] *MGH Capit.* I, no. 136 (817), cc. 7–8, p. 272.
[36] *MGH Capit.* I, no. 136 (817), c. 13, p. 272.
[37] *MGH Capit.* I, no. 136 (817), cc. 14–17, pp. 272–3.
[38] *MGH Capit.* I, no. 141(819), c. 12, p. 290; c. 27, p. 291; no. 146 (820?), c. 4, p. 298, demanding that peace be made between brawlers (*rixantes*).

the world'.[39] Whilst the *Liber's* dedication celebrated Louis as a new Solomon its later chapters explored the implications of the identification, as Amalarius reminded Louis of the allegorical meaning of the period from Septuagesima to the fourth week before Easter. This matched the fourth age of the world, when David and Solomon ruled. David triumphed, and 'Solomon the eternal, ruled as peacemaker, of whom the Apostle said: "Christ rising again from the dead, dieth now no more, death shall no more have dominion over him"'.[40] Later Amalarius turned to a prayer we have already encountered, 'give us peace in our days'. No peace is safer, he noted, than when we obey the Lord's commandments, follow Solomon's wisdom, and 'turn away from evil and do good'.[41] Not for the last time would Louis have the words of the liturgy presented to him as a yardstick for his own behaviour.

Others in the 820s performed their own variations on the theme. In his richly allusive verses of early 829 on the statue of Theoderic set up by Charlemagne in the grounds of the palace at Aachen, the young Walahfrid Strabo, recently installed as tutor to Charles the Bald, celebrated Louis' reign as a new golden age, and the peaceful ways in which both tame and wild animals played together under Louis' rule.[42] In the future, suggested Walahfrid, he could envisage bears, elephants, rhinoceros, even tame dragons (*domiti dracones*) lying down with cows and sheep. This is, as Michael Herren has observed, an image of harmony with its reference points in both Isaiah and the Fourth Eclogue, albeit one pushed to an extreme level.[43] Was there a hint of mockery underlying Walahfrid's fantastical menagerie?

However idiosyncratic it might be, Walahfrid's poem harmonized with an emphasis present in other works of the late 820s, but it also betrayed an underlying anxiety and growing tensions over Louis' decision to redivide his territories to accommodate Charles. Later in the poem, Walahfrid addressed each of Louis' sons in turn—with the notable absence of Pippin I of Aquitaine—finally turning to his young charge, Charles:

[39] Amalarius, *Liber officialis*, ed. J. M. Hanssens, *Amalarii Episcopi Opera Liturgica Omnia* (Rome, 1948), II, c. 7, p. 21: 'Ipsi novo Salomoni felicitas. Pax mundi vos estis. Pio principi prosperitas. Domine, vitam ipsi concede. Vestra fides vos servet. Christus quem vos honoratis, ipse vos servet. Potestatem vestram Deus conservet. Deus pacificet regnum vestrum. Judith orthodoxae, nobilissimae atque prudentissimae Augustae salus per multos annos. Lumina pacis, Domine, serva. Lumina mundi, Domine, serva.' Nelson, 'Aachen', 8, 20–1

[40] *Lib. off.*, I.2.5, pp. 38–9.

[41] *Lib. off.*, III.29.12, p. 358.

[42] M. W. Herren, 'The "*De imagine Tetrici*" of Walahfrid Strabo: Edition and Translation', *Journal of Medieval Latin* 1 (1991), 118–39, whose text and translation I follow here. For commentary *idem*, 'Walahfrid Strabo's *De Imagine Tetrici*: an Interpretation', in R. North and T. Hofstra (eds), *Latin Culture and Medieval Germanic Europe*, Germania Latina I (Groningen, 1992), 25–42.

[43] Herren, '*De Imagine*', 126, lines 117–27, with commentary in *idem*, 'Interpretation', 29. Louis the German as Louis' namesake will enjoy comparable benefits: 'Yours in like measure is the grace of peace', p. 127, lines 135–6.

> Christ, grant that he follow in deeds, character, ability, life, virtue, triumph
> Peace, faith, goodness, spirit, speech, daring
> Right belief, counsel, success and loyal children
> Him whom he follows in name.[44]

If Walahfrid expressed anxieties about the future he also betrayed a quietly subversive cynicism about rulership itself. Early in the poem poet and muse ('Scintilla') walk through the Aachen palace grounds. Encountering the statuary group with Theoderic at its centre leads Walahfrid to ask whom it represents. 'Scintilla', in reply, offers an account of the miserly and proud king. At dawn, midday, and dusk, replies Walahfrid, he has seen doves perching on the stature. 'Scintilla' explains the doves represent the humble subjects of such haughty tyrants:

> Don't you see how lowly folk seem to love cruel tyrants?
> Not of course from their hearts, but for the sake of peace here and now.
> They seek their bread; they do not rest from building nests.[45]

A safe home and a full stomach, rather than any more airy ideas, were the real concerns of the majority. Something of a ninth-century Machiavelli, Walahfrid implied both were the results of effective rather than exemplary rulership.

ERMOLDUS NIGELLUS' EPIC OF PEACE

Others in the 820s offered extensive praise of Louis as a Solomonic ruler. Amongst their number we find a figure for whom Walahfrid seems to have had active contempt: the Aquitanian Ermoldus Nigellus.[46] Viewing the two side by side is an exercise in contrasting personalities and backgrounds. Walahfrid was the young and a rising star of the Carolingian intellectual scene, the newly appointed royal tutor to the infant Charles. Like Ermold, Walahfrid had provincial origins. He was Swabian. Walahfrid was an old boy of Reichenau and Hrabanus' Fulda with several literary successes under his belt, notably the *Visio Wettini*, and powerful backers. Ermold, by contrast, was a member of one of the less culturally distinguished of Carolingian courts, Pippin's, and the product of an unidentified monastery or school.[47] Walahfrid's rise shows the growing gravity of a new centre of political possibility—the young Charles. Ermold had made his way through an older political landscape. By his own account a participant with Pippin on the Breton campaign of 818, Ermold must have been at least a generation older than Walahfrid, and a generation too late to make the transition smoothly from the halls of Aquitanian palaces such as Angeac and

---

[44] Herren, '*De Imagine*', 136, lines 158–61.
[45] Herren, '*De Imagine*', p. 133, lines 49–51.
[46] Herren, '*De Imagine*', 119, 133.
[47] R. Collins, 'Pippin I and the Kingdom of Aquitaine', *CH* 363–89.

Doué to Ingelheim and Aachen in the way older Aquitanian courtiers who had worked under Louis, Benedict of Aniane, Helisachar, and Claudius of Turin, had done.

All three of Ermold's extant works—two verse epistles to Pippin of Aquitaine and his nearly 3,000-line, four-book epic in praise of Louis the Pious, the *Carmen in honorem Hludowici Christianissimi caesaris augusti* (*In honorem*)— were written in captivity in Strasbourg, sometime after summer 826 and before spring 829.[48] The precise circumstances behind Ermold's internal exile, within Louis' empire but far from his beloved *patria* of Aquitaine and Pippin's court, have remained unclear: Ermold is vague on the subject.[49] Nor for that matter do we know with any certainty if Ermold's calls for his exile's end were ultimately successful, though there is cautious reason to think that they were.[50] Sprawling and derivative, *In honorem* was a sustained piece of panegyric directed towards an emperor Ermold cast as both *pacificus* and *pius*, and whose very name, he claimed, revealed his abilities in war and in peace. 'Hludowicus', Ermold explained, derived from two sources, from the Latin verb *ludere*, 'to celebrate', for the Franks 'ought to celebrate in the benefits of his peace',[51] and from the Frankish phrase '*hluto wicgh*' meaning 'illustrious Mars'.[52] The Frankish etymology was warlike. That of the baptismally bestowed Latin version, peaceful. This tortuous association linked peace with Latinity and implicitly with entry to the Christian society, a theme Ermold would explore on a larger scale later in his poem. The two dyadic sets of identities (Christian/peaceful, Frankish/bellicose) fused in Louis as Christian emperor and Frankish king, the living embodiment of collective Frankish values.

Ermold characterized Louis as a Solomonic ruler both through explicit parallels, but also more subtly through the careful redeployment of source material. This can best be seen in *In honorem*'s second book. Here Ermold presented

[48] Godman *Poets*, 108, following *In honorem*, IV, lines 2332–3, p. 178. P. Depreux, 'La *pietas* comme principe de gouvernement d'après le Poème sur Louis le Pieux d'Ermold le Noir', in J. Hill and M. Swann (eds), *The Community, the Family and the Saint: Patterns of Power in Early Medieval Europe. Selected Proceedings of the International Medieval Congress, University of Leeds, 4–7 July 1994, 10–13 July 1995* (Turnhout, 1998), 201–24. His debt to earlier poets, classical and Carolingian, is laid bare by I. Ranieri, 'I modelli formali del "Carmen in honorem Hludowici Caesaris" di Ermoldo Nigello', *Acme. Annali della Facoltà di Lettere e Filosofia dell'Università degli Studi di Milano* 36 (1983), 161–214.
[49] *ARF s.a.* 826–7, pp. 170–4 on unrest in Aquitaine and the March. On Aquitaine in this period Collins, 'Pippin I', *CH*, 378–9; J. Martindale, 'The Kingdom of Aquitaine and the Carolingian *Fisc*', *Francia* 11 (1984), 136–7.
[50] A *cancellarius* Hermoldus attested three of Pippin's charters in the late 830s, and Leon Levillain at least was convinced that this was our man, *Recueil des actes de Pépin I et Pépin II, rois d'Aquitaine* (Paris, 1926), nos 28–30. The 'Astronomer', writing around 840, referred to an 'Abbot Ermold' carrying messages between Louis and Pippin some years previously, in 835; *Vit. Hind.* c. 53, p.498.
[51] *In honorem*, I, lines 80–5, p. 10.
[52] *In honorem*, I, lines 84–5, p. 10.

Louis' relationship with the pope typologically, the latter speaking to Louis using the words of the Queen of Sheba to Solomon, echoing the exegetical trope in the Song of Songs that the Queen of Sheba represented the Church.[53] Other analogies between Louis and Solomon were more explicit. Ermold's description of Louis' royal chapel at Ingelheim, a temple with a gold door and bronze door posts has numerous parallels with Solomon's own Temple, itself mentioned by Ermold within the space of a few lines.[54]

In honorem is one of the most important poetic sources, and certainly the densest, for Carolingian court culture.[55] That it was the work of a scholar attached to a provincial court who perhaps came nearest to the great palaces of the Middle Rhine only when he was brought from Aquitaine to be imprisoned is a fact too little remembered. Combining elements of biography, ethnography, and providential history, Ermold traced Louis' life across four books. Their main subjects can be briefly sketched. The first addressed Louis' early years in Aquitaine, his military expedition to Spain, his successful siege of Barcelona and his purging the city of its 'demonic' Saracen shrine.[56] Peace was fostered through physical purification, a theme developed in Ermold's account of the baptism of the Danish prince Harald Klak, his family, and entourage, as Louis convinced them to abandon their worship of 'empty idols' (*vana idola*). Elsewhere Ermold recounted Louis' correction of the bellicose Bretons' sham Christianity ('Christians in name only').[57]

Exile and poet, he might also be classed as a Carolingian scholar of comparative religion, identifying various forms of flawed belief in the world beyond Francia. In addition to displaying Louis' martial skills Ermold's first book also established a key theme of the poem, the idea of Louis as a disseminator of Christianity, through warfare, by diplomacy, by personal example, and patronage of mission and monastic reform. Across all four books Ermold framed Louis as an emperor who both widened and deepened Christianity. *In honorem* reveals, through the treatment of this very theme, Ermold's fascination with the imagery and symbolism of baptism as purification, as exorcism, as creation of community, and as an act of peacemaking, as Harald accepts Christianity,

[53] *In honorem*, II, lines 908–15, p. 72, citing III Kings X.4–5.
[54] Description of the chapel, *In honorem*, IV, lines 2068–70, p. 158, Solomon's Temple, lines 2095–9, p. 160. The bronze pillar of the Temple: IV Kings, XXV.13; golden doors of the Temple: II Paralip. IV.22.
[55] J. L. Nelson, 'The Lord's Anointed and the People's Choice: Carolingian Royal Ritual', in D. Cannadine and S. Price (eds), *Rituals of Royalty. Power and Ceremonial in Traditional Societies* (Cambridge, 1987), 137–80, reprinted in her *Frankish World*, 99–132.
[56] *In honorem*, I, lines 563–5, p. 46.
[57] For the political context of this see S. Coupland, 'From Poachers to Gamekeepers: Scandinavian Warlords and Carolingian Kings', *EME* 7.1 (1998), 85–114. K. L. Maund, '"A Turmoil of Warring Princes": Political Leadership in Ninth-Century Denmark', *Haskins Society Journal* 6 (1994), 29–47.

joining the *pax Christiana* overseen by Louis, heir of Constantine and Charlemagne.[58]

In honorem's second book opens with Louis' coronation as co-emperor, his assumption of full authority in 814, his subsequent coronation with Constantine's own crown in 816, and his interest in monastic reform. External affairs were the subject of book three, and the Franks' wars with the Breton king Murman, who refused to accept the peace Louis offered. Ermold's fourth and final book also addressed external affairs, detailing not only Ebbo of Rheims' mission to the Danes but also their reception at Ingelheim. This afforded Ermold the opportunity to offer his detailed descriptions of the wall paintings in the chapel, depicting figures and events from Old and New Testaments typologically split between two facing walls, and those in the royal hall, with their own distinct oppositional Orosian sequence of rulers both good and bad, Frankish and ancient.[59]

A central thread of Orosius' vision of history was the transformative triumph of Christianity and, with it, peace—an image of a world gradually improving. Ermold borrowed Orosius' philosophy as much as his historical information, for in his poem Ingelheim's wall paintings not only provide the narrative climax of his poem, they also occupy the centre of his vision of the Carolingian world. The historical scheme they depict, a history of the world in terms of the four successive Danielic empires, their rise and fall, of moral development, argued for the benefits of the Christianization of the empire and the improvement of human conditions over time. Heir to a sequence of Christian emperors, wearer of Constantine's crown, Louis is the 'most Christian' (*christianissimus*), adding new peoples and new territories to the Christian community. Through his actions Louis played his own part in a larger providential scheme. As new generations of pagans came under his sway he oversaw a new Christian empire, and a new Christian peace. These processes Ermold portrayed in considerable depth, describing Harald and his entourage's journey up the Rhine in a hundred white-sailed ships—an image heavily weighted with baptismal imagery—and into Francia.[60] Then they are received and conducted to Ingelheim. The two leaders eat together, Harald sitting beside Louis.[61] In a discussion of the nature of

---

[58] K. Hauck, 'Karolingische Taufpfalzen im Spiegel hofneher Dichtung Überlegungen zur Ausmalung von Pfalzkirchen, Pfalzen and Reichsklöstern', *Nachrichten der Akademie der Wissenschaften in Göttingen Philologisch-historische Klasse*, I (Göttingen, 1985), 1–97. On the notion that certain early medieval narratives 'enacted' principles of belief see Cramer, *Baptism*, 201–2; M. M. Walsh, 'The Baptismal Flood in the Old English *Andreas*: Liturgical and Typological Depths', *Traditio* 33 (1977), 137–58; C. B. Hieatt, 'The Harrowing of Mermedonia: Typological Patterns in the Old English *Andreas*', *Neuphilologische Mitteilungen* 77 (1976), 49–62.

[59] *In honorem*, IV, lines 2081–90, pp. 158–60; L. Nees, *A Tainted Mantle. Hercules and the Classical Tradition at the Carolingian Court* (Philadelphia, 1991), 270–7; W. Lammers, 'Ein Karolingisches Bildprogramm in der Aula Regia Von Ingelheim', in *Festschrift für H. Heimpel zum 70. Geburtstag am 19. September 1971* (Göttingen, 1972), III, 226–89.

[60] *In honorem*, IV, lines 2167–75, p. 166.

[61] *In honorem*, IV, lines 2176–83, p. 166.

baptism Harald reveals that Ebbo, sent to arrange the meeting, had explained the significance of the blood and the water that flowed from Christ's side, their baptismal symbolism,[62] and the meaning of the chrism.[63] Harald states that he recognizes God and rejects the metal idols the Danes had formerly worshipped.[64] Louis, in response to Harald's rejection of idolatry agrees to have him baptized. Louis receives Harald from the font; Judith performs the same task for Harald's queen. Both Frankish rulers dress their opposite number in white clothes. Louis' sons, Lothar and Louis, carry out the same tasks for Harald's sons.[65] Moving down the court hierarchy nobles perform the same function for their counterparts amongst Harald's leading men. At the lowest level of society members of an undifferentiated Carolingian crowd sponsor and dress their own equally undistinguished opposite numbers.[66] By overseeing baptism, Louis has snatched 'a nation from the jaws of the wolf'.[67] Now members of the Christian community, the Danes receive gifts from their new spiritual kinsfolk. Reborn as Christians and reclothed as Franks, the Danes return to the chapel. At this point in his narrative Ermold addresses Harald directly, comparing his forsaken idols unfavourably with the true Christian God.[68] The service over, the royal party reenters the secular sphere, dining for a second time. Franks and Danes enjoy the happy day as one.[69] Louis asks Harald to join him on a hunt and Harald agrees. After further feasting, the parties return for Vespers.[70] In the final sequence the Danish king acknowledges Louis' authority, swears loyalty, and is rewarded with weapons.[71]

Is this a credible account? Clearly there is a heavy symbolic overlay to the narrative and the conversations between Harald and Louis are hardly reportage. That said, the key processes the two kings undertake are all attested elsewhere in the ninth-century record as elements in peacemaking strategies between Scandinavians and their former enemies, Anglo-Saxon as well as Frank. As Janet Nelson has noted, liturgical solemnities (baptism, Mass) and secular ceremonies (giftgiving, feasting, the hunt) mesh tightly throughout Ermold's account.[72] Taken together, they provide a catalogue of processes of Carolingian acculturation, social and religious, through which the Church grows, peace between the ruling houses of Francia and Denmark is established, and a former enemy absorbs Frankish culture. These were activities with ideological purpose, and their careful

---

[62] *In honorem*, IV, lines 2205–7, p. 168.
[63] *In honorem*, IV, line 2209, p. 168.
[64] *In honorem*, IV, lines 2222–8, p. 170.
[65] *In honorem*, IV, lines 2245–6, p. 172.
[66] *In honorem*, IV, lines 2246–7, p. 172.
[67] *In honorem*, IV, line 2251, p. 172.
[68] *In honorem*, IV, lines 2324–6, p. 178.
[69] *In honorem*, IV, lines 2360–1, p. 180.
[70] *In honorem*, IV, line 2436, p. 184.
[71] *In honorem*, IV, lines 2492–501, pp. 188–90.
[72] Nelson, 'Royal Ritual', *Frankish World*, 121–2.

description by Ermoldus continued the same work on the page. Written by an imprisoned poet of suspect loyalty, Ermold's verse account of court culture was itself a demonstration of allegiance to the Carolingian imperial enterprise.

It was also an exercise in exegesis in the poetic mode. Ermold's account of Harald's baptism may be drawn from earlier texts, and it is a work that at points, such as in the imagery of the Danes' white-sailed boats on the Rhine, tips into high symbolism. But the image he offers is recognizable. More than this, Ermold's poem reminds us of the web of ideas that surround peace and peace-making—the associations of purification, exorcism, and the identification of bonds of peace and bonds of kinship—informed its actual elements, as well as providing rich imagery and associations to those who chose it as a theme for poetry and for literature. To understand this patterning more clearly let us examine, briefly, the subject of baptism. Charlemagne's request for a clear exposition on the subject in 811/12 had resulted in a range of responses. Thanks to the efforts of Susan Keefe, we have a strong sense of what baptism meant to the Carolingians.[73] Most agreed on certain key points: baptism was an act of purification, a casting out of evil and a rejection of the Devil.[74] One voice from this scholarly colloquy can be singled out. Leidrad of Lyons' thinking on baptism bears probably the closest parallel to Ermold's. He expressed the cate-chumen's rejection of the Devil and his works in these terms:

For the works of the Devil are profane rites which are furnished with idols: then murder, theft, rape, deceit, perjury, adultery, hostility, discord, anger, violence, dissent, and other things like this.[75]

Treating the Devil as the enemy of peace gave the exorcism of the catechumen direct relevance as a component of peacemaking. The association between idolatry and violence on the one hand, and Christianity and peace on the other, both so central to Ermold's view of the world, has its roots here. The purification of the catechumen was symbolized by his white clothing, newly baptized he was newly born into the peace and unity of the Church.[76] Leidrad described it thus:

---

[73] S. A. Keefe, *Water and the Word: Baptism and the Education of the Clergy in the Carolingian Empire*, (South Bend, IN 2002) I, 116–31.

[74] E.g. Theodulf of Orléans, *Liber de Ordine Baptismi*, PL 105, cols 223–40, c. 4, (*cur exorcizatur?*), col. 225; c. 5 (*cur catechumenus accipit salem?*), cols 235–6. Discussion in Cramer, *Baptism*, 87–8.

[75] Leidrad of Lyons, *Liber de sacramento baptismi*, PL 99, cols 853–72, c. 3, at 859: 'Opera enim diaboli sunt ritus profanus qui idolis exhibebatur; deinde homicidium, furtum, rapina, fraus, perjurium, adulterium, inimicitiae, discordiae, irae, rixae, dissensiones, et caetera huiusmodi.' On Leidrad see further the comments of Keefe, *Water*, I, 65–7. Translations cited here from Cramer, *Baptism*, 159–65.

[76] *MGH Epp.* IV, no. 143(798), p. 226 for Alcuin in baptismal clothing. See also Theodulf, *Liber*, c. 14, cols 234–5.

The world's sins cannot be purged without the water's flood: the moment the foulness is despatched, the dove of the Holy Spirit flies down to Noah just as it flies down to Christ in the Jordan, and announces world peace with the branch of healing and light.[77]

Leidrad went on to cite Ezekiel on baptism's purificatory powers, a pertinent gloss on Ermold's account of Louis' purgation of Saracen shrines and sponsorship of Danish converts: 'I shall gather you from every land, I shall pour clean water over you, and you will be cleansed from your wickedness.'[78] Baptism also drove out evil thoughts of adultery, fornication, and murder.[79] Leidrad's exegesis and Ermold's poetry both made this fundamental connection between baptism and peace. Exorcism was enacted by the destruction of Pharaoh's armies. Leidrad quoted Psalm LXXIII ('You have confirmed the sea in your virtue, in the waters you have smashed the dragons' heads').[80] His catalogue of baptismal prefigurations continued with Abraham and Isaac, and the belief that Solomon's kingdom took its name from a spring, suggesting that at the root of Israel's peace lay a form of collective baptism.[81] The Danes' crossing of the Rhine in one hundred white-sailed ships is questionable as actuality. However, the crossing of a river and the particular reference to the white sails hint that Ermold was using his account of Harald's physical journey into Christian, Frankish territory, as a symbol of the Danes' baptism and their entry into Christian spiritual space. Harald's leading position in the flotilla mirrored his leading position in the baptismal rite.[82]

'AGOBARDUS PAX SIT': THE POLEMICS
OF AGOBARD OF LYONS

All the figures we have looked at so far offer single perspectives, whether of abstract notions of royal power or snapshots of Louis' image as king. By contrast, Agobard of Lyon's career and writings stretch across nearly the whole span of Louis' reign.[83] Both hedgehog and fox, Agobard pursued a single theme across a number of subjects ranging from orthodox Christian practice and belief (Adoptionism, rural superstition, liturgical innovations) to the issue of the personality

---

[77] Leidrad of Lyons, *Liber de sacramento de baptismi*, PL 99, cols 853–72, c. 1, col. 855: 'Peccat mundus, et sine aquarum diluvio non purgatur: statimque columba Spiritus sancti expulso alite teterrimo, ita ad Noe, quasi ad Christum in Jordanem devolat, et ramo refectionis ac luminis pacem orbis annuntiat.'
[78] *Liber*, c. 1, col. 856, citing Ezek. XXXVI.24–5.
[79] *Liber*, c. 2, col. 858, citing Matt. XV.19.
[80] *Liber*, c. 1, col. 855, citing Ps. LXXIII.13.
[81] *Liber*, c. 1, col. 855.
[82] *In honorem*, IV, lines 2167–75, p. 166.
[83] L. Van Acker (ed.), *Agobardi Lugdunesis Opera Omnia*, CCCM 52 (Turnhout, 1981).

of law to attacks upon Lyons' Jewish communities following his appointment as bishop in 816.[84] His stance in the latter case played no small part in his estrangement from the emperor. Agobard's writings capture a crucial moment in the development of Carolingian political discourse, as ideas and terms that we have seen first emerge as elements in the language of rulership broadcast from the court in the later eighth century begin to be found in a broader, and often viciously critical, body of literature. Agobard's own career path was first as a hopeful partisan and later as an adversary to Louis.[85]

The letters and tracts he produced from the mid 810s until the late 820s took up the themes of peace and unity, repeatedly exhorting Louis the Pious to cultivate them.[86] By the early 830s Agobard had, most notably in the *Liber apologeticus*, turned against Louis. Once the former exemplar of Agobard's ideals of *pax*, *iustitia*, and *unitas* he became the enemy of all three.[87] His attitudes map the growing disillusionment that some, at least, felt towards Louis. An aggressive advocate of unity, Agobard's polemics betray a debt to St Paul's teachings on the mystical unity of the *corpus Christi*.[88] Indeed, the image of Christ as reconciler and macrocosm of the Christian society is pervasive in Agobard's thought, Ephesians II.14–18 in particular providing a scriptural reference point for unity, in works ranging from a theological exchange with Fredegisus to his assault upon the ordeal.[89]

Agobard's emphasis upon unity in Christ meant that it was less easy for him than for others to settle with approval into an attitude of praise to Carolingian reality. In 817, in the earliest phase of his episcopal career, he dispatched to Louis his infamous criticism of the empire's diversity of laws, and in particular Gundobad's, with its reliance upon personality of the law and use of the ordeal.[90] Some, at least, have seen in the work a response to Louis' proclamation on the *Ordinatio imperii* the same year, with its division of the empire, as much as any personal antipathy to judicial duels or particular laws bearing an Arian king's name. Diversity, Agobard argued, weakened the underlying peace and unity of the Carolingian realm. His solution was the replacement of all other laws in the empire by *Lex Salica*. If law was one means of binding a community, prayer was

[84] J. Cohen, *Living Letters of the Law. Ideas of the Jew in Medieval Christianity* (Berkeley, 1999), 67–71, 124–45; A. J. Zuckerman, 'The Political Uses of Theology: The Conflict of Bishop Agobard and the Jews of Lyons', in J. R. Sommerfeldt (ed.), *Studies in Medieval Culture* (Kalamazoo, MI, 1970), III, 23–51.

[85] See Agobard's letter to Adalard, Wala, and Helisachar, *MGH Epp.* V, no. 4(822), pp. 164–6, discussed in S. Airlie, 'Bonds of Power and Bonds of Association in the Court Circle of Louis the Pious', *CH*, 191–204, at 194.

[86] Boshof, *Agobard*, 38–54.

[87] Agobard, *Liber apologeticus Opera*, I, pp. 309–12, II, pp. 315–19.

[88] Boshof, *Agobard*, 42, 111–12.

[89] Agobard, *Adversus legem Gundobadi*, c. 3, p. 21; *Contra iudicium Dei*, c. 1, p. 31; *Contra obiectiones Fredegisi*, c. 2, pp. 281–300, c. 21, p. 299. Boshof, *Agobard*, 38–43.

[90] Agobard, *Adversus legem Gundobadi*, pp. 19–28.

another. Agobard stressed the Church and its rituals of solidarity, such as the recitation of the *Pater Noster*, as a force for peace and unity.[91] Prayer brought everyone together, regardless of race, circumstance, sex, or status. Unity in devotion fleetingly prefigured that of Heaven, a place of celestial brotherhood, eternal harmony and ordered unity.[92] In Agobard's high evaluation of the peace of the Church, and the intimations of heavenly peace defined by perfectly fixed relationships, we can glimpse a genuinely Augustinian attitude to peace in both its earthly and heavenly forms.[93] With it, perhaps, he expressed the implicitly subversive implication of such a position: that in prayer rather than in the peaceful rule of an earthly emperor lay the earthly intimation of Heaven. Later in the same tract, writing of the varieties of law within Louis' realm, Agobard again cited Paul's second letter to the Ephesians on Christ's union of the Old and the New Law, combining traditional Judaic law, set out in the Old Testament, with his own teachings: 'He is our peace, who has made two into one'.[94] Famously, in Agobard's hands this citation was directed at the particular circumstances of the Carolingian empire. The proliferation of earthly laws meant that to St Paul's roster of diverse identities (Gentile and Jew, barbarian and Scythian) overcome by universal union in Christ Agobard added some of the empire's subject peoples: Aquitanians and Italians, Burgundians and Alemanni. This multiplicity existed not only within regions or cities, but even in individual homes. Five men sitting together might each live subject to different law, observed Agobard, when it came to superficial temporal issues. Beneath such externals, however—in the realm of things perpetual—each held a common adherence to the law of Christ.[95]

There is no small irony in Agobard's attack upon 'Gundobad's law', and his claims of its supposedly divisive character. This was an attack upon a ruler who himself possessed considerable interest in notions of peace and unity, and whose own promulgation of 'milder laws' may well have been intended as part of a wider policy of fostering social cohesion between Burgundians and Romans.[96] If Gundobad's laws failed to win Agobard's approval he had warmer words for his counsellor, Avitus (*venerandus et sanctus vir*). In the *Liber adversus legem Gundobadi* Agobard included extracts from an otherwise lost dialogue between Gundobad and Avitus in which the latter made the case against ordeals and Gundobad's belief that God's judgement might be revealed by a battle's

---

[91] Agobard, *Adversus legem Gundobadi*, c. 2, pp. 19–20.
[92] Agobard, *Adversus legem Gundobadi*, c. 3, pp. 20–1.
[93] Agobard, *Adversus legem Gundobadi*, c. 6, p. 22.
[94] Agobard, *Liber*, c. 3, p. 21.
[95] Agobard, *Liber*, c. 4, p. 21. For divine law elsewhere in Carolingian thought see D. Ganz, 'The Predestination Debate', in M. Gibson and J. L. Nelson (eds), *Charles the Bald. Court and Kingdom*, 2nd edition (Aldershot, 1990), 283–302, at 290.
[96] Shanzer and Wood, *Avitus of Vienne*, 187–93 on this lost dialogue.

outcome.[97] More than that, those who possessed too keen a taste for war might themselves incur Divine disfavour as a direct result. Agobard quoted with evident approval Avitus' advice that would-be warriors reflect first upon the Psalmist's imprecation: 'Scatter Thou the nations that delight in wars (Ps. LXVII.31).'[98] Often, argued Avitus, the stronger or the more cunning party was victorious, not the just. War was no simple indicator of justice, nor warfare, even for a good cause, a righteous pursuit.[99] Avitus was not the only authority from whom Agobard drew in his polemic. To his arguments against legal plurality and the ordeal he appended a short *florilegium* of supporting scriptural passages, beginning once more with the much-favoured Ephesians II.14–18, each of which addressed themes such as peace, reconciliation, and right order, and to which he appended brief comments of his own.[100]

Agobard's polemics found a poor reception at court. By the early 830s, as rebellion and dissent gained ground and harmony became an increasingly distant prospect, personal antipathy fused with the broader political factionalism. In the growing dissent within the Carolingian house engendered by Louis' accommodation of Charles the Bald within the inheritance scheme, Agobard sided with Lothar, a party that was joined in 833 by Pope Gregory IV.[101] Rarely a reluctant royal correspondent, Agobard justified Gregory's involvement in a letter stressing, as the Pope himself would, that he had crossed the Alps to make peace. Liturgy again provided a paradigm of enacted unity, order, and collective belief as Agobard cited Pope Pelagius I's own citation of the words of the Roman Canon, reminding Louis of his obligation to protect the peace of the Church.[102] Similarly, Gregory IV had come to make peace.[103]

A second letter, written in Gregory's name but accepted by some as displaying Agobard's handiwork, looked less to papal precedent than to scripture and to patristic authority to justify Gregory's intervention.[104] Here, Gregory/Agobard drew from Gregory of Nazianzus, and Augustine's treatment of happy emperors.[105] Happy emperors were just, humble, merciful, and happy in the hope of the eternal kingdom. Louis was not, and was leading his people astray. The letter

---

[97] Agobard, *Liber*, c. 13, p. 27, discussed by Shanzer and Wood, *Avitus*, 187–93.

[98] Ibid.

[99] Ibid.

[100] *De divinis sententiis contra indicium Dei*, CCCM 52, 31–49 citing Luke II. 14; Ps. CXVIII. 165; Matt. V.9, p. 35. Other passages excerpted by Agobard that explicitly address peace include Matt. XXVI.52, Mark IX.49, p. 37; Jas III.14–8, 2 Tim. II.16–7, Rom. II.8–9, p. 39; I Cor. XIII.4–8, p. 42; 2 Cor. XIII.11, p. 42.

[101] On Gregory's participation in the rebellion see E. J. Goldberg, *Struggle for Empire: Kingship and Conflict under Louis the German, 817–876* (Ithaca, 2006), 69; J. Fried, 'Ludwig der Fromme, das Papsttum und die fränkische Kirche', *CH*, 266–70.

[102] *MGH Epp.*, V, no. 16, pp. 226–7.

[103] *MGH Epp.*, V, no. 16, p. 227.

[104] Van Acker accepts the letter as genuinely Gregorian, *Opera*, xxi–xxii, following the arguments of Boshof, *Agobard*, 225–8.

[105] *MGH Epp.*, V, no. 17(833), pp. 228–32.

was directed to the bishops still loyal to Louis, and presented the case for the superiority of papal over imperial authority (a rule over souls, not temporal flesh), reminding the Frankish bishops of the nature of that authority, and pointing out that any oath Gregory might have sworn to Louis was voided by his actions against the peace and unity of the kingdom.[106] Those claiming loyalty to Louis were flatterers when they ought to have been 'builders of the truth' (*aedificatores veri*). They were no better than liars.[107] The 831 redivision of the kingdom was the source of all dissent, and, furthermore, oath-breaking. Faith and peace had been driven out.[108] The letter argued for the peacemaking role of the papal expedition justifying Gregory's presence in Francia; making peace was part of a bishop's *ministerium*. Agobard/Gregory also evoked the idea of good-will:

Why had the bishops and their churches opposed him, when he had come on a mission of peace and unity, which were themselves Christ's gift and ministry? Did the Frankish bishops not know the song of the angels when they promised peace on earth to men of good will (Luke II.14)? The Apostle's words seemed apposite: 'Tribulation and anguish upon every soul of man that worketh evil' (Romans II.9). No less those of Proverbs: 'Arms and swords are in the way of the perverse' (Prov. XXII.5). The Frankish bishops were the perverse, as they attempted to stand in Gregory's way, 'we who are undertaking an embassy of peace'.[109]

Turning once more to the organic argument for unity, the letter continued: 'For whoever among you are limbs of Christ, you are not able to separate him from the body of the head, which is Christ', before launching into a complex treatment of the Spirit as ointment flowing from head to beard to tunic in the same way that the Holy Spirit joined all in peace.[110] Agobard mixed the scriptural symbolism of anointing with the language of *vincula pacis*, setting both within his own idiosyncratic extemporization on the Pauline trope of *ecclesia* as *corpus Christi*. If strained in execution we might discern behind the imagery a sense of the various scriptural treatments of peace, its imagery and types, and perhaps most importantly the degree to which these ideas flowed into one another.

If debate surrounds his involvement in Gregory's letter, the authorship of Agobard's most sustained polemic of the 830s, the *Liber apologeticus*—'two books on behalf of the sons of Louis the Pious against his wife, Judith' as it

---

[106] *MGH Epp.*, V, no. 17, p. 230.
[107] *MGH Epp.*, V, no. 17, p. 229.
[108] *MGH Epp.*, V, no. 17, p. 230.
[109] *MGH Epp.*, V, no. 17, p. 231: 'Quare mihi contrarii cum ecclesiis vestris esse debetis in legacione pacis et unitatis, quod Christi donum et ministerium est? An ignoratis angelorum cantu promissam esse pacem in terra hominibus bone voluntatis? per apostolorum autem tribulacionem et angustiam in omnem animam hominis operantis malum? Hic apparet, quod congruat vobis illud quod scriptura dicit: Arma et gladii in via perversi. Vos conamini obsistere perversitatibus vestris nobis, qui legacione fungimur pacis.'
[110] *MGH Epp.*, no. 17, p. 231, citing Ps. CXXXII.2.

might more properly be known—has gone without challenge. Agobard's broad-
side detailed what he saw as Judith's pernicious influence, and the pollution of
the palace caused by her misbehaviour.[111] The *Liber apologeticus* marks a new
willingness by Carolingian intellectuals to reflect not only publicly but also
negatively upon contemporary kingship. It was, after all, a tract intended not
to exhort but to denigrate the monarch, plotting divergences from the ideals of
christian rulership and exonerating the rebels' actions in consequence. Agobard
set out what Louis had failed to do: an emperor's task was to campaign beyond
the borders of the realm, against outside peoples, not to engage in disputes at the
heart of the kingdom.[112] To justify this view Agobard turned once more to the
index of liturgy, the ritualized creation of order and Christian peace, and quoted
directly from the text of a solemn mass for the emperor: 'in those solemn
speeches the Universal Church prays thus for emperors on the days of the
Lord's Passion, that God will make the barbarian nations subject to them'.[113]
Rather than expanding outwards in the pattern of the empire's formative years
Agobard saw Louis' kingdom in the 830s as a polity in contraction. Conflict on
the periphery had given way to trouble at the kingdom's very heart. This
corporeal metaphor of the kingdom, a sense of political and religious coherence
merging with the body of Christ, was pushed by Agobard into startling new
forms. Some of those causing trouble within the kingdom sought to rupture the
kingdom's guts.[114] Liturgy offered both an image of the healthy kingdom and
the cure for a sick one: Agobard advised everyone to pray. Collective worship
brought all together in Christ, even as the act of prayer enacted, fleetingly, a
collective ideal of imperial unity. Repeating the prayer's words later in the same
passage Agobard this time extended the quotation: 'We must also pray for our
most Christian emperor, that our God and Lord will make all barbarian nations
subject to Him for our perpetual peace.'[115] The hope was timely. Soon after
Agobard wrote, a sequence of raids upon the highly exposed, if resilient, northern
entrepôt of Dorestadt began.[116] For Agobard wars with outside enemies were
justified (*bella justa*), but those campaigns waged by Louis within the bounds of
empire, against 'the sons who love him', were not.[117] It fell to all those who loved
and feared God, and wanted a peaceful society to strive to heal the wounds the

[111] *Lib. apol.*, c. 2, p. 309. For palace as metonym for the kingdom see Nelson, 'Kingship and
Empire', 59.
[112] *Lib. apol.*, c. 3, p. 310.
[113] *Lib. apol.*, c. 3, p. 310.
[114] *Lib. apol.*, c. 3, p. 310.
[115] *Lib. apol.*, c. 3, p. 310: '... qui omnes pia mente perpendere debuerant quod dicitur in praedictis
orationibus, ubi sacerdos admonet, dicens: Oremus et pro Christianissimo imperatore nostro, ut Deus et
Dominus noster subditas illi faciat omnes barbaras nationes, ad nostram perpetuam pacem.'
[116] *AB s.a.* 834.
[117] *Lib. apol.*, c. 4, p. 311.

kingdom had suffered.[118] Truth, too, had been lost. Truth that, Agobard continued, citing Paul to the Ephesians, brought humanity closer to God.[119] Agobard sketched out his ideal state:

Therefore if that truth possessed the minds of all men of which we sing in the Psalms: 'Thou art near, Lord, and all Thy ways are truth' (Ps. CXVIII.151), even without rulers or princes the things of this world would remain peaceful in harmonious agreement.[120]

For Agobard truth was the key to order. Its absence in the Carolingians' world, however, had pitched it from peace and quiet into disorder.[121] For peace to return, Agobard taught, truth and peace had to be defended from their corrupters.[122] Only through God's grace had the conflict been settled.[123] Louis, he declared with vitriol, was the destroyer of the kingdom's peace through his decision to marry Judith.[124] His sons, for their part, sought—albeit through rebellion—to right the disorder and disturbances her presence had generated.[125]

Agobard's confrontational polemics and his earlier decision to support rebellion against Louis served, in his own eyes at least, the twin causes of unity and peace. In what was almost certainly his last work, a sixty-line acrostic poem, Agobard's restless quest for peace turned from the wider world and inwards, reflecting upon his own death and judgement.[126] The initials of its fourteen strophes spell out AGOBARDO PAX SIT ('Let there be peace for Agobard'). The phrase both echoed and privatized the words of the liturgy (*pax Domini sit semper vobiscum*). What had once been Agobard's index for all Christian society became a frame for understanding his own circumstances in a poem that meditated upon God the almighty, witness, judge, and supreme dispenser of just punishment. In the end, the universal precepts of the Christian life and collective Christian law gave way to the solitary figure of the bishop of Lyons.[127]

---

[118] *Lib. apol.*, c. 6, p. 312.

[119] *Lib. apol.*, c. 7, p. 315.

[120] *Lib. apol.*, c. 7, p. 315: 'Si ergo illa veritas de qua et in psalmis cantamus; "Prope es tu, Domine, et omnes viae tuae veritas", omnium hominum mentes possideret, etiam sine rectoribus et principibus res mundi concordi societate pacatae manerent.'

[121] *Lib. apol.*, c. 7, p. 315.

[122] *Lib. apol.*, c. 7, p. 316.

[123] *Lib. apol.*, c. 8, p. 315.

[124] *Lib. apol.*, c. 8, pp. 315–16.

[125] *Lib. apol.*, c. 8, p. 316: 'Cumque talibus incrementis viderent hii, quibus cure erat de statu et honore regni, ac tranquillitate pacis et quiete populi, dehonestari palacium, obscurari claritatem regni et ad ignominiam deduci nomen regnantium, coeperunt queri et murmurare ac dolere et deplorare.'

[126] *CM* 52, no. 26, pp. 371–3. Commentary: L. Van Acker, 'Notice sur le poème rythmique *Agobardo pax sit*', *RB* 88 (1978), 291–5, discussing attribution at 292–3.

[127] Boshof, *Agobard*, 321–2.

Unity found its ultimate reduction—the individual soul's judgement for fitness
for admission to the eternal peace of the Heavenly Jerusalem.

'THE BUSINESS OF A KING . . .' : THE SONG
OF COUNT TIMO

Perhaps mercifully not all commentators on the troubled years of the early 830s
were as intense as Agobard. We encountered the anonymous author of the Song
of Count Timo (*Carmen de Timone comite*) at the very beginning of this book,
and now we can set him in his proper landscape. Composed in 834, the 'Song'
was dedicated to Louis the German and composed either by a member of
Freising's episcopal *familia* or the nearby monastery of Weihenstephan.[128] The
context of the poem's composition is specific. In the wake of his restoration Louis
the Pious had ordered that royal legates be sent out across the kingdom to ensure
order had indeed been fully restored after Lothar's rebellion. Louis the German's
eye for the choice of legate for Bavaria fell on Timo, a member of an aristocratic
family with substantial holdings around Freising.[129] The poem combined general praise with specific criticisms of Timo's belief in the efficacy of the ordeal and
his evident lack of belief in being respectful of the church of Freising, its first
bishop and patron St Corbinian. Timo had let his dog drink from the saint's holy
spring and the dog then paid the price for its master's disrespect. It dropped
dead.[130] As we've seen, the song's author had spelled out, in the bluntest terms,
the basics of kingship:

> The business of a king, believe me, is to restrain the harmful,
> And to raise the heavy yoke from innocent necks.
> For the business of a king is wholly to support peace,
> And to wield, with a discerning hand, a kingdom's sceptre.[131]

The anonymous poet went on to offer up a brief selection of biblical exemplars
starting with David and including Job, Moses, and Joseph.[132] The Freising poet
shared with Agobard contempt for the notion that ordeals revealed the truth,
arguing that such results were against reason (*ratio*). If it were that easy to reveal

---

[128] *MGH Poetae* II, 120–4. Discussion: W. C. Brown, *Unjust Seizure: Conflict, Interest, and
Authority in an Early Medieval Society* (Cornell, 2001), 1–4; Anton, *Fürstenspiegel*, 245–7.

[129] Goldberg, *Struggle*, 209 n. 115; K. L. Roper Pearson, *Conflicting Loyalties in Early Medieval
Bavaria: a View of Socio-Political Interaction 680–900* (Aldershot, 1999), 197–8.

[130] Brown, *Unjust Seizure*, 1–6. For contemporary anxieties about dogs in holy space see Meens,
'Politics', 348.

[131] *MGH Poetae* II, p. 121, lines 13–16: 'Regia, crede mihi, res est inhibere nocentes, /
Insontumque gravi colla levare iugo. / Regia prorsus enim res est succurrere paci. / Discreta et
regni sceptra movere manu.'

[132] *MGH Poetae* II, p. 121, lines 17–40.

right from wrong, he noted wisdom would be unnecessary.[133] And wisdom, the poet had already made clear, was one of the core attributes of a good king:

> A state is happy when he who rules it is one
> Who has sense, or at least rules himself sensibly.
> For the wise king is one seen as the people's support.
> Happy is the land in which a wise king rules well.[134]

Wisdom was the key to order, and to war's end, including the civil unrest that had recently wracked the Carolingian world:

> The salvation of the world is ensured by the collective advice of many wise men,
> And now war's end has been achieved.[135]

A king was to rule rightly and wisdom, the poet implied, was also needed by those who sought to follow his will and keep order in his realm. This is not, even by ninth-century standards, sophisticated political theory. But its value lies in its pithiness. The Freising author offered an image of kingship reduced to its essence: preventing injury, protecting the people, upholding the peace. If not quite a Carolingian equivalent of the politicized peasantry of thirteenth-century Peatling Magna made famous by Powicke, this poem is, as Warren Brown has rightly observed, a rare glimpse of the political engagement of the ruled with the methods of the rulers from outside the established centres of power and scholarship.[136] The anonymous poet doubted Timo's forensic rigour, and disapproved of his lack of respect for the purity of the local healing spring, but he was certain about the job of a king. It was to fulfil the role for which Charlemagne had been acclaimed, and that Smaragdus and others set out as a king's responsibility: to make and keep the peace.

LAMENTING LOST PEACE: FLORUS OF LYONS' AUGUSTINIAN VISION

The 840s opened with the *Brüderkrieg* and the horrors of Fontenoy, a battle that confounded order and the ties of kinship that earlier commentators had stressed were so central to earthly peace, pitching 'brother against brother, nephew against

---

[133] *MGH Poetae* II, p. 122, lines 77–8: 'Haud opus est ratio, sapientia nulla necesse est, / Totus in ambiguum sermo loquax teritur.'

[134] *MGH Poetae* II, p. 122, lines 41–4: 'Publica res tunc est felix, quando inperat ille / Qui sapit, aut certe qui regit ipse sapit. / Rex sapiens stabilimentum quia plebis habetur, / Terra beata, regit quam bene rex sapiens.'

[135] *MGH Poetae* II, p. 122, lines 47–8: 'Iuncta salus orbi multorum cum sapientum / Consiliis et iam bella patrata silent.'

[136] Brown, *Unjust Seizure*, 4. On Powicke, J. M. Wallace-Hadrill, and Peatling Magna see M. Wood, 'Peatling Magna: August, 1265', in *idem, In Search of England. Journeys into the English Past* (London, 1999), 247–69, at 247–50.

uncle' and leaving a bitter legacy.[137] The poet Angilbert claimed that the date of
the battle itself deserved to be reviled: 'Let it not be counted in the cycle of the
year'.[138] Whatever suspicion contemporary historians might harbour towards
master narratives, Carolingian authors were wedded to them; narratives of salvation, redemption and, as we move into the middle years of the ninth century,
political decline. In the 840s we encounter a further generation of commentators
for whom peace was neither to be celebrated nor debated, but lamented.

Several of Agobard's key concerns re-emerge in the writings of his student,
Florus, in particular in his *Querela de divisione Imperii,* a poetic reflection on the
destruction of the 840s, composed in early 842.[139] Yet whilst Florus' thought
carries traces of Agobard's influence, it also displays significant differences. At
least a generation younger than his teacher, for Florus the image of Charlemagne's reign had already frozen into an image of a lost golden age. 'All the
goodness of peace', he wrote, 'is ripped apart by bitter hatreds'.[140] In his
polemics Agobard drew upon the political lexicon of Charlemagne's day to
transform a rhetoric of ideals and virtues into an index of political criticism.
For all his ire, for Agobard such states remained within reach, and correctives
remained possible: a peaceful and ordered empire still attainable. In its own way
Florus' verse was underpinned by an equally acute sense of the achievements of
Charlemagne's day and the public forms of their celebration. His conviction that
a contemporary ruler might match such past achievements was, however, less
firmly held than it had been by Agobard. For the latter, the failure to do so lay
with Louis personally. For Florus, the goals of peace and order seemed beyond
reach. He was not a lone pessimist. Similar sentiments are to be found in the later
books of Nithard's *Histories* and in the commentaries of Hrabanus Maurus,
Haimo, and Paschasius Radbertus on Jeremiah and Lamentations.[141] It is too

---

[137] *MGH Poetae,* II, p. 138, lines 5–6: 'frater fratri mortem parat, nepoti avunculus; / filius nec
patri suo exhibet quod meruit.' J. L. Nelson, 'The Search for Peace in a Time of War, the
Carolingian *Brüderkreig, 841–843*', in J. Fried (ed.), *Träger und Instrumentarien des Friedens im
hohen und späten Mittelalter,* VuF 43 (1996), 87–114. For Nithard's allusion to *odia fraterna,
Histoire,* I.6, p. 28.
[138] *MGH Poetae* II, p. 139, lines 7–8: 'Maledicta dies illa, nec in anni circulo / numeretur, sed
radatur ab omni memoria.'
[139] *MGH Poetae* II, p. 559–64. On Florus' career and particularly his interest in Augustine see
C. Charlier, 'Les manuscrits personnels de Florus de Lyons et son activité littéraire', *Mélanges
E. Podechard* (Lyons, 1945), 71–84. Boshof has argued that Florus' thought was essentially an
epilogue to the polemics of the 830s: *idem,* 'Einheitsidee und Teilungsprinzip in der Regierungszeit
Ludwigs der Frommen', *CH,* 161–89, at 189. See also Boshof's discussion of the poem, 312–13.
Alternatively, Godman, *Poets,* 149–52, at 149.
[140] *MGH Poetae* II, p. 560, line 11: 'Omne bonum pacis odiis laniatur acerbis'. See K. Zechiel-
Eckes, *Florus von Lyon als Kirchenpolitiker und Publizist. Studien zu Persönlichkeit eines karolingischen
'Intellektuellen' am Beispiel der Auseinandersetzung mit Amalarius (835–838) und des
Prädestinationsstreits (851–855)* (Stuttgart, 1999), 15–16.
[141] Nithard, *Historiarum,* IV, c. 7, pp. 49–50, on Nithard's pessimism see J. L. Nelson, 'Public
Histories and the Private History in the Work of Nithard', *P&R,* 223–6, esp. 225, and S. Airlie,
'The World, the Text and the Carolingian: Royal, Aristocratic and Masculine Identities in Nithard's

simplistic to see exegetical interests as a kind of seismograph of wider concerns, but it is suggestive that in the 840s and 850s scholars turned to Jeremiah's account of Israel after Jerusalem's fall to Nebuchadnezzar and the Temple's destruction, when the reigns of David and Solomon grew increasingly distant. All might be read as symptoms of what David Ganz has termed the growing pessimism of the Carolingian humanists.[142]

Florus' *Querela*, often cited by those seeking Carolingian self-awareness of decline, might equally be read as complement and counterpoint to Cathwulf's Pseudo-Cyprianic invocation of the positive cosmic consequences of Charlemagne's rule. For Florus, like Cathwulf some sixty years before, the natural world responded to Frankish power. But for Florus the response was not an acceptance and adherence to right order, but rather a horror at its loss. Mountains, valleys, woods and rivers, springs and cliff sides grieved for the Frankish people.[143] With good reason, for Florus offered an image of moral and social collapse. Nuns, the poor, even scholars: none was safe from the violence of the nobility.[144] *Sanguine terra madet*: the earth was sodden with blood.[145] The words were Virgil's, from his account of the war in Italy between Aeneas' Trojans and the Latins led by Turnus. Earlier Carolingian poets had used Virgil's words as he himself had, to praise earthly power and to set it in a wide frame. Florus deployed them to lament their failings.[146] His vision of the lost Carolingian idyll is of a world of a single *princeps* and *populus*, where law and good judgement held sway, a place of learning and piety where the citizens (*cives*) lived in peace, and the collective *virtus* of the Carolingian armies held back enemies.[147] Florus expressed no doubt that this image of a past era of peace was anything less than accurate but he was not unaware of the possibilities of the disjunction between rhetoric and reality. Celebrations after Verdun were hollow for Florus. 'Peace they call it', he wrote, 'where there are none of the rewards of peace.'[148] The peace brought about by

---

Histories', in Wormald and Nelson, *Lay Intellectuals*, 51–76. Hrabanus Maurus, *Expositionis super Jeremiam prophetam libri viginti*, PL 111, cols 793–1272; Paschasius Radbertus, *Expositio in Lamentationes Hieremiae libri quinque*, ed. P. Beda, CCSL 85 (Turnhout, 1988). On both see E. A. Matter, 'The Lamentations Commentaries of Hrabanus Maurus and Paschasius Radbertus', *Traditio* 38 (1982), 137–63.

[142] Ganz, 'Predestination Debate', 286. On the anxieties and disillusionment that followed in the wake of Fontenoy, and their manifestation in a collection of scriptural passages preserved in two manuscripts from Cambrai and Corbie, P. Finsterwalder, 'Eine Parteipolitische Kundegebung eines Anhängers Lothars I', *NA* 47 (1928), 393–415.

[143] *MGH Poetae* II, pp. 559–60.

[144] *MGH Poetae* II, p. 560, lines 13–40.

[145] *MGH Poetae* II, p. 560, line 23.

[146] Aen. 12.691. On a later reuse see T. Andersson, 'Blood on the Battlefield: A Note on the Ludwigslied v. 49', *Neophilologus* 56.1 (1972), 12–17, discussing Florus at 15–17.

[147] *MGH Poetae* II, p. 561, lines 41–4.

[148] *MGH Poetae* II, p. 562, lines 11–2: Et pacem vocitant, nulla est ubi gratia pacis.'

the division of the empire was not true peace. But how could there be peace, asked the student of Agobard, without unity?[149]

Florus' condemnation belongs to a longer tradition: a more durable Augustinian suspicion of facades and false substance. By the 840s, it might be said, holes were beginning to show in the fabric of Carolingian political rhetoric. Flours' response was an equally crafted anti-rhetoric of disorder.

> The kingdom has equally lost the name and the honour of empire,
> The united kingdom has fallen into three lots.
> For there is no one at all who is recognized as emperor,
> For a king there is a petty king. For a kingdom, broken pieces of a Kingdom.[150]

The people from all over the Carolingian territory, distinguished by Florus through the rivers that ran through their regions—the Danube, Rhine, Rhône, Loire, and Po—once joined together in *concordia* were now divided by broken treaties and sad divisions.[151] Theodulf had used these rivers to limn the expanse of Charlemagne's authority. For Florus they delineated the fractures in the Carolingian world. Florus' poem closed, like Agobard before him, with its author turning his gaze away from the landscape of divided Francia towards heaven, and its gates of peace: what man could not vouchsafe, God alone could give. The coming of the Heavenly Kingdom, he wrote, would bring true peace for those who had been faithful and loving to Him, amongst whom Florus counted himself. He closed his lament with an address to God, a variation on a familiar Gregorian theme:

> Plucked from the black waves of the sea
> Coming to the port of peace through your skilful piloting,
> We may pluck sweet fruit grown from sad seed,
> And sing again in perpetual praise of Your triumphs.[152]

Whilst less overtly political, Florus' other verses reveal a similar sense of the lost peace of the past. His verses on the translation of the relics of the saints Cyprian, Pantaleon, and Speratus to Lyons tell a similar story with an opening image of Charlemagne, '*rector magnificus, piusque princeps*', dispatching a party to recover the neglected relics of the saints from Carthage, a city fallen into ruin and under barbarian domination, at a time while peace and quiet prevailed in

---

[149] Zechiel-Eckes, *Florus*, 15–16, 64, 156–8.

[150] *MGH Poetae* II, p. 561, lines 73–6: 'Perdidit imperii pariter nomenque decusque, / Et regnum unitum concidit sorte triformi, / Induperator ibi prorsus iam nemo putatur, / Pro rege est regulus, pro regno fragmina regni.'

[151] *MGH Poetae* II, p. 562, lines 85–8.

[152] *MGH Poetae* II, p. 564, lines 169–72: 'Quatinus erepti pelagi de fluctibus atris / Teque gubernante iam portum pacis adepti / Carpamus dulcem tristi de semine frugem / Perpetuaque tuos recinamus laude triumphos.'

Francia.[153] Pippin's revised prologue to *lex Salica* had stressed the superiority of the Franks' veneration of the martyrs over that of the Romans. Florus felt comparably with regard to the contemporary Christian community in Carthage.[154] Carolingian Lyons was, perhaps, an apposite resting place for the bones of one of the early Church's great advocates of unity, whose name—perhaps for that very reason—had become attached to *de XII abusivis*, with its own influential vision of order.[155]

Something of this can be seen in his exposition of the Mass of the later 830s in which he explored the liturgical salutations. The greeting 'Pax vobsicum', for example, referred not to peace in the human realm but in a higher sense—as the Angel greeted Daniel, and the Apostles each other, and this was an appropriate greeting for the bishops, their heirs.[156] This peace, Florus explained, was neither worldly nor fallen, but divine and eternal. It was the peace that reconciled man to God, that fortified man against the temptations of the Devil and earthly enemies, and fostered bonds of love with those close.[157] Expounding the meaning of the *Vere dignum*, the preface to the Mass, Florus explored Christ's role as mediator and as reconciler, between mankind and the angels, and mankind and God, 'making peace through the blood of His Cross'. Florus offered his readers Augustine's vision of the world to come, of a Heavenly Jerusalem comprising all the faithful since the world's beginning, together with the legions and armies of the angels, one city under one king, 'like a kind of province under one governor' happy in perpetual peace and security, praising God, joyfully, eternally.[158]

In a later chapter Florus addressed the nature of the Church itself, drawing from Isidore's exploration of *ecclesia* stressing both its universality and the need for the peace that it enjoys to be both internal, freedom from heresy and schism, and external, freedom from outside persecution. Florus quoted St Paul:

'And the peace of God, which surpasseth all understanding, keep your hearts and minds in Jesus Christ.' (Phil. IV.7) And He advises the whole Church to pray, when he says: 'I desire therefore, first of all, that supplications, prayers, intercessions and thanksgivings be made for all men.' (I Tim II.1) And, a little later: 'that we may lead a quiet and a peaceable life in all piety'. It is asked of Almighty God that he should deign to watch over, unite and govern it. For He is the true guardian of His people, that is the true Israel, of which the psalm is sung: 'Behold, he who guards Israel has neither slept, nor will

---

[153] *MGH Poetae* II, pp. 544–5. On the cult of Cyprian see M. Handley, 'Disputing the End of African Christianity', in A. Merrills (ed.), *Vandals, Romans and Berbers: New Perspectives on Late Antique North Africa* (Aldershot, 2004), 291–310, esp. 304–6; C. Courtois, 'Réliques carthaginoises et légende carolingienne', *Revue de l'histoire des religions* 129 (1945), 57–83.

[154] That such a community did indeed exist is argued, convincingly, by Handley, 'Disputing'.

[155] For Cyprian's influence upon Florus' thought Zechiel-Eckes, *Florus*, 200–4, 224.

[156] *De expositione Missae*, PL 119, cols 15–72, here c. 13, cols 26–8. For Florus' reliance upon earlier works in the composition of the work: J.-P. Bouhout, 'Fragments attribués à Vigile de Thapse dans l'Expositio missae de Lyon', *REA* 21 (1975), 302–16.

[157] *De Ep. miss.* c. 13, PL 119, col. 27.

[158] *De Ep. miss.* c. 25, PL 119, col. 35.

slumber'. (Ps. CXX.3–4). And again: 'Unless the Lord has guarded the city, he who guards it watches in vain.' (Ps. CXXVI.1) It appears, however, that uniting is pacifying and guarding is ruling because God unites his Church by pacifying and pacifies it by uniting, and rules it by guarding and guards it by ruling.[159]

Later Florus offered an extended treatment of prayers for peace beginning by establishing their scriptural basis with the words the Lord spoke to the captive Israelites through the Prophet Jeremiah: 'And pray for the peace of the city to which I have caused you to be carried away, for in the peace therefore shall be your peace. (Jer. XXIX. 7)' The earthly kingdom in which all Christians found themselves was itself a kind of Babylon.[160]

Explaining the prayer '*Da propitius pacem in diebus nostris*', Florus invoked the figure of Hezekiah. 'He said "Let there be peace and truth in my days,"' Florus explained. 'Peace, that the tranquillity of the kingdom would not be disturbed by enemies, and truth, that in that peace itself the worship of God, the truth of religion, will be preserved.'[161] Returning to Paul's injunction on the need to pray for quiet and tranquillity, Florus explained that 'quiet and tranquillity relate to peace, piety to the religion of divine worship. And so, therefore, the Church prays for peace to exist in our days, as others after us, and yet others after them, right on until the end of the world, will pray in the same way.'[162] But when peace is asked for, cautioned Florus in his exposition of the symbolism of the *Pater Noster*:

God's help and mercy are vital that we might be free from sin and safe from all disturbance, for peace which is in the service not of divine religion but earthly greed, is not the peace of the Just, but of the Unjust of whom the Psalmist said: 'Because I had a zeal on occasion of the wicked, seeing the peace of sinners' (Ps. LXXII.3).

Florus set out the sharp division between the treacherous and inherently limited nature of earthly peace and its slippery symbols, and the unchanging character of heavenly peace, manifest not in political communities but intimated in the liturgically constituted community of worshippers. Here he spliced the words of Augustine, mediated through Prosper, with Bede's from his commentary on the seven Catholic epistles.[163]

---

[159] *De Ep. miss.* c. 46, PL 119, col. 45.

[160] *De Ep. miss.* c. 85, PL 119, col. 69.

[161] *De Ep. miss.* c. 86, col. 69: 'Quod ergo dicit Ecclesia: Da propitius pacem in diebus nostris, manifeste juxta exemplum quod in Isaia legitur, hoc facit. Cum enim praedixisset idem propheta Ezechiae regi nostro venturae captivitatis mala, compunctus respondit: Bonum verbum Domini quod locutus est; fiat tantum pax et veritas in diebus meis (Is. XXXIX.8), videlicet futura humiliter, Dei judicio reservans, de praesenti vero quod ad suam et populi sui salutem pertinebat, deprecans: Fiat, inquit, pax et veritas in diebus meis: pax, ne regni tranquillitas ab hostibus turbaretur; veritas vero, ut in ipsa pace Dei cultus, religionis veritas, servaretur.'

[162] *De Ep. miss.*, c. 86, col. 70: 'Ita ergo et Ecclesia deprecatur pacem fieri in diebus nostris, quod et post nos alii, et post ipsos alii usque ad consummationem saeculi utique similiter orabunt.'

[163] Prosper, *Liber sententiarum*, CCSL 121, c. 373, p. 356, also excerpted by Florus in his Expositio on St Paul, PL 119, col. 284. For Bede see D. Hurst (ed.), *In epistulas septem catholicas*

For what is the Peace of the Lord, unless it is Christ's peace? The peace of Christ, however, has no temporal end, and it is itself the perfection of all devoted action and intention. On account of this peace we believe and hope in Him, and we are inflamed with his love, as much as he bestows, on account of this peace we bravely endure all tribulation that we might rule in it happily without tribulation. For true peace produces unity, beacause he who clings to the Lord is of one spirit. With peace therefore prayed for, beginning with the priest, the whole Church gives itself mutually the kiss of peace so that, with all united by true peace, there should be the peace of God amongst them, as is said in the Psalm: 'And his place is made in peace' (Ps. LXXV.3). And may it be fulfilled in the Church what the Psalmist says elsewhere: 'God is in his holy place, God makes the unanimous dwell in his house' (Ps. LXVII.6–7). And this the Church preserves from the Apostolic tradition, the Church of which the same Apostles often said: 'Greet one another in a holy kiss' (Rom. XVI.16), that is a true kiss, a peacemaking kiss, a dove-like kiss, not false and deceitful like the one Joab used to kill Amasia, like Judas in betraying the Saviour, like that used by those 'who speak peace with their nearest whilst harbouring evil in their hearts' (Ps. XXVII.3). They therefore greet one another with a holy kiss who do not love with words or tongue but in actuality and in truth.[164]

If one were to see a pattern in Florus' vision one might say that political unrest drove him from any easy notion of an earthly peace, and from the successors of Charlemagne who might claim to provide it, and instead towards Christ, the true Prince of Peace. Just as the disruptions of the later fourth and early fifth centuries put paid to an optimistic celebration of earthly imperial authority and the peace of the Church, so the events of the middle years of the ninth century had in their turn driven Florus, like Agobard in his final years, into an Augustinian distance from the fallen world, and towards a focus upon the peace of the Heavenly Jerusalem and its *vestigia* in the world.

CCSL 121 (Turnhout, 1983), II.5. On this passage, and its ascription by Florus to Vigilius, Bouhot, 'Fragments', 315.

[164] *De Ep. miss.* c. 86, col. 71: 'Quid est autem pax Domini, nisi pax Christi? Pax autem Christi finem temporis non habet, et ipsa est omnis piae actionis intentionisque perfectio. Propter hanc pacem in eum credimus et speramus, et amore ipsius, quantum donat, accendimur: propter hanc denique omnem tribulationem fortiter toleramus, ut in ea feliciter sine tribulatione regnemus. Vera enim pax unitatem facit, quoniam qui adhaeret Domino unus spiritus est. Imprecata igitur pace, incipiens a sacerdote, dat sibi mutuo omnis Ecclesia osculum pacis, ut, omnibus vera pace unitis, fiat in eis locus Dei, sicut dicitur in psalmo: Et factus est in pace locus eius (Ps. LXXI.13). Et impleatur in Ecclesia quod alibi Psalmista dicens: Deus in loco sancto suo, Deus inhabitare facit unanimes in domo (Ps. LXVII.17). Et hoc utique ex traditione apostolica servat Ecclesia, cui frequenter ab eiusdem apostolis dicitur: Salutate invicem in osculo sancto (Rom. XVI.16), id est osculo vero, osculo pacifico, osculo columbino, non ficto et subdolo, quali usus est Joab ad occidendum Amasiam, quali Judas ad tradendum Salvatorem, quali utuntur hi qui loquuntur pacem cum proximo suo, mala autem in cordibus eorum. Illi ergo osculo sancto salutant invicem qui non diligunt verbis nec lingua, sed opere et veritate.'

DHUODA OF SEPTIMANIA

Schooled in the ideological microclimate of Agobard's Lyons and steeped in Augustine's writings, Florus' attitudes to the world of the early 840s is perhaps not surprising. That they were to some extent shared by his contemporary, Dhuoda, wife of Bernard of Septimania, raises substantial questions about the degree to which higher learning pervaded elite lay Carolingian society.[165]

Dhuoda recorded that she had begun writing her *Liber manualis* for her son William on 30 November 841 (the first day of Advent), finishing it on 2 February 843, the feast of the Purification of the Virgin. In the *Liber* Dhuoda set out both to shape William's perception of his own familial past—to reinforce familial duties, and cement obligations of remembrance—and to guide him in his life as both a Christian and, more specifically, as a son 'commended' into the hands of Charles the Bald. As the son of a troublesomely independent father William stood as a pledge for his father's good conduct, one whose own future loyalty might be bolstered through his integration into the networks of Charles' court. Distant from the physical halls of power she may have been but Dhuoda nevertheless knew something of the real processes of the Carolingian court at work, and sought to guide her son through them.

Dhuoda's notion of peace was a complex one. At its deepest level she expressed a profound sense of the limited nature of earthly rule: 'In this world the way we talk is as if we might put whatever we please in our power, when it isn't so. For those who make their way in the world say, "This is *my* kingdom", and "In my whole kingdom", because they fail to consider that the kingdom is the Lord's, and everything that passes through it.'[166] Earthly power was temporary, a lesson Dhuoda pointed out to William was evident in the history of his clan.[167] Even more fundamental was the fleeting nature of life itself. It was as fragile as a cobweb.[168] This core sense drove her insistence upon the prevailing need for her son to live a good Christian life, in the process ensuring his entry into the one kingdom that would not fall, and under the rule of the only king whose power was without end. Dhuoda was direct in her portrait of the true ruler: 'His is the power, the kingdom and the power to command. The most holy Daniel said firmly of the power and the kingdom: "His power is an

[165] *Lib. man.* XI.2, p. 238. J. L. Nelson, 'Dhuoda', *Lay Intellectuals*, 106–20, esp. 116–19.
[166] *Lib. man.* I.5, p. 64: 'Usus locutionis nostrae in saeculo talis est, ut cuiuslibet rem in nostram vertamur potestatem, cum non sit ita. Contendit quis in saeculo et dicit: "Meum est regnum" et "in toto meo regno", et non considerat quia Domini est regnum et omnium currentium in eo.'
[167] *Lib. man.* I.5, p. 66.
[168] *Lib. man.* V.1, p. 166.

enduring power that shall never be withdrawn, and his kingdom shall not be destroyed"'.[169]

Their own age, however, was one in which strife prevailed. Dhuoda quoted St Paul: 'The days are evil' (Eph. V.16).[170] And she feared William would himself be touched by that evil. Nevertheless, she reminded him later in the handbook, God had chosen to raise Charles the Bald and his brothers as kings, and William was to bear his responsibilities and place in the kingdom's order with patience. She offered the hope that God, the Highest King, might preserve agreement and harmony between them, and that together they might follow in their own day in the tradition of peace of their forefathers'.[171] William was himself to pray for 'kings and those of the highest position' that they might uphold the universal Church's firm faith in Christ, and order the earthly kingdom in peace in such a way that they might attain the heavenly kingdom'.[172] To navigate successfully through this landscape it was vital that William follow a rigorous Christian life. In a fashion analogous to the way in which contemporary theorists of kingship placed a king's right relationship to God at the centre of their visions of royal success and collective prosperity, Dhuoda saw William's personal piety as the key to his success in the political life of a far from perfect earthly kingdom. Dhuoda offered concrete advice on how William might both deepen his personal faith and better understand the governing principles to which all kingdoms in *saeculum* were susceptible: acquire a library, use it to deepen your understanding of faith, pray and love God. Were William to do so, God would give him wealth, and 'convert all his enemies to peace' (Prov. XVI.7).[173] As for other Carolingian theorists, humility was crucial. 'The Lord causes those who share His humility to climb up step by step to find peace in Heaven.'[174] If William was both humble and peaceful, his mother counselled, he was certain to receive at least some of the gifts of the grace of the Holy Spirit.[175] He should control his anger and, as much as possible, have peace with all men.[176] It was at this point that Dhuoda offered a short set of verses related to both Smaragdus' verses of peace and, ultimately, to the prayer on peace from the seventh-century Pseudo-Eugenian work on lay virtues:

---

[169] *Lib. man.* I.5, p. 66: 'Deus universorum ipse est; ipsius est potestas regnumque et imperium. De qua potestate et regno sanctissimus Danihel firmiter dicit: "Potestas eius, potestas aeterna quae non auferetur et regnum quod non corrumpetur (Dan. VII.14).'

[170] *Lib. man.* IV.2, p. 130.

[171] *Lib. man.* III.8, p. 106: 'Faciat eos omnipotens Almus Rexque fortis atque praeclarior Summus, conformes atque concordes, genitorumque more pacem sequaces hoc praesenti in saeculo . . .'.

[172] *Lib. man.* VIII.5, p. 198: 'Pro regibus et cunctis sublimibus illorum, ut firmam in Christo teneant religionem universalis Ecclesiae, regnumque terenum ita cum pace disponant ut illum acquirant coelestem.'

[173] *Lib. man.* I.7, p. 68.

[174] *Lib. man.* IV.3, p. 132.

[175] *Lib. man.* IV.3, p. 134.

[176] *Lib. man.* IV.7, pp. 144–6.

> Peace restrains anger.
> A quarrel fears peace.
> Untroubled peace rests far and wide.[177]

Be like Moses, Dhuoda counselled, like the anonymous author of the verses on Timo, the leader who always kept his anger in check and lived tranquilly and healthily, until his peaceful death.[178]

REGIMES OF FRATERNAL PEACE

Whilst the figure of Moses may not have been uppermost in their minds, over the course of the ninth century Carolingians rulers repeatedly prescribed formalized scripts for peaceful interaction. In the text of his 806 *divisio* Charlemagne had encouraged his sons to strive to defend their frontiers and maintain peace and *caritas* with each other. Further, he forbade them to invade each other's territory under any pretext, nor to receive his brother's man, and to present a common front to enemies.[179] Disputes over shared borders that could not be settled by witness testimony were to be decided through the ordeal of the cross, but never by violence or on the field of battle.[180] Louis' *Ordinatio Imperii* developed these injunctions by setting out concrete processes intended to sustain 'everlasting peace (*pax perpetua*) between his sons for the benefit of all Christian people'.[181] Together or individually, Pippin and Louis were to meet with Lothar annually to discuss matters that demanded collective attention in the interests of the common good and for the maintenance of everlasting peace. If indisposed, ambassadors were to deputize.[182] The two younger brothers were to bring gifts for Lothar, and he was to reciprocate; as the eldest, his gifts were to be the finer.[183] All decisions about war and peace ultimately lay with him, and it was to him also that the embassies of foreign peoples were to be directed.[184] (As in Einhard's vision of the Merovingian court of the late 740s, outsiders would be presented with a single face of Frankish rule, regardless of domestic political complexities.[185]) The lack of an extant text of the full terms of the treaty of Verdun's territorial division of 843 precludes any firm conclusions on what, if any, strictures were agreed for regulating intra-Carolingian political communication, though the subsequent behaviour of its royal participants

---

[177] *Lib. man.* IV.7, p. 146: 'Pax comprimit iram / Litis metuit pacem / Pax secura / per ampla quiescit / Consors amica.'
[178] *Lib. man.* IV.7, p. 148.
[179] *MGH Capit.* I, no. 45 (806), *pref.* cc. 6–10, pp. 127–8.
[180] *MGH Capit.* I, no. 45 (806), c. 14, p. 129.
[181] *MGH Capit.* I, no. 136 (817), *pref.*, p. 271.
[182] *MGH Capit.* I, no. 136 (817), c. 4. p. 271.
[183] *MGH Capit.* I, no. 136 (817), cc. 4–5, p. 271.
[184] *MGH Capit.* I, no. 136 (817), cc. 7–8, p. 272.
[185] Einhard, *Vita Karoli*, I.1, pp. 2–4.

shows considerable continuities with these early methods of formalizing political harmony.[186] Beginning in 844 Lothar, Louis, and Charles, and later their sons, would follow Louis' injunctions, coming together at royal villas and other sites sometimes supplemented by church councils, to renew their political bonds and to address matters of joint concern.

THE STRASBOURG OATHS

The immediate blueprint for the form of these meetings came from Charles and Louis' Strasbourg summit of February 842, famously recorded in Nithard's *Histories*.[187] Nithard's account is well studied, and a full exposition need not concern us here. Some issues are, however, pertinent to address. The first is that the vernacular was used twice at Strasbourg, Nithard only offering a transcription of the latter instance, the texts of the oaths sworn. However, Louis, and Charles, following in age order, began by addressing their own armies in their own tongues (German for Louis, Romance for Charles). In this public performance of alliance, they made clear—and clarity was the goal—their purpose for entering in to the compact, and the justification for their actions. Lothar had waged pre-emptive war, 'neither brotherhood, nor faith, nor any other argument could make for peace with justice'.[188] This intransigence had forced the brothers to take up arms, and by so doing to put the matter in the hands of God. Victory was won at Fontenoy, but Charles and Louis had held back, and 'moved by brotherly love and compassion for our Christian people', had mercifully allowed Lothar's fleeing army to escape. Lothar had then renewed his hostility, driving the two brothers even closer together. Not, as they made clear to their respective troops, because of greed (*cupiditas*) but in order to achieve peace and preserve the general welfare.[189] Both brothers offered their respective supporters clear justifications for their actions, and rejected implicit alternatives, chief among them self-interest. Such efforts hint at the need both to

---

[186] F. Ganshof, 'On the Genesis and Significance of the Treaty of Verdun (843)', in F. Ganshof, *The Carolingians and the Frankish Monarchy. Studies in Carolingian History*, trans. J. Sondheimer (Ithaca, NY, 1971), 289–302.

[187] S. Airlie, 'The World, the Text'; J. L. Nelson, 'Public Histories and Private History in the Work of Nithard', *Speculum* 60 (1985), 251–93, and reprinted in J. L. Nelson, *Politics and Ritual in Early Medieval Europe* (London, 1986), 195–237. The literature on the oaths is extensive. Entry points include J. Beer, 'The Strasbourg Oaths', in *Early Prose in France: Contexts of Bilingualism and Authority* (Kalamazoo, MI, 1992), 15–29; K. Gärtner and G. Holtus, 'Die erste deutsch-französische "Parallelurkunde". Zur Überlieferung und Sprache der Straßburger Eide', in *eidem, Beiträge zum Sprachkontakt und zu den Urkundensprachen zwischen Maas und Rhein*, Trierer Historische Forschungen 29 (Trier, 1995), 97–127.

[188] Nithard, *Historiarum libri* IV, III.5, p. 102. English translation: P. E. Dutton, *Carolingian Civilization*, 2nd edition (Peterborough, ON, 2004), 320–3, which I draw upon here.

[189] Ibid.

refute grumblings in circulation amongst their own men and to address potential unrest in the ranks.[190]

What, then, of the brothers' rationale to their war-weary and potentially
restive armies? Paramount was their shared wish that their actions be read as
those of just, peacekeeping kings, mindful of the common good, fair in their
dealings, loyal to the obligations of brotherhood, respectful of God's will,
fighting for peace, and merciful in victory. In short, a Carolingian ideal in action.
Lothar, restrained neither by religion, nor kinship, nor the demands of justice,
was unwilling to settle for peace on any grounds, and lacked respect even for
God's judgement manifest on the field of battle. Lothar was their very antithesis.
Nithard chose the words of his Latin account of Louis' apology carefully. Rather
than the measured violence of the justly motivated younger brothers, Lothar's
lacked any higher goal and was wholly destructive: 'he is ruining our people by
fire, plunder and slaughter'.[191] The phrase was knowingly evocative and, in its
echoing of an earlier historical work, politically resonant. At various points in his
Histories Nithard drew from a number of earlier works, both classical (Sallust)
and Carolingian, including Einhard's *Life* of Charlemagne, and the revised
Annales regni Francorum. In the former Einhard had used the same trio in his
account of Charlemagne's wars against the Saxons, fierce demon-worshippers,
opposed to Christianity, respectful of the laws of neither man nor God. Along
the common border with the Franks, he wrote, 'murder, theft and arson
constantly occurred' (*in quibus caedes et rapinae vel incendia vicissim fieri non
cessabant*).[192] Nithard's point, and perhaps Louis', too, was a blunt one: Louis
and Charles behaved like good Christian Carolingians, true grandsons of Charlemagne; their behaviour echoed the latter's image given by Nithard.[193] Lothar,
conversely, was like the godless Saxons against whom Charlemagne had long
fought, and whose eventual subjection Nithard counted as his greatest achievement.[194]

The high ideals and binary ethnic morality of Charlemagne's day had given
way to something far more complex. To give support that this was more than
simply rhetoric (in whatever language) Nithard followed his account of the oaths
with his famous tableaux of Louis and Charles' fraternal love, their indivudal
merits overshadowed by 'the sacred and venerable *concordia* that existed between
them'.[195] They ate together, slept in the same house, exchanged possessions, and
handled any business with the same fraternal generosity. Even their armies
engaged in well-disciplined exercises, free from injury or abuse: bloodless war

[190] Goldberg, *Struggle*, 105–6.
[191] Nithard, *Historiarum*, III.5, p. 102: '. . . et populum nostrum incendiis rapinis cedibusque
devastat.'
[192] Einhard, *Vita Karoli*, I.7, pp. 9–10.
[193] Nithard, *Historiarum*, IV.7, pp. 142–4.
[194] Nithard, *Historiarum*, I.1, p. 4.
[195] Nithard, *Historiarum*, III.6, p. 110.

games of the kind Ennodius had described Theoderic's Goths pursuing over three centuries earlier. Louis' and Charles' forces were more ethnically diverse than Theoderic's but competed with common course. Nithard noted not only that the participating sides were ordered along ethnic lines, but that they comprised groups once considered the Franks' most indefatigable enemies, including Saxons and Gascons. That apart, all three represented a common ideal, peaceful warrior kings overseeing well-ordered but similarly pacific armies.

CONVENTUS, COLLOQUIA, PAX, AMICITIA

The family summits that followed the pattern Nithard set out in his *Histories* offered a new theatre for the broadcast of images of peaceful rulership, in which legislative language and the expectations of earlier divisions came together with a strong dose of Pauline *caritas*. They also generated a new sub-genre, the fraternal treaty. Some fifteen such documents survive from the ninth century, a fraction of the fifty-five agreements recorded in Carolingian historical narratives between about 840 and 881.[196] We might loosely term these agreements treaties, but the extant texts use a range of terms, *conventus, colloquium, placitum, or, more abstractly, pax, amicitia, concordia*.[197] Their form was equally varied, though Reinhard Schneider, in what remains the closest study of these intra-Carolingian agreements, has identified a cluster of recurring features, including publicly and sequentially stated agreed terms (*adnuntiationes*), and supporting oaths.[198] As at Strasbourg, the vernacular was occasionally deployed, such as at Koblenz in June 860, when both Louis the German, Charles the Bald and Lothar II spoke in various permutations of *Romana* and *Theodisca*. Of the fifteen extant 'family' treaties, six were tripartite agreements, whilst nine were two-way compacts. Some, particularly in the 840s and 850s between Charles and Louis and the sons of Lothar, were genuine familial meetings intended to underpin a fragile balance of power, and continued to meet Louis' wishes for collective communication. Others were primarily political redivisions, such as the treaty of Meersen in August 870 reapportioning Lotharingia between Charles the Bald and Louis the German. Others, again, were peace treaties in the truest sense, following open war, most notably the Koblenz treaty of 860, following the latter's failed invasion.

These treaties punctuate the political history of the Carolingian world in the ninth century. In general terms, the years after Verdun in 843 were relatively

[196] R. Schneider, *Brüdergemeine und Schwurfreundschaft: Der Auflösungprozeß des Karolingerreiches im Spiegel der caritas-Terminologie in den Verträgen der karlingischen Teilkönige des 9. Jahrhunderts* (Lübeck, 1964), 178–84.
[197] A. Kosto, 'The *convenientia* in the early Middle Ages', *Medieval Studies* 60 (1998), 1–54, esp. 19–23.
[198] Schneider, *Brüdergemeine*, 19–29.

free from intra-Carolingian strife, though not from external attack nor from internal unrest. It was in fact the latter that was frequently the fuse threatening to ignite new conflicts. From the earliest post-Verdun meeting held at Thionville in October 844 there were already problems.[199] Earlier in the year, Adalard, a former seneschal and supporter of Charles had crossed the floor to Lothar, whose opposition to Charles seems to have settled into a latent dislike. Lothar gave Adalard new *honores*.[200] Part of a powerful network of loyalties within West Francia, Adalard's defection threatened West Frankish stability, Verdun's equilibrium, and set a dangerous precedent. Earlier in the year some of Charles' army (including Nithard) had been wiped out in an ambush by a party that included Dhuoda's son, William, whilst on their way to subdue a still rebellious Pippin II. At the Thionville meeting the three brothers overtly addressed those who threatened their collective *concordia*, naming Pippin explicitly, and renewed their mutual commitment to the laws of brotherhood and love (*fraternitatis et caritatis iura*).[201] A concurrently running synod voiced its own collective support for the brothers' continued custodianship of the peace.[202] Further meetings took place between the three brothers, at Meersen (847, 851) when again they addressed issues involving unfaithful *fideles* threatening to disturb harmony, and between Lothar and Louis at Koblenz in 848. Louis and Charles met without Lothar at Péronne in 849, and infrequently thereafter down to 855, though relations between the two soured over time.[203] This estrangement left them susceptible to exploitation by disaffected subjects. In 853, 856, and in 858 Aquitanian factions repeatedly appealed to Louis for help against Charles. These requests led to a fully fledged invasion of West Francia in 858 that ultimately failed, less for military reasons than because Hincmar of Rheims mustered Aquitaine's bishops against Louis and withheld support. Louis' occupation crumbled. At Koblenz, he, together with Lothar II met with Charles the Bald to be reconciled, reaffirming their commitment to peaceful brotherhood.[204]

Lothar I's death in 855 added three new players and thus vastly more complex political permutations were possible. Louis II inherited Italy and the imperial title, Lothar II, Lotharingia. Lothar's youngest son, Charles, ruled Provence. By the later 850s an initial configuration of allegiances between Charles the Bald and Lothar II, and Louis the German and Louis II had emerged. The 860s saw Charles dealing with Viking attacks by tribute, arms, and fortifications and issuing major legislation. Charles and Louis, together with their sons, came together in February 865 at Tusey on the Meuse, part of their nephew Lothar II's territory. The resulting *conventus* drew particularly heavily from earlier treaties, referencing both that of Meersen

---

[199] *AB s.a.* 844, p. 48. *AX s.a.* 844, pp. 13–14.
[200] Goldberg, *Struggle*, 150–1; Nelson, *Charles*, 143–4.
[201] *AB s.a.* 844, p. 48.
[202] *MGH Conc.* III, no. 6 (844), pp. 27–35.
[203] *MGH Capit.* II, no. 204 (847), pp. 68–71; no. 205 (851).
[204] *MGH Capit.* II, no. 242 (860), pp. 152–8.

(851) but also revisiting the terms of Koblenz five years previously.[205] In 867 and 868 they met again, both times in Metz, again in Lothar's kingdom. This time their shared sense of avuncular entitlement stretched beyond scheduling their summit meetings in Lothar's domain to the prospect of wholesale possession: the agreement they reached was a potential division of Lotharingia. The agreement's wording echoed that of the Strasbourg Oaths over a quarter century earlier.[206]

Lothar II's death in 869 precipitated Charles the Bald's swift seizure of Lotharingia (he had tried in 860, but failed) and was the path that led to his coronation in Metz that autumn, where this book began. Charles' attempt to hold Lotharingia failed. The following year, it was split with Louis the German at Meersen, for whom the 860s had been a decade punctuated by rebellions by his sons. In 865 the ageing Louis had divided his own territories amongst them. The epitaph above his tomb, raised perhaps by the eldest heir, Louis the Younger, spoke of his sons as 'a triple-stranded rope', binding his kingdom and preventing dissolution. In November 876, shortly after Louis the German's death, his three sons emulated the fraternal practice of the previous generation. They convened at the charged site of the Ries, where Louis had won a key victory over Lothar's army in 841 and where on its anniversary in 857 they had first subscribed to a diploma of their father. The brothers, led by the eldest, Louis the Younger, affirmed their commitment to realizing Louis' own division of his territories.[207]

When unity returned to the Carolingian territories it did so not because of mutual cooperation but because of mortality. By January 882 only one of Louis' sons still lived: Charles III, and it was to him that all Louis' lands passed. In December 884 Carloman II, son of Louis the Stammerer, grandson of Charles the Bald, was killed whilst hunting. In May 885 Charles was crowned king of West Francia; until his death Charlemagne's empire was briefly reassembled under a single ruler.

The language and practices established by the Carolingian treaties would outlive Carolingian authority itself. The treaty between Charles the Simple and the first Ottonian king, Henry the Fowler, at Bonn in November 921 was, as Gerd Althoff has noted, in very many respects a continuation of practice established in the previous decades.[208] An initial exchange of envoys led to the two kings coming together on either side of the Rhine—the frontier of their respective territories—on their own ships, accompanied by their respective entourages. The two rulers then transferred themselves to a third boat, moored midstream, where proceedings were formally concluded and oaths sworn on

---

[205] *MGH Capit.* II, no. 244 (865), c. 2, p. 166. Reference to Koblenz was also made in no. 243 (862), c. 9, p. 164; Louis II, *adnunt.*, c. 1, p. 163.

[206] Nelson, *Charles*, 217.

[207] Goldberg, *Struggle*, 99–101, 195, 336–7.

[208] G. Althoff, *Family, Friends and Followers. Political and Social Bonds in Early Medieval Europe*, trans. C. Carroll (Cambridge, 2004), 80–2. K. Schmid, 'Unerforschte Quellen aus quellenarmer Zeit. Zur *amicitia* zwischen Heinrich I. und dem westfränkischen König Robert im Jahre 923', *Francia* 12 (1984), 119–47.

relics, by which they agreed to adhere to the laws of friendship.[209] What had begun as family politics became the practice of European kings.

SOLOMON'S RETURN: CHARLES THE BALD

It was in the circles around Charles the Bald's court, more than anywhere else in the Carolingian world after Verdun, that we see many of the ideas and imagery explored in previous pages come together with renewed vigour. And with this moment we come full circle and return to the figure we encountered at our beginning, Charles, crowned king of Lotharingia in autumn 869, 'Holding the paternal sceptre, a peacemaker, like Solomon'.[210]

Why, we must ask, was it at Charles' court that we seem to see the triumph of Solomonic kingship and the image of the peaceful king? Part of the answer lies in the pervasiveness of the public rhetoric of peace evident in the fraternal treaties, coupled with the particular susceptibility of Charles and his circle to the power of that rhetoric. After all, Louis the German's court, in contrast, constructed a model of kingship that was far less eirenic and far more self-consciously martial during the same period: a world of iron, not, as we shall shortly see, of lilies.[211] Geographic determinism has long been out of favour as an explanatory device, at least beyond the pages of Western Civilization text-books devoted to presenting the diversity of ancient Near Eastern cultures in manageable terms. Nevertheless, Chris Wickham's recent work has made a powerful case for the complex relationship of social power to landscape, and the role of systems of exploitation, trade, and communication in the formation of political communities.[212] Even without recourse to a model as sophisticated as Wickham's, the continued existence in East Francia of an unstable eastern frontier across which aggressive campaigns could be launched and defence against counter incursions sustained, generated distinctive parameters within which Louis' kingship developed.[213]

Western Francia's longest border, by contrast, was with Carolingian Lotharingia, and expansionist eastern ambitions had to be pursued by methods other

---

[209] *MGH Constitutiones* I, ed. L. Weiland (Hanover, 1893), no. 1 (921), pp. 1–2. G. Koziol, 'Charles the Simple, Robert of Neustria, and the *vexilla* of Saint-Denis', *EME* 14.4 (2006), 355–90, esp. 385–6.

[210] *Carm.* no. 12, p. 28, lines 11–12.

[211] Goldberg, *Struggle*, pp. 45–7, 195–7 ' "More Devoted to the Equipment of Battle Than the Splendor of Banquets": Frontier Kingship, Martial Ritual, and Early Knighthood at the Court of Louis the German', *Viator* 30 (1999), 41–78.

[212] C. Wickham, *Framing the Early Middle Ages: Europe and the Mediterranean, 400–800* (Oxford, 2005).

[213] Goldberg, *Struggle*, 12, 119–46; *idem*, 'Ludwig der Deutsche und Mähren: eine Studie zu karolingischen Grenzenkriegen im Osten', in W. Hartmann (ed.), *Ludwig der Deutsch und seine Zeit* (Darmstadt, 2004), 67–94.

than annual *razzia*. Charles did have to contend with Viking attacks, handing them through a combination of tribute-giving, treaties, and innovative fortifications.[214] Charles' wars were largely reactive, in the service of Frankish security, and there was little glory and less profit in defensive war, save that it won peace.[215] Consequently Charles' circumstances more closely resembled those of his father, in whose reign, as we have seen, a Solomonic model of rulership took on heightened importance. This last point is worth stressing, for there has been a tendency to view this as primarily the product of Charles' reign.[216] As we have seen, the model already had a complex history by the mid ninth century, though circles in and around Charles' court undoubtedly afforded it greater emphasis.

The final factor is Charles himself, the best educated and most intellectually engaged of Carolingian rulers, and one with the strongest apprehension of his grandfather's legacy.[217] One of Charles' tutors, as we have seen, was Walahfrid, whose interest in political harmony we have already encountered, and who was one of the first, though not the last, to stress the relevance of Charlemagne's achievements to the grandson who bore his name. Charles was also the indirect recipient of the learning amassed in Freculf of Lisieux's ambitious world chronicle: the second of its two volumes carried a dedication to Judith, whom Freculf invited to recall Bathsheba, mother and teacher of Solomon, the wisest king of their age, as she, in her turn, taught the young Charles.[218] With Judith's advice and direction Charles could use Freculf's text like a mirror, examining what, as a king, he should do and what he ought to avoid.[219] Freculf's histories set out the pattern of war and peace in ages past. Amazons, the Persian wars, the manoeuvring after Alexander's death, and the Punic wars were all present.[220] He also offered the young king an extended account of the synchrony of Augustus' rule and Christ's birth, stressing the quality of peace Augustus had achieved. He had even succeeded in subduing the Sarmatians, Charles was told, a people so barbarous that they were unable even to grasp the concept of peace.[221] Christ

---

[214] J. L. Nelson, 'England and the Continent in the Ninth Century: II, The Vikings and Others', *TRHS*, 6th series, 13 (2004), 1–28; *eadem*, 'The Frankish Empire', in P. H. Sawyer (ed.), *The Oxford Illustrated History of the Vikings* (Oxford, 1997), 134–55.

[215] S. Coupland, 'The Carolingian Army and the Struggle against the Vikings', *Viator* 35 (2004), 49–70; *idem*, 'The Frankish Tribute Payments to the Vikings and their Consequences', *Francia* 26.1 (1999), 57–75, with references; Nelson, *Charles the Bald*.

[216] Pratt, *Alfred*, 160–353–4; Staubach, *Rex Christianus*, II; E.H. Kantorowicz, 'The Carolingian King in the bible of San Paolo fuori le mura', *Selected Studies*, 81–94.

[217] W. Diebold, '"*Nos quoque morem illius imitari cupientes*": Charles the Bald's Evocation and Imitation of Charlemagne', *Archiv für Kulturgeschichte* 75 (1993), 271–300.

[218] Freculf, *Historiarum* XII, ed., M. I. Allen, *Frechulfi Lexoviensis Episcopi Opera Omnia* CCCM 169 (Turnhout, 2002), II, *prolog.*, pp. 435–7, at 436–7.

[219] Freculf, *Historiarum* II, *prolog.*, p. 436. Nelson, *Charles* 80–5.

[220] Freculf, *Historiarum* I.2.25 (Amazons), p. 133; I.4.6 (Xerxes), pp. 217–21; I.4.12 (Artaxerxes), pp. 227–8; I.4.19–28 (Alexander's conquests and the aftermath of his death); I.5.2–7 (Punic wars, Hannibal), II.5.22–3 (the Gothic wars), pp. 719–20, amongst many other examples.

[221] Freculf, *Historiarum*, I.7.16, p. 415. The notion came from Jordanes, *Romana*, ed. T. Mommsen, *MGH AA* V.1 (Berlin, 1882), 246, p. 32.

came into the world at a time when the whole world was peaceful to a miraculous and unheard of degree.[222]

Charles, in tandem with his constant adviser, Hincmar of Rheims, possessed a vision of kingship of his own.[223] Charles' patronage of learning made him a beacon for those in search of patronage. Reading through the hyperbole, Heiric of Auxerre's words crystallize this process in action: 'Ireland, despising the dangers of the sea is migrating almost as a whole with her crowds of philosophers to our shores. The more learned a man is the more likely he is to sentence himself to exile that he may serve the wishes of our most wise Solomon'.[224] Images of rulership developed at court were taken up and projected back by individuals and those allied with institutions wishing to speak in the idiom of central power.

Inheritances mattered, but Charles' reign also witnessed innovations. In 848 Charles was anointed and crowned as King of Aquitaine, initiating a sequence of coronations in 856, 866, 869, and 877 overseen by Hincmar of Rheims. The *ordines* he produced for these occasions, were assemblages of pre-existing prayers and apposite blessings for king and queen alike, with evocations of Old Testament imagery and their attendant patterns of hierarchy and obligation. As we have seen, by the 840s the Carolingian lexicon of *convenientia*, peace and concord, *caritas* and mutual support, had emerged. Of even longer standing was the importance of consensus between a king and aristocrats, his faithful men. In 843, Charles and Hincmar brought the two together in a new configuration, applying this language to the king's relationship to his *fideles* in the agreement enshrined in the capitulary of Coulaines.[225] In a close reading of this text, which describes itself as a *foedus concordiae*, Janet Nelson has heard not only the echoes of the longer capitulary tradition but also traces of Augustine, not least in the goal of the agreements, *tranquillitas*.[226] Coulaines' complexities cannot detain us here, but its implications must be clear. From early in his reign Charles, guided by Hincmar here as he would be until his death, viewed his kingdom as a community of distinct groups, bound together by mutual obligations and sharing a common responsibility to uphold the peace of the kingdom. The face of the peaceful ruler celebrated in Metz in 869 was already discernible in 843.

---

[222] Freculf, *Historiarum*, II.1.2, pp. 440–2: '…quando totus sub una pace mundus mirabili modo et praecedentibus saeculis inaudito quiescebat…'.

[223] J. L. Nelson, 'Charles le Chauve et les utilisations du savoir', in D. Iogna-Prat, C. Jeudy, and G. Lobrichon (eds), *L'école carolingienne d'Auxerre de Murethach à Remi, 830–908* (Paris, 1991), 37–54; J. M. Wallace-Hadrill, 'Charles the Bald: A Carolingian Renaissance Prince', *PBA* 64 (1978), 155–84.

[224] Heiric of Auxerre, *MGH Poetae* III, p. 429, lines 24–6.

[225] *MGH Conc.* III, no. 3 (843), 10–17.

[226] J. L. Nelson, 'The Intellectual in Politics: Context, Content and Authorship in the Capitulary of Coulaines, November 843', in L. Smith and B. Ward (eds), *Intellectual Life in the Middle Ages: Essays Presented to Margaret Gibson* (London, 1992), 1–14; P. Classen, 'Die Verträge von Verdun und Coulaines, 843, als politische Grundlagen des westfränkischen Reiches', *HZ* 196 (1963), 1–35.

Contemporaries recognized it. The First Bible of Charles the Bald, also known as the Vivian Bible, produced at St-Martin, Tours in the early 840s contains a sequence of verses Paul Dutton and Hubert Kessler have convincingly identified as the work of Audradus Modicus, a member of the community of St-Martin and future suffragan bishop of Sens.[227] They have also argued for a specific context for its preparation and presentation to Charles: December 845, when it was expected that the king and his entourage would assemble at the monastery for Christmas as they had in previous years.[228] In his evocation of biblical types—notably David—and his extended description of the key figures and episodes of scripture, from Moses and Joshua through to Revelation, Audradus revealed himself as a poet with a firm grasp of the themes, forms, and motifs of the poets of Charlemagne's day.[229] The lessons of Solomon's reign, however, were clearly important for Audradus and, by implication, for Charles. Who was richer in glittering wealth than Solomon, asked Audradus? Such riches were but the by-product of a different kind of wealth, *dives sapientia*, the wealth of wisdom that made him outstanding amongst all kings.[230] Charles also was 'to love, seek and grasp wisdom for its own sake'.[231] But wisdom, and the riches that it brought, was not the ultimate Solomonic goal:

> Yet this wisdom was [still] not able to contain more than itself.
> Therefore the threefold God [is] true peace or true wisdom.
> Beyond which there is no praise or perfect poetry.[232]

Audradus' dedication closed with the evocation of a trio of biblical figures whom Charles resembled—he was powerful like David, in blessed intelligence like Solomon and in appearance like Joseph—and a final peroration of hope.[233]

> May you have distinction, peace, order, adornment, patience, a kingdom,
> And all prosperity without end. Farewell.[234]

Audradus' verses in the First Bible were formal pieces, consciously set within an established tradition of verse for Carolingian kings. He did, however, allow

---

[227] P. E. Dutton and H. L. Kessler, *The Poetry and Paintings of the First Bible of Charles the Bald* (Ann Arbor, MI, 1997), 7–21, with edition and translation (cited here) at 104–21.

[228] Dutton and Kessler, *Poetry*, pp. 21–6.

[229] Dutton and Kessler, *Poetry*, pp. 51–2.

[230] Dutton and Kessler, *Poetry*, pp. 110–11, lines 179–82: 'Quisquis es instructus mundanis usibus hisce, / Quis Salomone opibus ditior emicuit? / Hoc concessa cui dives sapientia fecit. / Regibus ac cunctis hunc ea praeposuit.'

[231] Dutton and Kessler, *Poetry*, pp. 112–13, lines 183–4: 'Tu quoque, qui es humilis, prudens—intentio sancta—/ Se propter sophiam dilige, posce, cape.'

[232] Dutton and Kessler, *Poetry*, pp. 112–13, lines 186–8: 'Se tamen haec sophia plus nec habere quiit. / Ergo deus trinus pax seu sapientia vera: / Ultra non laus nec versificalis apex.' The translation is Dutton's with minor emendation.

[233] Dutton and Kessler, *Poetry*, pp. 112–13, lines 195–6: 'Vi David, intellectu Salomon benedicto, / In specie Ioseph. . . .'

[234] Dutton and Kessler, *Poetry*, pp. 112–13, lines 199–200: 'Sit tibi honor, pax, ordo, decus. patientia, regnum, / Prosperitas omnis et sine fine. Vale.'

himself a brief flash of wit, a moment more reminiscent of Luxorius than anyone else, in the penultimate *titulus* verse that preceded the volume's presentation miniature. Charles' name and honour, Audradus claimed, would be long-lasting:

> The Bretons will become settled, and the cat become peaceful to the mouse,
> Before your renown and honour fail.[235]

Neither event Audradus clearly viewed as imminent. The reference, as Dutton and Kessler have made clear, had a contemporary political context. 844 had seen Nominoë lead a raid into Neustria—an early and serious sign that the Franks' neighbours were themselves adjusting to the realities of a divided Carolingian world.

In the weeks leading up to Christmas 845 Charles was campaigning with little success against the increasingly aggressive Bretons, a campaign which reached its nadir with his defeat at the battle of Ballon.[236] Under the circumstances it might not have been the most sensitive comment but the verse must have been composed and copied either before or during the campaign.[237] Finally, Audradus moved on to a general exhortation ('Let the whole world join with me . . . ') for all to pray that Charles live happily, powerfully and vigorously, possessing peace and prosperity.[238]

Viewed as a moment in Charles' reign as a whole, the defeat at Ballon was a relatively minor setback, but at the time it caused concern amongst his supporters.[239] Lupus of Ferrières, a resolute supporter of the king, sent a letter of commiseration in which he exhorted Charles to trust less in his advisors and more in God.[240] He reminded Charles that Solomon had asked God especially for wisdom: 'so that he might rule the people of Israel and he reigned over them in the greatest peace for a long time'.[241] Here, as elsewhere, Charles was less the propagator of an image of Solomonic rule so much as its intended target.

Lupus' letters betray sustained concern about Charles as a ruler. Already in the opening months of the 840s an absent Lupus had written to Charles assuring him that he was praying that the king would enjoy 'good health, bloodless victory and everlasting peace', amongst other gifts, and that those qualities would allow Charles not only to rule on earth, but also, through good rulership, to attain the heavenly kingdom.[242] It was a theme to which he would

[235] Dutton and Kessler, *Poetry*, p. 118, lines 35–6: 'Ante Brito stabilis fiet vel musio muri / Pax bona, quam nomen desit honosque tuum.'
[236] J. M. H. Smith, *Province and Empire: Brittany and the Carolingians* (Cambridge, 1992), 94–7.
[237] Dutton and Kessler, *Poetry*, pp. 25–7, 100.
[238] Ibid., *Poetry*, pp. 118–19.
[239] Nelson, *Charles*, 147.
[240] T. F. X. Noble, 'Lupus of Ferrières in His Carolingian Context', in Callendar Murray, 232–50. Translations that follow are either those of G. W. Regenos, *The Letters of Lupus of Ferrières* (The Hague, 1966), or are heavily dependent upon them.
[241] *Ep.* 46, ed. Levillain, I, pp. 192–7, at 196.
[242] *Ep.* 22, ed. Levillain, I, 112–14, at 112.

return.[243] Writing to Lothar in late August or early September he closed with similar sentiments:

May our Lord and Saviour long keep you alive and in good health for the care and peace of the Christian people, whom He has redeemed, and may He crown you with everlasting glory in the life to come.[244]

Sometime earlier that year Lupus had sent Charles a curt letter of advice, offering him a set of precepts to be observed, 'that you might reign peacefully and happily'.[245] Daily prayer, political self-confidence, evenhandedness in judgement: all were vital. Lupus counselled that Charles ought to associate with the good, love the truth, and be humble. Through these means, amongst others, Charles might please God and win his support. 'And after a laborious temporal reign you will gain the eternal and truly peaceful kingdom'.[246]

At various moments in this book we have touched upon perceptions of peace anchored in neither abstract political ideals nor wide social theory so much as in immediate individual experience. Lupus' letters, also, preserved several such engagements. Writing to Marcward of Prüm, Lupus recalled his narrow escape 'from almost certain death' whilst accompanying Charles the Bald on campaign in Aquitaine in summer 844. The defeat of Ballon had not been unprecedented. At Angoulême in mid-June Charles' forces had been ambushed by Pippin.[247] Many were killed, including Nithard. Lupus was taken prisoner, though eventually released through the intercession of Count Turpio of Angoulême. Whilst his letters to kings ended with a reflection of earthly rule and its fruits, here Lupus closed with more intimate reflections upon personal peace. The vines that produced the better wine at Ferrières had failed to produce the previous year.[248] But there was an abundance of other things, and through God's grace the community of Ferrières was enjoying at least some little peace (*aliquantula pacis*).[249]

Like several other figures we have encountered, Lupus had a clear sense of travel's dangers. Writing to one 'Reg.' sometime between 856 and 858, a time of deep unrest in West Francia, Lupus counselled him to chose his route with great care, for brigandage was rife. 'Reg.' was also counselled to seek out a travelling party of sufficient number and strength that, if

---

[243] *Epp.* 19, 78, ed. Levillain, I, 104; II, 24–36.

[244] *Ep.* 29, ed. Levillain I, 36. Regenos, *Letters*, 45.

[245] *Ep.* 31, ed. Levillain I, 140–6, at 140: 'Ut pacifice feliciterque regnetis, observanda vobis fideli devotione collegi.' On Lupus' advice on rulership, Anton, *Fürstenspiegel*, 248–53.

[246] *Ep.* 31, ed. Levillain, I, 146: 'Haec studiose custodientes, Deo et bonis quibusque placebitis; rebelles, Deo ut credimus pro vobis pugnante, comprimetis atque vincetis et post regnum temporale atque laboriosum consequemini sempiternum et vere quietum.'

[247] *Ep.* 35, ed. Levillain, I, 154–8. *A.B. s.a.* 844, pp. 58–9. Nelson, *Charles*, 141.

[248] *Ep.* 35, ed., Levillain, I, 158.

[249] *Ep.* 35, ed., Levillain, I, 158.

attacked, it might defend itself a adequately.[250] It was a long time since the capitulary of Herstal.

That year Lupus was also hard at work in a more public role, serving as secretary for the synod that assembled at Ver in December 844. Collective authority permitted a firmer tone. The synod called for Charles to reflect upon his faith, reminding him that power lay in God's hands 'and He will give it to whomsoever it shall please him. (Dan. IV.14)' David, Hezekiah, and Charlemagne himself were offered as models.[251]

By 846 Lupus had more pressing matters on his mind than the lack of good-quality wine. Writing again to Charles he lamented the hardships that had arisen as a result of Charles' gift of the cell of St-Josse to Odulf, and the consequent privation it created.[252] This was such that the Ferrières community could not carry out their pastoral duties though, Lupus was quick to add, they still prayed for Louis and Judith. Charles had promised to return the property to Lupus' community. That he had failed reflected poorly on him:

Indeed, it does not befit your nobililty and morality, which ought to be a model for all, to do otherwise, and surely it is not conducive to your own salvation and the peace of the state.[253]

Lupus held firm views on the high standards to which Carolingian kings should be held. He had equally strong ones on the low standards to which other peoples' rulers fell. In a letter of 850 to Nominoë, ruler of the Bretons by God's obscure but undoubtedly just choice, Lupus offered a series of criticisms of his rule that amount to a negative exemplar of kingship.[254] Whilst good rule would ensure the Franks' rulers would find their way to heaven, Nominoë's misrule, his mistreatment of the Church (not least his convening of a synod and replacement of all senior personnel), and the violence of his rule, endangered his own hopes of salvation. Not all who claimed to be Christians acted like Christians, commented Lupus. Actions, not words, mattered.

Lupus' fullest view on peace addresses neither kings nor his own circumstances, but the duties of members of the Church. Once again the context is specific: Louis the German's invasion of Charles' kingdom. Lupus remained loyal to Charles. Notoriously, Wenilo, bishop of Sens, did not, giving both

---

[250] *Ep.* 101, ed. Levillain, II, 124. Elsewhere, in a sequence of lettters written to churchmen in York, Lupus would write of the difficulties of maintaining communication during times of disturbance, *Epp.* 86, 88, II, II, 75–6, 78–80.

[251] *MGH Conc.* III, no. 7 (844), 36–44.

[252] *Ep.* 49, ed. Levillain, I, 202–8. The campaign to reclaim St-Josse would occupy Lupus for several years, see Noble, 'Lupus', 232–50, esp. 237–40.

[253] *Ep.* 49, ed. Levillain, I, 208: 'Namque nec aliter decet vestram nobilitatem atque probitatem, quae omnibus imitabilis esse debet, nec vero aliter convenit vestrae saluti atque reipublicae paci.'

[254] *Ep.* 81, ed. Levillain, II, 56–64.

practical and spiritual support to Louis.[255] Lupus' letter has been regarded as a text written by him on Wenilo's behalf for distribution amongst his parish priests, but might equally be read as Lupus' own response to his fellow churchmen's treasonous support of Louis the German.

Let there be no factions, no conspiracies among us who call upon God the Father, to whom the bishops say: 'Peace be unto you', and for whom all the priests in unison pray: 'Graciously grant us peace in our days', and 'May the peace of the Lord be always with you' and to whom God deems it proper to promise: 'Blessed are the peacemakers, for they shall be called the children of God' (Matt. V.9).... Let us renounce altogether pillaging and plundering, for they are utterly opposed to the Christian way of life and keep wretched men from the kingdom of God. The apostle indeed speaks out against these in the following words: 'Nor shall thieves inherit the kingdom of God' (I Cor. VI.10). Out of fear and love of God let us give up personal gain, let us earnestly and united look out for the good of the community and state, so that as we strive to provide tranquillity for the faithful, we may regain strength to resist the unfaithful and obtain from Him who is omnipotent the blessings of each peace, that is to say, the peace which we can have now and that other perfect peace which will be given to the elect. But let none of us forget that saying which has been tested and held by all the wisest men down to our present age that 'through concord small states increase, but through discord the largest fall.'[256]

Lupus' last words were Sallust's, a reminder of past lessons of the danger of political unrest. Einhard had reached for Suetonius when he wished to find both models and material for praising the new emperor, Charlemagne. In the world of the mid-ninth century with its multiple kingdoms and regional factions eager to play one king off against another it was Sallust, historian of the Catiline conspiracy, noble ambitions and political rivalries, who offered a model for thinking about the present.[257]

---

[255] For the accusations levelled by Charles against Wenilo see *MGH Conc.* III, no. 47 (859), pp. 464–70, and Goldberg, *Struggle*, 254–5.

[256] 'Nullae sint factiones, nullae conspirationes inter nos, qui patrem invocamus Deum, quibus dicunt pontifices: "pax vobis", et pro quibus omnes concorditer orant sacerdotes: "Da propitius pacem in diebus nostris", et: Pax Domini sit semper vobiscum, et quibus polliceri dignatur: "Beati pacifici, quoniam filii Dei vocabuntur" Illa comminatio eius non videatur nobis contemptibilis... Praedas et rapinas conversationi christianae nimis contrarias et a regno Dei miserrimos excludentes paenitus deponamus. Contra hos enim sic sermo apostolicus fremit: Neque rapaces regnum possidebunt. Pro Dei timore atque amoro lucra propria intermittamus, bono communi et publico certatim et unanimiter consulamus, ut, dum tranquillitatem fidelibus praestare nitimur, et vires resistendi infidelibus recuperemus et ab eo, qui est omnipotens, utriusque pacis, id est et qualis nunc esse potest, et illius consummatae, quae solis electis dabitur, gaudia consequamur. Illud autem neminem nostrum fugiat, quibusque doctissimis usque ad nostram aetatem probatum et creditum, quia "per concordiam parvae res crescunt, per discordiam vero maximae dilabuntur..."' *Ep.* 94, ed. Levillain, II, 104–6. Regenos, *Letters*, 114, with minor emendations.

[257] Nithard's debt to Sallust is signalled by Nelson, 'Public Histories', 195–238, at 201 n. 24, citing the comments of David Ganz, and examined in depth by Matthew Gillis of Furman University, to whose research I am indebted.

HINCMAR OF RHEIMS

It is impossible to conceive of the political and intellectual landscape of the ninth century without Hincmar of Rheims. His career as theorist, author, and framer of royal law stretched from the mid 830s to the 880s. Longevity, productivity, and political centrality make his work substantial and significant. Hincmar was an experienced polemicist, contributing to both the debates sparked by Gottschalk's avowal of *predestinatio gemina* and Lothar II's divorce struggle. His contribution to the latter, the monumental *de Divortio*, carried sustained commentary upon kingship, both good and bad, supported by an exhaustive marshalling of authorities.[258] As the drafter of capitularies that set out a political vision of order—as did his revision of Adalhard of Corbie's *de Ordine Palatii*—Hincmar's works are characterized by a clear image of kingship and Christian society, and within it, the commanding figure of the bishop.[259] The latter is a powerful, if often implicit, presence in the sequence of royal *ordines* he composed for the West Frankish house. Exegesis is less of a presence in Hincmar's canon; theological exposition took the form of contributions to wider debate, rather than serving as an end in itself. Occasionally, however, Hincmar did work as expositor. In his *Ferculum Salamonis* of 853–6, a verse exploration of Solomon's litter, Hincmar responded to Charles' query on lines from the Song of Songs and offered the king an elaborate *carmina figurata* (with supporting *explanatio*), which drew from Bede's work. Even here, however, polemic had a place: the Christological typologies Hincmar explored that linked Solomon to Christ, royal litter to Second Coming, were assertions of the power of Christ as reconciler, the need for grace, and an implicit refutation of Gottschalk's arguments for Predestination.[260]

With Louis the German's invasion of West Francia in 858 Hincmar's attention was directed from the defence of religious orthodoxy to that of the kingdom itself. Summoned by Louis to a synod at Rheims Hincmar stalled and rapidly organized an alternative synod of his own at Quierzy in November, whilst despatching a written rebuke to Louis.[261] In it, Hincmar attacked the invasion, repeatedly emphasizing that Louis would, in due course, be called to account for his actions before God. Louis claimed to be concerned with the West Frankish church and the welfare of the Christian people, but Hincmar was unconvinced. Those who asserted they acted in the name of peace, the welfare of the Church

---

[258] *De Divortio Lotharii Regis et Theutbergae Reginae*, ed. L. Böhringer, *MGH Conc.* IV.1 (Hanover, 1992), Responsio no. 7, 259–61, for example, drawing upon *de XII abusivis*.

[259] The literature on Hincmar's view of kingship is extensive: Nelson, 'Kingship, Law and Liturgy in the Political Thought of Hincmar of Rheims', *P&R*, 133–71; Anton, *Fürstenspiegel*, 281–354; Devisse, *Hincmar*, 671–724.

[260] Hincmar, *Ferculum Salamonis*, PL 125, cols. 817–34. Chazelle, *Crucified*, 155. B. Taeger, 'Ferculum Salomonis', *DA* 33 (1977), 153–67.

[261] *MGH Conc.* III, no. 41 (858), 407–27.

and people, and brotherly love, but whose actions revealed other goals carried
poison in their honeyed words.[262] Hincmar quoted the Psalmist's words on
those, 'who speak peace with their neighbour, but evils are in their hearts' (Ps.
XXVII.3).[263] The reality was something different: Christian against Christian,
Christian king against Christian king, brother against brother, all against earthly
and divine law. Hincmar and his fellow bishops had patiently sought a viable
peace but failed, 'behold trouble' (Jer. XIV.19).[264] Hincmar rebutted any
justification of Louis' invasion as itself an attempt to establish peace and order.
If he'd come to make peace he would have been better to have done so 'by
peacefully keeping the peace that came from God, the author of peace'. If Louis
wished to drive out discord and restore *caritas* his behaviour ought to bear
witness to what Christ taught through St Paul: '*Caritas* is not ambitious, deals
not perversely, nor seeks its own, nor rejoices in iniquity but rejoices rather with
the truth, which is from a pure heart, and a good conscience, and an unfeigned
faith (I. Cor. XIII.4–6, I Tim. I.5).'[265] A Christian king ought to protect the
Church, and maintain peace and tranquillity. These were the same goals as the
bishops, followers and preachers of peace. 'We hope for and we seek peace and
quiet, not quarrels and wars', reiterated Hincmar towards the letter's end. The
bishops' weapons were spiritual—excommunication—rather than carnal, and
their armour similarly elevated, their feet shod with the preparation of the gospel
of peace, wearing the breastplate of justice, the helmet of salvation, their loins
girded with truth (Eph. VI.14–17).' Hincmar finally brought to a close his lesson
on kingship (and on other issues) with the same image of the Church on a stormy
sea (*id est saeculo naufragoso*) he had used in 843 at Coulaines, hoping, as he had
there, that right action might see it returned to some small tranquillity (*redeat
quantulacunque tranquillitas*).[266]

Perhaps Hincmar's most extensive treatment of peace, its character, its creation, and enforcement is to be found in his late work, 'On the Character of the
King and the Ministry of Rulership' (*De Regis Persona et Regio Ministerio*),
written around 873 for Charles the Bald, and the nearest thing in the Hincmarian
canon to a conventionally conceived *Fürstenspiegel*.[267] In this 'little book of
sententiae', composed at Charles' apparent request, Hincmar gathered familiar
passages from scripture and elsewhere: Augustine's letters and the *City of God*
together with works by Ambrose and Gregory the Great, *de XII abusivis* (here-
ascribed to Cyprian), and many others.[268] Questions on the proper royal position
on warfare, the morality of killing in battle, and the thorny issue of royal

---

[262] *MGH Conc.* III, no. 41 (858), c. 4, p. 410.
[263] *MGH Conc.* III, no. 41 (858), c. 4, p. 411.
[264] *MGH Conc.* III, no. 41 (858), c. 5, p. 411.
[265] *MGH Conc.* III, no. 41 (858), c. 5, p. 412.
[266] *MGH Conc.* III, no. 41 (858), c. 15, pp. 426–7. Nelson, 'Intellectual', 163, 168.
[267] *De Regis Persona et Regio Ministerio*, PL 125, cols 833–56. Anton, *Fürstenspiegel*, 291–2.
[268] *De Regis*, pref., col. 833; c. 1.

judgement were either of particular concern to Charles, or thought by Hincmar to
be so, and he gave them particular attention.[269] If Charles ruled as he ought,
Hincmar affirmed, the frontiers of his kingdom would be peaceful.[270] On the issue
of war Hincmar turned to Augustine.[271] A king had, on occasion, to recognize that
war was an unavoidable necessity. But it was to be waged with the clear intention of
suppressing discord and restoring peace, not for base earthly advantage.[272] Hincmar advised Charles that when the time for battle drew near he should remind the
army assembled around him of Judas Maccabeus' words before the battle of
Emmaus: 'Be not greedy of the spoils: for there is war before us'.[273] Later in his
libellus Hincmar offered Charles a passage from Augustine's letter to Count
Boniface of 417 on the issue of 'just war' and the responsibilities of a soldier.[274]
Like Boniface, Charles was comforted by his bishop advisor that military service
was fully compatible with Christian life. (Had John the Baptist not told the
soldiers he baptized to be content with their pay?) Each person in society possessed
their own gift, and their own consequent responsibilities. Members of the
Church's upper orders prayed for secular society, and by so doing fought against
invisible enemies. Those lower down, like the lay warriors Boniface and Charles,
fought, in turn, on the Church's behalf, against rather more tangible 'visible
barbarians' (*visibiles barbaros*). Augustine clearly had Boniface's enemies along
the Numidian frontier in mind when he wrote.[275] Hincmar presumably had a
rather different set of 'barbarians'—the Vikings—in his. Charles ought to desire
peace, but realize that war was sometimes necessary. Moreover, God permitted it
out of necessity: in order that peace might be maintained. Peace was not sought
that war might be stirred up, but rather war waged that peace be attained.
Augustine (and, implicitly, Hincmar) dissolved the conventional, oppositional
binary: one must be a peacemaker when waging war, as through conquest the
defeated might be led back to the beneficial state of peace. The ubiquity of this
notion in discussions on 'just war' in the Middle Ages has perhaps had the effect of
seeming less arresting than it may have appeared in the later ninth century, if not
at other times too.[276] That Hincmar himself may have felt that this Augustinian
perspective needed additional corroboration is hinted at by his decision to close
this chapter on war fought for the goal of peace by invoking one further authority,

[269] *De Regis,* cc. 8–15, 24–6, on war, cols 840–4, 850–1; cc. 16–23, 27–33, justice, judgement
and impartiality, cols 844–9, 851–6. Devisse, *Hincmar,* I, 530–1.
[270] *De Regis,* c. 8, col. 840: 'Qui si bene direxit vias suas, et studia sua coram eo qui est Rex
regum, necessario pacatos regni sui fines possidebit'.
[271] Devisse, *Hincmar,* III, pp. 1358–63. Nelson, 'Coulaines', 168.
[272] *De Regis,* c. 8, col. 841.
[273] *De Regis,* c. 8, col. 841. Anton, *Fürstenspiegel,* pp. 298–9. Devisse, *Hincmar,* III, pp. 1116–18.
[274] *De Regis,* c. 10, col. 842, quoting Augustine, *Ep.* 189, CSEL 57, 131–7, at 135.
[275] For Boniface's career see J. S. Alexander, 'The Goths in St. Augustine's De Correctione
Donatisarum (= 185)', in E. A. Livingstone (ed.), *Studia Patristica* 33 (1996), 11–15.
[276] R. A. Markus, 'Saint Augustine's Views on the Just War', SCH 20 (1983), 1–13; F. H.
Russell, *The Just War in the Middle Ages* (Cambridge, 1977), 16–32.

Jerome, in the act of invoking another, holy writ: 'We read in Paralipomenon that the sons of Israel went into battle with peaceful minds, fighting not out of a desire for victory but rather to attain peace.[277] And, when that peace was won, Hincmar made clear in a later chapter, it came from God. (He did not send 'Victory', explained Augustine in Hincmar's source text, because she did not exist, but He did send His angel).[278] Agobard and others may have poured scorn upon the notion of trial by battle but Hincmar, drawing upon the fragmentary letter assigned to Augustine known as *Gravi de pugna*, had few qualms in making the case to Charles. God looked down from heaven, he quoted. He awarded the palm of victory to the just.[279]

'THE LILIES OF PEACE AND WAR'S ROSES': SEDULIUS SCOTTUS

The final figure from the age of Charles the Bald is the one we first met in this book's opening pages, the Virgil of Charles' Metz 869 coronation, the Irish scholar, Sedulius Scottus. As we saw, Sedulius was a scholar of wide-ranging ability, producing commentaries, grammatical works, verse in various forms for a range of purposes, and a single political tract, his *Liber de rectoribus Christianis*. Sedulius' continental career stretched from the 840s to around 870. It is, in its own way, an exercise in the complex politics and multiple layers of power and patronage during these years, and Lotharingia's place within these patterns.[280] Unlike many earlier scholars, and some contemporaries, Sedulius never enjoyed the consistent patronage of a single ruler. In strict terms he did not enjoy the direct patronage of any king. The bishop of Liège was Sedulius' primary patron, and he seems to have served as tutor and house poet of the episcopal *familia* of St-Lambert, Liège, under the successive patronage of Bishops Hartgar and Franco.[281] He may, however, have spent at least some time south of the Alps. He had evident connections with northern Italian Irish communities and the circles around Sant'Ambrogio in Milan where he seems to have enjoyed a reputation as a scholar, manifest in his presence as an authority in the margins of Bern, Burgerbibliothek 363 ('the 'Bern Horace'), and where his poetry seems

---

[277] *De Regis*, c. 10, col. 842, citing (from memory?) Jerome, *Ep.* 112, CSEL 55, 367–93, at 369, referencing I Paral.XII.17–8.

[278] *De Regis*, c. 10, col. 842.

[279] *De Regis*, c. 13, col. 843, citing Pseudo-Augustine, *Ep.* 13, PL 33, col. 1098.

[280] Above, 2–8, with references.

[281] *Carm.*, no. 1 (Hartgar), pp. 3–4; no. 4 (Hartgar), pp. 8–9; no. 10 (Hartgar), p. 25; no. 16 (Hartgar, *planctus*), pp. 35–6; no. 49 (Hartgar), p. 87; no. 53 (on behalf of Hartgar to Eberhard), pp. 90–1; no. 18 (Franco), p. 37; no. 33 (Franco), p. 61; no. 34 (Franco), pp. 62–3; no. 66 (Franco), pp. 107–8.

to have found at least one emulator.[282] The politics of Lotharingia and the demands they placed upon the bishop of the important northern see of Liège dictated the occasions and the recipients of Sedulius' verse. They also directed its tone and content. At moments in the 850s and 860s he presented formal verse for Charles the Bald, Louis the German (and on occasion for the pair), and Lothar I, as well as to other members of the Carolingian elite, notably Eberhard of Friuli.[283] Free from a consistent audience, and hence, perhaps, the pressure of constant novelty, Sedulius had few qualms about recycling material, presenting variations on certain favoured motifs to different recipients. This had less to do with opportunism—of a 'man with his eye on the main chance', in Peter Godman's words—and rather more to do with Sedulius' own self-confidence as a poet possessed of favoured themes, writing political verse for presentation by a bishop navigating the shifting ground of ninth-century Carolingian politics.

We have already seen something of Sedulius' verse in his poem for the Metz coronation of 869, and how its themes meshed with the idealized vision of the assembled bishops (as scripted by Hincmar) of a successor to Lothar II. Peace, however, is so strong a theme in Sedulius' verse and political theorizing that some have seen it demanding particular explanation, finding their answer in his Irish origins and consequent debt to Irish theories of kingship.[284] The growing awareness that the extant *tecosca* literature was itself a complex archaizing synthesis of legendary figures and visions of the pre-Christian past and scriptural, often proverbial, notions of rulership undermines those who have seen Sedulius as a ninth-century advocate of genuinely archaic notions of rulership. Similarly, at least one of the Irish works upon which he drew, *De XII abusivis*, was well established amongst the battery of Carolingian political authorities by the 840s, and was thus potentially accessible through intermediary texts of clearly non-Irish provenance.[285] That said, it is clear that Sedulius possessed an interest in peaceful rule in general terms that might be said to be congruent with interests found in the early Irish record, not only kingship tracts, but also, for example, the seventh-century *Cain Adomnáin* and Irish texts that the are amongst the sources upon which he drew for descriptions of the peaceful king, in particular the *Proverbia grecorum*. Other influences were also at work. Sedulius was a close reader of Augustine, and the impact of his thought is also apparent in Sedulius'

---

[282] H. Hagen, *Codex Bernensis 363 phototypice editus, Codices graeci et latini photographice depicti* 2 (Leiden, 1897). Studies of the manuscript as a whole include S. Gavinelli, 'Per un'enciclopedia Carolingia (codice Bernese 363)', *Italia Medioevale e Umanistica* 26 (1983), 1–25; J. Contreni, 'The Irish in the Western Carolingian Empire (According to James F. Kenney and Bern, Burgerbibliothek 363)', *IuE*, 758–98.

[283] Kershaw, 'Eberhard', 77–105, sketches this particular relationship.

[284] M. E. Moore, 'La monarchie carolingienne et les anciens modèles irlandais', *Annales HSS* 51 (1996), 307–24, esp. 311–12; L. Mair Davies, 'Sedulius Scottus': *Liber de Rectoribus Christianis*, a Carolingian or Hibernian Mirror for Princes?', *Studia Celtica* 26–7 (1991–2), 34–50. Kelly, 'Hiberno-Latin Theology', *IuE*, II, 549–67.

[285] Anton, 'Pseudo-Cyprian', *IuU*, II, 568–617.

surviving works in his sense not only of the impermanence of earthly peace, but also its character.[286] Wise rulers, wrote Sedulius, in one of the central passages of the *Liber de Rectoribus Christianis*, strove to expand, order, and rule through bonds of peace since, he continued, quoting directly from *De Civitate Dei*, the peace of all things was the tranquillity of order.[287] Augustine influenced Sedulius not only to place notions of right order near the centre of his political vision, but also to underscore the limits of earthly authority. Consequently, successful rule came about as much through the recognition by wise rulers that their own elevated place in the univeral hierachy was the result of divine mandate as by their own limited skill in governance. Within this framework Sedulius drew exemplars both good and bad from sources as diverse as the *Scriptores Historiae Augustae*, Bede, and Boethius, from whom he probably borrowed both the *Liber*'s prosimetric form and the image of fortune's wheel.

From these source materials Sedulius crafted his brief, heavily historical guide to rulership. Comprising a preface and twenty chapters written in alternating prose and verse (each chapter ended with a verse paraphrase) the *Liber de rectoribus Christianis* lacks a named dedicatee.[288] Whilst Lothar II and Charles the Bald have been suggested as possible recipients, and dates between 855 and 870 offered for its composition, Nicholas Staubach has argued, to general agreement, for its composition for Charles the Bald in 869, against the backdrop of his accession to Lotharingia.[289] In addition to its political content and its potential 'propaganda' use, Sedulius' apparent relationship to Franco of Liège, and the latter's involvement in the coronation and importance as a powerful Lotharingian supporter of Charles the Bald, ought to remind us that the work's composition was a potential statement of political allegiance in itself.

Across its twenty chapters Sedulius set out lessons in rulership, self-governance, the crucial importance of a ruler's right relationship to God, the paramount need for prayers before and after battle, and with them the recognition that all power and all victories come from God rather than human endeavour. The pitfalls of kingship ('why princes become evil'), the consequences of poor counsel, and the need for the king both to support the Church and to accept

---

[286] Direct quotation by Sedulius of Augustine's words include *LdRC*, c. 9, p. 47: 'tantum est enim pacis bonum, ut etiam in rebus terrenis atque mortalibus nihil gratius soleat audiri, nihil desiderabilis concupisci, nihil postremo possit melius inveniri', see *De Civ. Dei* XIX.11, pp. 674–5; *LdRC*, c. 12, p. 54, quoting *De Civ. Dei* XIX.6, pp. 670–1; *LdRC*, c. 19, pp. 84–5 contains repeated allusions to the two kingdoms. Bonnaud-Delamare, *L'idée*, 274–7, esp. 274; Anton, *Fürstenspiegel*, 263. H. Tiralla, *Das augustinsiche Idealbild der christlichen Obrigkeit als Quelle der 'Fürstenspiegel' des Sedulius Scottus und Hincmar von Reims* (Greifswald, 1916), 52–6.

[287] *LdRC*, c. 17, p. 77: 'Prudens itaque dominator per pacis connexionem studet semper amplificare, ordinare atque gubernare imperium, cum pax sit omnium rerum tranquillitatis ordinis et connexio et incrementum regiae potestatis.'

[288] Godman, *Poets*, 160–1.

[289] Staubach, *Rex Christianus*, 105–88, makes the case for an 869/70 dating, and the attendant political context. See also J. L. Nelson, 'Early Medieval Rites of Queen-making and the Shaping of Medieval Queenship', in A. Duggan (ed.), *Medieval Queenship* (London, 1997), 304–5.

guidance and correction from its leaders were all discussed, supported by numerous examples, good and bad, drawn from Sedulius' studies.

Above all, self-rule and a righteous acknowledgement of God were the engines
behind Sedulius' vision of kingship. Solomon was the key model here: his
building of the Temple and his many sacrifices to God a paradigm of the ideal
peaceful ruler's own constant support for the Church.[290] Sedulius' sense of the
limits of earthly authority, and the ephemerality of the peace it might achieve
were set out in the *Liber*'s third chapter, 'With what skill and assiduity a temporal
kingdom can be made steadfast'.[291] Earthly peace, Sedulius stressed, was evanescent and earthly kingdoms impermanent. Only the true kingdom would endure,
and the best that could be achieved in the earthly realm was that it might reveal a
little likeness (*similitudinem*) of the eternal kingdom.[292] The ruler's skills might
at best hold a kingdom in some semblance of stability (*ad aliquam stabilitatis
effigiem*), though this was itself dangerous for it allowed dissent to develop. He
drove the point home with Boethius' image of Fortune's wheel.[293] Earthly peace
when it came about did so through the efforts of rulers, whose effective rule
served to maintain a right relationship with God. History again provided lessons
about peaceful rulers, emperors who had followed Ephesians II.14, and 'placed
their hearts in God's hand'. Grace was the counter-gift for their trust.[294] Sedulius
moved on to sketch out the character of the relationship between the ruler's inner
spiritual state and wider society. He thought in terms of widening social spaces
with the king at their centre. The wise and pious king first ruled himself, then his
family and household, and finally, the people entrusted to him.[295] This tripartite
model, drawn from St Matthew, recurred elsewhere in the *Liber*, albeit in a more
abstracted form.[296] A king ought to adhere at all times to a threefold rule of
peace (*trinam pacis regulam*)—'that is above himself, inside himself, and beside
himself'. Sedulius unpacked what this meant in practice: the king ought to be
at peace with God, within himself and with those near to him.[297] Sedulius had

---

[290] *Liber*, c. 1, pp. 21–5.
[291] *Liber, incip.*, p. 20. 'Qua arte et industria momentaneum regnum stabiliri potest'.
[292] *Liber*, c. 3, p. 28: 'Quanta quoque mala sub ficto nomine pacis proveniunt, quis explicare
potest, cum etiam illa pax, quae stabilis ac firma inter bonos esse credebatur, interdum per prava
malorum consilia in exitiosas discordiarum tempestates transfertur, unde et inormis instabilitas in
pace transitoria videtur.'
[293] *Liber*, c. 3, pp. 27–30.
[294] *Liber*, c. 4, p. 32. Hellmann noted that the phrase also echoed *Historia Tripartita* VII.3, and
it has its root in *Prov* xxi. 1, see Anton, *Fürstenspiegel*, 357–8. On Valentinian see also *Liber* c. 11,
p. 52.
[295] *Liber*, c. 5, p. 34: 'Rex pius et sapiens tribus modis regendi ministerium gerit. Nam primo se
ipsum, quomodo in superioribus ostendimus, secundo uxorem propriam et liberos suosque
domesticos, tertio populum sibi commissum rationabili et glorioso moderamine regere debet.'
Self-control is the main theme of *Liber*, c. 13, pp. 75–6.
[296] Matt. XXII.37–9.
[297] *Liber*, c. 9, p. 47: 'Quem trinam pacis regulam conservare oportet, hoc est supra se, in se,
iuxta se, quia erga Deum et in se ipso et circa proximos debet esse pacificus.'

invoked a comparable, but fourfold, set of categories in his commentary on Matthew V.9, taking his lead from Jerome:

They are peacemakers, who first make peace within their own heart and then between disagreeing brothers. For how are you able to bring peace to others, when in your own heart there are wars of vices? There are four ways to make peace: the first between ourselves and God, the second between our body and spirit, the third between us and those closest to us and, fourthly, between ourselves and our enemies.[298]

The commentary's final category of peacemaking—with one's enemies—is conspicuously absent from the *Liber*'s threefold rule. It is implicit, however, in the advice Sedulius offered on how a king ought to deal with earthly enemies. Only if an enemy had refused the peace that a Christian ruler first offered was it justifiable to attack.[299] Terms of peace, Sedulius made clear, were not to be refused. Peace, after all, was the ultimate goal of a good ruler. Looking again to the past, Sedulius noted those who overcame their foes because they, like Moses, had prayed and been rewarded with divine aid: rest, deliverance, peace and victory, all rested in God's hands alone.[300] The righteous ruler recognized this debt, acknowledging it through a programme of thanksgiving and hymns of praise.[301]

The *Liber*'s ninth chapter took up these ideas, addressing the peacemaking and clement king (*rex pacificus atque clemens*).[302] Listing 'the seven most beautiful things in God's creation', Sedulius placed a peace-loving king ruling in full splendour as the last item.[303] This list otherwise comprised natural phenomena: the sky, the sun and moon, fruitful fields, and the sea reflecting back the order of the heavens.[304] Chapter nine also revived the theme of peace within the royal household. Here, however, Sedulius collapsed the distinction between the court and the inner life of the king. The king's heart was itself an *aula*, the palace of Christ, 'since Christ is peace and desires to dwell in peace'.[305] Sedulius gave some insight into the actual means by which good relations were maintained by the king with those around him through generosity, justice, and

---

[298] *Kommentar zum Evangelium nach Matthäus*, ed. B. Löfstedt, Vetus Latina: Aus der Geschichte der lateinischen Bibel 19 (Freiburg, 1991), I.1, 139–40.

[299] *Liber*, c. 17, p. 77.

[300] *Liber*, c. 15, p. 66: 'Unde, si quando bellici rumores crebrescant, non tam in armis corporalibus et fortitudine confidendum, quam assiduis ad Dominum orationibus est insistendum Deique sunt imploranda suffragia, cuius in manibus consistit salus, pax atque victoria . . .'.

[301] *Liber*, c. 18, p. 21, entitled '*Gratiarum actiones ac benivola vota post pacem seu victoriam Deo reddenda*', the text of the chapter follows at 80–4. See McCormick, *Victory*, 349, 355–6.

[302] *Liber*, c. 9, p. 20.

[303] *Liber*, c. 9, pp. 46–9.

[304] *Liber*, c. 9, p. 46.

[305] This linkage of Christ as peace and the king as arbiter of peace points the way towards the development of a Christological conception of kingship; the connection is also implicit in the poem at the end of c. 9, lines 11–12, p. 49, where the king is compared to the Trinity.

charity: 'a just and peaceable king distributes gifts with a happy face, admin-
isters justice fairly, and attends to the needs of the poor and the sick'.[306] Several
similarly epigrammatic statements followed. Peace was the highest state possible on earth, stated Sedulius. Nothing was more pleasurable, desirable, or
beneficial.[307]

The *Liber* reveals both the nature of Sedulius' thought on peace and something of the influences that shaped it. By turning to the *Collectaneum Miscellaneum* (hereafter *Collectaneum*) we can see these influences more clearly.[308] This a
substantial work, containing as it does some 3500 individual excerpts of varying
lengths and running, in its modern edition, to nearly four hundred pages.[309] It
has sometimes been seen as Sedulius' 'notebook', serving as a distillation of his
reading, a compendium of ideas, imagery, and aphorisms to be used in the
classroom context or as raw material for polished works.[310] It is true that several
of the excerpts contained in the *Collectaneum* occur elsewhere in Sedulius'
writings, in particular the *Liber de rectoribus Christianis*.[311] However, the relationship between *florilegium* and political tract ought not to be seen as simply
that of a roughly assembled sourcebook and a polished composition.[312] Comprising several carefully compiled thematic sequences of extracts, the

---

[306] *Liber*, c. 9, p. 46: 'Rex etenim iustus et pacificus laeta facie bona dividit, et uniuscuiusque causam diligenter meditatur, et infirmos et pauperes populi non despiciens'. The *Liber* contains several references to the importance of the king's expression in performing his royal duties, see also *Liber*, c. 13, p. 61, lines 24–7: 'Miscat tus ergo menti / Flagrans odore pacis / Dux fiat ac serenus / Grato nitente vultu.' The key to Sedulius' emphasis upon the importance of the king's appearance lies in the *Collectaneum*, XIII.xxxvii.13, p. 26: *SALEMON: In hilaritate vultus regis vita et clementia eius, quasi ymber serotinus*, taken from Prov. XVI.15.

[307] *Liber*, c. 9, p. 47: '. . . in rebus terrenis atque mortalibus nihil gratius soleat audiri, nihil desiderabilius concupisci, nihil postremo possit melius inveniri' (citing *De Civ. Dei* XXII.11).

[308] Sedulius Scottus, *Collectaneum Miscellaneum*, ed. D. Simpson, CCCM 67 (Turnhout, 1988), best approached with the additional indices of F. Dolbeau, *Supplementum*, CCCM 67 (Turnhout, 1990), and see Dolbeau's comments in 'Recherches sur le *Collectaneum Miscellaneum* de Sedulius Scottus', *ALatMA* 48–9 (1988–89), 47–84. See Hellman's comments, *Sedulius*, 92–117. Carolingian *florilegia* discussed by M. Garrison, 'The Collectanea and medieval florilegia', in M. Bayless and M. Lapidge (eds), *Collectanea Pseudo-Bedae*, Scriptores Latini Hiberniae 14 (Dublin, 1998), 42–83; R. McKitterick, *The Frankish Church and the Carolingian Reforms, 789–895* (London, 1977), 155–83.

[309] B. Löfstedt, 'Zum Collectaneum des Sedulius Scottus', *Acta Classica: Verhandelinge van die Klassieke Vereniging van Suid-Afrika* 32 (1989), 111–17.

[310] Simpson, *Collectaneum*, pp. xxii, xx–xxiv.

[311] Hellmann, *Sedulius*, 109–17. The relationship between the two works is explored within the specific context of one work, Bede's *Historia ecclesiastica*, in Kershaw, 'English History', 131–9.

[312] For a discussion of the actual logistics of assembling excerpts and the nature of early medieval notebooks see M. Lapidge, 'The Origins of the *Collectanea*', in M. Bayless and M. Lapidge (eds), *Collectanea Pseudo-Bedae*, 1–12, at 6 n. 13 and the same issues addressed by Garrison, 'Florilegia', 50–1. Evidence for Sedulius working through his sources and marking up passages that would eventually find their way into the *Collectaneum* was first identified by L. Traube, *O Roma nobilis: philologische Untersuchungen aus dem Mittelalter*, Abhandlungen der philosophisch-philologischen Classe der königliche bayerischen Akademie der Wissenschaften 19 (Munich, 1891), 364–4, and see Simpson's assessments of Sedulius' working methods, *Collectaneum*, pp. xxi–xxii.

Collectaneum was clearly the result of considerable formal organization.[313] Several of these are miniature *florilegia* within the larger work, perhaps betraying the incorporation of earlier collections into the *Collectaneum*'s master text.[314] If the *Collectaneum* was prefaced by a dedication letter this has been lost.[315] The volume and diversity of its entries together with the lack of a single, coherent focus set it apart from contemporary collections such as those by Paulinus of Aquilea or Heiric of Auxerre.

Indeed, the wealth and diversity of the *Collectaneum* means that any attempt to recover a sense of Sedulius' special interests from the subjects under which he collected extracts runs the risk of foundering on the sheer volume of entries, overemphasizing one strand amongst very many. From his poetry and political thought, however, we can see Sedulius' fascination with peace in its manifold forms. What did Sedulius make of its treatment by earlier scholars, and what relationship can be established between the apparent influences and borrowings in the *Liber* and the evidence of his compilation? Sedulius' excerpts display the diversity of definitions of peace with particular clarity, ranging from pithy Irish wisdom (disputes that are not settled never will be—you can't make peace when your're dead), to an account of the benefits of a society at peace: 'in peace many things come together: love of neighbours, knowledge of God, scorn for the Devil, the presence of angels, serenity in the present, healing in the future, and so forth.'[316]

The *Collectaneum*'s opening contains the so-called *proverbia grecorum*, a collection of wisdom statements that circulated in various forms.[317] The scattering of Greek terms and title—perhaps a claim to antiquity and scholarly authority comparable to the ascription of Old Irish wisdom texts to semi-mythical judges and kings—are embellishments to a work probably composed in Ireland in the seventh century in a strong scholastic context.[318] Its debt to scriptural models is substantial, with the Book Proverbs unsurprisingly exerting

[313] Dolbeau, 'Recherches', 49–51.
[314] *Collectaneum*, XXV, pp. 157–89; LXXX, pp. 314–56. Garrison, 'Florilegia', 62–3.
[315] That the complete work survives only in a single twelfth-century MS Kues 52 (s.xii²) makes this unverifiable. The prefatory letter to the *Proverbia* was once considered to have been Sedulius' own; see D. Simpson, '*Proverbia Grecorum*', *Traditio* 43 (1987), 1–22, at 1–2, 5–6, suggesting a late seventh- or early eighth-century dating.
[316] *Collectaneum* XXV.i.1, p. 158. The second sentence shared this Irish context of composition, a fact attested by its inclusion in the *Collectio Canonum Hibernensis*; see *Collectio Canonum Hibernensis*, ed. F. W. H. Wasserschleben (Leipzig, 1885), *Die Irische Kanonensammlung*, 2nd edition, XXI.8, p. 64.
[317] C. D. Wright, 'The Prouerbia Grecorum, the Norman Anonymous, and the Early Medieval Ideology of Kingship: Some New Manuscript Evidence', in G. Wieland, R. G. Arthur and C. Ruff (eds), *Insignis Sophiae Arcator: Medieval Latin Studies in Honour of Michael Herren* (Toronto, 2006), 193–215, H. H. Anton, 'Königsverstellungen bei Iren und Franken im Vergleich', in F.-R. Erkens (ed.), *Das Frühmittelalterliche Konigtum, Ideelle und religiöse Grundlagen, Ergänzungsbände zum Reallexikon der germanischen Alterumskunde* 49 (Berlin, 2005), 270–80.
[318] Simpson, '*Proverbia*', 9.

particularly deep influence.[319] 'Paradise at hand', noted Sedulius, 'is a just and
peaceful king. Hell on earth a king who is voracious, impious and oppressive'.[320]

Of all the *Proverbia*'s passages that fed into the *Liber* the most important is its
forty-third, which became Sedulius' own treatment of the 'just and peaceable
king':[321]

For the peaceful king shares out gifts with a cheerful countenance and diligently considers
every petition, the sick and the powerless are not held in contempt. Truthful judgements are
passed with the counsel of the wise and experienced. The impious king has the character of a
lion, replying sharply to everyone, causing malice for everyone and never taking wise
counsel. The good are cast down and the bad exalted. His days will be shortened and his
memory will perish with a noise, for he has sinned more than he could.[322]

Several scriptural proverbs lie behind this short passage, including Psalms
XVI.15, XXIX.14, and XXIX.24.[323] If the seventh-century dating is correct,
the *Proverbia*'s image of the happy, gift-giving ruler would be the earliest extant
insular image of the peacemaking king. The *Collectaneum* also confirms the
Augustinian basis of Sedulius' thought, with Sedulius entering some of the
familiar definitions at various stages, including Augustine's maxims on *pax
domestica*,[324] and on peace as tranquil order, in a section headed 'On Fear,
Peace and Patience'.[325] All three Augustine excerpts came from the opening of
De Civ. Dei XIX. 13.[326] Rubbing shoulders with them, however, was an extract
from a very different work, Statius' *Thebaid.*[327] This first-century epic recounted
the struggle between Oedipus' sons Eteocles and Polynices for the throne of
Thebes, the agreements they made and broke, and the *odia fraterna* that characterized their relationship. 'Peace', Sedulius transcribed 'is won with savage
weapons'.[328]

---

[319] Simpson, '*Proverbia*', 8. Moore, 'La monarchie carolingienne' 307–24, presents a variant on
this, seeing kingship in these texts as a fusion of pre-Christian material and OT models; see esp.
311–12.
[320] *Collectaneum*, I.64, p. 9: 'Paradisus in prope rex iustus et pacificus, infernus presens et vorax
rex impius et iniquus'.
[321] *Collectaneum*, XIII.37, pp. 124–6.
[322] *Collectaneum*, I.43, p. 7: 'Rex pacificus laeta facie bona dividit et uniuscuiusque causam
diligenter meditatur, etiam infirmos et pauperes populi non despiciens; cum seniorum iudicio et
consilio verax iudicia loquitur. Rex impius leonis personam habens ad omne responsum acriter
verbum nequam sine prudentium consilio cum omni malitia profert, bonos humilians malosque
exaltans. Dies eius adbreviabuntur et eius memoria cum sonitu peribit; peccavit enim plus quam
potuit.'
[323] The latter two also compiled beneath the heading *De Regibus*, *Collectaneum*, XIII, 37, pp.
124–6.
[324] *Collectaneum*, LX.3. *De Civ. Dei* XIX, c. 13, pp. 678–9.
[325] *Collectaneum*, LXXX.19, pp. 338–9.
[326] *Collectaneum*, LXXX.19.6–9, p. 339. *De Civ. Dei* XIX, c. 13, pp. 678–9.
[327] *Collectaneum*, LXXX.xix. 7, p. 339.
[328] *Collectaneum*, LXXX.xix.7, p. 339: 'Saevis pax queritur armis'. Statius *Thebaid*, VII, lines
554–5.

Peace was also a recurrent theme of Sedulius' celebratory verse, written for various members of the Carolingian royal house—Lothar, Charles, Louis the German, and the latter two jointly—across the period when he was resident in Liège, though absolute dating is not always possible to establish for Sedulius' stylized poems. His tendency to reuse favoured images and phrases, together with the timeless ideal that his poems present, further militate against fixing his verse with high specificity. Certain themes dominate Sedulius' occasional verse: the celebration of military victories (whether by kings, nobles, or bishops), the reception of kings and return of favoured figures (his early patron, Hartgar, Eberhard of Friuli) to various Lotharingian centres (Metz, Xanten).[329] Lothar, Charles, and Louis are also addressed at various moments as Solomon, Sedulius' favourite image of rulership, and virtually all kings for whom he wrote are praised for their peacemaking qualities.[330] For example, in his verse to the young Lothar II on the occasion of his reception, together with his brother Louis II, at Xanten, probably from the late 840s: 'He who is the "Alpha" and will also be the "Omega of Peace" has blessed your peaceful kingdom. Peace shines in the period between', wrote Sedulius, conscious even here of the prescribed character of earthly rule, its temporal limits poetically framed by the Alpha and Omega, twin symbols of God's eternity.[331] Sedulius wrote two poems explicitly about peace-making, the first a poem extolling the glories of Louis the German,[332] and the subsequent conversion of the Vikings, the second an *adventus* poem for the meeting between Louis and Charles.[333] Sedulius' poetry expressed the successful ruler's accomplishments in war and peace through the use of floral imagery; peace was represented by the lily and war by the rose.[334] Of the two it is the lily in particular which serves as a constant symbol of kingship. Celebrating the birth of Charles of Provence in 845 Sedulius delivered one of his frequent floral injunctions: 'Bring white lilies, strew your blooms, look! The brilliant-white prince has come'.[335] The adult Lothar was praised in a similar way: 'You love the lilies of

---

[329] Amongst others: military victories: *Carm.* no. 8 (Hartgar's victory over vikings), 21–2; *Carm.* no. 25 (Louis' II's return from Italy), 48–9; *Carm.* no. 39 (Eberhard's return), 68–70; receptions: *Carm.* no. 2 (Hartgar's return), 5–6; *Carm.* no. 6 (Hartgar's return from Rome), 15–19; *Carm.* no. 18 (Franco's arrival in Liège), 37; *Carm.* 12, (Charles reception), 28–30; *Carm.* no. 15 (Charles and Louis' joint arrival), 32–3; *Carm.* no. 24 (Lothar), 47.

[330] *Carm.* no. 12 (Charles), 28–30; no. 20 (Lothar), 39–40; no. 26 (Lothar), 50; no. 28 (Charles), 51–3; *Carm.* no. 30 (Louis the German), 55–7; no. 54 (Lothar), 92; no. 59 (Lothar), 99.

[331] *Carm.* no. 24, p. 47, lines 17–18: 'Pacificum vestri regnum sacraverat alpha, / Pax nitet in mediis, omega quoque pacis erit.'

[332] *Carm.* no. 30, pp. 55–7.

[333] *Carm.* no. 15, p. 32.

[334] See also Sedulius' dedicatory poem on Vegetius given to Eberhard, *Carm.* no. 53, pp. 90–1, at p. 90, lines 1–2. Meyers noted similar imagery in Aldhelm, *Aenigmata*, p. 100, line 15.

[335] *Carm.* no. 22, lines 11–12, p. 44: 'Candidus ecce venit: candentia lilia ferte; / Spargite vos flores: candidus ecce venit.'

peace mixed with the roses of war, this brilliant-white ruler loves the lilies of peace'.[336]

The pairing of royal authority and the lily was not wholly new to Carolingian culture. In the Book of Kings the lily was a decorative motif in Solomon's temple, an association that Schramm saw behind the introduction of the lily into Carolingian political symbolism.[337] Roses and lilies led the list of plants that royal stewards were instructed to cultivate on royal estates in the capitulary *de Villis*, their prominence suggesting they already possessed royal associations.[338] The anonymous monastic theorist behind the St-Gall plan (*c.* 820) envisaged them growing in adjacent beds by the doctor's house, whilst Walahfrid, writing his *Hortulus* ('the Little Garden') in the earlier 840s, also imagined the two growing side by side.[339] Walahfrid acknowledged their respective medical properties but closed his poem with an exploration of their symbolism.[340] The lily symbolized chastity, purity, virginity, and innocence, wrote Walahfrid, evoking its Marian associations.[341] The rose—its crimson Germany's own indigenous equivalent to the imperial purple of the East—represented Christ's blood, his sacrifice, and that of the martyrs of the Church.[342] Paired, the two were also symbols of war and peace.[343]

Sedulius, however, both developed and personalized the imagery. This reached its fullest form in his dialogue poem between the two.[344] Peter Godman has read this poem as merely 'a comedy of manners' lacking a political, allegorical, or elegiac purpose.[345] Read against Sedulius' poems on kingship, however, as perhaps it ought to be, the *certamen* of the flowers presents itself as poetic debate between war and peace as royal functions, an allegorical debate on kingship.[346]

The rose speaks first. She argues for her superiority on the grounds of her royal colour, purple (*purpura*). Purple makes kings, it is the glory of rulership.[347] Kings find white worthless.[348] The lily in reply mocks the rose: is her conscience bothering her? Why had her face turned shameful red? The rose replies presenting herself in martial terms, armed with thorns, and equipped with God-given

---

[336] *Carm.* no. 59, lines 29–30, p. 99: 'Lilia pacis amat bellorum mixta rosetis, / Candidus hic rector lilia pacis amat.'

[337] III Kings VII.19–26. P. E. Schramm, 'Die Kronen des frühen Mittelalters', *Herrschaftzeichen und Staatsymbolik, MGH Schriften* XIII.2 (Stuttgart, 1955) II, 317–417.

[338] *MGH Capit.* I, no. 128 (?800), 250–7, c. 70, p. 90.

[339] Walahfrid Strabo *Hortulus*, ed. E. Dümmler, *MGH Poetae* II, no. 4, 335–50, at 349, lines 405–6.

[340] Walahfrid Strabo *Hortulus*, p. 344, lines 258–61 (the lily); p. 349, lines 543–4.

[341] Walahfrid Strabo *Hortulus*, p. 349, lines 405–21.

[342] Walahfrid Strabo *Hortulus*, pp. 348–9, lines 395–401; p. 349, line 405.

[343] Walahfrid Strabo *Hortulus*, p. 344, line 422; p. 349, lines 415–28.

[344] *Carm.* no. 81, pp. 127–9. Düchting, *Sedulius*, 205–8.

[345] Godman, *Carolingian Poetry*, 54, recapitulated at 282–3.

[346] On the difficulties of trying to recover the allegorical meaning of Sedulius' work see J. Ziolkowski, *Talking Animals* (Philadelphia, PA, 1995), 69–78.

[347] *Carm.* no. 81, p. 127, line 5: 'Purpura dat regnum, fit purpura gloria regni'.

[348] *Carm.* no. 81, p. 127, line 6: 'Regibus ingrato vilescunt alba colore.'

armour to protect her rosy face.[349] The lily responds by stressing her virtues. Her crown is of gold, not thorns. Milk flows in profusion from her breasts, and she is called the blessed mistress amongst plants.[350] At this point 'Spring' intervenes, reminding them that they are sisters, and reconciling them with the kiss of peace. The rose shines with glory, Spring agrees, but the lily commands the shining sceptres of kingdoms.[351] Harmony is finally restored between the sisters, but of the two it is the lily that emerges as the superior.[352] In closing, Spring echoes Jerome's influential colour typology: roses were the martyrs' colours whilst the lilies' white was the Virgin's.[353]

Sedulius' imagery may have developed pre-existing themes, albeit in idiosyncratic ways, but it was timely. Whilst the origin of the fleur-de-lys has been one of the more contentious topics in the history of royal regalia and state symbolism it is generally agreed that it is in the mid-ninth century, and in particular during the reign of Charles the Bald, that the lily emerges as a significant element in the iconography of rulership.[354] One might also add that another tradition of lilies and crowns was in existence in the ninth century, within Lotharingia and near to the northern Italian circles with which Sedulius had a clear connection: the so-called 'iron crown' of Monza, the complex history of which is slowly beginning to be unravelled through high technology, which has revealed a phase of reworking in the Carolingian period bearing close parallels with comparable artistry, including that on the golden altar of Sant'Ambrogio, Milan. The floral and foliage decoration on several plaques of the Monza crown can be interpreted, quite plausibly, as roses and lilies.[355]

Fêted as a new Solomon, a *rex pacificus* of the later ninth century, there is some evidence that this image made its way into the self-image Charles projected from the royal court. In a letter to Hadrian II in 872, Charles denounced the synod of Douzy's refusal to recognize the deposition of Hincmar of Laon and with it, he clearly felt, his own authority.[356] Whilst many have seen the hand of Hincmar of

[349] *Carm.* no. 81, p. 128, line 24.
[350] *Carm.* no. 81, p. 128, line 28: 'Sic holerum dominam me dicunt esse beatam.': a faint echo of Matt. V.9?
[351] *Carm.* no. 81, p. 128, lines 36–7: 'O rosa pulchra, tace! Tua gloria claret in orbe, / Regia sed nitidis dominentur lilia sceptris'.
[352] C. Stancliffe, 'Red, White and Blue Martyrdom', in R. McKitterick, D. Whitelock, and D. Dunville (eds), *Ireland in Early Medieval Europe. Studies in Memory of Kathleen Hughes* (Cambridge, 1982), 21–47, with extensive references; at 26–30.
[353] Stancliffe, 'Red'.
[354] Schramm, 'Krone', 412–15.
[355] *The Iron Crown and Imperial Europe*, ed. G. Buccellati, T. Parks, J. Snapp, and A. Ambrosioni (Milan, 1995–9), 2 volumes, offers an exhaustive treatment of recent research and past hypotheses.
[356] *MGH Conc.* IV, no. 37 (871), pp. 533–47. For scholarship on the letter and the wider context of the issues surrounding Hincmar of Laon see M. E. Sommar, 'Hincmar of Rheims and the Canon Law of Episcopal Translation', *The Catholic Historical Review* 88.3 (2002), 429–44, with references.

Rheims behind this letter, Janet Nelson has claimed it as the voice of Charles himself.[357] If so, it reveals a sensibility shaped by the authority of scripture and conscious of the needs of inner peace:

We read in Paralipomenon that the sons of Israel went forth into battle with a peaceful mind because they fought, not out of vengeful spite but to gain peace. We say this, because you force us, dishonoured as we are by letters from you which are unfitting to the royal power—to write to you otherwise than we should have wished, but still with a peaceful mind.[358]

Charles went on to invoke his lineage for Hadrian; he was the successor to his father and grandfather and thus to 'the title and dignity of a king'.[359] Charles' words evoked this lineage somewhat more allusively. His apparently 'peaceful mind' (*mente pacifica*) when composing his response to the synod of Douzy's ruling itself echoed the peaceful and pious mind (*pacifico pie mentis*) with which his grandfather, Charlemagne, had also reflected upon the bond that linked the Franks to God in the *Admonitio generalis*' opening statement, nearly a century earlier.

'AN APOSTLE AMONGST THE APOSTLES': POPE NICHOLAS I PREACHES PEACE

As we have seen, peace was a recurrent theme in Carolingian relations with the Papacy, a mainstay of the diplomatic language developed from Pippin III's day forward, and a crucial goal at various points in their interaction, whether in terms of Charlemagne bringing order to a factionalized Rome or Gregory IV's ineffectual involvement in the turmoil of the 830s.

Few occupants of St Peter's see, however, matched Nicholas I (858–67) either in the confidence he invested in his *auctoritas* or the vigour and range with which he applied it. In this respect, as Regino of Prüm noted in the early tenth century.[360] Like his sixth-century predecessor, Nicholas expended considerable energy in counselling and keeping the peace across western Europe. The *Liber*

---

[357] Nelson, *Charles*, 235–8. This view has not been universally accepted, Sommar, 'Hincmar', p. 430, n. 3.

[358] *MGH Conc.* IV, no. 37 (871), p. 533: 'Legimus in libro Paralypomenon filios Israhel mente pacifica isse ad prelium, quia non livoris vindicta, sed obtinendae pacis gratia dimicarunt. Quod eorsum dicimus, quia cogitis nos indecentibus potestati regie litteris vestris inhonoratum, inconvenientibus episcopali modestie vestrae mandatis gravatum, contumeliis et obprobriis dehonestatum, aliter quam vellemus mente pacifica vobis rescribere . . .' Translation: Nelson, *Charles*, 236.

[359] *MGH Conc.* IV, no. 37 (871), p. 533.

[360] Regino, *Chronicon*, ed. F. *MGH* SRG 50 (Hanover, 1890), *s.a.* 868, p. 94.

pontificalis remembered his involvement in the Lotharingian divorce as one who sought, through the mediation of his legate Arsenius of Orte, 'to maintain peace and concord between the kings of the Gauls, so as to join them together, with peace restored, in the bosom of the Holy Church, without resistance ... '.[361] Others were not so positive. 'He numbers himself an Apostle amongst the Apostles', sniped Gunther of Cologne, 'he makes himself emperor of the whole world'.[362] Nicholas was not beyond adopting Gregorian imagery, albeit with a twist. In an acidic letter of late 861, against a backdrop of Viking attacks, Nicholas I wrote to Hunfrid, incumbent of the dangerously exposed northern bishopric of Thérouanne, close to Quentovic, addressing the question of whether a bishop could abandon his see in the face of Viking attack. Nicholas was firm. It is dangerous for a ship's lookout to abandon his post when the sea is tranquil, how much worse when a storm rages?[363] Nor, for that matter, he added, could a cleric who killed a pagan progress in the Church's hierarchy.[364] It was, in any case, as absurd for a cleric to shoulder arms and go off to battle as it was shameful and dangerous for a layman to say Mass and give out the body and blood of Christ.[365] Such views were, perhaps, easier to write from behind the Leonine walls than they were to receive on Francia's exposed northern coast.

Like Gregory, the theme of peace was a concern to which Nicholas would frequently return, and one he explored, like his predecessor, in letters to a number of contemporary rulers. Commenting to Salomon of Brittany on the treaty he had established between the Bretons and Charles the Bald in 862, and the attendant need to normalize ecclesiastical relations, Nicholas confidently promised the Breton duke that once irregularities had been ironed out 'there will be peace and concord, and all lawful order in your kingdom'.[366] Fostering mission in a letter of 864, Nicholas exhorted the Danish king Horic to abandon the worship of his 'deaf, dumb and blind' man-made idols for Christianity. He held out the promise of the Eternal Kingdom with its endless peace, a far cry from earthly kingdoms, constantly shaken by war, where life and power were fleeting.[367]

The perceived discrepancies between the behaviour of pagan and Christian kings meant that the former, if joining the ranks of the latter, needed instruction.

---

[361] *LP* II, 163.

[362] *AB s.a.* 864, p. 68: 'Nam, quamvis domnus Nicolaus, qui dicitur papa et qui se apostolum inter apostolos adnumerat totiusque mundi imperatorem se facit ... '. For Gunther's position and perspective, W. Georgi, 'Erzbischof Gunthar von Köln und die Konflikte um das Reich Lothars II. Überlegungen zum politischen und rechtlichen Köntext der Absetzung durch Papst Nikolaus I. im Jahre 863', *Jahrbuch des Kölnischen Geschichtesvereins* 66 (1995), 1–33.

[363] *MGH Ep.* IV, no. 104, pp. 612–14, at 613.

[364] *Ibid.*

[365] *MGH Ep.* IV, no. 104, p. 613.

[366] *MGH Epp.* VI, no. 107 (862), pp. 620–2, at 622.

[367] *MGH Epp.* VI, no. 27 (863), pp. 293–4.

Nicholas' best-known letter is the reply he sent in November 866 to the Bulgar Khan Boris, who had sent him a list of over one hundred questions on matters ranging from marriage policy and bodily pollution to differences between the practices of the western and eastern churches. Practical matters were also addressed, questions of law, frontiers, crimes of *lèse-majesté*. Some of these seem to have been raised by his unease at the pressured conversion to Christianity he had undergone following his defeat by a Byzantine army in 864. This attack had itself been precipitated by Boris' acceptance of Latin Christianity through the initiatives of Louis the German.[368] Soon after, Boris received a substantial tract from Photios, setting out the patriarch's vision of the ideal *archon*.[369]

Nicholas' response to the Bulgar Khan's questions on the appropriate behaviour for a Christian king can be read as a further example of a ninth-century *speculum principis*, but with one vital difference. In his letter Nicholas sought to offer a papal perspective on problems the ruler himself had raised, and wished to be given an authoritative response. Consequently, Nicholas offered ideals in his letter, but ideals moored in the tangible concerns of a ruler dealing with Byzantine military and religious pressure. That said, he was not beyond using Boris' practical enquiries—can I still execute those I find ill-prepared for battle?—as a springboard for allegory: spiritual arms are good works, a man's soul is his horse (*Porro equus animus intelligitur*).[370] Boris' duty was to protect the Church, keeping it peaceful and without diminution (*pacatam et sine diminutione*), though Nicholas was also explicit on the matter of standards—the cross, not a horse's tail on a pole was preferred—and the vital importance of prayer before battle.[371] In this and other responses, not least Nicholas' insistence that Boris listen to the Church and more specifically to his bishops, his thoughts bear general similarities with those of his contemporaries. Could the Bulgars wage war during Lent? Boris asked. Unless compelled by circumstance, replied Nicholas, it was best the Bulgars avoided war at all times, though when it was necessary to defend his *patria* and the Church, they could.[372] Tangible anxiety might be discerned behind some of Boris' questions. What if a messenger announced that

---

[368] *MGH Epp.* VI, no. 99 (November, 866), pp. 568–600. Commentary: P. A. Holmes, 'Nicholas I's "Reply to the Bulgarians" Revisited', *Ecclesia Orans* 7 (1990), 131–43; M. M. Sheehan, 'The Bishop of Rome to a Barbarian King on the Rituals of Marriage', in J. Farge (ed.), *Marriage, Family, and Law in Medieval Europe: Collected Studies* (Cardiff, 1996), 278–91; R. E. Sullivan, 'Khan Boris and the Conversion of Bulgaria: a Case Study of the Impact of Christianity on a Barbarian Society', *Studies Studies in Medieval and Renaissance History* 3 (1966), 55–139.

[369] *Photii Patriarchae Constantinopolitani Epistulae et Amphilochia*, eds, B. Laoudas and L. Westerink (Leipzig, 1983), I, 1–39. An English translation, drawing from earlier editions, is D. Stratoudaki White and J. R. Berrigan, *The Patriarch and the Prince* (Brookline, MA, 1982).

[370] *MGH Epp.* VI, no. 99 (866), c. 40, p. 582.

[371] *MGH Epp.* VI, no. 99, c. 33, p. 580.

[372] *MGH Epp.* VI, no. 99, c. 46, p. 585: 'Et ideo, si nulla urguet necessitas, non solum quadragesimali, sed omni tempore est proeliis abstinendum.'

battle had been joined once prayers had actually begun?[373] The scenario was not as unlikely as it might at first seem, particularly in light of injunctions for prayers to be said immediately before battle. In fact, just this situation would occur in southern England in summer 871 just before the battle of Assandun. Asser wrote approvingly of Alfred's elder brother Æthelred I's decision to finish Mass before rallying his troops. Nicholas would have approved, for he advised the same course of action to the Khan. Victory is the result more of prayer than force of arms. Stay and pray.[374]

Several chapters of Nicholas' reply directly addressed Boris' concerns about making, and keeping, peace with those around him. Like nowhere else in the later ninth century we see a new member of the family of kings attempting to understand what obligations membership brought with it. How, asked Boris, ought he to establish and maintain (*firmare et custodire*) peace with a people who wish to have peace with him? Nicholas replied that he ought not to refuse peace with anyone, citing Hebrews XII.14 ('Pursue peace with everyone') and Romans XII.18 ('Have peace with all men'), statements of ideal behaviour within the community of the Church.[375] Nicholas emphasized Paul's use of 'all': nobody was exempt from the peace. He was, however, as aware as Boris of the Bulgars' precarious political balancing act between Byzantium and the West, and doubtless also aware of Michael III's enforced peace of 864 when Boris had been baptized and Michael made his godfather. Perhaps for that reason he qualified Paul's universal statement with the observation that the precise means by which it was established and maintained depended upon the customs and the words (*mores et verba*) of the people in question. Peace, Nicholas cautioned, could be as destructive (*perniciosa*) as it was praiseworthy (*laudabilis*). Put Christ first in any treaty you enter into, he advised, and do not make peace with those who lack the Peace of Christ, nor with those who would make peace that they might commit crimes more freely. Here, Nicholas was genuinely like Gregory the Great, fully alive to the dangers of earthly peace for the wrong reasons, and the dangers such a peace posed to faith and social order. It was precisely the tie created by the 864 treaty with Byzantium that concerned Boris in the next question he sent to Nicholas. If a peace treaty had been made with a Christian people by oath, but later the same Christian people wish to break their oaths and attack, would it be lawful to attack them first?[376] Nicholas counselled tolerance, but added a codicil: if a clause was included in the treaty which stipulated that it was nullified by an act of aggression by either party then, yes, war was legitimate. Once again, however, he hedged. Ask your bishop, he advised, as he would know

---

[373] *MGH Epp.* VI, no. 99, c. 74, p. 593.
[374] *De rebus,* c. 37, pp. 28–9.
[375] *MGH Epp.* VI, no. 99 (866), c. 80, p. 594.
[376] *MGH Epp.* VI, no. 99 (866), c. 81, p. 594.

the specifics of the matter. Generally, however, Boris ought to pray for things to be peaceful.

This last question has an interesting coda. Around 905 a later emperor, Leo VI the Wise—Byzantium's own Solomonic king—reflected upon the same issue from the opposite perspective, concluding in his *Taktika* that, 'since the Bulgars have accepted peace in Christ and share the same faith as the Romans, we do not think it right to arm ourselves against them. Defence against them lies in God's hands.'[377]

Boris' final question on foreign relations turned from peace with Christian peoples to peace with pagans. Although citing St Paul's injunction that light should not commune with darkness Nicholas conceded that, under certain circumstances, it was acceptable for a Christian king to enter into pacts or friendship treaties with foreigners or the faithless (*cum alienigenis et infidelibus*). First, if by so doing the intended goal was the spreading of the faith, and second, if they were engaged to perform servile tasks.[378]

Whilst Breton, Danish, and Bulgar kings received exhortations to peace during Nicholas' pontificate he also directed them towards Carolingian rulers. In a letter of 865, in direct response to Charles the Bald's aggression towards Louis II, again delivered by the indefatigable Arsenius, Nicholas offered Charles as intense a disquisition on the importance of peace as any we have. Paul's words, Nicholas began, were also his: 'My little children, of whom I am in labour again, until Christ be formed in you' (Gal. IV.19). Charles' inner life was the focus of Nicholas' first attack. He ought to take Christ into his very insides, and rip the thorn bush of hatred from his heart.[379] Christ was our peace, 'who has made two into one', he reminded Charles: 'God was *caritas*' (John I.4). There is no doubt, Nicholas continued, that the man who possessed neither peace nor *caritas* within himself drove Christ from his heart. The absence of peace within Charles' mind and the divisions its absence fostered, lay at the root of the wider political unrest. Christ, who was complete peace, complete justice, complete truth would not live in a divided mind, and Charles' mind was divided.[380] He, should, therefore,

---

[377] H. Chadwick, *East and West: the Making of a Rift in the Church: from Apostolic Times until the Council of Florence* (Oxford, 2003), 110. For the *Taktika*'s composition in the aftermath of the Byzantino-Bulgarian wars of 894–6 see S. Tougher, *The Reign of Leo VI (886–912). Politics and People* (Leiden, 1997), 168–73. For Leo, the Bulgars, and the celebration of peace R. J. H. Jenkins, 'The Peace with Bulgaria (927) Celebrated by Theodore Daphnopates', in P. Wirth (ed.), *Polychronion. Festschrift F. Dölger zum 75. Geburtstag* (Heidelberg, 1966), 287–303.

[378] *MGH Epp.* VI, c. 82, pp. 594–5: 'Inveniuntur autem nonnulli sanctorum et fidelium cum alienigenis et infidelibus pacta et amicitiae foedera contraxisse diversa, sed eos non tanquam infidelitatem eorum et superstitionem adprobantes coluisse, sed tamquam in angarias diversis usibus implicasse et praecipue in terrenis eos quaestibus et servilibus occupasse.'

[379] *MGH Epp.* VI, no. 33 (865), pp. 302–5, at 302.

[380] *MGH Epp.* VI, no. 33 (865), p. 302.

become a son of peace. Charles should foster justice, embrace *caritas*.[381] 'Follow peace with all men', counselled Nicholas, in full apostolic flight (Heb. XII.14) 'as much as is in you, have peace with all men' (Rom. XII.18). How much more important, Nicholas asked, turning obliquely to the events of 865, and how much better to be at peace with those to whom one was related by blood?[382] Nicholas made clear that not only was he concerned that Charles rule correctly, but also that his days should pass in the greatest peace. He should consider the lessons of the Beatitudes. Shifting, as he would do when writing to Boris, between Christian precept and legal process, Nicholas counselled Charles to abide by his sworn agreement with his nephew, Louis II, reminding him that it served as a symbol of his faith to the peoples around. 'Stay your sword', he commanded, and prevent the terrible bloodletting it threatened to cause.[383] 'Cease your anger, let your hatred be settled, your quarrels calmed, and rip out all your enmity by the roots'.[384] Augustinian order was the final base for his argument. Everyone ought to be content with their lot. A king by the grace of God, Louis II had his own divinely apportioned place in the hierarchy. Charles ought to let *iustitia, caritas*, and *concordia* rule him, rather than a hunger for glory or arrogance, then the highest summit of peace will be achieved. It was peace that Christ left to man, '"*my* peace"', stressed Nicholas, 'not "my love of the world"'. Nicholas added: 'not as the world giveth, do I give unto you' (John XIV.27). What we should learn from this, he added, 'Saint Augustine has beneficially and brilliantly set out.'[385]

As we have seen, other Carolingian intellectuals in the middle decades of the ninth century had independently anticipated Nicholas' advice, looking to Augustine to give shape to their understanding of the rapidly shifting political world in which they lived. This they did in a fashion so diverse as to confound any easy notion of a shared understanding of Augustine's thought of the kind once postulated by scholars of early medieval political thought.[386] No less diverse were the treatments of peace and power of which they formed part, from Dhuoda's advice to her son, a small cog with an uncertain place in the Frankish political machine, and the Bavarian poet's plain vision of good government manifest in local law and order through to the more elevated,

---

[381] *MGH Epp.* VI, no. 33 (865), p. 302.
[382] *MGH Epp.* VI, no. 33 (865), p. 302.
[383] *MGH Epp.* VI, no. 33 (865), pp. 302–3
[384] *MGH Epp.* VI, no. 33 (865), p. 302.
[385] *MGH Epp.* VI, no. 33 (865), p. 303.
[386] H.-X. Arquillière, *L'Augustinisme politique. Essai sur la formation des théories politiques du moyen-âge* (Paris, 1934, revised 1955), a major influence on Bonnaud-Delamare's *L'idée de paix*. On Arquillière's model see J. Contreni, 'Carolingian Era, Early', D. Kries, 'Political Augustinianism', *Augustine through the Ages*, 124–9; 657–8; P. Brezzi, 'Considerazioni sul cosidetto "Agostinismo politico" (alto) medioevale', *Augustinianum* 25 (1985) 235–54; T. Renna 'The Idea of Peace in the West, 500–1150', *Journal of Medieval History* 2.6 (1980), 143–68, esp. 162.

liturgically based vision of Florus, and Sedulius' mix of praise and practicality. Collectively, they attest to the intensity with which political conversation and commentary was conducted in the ninth century, the depth of engagement with ideas and texts old and new, and the richness of the Carolingian political imagination.

5

'The Wise Must Hold Meetings with the Wise':[1] Anglo-Saxon England

We have already encountered Anglo-Saxon treatments of peace and peaceful rulership at several earlier points, in Bede's evident interest in peaceful rule and the figures of Solomon and Edwin, in his contemporary Tatwine's canopy-dwelling Saxon squirrel '. . . avoiding by such swift pace the period of war', and in the contributions of Cathwulf and Alcuin to the political thought of the Carolingian world.[2] For all the connections that linked England and the continent there are distinct differences between the two, not least in the matter of sources. Before the tenth century we lack Anglo-Saxon equivalents comparable to the substantial Carolingian *specula* of Smaragdus or Sedulius, nor do we have surviving polemics and apologetics such as those that events in Louis the Pious' reign generated. When, late in Æthelred's reign, we see comparable works emerge they do so under clear Carolingian influence and at a time when Viking attack and internal misrule precipitated both a crisis of confidence in central authority and in the specific delegatory character of Æthelred's leadership. 'By what means shall peace and comfort come to God's servants and God's poor, other than through Christ and through a Christian king?' Wulfstan would ask in his fragmentary sets of observations on Christian society collectively known as the *Institutes of Polity*.[3] Remarkably, of course, the most sustained vision of kingship we have from before AD 900 seemingly comes from a king himself, the Old English translations produced at Alfred's court in the latter half of his reign.[4]

---

[1] 'Þing sceal gehegan / frod wiþ frodne. Biþ hyra ferð gelic. / Hi a sace semaþ, sibbe gelærað, / þa ær wonsælge awegen habbað.' 'Wise men must hold meetings together. Their minds are similar. / They always settle disputes and counsel peace, / Which unfortunate men have previously disturbed', *Maxims* I, lines 18–21, *ASPR* III, p. 157. Translation from T. A. Shippey, *Poems of Wisdom and Learning in Old English* (Cambridge, 1976), 64–5.

[2] Tatwine, *Aenigmata*, no. 17, p. 184.

[3] M. Swanton, *Anglo-Saxon Prose* (London, 1975), 125–38, at 127. R. Trilling, 'Sovereignty and Social Order: Archbishop Wulfstan and the *Institutes of Polity*', in J. Ott and A. Trumbore Jones (eds), The Bishop Reformed: Studies of Episcopal Power and Culture in the Central Middle Ages *(Aldershot, 2007)*, 58–85, esp. 60–78.

[4] For arugments about Alfredian authorship see D. Pratt, 'problems of authorship and audience in the writings of King Alfred the Great,' *Lay Intellectuals*, 162–191, responding to M. Godden, 'Did King Alfred write anything?', *Medium Ævum* 76 (2007), 1–23.

ALDHELM, WEALDHERE, AND BEDE

The earliest piece of political advice to an Anglo-Saxon king, Gregory the Great's letter to Æthelberht of Kent in June 601 offered little beyond Gregory's reminder of Æthelberht's obligations as a Christian king, the opportunities the role offered for achieving fame (a favoured strategy when writing to convert kings), and a reminder of the need for both humility and mindfulness of eventual judgement.[5] By the close of the seventh century, however, we can see Anglo-Saxon churchmen offering political advice with an emphasis upon their responsibility for peace. Aldhelm, writing to Geraint, king of Dumnonia sometime between the mid 680s and 706, and hence in the wake of the Synod of Whitby, expounded at some length on Geraint's duty as a king to ensure that the Church under his rule adhered to Roman orthodoxy, correct paschal observance, and tonsorial style established in 664.[6] Aldhelm's bigger theme was the unity of the Church, and implicitly Geraint's responsibility for it where he ruled. His appeal was to the peace of the Church: 'Much peace have they that love thy law and to them there is no stumbling block' (Ps. CXVIII.165). Aldhelm drove his point home through a chain of biblical extracts, reminding him that peace is the mother of Catholics and the authoress of the children of God, culminating with Psalm CXXI: 'Let peace be in thy strength and abundance in thy towers'. Aldhelm offered to the Dumnonian king the same exhortation that Avitus had provided Gundobad, casting Geraint in the long-standing role of the ruler as the protector of the Church, guardian of orthodoxy, and keeper of its peace.[7]

When letters counselling peace were not sufficient, Anglo-Saxon churchmen of the later seventh century acted like their continental counterparts and attempted to keep it. At various points in the *Historia ecclesiastica* Bede cited instances of shuttle diplomacy, such as in 679 when Theodore of Canterbury succeeded in convincing Ecgfrith of Northumbria and Æthelred of Mercia to come to terms. For Bede, Theodulf's achievement was all the more impressive not only because of the warlike character of each king's subjects, but also because driving the war was a feud between the two royal houses—Æthelred's much-loved brother Ælfwine had been slain in a previous clash. Theodore, however, had been able to cement peace by convincing the Mercians to pay the full *wergeld* for the atheling's death.[8]

Whilst much of the evidence we have for actions such as these is necessarily anecdotal, a remarkable survival brings us closer to the actual processes themselves. This is the original 'letter close' sent by Wealdhere, East Saxon Bishop of

---

[5] Gregory, *Ep.* XI.37.
[6] M. Lapidge, 'The Career of Aldhelm', *ASE* 36 (2007), 15–69, at 66–7.
[7] *Aldhelm, The prose works*, trans. M. Lapidge and M. Herren (Ipswisch, 1979), 155–60, at 156. Text: *Aldhelmi Opera*, ed. R. Ehwald, *MGH AA 15* (Berlin, 1919), Ep. 4, pp. 480–6, at 482.
[8] *HE* IV.21.

London, to Berhtwald of Canterbury, in which he discussed the repeated attempts to settle mounting disagreement (*discordia, iurgia*) between Ine of Kent and Sigeheard and Swæfred of the East Saxons, the result of the latter's growing ambitions in Surrey.[9] A meeting had been arranged at Brentford with a view to settling relations, and Wealdhere's presence was requested. Wealdhere, therefore, was writing to ask permission from the Archbishop for him to be in communication with the West Saxons, and in particular their bishop, Hædde of Winchester, in breach of Berhtwald's instruction the previous year that, until irregularities in West Saxon episcopal ordination were amended, no communication should take place with Wessex.[10] In the course of his explanation Wealdhere indirectly reveals something of the means by which peace had been sought between the two sides. As elsewhere in the early medieval West a core component of the settlements was an agreement by one side (in this case the East Saxons) to expel any exiles they harboured from the opposing side. The forthcoming meeting at Brentford was intended as an opportunity not only to settle issues for all but also to make satisfactory amendments—presumably *wergeld* payments—by law for offences caused.[11] In many ways the terms both sides had sought both before and at Brentford—expulsion of exiles, arrangement of reparations, collective decision-making—resembles in its general outline the provisions for establishing *wergeld* equivalences and preventing defection that Alfred was to draw up with Guthrum nearly two centuries later. In the very peace strategies he pursued with Alfred, as much as his adoption of Christianization, promulgation of laws, and issue of coinage, the East Anglian king was working within established Anglo-Saxon patterns. Wealdhere expressed to Berhtwald the hope that he might reconcile the two *regna*, 'as if he were a peace hostage' (*quasi obses pacis*), a telling analogy between his own difficult position, the allusion's casual character hinting at the familiarity of the position, and the tensions it created. Wealdhere's letter makes clear that both sides afforded him considerable authority and latitude in brokering a peaceful solution. Both sides had agreed to abide by the conditions of the treaty that he and the West Saxon bishop would peacefully and unanimously agree upon.[12]

If, ultimately, this letter reveals more about the continued importance of bishops as diplomats and peacekeepers in the post-Roman West than it does about peaceful rulers per se, it is nevertheless a vital reminder that in addition to any formal, written admonitions to be peaceful Anglo-Saxon bishops may also have delivered many orally in dealings with neighbouring kings. (What arguments, one might wonder, did Theodore muster, and how, when trying to calm

---

[9] P. Chaplais, 'The Letter from Bishop Wealdhere of London to Archbishop Brihtwold of Canterbury: the Earliest Original "Letter Close" Extant in the West', in *idem, Essays in Medieval Diplomacy and Administration* (London, 1981), 3–23, text at 22–3.

[10] Chaplais, 'Letter', 22.

[11] Ibid.

[12] Chaplais, 'Letter', 23.

tensions between Ecgfrith and Æthelred?) However, it also reveals what might otherwise have gone unnoticed: that in the early eighth century the kings of Wessex and the East Saxons were themselves willing to commit to repeated attempts to establish peaceful relations between their respective kingdoms, and were prepared as part of that process both to involve churchmen, like Wealdhere of London, with interests in the settlement, and to give them considerable freedom to establish peace between them. Bishops could be *pacifici* precisely because the kings with whom they treated were willing to countenance the creation of such a peace.

One churchman whom we can probably discount from the role of active peacemaker in the vein of Wealdhere and Berhtwald is Bede, whose life was characterized by intense stasis within the secure precincts of Monkwearmouth, his home since childhood.[13] In his homily on the monastery's patron, the indefatigable Biscop, he expressed gratitude that Biscop's willingness to risk the roads of seventh-century Europe meant that he, and his fellows, could 'be at peace within the cloisters of the monastery,' free and safe to serve Christ.[14] He was also aware that it came less easily to other sections of society. Explaining Ahab's rebuke to the demand of unconditional surrender by Israel made by Benedad, the feared and mighty king of Syria in III Kings XX.11, 'Let not the girded boast as though he were ungirded', Bede expounded that what Ahab meant was: do not boast or set terms before the battle has been won. Only when a battle has been won can a conqueror be truly called 'ungirded', 'because only when arms have been put down might he properly enjoy the leisure of a longed-for peace'.[15] In keeping with the plain, historical treatment of the commentary as a whole Bede even offered a remarkable image of Israelite rest and recuperation: unbelted a warrior might perhaps take a bath, rest in bed, change clothes.[16]

We need not revisit Edwin here, save, perhaps, to note that the same awareness of the potential dangers of travel underpins Bede's vision of Biscop's travels. What of Bede's wider vision of peace? In his exegesis on the Temple and the Tabernacle, and elsewhere when he dwelt upon the christological symbolism of Solomon's litter, Bede offered extended explorations of biblical Solomonic materials, emphasizing Solomon as a prefiguration of Christ, his peaceful kingdom in its own way a prefiguration of the eternal peace of the heavenly kingdom and the Temple as an image of the holy universal Church. In his treatment of

---

[13] *HE* V.24.

[14] Bede, *Homiliae Evangelia*, ed. D. Hurst, CCSL 122 (Turnhout, 1955), I.13, pp. 91–2; see L. Martin, 'Homily on the Feast of St. Benedict Biscop by the Venerable Bede', *Vox Benedictina* 4.1 (1987), 81–92; W. T. Foley and A. Holder (trans.), *Bede: A Biblical Miscellany*, TTH 28 (Liverpool, 1999), xv.

[15] Bede, *In Regum librum XXX quaestiones*, ed. David Hurst CCSL 119 (Turnhout, 1962), XVII, pp. 310–1. Translation: Foley and Holder, *Miscellany*, 81–143, at 117.

[16] Ibid.

Proverbs (Solomon's own words) Bede further presented Solomon's identity as a teacher of wisdom, 'a doctor of the Anglo-Saxon church', and, on one recent opinion, nothing less than an image of Bede himself.[17]

In the *Historia ecclesiastica* Bede offered a broader vision of peace. As much as it was to be wished for, it brought concrete dangers. In the wake of Germanus' Alleluia victory Britain was spared further external attack, Bede wrote, but following Gildas Bede saw that this peace had hazards of its own. Whilst the actions of the earlier generation of kings, priests, private men, and nobles (*reges, sacerdotes, privati et optimates*) had been tempered by an awareness of external dangers, those coming to power subsequently, knowing only the present peaceable state of things, had little reason to limit their behaviour.[18] For Bede, the notion that times of peace brought potential danger was not simply a past lesson but a present truth. In the *Historia*'s final historical chapter he sketched contemporary conditions, enumerating the English kingdoms' current leaders, and voiced his deep uncertainty about Northumbria's fate under Coenred. Recent developments included a peace treaty with the Picts who, in return, themselves enjoyed the peace and truth of the Church. The Irish and the British were similarly quiescent. But Bede was wary:

In these pleasing times of peace and serenity, many of the Northumbrian people, as many nobles as ordinary folk, have lain aside their weapons and are concerned to take the tonsure and to dedicate themselves and their children to monastic vows, rather than the practice of martial discipline. What the outcome of this will be, a later age will see.[19]

This passage has often been seen, with good reason, as the companion piece to the fuller criticism of mispursued monastic practice and its weakening of Northumbria's defences in his letter to Ecgberht.[20] Within the context of the passage itself, however, with its description of a fragile and unsteady political equilibrium in the British Isles, we are left with an attitude strikingly evocative of Gregory's sense of peace's dangers: the false security (*vanae securitatis*) that was, in Robert Markus' words, 'the enemy of effort'.[21] Bede had a clear notion of the very different duties of lay and monastic life. When muddled, both estates suffered. Pious kings prayed, but they also fought. As Bede made clear in his Commentary on Ezra and Nehemiah, a work almost certainly produced late in

---

[17] A. Moss, 'Proverbs with Solomon: A Critical Revision of the Pre-Critical Commentary Tradition in the Light of a Biblical Intertextual Study', *Heythrop Journal* 43.2 (2002), 199–211, esp. 200–2.

[18] *HE* I.22.

[19] *HE* V.23: 'Qua adridente pace ac serenitate temporum, plures in gente Nordanhymbrorum, tam nobiles, quam privati, se suosque liberos, depositis armis, satagunt magis, accepta tonsura, monasterialibus adscribere votis, quam bellicis exercere studiis. Quae res quem sit habitura finem, posterior aetas videbit.'

[20] 'Epistola ad Ecgbertum Episcopum', ed. C. Plummer, *Venerabilis Baedae Opera Historica* (Oxford, 1896), I, 405–23, discussed Blair, Church, 101–7.

[21] R. A. Markus, *Gregory the Great and His World* (Cambridge, 1997), 54.

Bede's life and whose concern with reform has been powerfully affirmed by Scott DeGregorio to have possessed contemporary force, it was the task of kings, and implicitly their armed followers, to protect the Church.[22] Darius the Great, Persian supporter of the Second Temple's construction and author of laws protecting its peace, offered contemporary rulers an ancient model to emulate. 'This occurs', Bede continued, 'in the same way now, in the Holy Church when terrestrial powers that have been converted to the faith issue public edicts for the establishment of the Church and, since the Lord aids the Church and puts all its enemies under its feet, desire that it should enjoy restful calm and peace.'[23]

Some monasteries, at least, had an active part to play maintaining peace and security in Bede's highly ordered vision of society. In book III of the *Historia* Bede recounted Penda's refusal to accept the tribute offered by King Eanfrith as the price of peace between Mercia and Northumbria prior to the battle of the Winwæd in 654/5.[24] Osuiu's subsequent vow to offer the tribute (in the form of land grants for twelve monasteries) and his daughter to God was instead presented by Bede as the real reason behind Penda's destruction at the hands of the smaller Northumbrian army. Peace came properly from God, was the evident lesson, and it was to Him that offerings ought to be made for its assurance.[25] In an episode seized upon by scholars of land tenure but largely overlooked by those interested in the political implications of early English prayer, Osuiu fulfilled his vow. He dispatched his daughter to the nunnery at Hartlepool and gave twelve grants of land—of ten hides each, six in Deira, six in Bernicia—to the Church.[26] Freed from earthly military obligations the resources of these estates were directed towards the support of minsters 'to pursue heavenly warfare and to pray with unceasing devotion for the eternal peace of his people' (*supplicandumque pro pace gentis eius aeterna*).[27] Heavenly warfare and unceasing prayer: Osuiu's foundation resembles a Northumbrian version of St-Maurice, Agaune, with its own focus of constant prayer and transposed militarism.[28] Considering the connections between Anglian royal houses and Frankish monastic centres in

---

[22] S. DeGregorio, *Bede. On Ezra and Nehemiah'* TTH 47 (Liverpool, 2006), xxxvi–xliv, with references. Text: Bede, *In Ezram et Neemiam*, ed. D. Hurst, CCSL 119A (Turnhout, 1969), 235–392.
[23] Bede, *In Ezram*, II, p. 296. Translation: De Gregorio, *Ezra*, 91.
[24] *HE III.24*.
[25] For these themes elsewhere in Bede's thought, and some sense of their reception in the ninth century see Kershaw, 'English History' *Frankland*, 131–8, discussing Sedulius Scottus' use of the *Historia ecclesiastica*.
[26] Blair, *church*, 72–3, with discussion and references.
[27] *HE* III.24: '. . . in quibus ablato studio militiae terrestris, ad exercendam militiam caelestem, supplicandumque pro pace gentis eius aeterna, devotioni sedulae monachorum locus facultasque suppeteret.'
[28] Rosenwein, 'Agaune', 53–4.

the first half of the seventh century the resemblance may not be wholly coincidental.

Bede's vision of a peaceful society was that of a well-ordered Christian community in which all of its constituent elements (kings, monasteries, bishops) fulfilled their right responsibilities and in a way that created a unified harmonious whole. In general terms this sense of ordering might be said to carry Augustinian overtones.[29] If a primary influence can be identified at work upon Bede's thinking about peace in the world, however, it is perhaps that of Gregory the Great, whose own concerns for peace, personal, political, and liturgical, he explicitly acknowledged. In the *Historia*'s account of Gregory Bede drew from the *Dialogues* his admission of particular sadness at having to turn his back upon the peace of the contemplative life, whilst his citation of the *Libellus responsionum* brought with it Gregory's observation to Augustine that, by censuring the faults of others, one's own inner peace could be disturbed: good advice to a hesitant pastor with an unfamiliar flock.[30] Moreover, Gregory's interest in peace—as Bede almost certainly knew from the *Liber pontificalis*—was reflected the liturgy of the Christian West. Bede enumerated Gregory's additions: '. . . in the celebration of the Mass he added three quite perfect petitions: "And dispose our days in Thy peace and command us to be taken from eternal damnation, and to be numbered in the flock of Thine."'[31]

CREATING KINGSHIP: THE FIRST ENGLISH *ORDO*

Whilst prayers for rulers, as well as prayers for peace of a more conventional kind, have long been present in the early medieval liturgical canon, the earliest surviving evidence for their assembly, in combination with other dedicated elements, into coherent king-making rites comes from the ninth-century West Saxon kingdom. This text, the so-called First English *Ordo*, brought together several earlier royal blessings, including several found in two Carolingian 'Eighth-Century Gelasians', the Sacramentaries of Angoulême and Autun, with newer prayers containing considerable conceptual and terminological debts to earlier liturgies, Visigothic and North Italian, as well as Frankish.[32] Strictly

---

[29] A. Thacker, *Bede and Augustine of Hippo: History and Figure in Sacred Text*, Jarrow Lecture 2005 (Newcastle upon Tyne, 2007).

[30] *HE* II.1.

[31] *HE* II.1: 'Sed et in ipsa missarum celebratione tria verba maximae perfectionis plena superadiecit: "Disque nostros in tua pace disponas, atque ab aeterna damnatione nos eripi, et in electorum tuorum iubeas grege numerari."' On Bede's treatment of Gregory's additions D. Bullough, 'Roman books and Carolingian *renovatio*', in *idem, Carolingian Renewal: Sources and Heritage* (Manchester, 1991), 1–33, at 3, noting that these prayers were 'universal by the eighth century', with further references at 22 n. 7.

[32] *The Leofric Missal*, ed. N. Orchard, HBS 113–14 (London, 2002), I, 99–105; J. L. Nelson, 'The First Use of the Second Anglo-Saxon *Ordo*', in J. Barrow and A. Wareham (eds), *Myth,*

speaking, the text is that of a consecration rather than a coronation: no crown was used in the rite as it is recorded, the royal subject being invested rather with a helmet (*galea*), an element conventionally seen as an indicator of its antiquity as well as being emblematic of the *Ordo*'s martial theme.[33]

In one sense the First English *Ordo* might be seen as royal benediction by bricolage; comprised as it was from several discrete but cross-informing elements the *Ordo* effectively offered a condensation of current political ideals and pre-existing royal prayers. The text survives in three post-Conquest manuscripts, the so-called Leofric Missal, and the Egbert and Lanalet Pontificals, of which the first contains the text in a more skeletal form, lacking both the readings that precede it (Lev. XXVI.6–9, Matt. XXII.15–22), most of the rubrics and several prayers, including 'Deus qui populis',[34] but containing the offertory, communion and post-communion prayers, as well as other minor variations.[35] Leofric has recently been convincingly identified by Nicholas Orchard as a collection with a sacramentary produced for Plegmund of Canterbury (d. 909) at its core.[36] There is general agreement that this *Ordo* was assembled sometime before 856 when elements of it were re-used by Hincmar on the occasion of Æthelwulf's marriage to Charles the Bald's daughter Judith, and its possible use at Æthelwulf's coronation at Kingston in 838 mooted, but standing beyond proof.[37] In a recent reappraisal of her earlier reading, Janet Nelson concluded that the First *Ordo* was 'considered current' into the first decade of the tenth century and the first half of Edward the Elder's reign.[38] The implications of the *Ordo*'s potential use across seventy years, the sequential reigns of six members and three generations of the West Saxon house, are crucial to our understanding of the vision of kingship it contains. These were decades characterized by Viking attack and conquest, years in which West Saxon kingship was, if not reshaped by the experience, placed under sufficient pressure as an institution both to codify its character and identify its goals. We might, perhaps, see the ideological programme of the First English *Ordo* as a condensation or distillation of current political ideals in the face of

Rulership, Church and Charters. Essays in Honour of Nicholas Brooks (Aldershot, 2008), 117–26; eadem, 'The Earliest Surviving Royal *Ordo*: Some Liturgical and Historical Aspects', *P&R*, 341–60, esp. 344–56.

[33] Nelson, 'Earliest', 356–7.

[34] Nelson, 'Earliest', 354. R. A. Jackson, 'Who Wrote Hincmar's Ordines?', *Viator* 25 (1994), 31–52 argues for the prayer's adaption from a model in the Gregorian Sacramentary for Louis the Pious' restoration in 835.

[35] *Leofric Missal*, II, 429–32; Egbert Pontifical text in *Two Anglo-Saxon Pontificals*, ed. H. M. J. Banting, HBS 104 (London, 1989), 109–13; *The Lanalet Pontifical*, ed. G. H. Doble, HBS 74 (London, 1937), 59–63. L. G. Wickham Legg, *English Coronation Records* (London, 1901), 3–9, a synoptic edition drawing on all three. Nelson, 'First Use', 118–19; D. Pratt, *The Political Thought of King Alfred the Great* (Cambridge, 2007), 72–8.

[36] *Leofric Missal*, I, 99–105; Nelson, 'First Use', 118–23.

[37] Nelson, 'First Use', 118. This date first suggested by P. Wormald, 'The Ninth Century', in James Campbell (ed.), *The Anglo-Saxons* (Oxford, 1982), 140.

[38] Nelson, 'First Use', 121.

concrete circumstance. Nelson has highlighted its thematic congruencies with *De XII Abusivis* and the ideas of rule articulated by several eighth-century authors, Boniface, Cathwulf, and Alcuin, though some of those similarities might be seen as the result of a shared reliance upon Old Testament models.[39] Nor should some of the features of the text be seen as necessarily ancient. That it is a helmet rather than a crown with which the king in invested may say less about 'English-ness and antiquity' than an awareness of contemporary continental images of the king as *miles Christi*. There are suggestive parallels between elements of the First English *Ordo* and the dedicatory verse and image of Louis the Pious in Hrabanus Maurus' *De laudibus sanctae crucis* of the early 830s, in its own way a self-consciously 'antique' portrait.[40]

Several mutually interlocking themes are dominant in the First English *Ordo*, running through its constituent anthems, lessons, and prayers: the king as defender and protector of his people and vanquisher of their enemies and God, who is in turn his defender; the ruler's responsibility for peace for his people; his possession of the qualities (wisdom, piety) needed both to rule and to serve as an exemplar to his subjects, and the repeated hopes that the reign thus initiated would be blessed not only by the king's own health and longevity but by abundance and fertility throughout the realm. The martial character of the *Ordo* is established early. After the first prayer, the famous *Deus regnorum omnium*, the opening prayer of the Gelasian *Missa pro regibus* rendered here in its emended Carolingian variant, there followed a lesson from Leviticus XXVI.6–9 apt for wartime:

These are the words of the Lord: 'I will give you peace in your lands. You shall sleep, and none shall make you afraid. I will take away evil beasts, and the sword shall not pass through your land. You shall pursue your enemies, and they shall fall before you.'[41]

The succeeding prayers articulated the network of relationships of which the newly elected king was part. God had protected him since birth and the assembled participants prayed for the Lord's ongoing protection, that God's 'wall of Mercy' *(murus misericordiae)* would continue to shelter him from his enemies. They prayed also for the king's goodness to grow, thus ensuring that he remained worthy of continued divine favour, and that he would govern the people in his care with 'the blessings of peace and the excellence of victory'.[42] Protected by God and, in his turn, protector of his people, the king was also able to provide the support or correction demanded by discrete members of society: a help to his friends, a hindrance to his enemies, a comfort to the lowly, and so on, ensuring peace and

[39] Nelson, 'Earliest', 361–70, at 351.

[40] M. Perrin, 'Le représentation figurée de César-Louis le Pieux chez Raban Maur en 835: religion et idéologie', *Francia* 24.1 (1997), 39–64; E. Sears, 'Louis the Pious as *Miles Christi*: The Dedicatory Image in Hrabanus Maurus' *De laudibus sanctae crucis*', *CH*, 605–28.

[41] *Anglo-Saxon Pontificals*, 109; *Lanalet*, 59–60; Wickham Legg, *Coronation*, 4.

[42] *Leofric*, no. 2458, 429; *Anglo-Saxon Pontificals*, 109; *Lanalet*, 60; Wickham Legg, *Coronation*, 4.

security for his own particular homeland and moderately governing each of his subjects according to the measure of each, in a fashion reminiscent of Gregorian directives for pastoral responsibility.[43] Both the Lanalet and the Egbert versions of the *Ordo* agreed that it also fell to the king to be a peacekeeper for foreigners or travellers (*peregrinis pacificatio*). The Leofric Missal's text, however, offered him an alternative role: 'let him be a help or support for foreigners' (*peregrinis auxilium*): either way, there are shades of Bede's image of Edwin. Metaphorically all travelled on the road of truth, and it fell to the king to guide the flock given to him along its way, serving himself as an exemplar to his people of a righteous life, ruling always with peace and wisdom.[44]

Pax and *sapientia* were the qualities hoped for in the final petition, signalling the degree to which the first *Ordo* sought to evoke a Solomonic ideal.[45] Whilst Solomon was already present in one of the earlier Frankish prayers (*Benedic domine hunc presulem*), and deployed here by the *Ordo*'s anonymous creator as the prayer to be said as the sceptre was passed to the king by the assembled bishops and *principes*, his centrality to the conception of kingship in the first *Ordo* is worth stressing. Implicit at various points, Solomon as kingly model finally emerged overtly in the anthem; whilst the leading officiant poured the oil over the king's head, other bishops (*pontifices*) jointly anointed him: '*Unxerunt Salomonem...*' ('They anointed Solomon king, in Gihon, Zadok the priest and Nathan the prophet and going up they said, "May the king live forever"').[46]

The prayer that follows, '*Deus electorum fortitudo*', pursued this Solomonic theme of peace through a tripartite exploration of the oil's symbolism.[47] The text set out a typological sequence: the dove carried the olive branch to Noah, act and object symbolizing the return of peace to the world after the Flood's end (Gen. VIII.11), and with it the implicit renewal of the covenant. From Aaron onwards generations of priests, kings, and prophets had been anointed to rule the people of Israel (Lev. VIII.12). 'By the prophetic voice of David', the prayer continued, alluding to Psalm CIII.15, 'You foretold that the face of the Church should be cheered with oil'. Each instance found its reflection in the condition of the newly anointed king. The richness of the oil with which he was anointed both recalled the dove's olive branch and shared its symbolic meaning, a sign of God's blessing and sanctification. The new king, with the same simplicity as a dove, would bring

[43] *Leofric*, no. 2459, 429; *Anglo-Saxon Pontificals*, 109; *Lanalet*, 60: Wickham Legg, *Coronation*, 5.
[44] *Leofric*, no. 2459, 429; *Anglo-Saxon Pontificals*, 109; *Lanalet*, 60: Wickham Legg, *Coronation*, 5.
[45] Pratt, *Political*, 75–6.
[46] *Anglo-Saxon Pontificals*, 110; *Lanalet*, 60; Wickham Legg, *Coronation*, 5. Nelson, 'Earliest', 355.
[47] *Leofric*, no. 2460, 429–30; *Anglo-Saxon Pontificals*, 110; *Lanalet*, 60–1; Wickham Legg, *Coronation*, 5.

peace to his subjects. By so doing he himself ranked alongside Israel's own anointed rulers, the prayer went on to express the hope that he would in turn emulate the example of these predecessors, imitating Aaron in his diligent service to God, and following in the footsteps (*vestigia*) of those earlier rulers who were both knowledgeable in counsel and fair in judgement. Finally, the text returned to the Psalmist's image of oil 'making cheerful' the face of man. Initially, David's words had been taken to allude to 'the Church'; here, the face was the king's own: 'Give him, through the anointing of this oil a cheerful face, ready to rule the entire people', an allusion to Solomon's advice on royal deportment (Prov. XXVI.15). This exploration of the symbolism of royal anointing drew extensively from earlier prayers, in particular the Gelasian *Benedictio chrismatis* for Maundy Thursday, where several of the scriptural examples present in *Deus electorum fortitudo* occur.[48] Where the latter deviated markedly from its Gelasian forebear, however, was in the way in which these examples turned from the general symbolism of the oil to the very specific function of anointing a king—both active upholder and simultaneous symbol of earthly peace and his people's covenant with God. It is at this point that *Benedic domine hunc presulem* follows, reinforcing these themes through its imprecation that the king would be like David (ruling with sublimity) and Solomon:

Grant that, through your inspiration, he may rule his people with mercy and grant that he will establish and maintain a peaceful kingdom, like Solomon. Amen.

Subsequent blessings emphasized justice, prosperity, fear of God (the beginning of wisdom and an injunction made repeatedly by Solomon), and articulated the hope that the nations 'may keep faith with him' (*gentes illi teneant fidem*) and that his nobles 'may have peace and value charity' (*proceres sui habeat pacem diligantque caritatem*).[49] Invested with sceptre and helmet, the king was acclaimed, and the *principes* kissed him in an act once seen as 'feudal homage' and by Nelson as a 'ritual of recognition' but which, in the context of the previous blessing, the general pacific theme of the rite and the context of the act, might be seen as a kiss of peace, affirming both the king's peacemaking faculty, his wish for harmony with his nobles and in turn their good will towards him. In short, a formalized reaffirmation of the Christian community that included both ruler and ruled.[50]

The obligations of the latter were the focus of the *Ordo*'s final section, as it listed the three commands (*praecepta*) that a newly minted king was to charge his subjects with upholding, in what was effectively the first directive of the new reign :

[48] *Lib. Sacr. Rom.* no 386–8, p. 62. This prayer's dense web of associations and allusions is unravelled by Cramer, *Baptism and Change*, 211–15.

[49] *Leofric*, no. 2461, 430; *Anglo-Saxon Pontificals*, 110–11; *Lanalet*, 61; Wickham Legg, *Coronation*, 6.

[50] Nelson, 'Earliest', 359.

First, that the Church of God and all Christian people should keep true peace in Almighty God. Amen.
The second is that he should forbid all robbery and all unrighteous things to all orders. Amen.
The third is that he should enjoin in all judgements, justice and mercy, so that through this the gracious and merciful God might indulge us with His mercy. Amen.[51]

'GIF WE ÐA STILNESSE HABBAÞ . . .': PEACE IN KING ALFRED'S POLITICAL THOUGHT[52]

Perhaps few lives from the early Middle Ages combined a sense of the possibilities of peace with a first-hand awareness of its achievement and maintenance as that of Alfred the Great.[53] Born in 849 against a backdrop of intensifying Viking raids, Alfred's own life attests to both the rhythms of war and of peace in the early Middle Ages, as well as their effects. According to Asser, Alfred lamented that when he was a boy, having both the leisure and the aptitude to study, he had no teachers. As a king he had at least a few teachers and scribes, but his illnesses, the foreign and domestic concerns of royal power, and Viking

---

[51] Leofric, no. 2466, 432: 'Inprimis, ut ecclesia dei et omnis populus christianus veram pacem servent, in omnipotenti deo. R. Amen. | Aliud est, ut rapicitates et omnes iniquitates, omnibus gradibus interdicat. Amen. | Tertium est, ut in omnibus iudiciis aequitatem et misericordiam precipiat, ut per hoc nobis indulgeat misericordiam clemens et misericors deus. Amen.' P. Stafford, 'The Laws of Cnut and the history of Anglo-Saxon Royal Promises', *ASE* 10 (1983), 173–90; Nelson, 'Earliest', 359.

[52] 'If we have peace . . .', *King Alfred's West Saxon Version of Gregory's Pastoral Care*, ed. H. Sweet, EETS 45 (London, 1871), I, 6.

[53] Studies of Alfred's reign and works are substantial but recent key entries include Pratt, *Political Thought*; P. Wormald, 'Alfred (848/9–899)', *Oxford Dictionary of National Biography*, Oxford University Press, Sept 2004; online edn, Oct 2006 <http://www.oxforddnb.com/view/article/183>, accessed 21 Nov 2008; Karkov, *Ruler*, 23–52; the papers collected in T. Reuter (ed.), *Alfred the Great: Papers from the Eleventh-Centenary Conferences* (Aldershot, 2003); R. P. Abels, *Alfred the Great. War, Kingship and Culture in Anglo-Saxon England* (London, 1998); M. Kempshall, 'No bishop, no king: the ministerial ideology of kingship and Asser's Res gestae *Ælfredi*', in R. Gameson and H. Leyser (eds), *Belief and Culture in the Middle Ages: Studies presented to Henry Mayr-Harting* (Oxford, 2001), 106–27; N. Guenther Discenza, *The King's English: Strategies of Translation in the Old English Boethius* (New York, 2005); *eadem*, 'Wealth and Wisdom: Symbolic Capital and the Ruler in the Translation Program of Alfred the Great', *Exemplaria: A Journal of Theory in Medieval and Renaissance Studies* 13.2 (2001), 433–67; A. Scharer, *Herrschaft und Repräsentation. Studien zur Hofkultur König Alfreds des Großen* (Vienna, 2000); *idem*, 'The Writing of History at King Alfred's Court', *EME* 5.2 (1996), 177–206; A. J. Frantzen, *King Alfred* (Boston, 1986); J. L. Nelson, 'The Political Ideas of Alfred of Wessex', in A. Duggan (ed.), *Kings and Kingship in Medieval Europe* (London, 1993), 125–58; *eadem*, 'Wealth and Wisdom: the Politics of Alfred the Great', in J. Rosenthal (ed.), *Kings and Kingship*: Acta 11 (Binghamton, 1986), 31–52; *eadem*, '"A king across the sea": Alfred in Continental Perspective', *TRHS* 5th series 36 (1986), 45–68, all reprinted with the same pagination in her *Rulers and Ruling Families in Early Medieval Europe: Alfred, Charles the Bald, and Others* (Aldershot, 1999).

attacks made study impossible.[54] As Asser and the *Anglo-Saxon Chronicle* reveal, Alfred was involved in treaty-making and with the purchase of peace from Viking invaders on numerous occasions, giving tribute, offering or exchanging hostages, and swearing oaths, both as a member of the West Saxon *fyrd* whilst his elder brothers lived and, from 871, as king himself.[55] It was as king that Alfred entered into his treaty with Guthrum, the earliest extant vernacular treaty in the medieval West.[56] This respite allowed him both to reflect upon his role as ruler and to reorganize Wessex's defences as well as to revive Southumbrian learning.[57] Both, in their own way, served peace, or at least that was how Alfred, and some others, saw it. In a letter of around 886, which some have seen as reflecting Alfred's own words, Fulk of Rheims wrote to the West Saxon king, explaining that he gave thanks that God's love was kindled in Alfred's heart:[58]

... that illumined and similarly kindled by this, you administer strenuously the profit of the kingdom committed to you from above, both by striving for and defending its peace with warlike weapons and divine support, and by earnestly desiring with a religious heart to raise the dignity of the ecclesiastical order with spiritual weapons.[59]

Switching from Alfred's efforts to his own support of them, Fulk offered the familiar buttress of ecclesiastical support: the promise of prayer, echoing the words of the equally familiar prayer for peace 'in our days':

Hence we beseech the heavenly clemency with unwearied prayers, that he who had directed and kindled your heart to this, may cause you to have that wish by satisfying your desire with good things; in order that peace may increase for your kingdom and your

---

[54] Asser, *De rebus gestis Aelfredi*, ed. W. H. Stevenson, with additional material by D. Whitelock, *Asser's Life of King Alfred together with the Annals of St Neot Erroneously Ascribed to Asser* (Oxford, 1959), c. 25, pp. 21–2, and compare with Alfred's adaption of Augustine's description of reflective *otium*, Alfred, *Soliloquies*, ed. T. A. Carnicelli, *King Alfred's Version of St Augustine's Soliloquies* (Cambridge, MA, 1969), 49.

[55] R. Lavelle, 'The Use and Abuse of Hostages in Later Anglo-Saxon England', *EME* 14.3 (2006), 269–96; *idem*, 'Towards a Political Contextualization of Peacemaking and Peace Agreements in Anglo-Saxon England', in D. Wolfthal (ed.), *Peace and Negotiation: Strategies for Coexistence in the Middle Ages and the Renaissance* (Turnhout, 2000), 39–55; R. Abels, 'King Alfred's Peace-Making Strategies with the Vikings', *HSJ* 3 (1992), 23–34; T. Charles-Edwards, 'Alliances, Godfathers, Treaties and Boundaries', in M. Blackburn and D. N. Dumville (eds), *Kings, Currency and Alliances: History and Coinage of Southern England in the Ninth Century* (Woodbridge, 1998), 47–62.

[56] P. J. E. Kershaw, 'The Alfred-Guthrum Treaty. Scripting Accommodation and Interaction in Viking-Age England', in D. M. Hadley and J. D. Richards (eds), *Cultures in Contact: Scandinavian Settlement in England in the Ninth and Tenth Centuries* (Turnhout, 2000), 43–64.

[57] R. Gameson, 'Alfred the Great and the Destruction and Production of Christian Books', *Scriptorium* 49 (1995), 180–210.

[58] J. L. Nelson, '"... *sicut olim gens Francorum ... nunc gens Anglorum*": Fulk's Letter to Alfred Re-visited', in J. Roberts, J. L. Nelson, with M. Godden (eds), *Alfred the Wise. Studies in Honour of Janet Bately on the Occasion of her Sixty-fifth Birthday* (Cambridge, 1997), 135–44, at 141.

[59] Text: D. Whitelock and M. Brett et al. (eds), *Councils and Synods: with Other Documents Relating to the English Church*, (Oxford, 1964), 8–11. Translation (with emendation) from *EHD* I, no. 223, pp. 883–5. On this letter, Nelson, '"... *sicut olim*"', refuting her own earlier view that the letter was a Winchester forgery.

people in your days, and also that the ecclesiastical order—which, as you say, has fallen in many ways into ruins, whether by the frequent invasion and attack of pagans, by the great passage of time or the carelessness of prelates or the ignorance of those subject to them— may be reformed, improved and extended by our diligence and zeal as quickly as possible.

Alfred's 'warlike weapons' have been well studied, as has his vexed sense of the demands of divine support.[60] What might be said of his vision of peace? In the first instance that it was born from a tangible knowledge of its absence, in terms of both his troubled inner life and physical illness and in the wider world in which he found himself. In this respect, as much as in any more considered and selective aspects of his thought, Alfred bears some comparison with Gregory the Great. Alfred's debt to Gregory is clear and well delineated.[61] Gregory was, after all, the only author we know to have warranted two Alfredian translations.[62] The Old English translation of the *Pastoral Care*, Alfred's *Hierdeboc* ('the Shepherd Book'), is the first and the earliest of the sequence of Alfredian translations. In it, Gregory's concerns when faced with the troubled landscape of the late sixth century found new form.[63] The *Hierdeboc*'s prose preface set out Alfred's educational vision, driven by a sense of what had been lost:

> . . . very often it has come to my mind what men of learning there were formerly throughout England, both in sacred and secular orders, and how there were happy times then throughout England; and how the kings who had authority over this people, obeyed God and his messengers; and how they not only maintained their peace, morality and authority at home but also extended their territory outside: and how they succeeded in both war and in wisdom.[64]

---

[60] For his military reorganization and the institution of the burghal system see R. Abels, 'Alfred the Great, the *micel hæðen here* and the Viking Threat', in Reuter (ed.), *Alfred*, 265–79; R. Lavelle, *Fortifications in Wessex, c. 800–1066* (London, 2003). For Alfred's piety S. DeGregorio, 'Texts, *Topoi* and the Self: a Reading of Alfredian Spirituality', *EME* 13.1, (2005), 79–96; B. Raw, 'Alfredian Piety: the Book of Nunnaminster', in J. Roberts, J. L. Nelson, and M. Godden (eds), *Alfred the Wise. Studies in Honour of Janet Bately on the Occasion of her Sixty-fifth Birthday* (Cambridge, 1997), 145–54; P. J. E. Kershaw, 'Power, Prayer and Illness in Asser's *Life of Alfred*', *EME* 10.2 (2001), 201–24.

[61] A. Scharer, 'The Gregorian Tradition in Early England', in R. Gameson (ed.), *St Augustine and the Conversion of England* (Stroud, 1999), 187–201; A. Crépin, 'L'importance de la pensée de Grégoire le Grand dans la politique culturelle d'Alfred, roi de Wessex (871–899)', in J. Fontaine, R. Gillet, and S. Pellistrandi (eds), *Grégoire le Grand* (Paris, 1986), 579–87; J. Campbell, 'Asser's *Life of Alfred*', in C. Holdsworth and T. P. Wiseman (eds), *The Inheritance of Historiography, 350–900* (Exeter, 1986), 115–35. The Gregorian elements in Asser's life, and Asser's own involvement in the translation of the *Pastoral Care*, I touch on in 'Illness', 215–16.

[62] Bately, 'Canon', 114–19; Pratt, *Political Thought*, 134–49.

[63] Pratt, *Political Thought*, 193–213.

[64] Sweet, *Alfred's*, preface, 2. This translation, and all that follow unless otherwise stated, come from Keynes and Lapidge, *Alfred*, here 124.

Bede's account of the later seventh century—Theodore's era—has usually been seen as underlying this vision of a lost golden age.[65] Alfred went on to set out his intention of translating into English 'those books which it is most necessary for all men to know'. He had the scholars, but the precondition for this revival was 'that we have peace' (*gif we ða stilnesse habbað*).[66] Wisdom and learning fostered morality, piety, a right relationship with God and the benefits all brought, not least, happiness, security, and peace.[67] But equally, wisdom depended upon peace for its cultivation. The same sentiment is to be found later in the text. 'Peace', wrote Alfred, is 'the mother of all godly virtues', pointedly selecting *sibb* rather than *lufu* or any more commonly deployed synonym—as the word to translate Gregory's original *caritas*.[68]

The *Hierdeboc* was the first step back towards such a lost age, a return to what in his translation of Psalm II Alfred termed the right path (*rihtum wege*).[69] Its text, famously, follows Gregory's original very closely, a testament less to its unoriginality so much as the degree to which Gregory's thoughts resonated and had perhaps at a fundamental level informed Alfred's particular sense of himself as king.[70] The *Hierdeboc* faithfully replicated Gregory's teachings on the careful calibration of the inner and outer life of the ruler, and the range of approaches needed to oversee harmony within a disparate and often difficult flock. Alfred and his helpers repeated Gregory's dictum that a *rector*'s words should be wise and well chosen. If not, his intended message might be misunderstood, and dissent arise. 'Have salt in you, and have peace among you', counselled Gregory, explaining that 'salt' meant 'wisdom of speech'. The Alfredian text followed closely: '*Habbað ge sealt on eow, ond sibbe habbað betweoh eow*'.[71] The *Hierdeboc*, as in Gregory's own text, contains a deep-seated suspicion of the dangers of immoderate speech and its potential for social disruption. Some of Gregory's advice had particular resonances in Wessex in the late ninth century. For example, did Alfred and his helpers reflect upon his own repeated diplomacy with Danish raiders (and after 878, neighbours) when they recast into the vernacular Gregory's words on the subject of making peace with the wicked— 'when we unthinkingly join in friendship with evil men we join in their guilt'?

[65] Keynes and Lapidge, *Alfred*, p. 294 n. 2.

[66] Sweet, *Alfred's*, preface, 6.

[67] Nelson, 'Wisdom', 36.

[68] *Cur. Past.* III.23, p. 414. Sweet, *Alfred's*, XLVII, 359: '. . . sibb, ðe modor is ealra godra cræfta'. For the semantic range of *cræft* see Guenther Discenza, *King's*, 22, 105–22.

[69] P. P. O'Neill (ed.), *King Alfred's Old English Prose Translation of the First Fifty Psalms* (Cambridge, MA, 2001), 12. For Alfred's authorship see J. M. Bately, 'Lexical Evidence for the Authorship of the Prose Psalms in the Paris Psalter', *ASE* 10 (1982), 69–95.

[70] Bately, Canon, 110 n. 25 citing Whitelock's views that the fidelity of the translation, compared with the treatment of other texts was because: '. . . he was not in disagreement with the views expressed'.

[71] Sweet, *Alfred's*, XV, 92.

Or in his description of the evil king Ahab, whose friendship was almost the undoing of the otherwise spotless Jehoshaphat?[72] Occasionally, translation took the form not 'word for word' (*word be worde*) but 'sense for sense' (*andgit of andgite*).[73] For example, the *Hierdeboc* offered a significant reworking of Gregory's treatment of John XIV.27 (*Mine sibbe ic eow selle, ond minne sibbe ic læte to iow*), a passage which, in the original text was intended to elucidate the distinction between temporal earthly peace and its eternal heavenly form. Not for the last time in the Alfredian translations earthly temporality and heavenly permanence were set out with reference to contemporary land tenure. 'As if', the *Hierdeboc* explained, 'He had said: "I loan you this transitory peace, and I give you the lasting peace."'[74] The same distinction would recur in the OE *Soliloquies*' prefatory images of leased earthly habitation and the permanent place of the saved in Heaven.[75]

Other aspects of the Alfredian conception of peace can be found elsewhere in the translations. The Old English *Consolation* offered a vernacular remoulding of Boethius' Neoplatonic image of the ordered universe: God kept order, binding disparate elements together with unbreakable fetters (*unanbindendlicum racentum*), and preventing them from slipping away.[76] Should he decide to unbind these fetters order would cease: the elements of the cosmos would destroy each other, the universe would come to nothing.[77] On a lesser level the same principle functioned in earthly society, binding through friendship and marriage, bringing together friends and comrades, 'bound by concord and friendship'.[78] 'How blessed mankind would be', Alfred/Boethius went on, 'if their minds were as straight and as firmly established and ordered as the rest of creation is!'[79]

On a cosmic level, and on an earthly one, the OE *Boethius* taught that peace came through strong kingship. The belief that order was predicated upon effective rule led to the OE *Consolation*'s extended justification of the trappings of earthly power as the tools by which social order was kept. There are congruencies to be found between the treatment of government in Alfred's *Consolation* and in Sedulius Scottus' *Liber*. Both works emphasized the idea of art in rulership (*cræft* in its Old English formulation), an idea that incorporated both

---

[72] Sweet, *Alfred's*, XLVI, 353: 'Forðæm, ðonne we us unwærlice geðiedað to yfelra monna freondscipe, ðonne gebinde we us to hiera scyldum.'
[73] Sweet, *Alfred's*, preface, p. 7.
[74] Sweet, *Alfred's*, XLVI, 351: 'Swelce he cwæde: "Ic iow onlæne ða gewitendan, and ic eow geselle ða ðurhwiniendan."'
[75] Carnicelli, *Soliloquies*, 48.
[76] W. J. Sedgefield, (ed.) *King Alfred's Version of Boethius' De Consolatione Philosophiae* (Oxford, 1899), c. 25, pp. 57–8; c. 33, pp. 80–1, on which see A. F. Payne, *King Alfred and Boethius* (London, 1968), 24–5.
[77] Sedgefield, *Boethius*, c. 21, pp. 48–50, at 49.
[78] Sedgefield, *Boethius*, c. 21, p. 50.
[79] Sedgefield, *Boethius*, c. 17, pp. 40–1. R. Thomas, 'The Binding Force of Friendship in King Alfred's *Consolation* and *Soliloquies*', *Ball State University Forum* 29.1 (1988), 5–20.

the abstract ability to govern well alongside the concrete idea of physical creativi-ty.[80] In both cases the art of earthly rule had parallels with God's.[81] As we have seen, Sedulius emphasized the Solomonic aspects of rule and, like Alfred, stressed the importance of wisdom.[82] Both the OE *Boethius* and the *Liber* placed a heavy emphasis upon royal self-rule.[83] And both works developed Boethius' original wheel of Fortune motif.[84] Finally, both the *OE Boethius* and *Liber* shared an understanding of the desire of all things for reconciliation with God, and ultimate peace. Alfred identified peaceful rest and security with God himself: 'There is no created thing which does not wish that it could arrive once more at its source, namely at peaceful rest and security. This rest is with God. Indeed it is God.'[85]

Of all late ninth-century writings the OE *Orosius* has perhaps been the least examined by scholars of Anglo-Saxon ruler representation, despite its rich reinterpretation of the actions and qualities of historical figures.[86] The precise character of the OE *Orosius'* relationship to Alfred's circle is unclear, although it has been generally viewed as a work with close connections to Alfred's court, not least because Alfred is himself a presence in the work as interlocutor to the Norwegian chieftain and trader, Ohthere, whose accounts of his northern travels constitutes one of the two original additions to the core text.[87] It is Ohthere who, much like his contemporary Bernard the Monk whom we encountered at the beginning of this book, provides an insight into the changing topographies of peace and order. He recounted to Alfred his unwillingness, in the course of his exploration to the far north, to sail past a certain river into heavily cultivated territory, for fear of *unfrið*, 'un-peace'—conflict with a people with whom

---

[80] *Cræft* in the OE *Boethius*: c. 14, p. 30; c. 17, pp. 40–1; the transitoriness of what is accomplished by earthly craft exemplified by Wayland the Smith, c. 19, p. 46. Art in the *Liber*: verse preface, lines 1–3, p. 19; c. 3, pp. 27–30. Guenther Discenza, *King's English*, 105–22; P. Clemoes, 'King Alfred's Debt to Vernacular Poetry: the Evidence of *ellen* and *cræft*', in M. Korhammer (ed.), *Words, Texts and Manuscripts: Studies in Anglo-Saxon Culture Presented to Helmut Gneuss on the Occasion of his Sixty-fifth Birthday* (Woodbridge, 1992), 213–38.

[81] *Liber* c. 3, p. 29.

[82] *Liber* verse preface, line 5, p. 19; c. 4, pp. 30–3; c. 13, pp. 58–62.

[83] *Liber* c. 2, pp. 25–7, and the epigrammatic first line of its closing verse, l. 1, p. 27: 'Qui regit affectus animi, rex iure vocatur'. *Boethius*, c. 29, p. 67; c. 31, pp. 70–1.

[84] *Liber* c. 3, pp. 27–8. Sedgefield, *Boethius*, c. 39, pp. 128–9.

[85] Sedgefield, *Boethius*, c. 25, p. 57: 'Nis nan gesceaft gesceapen ðara þe ne wilnige þæt hit þider cuman mæge þonan þe hit ær com, þæt is to ræste and to orsorgnesse. Seo ræst is mid Gode, and þaet is God.' Translation from Keynes and Lapidge, *Alfred*, 133.

[86] On the Old English *Orosius'* relationship to the core Alfredian translations, Bately, 'Canon', 109. D. Whitelock, 'The Prose of Alfred's Reign', in E. G. Stanley (ed.), *Continuations and Beginnings: Studies in Old English Literature* (London, 1966), 67–103.

[87] *Orosius*, I.1, pp. 12–16. For Ohthere's travels, the OE text and the contexts for both, see the papers collected in J. Bately and A. Englert (eds), *Ohthere's Voyages. A late 9th-Century Account of Voyages along the Coasts of Norway and Denmark and its Cultural Context* (Roskilde, 2007).

Ohthere had established no treaty and from whom he could not expect peaceful
interaction.[88]

The classical past down to Rome's sack in 410, rather than the Scandinavian
present, is the main subject of the OE *Orosius*. The translator recast Orosius'
central lesson in vernacular terms, that the *pax Romana* was part of a divine plan
in the synchrony of Christ's birth and Augustus' establishment of universal peace
(*eall moncynn ane sibbe hæfde*). The gates of Janus were closed, their locks rusted
shut (*loca rustega*) as never before.[89] 'In that same year', the text continued, 'He
was born who brought peace to the world, that is our Lord and Saviour Christ'.[90]
The Incarnation signalled a shift in human behaviour.

How blindly many speak of Christianity, that now it is worse than it once was, and
either don't know or choose not to remember what happened before Christianity, when
no people would voluntarily ask for peace from another, except when need made them,
nor when any people might, from another, obtain peace, with either gold or silver, or at
any price, without being subject to them. But since Christ was born, who is the love and
peace of all the earth, not only can men put themselves out of subjection with money,
but nations are also at peace with each other without slavery. How can you think that
men had peace before Christianity, when even their women did such mainfold evils
upon the earth?[91]

The OE *Orosius* made clear that conversion to Christianity changed attitudes
towards peacemaking, as he showed in his account of Claudius' fate, after Peter
had begun preaching in Rome. 'But after the Romans had received Christianity,
they were so gentle and pacific that they all forgave the emperor and all who
were of that family.'[92] Christ's coming also transformed non-Romans. Even
traditionally bellicose Dalmatian tribes became reluctant to attack Rome after the
Incarnation, another sign of a changed world.[93]

Orosius' anonymous translator(s) paid particular attention to the qualities
and abilities of Rome's emperors, adding explanations to subjects that might

---

[88] *Orosius*, I.1, p. 14. Fell, 'Unfrið'.

[89] *Orosius*, V.14, p. 132.

[90] *Orosius*, V.14, p. 132: 'On þæm ilcan gere þe þis eall gewearð—þæt wæs on þæm twæm ond
feowerteoþan wintra Agustuses rices—þa wearð geboren se þe þa sibbe brohte eallre worolde, þæt is
ure Dryhten Hælende Crist.'

[91] *Orosius*, I.10, p. 31: 'Hu blindlice monege þeoda sprecað ymb þone cristendom, þæt hit nu
wyrse sie þonne hit ær wære, þæt hie nellað ge þencean oþþe ne cunnon, hwær hit gewurde ær þæm
cristendome, þæt ænegu þeod æt oþerre mehte frið begietan, oððe id golde, oððe mid seolfre, oððe
mid ænige feo, buton he him underþiedd wære. Ac siþþan Crist geboren wæs, þe ealles
middangeardes is sibb and frið, nales þæt an þæt men hie mehten aliesan mid feo of þeowdome,
ac eac þeoda him betweonum buton þeowdome gesibbsume wæron. Hu wene ge hwelce sibbe þa
weras hæfden ær þæm cristendome, þonne heora wif swa mongfeald yfel donde wæron on þiosan
middangearde?'

[92] *Orosius*, VI.4, pp. 136–7 at 136: 'Ac mid þon þe hie þæs cristendomes onfengon, hie wæron
swa geþwære ond swa gesibsume þæt hie ealle forgeafon þæm casere þa fæhþe þe his mæg hæfde wið
hie ær geworht, ond he forgeaf him eallum þæt unryht ond þæt facn þæt [hie] him don þohte.'

[93] *Orosius*, VI.4, p. 136.

otherwise be opaque to a ninth-century audience.[94] 'All the world', the OE *Orosius* recounted of the *pax Augusta*, chose Augustus' *frið und his sibbe*.[95] At points the original content was considerably embellished. The OE *Orosius'* image of Julius Caesar, in particular, departs significantly from the original text, emphasizing his mercifulness, generosity, and courage in the face of over-whelming odds, and, following his eventual victory over his enemies, his revision of Rome's laws.[96] The parallels with Alfred's own experiences in the 870s and 880s hardly need spelling out.[97] Julius Caesar was not the only figure to be remodelled. Theodosius' peacefulness, too, was given added emphasis.[98] More extensively treated than either, however, was Alaric, who became, in the OE *Orosius*, 'the most Christian and merciful king' ('*se cristena cyning ond se mildesta*'), overseeing a remarkably bloodless sack of Rome—no man slain, no house torched.[99] This transformation has puzzled some. Harris noted, rightly, that his re–creation as a positive figure was bought at the cost of Orosius' internal logic.[100] A Christian, merciful, peace-loving warrior: intriguingly all were qualities with a place in the Alfredian self-image. To some degree no less was Gothic ethnicity itself. According to Asser, Alfred's maternal grandfather, Oslac, was himself 'a Goth by race'.[101]

And what of Asser? As in continental biographies, Asser's *Life of Alfred* contains potent images of rulership. A key passage for Asser's conception of Alfred's kingship is chapter 91 of the *Life*, another inexplicably underexploited source. Asser's image of Alfred is of one wracked by illness, Christ-like in his suffering, whose bodily sufferings paralleled those of his kingdom:

The nails of many tribulations have transfixed King Alfred even though he is invested with royal authority. From his twentieth year until his forty-fifth, which is now in course, he has been plagued continually with the savage attacks of some unknown disease, such that he does not have even a single hour of peace in which does not suffer from the disease or else is gloomily dreading it, and is driven almost to despair.

---

[94] Bately, *Orosius*, pp. xcviii–xcc; *eadem*, 'The Classical Additions in the Old English Orosius', in P. Clemoes and K. Hughes (eds), *England before the Conquest. Studies in Primary Sources Presented to Dorothy Whitelock* (Cambridge, 1971), 237–51. For the possible Cornish identity of the translator, see A. Breeze, 'Cornish *Donua* "Danube" and the Old English Orosius', *N&Q* 39 (1992), 431–3; *idem*, 'Cornwall and the Authorship of the Old English Orosius', *N&Q* 38 (1991), 152–4, and the reply of P. Kitson 'The Dialect Position of the Old English Orosius', *Studia Anglica Posnaniensia* 30 (1996), 3–35.

[95] *Orosius*, VI.4, p. 136.

[96] *Orosius*, V.12, pp. 126–9, noted by Bately, *Orosius*, p. xcix.

[97] The connection between the OE *Orosius* and the *ASC* established by Bately, *Orosius*, pp. lxxxiii–lxxxvi.

[98] *Orosius*, VI.35, p. 153.

[99] *Orosius*, VI.38, p. 156. Compare with the description of Tiberius' mercy, VI.2, p. 134.

[100] S. J. Harris, 'The Alfredian *World History* and Anglo-Saxon Identity', *JEGP* 100 (2001) 482–510, at 503.

[101] Asser, *Rebus*, c. 2, p. 4. On this passage see M. Godden, 'The Anglo-Saxons and the Goths: Rewriting the Sack of Rome', *ASE* 31 (2002), 47–68, at 68.

Moreover, he was continually disturbed, not without reason, by the relentless attacks of foreign peoples, which he continually sustained from land and sea without any moment of peace.[102]

Such christomimetic imagery, frequently under-emphasized by many commentators, aligns Asser's image of Alfredian kingship more closely with Thegan's portrait fo Louis, perhaps, than Einhard's Charlemagne. In a bravura piece of political (and politicized) exegesis Asser framed Alfred's illness as a powerful legitimizing phenomenon, manifesting both his Christ-like suffering, and therefore his exalted position, and his identity as a true ruler, one whose personal passion was ultimately inseparable from the attacks suffered by the polity over which he ruled.[103] Christ's sacrifice on the Cross, undertaken as a way of reconciling man to God, was paralleled by Alfred's responsibility for his subjects and the duties he undertook for their earthly protection.[104] The remainder of the passage addressed these duties, outlining Alfred's achievements as ruler, but more particularly as a maker: the rebuilder of towns and cities, the patron of gold- and silversmiths, and the constructor of royal halls.[105] Alfred, like Solomon, was a builder.[106] Asser's image of rulership realized through craft carries strong echoes of the OE *Boethius'* depiction of the necessary tools of rulership, and its emphasis, both literal and metaphorical, on the place of *cræft* for its execution. Once again we can see a thematic convergence in Asser's *Life* and the *Boethius*. A final parallel remains to be drawn out from this passage. It shares the *Boethius'* vision of peace as the product of strong rule. While the image of God in the *Boethius* was of a strong ruler keeping the cosmos from collapsing into chaos, in his depiction of Alfred Asser presented an earthly ruler maintaining order amidst one type of earthly chaos: that of the embattled society over which Alfred ruled. 'And what of the mighty disorder and confusion of his own people—to say nothing of his own malady—who would undertake of their own accord little or no work for the common needs of the kingdom?'[107]

Alfred's association with peace and wisdom also passed into later culture. The Solomonic aspects of Alfred's kingship became, literally, proverbial. In the twelfth century a series of Middle English alliterative aphorisms were ascribed

---

[102] Assei, *Rebus*, c. 91, pp. 76–9.

[103] On Alfred's bodily illness see D. Pratt, 'The Illnesses of King Alfred the Great', *ASE* 30 (2001), 39–90; A. Scharer, 'König Alfreds Hof und die Geschichtsschreibung: Einige Überlegungen zur Angelsachsenchronik und zu Assers De rebus gestis Ælfredi', in A. Scharer and G. Scheibelreiter (eds), *Historiographie im frühen Mittelalter* (Vienna, 1994), 443–58, esp. 456–8.

[104] On ninth-century attitudes to the Passion, see B. C. Raw, *Anglo-Saxon Crucifixion Iconography* (Cambridge, 1990), 59–60, with references to prayers collected in the *Books* of *Cerne* and *Nunnaminster*, both of which have connections with the late ninth-century West-Saxon court. On the former M. Brown, *The Book of Cerne. Prayer, Patronage and Power in Ninth-Century England* (London, 1996). The relationship of the prayers to the Alfredian translations is explored by Raw, 'Alfredian Piety', 145–54.

[105] Asser, *Rebus*, cc. 91–2, pp. 77–80.

[106] III Kings V.18; VI.14; VII.1, 48; IX.1–10, 17, 24.

[107] Asser, *Rebus*, c. 91, p. 79.

to him, setting out lessons in right rule and good conduct whilst Symeon of Durham, writing in the *Historia Regum*, offered a portrait that continued the tradition of Asser's christomimetic peacemaker, borrowing the words from III Kings X.23, words also present in the Antiphons for Christmas Eve's Vespers, to acclaim the coming of Christ, King of Peace: 'Alfred, *rex pacificus*, was glorified above all the kings of the earth'.[108]

---

[108] *The Proverbs of Alfred: An Emended Text*, ed. O. Arngart (Lund, 1978). Symeon of Durham, *Historia Regum*, ed. T. Arnold, *Rolls Series* 75–6 (London, 1882–5), II, *s.a.* 885, p. 88. For the use of III Kings X.23 as part of the Advent Office see R. Boeing, *Anglo-Saxon Spirituality: Selected Writings* (Mahwah, NJ, 2001), 308–12, with references.

Conclusion

As we saw in the opening sections of this book, the relationship between peace and rulership already had a long and tangled history by the late fifth century. Its history after the year 900 would be no less complex. Peacemaking as a part of rulership continued to engage theorists, propagandists, and polemicists until the waning of monarchy as the dominant form of European government. In the same years when Shakespeare's characters were offering the divergent opinions that preface this book, James VI and I was styling himself *rex pacificus*, seeking to elicit parallels with Solomon, and receiving panegyrics that called him 'a new Augustus' and a 'King of Peace and Plentie'.[1] Any study that sought to chart the theme of this book through the intervening centuries would follow a path into Ottonian Germany, and particularly the political language of Otto III's brief *renovatio*, Capetian France and the Anglo-Norman world, and thread through the polemical thickets of the Investiture Controversy, where texts like the *Liber de unitate ecclesiae conservanda*, the late eleventh-century tract compiled in support of Henry IV, offered visions of the king as peacemaker and peacekeeper that drew extensively upon earlier sources.[2] It would further demand engagement with tracts such as Marsilius of Padua's *Defensor pacis*, the early fourteenth-century work that opened by quoting Cassiodorus' views on peace and tranquillity from the *Variae*, and the *Quaestio de potestate papae* (*rex pacificus*), as well as with an ever-multiplying body of letters, treaties, sermons, and historical works, in addition to addressing, as I have here, those moments when later rulers would place notions of peace at the centre of their own ideological programmes.[3]

---

[1] M. Smuts, 'The Making of *Rex Pacificus*: James VI and I and the Concept of Peace in an Age of Religious War', in D. Fischlin and M. Fortier (eds), *Royal Subjects: Essays on the Writings of James VI and I* (Detroit, MI 2002), 371–88.

[2] E.g. *Liber de unitate ecclesiae conservanda*, ed. W. Schwenkenbecher, *LdL*, II, 173–284, I.3, pp. 186–8; II.10, pp. 221–2; II.36, pp. 263–4. Commentary: I. S. Robinson, *Authority and Resistance in the Investiture Contest: The Polemical Literature of the Late Eleventh Century* (Manchester, 1978), 89–113.

[3] Marsilius of Padua, *The Defender of the Peace*, ed. and trans. A. Brett (Cambridge, 2005), citing Cassiodorus on tranquillity at I.1, p. 3. For Marsilius' thought see G. Garnett, *Marsilius of Padua and 'the Truth of History'* (Oxford, 2006), for *rex pacificus* see R. W. Dyson, *Quaestio de Potestate Papae (Rex Pacificus): An Enquiry into the Power of the Pope. A Critical Edition and Translation* (Lampeter, 1999).

Whilst it is a task I happily leave to those qualified to undertake it, in closing it is worth considering briefly the longer legacy of the developments we have seen in previous chapters, not least because it serves to situate these developments within a broader sweep of medieval history, and as a reminder that the peaceful kings, the *reges pacifici* of the early Middle Ages, lived on in the political imaginations of later cultures.

In 888, after the death of Charles the Fat, Rudolf was elected and crowned king at St-Maurice, Agaune, the monastic foundation that, some four centuries earlier, had played its part in a distinctive Burgundian culture of royal peace and prayer. This briefly resurgent Burgundian kingdom survived until 1032, when Rudolf III's death without heirs allowed the Salian Conrad II to make it the third kingdom over which he ruled. From 925 to 993, however, Burgundy lay under the rule of Conrad the Pacific. 'Few European rulers of any period', Tim Reuter observed, 'can have left as little trace in the record after reigning for nearly sixty years . . .'.[4] The origin of his byname is unknown.[5] It may well be contemporary, for evidence certainly survives that shows post-Carolingian rulers in Burgundy styling themselves with variations on *rex pacificus* as, for example, in the titles of Rudolf I's confirmation of a grant to Cluny of September 927 (*gratia Dei pacificus, augustus et invictus rex*).[6] The echoes of 800's coronation carried far. Rudolfine Burgundy existed, as Gibichung Burgundy had, in the lengthening shadow of neighbouring power. In the case of the Rudolfines that power was Otto I's, and there, in a political world of repressed violence and high political tension we also find peaceful rulership celebrated. In the 960s Hrotsvitha of Gandersheim commemorated the dynasty's successes in establishing on earth a peace reflecting that of Heaven:

To him the *Rex Pacificus*, Christ, had given from Heaven civil peace during the time of his life; and he also held the heights of kingship with a happy omen, unless I am mistaken, ten years of passing time plus twice three, very happily spent.[7]

Under Conrad II and his son Henry III, Burgundy would continue to be ruled by kings conscious of both the Carolingian political inheritance and the importance of peace as a key element of it. Wipo, member of the Salian royal chapel, would write the biography of the father and tutor the son.[8] In the late 1020s,

---

[4] T. Reuter, 'Introduction', *NCMH*, III, 3.

[5] R. Poupardin, *Le royaume de Bourgogne (888–1038). Étude sur les origines du royaume d'Arles* (Paris, 1907), p. 67 n. 3.

[6] *Recueil des Chartes de l'Abbaye de Cluny*, ed. A. Bruel (Paris, 1876), I, no. 285 (927), p. 281. See also Rudolf III's grant of rights to the canonry of St-Anatole, Salins-les-Bains, as 'rex pacificus ac clementissimus', *Die Urkunden der burgundischen Rudolfinger*, eds T. Schieffer and H.E. Mayer, *MGH Regum Burgundiae e Stirpe Rudolfina Diplomata et Acta* (Munich, 1977), no. 122 (1029), 294–5.

[7] Hrotsvitha of Gandersheim, *Gesta Ottonis*, ed. P. Winterfeld, *MGH SRG* 34 (Hanover, 1902), p. 205, lines 17–21: 'Huic rex pacificus dederat de sidere Christus / Eius civilem vitae per tempora pacem; / Omine felici tenuit quoque culmina regni, / Ni fallor, denos labentis temporis annos / Necnon bis ternos multum feliciter actos.'

[8] For Wipo's writings and career see S. Bagge, *Kings, Politics, and the Right Order of the World in German Historiography c. 950–1150* (Leiden, 2002), 189–230, with substantial references to earlier

when Henry was an adolescent, Wipo had offered him a collection of *proverbia* bearing a greeting which would prove to be a programmatic statement for author and recipient alike: 'Peace to Henry, friend of God!'[9] The *proverbia* that followed pared the ideal of educated, humble, and peaceful rulership to its barest: digestible maxims for one starting out on the path to rulership.

On Christmas Day 1041, Wipo presented Henry III with his *Tetralogus*, a fusion of panegyric and political admonition in which he adopted four personae ('Wipo', the Muses, Law, and Grace) lauding Henry as 'the peace of the world' (*pax orbis*), resonant terms on a date so heavy with historical and christological associations.[10]

> If we ask for peace, you, king, will provide it!
> If we want war, you, king, will start it![11]

With a humble mind and love of piety, Wipo confidently predicted, Henry would spread peace throughout the world.[12] By ensuring this, Wipo noted, offering the young Salian the same incentives of honour and reputation Gregory the Great had held out some four hundred years before to the Visigoth Reccared, Henry would win enduring fame and be remembered as the friend of peace (*amicus pacis*).[13] Appropriately he also took the opportunity to remind him that he was, through Gisela, his mother, a descendant of Charlemagne.[14] When the time arrived and the boy came to power there would be days of endless peace.[15] Wipo's closing peroration drove the point home:

> Now, let the peace and mercy of Christ be given to you as King.
> May you, prince of the world, be strong in the responsibility of Christ.
> May you, lord of the kingdom, live in everlasting peace!
> So wishes your servant Wipo, with a faithful heart.[16]

What we can see of Henry's activities as a ruler strongly suggest that he sought to apply at least some of Wipo's lessons. In addition to dealing effectively with neighbouring peoples, including the Hungarians and the Bohemians, in war

---

studies and for Conrad's reign, H. Wolfram, *Conrad II, 990–1039. Emperor of Three Kingdoms*, trans. D. A. Kaiser (Philadelphia, 2006).

[9] *Proverbia*, ed. H. Bresslau, *MGH SRG* 61 (Hanover, 1915), 66–74, at 66.

[10] *Tetralogus*, ed. H. Bresslau, *MGH SRG* 61 (Hanover, 1915), 75–86, at p. 78, line 96: 'Salve, pax orbis, mundi fortissima turris . . .'.

[11] *Tetralogus*, p. 78, lines 79–80: 'Si petimus pacem, tu, rex, praestaveris illam, / Si cupimus bellum, tu, rex, commiseris illud . . .'.

[12] *Tetralogus*, p. 79, line 132: 'Mens humilis, pietatis amor, pax missa per orbem.'

[13] *Tetralogus*, p. 77, lines 70–1: 'Tertius Heinricus fuit olim pacis amicus. / Fama sui meriti superabit tempora mundi.'

[14] *Tetralogus*, p. 80, lines 157–60.

[15] *Tetralogus*, p. 80, line 174: 'Cum dominis rerum sit pax sine fine dierum!'

[16] *Tetralogus*, p. 86, lines 323–6: 'Nunc tibi sit regi pax et clementia Christi; / Tu, princeps orbis, sis Christi munere fortis, / Tu, dominus regni, vivas in pace perenni! / Sic vult Wipo tuus cum fido pectore servus.'

and by treaty, Henry pursued a particular vision of peace at home. At the synod of Constance in 1043 he even preached to the assembled magnates, in what one contemporary annalist recorded as 'a brilliant sermon', admonishing them to be peaceful.[17] It was an injunction he would repeat on several subsequent occasions, exhorting his subjects to keep the peace, and to forsake animosity with their enemies.[18] Such seemingly intense attempts to realize peace on earth, with their apparent overtones of the German emperor as preacher and prince of peace sat ill with some contemporaries. The Augustinian sensibilities of the abbot of Gorze, Siegfried, were offended by Henry's presumptuous notion that an earthly king might establish any kind of 'true peace' in a fallen world.[19]

In the early eighth century Bede had offered an image of Edwin's peace as proverbial, a state of such novelty that it passed into collective memory and slipped into myth. In his *Gesta* of Conrad II, dedicated to 'King Henry III, the Pious, the Peaceful', Wipo also presented Conrad's peace as a thing of wonder to his subjects.[20] They believed, he claimed, that, 'every day was more outstanding than the day before for the fastness of peace, more dear for the grace of benevolence, more honoured for regal judgement.'[21] Similarly, Conrad's decision to grant Burgundy to Henry in 1038 had elicited a response little short of ecstasy from the Burgundians: 'The people were shouting and saying that peace would beget peace if the king reigned with Caesar.'[22] Wipo constantly stressed the dependency of peace upon the proper administration of law: old themes indeed, and old themes for Wipo personally. His first words of advice to the young Henry in the *Proverbia* had set the agenda: 'It is fitting for a king to learn the law'.[23] Conrad's travels through Frisia and Franconia in 1038 were marked by him confirming peace and making law.[24] Conrad's successful ordering of his empire had led him to be able to

[17] *Annales Sangallenses maiores*, ed. G. Pertz, *MGH SS* 1 (Hanover, 1826), *s.a.* 1043, p. 85: 'In quarto autem die . . . ipse gradum cum pontifice facundus orator ascendit, et luculento sermone populum ad pacem cohortari coepit . . .'.
[18] T. Reuter, 'Contextualizing Canossa: Excommunication, Penance, Surrender, Reconciliation', in J. L. Nelson (ed.), *Medieval Polities and Modern Mentalities* (Cambridge, 2006), 147–66, at 159–60; Hamilton, *Penance*, 177–80.
[19] W. von Giesebrecht, *Geschichte der deutschen Kaiserzeit*, 5th edition (Leipzig, 1885), II, 714–18.
[20] *Gesta Chuon.*, c. 1, p. 12: 'Ad extremum rex Heinricus tertius, pius, pacificus, linea iustitiae, bello et pace eandem Burgundiam temperavit cum magnificentia; ubi quae divina providentia tam pacis quam belli consiliis, conciliis et conventibus, quibus interdum ipse interfui, peregit, alias commemorabo.' Translation here and below drawn from T. E. Mommsen, K. F. Morrison, trans., *Imperial Lives and Letters of the Eleventh Century* (New York, 1962), 52.
[21] *Gesta Chuon.*, c. 6, pp. 27–9: 'Fama eius vires de virtutibus sumpsit; hodie quam heri pro tenore pacis praestantior, pro benevolentiae gratia carior, pro regali censura honoratior habitus est ab omnibus.'
[22] *Gesta Chuon.*, c. 38, p. 58: 'Quem episcopi cum caeteris principibus in ecclesiam sancti Stephani, quae pro capella regis Solodoro habetur, deducentes hymnis et canticis divinis Deum laudabant populo clamante et dicente, quod pax pacem generaret, si rex cum caesare regnaret.'
[23] *Proverbia*, p. 66, line 1: 'Decet regem discere legem'.
[24] *Gesta Chuon.*, c. 38, p. 58: 'Pacem firmando, legem faciendo revisit'.

'reap the rich fruits of peace' (Eccles. I.22).[25] Wipo's Conrad—again like Bede's
Edwin some three centuries earlier—kept the peace of his kingdom through
constant movement: 'by this progress', Wipo wrote, 'he bound the realms very
firmly in a bond of peace and in royal guardianship.'[26] Above all, Wipo's portrait of
Conrad delineates a king in control, cementing peace, and upholding right order. It
is also a portrait in which the image of Conrad, father to the young Henry, was
repeatedly framed by reference to his earlier ancestor, Charlemagne. Wipo blended
notions of succession and stability with an image of inherited instruments of war
that carried memories of their earlier owners—a notion perhaps familiar to any
member of the eleventh-century martial elite: 'Conrad's saddle', he wrote, 'has
Charlemagne's stirrups' (*Sella Chuonradi habet ascensoria Caroli*).[27] For Wipo, as
for others, Charlemagne ruled over an age of peace and harmony that presaged
Conrad's own.[28] Wipo's connection of Charlemagne and Conrad II, it might be
said, verged on a form of secular, imperial typology, Carolingian and Salian linked
across time. The *Gesta* might also be read as an invitation to Henry to engage in a
double imitation: firstly, of his father and secondly, of his father's own model (and his
ancestor), Charlemagne. In this, and like other texts we have encountered in past
pages, Wipo's *Gesta* was history in the service of royal exemplarity: looking back to
past peace and, by expounding the circumstances by which peace and concord
had been brought about, seeking to stress to a ruler in the present the importance
of ensuring it in his own day.[29]

The *Gesta*'s final, fortieth chapter, the only one written entirely in verse,
encapsulated Wipo's elegiac view of the empire under Conrad.[30] He was the
replenisher of peace in Franconia, he wrote, the upholder of law, dissent's suppresser:

> The emperor never delayed. He brought peace everywhere.
> He carried war to the pagans lest they harm Christians.[31]

This intense emphasis upon peace at Henry III's court, manifest in Wipo's
writings and Henry's own political activities, has puzzled some. 'It is difficult',
Stefan Weinfurter has written, 'to pinpoint the propelling forces behind this
ideology of peace', before offering as its possible origins both the influence of the

[25] *Gesta Chuon.*, c. 38, p. 57.
[26] *Gesta Chuon.*, c. 6, p. 29.
[27] *Gesta Chuon.*, c. 6, p. 28.
[28] K. Schnith, 'Recht und Friede. Zum Königsgedanken im Umkreis Heinrichs III', *HJ*, 81 (1962), 22–57, at 44.
[29] Schnith, 'Recht und Friede', 24–6.
[30] *Gesta Chuon.*, c. 40, pp. 60–2. The numerical significance of the work's forty chapters cannot be wholly discounted. Forty years was the number of years repeatedly referred to as the length of reigns of peace in the Old Testament: see Judg. III.11, V.11, VIII.28.
[31] *Gesta Chuon.*, c. 40, p. 62, line 43: 'Nil moratus imperator, pacis ubicumque dator, / Bellum, intulit paganis, ne nocerent christianis'. On the peace Conrad II established see also *Gesta Chuon.*, c. 2, pp. 13–14. For another elegiac view of a peaceful past, this time that of Henry III viewed from Henry IV's reign, c. 1106/7, see the *Vita Heinrici IV Imperatoris*, ed. W. Eberhard, *MGH SRG* 58 (Hanover, 1899), c. 2, p. 40.

'Peace of God' movement and the broader notion of Salian kingship as an act of sustained *imitatio Christi*, together with the continued need for a Salian king to be, in his own time, a tangible peacekeeper maintaining social order and defending the homeland.[32] Other scholars have also noticed that in the early decades of the eleventh century peace was a central theme. Richard Landes, writing of the peace councils and the 1024 meeting between Robert the Pious and Henry II noted that in these years 'peace ideology became the transcendent idiom', explaining that phenomenon, if I understand him correctly, again, chiefly through the deep impact of the 'Peace of God' movement upon the political language of the early eleventh century.[33]

The Salian interest in peace was certainly not an isolated incident in the early eleventh century. In West Francia, for example, Wipo's contemporary Fulbert of Chartres, writing to Robert the Pious in late 1024, explained that he was delighted that Robert intended to meet his leading nobles to address the kingdom's peace. That it was to take place in Orléans, a city under interdict, he added, filled him with remorse, for the bishops at his assembly would be unable to celebrate Mass.[34] For his part Fulbert had no doubt about the needs of the common man. 'Of all that common men regard as life's greatest blessings', he explained, 'they normally prize peace and plenty'.[35]

As we have seen repeatedly, this idiom of peace was far from novel. Henry III, at least, and Wipo also, might both have explained its deployment in terms of received notions of the obligations of rulership: Charlemagne made peace, Conrad had too. It fell to Henry to continue that tradition, striving through good government to follow their examples. Peace had been a component of post-Roman political language long before the 1020s, in the same way that churchmen had, long before the first peace meeting at Le Puy in 975, taken responsibility for peace and, implicitly, the protection of the innocent. That, after all, had been precisely the intentions of Adomnán at Birr in 697, when he gathered the great and the good to agree to limit violence and won Bede's remembrance as a 'champion of peace and unity'.[36] The primary difference between the emphasis upon peace in some parts of the medieval West in the early years of the eleventh century and what had gone before was that magnates began to claim responsibility for the peace themselves. In the centuries from Romulus Augustulus' deposition to the final decades of the Carolingian world, peace had been the province of kings and emperors. This was a phenomenon

[32] S. Weinfurter, *The Salian Century: Main Currents in an Age of Transition*, trans. B. M. Bowlus (Philadelphia, 1999), 101.

[33] R. Landes, 'Introduction', *Peace*, 6.

[34] Fulbert of Chartres, *The Letters and Poems of Fulbert of Chartres*, ed. and trans. F. Behrends (Oxford, 1976), 171.

[35] Fulbert of Chartres, *Letters and Poems*, 265.

[36] A point first made, to my knowledge, by A. Smyth, *Warlords and Holy Men: Scotland AD 80–1000* (Edinburgh, 1984), 131–2.

that they, and those around them, recognized. From Gibichung Burgundy to Lombard Italy and Merovingian Francia, kings showed considerable concern with issuing edicts, minting coins with peace-based legends and being made the subject of panegyric verse that stressed peaceful qualities in both their own personalities and their reigns. On occasion, as in the case of the Burgundian king Gundobad, Alfred, Charlemagne, and Charles the Bald, it is even possible to see rulers with an immediate personal interest in the theme.

Henry and Wipo teach an important lesson about the legacy of peace in the early medieval political imagination. Where royal power remained strong or even grew in the decades after 900, so too did the presence of the figure of the peaceful king. Charlemagne and, to a lesser degree, other peaceful kings were remembered, not simply as the focus for scholarly remembrance, but also as exemplars for would-be peacemaking kings in an ever-renewing present. When and where royal authority failed, as it did in parts of central and southern France in the decades around the turn of the millennium, in places where kings could no longer keep the peace or, perhaps more importantly, make a convincing claim that they could, we see the development of a movement in which others took on the position themselves. Some were bishops but others were local figures of secular authority— lords and castellans—who no longer worked as agents for peace, but seemed now to wish to be seen as the originators of that peace. And where peacemaking kings were in short supply and peacemaking bishops and lords appeared, so, often, did the crowd who could demand peace from God directly, as in Ralph Glaber's famous account of the crowds chanting 'Pax! Pax! Pax!' and raising their hands heavenwards, a demand offered up, not a bequest to be passed down.[37] In the early Middle Ages, covenants with God were matters for kings. Indeed, the centuries I have looked at here comprise an age of kings, and of politics conceived of almost exclusively in terms of kingship. The eleventh century, with the peace councils in its early decades, the steady growth of the reform movement, and the intense polemics of Investiture at its close, is also a crowded one: the world of the *populus*.

In places where kingship was strong and in places where it was weak we see the idiom of peace employed. It is hard in either case not to see its prevalence linked to its presence in the political imagination and its fundamental place in the political discourse of earlier centuries. In one sense this study has sought to examine the deep background to the 'propelling forces' that shaped conceptions of medieval kingship, underscoring the degree to which ideas of peace informed notions of rulership from the earliest days of post-Roman rule.

[37] Landes, 'Introduction', *Peace*, 17–18; K. G. Cushing, *Reform and the Papacy in the Eleventh Century: Spirituality and Social Change* (Manchester, 2005), 40–52; R. I. Moore, 'Family, Community and Cult on the Eve of the Gregorian Reform', *TRHS* 5th series 30 (1980), 49–69; L. MacKinney, 'The People and Public Opinion in the Eleventh-Century Peace Movement', *Speculum* 5.2 (1930), 182–206.

These fleeting glimpses of the world of the tenth and eleventh centuries can only hint at the complexities of the periods beyond my end point. As we have also seen, the need for a ruler to ensure peace and the legitimacy that accrued from effective peacekeeping were hardly ideas peculiar to the early medieval West, and we have briefly seen comparable concerns expressed both in the Islamic and Byzantine worlds, and also in places newly emergent in early medieval Christian culture: the fledgling Viking kingdom of East Anglia and Boris' Bulgaria. By understanding how it found expression, and how that expression was elaborated in early medieval Europe in the period between the sixth and the eleventh centuries we might come to understand a little better what was distinctive about the political cultures of the post-Roman West. In voices as disparate as Avitus, Sedulius, Alfred, and Nicholas I, and in rare surviving treaties, epic poems, prayers, and on coins we find our answers.

What conclusions can be drawn as we reach our end? The first, and the most important—if at first sight perhaps the most banal: the sheer pervasiveness of the theme of peaceful rulership across the early medieval period. There is no a priori reason why this particular notion ought to have been articulated by so many post-Roman regimes. And yet we see it turned to repeatedly. The basic explanation for this phenomenon lies in the constant necessity for kings to have their authority recognized and their regimes acknowledged on some level as legitimate. The limits of coercion meant that early barbarian rulers needed to present themselves as upholders of Roman peace. In a sense this was the culmination of a long tradition: barbarian leaders had been doing just that as federates and auxiliaries in Rome's armies since the early Principate. In the sixth century we see this in the image of authority propounded by Cassiodorus on behalf of Theoderic, and in the various ways through which Frankish, Gothic, and Burgundian rulers associated themselves with the languages and methods of late Roman peacekeeping, whether through the maintenance of local policing systems—the Merovingians' *centenarii*—through the deployment of a political rhetoric that invoked notions of civic order (such as Ostrogothic *civilitas*), or by the occasional coin issues that offer us the most condensed and accessible insights to new rulers' claims on old civic qualities. This process was not a one-sided affair, for members of the old provincial aristocracy were also involved in the process: Cassiodorus, perhaps most obviously, but also the Gallo-Roman legists in sixth-century Gaul who were responsible for drafting these new codes and translating their kings' authority into parsable late Roman terms. Other readings of these political circumstances were possible: Salvian and Victor of Vita, for whom Roman peace and that of the Catholic Church went together, both lamented the loss of peace even as a new generation of rulers began to affirm its continued vitality under their tutelage. In Visigothic Spain similar concerns to engage with late Roman urban elites led not only to the application of law-codes as a means for asserting authority, but also to the exploitation of a strong conciliar tradition. The responsibility of royal power to defend and protect the Church—part of the conciliar 'contract' between Church and ruler since Constantine and reaffirmed by a succession of popes (including Gregory the Great in his letters to Maurice)— created a theatre in which royal peacekeeping, with its attendant claims to legitimacy, could be asserted by Toledan rulers. Visigothic Spain is where we also see the development of new liturgical aspects of rulership, and where, as a part of this process, we see royal anointing develop by the 670s. Whilst a clear connection is far from apparent, it is striking that this same period saw, in Eugenius II, a poet for whom peace was a particularly important commodity.

By the later Merovingian period a Roman political lexicon was rivalled by one drawn from scripture. In this respect when peace was evoked it was less that of the late Roman state, with its own legacies of Augustan authority, and more that of Israel: the *Liber historiae Francorum*'s image of Dagobert was peaceful like Solomon, not Augustus. Under Charlemagne we see not only the development of an intensified legislative process but an increasing willingness on the part of poets and scholars to frame him in biblical terms. David is the dominant model, but Solomon is far from absent, not least in Alcuin's writings. The image of Charlemagne as peacemaker is apparent in Frankish *laudes* from the 790s and we have seen it articulated in the acclamation of Christmas Day 800. I have argued that whilst the term itself draws upon Italian diplomatic practice and Byzantine precedent, its application reflects both longer-term Frankish notions of rulership and some specific circumstances, Charles' imperial achievements by conquest and his more immediate restoration of order to factionalized Rome. That the title of *pacificus* mattered to him was apparent by its use in titulature and in his concern to maintain peace within those territories even after his death through the systems enshrined in the *divisio* of 806. This developed emphasis upon peacemaking as a quality of the Carolingians is apparent in the *Annales Mettenses priores*. By the accession of Louis the Pious in 814, notions of the emperor as a force of peace and the Carolingian ruler as a Solomonic figure were all in place. The heavy emphasis that had been placed upon Charlemagne as David naturally led, typologically, to ideas of his son as Solomon, an idea in any case already sanctioned by its use in praise of Charlemagne at various earlier moments. The lack of sustained military campaigning gave his reign additional claim on the idea of its ruler as a man of peace, not war. So, too, did the increased emphasis upon humility and qualities that have sometime been labelled as 'monastic', but which might better be seen as the development of an increasingly christomimetic model of rulership. The intensification of the christomimetic aspects of rulership brought with it the associations explored in the first chapter of this book, of Christ as a peacemaker, whilst reinforcing the power of Solomonic associations retroactively, Solomon as a type of Christ. This, however, was only one trajectory in Louis' reign. Increasing discontent over his rule, crystallizing around resentment over his redivison of his territories following the birth of Charles the Bald, led to both rebellion and written polemics that seized upon the language of rulership articulated under Charlemagne to offer fierce criticism of Louis' rule.

Louis' death in 840 was followed by open war between his three surviving sons. Inherited notions of peace, and the expectations of correct rulership based upon the image propounded by Charlemagne and his supporters, shaped the ways in which intra-familial polemics were couched in the period 840–3, both by the brothers and their partisans.

In the later ninth century we see the image of Solomonic rulership propounded with renewed vigour at the court of Charles the Bald, and explored in the works of Sedulius Scottus for whom it is a dominant theme of poetry and prose. The later ninth century gives us other visions of peaceful rulership: that of Alfred the Great, whose own life was dictated by the demands of war and peace, and Pope Nicholas I, whose lessons on rulership complement those emerging from the court circles north of the Alps. By the close of the ninth century the development of king-making *ordines*, with prayers for peaceful rule and expectations of rulers imitating Solomon, together with a substantial corpus of historical, political, and literary works would ensure that later generations like those of Conrad II, Henry III, and the scholars that surrounded them, would inherit a strong sense of the importance and associations of the *rex pacificus*.

When men and women thought and wrote about power in the early Middle Ages—what it was, what it should be, what it had been—peace was never far from their thoughts. It informed the words they wrote, and also how they thought those words would be read. In that spirit, I will add a final voice to the colloquy, that of Theodulf of Orléans:[38]

> *Finis adest operi: his, quibus est peragentibus actum,*
> *Sit pax, vita, salus et tibi, lector, ave!*

---

[38] *MGH Poetae*, I *carm.* 41.4, p. 540: 'The end of the work is here. To those by whose effort it has been completed, and to you, reader, let there be peace, life and salvation. Farewell!'

Select Bibliography

Limits of space make a comprehensive bibliography of all secondary scholarship cited in the previous chapters impossible. Full references to these works are, however, given in the relevant footnotes. The works listed below consequently comprise a core bibliography of studies selected either on grounds of their frequent citation, centrality to the key themes of the book, or particular importance to the arguments presented above.

Abels, R., 'King Alfred's Peace-Making Strategies with the Vikings', *Haskins Society Journal* 3 (1992), 23–34.
—— 'Paying the Danegeld: Anglo-Saxon Peacemaking with Vikings', in Philip de Souza and John France (eds), *War and Peace in Ancient and Medieval History* (Cambridge, 2008), 173–92.
Althoff, G., 'Der frieden-, bündnis- und gemeinschaftsstiftende Charakter des Mahles im früheren Mittelalter', in I. Bitsch, T. Ehlert, and X. von Ertzdorff (eds), *Essen und Trinken in Mittelalter und Neuzeit* (Sigmaringen, 1987).
—— *Verwandte, Freunde und Getreue. Zum politischen Stellenwert der Gruppenbindungen im früheren Mittelalter* (Darmstadt, 1990).
—— *Spielregeln der Politik im Mittelalter: Kommunikation in Frieden und Fehde* (Darmstadt, 1997).
—— 'Zur Bedeutung symbolischer Kommunikation für das Verständnis des Mittelalters', *FmSt* 31 (1997), 370–89.
—— *Family, Friends and Followers. Political and Social Bonds in Early Medieval Europe*, trans. C. Carroll (Cambridge, 2004).
Anton, H. H., *Fürstenspiegel und Herrscherethos in der Karolingerzeit*, Bonner Historische Forschungen, 32 (Bonn, 1968).
—— 'Zum politischen Konzept karolingischer Synoden und zur karolingischen Brüdergemeinschaft', *HJ* 99 (1979), 55–132.
—— 'Pseudo-Cyprian: *De duodecim abusivis saeculi* und sein Einfluss auf den Kontinent, insbesondere auf die karolingischen Fürstenspiegel', in H. Löwe (ed.), *Die Iren und Europa im früheren Mittelalter* (Stuttgart, 1982), II, 568–617.
Baldus, C., '*Vestigia pacis*. The Roman Peace Treaty: Structure or Event?', in R. Lesaffer (ed.), *Peace Treaties and International Law in European History* (Cambridge, 2004), 103–46.
Barnes, T. D., 'Lactantius and Constantine', *JRS* 63 (1973), 29–46.
—— *Constantine and Eusebius* (Cambridge, MA, 1984).
—— *Athanasius and Constantius: Theology and Politics in the Constantinian Empire* (Cambridge, 1993).
—— 'Emperors, Panegyrics, Prefects, Provinces and Palaces (284–317)', *Journal of Roman Archaeology* 9 (1996), 532–45.
Barnish, S. J., 'The *Anonymous Valesianus* II as a Source for the Last Years of Theodoric', *Latomus* 42 (1983), 572–96.
Barros-Dios, I., 'Pax, Lux, Lex, Rex', in D. Buschinger and W. Spiewok (eds), *Die Ritterorden im Mittelalter – Les Ordres Militaires au Moyen Âge* (Greifswald, 1996), 31–45.

Becher, M., *Eid und Herrschaft: Untersuchungen zum Herrschaftsethos Karls Des Grossen* (Sigmaringen, 1993).

—— 'Karl der Große und Papst Leo III', in C. Stiegemann and M. Wemhoff (eds), *799, Kunst und Kultur der Karolingerzeit: Karl der Grosse und Papst Leo III. in Paderborn 799* (Mainz, 1999), I, 22–36.

—— 'Die Kaiserkrönung im Jahre 800. Eine Streitfrage zwischen Karl dem Großen und Papst Leo III', *Rheinische Vierteljahrsblätter* 66 (2002), 1–38.

—— and Jarnut, J., *Der Dynastiewechsel von 751: Vorgeschichte, Legitimationsstrategien und Erinnerung* (Düsseldorf, 2003).

Beer, J., 'The Strasbourg Oaths', in *Early Prose in France: Contexts of Bilingualism and Authority* (Kalamazoo, MI, 1992), 15–29.

Benko, S., 'Virgil's Fourth Ecologue in Christian Interpretation', *Aufstieg und Niedergang der römischen Welt* 31.1 (1980), 646–705.

Berlinger, L., *Beiträge zur inoffiziellen Titulatur der römischen Kaiser. Eine Untersuchungen ihres ideengeschichtlichen Gehaltes und ihrer Entwicklung* (Breslau, 1935).

Bernhardt, J., 'Concepts and Practice of Empire in Ottonian Germany (950–1024)', in B. Weiler and S. MacClean (eds), *Representations of Power in Medieval Germany, 800–1500* (Turnhout, 2006), 141–63.

Bertoldi, M. E., 'L'area archaeologica di San Lorenzo in Lucina a Roma', *Bolletino di Archaeologia* 13–15 (1992), 127–34.

—— *S. Lorenzo in Lucina, Chiese Di Roma Illustrate 28* (Rome, 1994).

Beskow, P., *Rex Gloriae: The Kingship of Christ in the Early Church*, trans. E. J. Sharpe (Stockholm, 1962).

Beumann, H., '*Unitas ecclesiae-unitas imperii-unitas regni*. Von der imperialen Reichseinheitsidee zur Einheit der regna', *Settimane* 27 (Spoleto, 1981), 531–71.

Bietenhard, H. and Stamm, J. J., *Der Weltfriede im Alten und Neuen Testament* (Zurich, 1959).

Binding, K., *Das burgundisch-romanische Königreich (von 443–532 n.Chr.): eine reichs- und rechtsgeschichtliche Untersuchung* (Leipzig, 1868).

Bonnaud-Delamare, R., *L'idée de paix à l'époque carolingienne* (Paris, 1939).

Boshof, E., *Erzbischof Agobard von Lyon. Leben und Werk*, Köln Historische Abhandlungen 17 (Cologne, 1969).

—— 'Einheitsidee und Teilungsprinzip in der Regierungszeit Ludwigs der Frommen', in P. Godman and R. Collins, (eds), *Charlemagne's Heir: New Perspectives on the Reign of Louis the Pious (814–840)* (Oxford, 1990), 161–89.

Bovendeert, J., 'Royal or Monastic Identity? Smaragdus' *Via regia* and *Diadema monachorum* Reconsidered', in R. Corradini, R. Meens, C. Pössel, and P. Shaw (eds), *Texts and Identities in the Early Middle Ages* Forschungen zur Geschichte des Mittelalters, 12 (Vienna, 2006), 239–51.

Brandes, J., '*Tempora periculosa sunt*. Eschatologisches im Vorfeld der Kaiserkrönung Karls des Grossen', in R. Berndt (ed.), *Das Frankfurter Konzil von 794. Kristallisationspunkt karolingischer Kultur* (Mainz, 1997), 49–79.

Breen, A., 'Pseudo-Cyprian *De Duodecim abusivis saeculi* and the Bible', in P. Ní Chatháin and M. Richter (eds), *Irland und die Christenheit: Bibelstudien und Mission / Ireland and Christendom: The Bible and the Missions* (Stuttgart, 1987), 230–45.

—— 'The Evidence of Antique Irish Exegesis in Pseudo-Cyprian, *de duodecim abusivis saeculi*', *PRIA* C 87.4 (1987), 71–101.

—— 'The Date, Provenance and Authorship of the Pseudo-Patrician Canonical Materials', *ZfRGKA* 81 (1995), 83–129.

—— '*De XII Abusivis*: Text and Transmission', in P. Ní Chatháin and M. Richter (eds), *Ireland and Europe in the Middle Ages: Texts and Transmission/Irland und Europa im früheren Mittelalter: Texte und überlieferung* (Dublin, 2005), 78–94.

Brown, W. C., 'The Idea of Empire in Carolingian Bavaria', in S. MacClean and B. Weiler (eds), *Representations of Power in Medieval Germany 800–1500* (Turnhout, 2006), 37–56.

Buc, P., 'Ritual and Interpretation: the Early Medieval Case (with an Edition of the Chronicle of Moissac)', *EME* 9.2 (2000), 183–210.

—— 'Political Rituals and Political Imagination in the Medieval West from the 4th century to the 11th', in P. Linehan and J. L. Nelson (eds), *The Medieval World* (London, 2001), 189–213.

—— *The Dangers of Ritual. Between Early Medieval Texts and Social Scientific Theory* (Princeton, 2002).

—— 'The Monster and the Critics: a Ritual Reply', *EME* 15.4 (2007), 441–52.

Bujard, J., 'L'inscription de Gondebaud et la Porte du Bourg-De-Four à Genève', *Nos Monuments d'Art et d'Histoire* 34 (1983), 306–13.

Bullough, D. A., 'Hagiography as patriotism: Alcuin's York Poem and the Early Northumbrian *vitae sanctorum*', in E. Patlagean and P. Riché (eds), *Hagiographie, cultures et sociétés, IVᵉ-XIIᵉ siècles : Actes du Colloque organisé à Nanterre et à Paris, 2–5 mai 1979* (Paris, 1981), 339–59.

—— 'Roman Books and Carolingian *renovatio*', in D. A. Bullough *Carolingian Renewal: Sources and Heritage*, (Manchester, 1991), 1–38.

—— *Carolingian Renewal: Sources and Heritage* (Manchester, 1991).

—— *Friends, Neighbours and Fellow-Drinkers: Aspects of Community and Conflict in the Early Medieval West*, H. M. Chadwick Memorial Lecture 1 (Cambridge, 1991).

—— 'What has Ingeld to do with Lindisfarne?', *ASE* 22 (1993), 93–125.

—— 'Alcuin and Lay Virtue', in L. Gaffuri and R. Quinto (eds), *Predicazione e società nel Medioevo: riflessione etica, valori e modelli di comportamento / Preaching and Society in the Middle Ages: Ethics, Values and Social Behaviour: Proceedings of the XII Medieval Sermon Studies Symposium, Padova, 14–18 Juglio 2000* (Padua, 2002), 71–91.

—— *Alcuin: Achievement and Reputation* (Leiden, 2004).

—— 'Was there a Carolingian Anti-War Movement?', *EME* 12.4 (2004), 365–76.

Burt, D. X. 'Peace', in J. C. Cavadini and A. D. Fitzgerald (eds), *Augustine through the Ages: An Encyclopedia* (Grand Rapids, MI, 2005), 629.

Callu, J. P., '*Pax et Libertas*: une légende monétaire de Théodebert Iᵉʳ', in P. Bastien (ed.), *Mélanges de numismatique d'archéologie et d'histoire offerts à Jean Lafaurie* (Paris, 1980), 189–99.

Carney, J., 'Sedulius Scottus', in R. E. McNally (ed.), *Old Ireland* (New York, 1965), 230–5.

Cary-Elwes, C., 'Peace in the City of God', *La Ciudad de Dios* 167 (1955), 417–33.

Caspari, W., *Vorstellung und Wort 'Friede' im Alten Testament*, Beiträge zur Förderung Christlicher Theologie 14 (Erlangen, 1910).

Castellanos, S., 'The Significance of Social Unanimity in a Visigothic Hagiography: Keys to an Ideological Screen', *Journal of Early Christian Studies* 11.2 (2003), 387–419.

Castriota, D., *The Ara Pacis Augustae and the Imagery of Abundance in Later Greek and Early Roman Imperial Art* (Princeton, PA, 1995).

Charles-Edwards, T. M., 'Alliances, Godfathers, Treaties and Boundaries', in M. A. S. Blackburn and D. N. Dumville (eds), *Kings, Currency and Alliances: History and Coinage of Southern England in the Ninth Century* (Woodbridge, 1998), 47–62.

Charlier, C., 'Les manuscrits personnels de Florus de Lyon et son activité littéraire', *Mélanges E. Podechard* (Lyons, 1945), 71–84.

—— 'La compilation augustinienne de Florus sur l'Apôtre', *RB* 57 (1947), 132–86.

Chester, A., 'The Concept of Peace in the Old Testament', *Theology* 92 (1989), 466–81.

Chydenius, J., *Medieval Institutions and the Old Testament*, Societas Scientiarum Fennica: Commentationes Humanarum Litterarum 37.2 (Helsinki, 1965).

Classen, P., '*Romanum gubernans imperium*: Zur Vorgeschichte der Kaisertitulatur Karls des Grossen', *DA* 9 (1951), 103–21.

—— 'Die Verträge von Verdun und Coulaines 843 als politische Grundlagen des westfränkischen Reiches', *HZ* 196 (1963), 1–35.

—— *Kaiserreskript und Königsurkunde: diplomatischer Studien zum Problem der Kontinuität zwischen Altertum und Mittelalter* (Thessalonika, 1977).

—— *Karl der Große, das Papsttum und Byzanz. Die Begründung des karolingischen Kaisertums*. Beiträge zur Geschichte und Quellenkunde des Mittelalters 9 (Sigmaringen, 1988).

Coady, C. A. J. and Ross, J., 'St. Augustine and the Ideal of Peace', *American Catholic Philosophical Quarterly* 74 (2000), 153–61.

Cocchi Ercolani, E., 'La propaganda di pace attraverso la monetazione nell' ultimo secolo della Repubblica', *Rivista Italiana di Numismatica e Scienze Affini* 74 (1972), 76–8.

Codoñer Merino, C., 'The Poetry of Eugenius of Toledo', in F. Cairns (ed.), *Papers of the Liverpool Latin Seminar* 3 (Liverpool, 1981), 323–42.

Coleman, V., 'Domestic Peace and Public Order in Anglo-Saxon Law', in J. Woods and D. A. E. Pelteret (eds), *The Anglo-Saxons, Synthesis and Achievement* (Waterloo, ON, 1985), 49–56.

Collins, R., 'Julian of Toledo and the Royal Succession in Late Seventh-Century Spain', in P. H. Sawyer and I. N. Wood, (eds), *Early Medieval Kingship* (Leeds, 1977), 30–49.

—— 'Theodebert I, *Rex Magnus Francorum*', in P. Wormald (ed.), *Ideal and Reality in Frankish and Anglo-Saxon Society Presented to J. M. Wallace-Hadrill* (Oxford, 1983), 7–33.

—— 'Pippin I and the Kingdom of Aquitaine', in R. Collins and P. Godman (eds), *Charlemagne's Heir: New Perspectives on the Reign of Louis the Pious (814–840)* (Oxford, 1990) 363–89.

—— 'Julian of Toledo and the Education of Kings in Late Seventh-Century Spain', in *idem, Law, Culture, and Regionalism in Early Medieval Spain* (Aldershot, 1992), III 1–22.

—— 'Queens-Dowager and Queens-Regent in Tenth-Century León and Navarre', in J. C. Parsons (ed.), *Medieval Queenship* (New York, 1993), 79–92.

—— 'Deception and Misrepresentation in Early Eighth-Century Frankish Historiography: Two Case Studies', in J. Jarnut, U. Nonn, and M. Richter (eds), *Karl Martell in Seiner Zeit* (Sigmaringen, 1994), 227–48.

—— 'The "Reviser" Revisited: Another Look at the Alternative Version of the *Annales regni francorum*', in A. C. Murray (ed.), *After Rome's Fall: Narrators and Sources of Early Medieval History. Essays Presented to Walter Goffart* (Toronto, 1998), 191–213.

—— 'Continuity and Loss in Medieval Spanish Culture: the Evidence of MS Silos Archivo Monástico 4', in R. Collins and A. Goodman (eds), *Medieval Spain: Culture, Conflict and Coexistence. Studies in Honour of Angus McKay* (Basingstoke, 2002), 1–22.

—— *Visigothic Spain, 409–711* (Oxford, 2004).

—— 'Charlemagne's Imperial Coronation and the Annals of Lorsch', in J. Story (ed.), *Charlemagne. Empire and Society* (Manchester, 2005), 52–70.

Conlin, D. A., *The Artists of the Ara Pacis: The Process of Hellenization in Roman Relief Sculpture* (Chapel Hill, NC, 1997).

Contreni, J., 'Carolingian Era, Early', and J. Kelly, 'Carolingian Era, Late', in John C. Cavadini and Allan D. Fitzgerald (eds), *Augustine through the Ages: An Encyclopedia* (Grand Rapids, MI, 1999), 124–9, 129–32.

—— 'The Irish in the Western Carolingian Empire (According to James F. Kenney and Bern, Burgerbibliothek 363)', in H. Löwe (ed.), *Die Iren und Europa im früheren Mittelalter* (Stuttgart, 1982), II, 758–98.

Cramer, P., *Baptism and Change in the Early Middle Ages, c.200–c.1150* (Cambridge, 1993).

Crépin, A., 'L'importance de la pensée de Grégoire le Grand dans la politique culturelle d'Alfred, roi de Wessex (871–899)', in J. Fontaine, R. Gillet, and S. Pellistrandi (eds), *Grégoire le Grand* (Paris, 1986), 579–87.

Dagron, G., *Emperor and Priest. The Imperial Office in Byzantium*, trans. J. Birrell (Cambridge, 2003).

Davies, L. M., 'Sedulius Scottus: *Liber de Rectoribus Christianis*, a Carolingian or Hibernian Mirror for Princes?', *Studia Celtica* 26–7 (1991–2), 34–50.

—— 'Sedulius Scottus (fl. 840x51–860x74)', *Oxford Dictionary of National Biography* (Oxford, 2004) <http://www.oxforddnb.com/view/article/50134>, accessed 27 March 2007.

Debrohun, J. B., 'The Gates of War (and Peace): Roman Literary Perspectives', in K. A. Raaflaub (ed.), *War and Peace in the Ancient World* (Oxford, 2007), 256–78.

De Clerck, P., 'L'ange de paix', in K. G. Cushing and R. F. Gyug (eds), *Ritual, Text and Law. Studies in Medieval Canon Law and Liturgy Presented to Roger E. Reynolds* (Aldershot, 2004), 11–22.

De Grummond, N., 'Pax Augusta and the *Horae* of the *Ara Pacis Augustae*', *American Journal of Archaeology* 94 (1990), 663–77.

Dekkers, E., 'Quelques notes sur des florilèges augustiniens anciens et médiévaux', *Augustiniana* 40–1 (1990), 27–44.

Depreux, P., 'La *pietas* comme principe de gouvernement d'après le Poème sur Louis le Pieux d'Ermold le Noir', in J. Hill and M. Swann, *The Community, the Family and the Saint: Patterns of Power in Early Medieval Europe. Selected Proceedings of the International Medieval Congress, University of Leeds, 4–7 July 1994, 10–13 July 1995* (Turnhout, 1998), 201–24.

Deshman, R., '*Christus Rex et Magi Reges*: Kinship and Christology in Ottonian and Anglo-Saxon Art', *FmSt* 10 (1976), 367–405.

—— 'The Exalted Servant: The Ruler-Theology of the Prayer Book of Charles the Bald', *Viator* 11 (1980), 385–417.

De Souza, P., '*Parta victoriis pax*: Roman Emperors as Peacemakers', in P. De Souza and J. France (eds), *War and Peace in Ancient and Medieval History* (Cambridge, 2008), 76–106.

Díaz y Díaz, M. C., 'Titulaciones regias en la monarquia visigoda', *Revista Portuguesa de Historia* 16 (1976), 133–41.

—— 'Literary Aspects of the Visigothic Liturgy', in E. James (ed.), *Visigothic Spain: New Approaches* (Oxford, 1980), 61–76.

Diebold, W. J., '*Nos quoque morem illius imitari cupientes*: Charles the Bald's Evocation and Imitation of Charlemagne', *Archiv für Kulturgeschichte* 75 (1993), 271–300.

—— 'Ruler Portrait of Charles the Bald in the S. Paolo Bible', *Art Bulletin* 76 (1994), 6–18.

Dinkler, E., 'The Early Christian Conception of Peace', in P. B. Yoder and W. M. Swartley (eds), *The Meaning of Peace* (Louisville, 1992), 164–212.

—— 'Power, Skill and Virtue in the Old English *Boethius*', *ASE* 26 (1997), 81–108.

—— 'Wealth and Wisdom: Symbolic Capital and the Ruler in the Transformational Program of Alfred the Great', *Exemplaria: A Journal of Theory in Medieval and Renaissance Studies* 13.2 (2001), 433–67.

Doherty, C., 'Kingship in Ireland', in E. Bhreathnach (ed.), *The Kingship and Landscape of Tara* (Dublin, 2005), 3–31.

—— 'Ireland and Rome in the Seventh Century', in É. Ó Carragáin and C. Neuman de Vegvar (eds), *Roma Felix—Formation and Reflections of Medieval Rome* (Aldershot, 2007), 277–86.

Dolbeau, F. 'Recherches sur le *Collectaneum Miscellaneum* de Sedulius Scottus', *AlatMA* 48–9 (1990), 47–84.

Donahue, T. O., '*Cert cech ríg co réil*', in B. Osborn and C. Marstrander (eds), *Miscellany presented to Kuno Meyer* (Halle, 1912), 258–77.

—— 'Advice to a Prince', *Ériu*, 9 (1923), 43–54.

Drabek, A. M., 'Der Merowingervertrag von Andelot aus dem Jahr 587', *MIÖG* 78 (1970), 34–41.

Drögereit, R., 'Kaiseridee und Kaisertitel bei den Angelsachsen', *ZfRG GA* 69 (1952), 24–73.

Düchting, R., *Sedulius Scottus. Seine Dichtungen* (Munich, 1968).

Dümmler, E., 'Ermahnungsschreiben an einen Karolinger', *NA* 13 (1887), 191–6.

Dutton, P. E., *The Politics of Dreaming in the Carolingian Empire* (Lincoln, NE, 1993).

—— *Carolingian Civilization: A Reader*, 2nd edition (Peterborough, ON, 2004).

—— and Kessler, H. L., *The Poetry and Paintings of the First Bible of Charles the Bald* (Ann Arbor, MI, 1997).

Dyer, J., 'Roman Processions of the Major Litany (*litaniae maiores*) from the Sixth to the Twelfth Century', in E. Ó Carragáin and C. Neuman de Vegvar (eds), *Roma Felix: Formation and Reflections of Medieval Rome* (Aldershot, 2007), 113–58.

Ebenbauer, A., 'Fróði und sein Friede', in H. Birkhan (ed.), *Festgabe für Otto Höfler zum 75. Geburtstag, Philologica Germanica* 3 (Vienna, 1976), 128–81.

—— *Carmen Historicum: Untersuchungen zur historischen Dichtung im karolingischen Europa* I, *Philologica Germanica* 4 (Vienna, 1978).

Eberhardt, O., *Via Regia. Der Fürstenspiegel Smaragds von St. Mihiel und seine literarische Gattung* (Munich, 1977).

Eshelman, L., 'Weavers of Peace, Weavers of War', in D. Wolfthal (ed.), *Peace and Negotiation: Strategies for Coexistence in the Middle Ages and the Renaissance* (Turnhout, 2000), 15–37.

Ewig, E., 'Das Bild Constantins des Großen in den ersten Jahrhunderten des abendländischen Mittelalters', *HJ* 75 (1955), 1–46.

—— 'Zum christlichen Königsgedanken im Frühmittelalter', in T. Mayer (ed.), *Das Königtum, VuF* 3 (Sigmaringen, 1956), 7–73.

Fanning, S., 'Clovis Augustus and Merovingian *imitatio imperii*', in K. Mitchell and I. Wood (eds), *The World of Gregory of Tours* (Leiden, 2002), 321–35.

Farmer, S. and Rosenwein, B. H., *Monks and Nuns, Saints and Outcasts: Religion in Medieval Society* (Ithaca, 2000).

Fasoli, G., 'Pace e Guerra nell' Alto Medioevo', in F. Bocchi, A. Carile, and A. Pini (eds), *Scritti di Storia Medievale* (Bologna, 1974), 79–104.

Favreau, R., *Historie politique du royaume burgonde (443–534)* (Lausanne, 1997).

—— '"Rex, Lex, Lux, Pax": jeux de mots et jeux de lettres dans les inscriptions médiévales', *Bibliothèque de l'École des chartes* 161.2 (2003), 625–35.

Fell, C. E., '*Unfrið*: An Approach to a Definition', *Sagabook of the Viking Society for Northern Research* 21 (1982–3), 85–100.

Finsterwalder, P., 'Eine Parteipolitische Kundegebung eines Anhangers Lothars I', *Nachrichten der Akadamie der Wissenschaften in Göttingen I: Philologisch-historische Klasse* 47 (1928), 393–415.

Fitzgerald, A. and Cavadini, J. C., *Augustine Through the Ages: An Encyclopedia* (Grand Rapids, MI, 1999).

Folz, R., 'Tradition hagiographique et culte de Saint Dagobert, roi des Francs', *MA* 69 (1963), 17–33.

—— *The Concept of the Empire in Western Europe from the Fifth to the Fourteenth Century*, trans. S. A. Ogilvie (London, 1969).

—— *The Coronation of Charlemagne, 25 December 800* (London, 1974).

—— *Les saints rois du Moyen Âge en Occident (VIᵉ–XIIIᵉ siècles)*, Subsidia Hagiographia 68 (Brussels, 1984).

Fontaine, J., 'La homilía de San Leandro ante el Concilio III de Toledo: temática y forma', *Concilio III De Toledo: XIV Centenario, 589–1989* (Toledo, 1991), 249–70.

Formin, M., '*Tecosca Cormaic*: the Compilation of a Wisdom-Text', <http://www.celt.dias.ie/publications/tionol/maximfomin03.pdf>.

Fouracre, P., 'Merovingian Historiography and Merovingian Hagiography', *Past and Present* 127 (1990), 3–38.

—— 'Carolingian Justice: the Rhetoric of Improvement and the Contexts of Abuse', *La giustizia nell'alto Medioevo (secoli V–VIII): 7–13 Aprile 1994*, Settimane 42, 771–803.

—— 'The Long Shadow of the Merovingians', in J. Story (ed.), *Charlemagne. Empire and Society* (Manchester, 2005), 5–22.

Fouracre, P. and Davies, W. (eds), *Property and Power in the Early Middle Ages* (Cambridge, 1995).

Fouracre, P. and Gerberding, R., *Late Merovingian France: History and Hagiography, 640–720* (Manchester, 1996).

Frantzen, A. J., *King Alfred* (Boston, 1986).

Fridh, A. J., *Terminologie et formules dans les Variae de Cassiodore: études sur le développement du style administratif aux derniers siècles de l'antiquité*, Studia graeca et latina Gothoburgensia 2 (Stockholm, 1956).

Fried, J., 'Der karolingischen Herrschaftverband im 9. Jhdt zwischen "Kirche" und "Königshaus"', *HZ* 235 (1982), 1–43.

—— 'Ludwig der Fromme, das Papsttum und die fränkische Kirche', in P. Godman and R. Collins (eds), *Charlemagne's Heir. New Perspectives on the Reign of Louis the Pious (814–840)* (Oxford, 1990), 266–70.

—— 'Papst Leo III besucht Karl den Großen in Paderborn oder Einhards Schweigen', *HZ* 272 (2001), 281–326.

Ganshof, F. L., *Feudalism*, trans. P. Grierson, 3rd edition (London, 1964).

—— 'On the Genesis and Significance of the Treaty of Verdun', in *The Carolingians and the Frankish Monarchy. Studies in Carolingian History*, trans. J. Sondheimer (London, 1971), 289–302.

—— 'The Use of the Written Word in Charlemagne's Administration', in *The Carolingians and the Frankish Monarchy*, trans. Janet Sondheimer (London, 1971).

Ganz, D., 'The Predestination Debate', in M. Gibson and J. L. Nelson (eds), *Charles the Bald. Court and Kingdom*, 2nd edition (Aldershot, 1990), 283–302.

—— 'Einhard and the Characterization of Greatness', in J. Story (ed.), *Charlemagne. Empire and Society* (Manchester, 2005), 38–51.

Garipzanov, I. H., 'Communication of Authority in Carolingian Titles', *Viator* 36 (2005), 40–80.

—— *The Symbolic Language of Authority in the Carolingian World (c.751–877)* (Leiden, 2008).

Garrison, M., 'The Emergence of Carolingian Latin Literature and the Court of Charlemagne (780–814)', in R. McKitterick (ed.), *Carolingian Culture: Emulation and Innovation* (Cambridge, 1993), 111–40.

—— 'The English and the Irish at the Court of Charlemagne', in P. L. Butzer, M. Kerner, and W. Oberschelp (eds), *Karl der Grosse und sein Nachwirken 1200 Jahre Kultur und Wissenschaft in Europa* (Turnhout, 1997), 97–124.

—— 'The Social World of Alcuin: Nicknames at York and the Carolingian Court', in L. A. J. R. Houwen and A. A. MacDonald (eds), *Alcuin of York: Scholar at the Carolingian Court: Proceedings of the Third Germania Latina Conference held at the University of Groningen, May 1995* (Groningen, 1998), 58–79.

—— 'Letters to a King and Biblical Exempla: the Examples of Cathwulf and Clemens Peregrinus', *EME* 7.3 (1998), 305–28.

—— 'The Franks as the New Israel? Education for an Identity from Pippin to Charlemagne', in Y. Hen and M. Innes (eds), *The Uses of the Past in the Early Middle Ages* (Cambridge, 2000), 114–61.

—— 'The Bible and Alcuin's Interpretation of Current Events', *Peritia* 16 (2002), 68–84.

—— 'The *Missa pro principe* in the Bobbio Missal', in Y. Hen and R. Meens (eds), *The Bobbio Missal: Liturgy and Religious Culture in Merovingian Gaul* (Cambridge, 2004), 187–205.

—— 'Quid Hinieldus cum Christo?' in K. O'Brien O'Keeffe and A. Orchard (eds), *Latin Learning and English Lore: Studies in Anglo-Saxon Literature for Michael Lapidge* (Toronto, 2005), I, 237–59.

Geary, P. J., 'Ethnic Identity as a Situational Construct in the Early Middle Ages', *Mitteilungen der anthropologischen Gesellschaft in Wien* 113 (1983), 15–26.

—— 'Extra-Judicial Means of Conflict Resolution', *Settimane du Studio* 42 (1995), 569–601.

George, J., 'Poet as Politician: Venantius Fortunatus' Panegyric to King Chilperic', *Journal of Medieval Studies* 15 (1989), 15–18.

—— *Venantius Fortunatus: The Role of a Latin Poet in Merovingian Gaul* (Oxford, 1992).

—— 'Panegyric in Merovingian Gaul', in M. Whitby (ed.), *The Propaganda of Power: the Role of Panegyric in Late Antiquity* (Leiden, 1998), 225–46.

—— 'Vandal Poets in their Context', in A. H. Merrills (ed.), *Vandals, Romans and Berbers: New Perspectives on Late Antique North Africa* (Aldershot, 2004), 133–43.

Gerberding, R. A., *The Rise of the Carolingians and the Liber historiae Francorum* (Oxford, 1987).

Gil, J., 'Los terrores del año 800', in *Actas del Simposio parael estudio de los codices del 'Comentario al Apocalipsis' de Beato de Liebana* (Madrid, 1978).

Gillett, A., 'The Purpose of Cassiodorus', in A. C. Murray (ed.), *After Rome's Fall: Narrators and Sources of Early Medieval History: Essays Presented to Walter Goffart* (Toronto, 1998), 37–50.

—— *Envoys and Political Communication in the Late Antique West, 411–533* (Cambridge, 2003).

Goar, J., *Euchologion sive rituale graecorum* (Venice, 1730, reprinted Graz, 1960).

Godden, M., 'The Anglo-Saxons and the Goths: Rewriting the Sack of Rome', *ASE* 31 (2002), 47–68.

Godman, P., *Poets and Emperors: Frankish Politics and Carolingian Poetry* (Oxford, 1987).

—— and Collins, R., *Charlemagne's Heir: New Perspectives on the Reign of Louis the Pious (814–840)* (Oxford, 1990).

—— Jarnut, J., and Johanek, P. (eds), *Am Vorabend der Kaiserkrönung. Das Epos 'Karolus Magnus et Leo papa' und der Papstbesuch in Paderborn 799* (Berlin, 2003).

Goebel, J., *Felony and Misdemeanor: A Study in the History of English Criminal Procedure* (New York, 1937).

Goffart, W., 'From *Historiae* to *Historia Francorum* and Back Again: Aspects of the Textual History of Gregory of Tours', in J. J. Contreni and T. F. X. Noble (eds), *Religion, Culture, and Society in the Early Middle Ages: Studies in Honor of Richard E. Sullivan* (Kalamazoo, 1987), 55–76.

—— *The Narrators of Barbarian History (A.D. 550–800): Jordanes, Gregory of Tours, Bede, and Paul the Deacon* (Princeton, NJ, 1988).

—— *Rome's Fall and After* (London, 1989).

Goldberg, E. J., 'Ludwig der Deutsche und Mähren: eine Studie zu karolingischen Grenzenkriegen im Osten', in W. Hartmann (ed.), *Ludwig der Deutsch und seine Zeit* (Darmstadt, 2004), 67–94.

—— *Struggle for Empire: Kingship and Conflict under Louis the German, 817–876* (Ithaca, 2006).

—— ' "More Devoted to the Equipment of Battle Than the Splendor of Banquets": Frontier Kingship, Martial Ritual, and Early Knighthood at the Court of Louis the German', *Viator* 30 (2006), 41–78.

Gorman, M., 'Wigbod and Biblical Studies under Charlemagne', *RB* 107 (1997), 40–76.

—— 'The Commentary on Kings of Claudius of Turin and its Two Printed Editions (Basel 1531); (Bologna 1755)', *Filologia mediolatina* 4 (1997), 99–13.

—— *The Manuscript Traditions of the Works of St Augustine* (Florence, 2001).

Green, D. H., *Language and History in the Early Germanic World* (Cambridge, 1998).

—— 'Three Aspects of the Old Saxon Biblical Epic, the *Heliand*', in D. H. Green and F. Siegmund (eds), *The Continental Saxons from the Migration Period to the Tenth Century: An Ethnographic Perspective* (Woodbridge, 2003), 247–63.

—— *The Continental Saxons from the Migration Period to the Tenth Century: An Ethnographic Perspective* (Woodbridge, 2003).

Grierson, P., 'Election and Inheritance in Early Germanic Kingship', *Cambridge Historical Journal* 7 (1941), 1–22.

Gruen, E. S., 'Augustus and the Ideology of War and Peace', in R. Winkles (ed.), *The Age of Augustus: Interdisciplinary Conference Held at Brown University April 30–May 2 1982* (Louvain, 1985), 51–72.

Hägermann, D., 'Reichseinheit und Reichsteilung. Bemerkungen zur *Divisio regnorum* 806 und zur *Ordinatio Imperii* 817', *HJ* 95 (1975), 278–307.

—— '"*Quae ad profectum et utilitatem pertinent*". Normen und Maximen zur "Innen- und Außenpolitik" in der *divisio regnorum* von 806', in J.-M. Duvosquel and E. Thoen (eds), *Peasants and Townsmen in Medieval Europe: Studia in honorem Adriaan Verhulst* (Ghent, 1995), 605–15.

Haldon, J., *Warfare, State, and Society in the Byzantine World, 565–1204* (London, 1999).

Hall, A., 'A Present, a Potentate and a Peaceweaver in *Beowulf*', *Studia Neophilologica* 78.1 (2006), 81–7.

Halsall, G., *Settlement and Social Organization: The Merovingian Region of Metz* (Cambridge, 1995).

—— 'Violence and Society in the Early Medieval West: An Introductory Survey', in *idem* (ed.), *Violence and Society in the Early Medieval West* (Woodbridge, 1997), 1–45.

Halsall, G. (ed.), *Violence and Society in the Early Medieval West* (Woodbridge, 1997).

—— 'Funny Foreigners: Laughing with the Barbarians in Late Antiquity', in *idem* (ed.), *Humour, History and Politics in Late Antiquity and the Early Middle Ages* (Cambridge, 2002), 89–113.

—— *Warfare and Society in the Barbarian West, 450–900* (London, 2003).

—— 'The Preface to Book V of Gregory of Tours' *Histories*: Its Form, Context and Significance', *HER* 122 (2007), 297–317.

Handley, M. A., 'Inscribing Time and Identity in the Kingdom of Burgundy', in S. Mitchell and G. Greatrex (eds), *Ethnicity and Culture in Late Antiquity* (London, 2000), 83–102.

—— *Death, Society and Culture: Inscriptions and Epitaphs in Gaul and Spain, AD 300–750*, BAR International Series, 1135 (Oxford, 2003).

—— 'Disputing the End of African Christianity', in A. Merrills (ed.), *Vandals, Romans and Berbers: New Perspectives on Late Antique North Africa* (Aldershot, 2004), 291–310.

Harries, J. and Wood, I. N., *The Theodosian Code: Studies in the Imperial Law of Late Antiquity* (London, 1993).

Harris, S. J., 'The Alfredian *World History* and Anglo-Saxon Identity', *JEGP* 100 (2001), 482–510.

Harrison, R. M., 'The Church of St. Polyeuctus in Istanbul and the Temple of Solomon', in O. Pritsak, C. Mango, and U. M. Pasicznyk (eds), *Okeanos: Essays Presented to Ihor Ševčenko on His Sixtieth Birthday by his Colleagues and Students*, Harvard Ukrainian Studies 7 (Cambridge, MA, 1984), 276–9.

—— *A Temple for Byzantium: The Discovery and Excavation of Anicia Juliana's Palace Church in Istanbul* (London, 1989).

—— 'From Jerusalem and Back Again: The Fates of the Treasures of Solomon', in K. Painter (ed.), *Churches Built in Ancient Times: Recent Studies in Early Christian Archaeology*, Occasional Papers from The Society of Antiquaries of London 16 (London, 1994), 239–48.

Hartmann, W., *Der Frieden im früheren Mittelalter. Zwei Studien* (Stuttgart, 1992).

Haselbach, I., *Aufstieg und Herrschaft der Karlinger in der Darstellung der sogenannten Annales Mettenses Priores. Ein Beitrag zur Geschichte der politischen Ideen im Reiche Karls des Großen*, Historische Studien 412 (Lübeck, Hamburg, 1970).

Hattenhauer, H., *Pax et iustitia*. Berichte aus den Sitzungen der Joachim Jungius-Gesellschaft der Wissenschaften 3 (Hamburg, 1983).

Hauck, K., 'Rituelle Speisegemeinschaft im 10. und 11. Jahrhundert', *Studium Generale* 3 (1950), 611–21.

—— 'Karolingische Taufpfalzen im Spiegel hofneher Dichtung. Überlegungen zur Ausmalung von Pfalzkirchen, Pfalzen und Reichsklöstern', *Nachrichten der Akademie der Wissenschaften in Göttingen. I: Philologisch-historische Klasse* 1(1985), 1–97.

Hays, G., ' "*Romuleis Libicisque Litteris*": Fulgentius and the "Vandal Renaissance" ', in A. H. Merrills (ed.), *Vandals, Romans and Berbers: New Perspectives on Late Antique North Africa*, (Aldershot, 2004), 125–6.

Head, T., 'The Development of the Peace of God in Aquitaine (970–1005)', *Speculum* 74.3 (1999), 656–86.

——, 'Peace and Power in France around the Year 1000', *Essays in Medieval Studies* 23 (2006), 1–17.

Head, T. and Landes, R. (eds), *The Peace of God: Social Violence and Religious Response in France around the Year 1000* (Ithaca, 1992).

Heather, P. J., *Goths and Romans, 332–489* (Oxford, 1991).

—— 'The Emergence of the Visigothic Kingdom', in J. Drinkwater and H. Elton (eds), *Fifth-Century Gaul: A Crisis of Identity?* (Cambridge, 1992), 85–94.

—— 'Theoderic, King of the Goths', *EME* 4.5 (1995), 145–73.

—— 'The Barbarian in Late Antiquity. Image, Reality, and Transformation', in R. Miles (ed.), *Constructing Identities in Late Antiquity* (London, 1999), 234–58.

Heinzelmann, M., *Gregory of Tours: History and Society in the Sixth Century*, trans. C. Carroll (Cambridge, 2001).

Hen, Y., *Culture and Religion in Merovingian Gaul, A.D. 481–751* (Leiden, 1995).

—— 'The Uses of the Bible and the Perception of Kingship in Merovingian Gaul', *EME* 7.3 (1998), 33–41.

—— 'The Annals of Metz and the Merovingian Past', in M. Innes and Y. Hen (eds), *The Uses of the Past in the Early Middle Ages* (Cambridge, 2000), 175–90.

——, *The Royal Patronage of the Liturgy in Frankish Gaul to the Death of Charles the Bald*, Subsidia 3 (London, 2001), 37–41.

Henry, P. L., 'The Cruces of *Audacht Morainn*', *ZCP* 39 (1982), 33–53.

Herbers, K., 'Papst Nikolaus I. und Patriarch Photios: Das Bild des byzantinischen Gegners in lateinischen Quellen', in O. Engels and P. Schreiner (eds), *Die Begegnung des Westens mit dem Ostens. Kongreßakten des 4. Symposions des Mediävistenverbandes in Köln 1991 aus Anlaß des 1000. Todesjahres der Kaiserin Theophanu* (Sigmaringen, 1993), 51–74.

Herren, M. W, 'The "De Imagine Tetrici" of Walahfrid Strabo: Edition and Translation', Journal of Medieval Latin 1 (1991), 118–39.

—— 'Walahfrid Strabo's *De Imagine Tetrici*: an interpretation', in R. North and T. Hofstra (eds), *Latin Culture and Medieval Germanic Europe, Germania Latina I* (Groningen, 1992), 25–42.

Hillgarth, J. N., 'Coins and Chronicles: Propaganda in Sixth-Century Spain and the Byzantine Background', *Historia* 15 (1966), 483–508.

—— 'Historiography in Visigothic Spain', *Settimane di studio* 17 (1970), 261–311.

—— 'Influence de la *Cité de Dieu* de Saint Augustin au Haut Moyen Age', *Sacris Erudiri* 24 (1985), 1–24.

—— 'Eschatalogical and Political Concepts in the Seventh Century', in J. Fontaine and J. Hillgarth (eds), *The Seventh Century: Change and Continuity* (London, 1992), 212–35.

Hirst, S., *The Prittlewell Prince: The Discovery of a Rich Anglo-Saxon Burial in Essex* (London, 2004).

Hiscock, N., 'The Aachen Chapel: A Model of Salvation', in P. L. Butzer and D. Lohrmann (eds), *Science in Western and Eastern Civilization in Carolingian Times* (Basel, 1993), 115–26.

Hoffmann, H. H., *Untersuchungen zur karolingischen Annalistik* (Bonn, 1958).

—— '*Serenissimus*. Ein fürstliches Prädikat in fünfzehn Jahrhunderten', *HJ* 80 (1960), 240–51.

Holliday, P. J., 'Time, History and the *Ara Pacis Augustae*', *The Art Bulletin* 72.4 (1990), 547–57.

Holmes, P. A, 'Nicholas I's "Reply to the Bulgarians" Revisited', *Ecclesia Orans* 7 (1990), 131–43.

Houwen, L. A. J. R. and Macdonald, A. A., *Alcuin of York: Scholar at the Carolingian Court: Proceedings of the Third Germania Latina Conference held at the University of Groningen, May 1995* (Groningen, 1998).

Hughes, K., *Constructing Antichrist: Paul, Biblical Commentary, and the Development of Doctrine in the Early Middle Ages* (Washington DC, 2005).

Hummer, H., 'Politics and Power', in E. English and C. Lansing (eds), *Companion to the Medieval World* (Oxford, 2009), 36–67.

Innes, M., *State and Society in the Early Middle Ages: The Middle Rhine Valley, 400–1000* (Cambridge, 2000).

—— ' "He never even allowed his white teeth to be bared in laughter": the Politics of Humour in the Carolingian Renaissance', in G. Halsall (ed.), *Humour, History and Politics in Late Antiquity and the Early Middle Ages* (Cambridge, 2002), 131–57.

—— ' "A place of discipline": Aristocratic Youth and Carolingian Courts', in C. Cubitt (ed.), *Court Culture in the Early Middle Ages* (Turnhout, 2003), 59–76.

—— 'Land, Freedom and the Making of the Early Medieval West', *TRHS*, 6th series, 16 (2006), 39–74.

Jaeger, S., ' "Seed-sowers of Peace": The Uses of Love and Friendship at Court and in the Kingdom of Charlemagne', in M. F. Williams (ed.), *The Making of Christian Communities in Late Antiquity and the Middle Ages* (London, 2005), 77–92.

James, E., ' "*Beati Pacifici*": Bishops and the Law in Sixth-Century Gaul', in J. Bossy (ed.), *Disputes and Settlements: Law and Human Relations in the West* (Cambridge, 1983), 25–46.

Jamison, C. P., 'Traffic of Women in Germanic Literature. The Role of the Peace Pledge in Marital Exchanges', *Women in German Yearbook* 20 (Lincoln, 2004), 13–36.

Jaski, B., 'Early Medieval Irish Kingship and the Old Testament', *EME* 7.2 (1998), 329–44.

De Jong, M., 'Power and Humility in Carolingian Society: the Public Penance of Louis the Pious', *EME* 1.1 (1992), 29–52.

—— 'Old Law and New-found Power: Hrabanus Maurus and the Old Testament', in J. W. Drijvers and A. A. MacDonald (eds), *Centres of Learning. Learning and Location in Pre-Modern Europe and the Near East* (Leiden, 1995), 161–76.

—— 'Adding Insult to Injury: Julian of Toledo and His *Historiae Wambae*', in P. Heather (ed.), *The Visigoths. From the Migration Period to the Seventh Century* (Woodbridge, 1999), 373–402.

—— 'The Empire as *ecclesia*: Hrabanus Maurus and Biblical *historia* for Rulers', in Y. Hen and M. Innes (eds), *The Uses of the Past in the Early Middle Ages* (Cambridge, 2000).

—— 'Exegesis for an Empress', in E. Cohen and M. de Jong (eds), *Medieval Transformations. Texts, Power, and Gifts in Context* (Leiden, 2000), 69–100.

—— 'Charlemagne's Church', in J. Story (ed.), *Charlemagne, Empire and Society* (Manchester, 2005), 103–35.

Jussen, B., *Spiritual Kinship as Social Practice: Godparenthood and Adoption in the Early Middle Ages* (Newark, DE, 2000).

Kaczynski, B. M., *Greek in the Carolingian Age: The St. Gall Manuscripts* (Cambridge, MA, 1988).

—— 'Edition, Translation and Exegesis: The Carolingians and the Bible', in R. E. Sullivan (ed.), *The Gentle Voices of Teachers: Aspects of Learning in the Carolingian Age* (Columbus, OH, 1995), 171–86.

Kahler, H., 'Die *Ara Pacis* und die Augusteische Friedensidee', *Jahrbuch des Deutschen Archälogischen Instituts* 69 (1954), 68–100.

Kamp, H., *Friedensstifter und Vermittler im Mittelalter* (Darmstadt, 2001).

Kantorowicz, E. H., '"The King's Advent" and the Enigmatic Panels in the Doors of Santa Sabina', *The Art Bulletin* 26.4 (December 1944), 207–31.

—— *The King's Two Bodies: A Study in Mediaeval Political Theology* (Princeton, 1957).

—— *Laudes Regiae; a Study in Liturgical Acclamations and Mediaeval Ruler Worship* (Berkeley, 1958).

—— 'The Carolingian King in the Bible of San Paolo fuori Le Mura', *Selected Studies* (Locust Valley, NY, 1965), 82–94.

—— *Selected Studies* (Locust Valley, NY, 1965).

Karkov, C., *The Ruler Portraits of Anglo-Saxon England* (Woodbridge, 2004).

Keefe, S. A., *Water and the Word: Baptism and the Education of the Clergy in the Carolingian Empire* (South Bend, IN, 2002).

Kelly, J. F., 'Hiberno-Latin Theology', in H. Löwe (ed.), *Die Iren und Europa im früheren Mittelalter* (Stuttgart, 1982), 549–67.

Kershaw, P. J. E., 'The Alfred-Guthrum Treaty. Scripting Accommodation and Interaction in Viking-Age England', in D. M. Hadley and J. D. Richards (eds), *Cultures in Contact: Scandinavian Settlement in England in the Ninth and Tenth Centuries* (Turnhout, 2000), 43–64.

—— 'Power, Prayer and Illness in Asser's *Life of Alfred*', *Early Medieval Europe* 10.2 (2001), 201–24.

—— 'Eberhard of Friuli, a Carolingian Lay Intellectual', in P. Wormald and J. L. Nelson (eds), *Lay Intellectuals in the Carolingian World* (Cambridge, 2007), 77–105.

—— 'English History and Irish Readers in the Frankish World', in D. Ganz and P. Fouracre (eds), *Frankland. The Franks and the World of Early Medieval Europe* (Manchester, 2008), 126–51.

Keynes, S. D., 'An Interpretation of the Pacs, Pax and Paxs Pennies', *ASE* 7 (1978), 165–73.

—— 'Anglo-Saxon Kingship', *History Today* 35 (1985), 38–43.

—— 'Royal Government and the Written Word in Anglo-Saxon England', in R. McKitterick (ed.), *The Uses of Literacy in Early Mediaeval Europe* (Cambridge, 1990), 226–57.

King, P. D., 'The Barbarian Kingdoms', in J. H. Burns (ed.), *The Cambridge History of Medieval Political Thought, c. 350–1450* (Cambridge, 1988), 123–53.

Klaniczay, G., 'Manichaean Kingship: Gnosis at Home in the World', *Numen* 29.1 (1982), 17–32.

—— *Holy Rulers and Blessed Princesses: Dynastic Cults in Medieval Central Europe*, trans. É. Pálmai (Cambridge, 2002).

Klinck, A. L., 'Anglo-Saxon Women and Law', *JMH* 8 (1982), 107–21.

Klinkenberg, A. M., 'Über karolingische Fürstenspiegel', *Geschichten des Wissenschaft und Unterricht* 7 (1956), 82–98.

Kornbluth, G. A., *Engraved Gems of the Carolingian Renaissance*, (University Park, PA, 1995).

—— 'The Seal of Alaric, *rex Gothorum*', *EME* 16.3 (2008), 299–332.

Kosto, A. J., 'The *convenientia* in the early Middle Ages', *Medieval Studies* 60 (1998), 1–54.

—— 'Hostages in the Carolingian World (714–840)', *EME* 11.2 (2002), 123–47.

Kottje, R., *Studien zum Einfluß des Alten Testaments auf Recht und Liturgie des frühen Mittelalters 6 bis 8 Jahrhundert*, Bonner Historische Forschungen 23, 2nd edition (Bonn, 1970).

Koziol, G., *Begging Pardon and Favour: Ritual and Political Order in Early Medieval France* (Ithaca, 1992).

—— 'The Dangers of Polemic: Is Ritual Still an Interesting Topic of Historical Study?', *EME* 11.4 (2003), 367–88.

—— 'Charles the Simple, Robert of Neustria, and the *vexilla* of Saint-Denis', *EME* 14.4 (2006), 355–90.

Krautheimer, R., *Corpus Basilicarum Christianarum Romae. The Early Christian Basilicas of Rome*, 5 vols (Vatican City, 1937–77).

—— *Three Christian Capitals: Topography and Politics* (Berkeley, 1983).

—— 'The Ecclesiastical Building Program of Constantine', in G. Bonamente and F. Fusco (eds), *Costantino il Grande dall'antichità all'umanesimo* (Macerata, 1992), 509–52.

Kulikowski, M., *Late Roman Spain and its Cities* (Baltimore, 2004).

La Rocca, C., 'Perceptions of an Early Medieval Urban Landscape', in P. Linehan and J. N. Nelson (eds), *The Medieval World* vol. 10 (London, 2001), 416–30.

Lammers, W., 'Ein Karolingisches Bildprogramm in der Aula Regia von Ingelheim', *Festschrift für H. Heimpel zum 70. Geburtstag am 19. September 1971* (Göttingen, 1972), 226–89.

Landes, R., 'Lest the Millennium be Fulfilled: Apocalyptic Expectations and the Pattern of Western Chronography, 100–800 CE', in W. Verbeke, D. Verhelst, and A. Welkenhuysen (eds), *The Use and Abuse of Eschatology in the Middle Ages* (Leuven, 1988), 137–211.

—— 'Between Aristocracy and Heresy: Popular Participation in the Limousin Peace of God', in T. Head and R. Landes (eds), *The Peace of God: Social Violence and Religious Response in France around the Year 1000* (Ithaca, NY, 1992), 184–219.

Lapidge, M., 'A Stoic Metaphor in Late Latin Poetry: the Binding of the Cosmos', *Latomus* 39 (1980), 817–37.

—— 'The Archetype of Beowulf', *ASE* 29 (2000), 5–41.

—— 'The Career of Aldhelm', *ASE* 36 (2007), 15–69.

Laufs, J., *Der Friedensgedanke bei Augustinus: Untersuchungen zum XIX. Buch des Werks 'De Civitate Dei'* (Wiesbaden, 1973).

Lavelle, R., 'Towards a Political Contextualization of Peacemaking and Peace Agreements in Anglo-Saxon England', in D. Wolfthal (ed.), *Peace and Negotiation: Strategies for Coexistence in the Middle Ages and Renaissance* (Turnhout, 2000), 39–55.

—— 'The Use and Abuse of Hostages in Later Anglo-Saxon England', *EME* 14.3 (2006), 269–96.

Leclerq, J., 'Smaragde et la grammaire chrétienne', *Revue de moyen âge latin* 4 (1948), 15–22.

Lee, A. D., 'Byzantine Treaties' in *idem, Information and Frontiers. Roman Foreign Relations in Late Antiquity* (Cambridge, 1993).

—— 'Treaties in Late Antiquity, in Philip de Souza and John France (eds), *War and Peace in Ancient and Medieval History* (Cambridge, 2008), 107–19.

Le Jan, R., 'La Sacralité de la Royauté Mérovingienne', *Annales ESC* 58.6 (2003), 1217–41.

Lenihan, D. A., 'The Just War Theory in the Works of Saint Augustine', *Augustinian Studies* (1988), 37–70.

Lerner, R. E., 'Refreshment of the Saints. The Time after Antichrist as a Station for Earthly Progress in Medieval Thought', *Traditio* 32 (1976), 97–144.

Leyser, K., *Medieval Germany and its Neighbours, 900–1250* (London, 1982).

—— 'The Tenth Century Condition', in *idem, Medieval Germany and its Neighbours 900–1250* (London, 1982), 1–9.

Liebschütz, J. H. W. G., '*Gens* into *regnum*: The Vandals', J. Jarnut, W. Pohl, and H.-W. Goetz (eds), *Regna and Gentes: The Relationship between Late Antiquity and Early Medieval Peoples and Kingdoms in the Transformation of the Roman World,* TRW 13 (Leiden, 2003), 55–83.

Llewellyn, P. A. B., 'Le contexte romain du couronnement de Charlemagne. Le temps de l'Avent de l'année 800', *MA* 96.2 (1990), 209–25.

Longtin, R., 'Constantine and Christianity: The Numismatic Evidence', *The Classical and Medieval Numismatic Society Journal* 1.2 (2000), 5–27.

Löwe, H., 'Eine Kölner Notiz zum Kaisertum Karls des Großen', *Rheinisches Vierteljahrs-blätter* 14 (1949), 7–34.

Lund, N., 'Peace and Non-Peace in the Viking Age', in J. E. Knirk (ed.), *Proceedings of the Tenth Viking Congress* (Oslo, 1987), 255–69.

Lynch, J., *God Parents and Kinship in Early Medieval Europe* (Princeton, 1986).

MacCormack, S. G., *Art and Ceremony in Late Antiquity* (Berkeley, 1981).

Mackinney, L., 'The People and Public Opinion in the Eleventh-Century Peace Movement', *Speculum* 5.2 (1930), 182–206.

Maclean, S., *Kingship and Politics in the Late Ninth Century: Charles the Fat and the End of the Carolingian Empire* (Cambridge, 2003).

—— 'Ritual, Misunderstanding and the Contest for Meaning: Representations of the Disrupted Royal Assembly at Frankfurt (873)', in *idem* and B. K. U. Weiler (eds), *Representations of Power in Medieval Germany, 800–1500* (Turnhout, 2006), 97–120.

—— 'Making a Difference in Tenth-Century Politics: King Athelstan's Sisters and Frankish Queenship', in P. Fouracre and D. Ganz (eds), *Frankland. The Franks and the World of Early Medieval Europe* (Manchester, 2008), 167–90.

Maclean, S. and Weiler, B. K. U. (eds), *Representations of Power in Medieval Germany, 800–1500* (Turnhout, 2006).

Majeska, G. P., 'The Emperor in his Church: Imperial Ritual in the Church of St. Sophia', in H. Maguire (ed.), *Byzantine Court Culture from 829 to 1204* (Washington DC, 1998), 1–11.

Manacorda, D., 'Trasformazioni dell'abitato nel Campo Marzio: L'area della "Porticus Minucia"', in L. Paroli and P. Delogu (eds), *La storia economica di Roma nell'alto Medioevo alla luce dei recenti scavi archeologici* (Florence, 1993), 31–53.

Mango, C. and Ševčenko, I., 'Remains of the Church of St. Polyeuktos at Constantinople', *DOP* 15 (1961), 243–7.

Markus, R. A., 'The Roman Empire in Early Christian Historiography', *The Downside Review* 81 (1963), 340–53.

—— 'Papal Primacy: Light from the Early Middle Ages', *Month* 229 (1970), 352–61.

—— *Saeculum: History and Society in the Theology of St. Augustine* (London, 1970).

—— 'Gregory the Great's Europe', *TRHS*, 5th series, 31 (1981), 21–36.

—— *Gregory the Great and his World* (Cambridge, 1997).

Martin, L., 'Homily on the Feast of St. Benedict Biscop by the Venerable Bede', *Vox Benedictina* 4.1 (1987), 81–92.

Martindale, J., 'The Kingdom of Aquitaine and the Carolingian *Fisc*', *Francia* 11 (1984), 136–7.

—— *Status, Authority and Regional Power* (Aldershot, 1997).

Mathews, T. F., *The Clash of Gods: A Reinterpretation of Early Christian Art*, 2nd edition (Princeton, 1999).

Matter, E. A., 'The Lamentations Commentaries of Hrabanus Maurus and Paschasius Radbertus', *Traditio* 38 (1982), 137–63.

—— *The Voice of My Beloved. The Song of Songs in Western Medieval Christianity* (Philadelphia, 1990).

—— 'The Apocalypse in Early Medieval Exegesis', in R. K. Emmerson and B. McGinn (eds), *The Apocalypse in the Middle Ages* (Ithaca, NY, 1992), 38–9.

Matthew, G., 'The Character of the Gallienic Renaissance', *JRS* 33 (1943), 65–70.

Maurin, L., 'Thuburbo Majus et la paix Vandale', *Mélanges d' archèologie et d' histoire offerts à Charles. Saumagne, Les Cahiers de Tunisie* 15 (1967), 225–54.

Mayr-Harting, H., *Ottonian Book Illumination: An Historical Study*, 2 vols (London, 1991).

—— 'Ruotger, Bruno and Cologne Cathedral Library', in L. Smith and B. Ward (eds), *Intellectual Life in the Middle Ages, Essays Presented to Margaret Gibson* (London, 1992), 1–14, 33–60.

—— 'Bede's Patristic Thinking as Historian', in A. Scharer and G. Scheibelreiter (eds), *Historiographie im frühen Mittelalter* (Vienna, 1994), 367–74.

—— 'Two Conversions to Christianity: the Bulgarians and the Anglo-Saxons', Stenton Lecture (Reading, 1994).

——, 'Charlemagne, the Saxons, and the Imperial Coronation of 800', *EHR* 444 (1996), 1113–33.

McClendon, C. B., *The Origins of Medieval Architecture: Building in Europe, A.D. 600–900* (New Haven, 2005).

McClure, J. 'Bede's Old Testament Kings', in D. Bullough and P. Wormald (eds), *Ideal and Reality in Frankish and Anglo-Saxon Society Presented to J. M. Wallace-Hadrill* (Oxford, 1983), 76–98.

McCone, K., *Pagan Past and Christian Present in Early Irish Literature* (Maynooth, 1990).

McCormick, M., 'The Liturgy of War in the Early Middle Ages: Crises, Litanies, and the Carolingian Monarchy', *Viator* 15 (1984), 1–23.

—— *Eternal Victory: Triumphal Rulership in Late Antiquity, Byzantium, and the Early Medieval West* (Cambridge, 1986).

—— 'Clovis at Tours, Byzantine Public Ritual and the Origins of Medieval Ruler Symbolism', in E. K. Chrysos and A. Schwarcz (eds), *Das Reich und die Barbaren* (Vienna, 1989), 155–80.

—— *Origins of the European Economy: Communications and Commerce, A.D. 300–900* (Cambridge, 2001).

—— Dutton, P. E., and Mayewski, P. A., 'Volcanoes and the Climate Forcing of Carolingian Europe, A.D. 750–950', *Speculum* 82 (2007), 865–95.

McGinn, B., *Visions of the End. Apocalyptic Traditions in the Middle Ages* (New York, 1979).

—— *Antichrist: Two Thousand Years of the Human Fascination with Evil* (New York, 2000).

McKitterick, R., *The Frankish Church and the Carolingian Reforms, 789–895* (London, 1977).

—— 'Charles the Bald (823–877) and his Library: the Patronage of Learning', *EHR* 95 (1980), 28–47.

—— *The Carolingians and the Written Word* (Cambridge, 1989).

—— (ed.), *The Uses of Literacy in Early Mediaeval Europe* (Cambridge, 1990).

—— 'Constructing the Past in the Early Middle Ages: The Case of the Royal Frankish Annals', *TRHS*, 6th series, 7 (1997), 101–30.

—— 'The Illusion of Royal Power in the Carolingian Annals', *EHR* 115 (2000), 1–20.

—— *History and Memory in the Carolingian World* (Cambridge, 2004).

—— *Perceptions of the Past in the Early Middle Ages* (Note Dame, IN, 2006).

McLynn, N. B., *Ambrose of Milan. Church and Court in a Christian Capital* (Berkeley, 1994).

Meeders, S., 'The early Irish Stowe Missal's Destination and Function', *EME* 13.2 (2005), 179–94.

Meens, R., 'Politics, Mirrors for Princes, and the Bible: Sins, Kings and the Well-being of the Realm', *EME* 7.3 (1998), 345–57.

Melzak, R., 'Antiquarianism and the Art of Metz', in R. Collins and P. Godman (eds), *Charlemagne's Heir: New Perspectives on the Reign of Louis the Pious (814–840)* (Oxford, 1990), 629–40.

Merrills, A. H., 'The Perils of Panegyric: The Lost Poem of Dracontius and its Consequences', in *idem, Vandals, Romans and Berbers: New Perspectives on Late Antique North Africa* (Aldershot, 2004), 145–6.

—— 'Vandals, Romans and Berbers: Understanding Late Antique North Africa', in *idem, Vandals, Romans and Berbers: New Perspectives on Late Antique North Africa* (Aldershot, 2004), 3–28.

—— (ed.), *Vandals, Romans and Berbers: New Perspectives on Late Antique North Africa* (Aldershot, 2004).

—— *History and Geography in Late Antiquity* (Cambridge, 2005).

Meyers, J. L., *L'Art de l'emprunt dans la poésie de Sedulius Scottus* (Paris, 1986).

Meyvaert, P., '"In the Footsteps of the Fathers": the Date of Bede's Thirty Questions on the Book of Kings to Nothelm', in W. E. Klingshirn and M. Vessey (eds), *The Limits of Ancient Christianity: Essays on Late Antique Thought and Culture in Honor of R. A. Markus* (Ann Arbor, MI, 1999), 267–86.

Miles, R., 'The *Anthologia Latina* and the Creation of Secular Space in Vandal Carthage', *Antiquité Tardive* 13 (Turnhout, 2005), 305–20.

Miller, E. P., 'The Politics of Imitating Christ: Christ the King and Christomimetic Rulership in Early Medieval Biblical Commentaries', unpublished Ph.D. (University of Virginia, 2001).

Mitchell, K. and Wood, I. N., *The World of Gregory of Tours* (Leiden, 2002).

Moore, M. E., 'La monarchie carolingienne et les anciens modèles irlandais', *Annales HSS* 51 (1996), 307–24.

Moore, R. I., 'Family, Community and Cult on the Eve of the Gregorian Reform', *TRHS*, 5th series, 30 (1980), 49–69.

—— *Theoderic in Italy* (Oxford, 1992).

Mordek, H., 'Karolingischen Kapitularien', in R. Kottje and H. Mordek (eds), *Überlieferung und Geltung normativer Texte des frühen und hohen Mittelalters*, Quellen und Forschungen zum Recht im Mittelalter 4 (Sigmaringen, 1986), 25–50.

Muhlberger, S., 'Eugippius and the Life of St. Severinus', *Medieval Prosopography* 17 (1996), 107–24.

Munitz, J. A., 'War and Peace Reflected in Some Byzantine Mirrors for Princes', in T. S. Miller and J. Nesbitt (eds), *Peace and War in Byzantium: Essays in Honor of George T. Dennis, S. J.* (Washington DC, 1995), 50–61.

Munzi, L., 'Compilazione e riuso in eta carolingia: il prologo poetica di Wigbodo', *Romano-barbarica* 12 (1992/3), 189–210.

Murray, A. C., *Germanic Kinship Structure: Studies in Law and Society in Antiquity and the Early Middle Ages* (Toronto, 1983).

—— 'From Roman to Frankish Gaul: *Centenarii* and *Centenae* in the Administration of the Frankish Kingdom', *Traditio* 44 (1988), 59–100.

—— 'Immunity, Nobility, and the Edict of Paris', *Speculum* 69.1 (1994), 18–39.

—— *Gregory of Tours. The Merovingians* (Toronto, 2006).

—— '*Pax et disciplina*: Roman Public Law and the Merovingian State', in T. F. X. Noble (ed.), *From Roman Provinces to Medieval Kingdoms* (London, 2006), 376–88.

Nees, L., *A Tainted Mantle. Hercules and the Classical Tradition at the Carolingian Court* (Philadephia, 1991).

Nelson, J. L., 'Kingship, Law and Liturgy in the Political Thought of Hincmar of Rheims', *EHR* 363 (1977), 241–79, Repr. in *eadem*, *P&R*, 133–71.

—— 'Inauguration Rituals', in P. Sawyer and I. N. Wood (eds), *Early Medieval Kingship* (Leeds, 1977), 50–71.

—— 'Public *Histories* and the Private History in the Work of Nithard', *Speculum* 60 (1985), 251–93.

—— '"A King across the Sea": Alfred in Continental Perspective', *TRHS*, 5th series, 36 (1986), 45–68.

—— *Politics and Ritual in Early Medieval Europe* (London, 1986).

—— 'The Earliest Surviving Royal *Ordo*: Some Liturgical and Historical Aspects', in J. L. Nelson (ed.), *Politics and Ritual in Early Medieval Europe* (London, 1986), 361–70.

—— 'Wealth and Wisdom: The Politics of Alfred the Great', in J. Rosenthal (ed.), *Kings and Kingship*, Center for Medieval and Early Renaissance Studies, State University of New York, Acta 11 (Binghamton, 1986), 31–52.

—— 'The Earliest Surviving Royal *Ordo*: Some Liturgical and Historical Aspects', in J. L. Nelson (ed.), *Politics and Ritual in Early Medieval Europe* (London, 1986), 341–60.

—— 'The Lord's Anointed and the People's Choice: Carolingian Royal Ritual', in D. Cannadine and S. Price (eds), *Rituals of Royalty. Power and Ceremonial in Traditional Societies* (Cambridge, 1987), 137–80.

—— 'Literacy in Carolingian Government', in R. McKitterick (ed.), *The Uses of Literacy in Early Mediaeval Europe* (Cambridge, 1990), 258–96.

—— 'The Last Years of Louis the Pious', in P. Godman and R. Collins (eds), *Charlemagne's Heir: New Perspectives on the Reign of Louis the Pious (814–840)* (Oxford, 1990), 147–59.

—— 'Charles le Chauve et les utilisations du savoir', in D. Iogna–Prat, C. Jeudy, and G. Lobrichon (eds), *L'école carolingienne d'Auxerre de Murethach à Remi, 830–908* (Paris, 1991), 37–54.

—— *Charles the Bald* (London, 1992).

—— 'The Intellectual in Politics: Context, Content and Authorship in the Capitulary of Coulaines, November 843', in L. Smith and B. Ward (eds), *Intellectual Life in the Middle Ages : Essays Presented to Margaret Gibson* (1992), 1–14.

—— 'The Political Ideas of Alfred of Wessex', in A. J. Duggan (ed.), *Kings and Kingship in Medieval Europe* (London, 1993), 125–58.

—— 'Kingship and Empire in the Carolingian World', in R. McKitterick (ed.), *Carolingian Culture: Emulation and Innovation* (Cambridge, 1993), 52–87.

—— Review of Head and Landes, *The Peace of God, Speculum* 69.1 (1994), 163–9.

—— 'Women at the Court of Charlemagne: A Case of Monstrous Regiment?' in J. Carmi Parsons (ed.), *Medieval Queenship* (Stroud, 1994), 43–61.

——, 'The Search for Peace in a Time of War: the Carolingian *Brüderkrieg*, 841–843', in J. Fried (ed.), *Träger und Instrumentarien des Friedens im hohen und späten Mittelalter*. VuF 42 (Sigmaringen, 1996), 87–114.

—— 'Kings with Justice, Kings without Justice: an Early Medieval Paradox', *La giustizia nell'Alto Medioevo (secoli IX–XI), Settimane di Studio* 44 (Spoleto, 1997), II, 797–826.

—— 'Early Medieval Rites of Queen-making and the Shaping of Medieval Queenship', in A. Duggan (ed.), *Medieval Queenship* (London, 1997), 301–15.

—— 'Violence in the Carolingian World and the Ritualization of Ninth-Century Warfare', in G. Halsall (ed.), *Violence and Society in the Early Medieval West* (Woodbridge, 1997), 90–107.

—— 'The Frankish Empire', in P. H. Sawyer (ed.), *The Oxford Illustrated History of the Vikings* (Oxford 1997), 134–55.

—— '"... *sicut olim gens Francorum... nunc gens Anglorum*": Fulk's Letter to Alfred Revisited', in J. Roberts, J. L. Nelson, with M. Godden (eds), *Alfred the Wise. Studies in Honour of Janet Bately on the Occasion of her Sixty-Fifth Birthday* (Cambridge, 1997), 135–44.

—— *Rulers and Ruling Families in Early Medieval Europe: Alfred, Charles the Bald and Others* (Aldershot, 1999).

—— 'Carolingian Royal Funerals', in F. Theuws and J. N. Nelson (eds), *Rituals of Power: From Late Antiquity to the Early Middle Ages* (Leiden, 2000), 131–84.

—— 'Good Kingship and Bad Kingship in the Early Middle Ages', *Haskins Society Journal* 8 (2000), 1–26.

—— 'The Voice of Charlemagne', in R. Gameson and H. Leyser (eds), *Belief and Culture: Studies in the Middle Ages. Studies Presented to Henry Mayr-Harting* (Oxford, 2001), 76–88.

—— 'Aachen as a Place of Power', in M. de Jong e van Rhijn and F. Theuws (eds), *Topographies of Power in The Early Middle Ages* (Leiden, 2001), 217–41.

—— 'England and the Continent in the Ninth Century: I, Ends and Beginnings', *TRHS*, 6th series, 12 (2002), 1–21.

—— 'England and the Continent in the Ninth Century: II, The Vikings and Others', *TRHS*, 6th series, 13 (2003), 1–28.

—— 'Review of Buc, *Dangers of Ritual*', *Speculum* 78.3 (2003), 847–51.

—— 'England and the Continent in the Ninth Century III: Rights and Rituals', *TRHS*, 6th series, 14 (2004), 1–24.

—— 'Gendering Courts in the Early Medieval West', in L. Brubaker and J. M. H. Smith (eds), *Gender in the Early Medieval World* (Cambridge, 2004), 185–97.

—— 'Presidential Address IV: Bodies and Minds', *TRHS*, 6th series, 15 (2005), 1–27.

—— 'Why Are There so Many Different Accounts of Charlemagne's Imperial Coronation?', in *eadem Courts, Elites, and Gendered Power in the Early Middle Ages. Charlemagne and Others* (Aldershot, 2007), XII, 1–27.

—— 'Charlemagne and Empire', in J. Davis and M. McCormick (eds), *The Long Morning of Medieval Europe. New Directions in Early Medieval Studies* (Aldershot, 2008), 223–34.

—— 'The First Use of the Second Anglo-Saxon *Ordo*', in J. Barrow and A. Wareham (eds), *Myth, Rulership, Church and Charters. Essays in Honour of Nicholas Brooks* (Aldershot, 2008), 117–26.

Neri, V., 'La legittimità politica del regno teodericiano nell'*Anonymi Valesiani Pars Posterior*', in A. Carile (ed.), *Teoderico e i Goti tra Oriente e Occidente* (Ravenna, 1995), 313–40.

Ní Dhonnchadha, M., 'The *Lex Innocentium*: Adomnán's Law for Women, Clerics and Youths, 697 A.D.', in M. O'Dowd and S. Wichert (eds), *Chattel, Servant or Citizen: Women's Status in Church, State and Society* (Belfast, 1995), 58–69.

—— 'Birr and the Law of the Innocents', in T. O'Loughlin (ed.), *Adomnán at Birr, AD 697. Essays in the Commemoration of the Law of the Innocents* (Dublin, 2001), 13–32.

Nicol, D. M., 'Byzantine Political Thought', *CHMPT*, 51–79.

Niederkorn-Bruck, M., Scharer, A., and Störmer, W., *Erzbischof Arn von Salzburg*, Veröffentlichungen des Instituts für Österreichische Geschichtsforschung 40 (Vienna, 2004).

Nikolov, S., 'The Pagan Bulgars and Byzantine Christianity in the Eighth and Ninth Centuries', *Journal of Historical Sociology* 13.3 (2000), 325–64.

Noble, T. F. X., 'The Monastic Ideal as a Model of Empire: the Case of Louis the Pious', *RB* 86 (1976), 235–50.

—— *The Republic of St. Peter: the Birth of the Papal State, 680–825* (Philadelphia, 1984).

—— 'From Brigandage to Justice: Charlemagne, 785–794', in C. Chazelle (ed.), *Literacy, Politics, and Artistic Innovation in the Early Medieval West: Symposium on Early Medieval Culture: Papers* (London, 1992), 49–75.

—— 'Tradition and Learning in Search of Ideology', in R. E. Sullivan (ed.), ' *The Gentle Voices of Teachers': Aspects of Learning in the Carolingian Age* (Columbus, OH, 1995), 227–60.

—— 'Lupus of Ferrières in his Carolingian Context', in A. C. Murray (ed.), *After Rome's Fall: Narrators and Sources of Early Medieval History: Essays Presented to Walter Goffart* (Toronto, 1998), 232–50.

—— *Images, Iconoclasm, and the Carolingians* (Philadelphia, 2009).

Noreaña, C. F., 'Medium and Message in Vespasian's *Templum Pacis*', *Memoirs of the American Academy in Rome* 48 (2003), 25–43.

Ó Corráin, D., 'Irish Law and Canon Law', in P. Ní Chatháin and M. Richter (eds), *Irland und Europa: die Kirche im Frühmittelalter* (Stuttgart, 1984), 157–66.

Oexle, O. G., 'Die Karolinger und die Stadt des heilige Arnulf', *FmSt* 1 (1967), 250–364.

O'Loughlin, T., (ed.) *Adomnán at Birr, AD 697. Essays in the Commemoration of the Law of the Innocents* (Dublin, 2001).

Opfermann, B., *Die liturgischen Herrscherakklamationen im Sacrum Imperium des Mittelalters* (Münster, 1953).

Otten, W., 'The Texture of Tradition: The Role of the Church Fathers in Carolingian Theology', in I. Backus (ed.), *The Reception of the Church Fathers in the West: From the Carolinguns to the Maurists* (Leiden, 1997), I, 1–51.

Overing, G., 'The Women of Beowulf', in P. Baker (ed.), *The Beowulf Reader* (New York, 2001), 219–60.

Oxford Dictionary of Byzantium, ed. A. P. Kazhdan, 3 vols (Oxford).

Palmer, A. with Rodley, L., 'The Inauguration Anthem of Hagia Sophia in Edessa: A New Edition and Translation with Historical and Architectural Notes and a Comparison with a Contemporary Constantinopolitan Kontakion', *BMGS* 12 (1988), 117–67.

Parker, K. I., 'Solomon as Philosopher King: the Nexus of Law and Wisdom in I Kings 1–11', *Journal for the Study of the Old Testament* 53 (1992), 75–91.

Patze, H., '*Iustitia* bei Nithard', *Festschrift für H. Heimpel zum 70. Geburtstag am 19. September 1971* (Göttingen, 1972), 147–65.

Paxton, F., 'History, Historians, and the Peace of God', in T. Head and R. Landes (eds), *The Peace of God: Social Violence and Religious Response in France around the Year 1000* (Ithaca, NY, 1992), 21–40.

—— 'Power and the Power to Heal. The Cult of St Sigismund of Burgundy', *EME* 2.2 (1993), 95–110.

—— 'Liturgy and Healing in an Early Medieval Saint's Cult: the Mass *In honore sancti Sigismundi* for the Cure of Fevers', *Traditio* 49 (1994), 23–43.

Pearson, B. A., 'Melchizedek in Early Judaism, Christianity and Gnosticism', in M. E. Stone and T. A. Bergren (eds), *Biblical Figures Outside the Bible* (Harrisburg, PA, 1998), 176–202.

Penndorf, U., *Das Problem der 'Reichseinheitsidee' nach der Teilung von Verdun (843). Untersuchungen zu den späten Karolingern* (Munich, 1974).

Perrin, M., 'Le représentation figurée de César-Louis le Pieux chez Raban Maur en 835: religion et idéologie', *Francia* 42.1 (1997), 39–64.

Peters, E., *The Shadow King: Rex inutilis in Medieval Law and Literature, 751–1327* (New Haven, 1970).

Phillips, L. E., 'The Kiss of Peace and the Opening Greeting of the Pre-Anaphoral Dialogue', *Studia Liturgica* 23.2 (1993), 177–86.

Pietri, C., 'Concordia apostolorum et *renovatio urbis* (culte des martyrs et propagande pontificale)', *Mélanges d'Archéologie et d'Histoire de l'École francaise de Rome* 73 (1961), 275–322.

Pohl, W., *Kingdoms of the Empire: The Integration of Barbarians in Late Antiquity* (Leiden, 1997).

—— 'The Empire and the Lombards: Treaties and Negotiations in the Sixth Century', in W. Pohl (ed.), *Kingdoms of the Empire: The Integration of Barbarians in Late Antiquity* (Leiden, 1997), 75–134.

—— 'Justinian and the Barbarian Kingdoms', in M. Maas (ed.), *The Cambridge Companion to the Age of Justinian* (Cambridge, 2005), 448–76.

Polomé, E. C., 'À propos de la déesse Nerthus', *Latomus* 13 (1954), 167–200.

Pontal, O., *Histoire des conciles mérovingiens* (Paris, 1989).

Pössel, C., 'The Magic of Ritual', *EME* 17.2 (2009), 111–25.

Poupardin, R., *Le royaume de Bourgogne (888–1038). Étude sur les origines du royaume d'Arles* (Paris, 1907).

Pratt, D. R., 'The Illnesses of King Alfred the Great', *ASE* 30 (2001), 39–90.

—— 'Persuasion and Invention at the Court of King Alfred the Great', in C. Cubitt (ed.), *Court Culture in the Early Middle Ages: The Proceedings of the First Alcuin Conference, Studies in the Early Middle Ages* 3 (Turnhout, 2003), 189–221.

—— *The Political Thought of King Alfred the Great* (Cambridge, 2007).

Prou, M., *Catalogue des monnaies français de la Bibliothèque Nationale: Les Monnaies Mérovingiennes* (Paris, 1892).

Rakob, F., 'Die Urbanisierung des Nördlichen Marsfeldes: Neue Forschungen im Areal des Horologium Augusti', in C. Pietri (ed.), *L'Urbs. Espace urbain et histoire (Ier siècle av. J.-C.- IIIe siècle ap. J.-C.): actes du colloque international organisé par le Centre national de la recherche scientifique et l'École française de Rome (Rome, 8–12 mai 1985)* (Rome, 1987), 687–712.

Ranieri, I., 'I modelli formali del "Carmen In Honorem Hludowici Caesaris" di Ermoldo Nigello', *Acme. Annali della Facoltà di Lettere e Filosofia dell'Università degli Studi di Milano* 36 (1983), 161–214.

Ratkowitsch, C., *Karolus Magnus—Alter Aeneas, Alter Martinus, Alter Iustinus. Zu Intention und Datierung des 'Aachener Karlsepos',* Wiener Studien. Beiheft 24, Arbeiten zur mittel- und neulateinischen Literatur 4 (Vienna, 1997).

Rehak, P., *Imperium and Cosmos. Augustus and the Northern Campus Martius* (Madison, WI, 2006).

Renna, T., 'The Idea of Peace in the West, 500–1150', *JMH* 2.6 (1980), 143–68.

—— 'Thoughts of Peace and Not of War', *Lutheran Theological Journal* 19 (1985), 65–72.

—— 'Zion and Jerusalem in the Psalms', in F. Van Fleteren and J. C. Schnaubelt (eds), *Augustine: Biblical Exegete* (New York, 2001), 279–98.

—— *Jerusalem in Early Medieval Thought, 400–1300* (Lewiston, 2002).

Reuter, T., 'Plunder and Tribute in the Carolingian Empire', *TRHS*, 5th series, 35 (1977), 75–94.

—— 'The End of Carolingian Military Expansion', in P. Godman and R. Collins (eds), *Charlemagne's Heir: New Perspectives on the Reign of Louis the Pious (814–840)* (Oxford, 1990), 391–405.

—— 'Pre-Gregorian Mentalities', *Journal of Ecclesiastical History* 45 (1994), 465–74.

—— (ed.), *Alfred the Great: Papers from the Eleventh-Centenary Conferences* (Aldershot, 2003).

—— 'The Insecurity of Travel in the Early and High Middle Ages: Criminals, Victims and their Medieval and Modern Observers', in J. L. Nelson (ed.), *Medieval Polities and Modern Mentalities* (Cambridge, 2006), 38–71.

—— 'Contextualizing Canossa: Excommunication, Penance, Surrender, Reconciliation', in J. L. Nelson (ed.), *Medieval Polities and Modern Mentalities* (Cambridge, 2006), 147–66.

—— '*Regemque, quem in Francia pene perdidit, in patria magnifice recepit*: Ottonian Ruler Representation in Synchronic and Diachronic Comparison', in J. L. Nelson (ed.), *Medieval Polities and Modern Mentalities* (Cambridge, 2006), 127–46.

Revel-Neher, E., '*Antiquus populus, novus populus*: Jerusalem and the People of God in the Germigny-des-Prés Carolingian Mosaic', in B. Kühnel (ed.), *The Real and Ideal Jerusalem in Jewish, Christian and Islamic Art: Studies in Honor of Bezalel Narkiss on the Occasion of his Seventieth Birthday* (Jerusalem, 1998), 54–66.

Reviron, J., *Les idées politico-religieuses d'un évêque du IXe siècle; Jonas d'Orléans et son 'De institutione regia'* (Paris, 1930).

Reydellet, M., *La royauté dans la littérature latine, de Sidoine Apollinaire à Isidore de Séville* (Rome, 1981).

—— 'La Bible miroir des princes, du IVe au VIIe siècle', in J. Fontaine and C. Pietri (eds), *Le monde latin antique et la Bible de tons les temps 2* (Paris, 1985), 431–53.

—— 'Théoderic et la *civilitas*', in A. Carile (ed.), *Teoderico e i Goti tra Oriente e Occidente* (Ravenna, 1995), 285–96.

Reynaud, J.-F., *Lugdunum christianum, Lyon du VIe au VIIIe s., topographie, nécropoles et édifices religieux* (Paris, 1998).

Reynolds, L. D. (ed.), *Texts and Transmissions. A Survey of the Latin Classics* (Oxford, 1983).

Riché, P., *Education and Culture in the Barbarian West, Sixth through Eighth Centuries*, trans. J. Contreni (Columbia, 1975).

—— 'La Bible et la vie politique dans le haut Moyen Âge', in *idem* and G. Labrichor (eds), *Le Moyen Âge et la Bible* (Paris, 1984), 385–400.

Rio, A., 'Freedom and Unfreedom in Early Medieval Francia: the Evidence of the Legal Formularies', *Past and Present* 193 (2006), 7–40.

—— 'High and Low: Ties of Dependence in the Frankish Kingdoms', *TRHS* 6.18 (2008), 43–68.

Roberts, M., 'Rhetoric and Poetic Imitation in Avitus' Account of the Crossing of the Red Sea (*De Spiritalis Historiae Gestis*, 5.371–702)', *Traditio* 39 (1983), 29–80.

—— 'Venantius Fortunatus' Elegy on the Death of Galswintha (*Carm.* 6.5)', in R. W. Matthisen and D. Shanzer (eds), *Society and Culture in Late Antique Gaul: Revisiting the Sources* (Aldershot, 2001), 298–312.

Rondet, H., 'Pax, tranquilitas ordinis', *La Ciudad de Dios* 167.2 (1956), 343–65.

Rohr, C., *Der Theoderich-Pangyricus Des Ennodius, MGH SuT* 12 (Hanover, 1995).

Rösch, G., *Onoma Basileias: Studien zum offiziellen Gebrauch der Kaisertitel in spätantiker und frühbyzantinischer Zeit*, Byzantina Vindobonensia 10 (Vienna, 1978).

Rosenblum, M., *Luxorius: A Latin Poet among the Vandals* (New York, 1961).

Rota, S., *Panegirico del clementissimo re Teoderico (opusc. 1)*, Biblioteca di Cultura Romanobarbarica 6 (Rome, 2002).

Rousseau, P., 'Visigothic Migration and Settlement, 376–418: Some Excluded Hypotheses', *Historia* 41 (1992), 345–61.

Rushworth, A., 'From Azuges to Rustamids: State Formation and Regional Identity in the Pre-Saharan Zone', in A. H. Merrills (ed.), *Vandals, Romans and Berbers: New Perspectives on Late Antique North Africa* (Aldershot, 2004), 77–98.

Saitta, B., *La civilitas di Teoderico. Rigore amministrativo, 'Tolleranza' religiosa e recupero dell'antico nell'Italia ostrogota* (Rome, 1994).

Saumagne, C., 'La paix vandale. À propos de documents relatifs à la domination vandale en Afrique', *Revue Tunisienne* (1930), 167–84, reprinted in *Les Cuhiers de Tunisie* 10 (1962), 417–25.

Shanzer, D., 'A New Edition of Sedulius Scottus's *Carmina*', *Medium Aevum*, 63 (1994), 104–17.

—— 'Two Clocks and a Wedding: Theodoric's Diplomatic Relations with the Burgundians', *Romanobarbarica* 14 (1996–7), 225–58.

Scharer, A., 'König Alfreds Hof und die Geschichtsschreibung. Einige überlegungen zur Angelsachsenchronik und zu Assers *De rebus gestis Aelfredi*', in A. Scharer and G. Scheibelreiter (eds), *Historiographie im frühen Mittelalter* (Vienna, 1994), 443–58.

—— 'The Writing of History at King Alfred's Court', *EME* 5.2 (1996), 177–206.

—— *Herrschaft und Repräsentation. Studien zur Hofkultur König Alfreds des Großen* (Vienna, 2000).

Scharf, J., 'Studien zu Smaragdus und Jonas', *DA* 17 (1961), 333–84.

Scharff, T., *Die Kämpfe der Herrscher und der Heiligen: Krieg und Historische Erinnerung in der Karolingerzeit* (Darmstadt, 2002).

Scheibe, F.-C., 'Alcuin und die *Admonitio Generalis*', *DA* 14 (1958), 221–9.

Scheja, G., 'Hagia Sophia und Templum Salomonis', *Istanbuler Mitteilungen* 12 (1962), 44–58.

Schieffer, R., 'Der Weg zur Kaiserkrönung 800', *Zeitschrift des Aachener Geschichtsvereins*, 104–5 (2002/3), 11–23.

—— 'Karl der Große, Eirene und der Ursprung des westlichen Kaisertums', in W. Pohl (ed.), *Die Suche nach den Ursprüngen. Von der Bedeutung des frühen Mittelalters* (Vienna, 2004), 151–8.

Schlesinger, W., 'Kaisertum und Reichsteilung: Zur *Divisio regnorum* von 806', in R. Dietrich and G. Oesreich (eds), *Forschungen zu Staat und Verfassung, Festgabe für Fritz Hartung* (Berlin, 1958), 9–51.

Schmid, K., 'Unerforschte Quellen aus quellenarmer Zeit. Zur *amicitia* zwischen Heinrich I. und dem westfränkischen König Robert im Jahre 923', *Francia* 12 (1984), 119–47.

Schmitz, G., 'The Capitulary Legislation of Louis the Pious', in R. Collins and P. Godman (eds), *Charlemagne's Heir: New Perspectives on the Reign of Louis the Pious (814–840)* (Oxford, 1990), 425–36.

Schneider, R., *Brüdergemeine und Schwurfreundschaft. Der Auflösungsprozeß des Karolingerreiches im Spiegel der caritas-Terminologie in den Verträgen der karlingischen Teilkönige des 9. Jahrhunderts* (Lübeck, 1964).

Schnith, K., 'Recht und Friede. Zum Königsgedanken im Umkreis Heinrichs III', *HJ* 81 (1962), 22–57.

Schork, R. J., *Sacred Song from the Byzantine Pulpit: Romanos the Melodist* (Gainesville, FL, 1995).

Schramm, P. E., *Die zeitgenössischen Bildnisse Karls des Grossen*, Beitragen zur kultur-geschichte des Mittelaters und Renaissance (Leipzig, 1928).

—— 'Das alte und das neue Testament in der Staatslehre und Staatssymbolik des Mittelalters', *Settimane de Studio* (Spoleto, 1963), 229–56.

—— 'Karl der Große als Kaiser im Lichte der Staatssymbolik (800–814)', in *idem*, Kaiser, Könige und Päpste: Gesammelte Aufsätze zur Geschichte des Mittelalters (Stuttgart, 1969), I, 264–302.

—— *Die deutschen Kaiser und Könige in Bildern ihrer Zeit, 751–1190*, rev. F. Mütherich et al., 2 vols (Munich, 1983).

—— and F. Mütherich, *Denkmale der deutschen Könige und Kaiser*, 2 vols (Munich, 1962).

Schreiner, K., 'Gerichtigkeit und Frieden haben sich geküßt (Ps. 84, 11): Friedensstiftung durch symbolisches Handeln', *TuI*, Johannes Fried (ed.), Vorträge und Forschungen 2/3 (Sigmeringen, 1996), 37–86.

Schütte, G., 'The Cult of Nerthus', *Saga Book of the Viking Society for Northern Research*, 8 (1913–14), 29–43.

Schwarz, A., 'The Settlement of the Vandals in North Africa', in A. H. Merrills (ed.), *Vandals, Romans and Berbers: New Perspectives on Late Antique North Africa* (Aldershot, 2004), 49–59.

Semmler, J., 'Das Klosterwesen im bayerischen Raum vom 8. bis zum 10. Jahrhundert', in E. Boshof and H. Wolff, (eds), *Das Christentum im bairischen Raum: Von den Anfängen bis ins 11. Jahrhundert*, Passauer Historische Forschungen 8 (Cologne, 1994), 291–324.

—— *Die Dynastiewechsel von 751 und die fränkische Königssalbung* (Düsseldorf, 2003).

Ševčenko, I., 'The Greek Source of the Inscription on Solomon's Chalice in the *Vita Constantini*', in *To Honor Roman Jakobson. Essays on the Occasion of his Seventieth Birthday* (The Hague and Paris, 1967), III, 1806–17.

Sheehy, M. P., 'The *Collectio Canonum Hibernensis*—a Celtic Phenomenon', in H. Löwe (ed.), *Die Iren und Europa im früheren Mittelalter* (Stuttgart, 1982), I, 525–35.

Shepard, J., 'Symeon of Bulgaria—Peacemaker', *Annuaire de l'Université de Sofia 'St. Kliment Ohridski'* 83 (1989), 9–48.

—— 'Manners maketh Romans? Young Barbarians at the Emperor's Court', in E. Jeffreys (ed.), *Byzantine Style, Religion and Civilization. In Honour of Sir Steven Runciman* (Cambridge, 2006), 135–58.

Shimahara, S., 'Peut-on parler de millénarisme à l'époque carolingienne? l'apport de quelques sources exégétiques', *Temas mediev* 14 (2006), 99–138.

Shippey, T. A., *Poems of Wisdom and Learning in Old English* (Cambridge, 1976).

Simon, E., 'Eirene und Pax: Friedensgöttinnen in der Antike', *Sitzungsberichte der Wissenschaften Gesellschaft an der Johann-Wolfgang-Goethe-Universität Frankfurt am Main* 24 (1988), 55–69.

Simpson, D., '*Proverbia Grecorum*', *Traditio* 43 (1987), 1–22.

—— 'Sedulius and the Latin Classics', in B. T. Hudson and V. Ziegler (eds), *Crossed Paths: Methodological Approaches to the Celtic Aspect of the European Middle Ages* (Lanham, MD, 1991), 25–38.

Sklute, L., '*Freoðuwebbe* in Old English Poetry', *Neuphilologische Mitteilungen* 71.4 (1970), 534–410.

Smalley, B., (ed.), *Trends in Medieval Political Thought* (Oxford, 1965).

Smith, J. M. H., *Early Medieval Rome and the Christian West: Essays in Honour of Donald A. Bullough* (Leiden, 2000).

Souçek, P., 'The Temple of Solomon in Islamic Art and Legend', in J. Gutmann (ed.), *The Temple of Solomon: Archaeological Fact and Medieval Tradition in Christian, Islamic, and Jewish Art* (Missoula, MT, 1976), 73–123.

Spörl, J., 'Augustinus - Schöpfer einer Staatslehrer?' *HJ* 74 (1955), 62–78.

—— '*Pie rex caesarque future!* Beiträge zum hochmittelalterlichen Kaisergedanken', in K. Lazarowich and W. Kron (eds), *Unterscheidung und Bewahrung, Festschrift für H. Kunisch* (Berlin, 1961), 331–53.

Sprengler, A., 'Die Gebete der Krönungsordines Hinkmars von Reims für Karl den Kahlen als König von Lothringen und für Ludwig den Stammler', *ZfKG* 53 (1950/1), 245–67.

Stafford, P., *Queens, Concubines and Dowagers. The King's Wife in the Early Middle Ages* (Athens, GA, 1983).

—— 'The Laws of Cnut and the History of Anglo-Saxon Royal Promises', *ASE* 10 (1983), 173–90.

Stancliffe, C., 'Red, White and Blue Martyrdom', in R. McKitterick, D. Whitelock, and D. Dumville (eds), *Ireland in Early Medieval Europe. Studies in Memory of Kathleen Hughes* (Cambridge, 1982), 21–47.

—— 'Kings who Opted Out', in D. Bullough and P. Wormald (eds), *Ideal and Reality in Frankish and Anglo-Saxon Society Presented to J. M Wallace-Hadrill* (Oxford, 1983), 154–76.

Stanley, E. G., 'On the Laws of King Alfred: the End of the Preface and the Beginning of the Laws', in J. Roberts, J. L. Nelson, and M. Godden (eds), *Alfred the Wise. Studies in Honour of Janet Bately on the Occasion of her Sixty-fifth Birthday* (Cambridge, 1997), 211–21.

Staubach, N., 'Sedulius Scottus und die Gedichte des Codex Bernensis 363', *FmSt* 20 (1986), 549–98.

—— *Rex Christianus: Hofkultur und Herrschaftspropaganda im Reich Karls Des Kahlen - Teil II: Grundlegung der 'religion royale'*, Pictura et Poesis, II/2 (Cologne, Weimar, and Vienna, 1993).

—— 'Die Rätsel des Sedulius Scottus. Bemerkungen zur Neuausgabe seiner Carmina', *Francia* 21.1 (1994), 213–20.

Steger, H., *David Rex et Propheta: König David als Vorbildliche Verkörperung des Herrschers und Dichters im Mittelalter, Nach Bilddarstellungen des Achten bis Zwölften Jahrhunderts*, Erlanger Buträge zur Sprach und Kunstwissenschaft 6 (Nuremberg, 1961).

Stephenson, P., *Byzantium's Balkan Frontier. A Political Study of the Northern Balkans, 900–1024* (Cambridge, 2000).

Stocking, R. L., *Bishops, Councils, and Consensus in the Visigothic Kingdom, 589–633* (Ann Arbor, MI, 2000).

Stoclet, A., 'From Baghdād to Beowulf: Eulogising "Imperial" Capitals East and West in the Mid-Eighth Century', *Proceedings of the Royal Irish Academy* 105.4 (2005), 151–95.

Story, J., 'Cathwulf, Kingship, and the Royal Abbey of Saint-Denis', *Speculum* 74 (1999), 1–20.

—— *Carolingian Connections. Anglo-Saxon England and Carolingian Francia, c. 750–870* (Aldershot, 2003).

Story, J. (ed.), *Charlemagne. Empire and Society* (Manchester, 2005).

Stroheker, K., *Der Senatorische Adel im Spätantike Gallien* (Tübingen, 1948).

Sullivan, R. E., *The Coronation of Charlemagne. What did it Signify?* (Boston, 1959).

—— 'Khan Boris and the Conversion of Bulgaria: a Case Study of the Impact of Christianity on a Barbarian Society', *Studies in Medieval and Renaissance History*, 3 (1966), 55–139.

Taft, R. F., 'The Dialogue before the Anaphora in the Byzantine Eucharistic Liturgy, I: The Opening Greeting', *Orientalia Christiana Periodica* 52 (1986), 299–324.

Tammasia, N., 'Sulla seconda parte dell'Anonimo Valesiano', *Archivio Storico Italiano* 71.2 (1913), 3–22.

Theuws, F., 'Introduction: Rituals in Transforming Societies', in F. Theuws and J. L. Nelson (eds), *Rituals of Power: From Late Antiquity to the Early Middle Ages* (Leiden, 2000), 1–15.

Throntveit, M. A., 'The Relationship of Hezekiah to David and Solomon in the Books of Chronicles', in S. L. McKenzie, G. N. Knoppers, and M. P. Graham (eds), *The Chronicler as Theologian. Essays in Honour of Ralph W. Klein* (London, 2003), 105–21.

Tiralla, H., *Das augustinsiche Idealbild der christlichen Obrigkeit als Quelle der 'Fürsten-spiegel' des Sedulius Scottus und Hincmar von Reims* (Greifswald, 1916).

Tougher, S., 'The Wisdom of Leo VI', in P. Magdalino (ed.), *New Constantines: The Rhythm of Imperial Renewal in Byzantium, 4th–13th Centuries* (Aldershot, 1994), 171–80.

—— *The Reign of Leo VI (886–912): Politics and People* (Leiden, 1997).

Traube, L., *O Roma nobilis. Philologische Untersuchungen aus dem Mittelalter*, Abhandlun-gen der Philosophisch-Philologischen Klasse der Königlich Bayerischen Akademie der Wissenschaften 19 (1891).

Treitinger, O., *Die oströmische Kaiser- und Reichsidee nach ihrer Gestaltung im höfischen Zeremoniell*, 2nd edition (Darmstadt, 1956).

Tricou, J., 'Légendes et symboles chrétiens des monnaies burgondes', *Studi di Antichità cristiana* 26 (1965), 551–5.

Trilling, R., 'Sovereignty and Social Order: Archbishop Wulfstan and the *Institutes of Polity*', in J. Ott and A. Trumbore Jones (eds), *The Bishop Reformed: Studies of Episcopal Power and Culture in the Central Middle Ages* (Aldershot, 2007), 58–85.

Tsirpanlis, C., 'The Imperial Coronation and Theory in *De cerimoniis aulae Byzantinae* of Constantine VII Porphyrogennitus', *Kleronomia* 4 (1972), 63–91.

Ullmann, W., *The Carolingian Renaissance and the Idea of Kingship* (London, 1969).

Unterkircher, F., *Die Glossen des Psalters von Mondsee (vor 788), Montpellier, Faculté de Médecine, MS 409 Spicitegium Friburgense* 20 (Freiburg, 1974).

Van Acker, L., 'Notice sur le poème rythmique *Agobardo pax sit*', *RB* 88.3–4 (1978), 291–5.

Valvirde Castro, M. R. V., *Ideología, simbolismo y ejercicio del poder real en la monarquía visigoda: un proceso de cambio* (Salamanca, 2000).

Voss, I., *Herrschertreffen im frühen und hohen Mittelalter. Untersuchungen zu den Begegnungen der ostfränkischen und westfränkischen Herrscher im 9. und 10. Jahrhundert sowie der deutschen und französichen Könige vom 11. bis 13. Jahrhundert* (Cologne, 1987).

Wadle, E., 'Heinrich IV. und die deutsche Friedensbewegung', in J. Fleckenstein (ed.), *Investiturstreit und Reichsverfassung, VuF* 17 (Sigmaringen, 1973), 141–73.

Walbank, F. W., 'Monarchies and Monarchic Ideas', in R. Ling (ed.), *New Cambridge Ancient History 7.1: The Hellenistic World to the Coming of the Romans* (Cambridge, 1984), 62–100.

Wald, E. T. D., *The Stuttgart Psalter, Biblia Folio 23*, Württembergische Landesbibliothek, Stuttgart (Princeton, 1930).

Wallace-Hadrill, A., 'The Emperor and His Virtues', *Historia* 30 (1981), 298–323.

—— 'Time for Augustus: Ovid, Augustus, and the *Fasti*', in P. Hardie, M. Whitby, and M. Whitby (eds), *Homo Viator: Classical Studies for John Bramble* (Bristol, 1987), 221–30.

Wallace-Hadrill, J. M., *Early Germanic Kingship in England and on the Continent* (Oxford, 1971).

—— 'The *Via Regia* of the Carolingian Age', in *idem, Early Medieval History*, (Oxford, 1975), 181–201.

—— 'Gregory of Tours and Bede: their Views on the Personal Qualities of Kings', in *idem, Early Medieval History* (Oxford, 1975), 96–114.

—— 'War and Peace in the Early Middle Ages', in *idem, Early Medieval History* (Oxford, 1975) 19–38.

—— 'Charles the Bald: A Carolingian Renaissance Prince', *PBA* 64 (London, 1978), 155–84.

—— *The Frankish Church* (Oxford, 1983).

Wallach, L., *Alcuin and Charlemagne: Studies in Carolingian History and Literature*, 2nd edition (Ithaca, NY, 1968).

Walsh, M. M., 'The Baptismal Flood in the Old English *Andreas*: Liturgical and Typological Depths', *Traditio* 33 (1977), 137–58.

Ward, P. L., 'An Early Version of the Anglo-Saxon Coronation Ceremony', *EHR* 57 (1942), 345–61.

Warner, D. A., 'The Cult of Saint Maurice: Ritual, Politics and Political Symbolism in Ottonian Germany', unpublished Ph.D. (UCLA, 1989).

—— 'Thietmar of Merseburg on Rituals of Kingship', *Viator* 26 (1995), 53–76.

—— 'Ideal and Action in the Reign of Otto III', *JMH* 25 (1999), 1–18.

—— 'Ritual and Memory in the Ottonian Reich: The Ceremony of *Adventus*', *Speculum* 76.2 (2001), 255–83.

—— 'The Representation of Empire: Otto I at Ravenna', in S. MacLean and B. K. U. Weiler (eds), *Representations of Power in Medieval Germany, 800–1500* (Turnhout, 2006), 121–40.

Watkins, C., '*Is tre fir flathemon*: Marginalia to *Audacht Morainn*', *Ériu* 30 (1979), 181–98.

Wattenbach, W. and Levison, W., *Deutschlands Geschichtsquellen im Mittelalter, Vorzeit und Karolinger*, 6 vols (Weimar, 1952–90).

Webster, L., '*Aedificia nova*: Treasures of Alfred's Reign', in T. Reuter (ed.), *Alfred the Great* (Aldershot, 2003), 79–103.

Welsh, A., 'Branwen, *Beowulf*, and the Tragic Peaceweaver Tale', *Viator* 22 (1991), 1–13.

Werner, K.-F., '*Hludovicus Augustus*: Gouverner l'empire chrétien – Idées et réalités', in P. Godman and R. Collins (eds), *Charlemagne's Heir: New Perspectives on the Reign of Louis the Pious (814–840)* (Oxford, 1990), 3–124.

Whitby, M., 'Byzantine Diplomacy: Good Faith, Trust and Co-operation in International Relations in Late Antiquity', in Philip de Souza and John France (eds), *War and Peace in Ancient and Medieval History* (Cambridge, 2008), 120–40.

Whitelock, D., 'The Prose of Alfred's Reign', in E. G. Stanley (ed.), *Continuations and Beginnings: Studies in Old English Literature* (London, 1966), 67–103.

—— 'Wulfstan *Cantor* and Anglo-Saxon Law', in A. H. Orrick (ed.), *Nordica et Anglica. Studies in Honour of Stéfan Einarsson* (The Hague, 1968), 83–92.

—— *From Bede to Alfred: Studies in Early Anglo-Saxon Literature and History* (Aldershot, 1980).

Wickham, C., *Framing the Early Middle Ages: Europe and the Mediterranean, 400–800* (Oxford, 2006).

Wiedemann, T. E. J., 'Between Men and Beasts: Barbarians in Ammianus Marcellinus', in J. D. Smart, I. S. Moxon, and A. J. Woodman (eds), *Past Perspectives. Studies in Greek and Roman Historical Writing* (Cambridge, 1986), 189–201.

Wielers, M., 'Zwischenstaatliche Beziehungsformen im frühen Mittelalter (Pax, Foedus, Amicitia, Fraternitas)', Habilitationsschrift (Münster, 1959).

Wilken, R. L., *The Spirit of Early Christian Thought: Seeking the Face of God* (New Haven, 2003).

Wilson, E., 'The Blood Wrought Peace: A Girardian Reading of *Beowulf*', *English Language Notes* 34 (1996), 7–30.

Wolfram, H., *Intitulatio* II (Wien, 1967).

—— *Conrad II, 990–1039. Emperor of Three Kingdoms*, trans. D. A. Kaiser (University Park, PA 2006).

—— and Schwarcz, A., *Annerkennung und Integration: Zu den wirtschaftlichen Grundlagen der Völkerwanderungszeit 400–600: Berichte des Symposions der Komission für Frühmittelalterforschung 7. bis 9. Mai 1986 Stift Zwettl, Niederösterreich* (Vienna, 1988).

Wood, I. N., 'Kings, Kingdoms and Consent', in I. N. Wood and P. Sawyer (eds), *Early Medieval Kingship* (Leeds, 1977), 6–29.

—— 'Ethnicity and the Ethnogenesis of the Burgundians', in H. Wolfram and W. Pohl (eds), *Typen der Ethnogenese unter besonderer Berüksichtigung der Bayern* (Vienna, 1990), 53–69.

—— 'The Code in Merovingian Gaul', in J. Harries and I. N. Wood (eds), *The Theodosian Code*, (Ithaca, 1993), 161–77.

—— *The Merovingian Kingdoms, 450–751* (London, 1994).

—— 'Avitus of Vienne, the Augustinian Poet', in R. W. Mathisen and D. Shanzer (eds), *Society and Culture in Late Antique Gaul: Revisiting the Sources* (Aldershot, 2001), 263–77.

—— '*Gentes*, Kings and Kingdoms—The Emergence of States: the Kingdom of the Gibichungs', in J. Jarnut, H.-W. Goetz, and W. Pohl (eds), *Regna and Gentes: The Relationship Between Late Antique and Early Medieval Peoples and Kingdoms in the Transformation of the Roman World*, TRW 13 (Leiden, 2003), 243–69.

—— 'Liturgy in the Rhône Valley and the Bobbio Missal', in Y. Hen and R. Meens (eds), *The Bobbio Missal: Liturgy and Religious Culture in Merovingian Gaul* (Cambridge, 2004), 206–18.

Woodruff, H., 'Illustrated Manuscripts of Prudentius', *Art Studies* 7 (1929), 33–79.

Wormald, P., 'The Ninth Century', in James Campbell (ed.), *The Anglo-Saxons* (Oxford, 1982), 132–57.

—— 'Foreword', in D. Bullough, R. Collins, and P. Wormald (eds), *Ideal and Reality in Frankish and Anglo-Saxon Society Presented to J. M. Wallace-Hadrill* (Oxford, 1983), ix–xii.

—— 'Celtic and Anglo-Saxon Kingship: Some Further Thoughts', in P. E. Szarmach and V. Darrow Oggins, (eds), *Sources of Anglo-Saxon Culture* (Kalamazoo, MI, 1986), 151–84.

—— 'In Search of King Offa's Law-Code', in I. N. Wood and N. Lund (eds), *People and Places in Northern Europe, 500–1600* (Woodbridge, 1991).

—— '*Engla Lond*: the Making of an Allegiance', *Journal of Historical Sociology* 7 (1994), 1–24.

—— 'Giving God and King His Due: Conflict and its Regulation in the Early English State', in *idem, Legal Culture in the Early Medieval West: Law as Text, Image and Experience* (London, 1999), 333–58.

—— *The Making of English Law: King Alfred to the Twelfth Century* (Oxford, 1999).

—— 'Bede, *Beowulf,* and the Conversion of the Anglo-Saxon Aristocracy', in *idem, The Times of Bede: Studies in Early English Christian Society and Its Historian,* ed. S. Baxter (Oxford, 2006), 30–100.

—— 'Alfred (848/9–899)', *Oxford Dictionary of National Biography,* Oxford University Press, Sept 2004; online edition, Oct 2006 <http://www.oxforddnb.com/view/article/183>, accessed 16 Oct 2007.

—— and Nelson, J. L. (eds), *Lay Intellectuals in the Carolingian World* (Cambridge, 2007).

Yannopoulus, P., 'Le couronnement de l'empereur à Byzance: rituel et fond institutionnel', *Byzantion* 61 (1991), 71–92.

Zechiel-Eckes, K., *Florus von Lyon als Kirchenpolitiker und Publizist: Studien zu Persönlichkeit eines karolingischen 'Intellektuellen' am Beispiel der Auseinandersetzung mit Amalarious (835–838) und des Prädestinationsstreits (851–855)* (Stuttgart, 1999).

Ziegler, K.-H., 'Conclusion and Publication of International Treaties in Antiquity', *Israel Law Review* 29 (1995), 233–49.

Zinn, G., 'Sound, Silence and the Word in the Spirituality of Gregory the Great', in R. Gillet, J. Fontaine, and S. Pellistrandi (eds), *Grégoire Le Grand* (Paris, 1986), 367–77.

Ziolkowski, J., 'Fighting Words: Wordplay and Swordplay in the *Waltharius*', in A. Harbus, K. E. Olsen, and T. Hofstra (eds), *Germanic Texts and Latin Models: Medieval Reconstructions* (Leuven, 2001), 29–52.

Index